PATIO LIVING

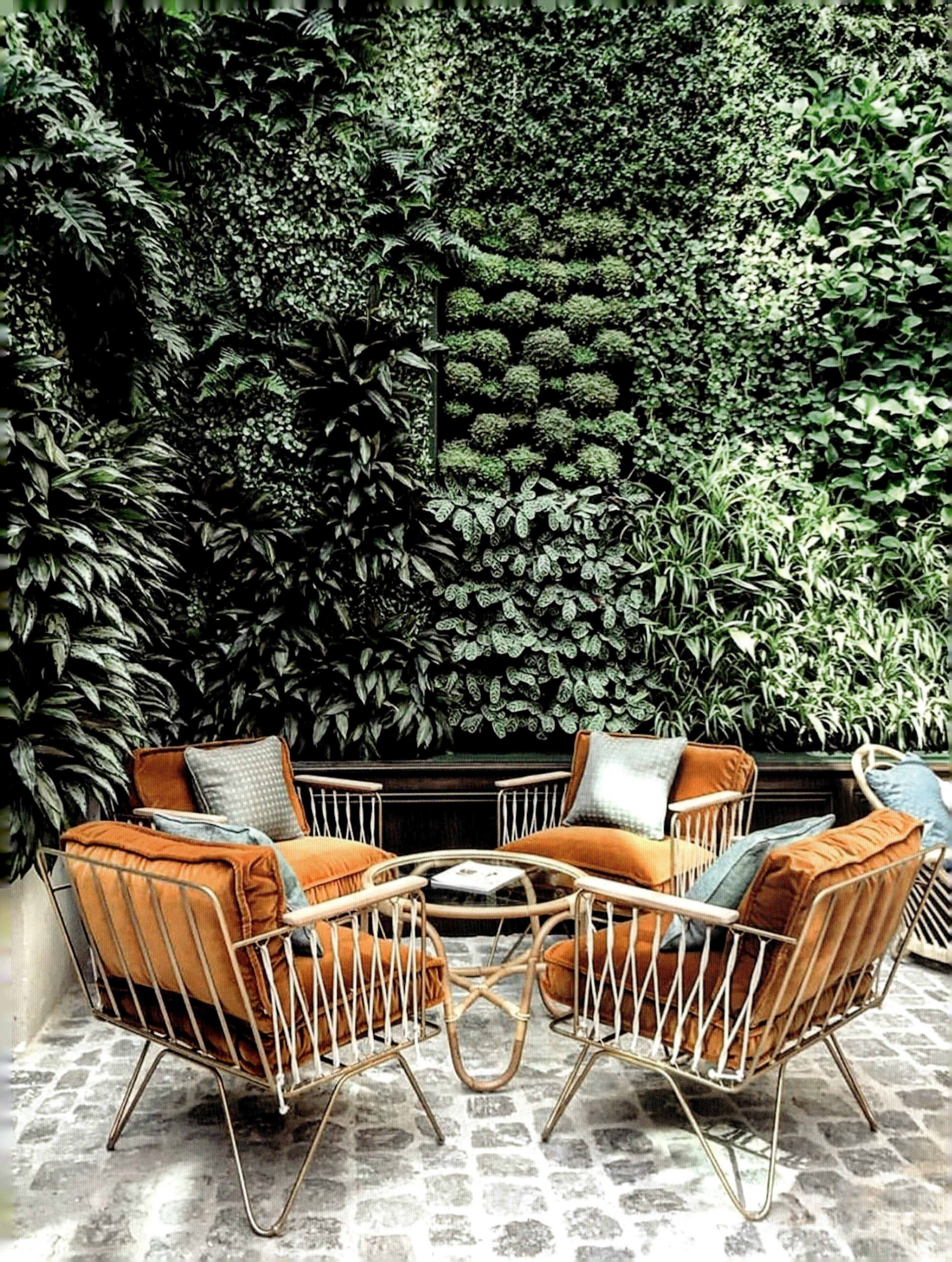

AGATA AND PIERRE TOROMANOFF

PATIO LIVING

SCHIFFER PUBLISHING
4880 Lower Valley Road • Atglen, PA 19310

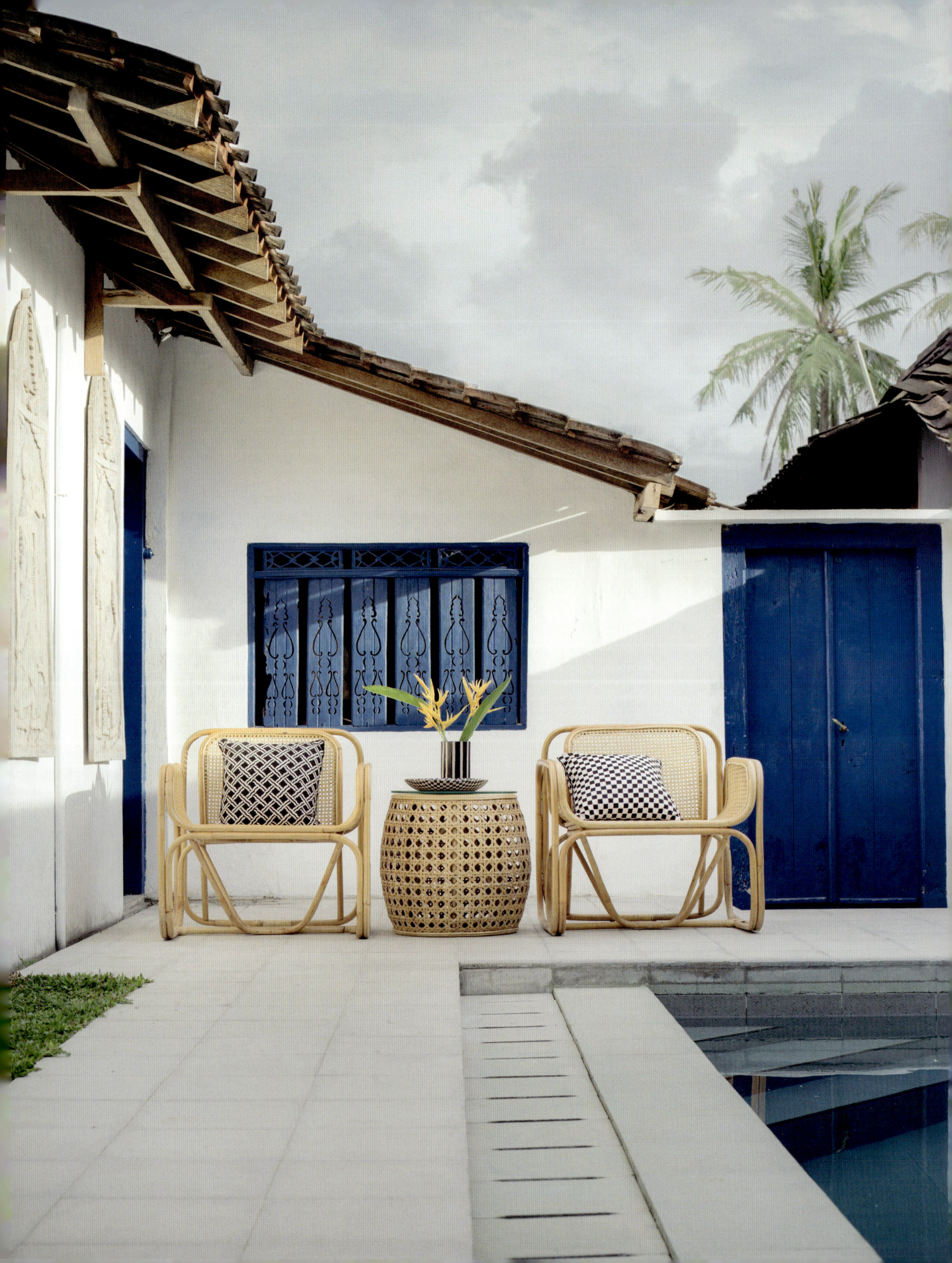

TABLE OF CONTENTS

INTRODUCTION

The concept of a patio house, with an inner courtyard providing both light and privacy, has been known since ancient times. Many Roman villas, including some in Pompeii, were built around a garden or a courtyard, with a peristyle—a porch adorned with columns—surrounding it and connecting the different parts of the house. This style of house quickly spread across the Roman Empire and became a part of local architecture in Spain, Portugal, and Northwest Africa in the Middle Ages. The influence is evident in Granada's Alhambra, as well as in the architecture of some medieval monasteries. Conventual buildings were often structured around a garden with a peristyle, as can be seen in remains of the spectacular Moissac Abbey in southwestern France. From the sixteenth century onward, during the Age of Exploration, patio houses spread around the globe thanks to Spanish and Portuguese colonization. They first made their way to the Americas, then to India and Southeast Asia, becoming elements of traditional architecture in many parts of the world.

A patio gives a house its heart. It is an oasis of tranquility, an inner garden, a communication hub, and, from a more practical perspective, a solution to divide up interior spaces. The latter is particularly valuable in houses inhabited by extended or multigenerational families, where patios play a crucial role in achieving a balance between common and private areas. A patio can be a courtyard or an inner court that is open to the sky, but also a recreational area typically paved and used as an outdoor dining space.

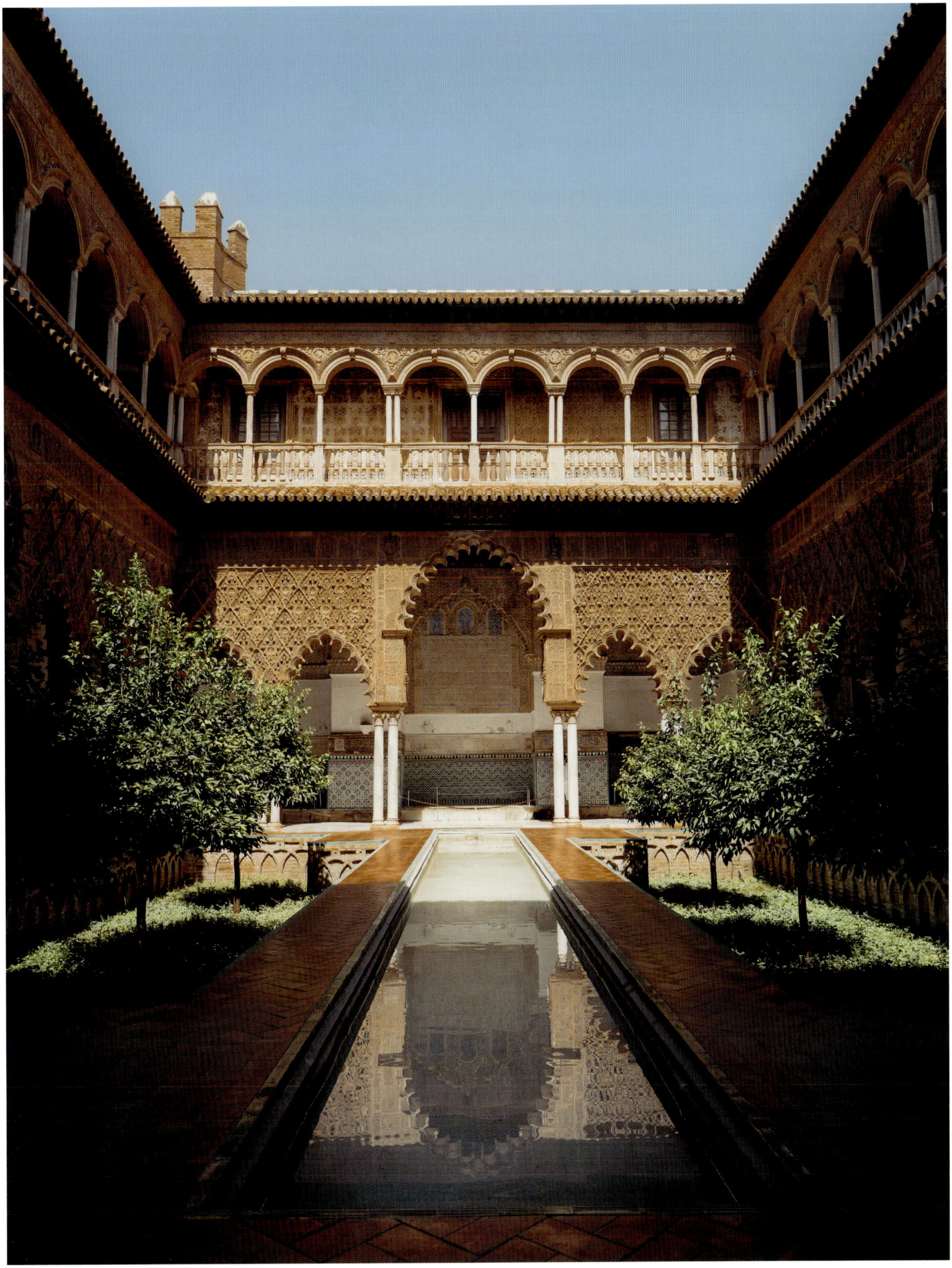

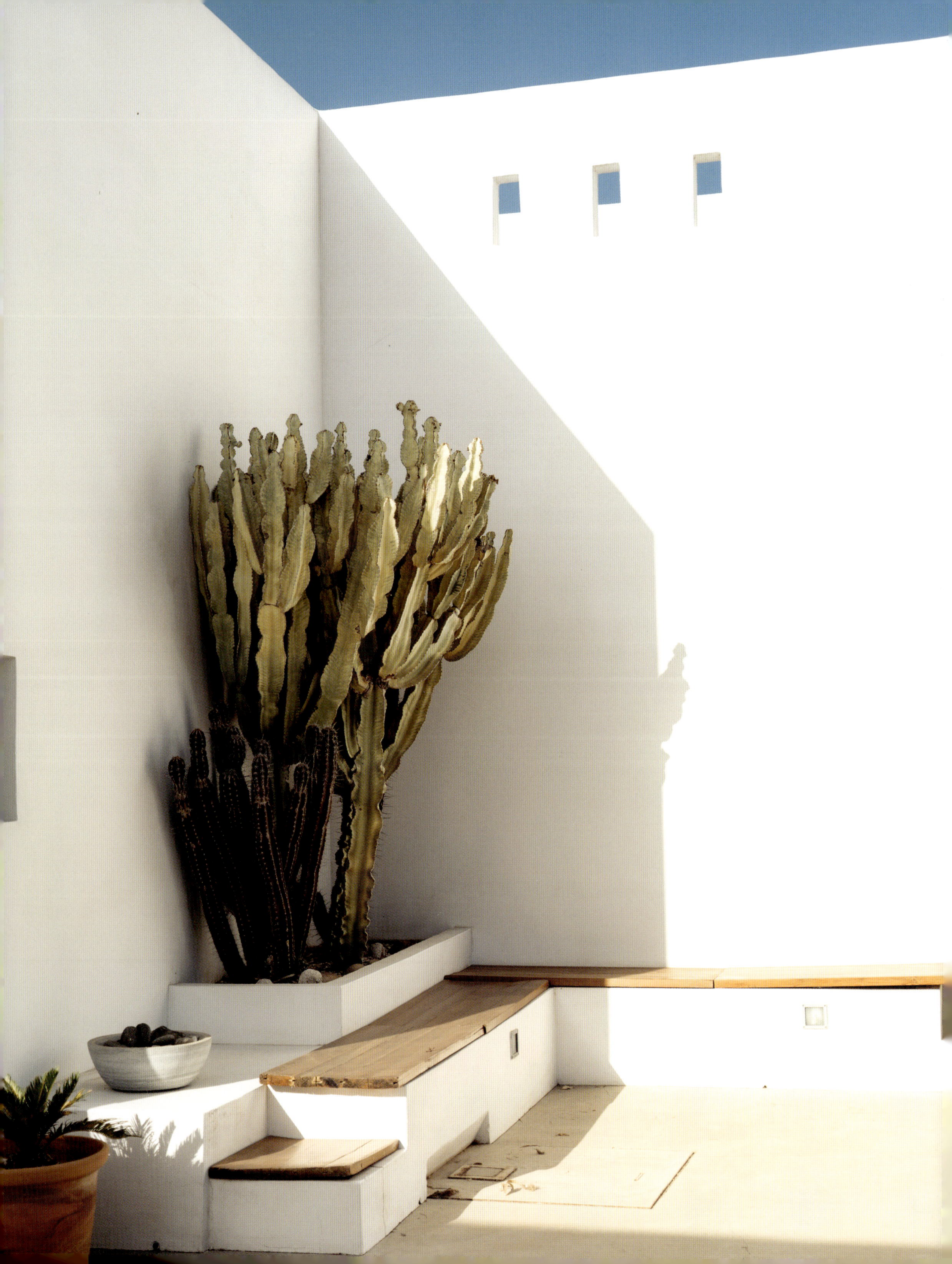

Depending on the chosen location, architects use patios in various ways to enhance the comfort of residents. In densely populated urban districts, where quiet outdoor spaces are scarce, patios primarily serve as private gardens that preserve tranquility. In more-residential areas surrounded by gardens, patios are seen as inviting meeting places and an extension of the interiors. Dwellings in remote areas often feature patios as a response to local weather conditions. These patios not only provide green spaces within the home but also offer protection against strong winds or excessive sun exposure.

To showcase the diversity of patio houses we have chosen examples from urban areas, as well as locations surrounded by nature. These selected patios emphasize intimacy, outdoor living, and togetherness. Our focus is on the role that patios play in the architecture of homes and the creative ways that architects integrate them with interior spaces. Adorned with specially chosen furniture and decor, patios exude a welcoming atmosphere and promote relaxation and socialization. The case studies featured in this book, beautifully captured in photographs, demonstrate how patios can easily become the heart of a residence.

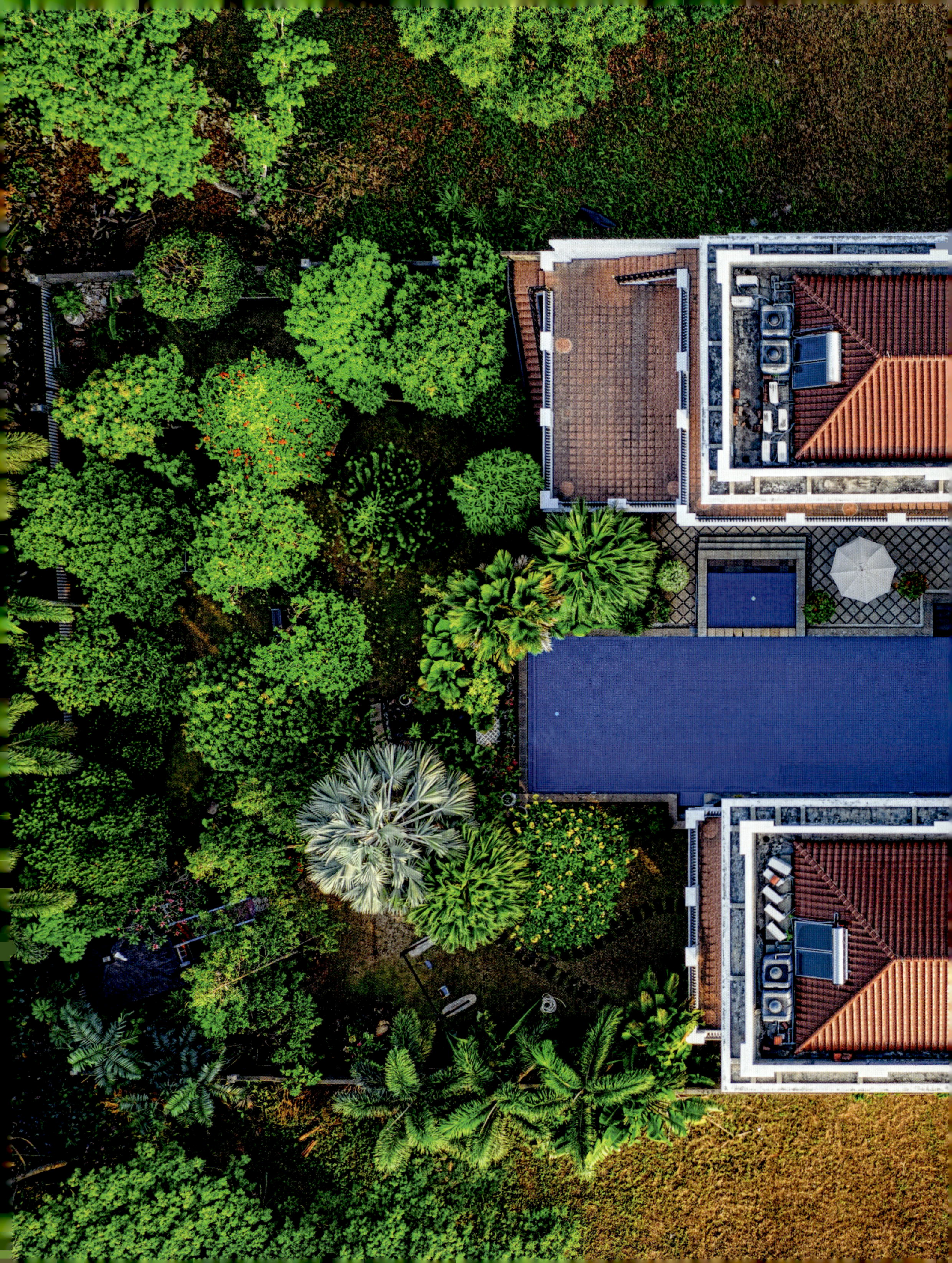

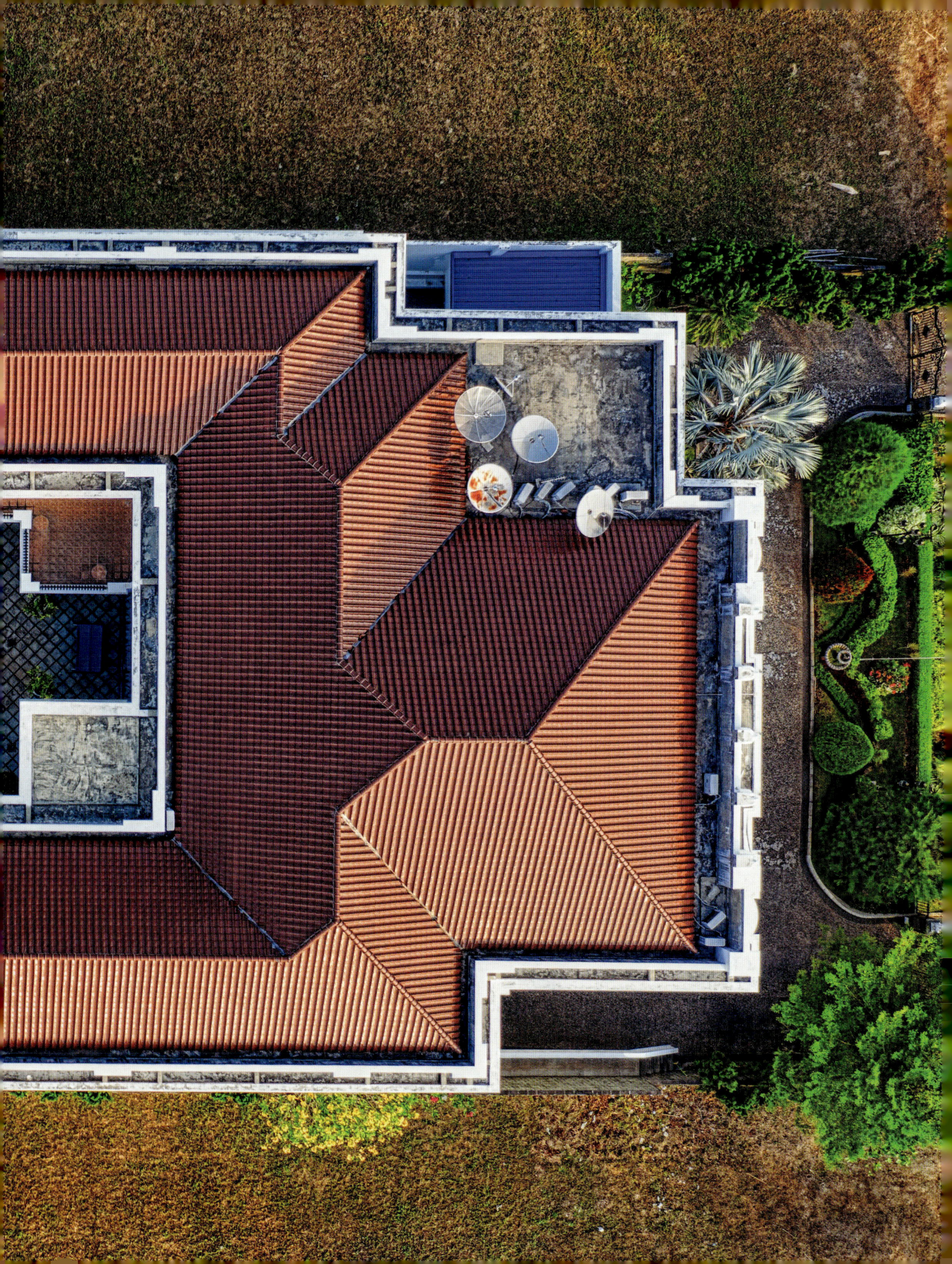

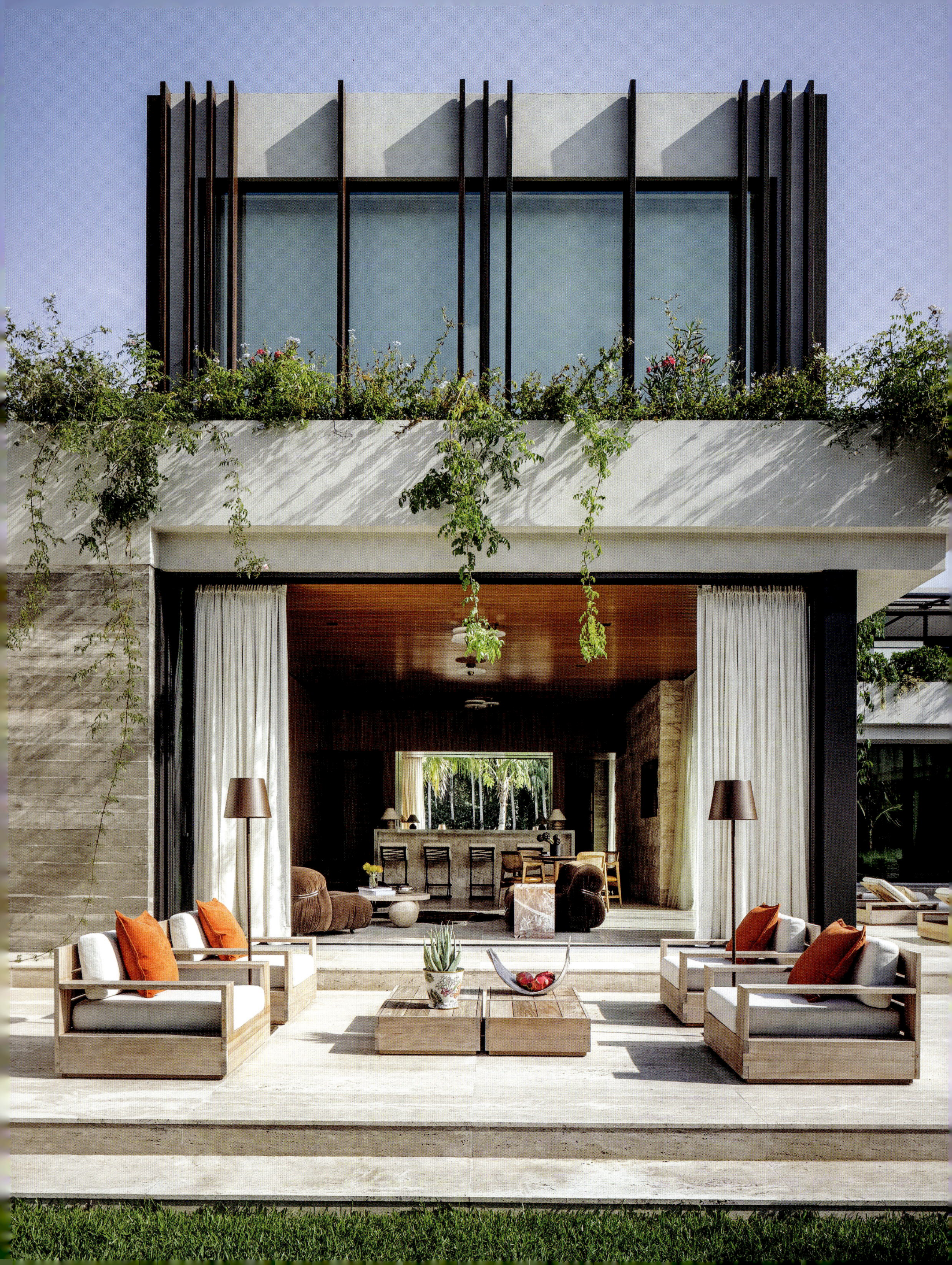

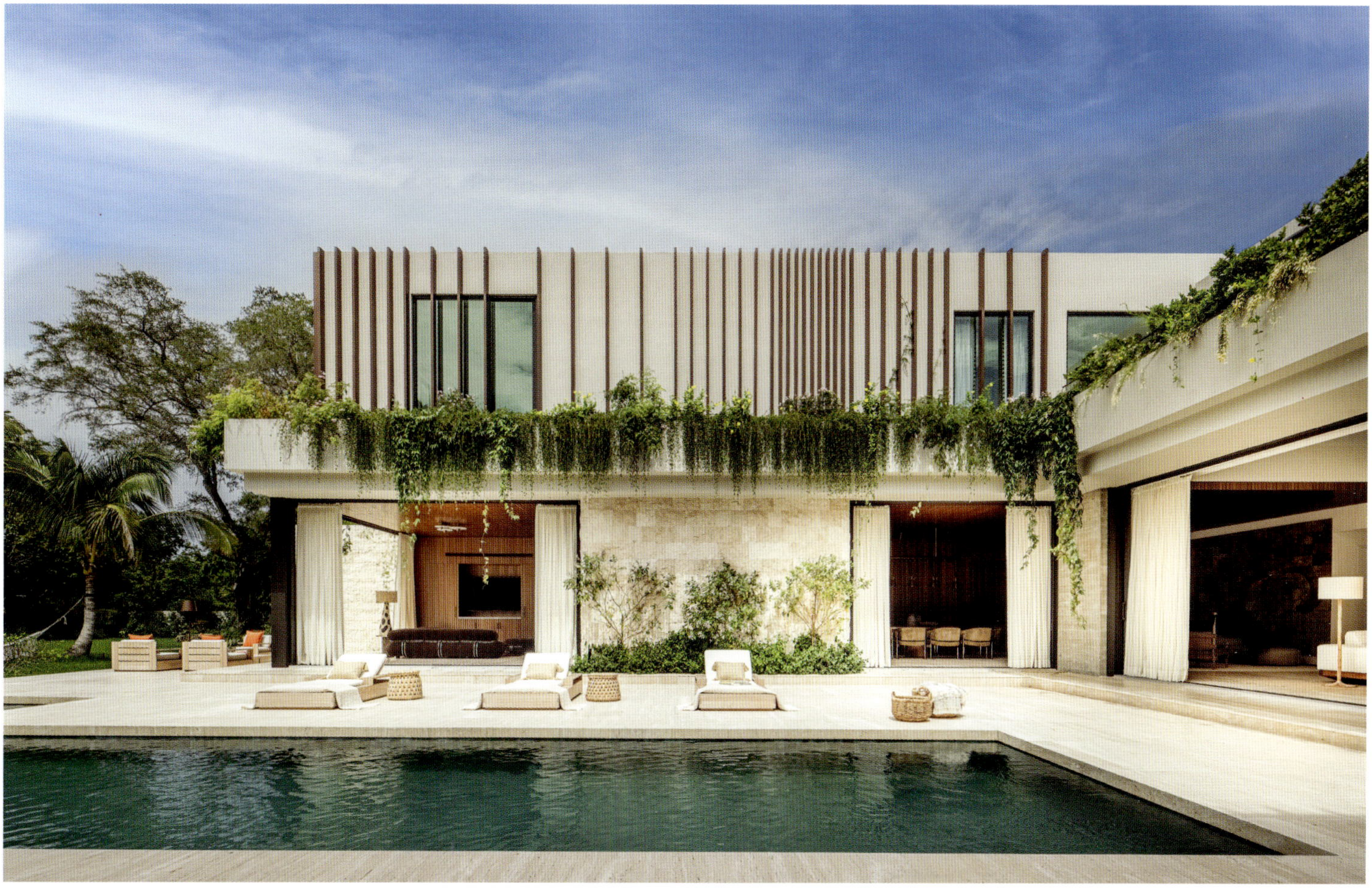

PROJECT: Angel Oaks
LOCATION: Miami, Florida, United States
YEAR: 2023
ARCHITECTS: STRANG
PHOTOGRAPHY: Kris Tamburello

Miami vibes meet Brazilian influences in this breathtaking residence in the shape of the letter H. The architects aimed for an orientation that would allow ample natural light into the interiors. What they achieved was the perfect composition to encompass a spacious and pleasant patio. Enveloped by the villa's three wings, this space is intimate but remains open to the lush adjoining garden. Floor-to-ceiling openings in the living and dining rooms on the first story connect the stylishly designed interiors with the expansive exterior area crowned with a swimming pool. One of the side wings of the house forms an outdoor kitchen, which enhances the fusion between inside and outside. The result is a highly relaxing combination of the intimacy of the interiors and the joy of the sunshine-flooded patio. The smoothness has been achieved not only by the entirely openable windows, but also thanks to the use of travertine flooring that crosses from the patio to the rooms.

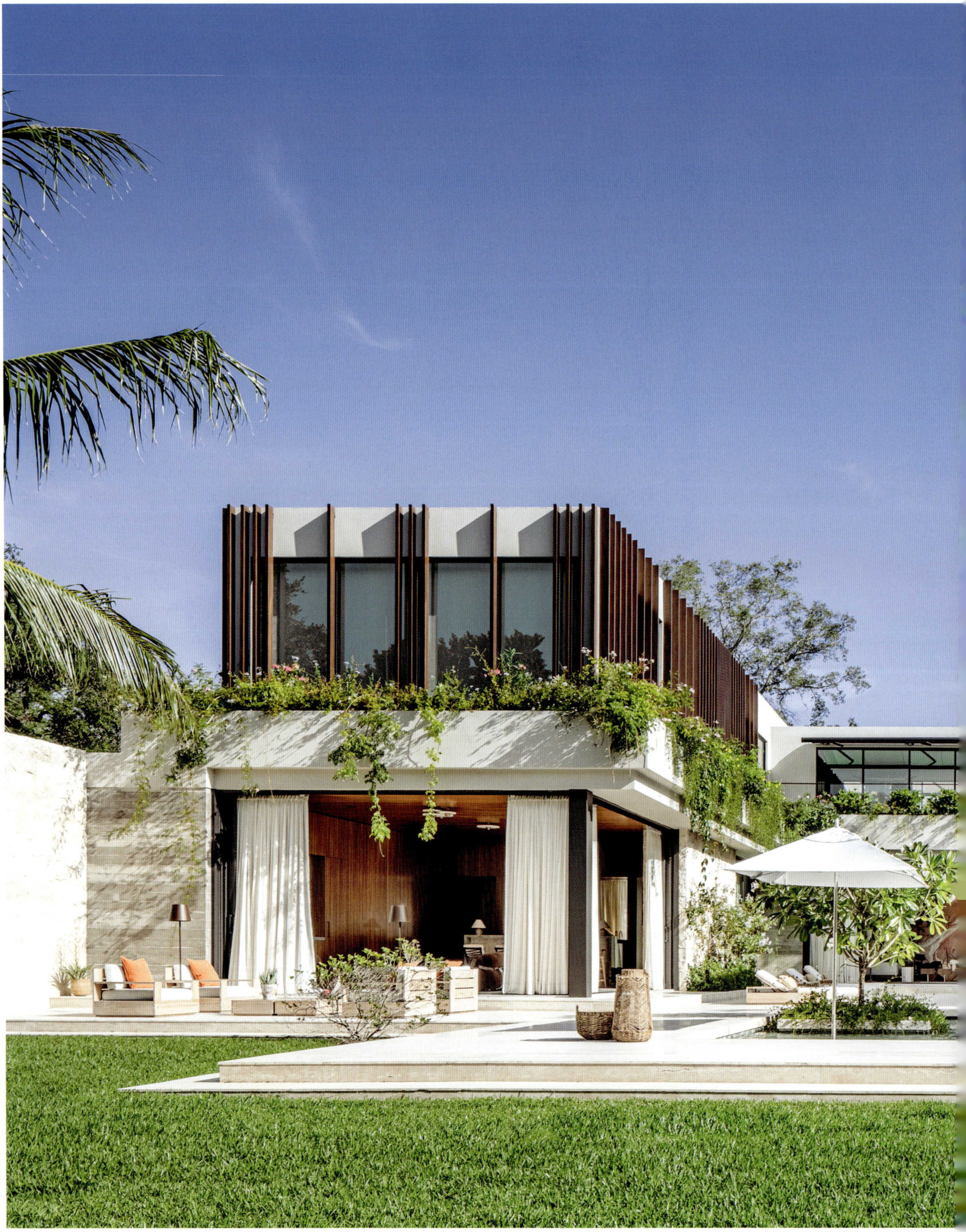

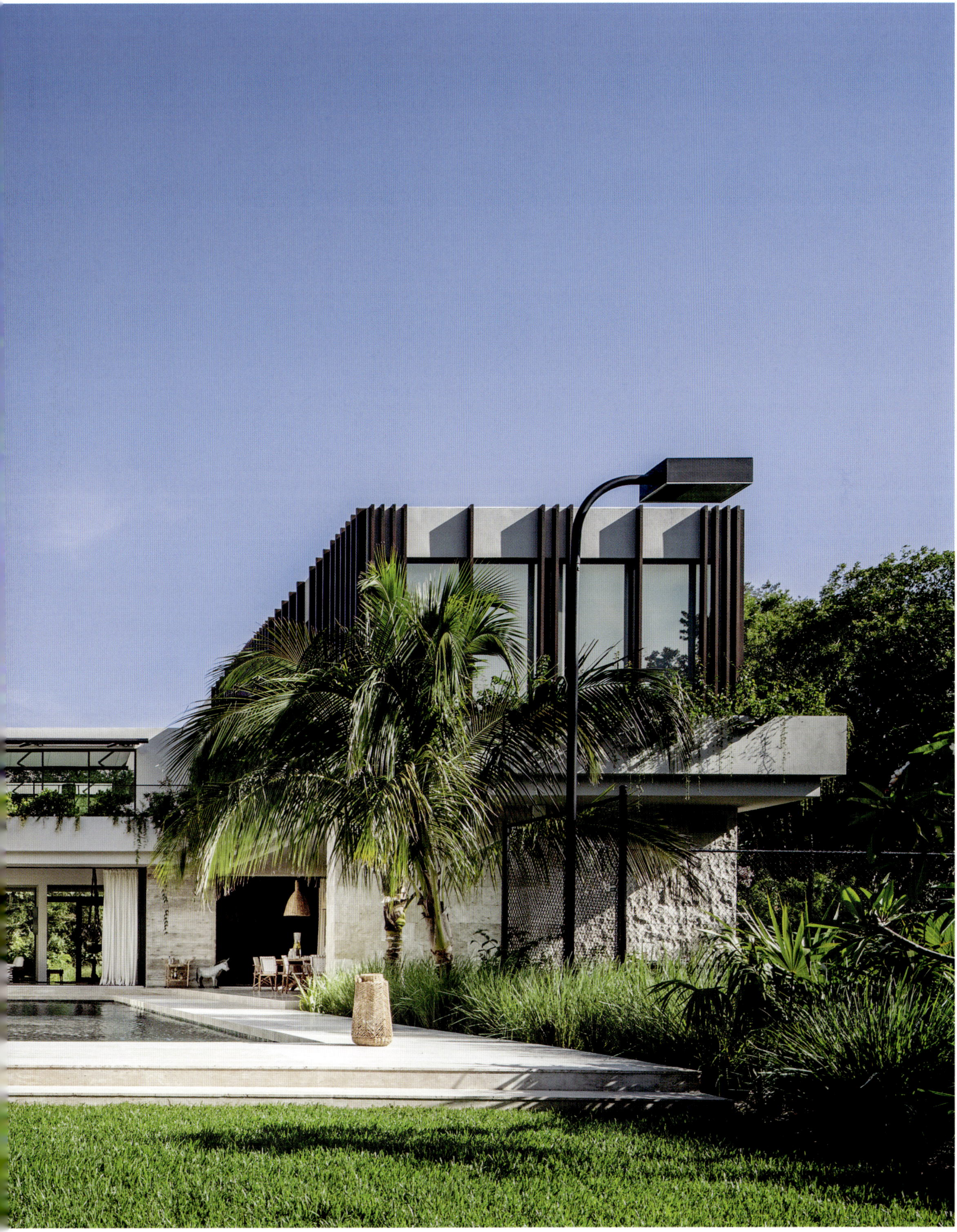

Travertine is one of many natural and environmentally friendly materials used in the house, including various kinds of wood, such as teak or oak. The earth tone color palette of the interiors harmoniously complements the play of organic textures. The interior design has been carefully planned to become a perfect scenery for the owner's vintage furniture, as well as artwork collections. Designing for a family of four from Brazil, the STRANG team, as they state, "paid careful attention to the clients' desires and way of life, creating a warm and inviting atmosphere that reflects their cultural heritage." The villa is spacious, but all its areas have been well connected both with each other and with the greenery around. STRANG collaborated with landscape architecture studio La Casona Garden to create an equally unique garden filled with native species. Interestingly, a portion of the property has been designated as a Certified Wildlife Habitat by the National Wildlife Federation.

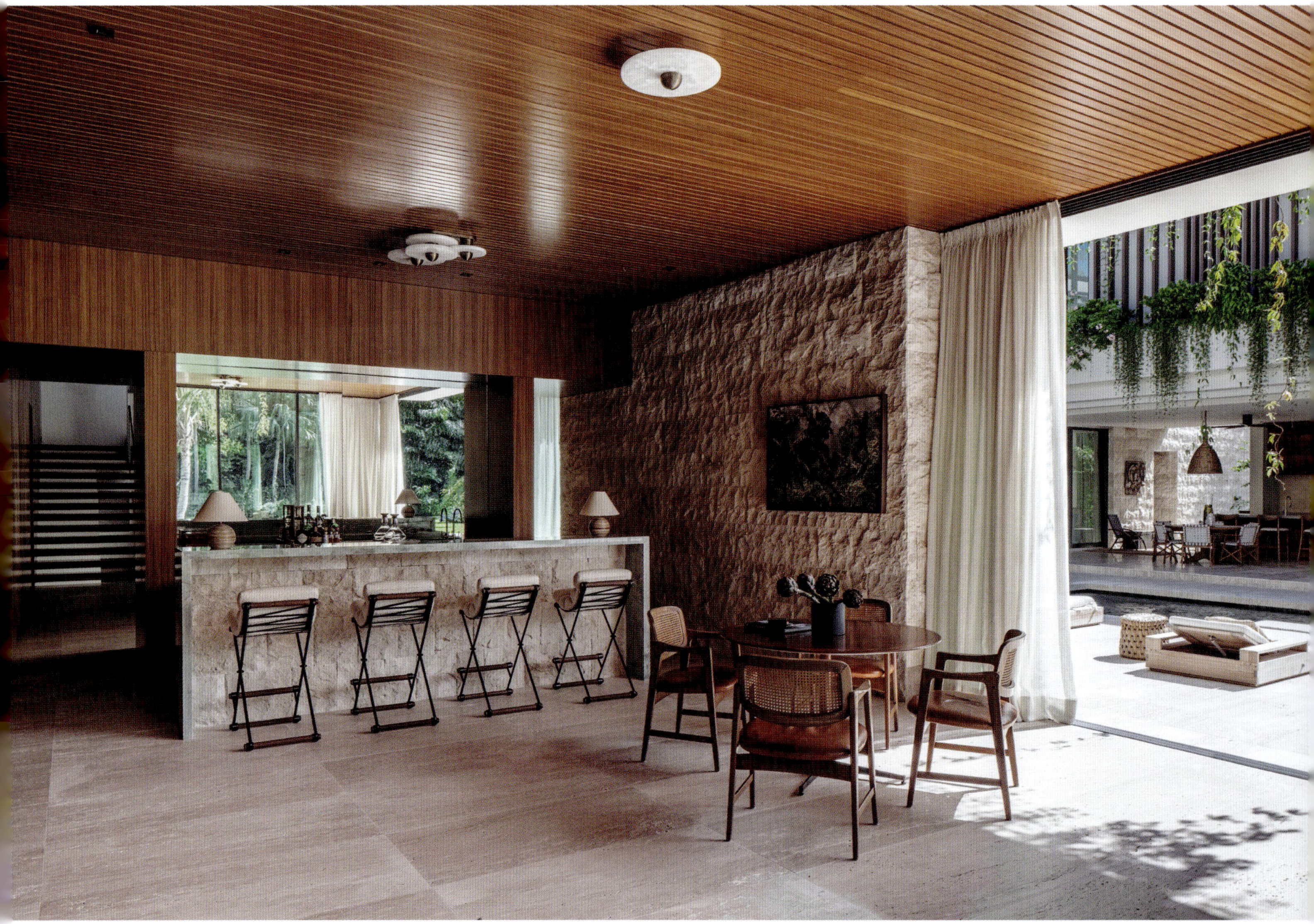

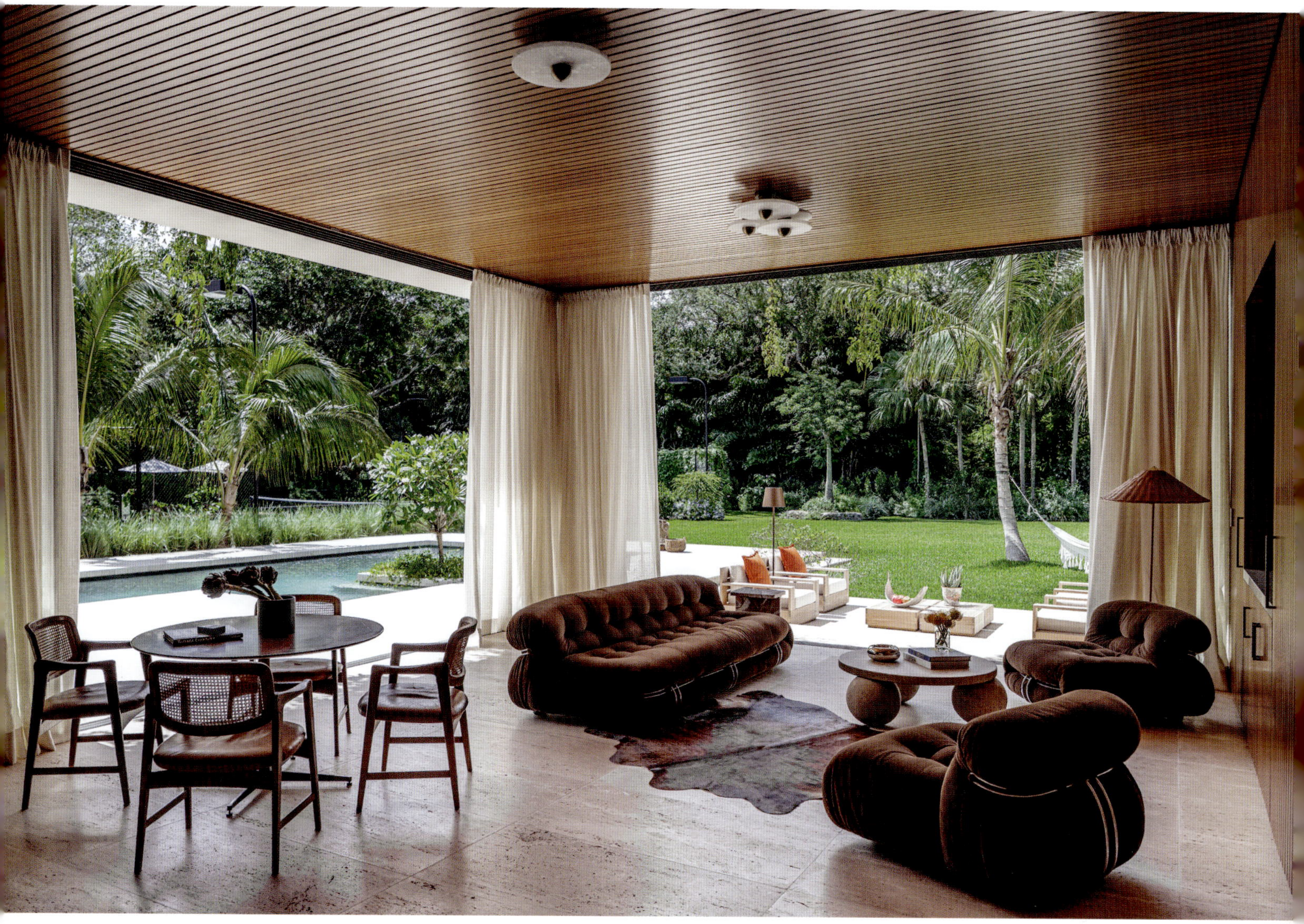

The most striking feature of the house is that all rooms on the first story are at the same time cozily embracing and smoothly open onto the inner patio, which invites entertainment. The second story of the house creates a stark visual contrast. Wrapped in vertical ipe wood fins, it is clearly the space devoted to privacy and calmness.

STRANG, with offices in Miami and Sarasota, is an architectural, interior-design, and landscape design firm pioneering the principles of environmental modernism. Working on residential architecture in some of the most extraordinary locations around the world, including the Caribbean Sea, Florida, Florida Keys, Colorado, the Bahamas, the Dominican Republic, and the United Arab Emirates, the team is inspired by modernism and reinventing it.

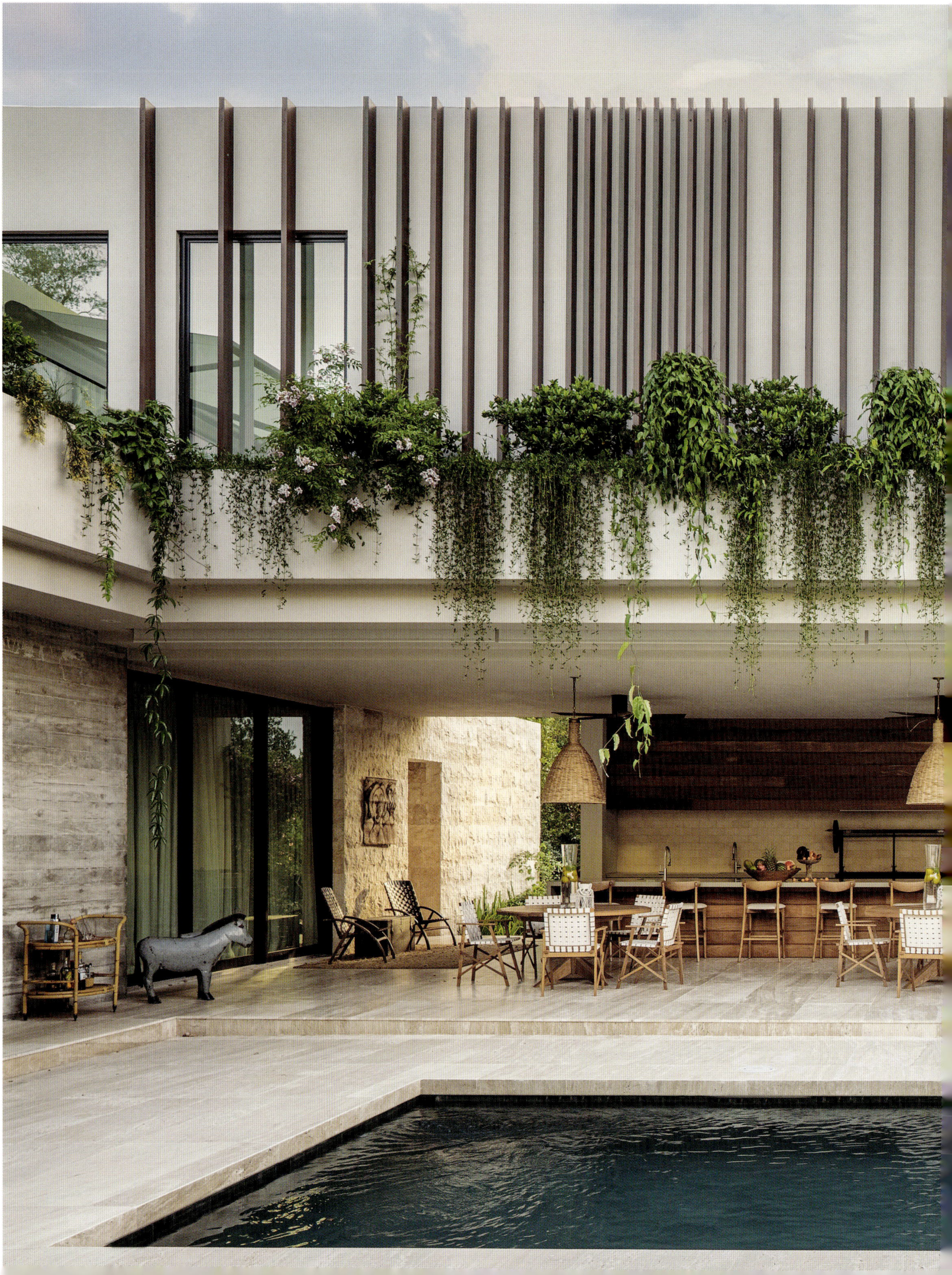

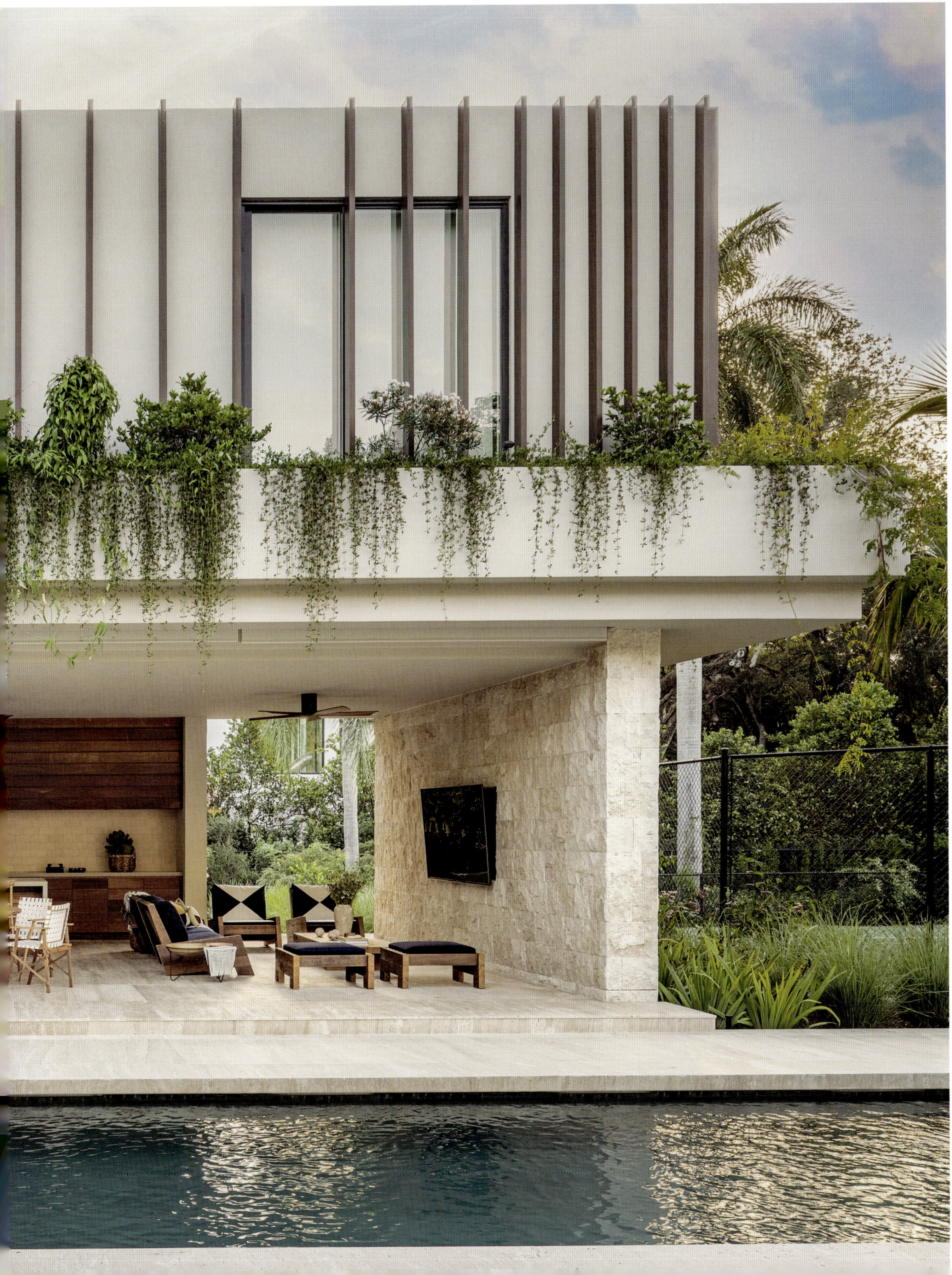

PROJECT: Carroll Gardens Townhouse
LOCATION: Brooklyn, New York, United States
YEAR: 2022
ARCHITECTS: Barker Architecture Office
PHOTOGRAPHY: Francis Dzikowski / OTTO

The Carroll Gardens Townhouse is an excellent example of a retrofit of a stylish townhouse to expand the kitchen, dining area, and children's rooms. The core of designing the extension was the preservation of the existing saucer magnolia tree, highlighted by the bluestone terrace embracing its base. The entrance to the patio on the first floor is partially covered by the expansive terrace on the second level, adding to the already comfortable atmosphere of the corner opening out onto the outdoor area. The entire space is glazed and is furnished with a large bookshelf and a rounded sofa, creating a seamless transition between the house and the back patio with a garden. The relaxation sphere extends throughout the yard, with lounging zones culminating in a comfortable cedar-clad bench. Numerous spots of greenery and trees create a unique hideaway from the hustle and bustle of the city.

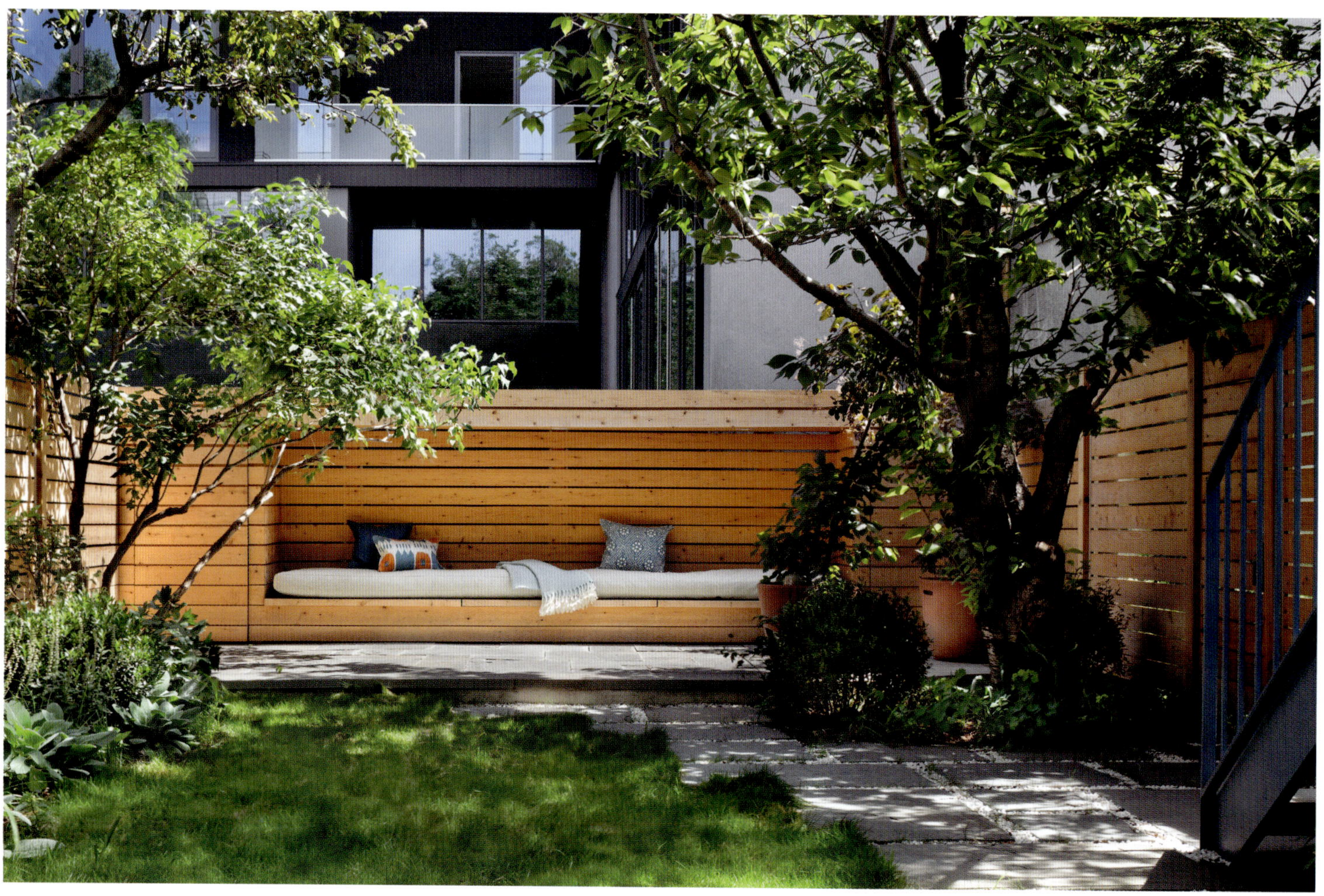

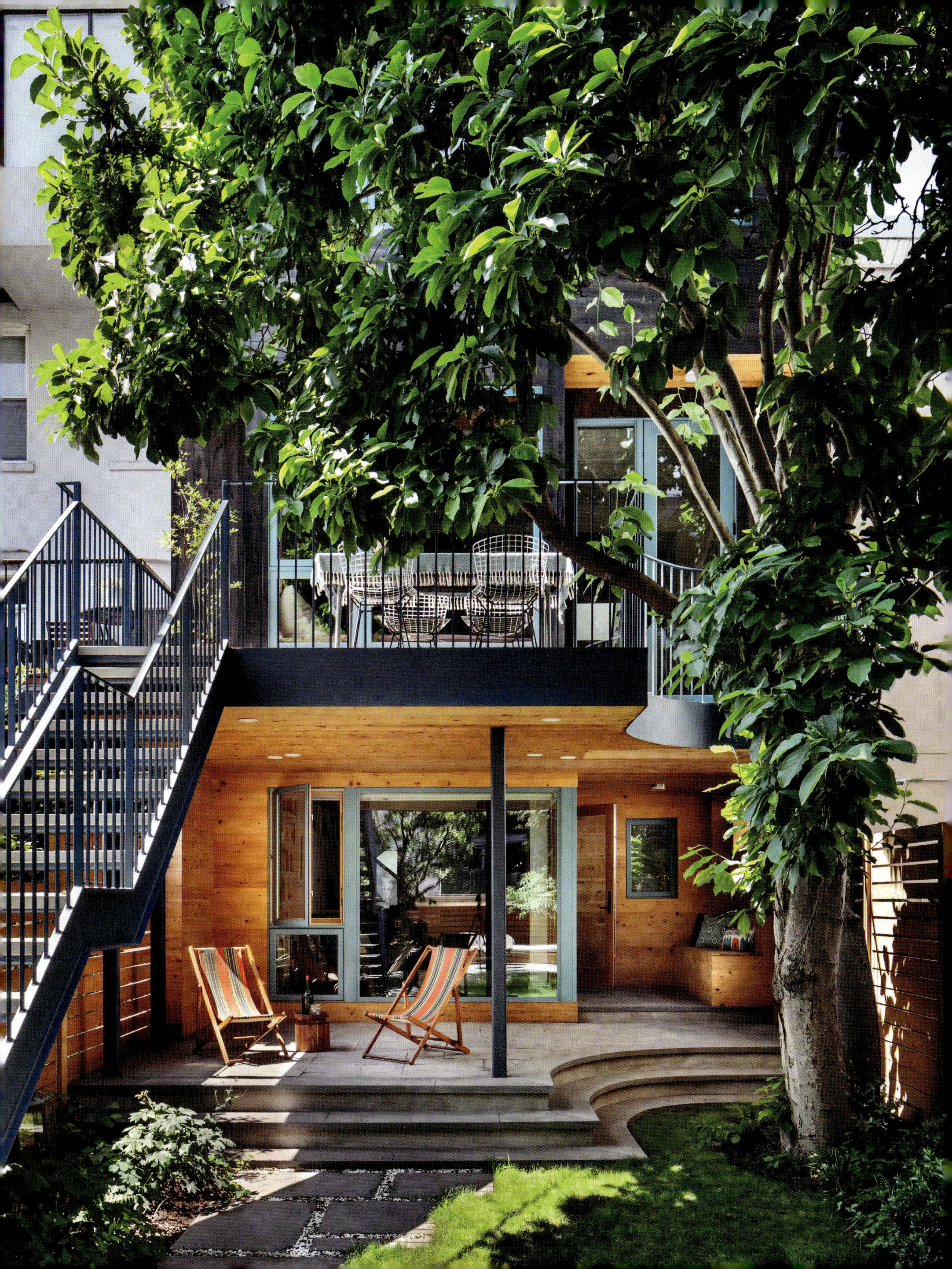

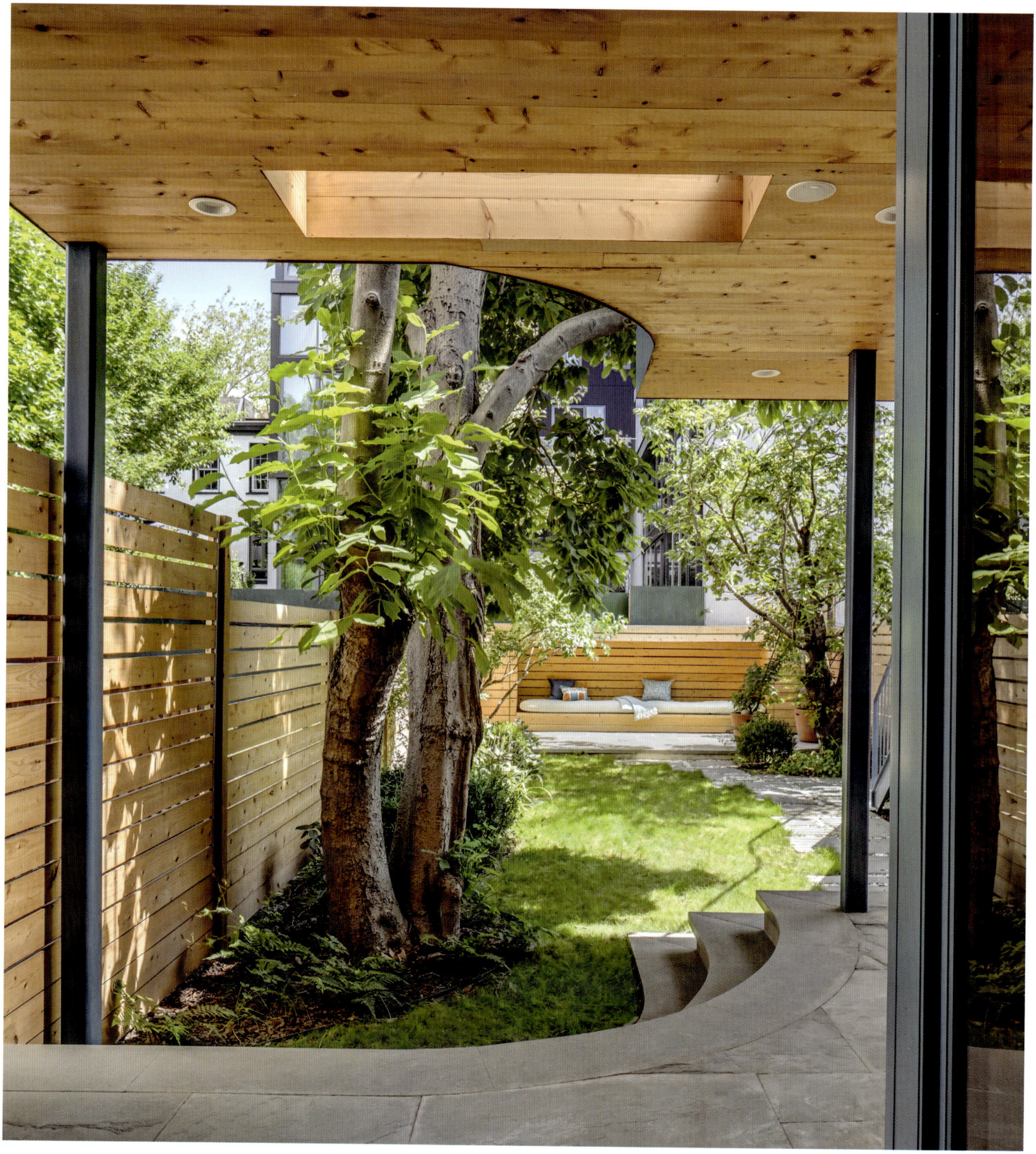

Barker Associates Architecture Office (BAAO) was founded in 2006 by Alexandra Barker. The studio's portfolio covers a wide range of projects, including architecture, with a focus on townhouses and residential developments as well as interior design and landscapes. Realizations in the New York area, the region, and internationally aim to bring design to broader communities, especially through the architects' designs for education.

The connected interiors are designed with bold colors and an interesting fusion of patterns and textures. On the second floor, the architects thoughtfully created a visual connection with the rear yard by adding a special bench overlooking it in the dining room in the new part of the house. The renovation made the house more spacious and comfortable, while the ingeniously designed exterior space acts as an additional extension to this lovely city residence.

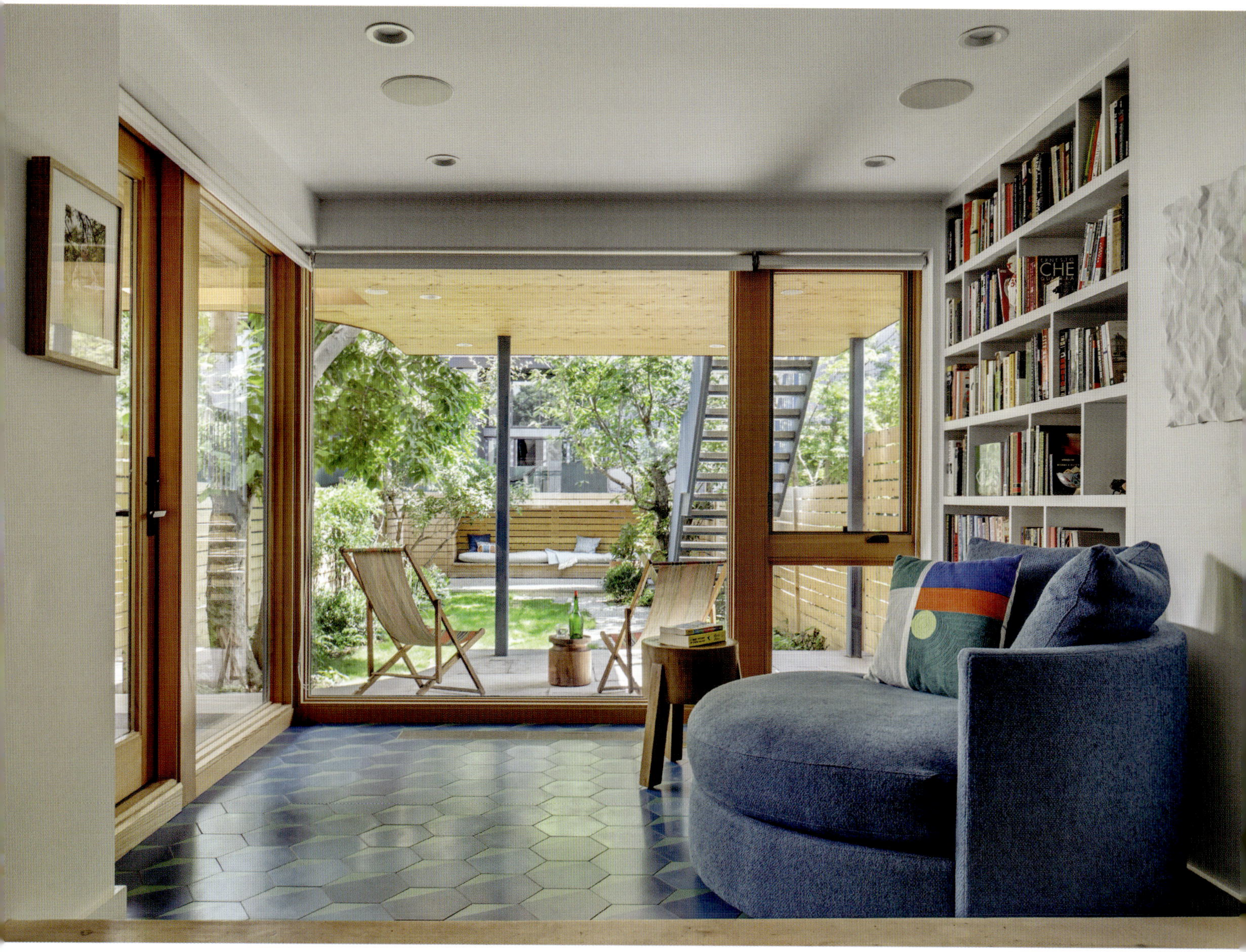

The interiors are connected with the rear yard on two levels: on the first floor through large openings in the reading area and on the second floor through expansive stairs running from the terrace, acting as an outdoor dining room.

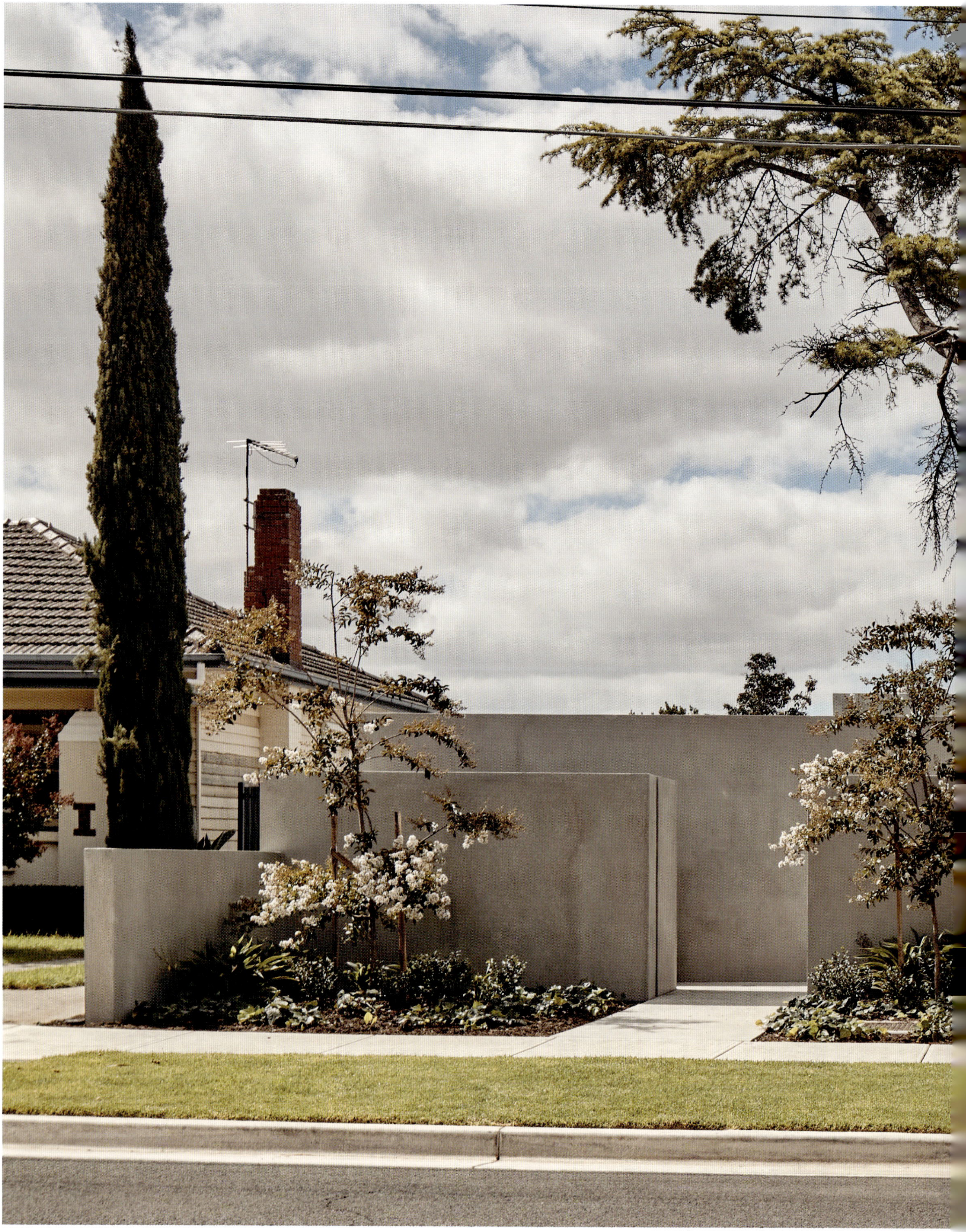

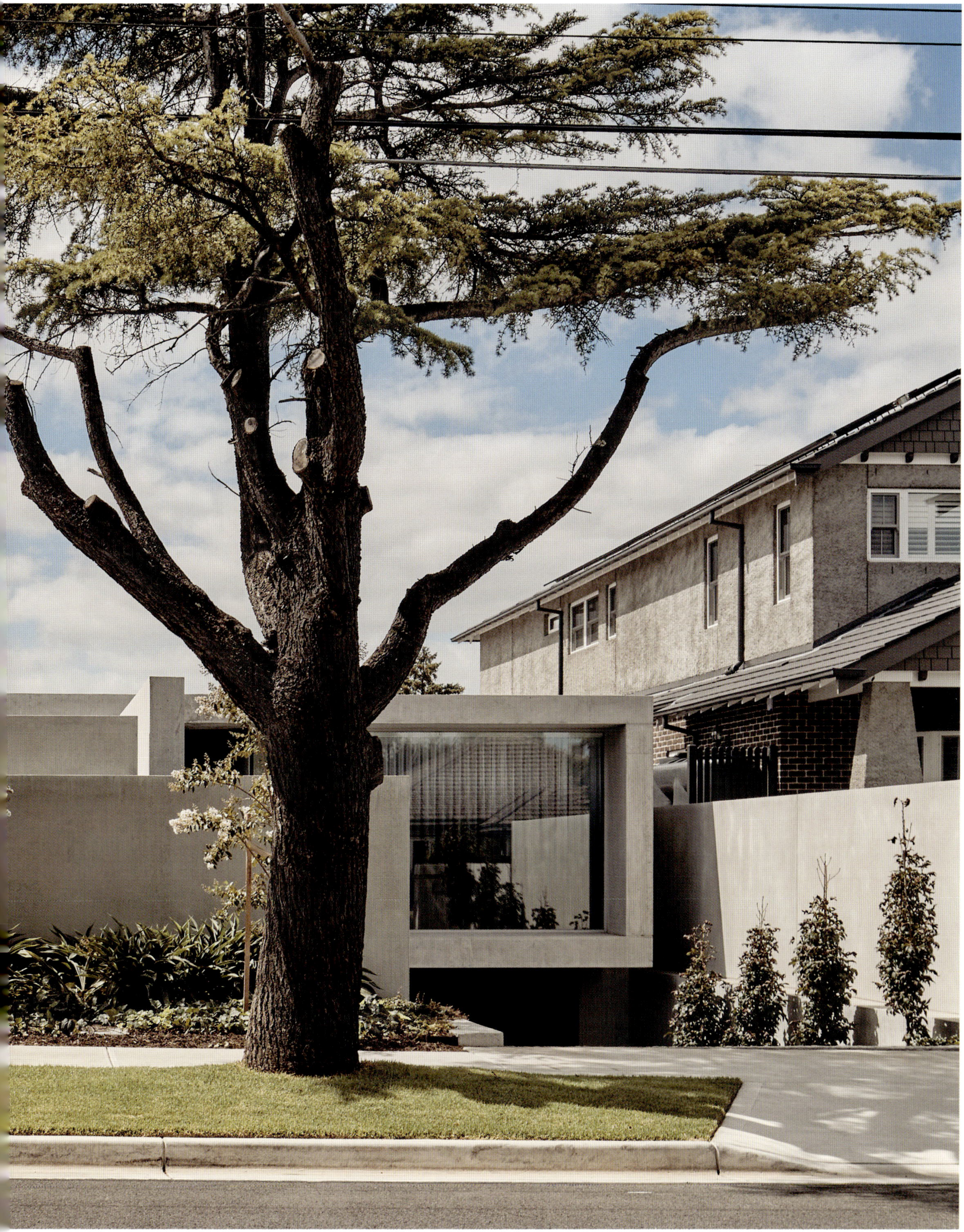

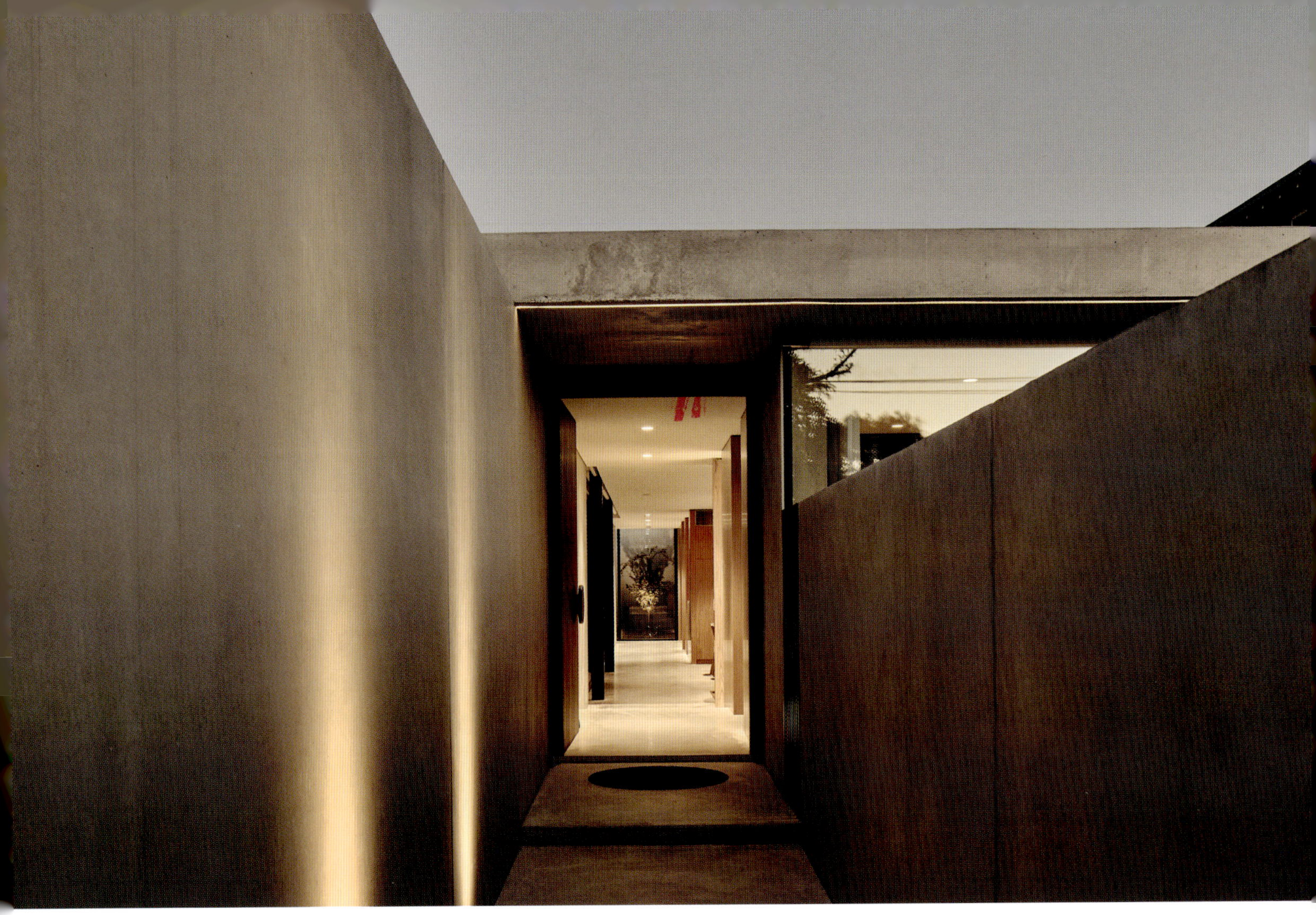

PROJECT: The Courtyard Residence
LOCATION: Melbourne, Australia
YEAR: 2022
ARCHITECTS: FGR Architects
PHOTOGRAPHY: Peter Bennetts

The Courtyard Residence is an excellent example of minimal style that is striking from the very entrance. The architects describe the Courtyard Residence as a rectangular origami made of concrete and glass. They emphasize that the project's ambition is to design a space that exudes calm expression, heightened experience, and seamless function. All these objectives have been successfully achieved with a touch of class and timeless elegance. From the street, the intriguing arrangement of concrete volumes creates a visual barrier that provides privacy for the inhabitants. At the heart of the house, the pure geometry of the walls surrounds an inner patio, creating an oasis of quietness that is entirely intimate. Large panes of polished concrete and the shimmering surface of the water form a geometric backdrop for relaxation and family life, carefully planned and devoid of any superfluous elements.

As described by the architects, the volume truly resembles an origami composition, unfolding most intriguingly around the patio. The walls, in a kind of geometric dance, gracefully embrace a private outdoor area in the middle of a big city.

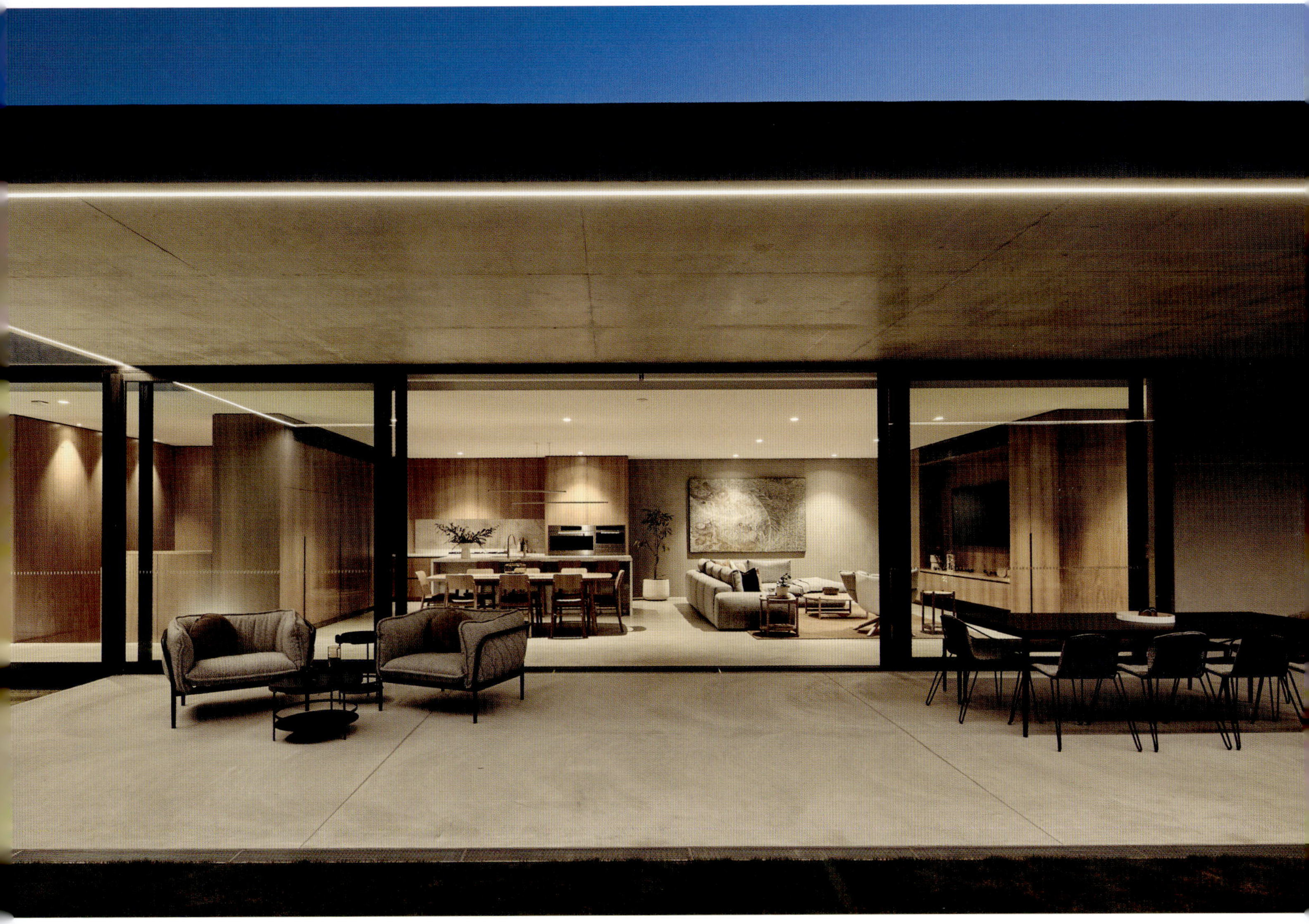

"FGR Architects obsesses over creating the best possible architecture for the human body, heart, and mind," reads the statement. The Australian studio, established in 2003 and led by Feray Raffoul, focuses on residential projects that enhance the owners' everyday life. With a focus on timeless elegance, the architects draw from minimalist style. Their main goal is to design beautiful and comfortable buildings by using raw, simple palettes and materials in unconventional ways, without unnecessary complications or waste.

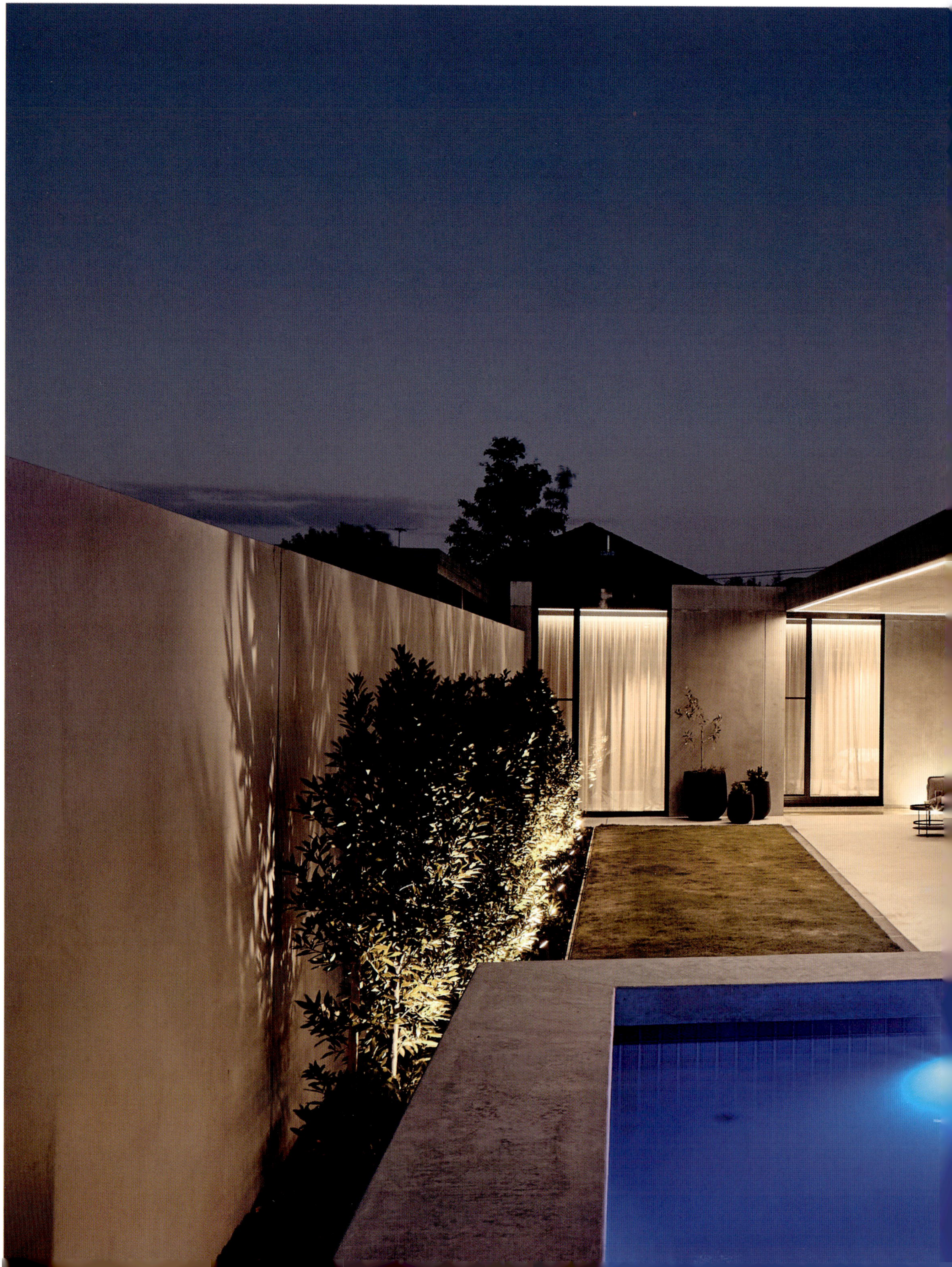

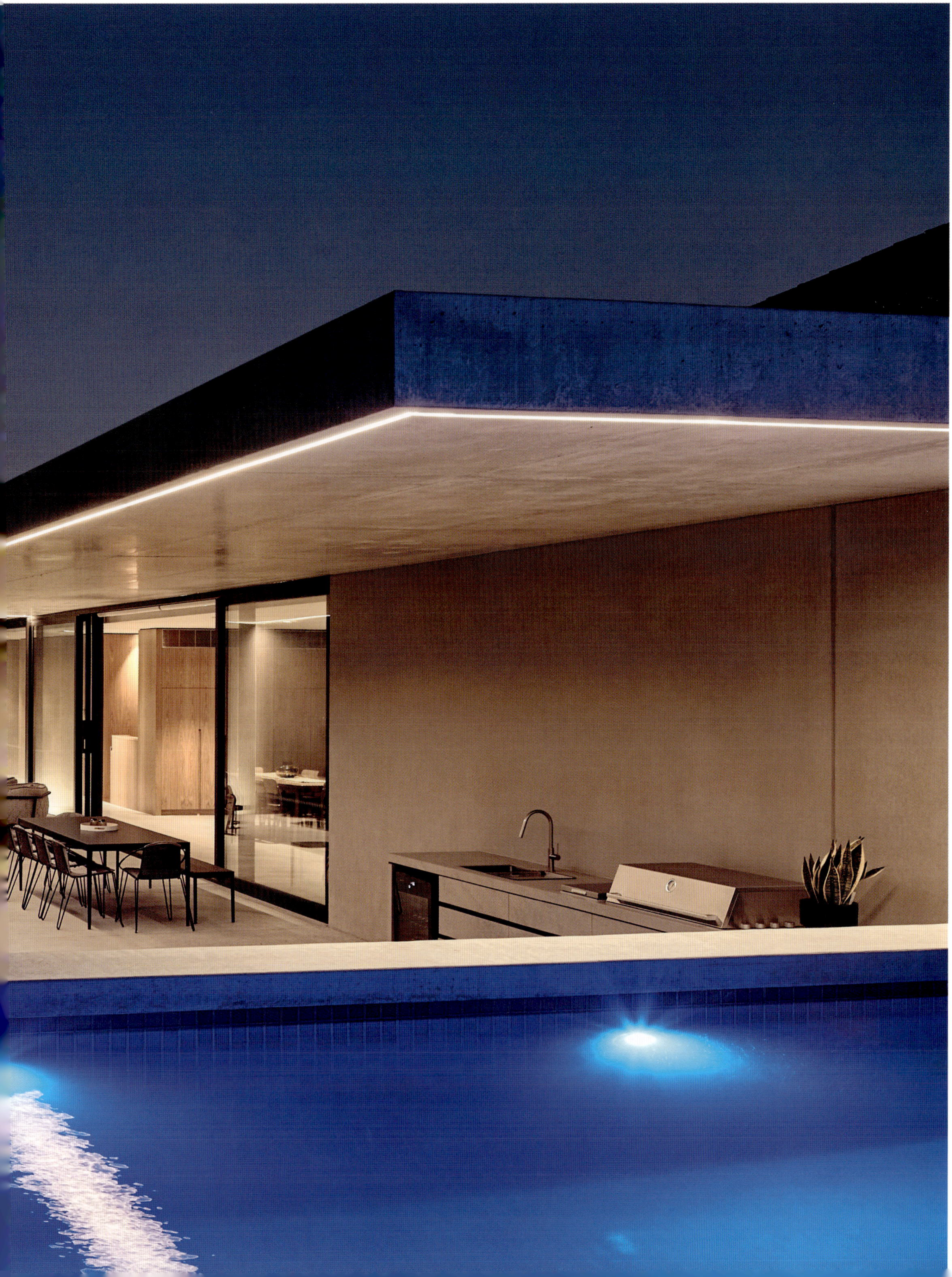

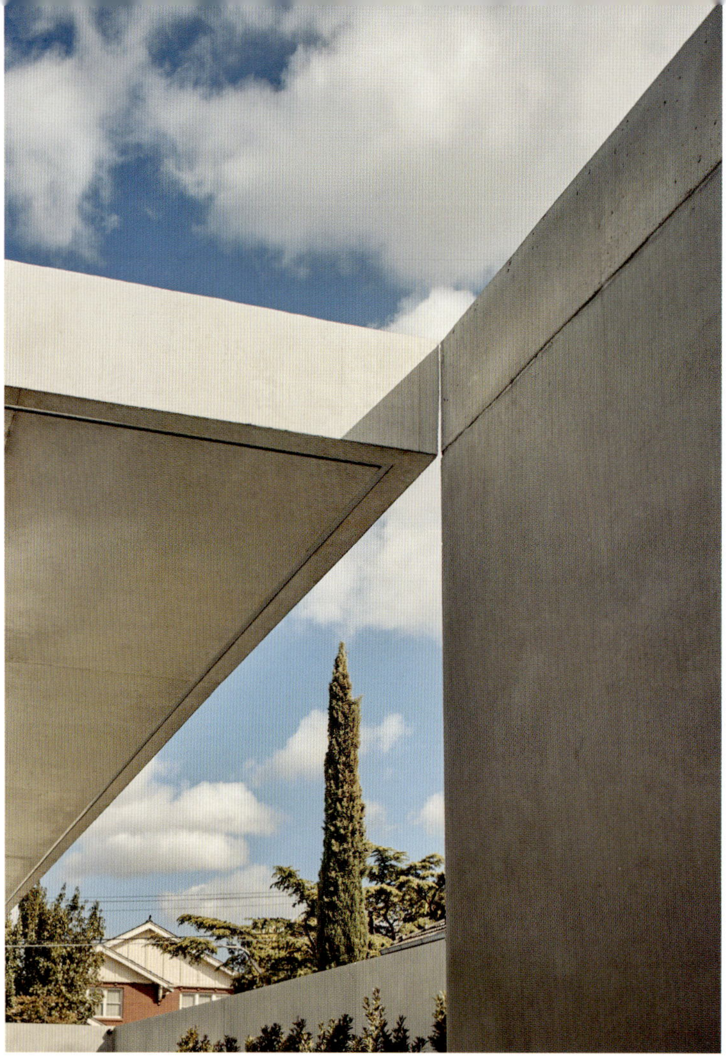

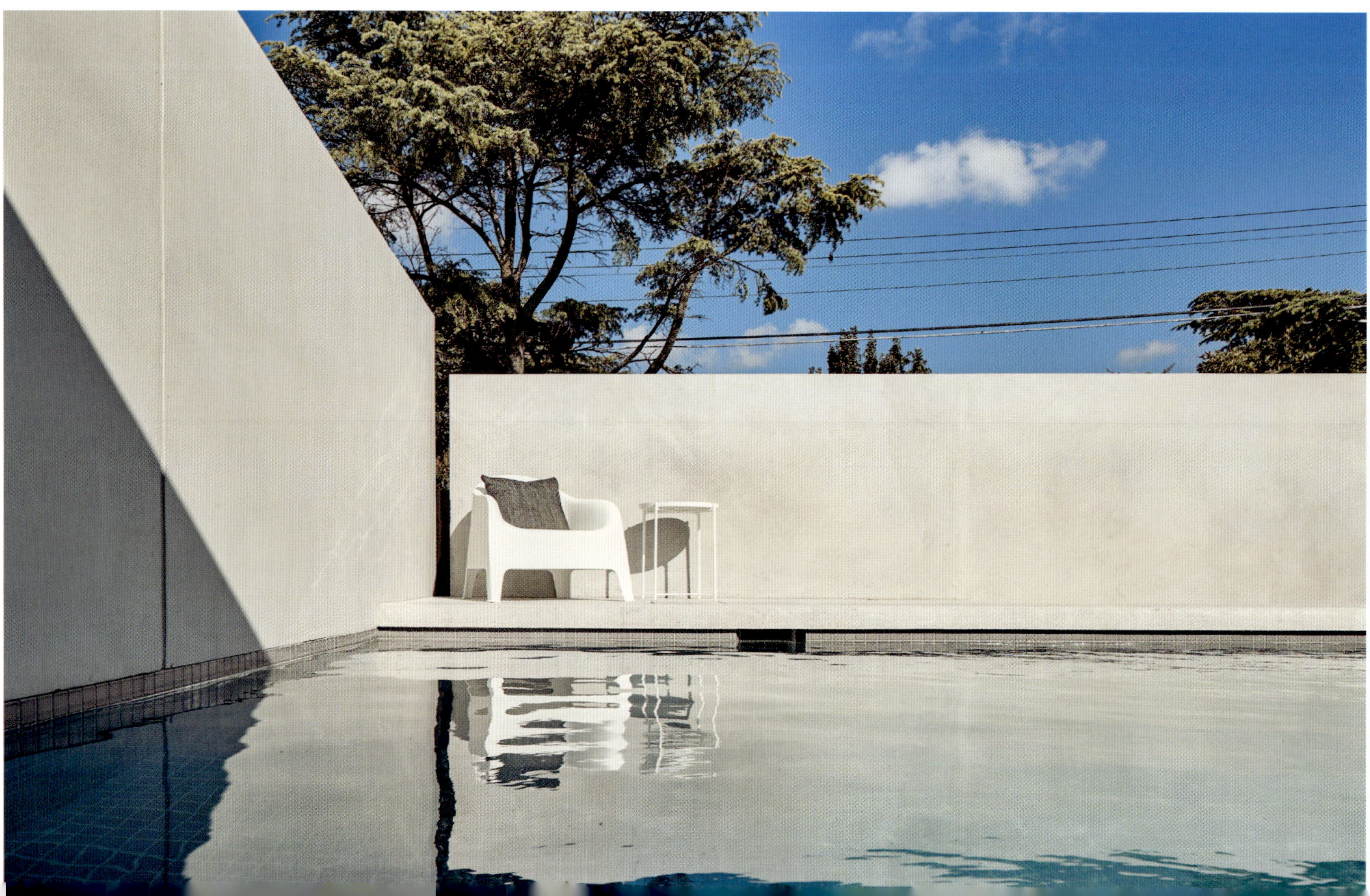

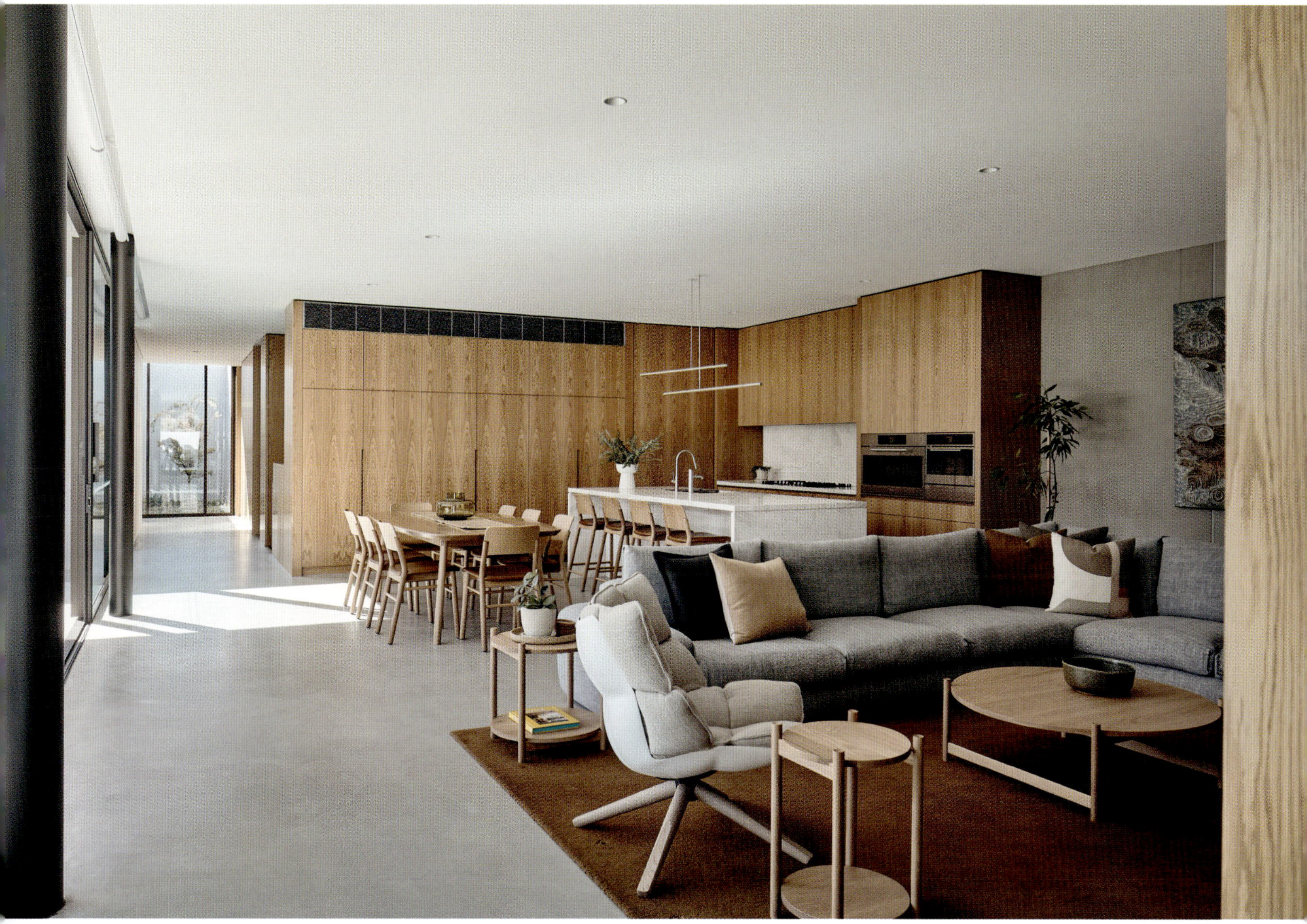

The minimalistic architecture is balanced by a neutral color palette and natural materials, with wood dominating the interior design. The juxtaposition of clean concrete structures with warm furnishings results in stylish and welcoming interiors. This effect is enhanced by the natural light that fills the rooms through large openings, seamlessly connecting the inside with the interior patio. The patio naturally becomes an extension of the house, with a roofed lounge area and an exterior kitchen with dining. Intertwined with greenery and an extensive pool, this space offers a compact yet comfortable outdoor experience that is completely private thanks to the concrete wrap.

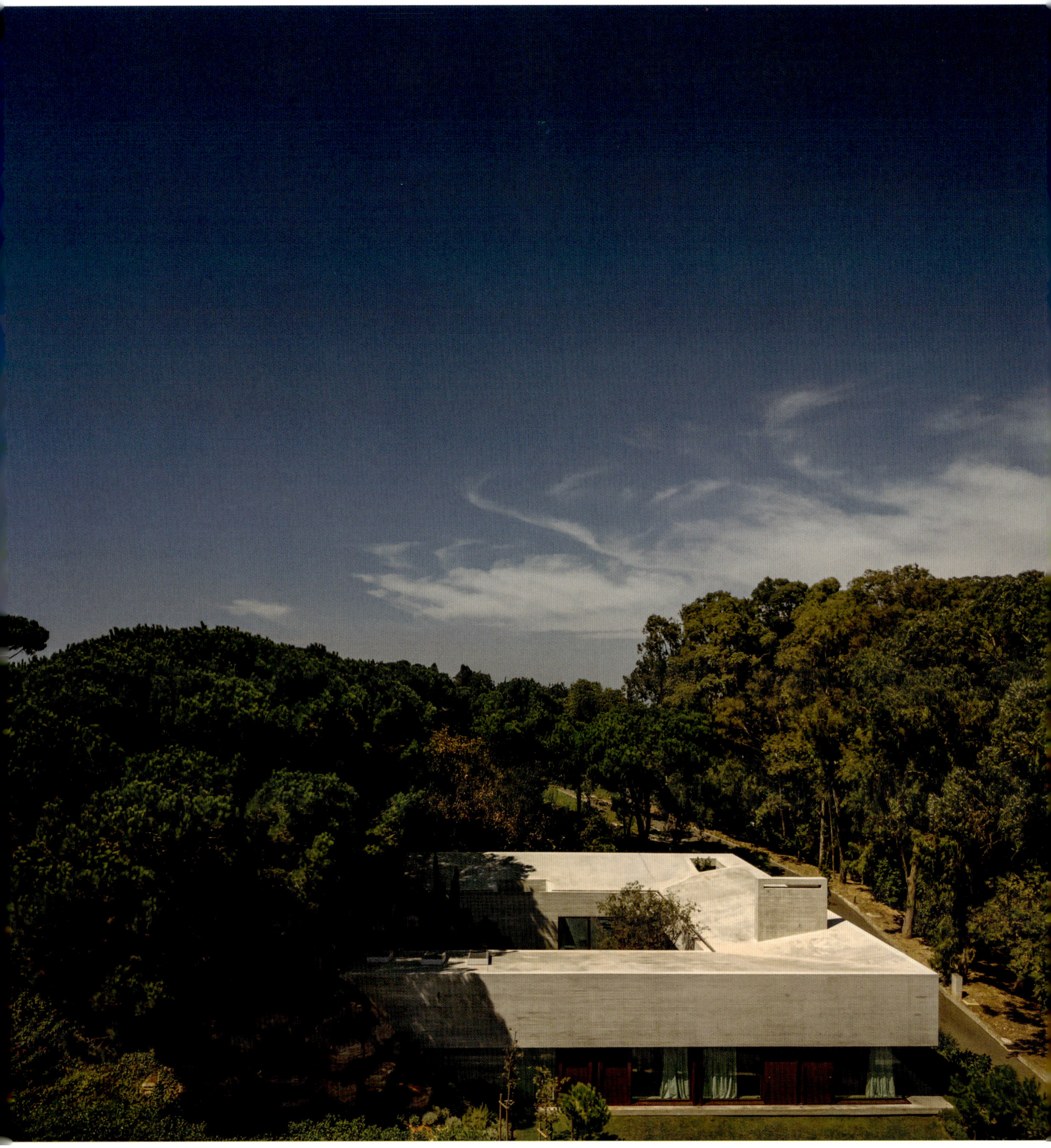

OODA was established in 2010 by Diogo Brito and Rodrigo Vilas-Boas, who were joined by Francisco Lencastre in 2011 and by João Jesus and Julião Pinto Leite in 2018. The five partners lead a team of sixty in offices in Porto and Lisbon. The studio's portfolio presents a large scope of projects ranging from single-family houses to hotels, institutional buildings, and master plans. The architects, as they state, "aim to challenge and change the traditional architectural model, leading to a more contemporary approach to the way of practice and promotion of architecture."

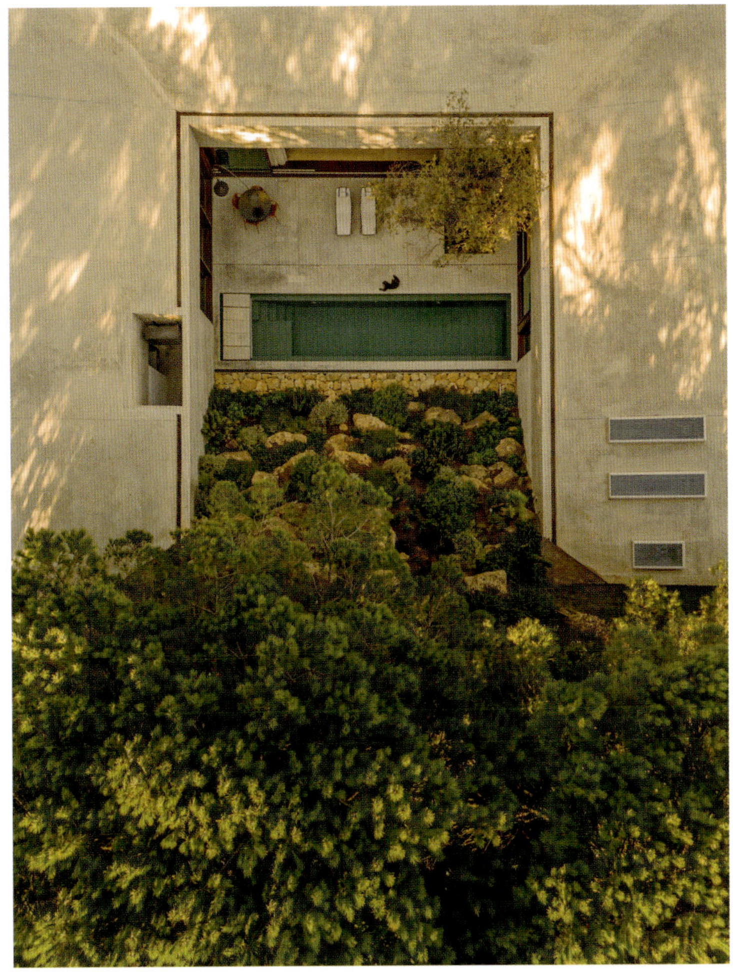

PROJECT: The Oeiras House
LOCATION: Oeiras, Portugal
YEAR: 2024
ARCHITECTS: OODA
PHOTOGRAPHY: Fernando Guerra

At the core of this project was the topography of the slope, which required the architects' flexible approach in designing the volume. As a result, the Oeiras House takes a U shape and is partly sunk into the incline of the terrain. Two of the three wings literally grow into the hill. This smooth connection was particularly important due to the fact that the hill is covered by dense greenery. The architects have managed to create a synergy between the natural and man-made environments. It is also an interesting example of how a patio can be the intermediary between the living space and the landscape. "Dense and strongly anchored on the slope, the mass levitates to let the soil flow and progress between the exterior and the center of the patio, with the unity and continuity of the vegetation," comment the architects.

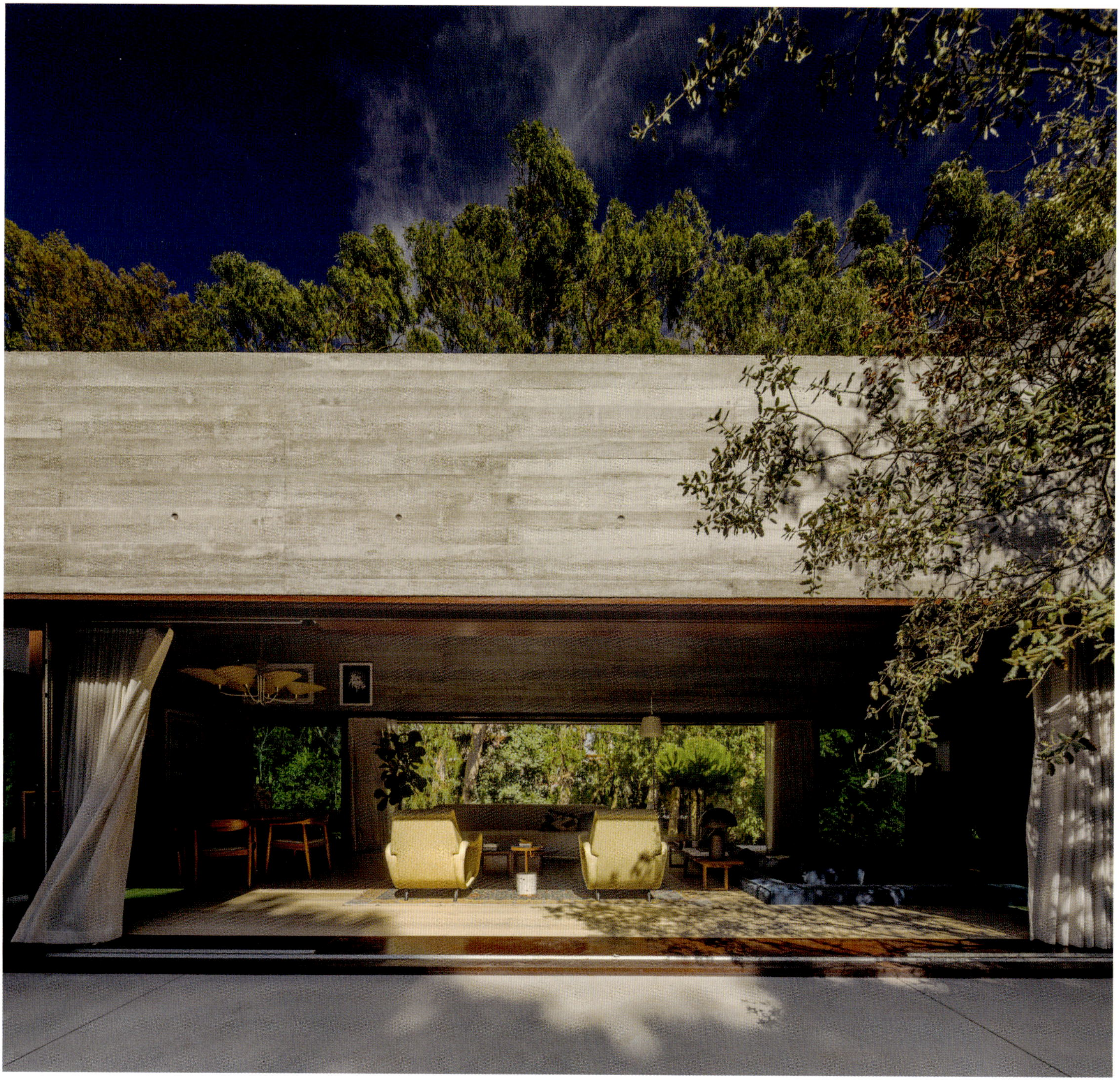

What is striking in the Oeiras House is the compact and distinctive form of the roof, which overhangs the thinner and largely glazed base of the volume. The openings connect the interiors with the street level but also open them to the patio. The central and partly buried courtyard becomes an embracing space that is both cozy and accessible from most of the interiors and remains open to the surrounding nature. Implanted in this striking seaside location, the house received a highly distinctive shape yet is well harmonized with the context. The wings, which clearly divide social and private spaces, embrace the patio in a way that invites the vegetation to become part of the interiors. There is even a tree planted on the surface of the courtyard, as a continuation of the landscape. The inhabitants' comfort in this quiet and green space is additionally enhanced by the pool.

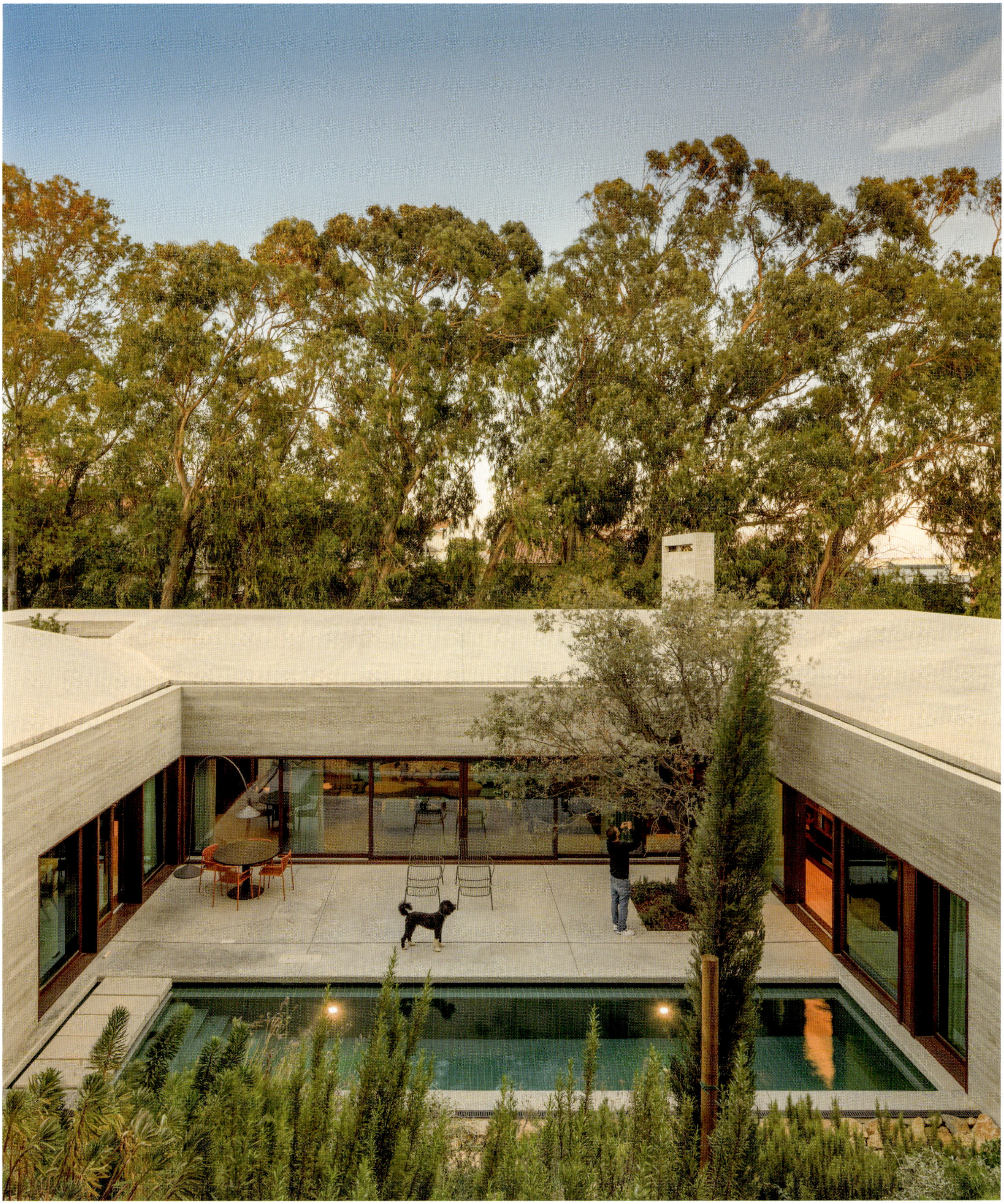

The patio visually connects the interiors of the everyday living area with the greenery of the slope, creating an inviting and relaxing space for the residents.

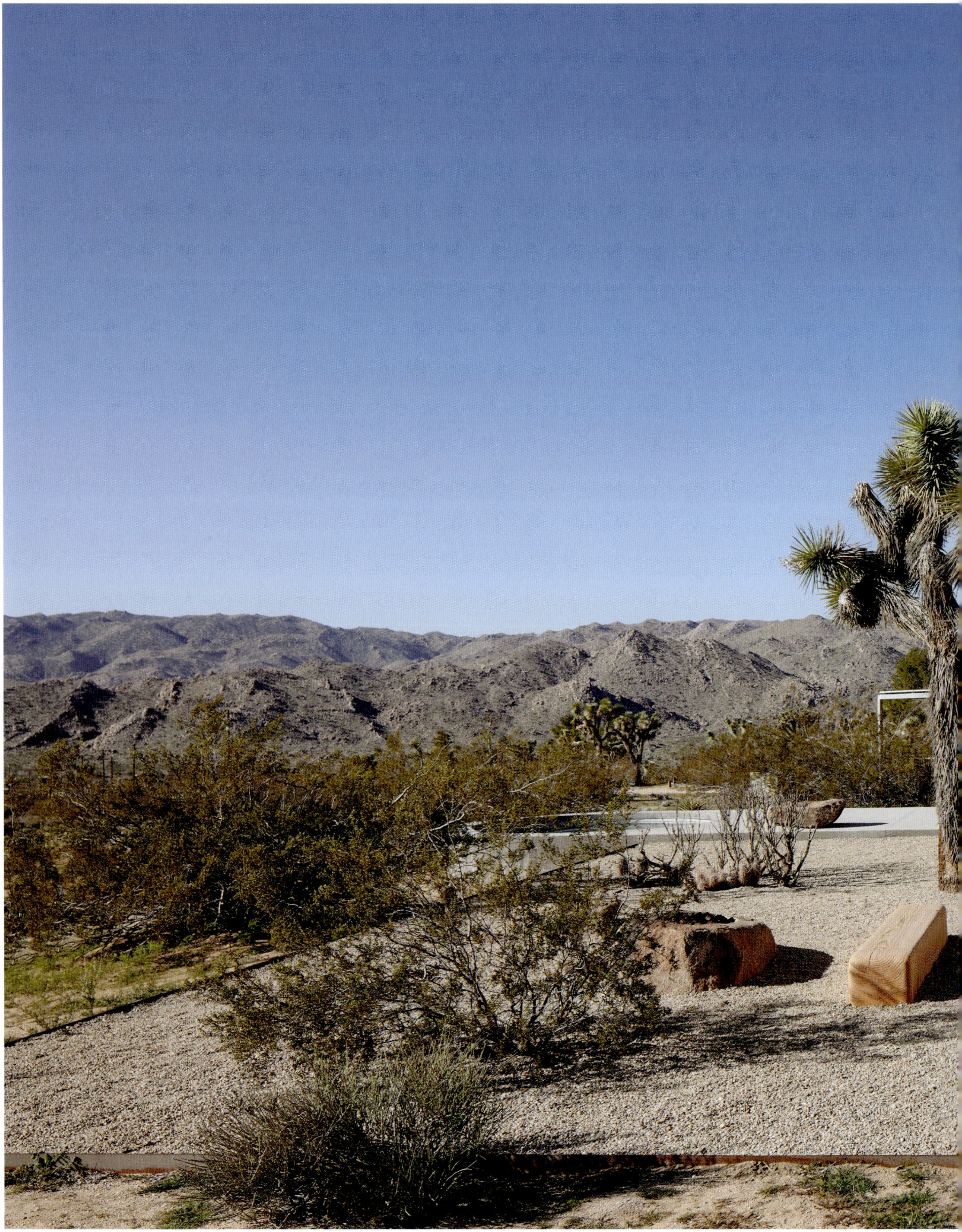

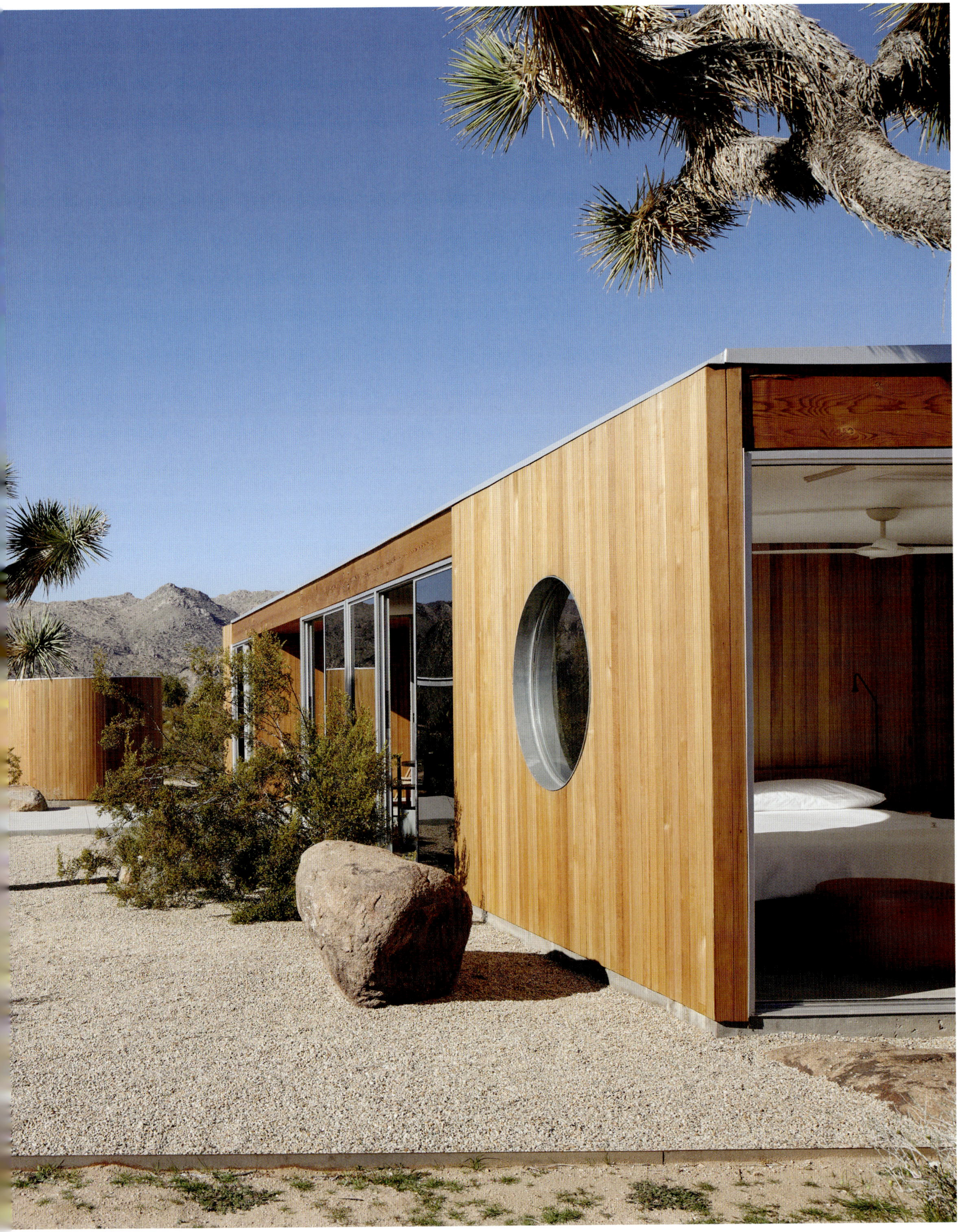

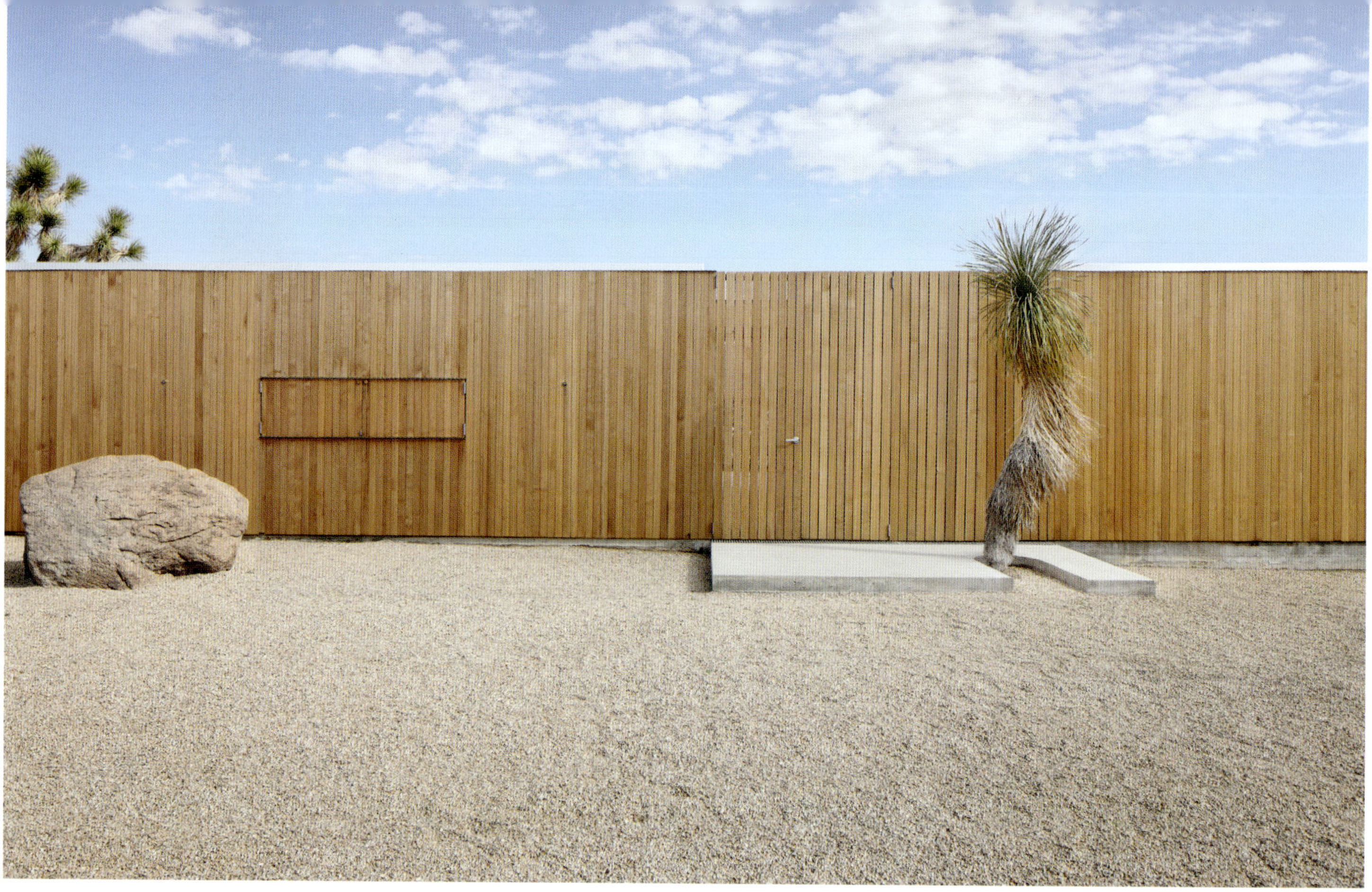

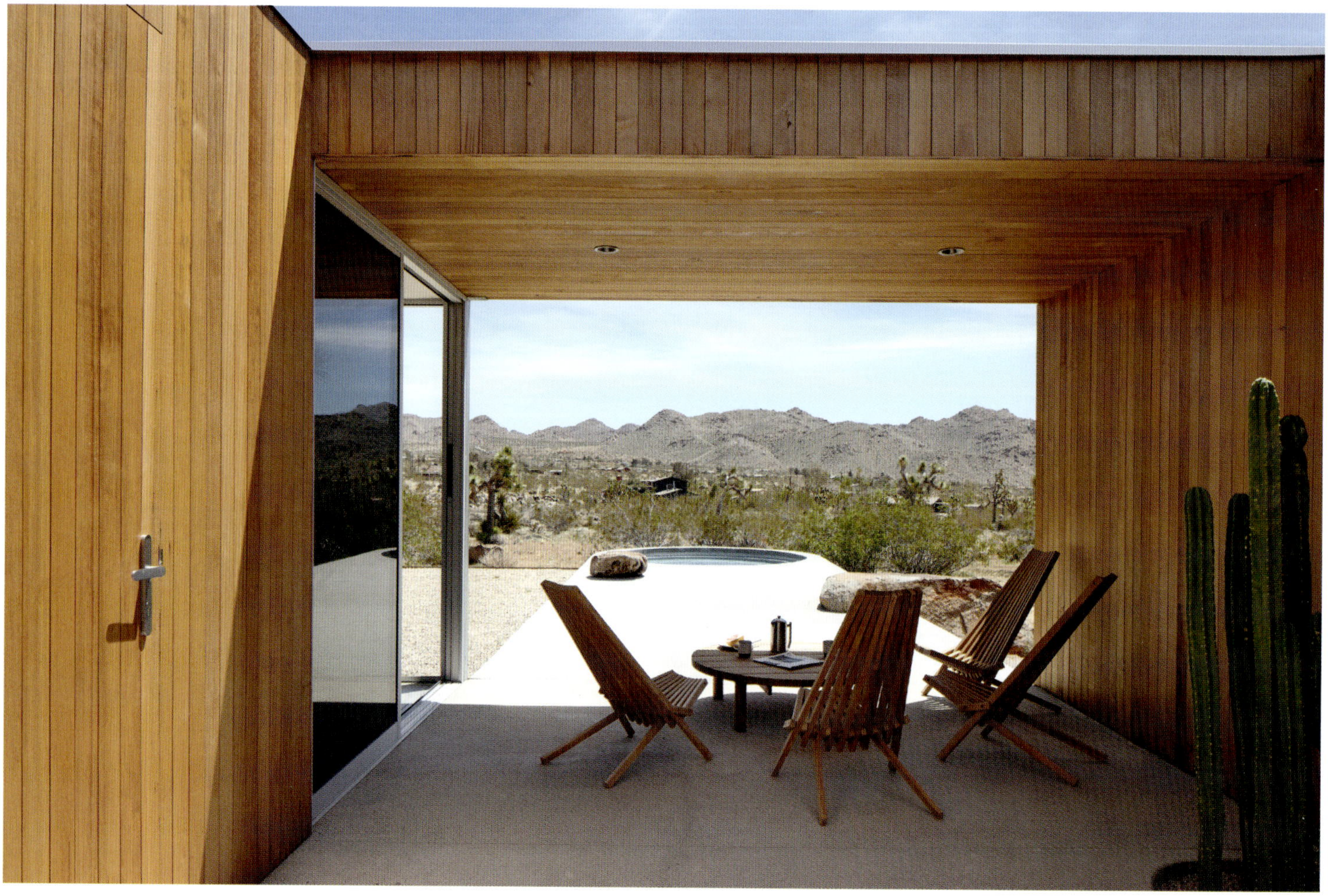

PROJECT: The Landing House
LOCATION: Joshua Tree, California, United States
YEAR: 2023
ARCHITECTS: Industry of All Nations
PHOTOGRAPHY: Ye Rin Mok

An important part of the Industry of All Nations (IOAN) brand DNA is utilizing ancestral methods paired with modern practices in manufacturing everyday goods. The team employed this approach, equally successful, in envisioning the Landing House, located on the premises of Joshua Tree National Park in California. Fernando Gerscovich of IOAN, a Buenos Aires-born architect, designed it together with his brothers Juan Diego and Patricio as a comfortable retreat in the desert environment, in a very sustainable manner. "We were determined to minimize disruptions of the natural landscape, so our design focused on integration that wouldn't disturb the surrounding plants and natural geography of the land," the team firmly states. Available as a vacation rental, the house is accessible through a private road leading up to the horizontal wall, entirely concealing the volume (and the view). The entrance doors are a kind of magic, since in crossing it, one not merely enters the house but also steps into the desert scenery.

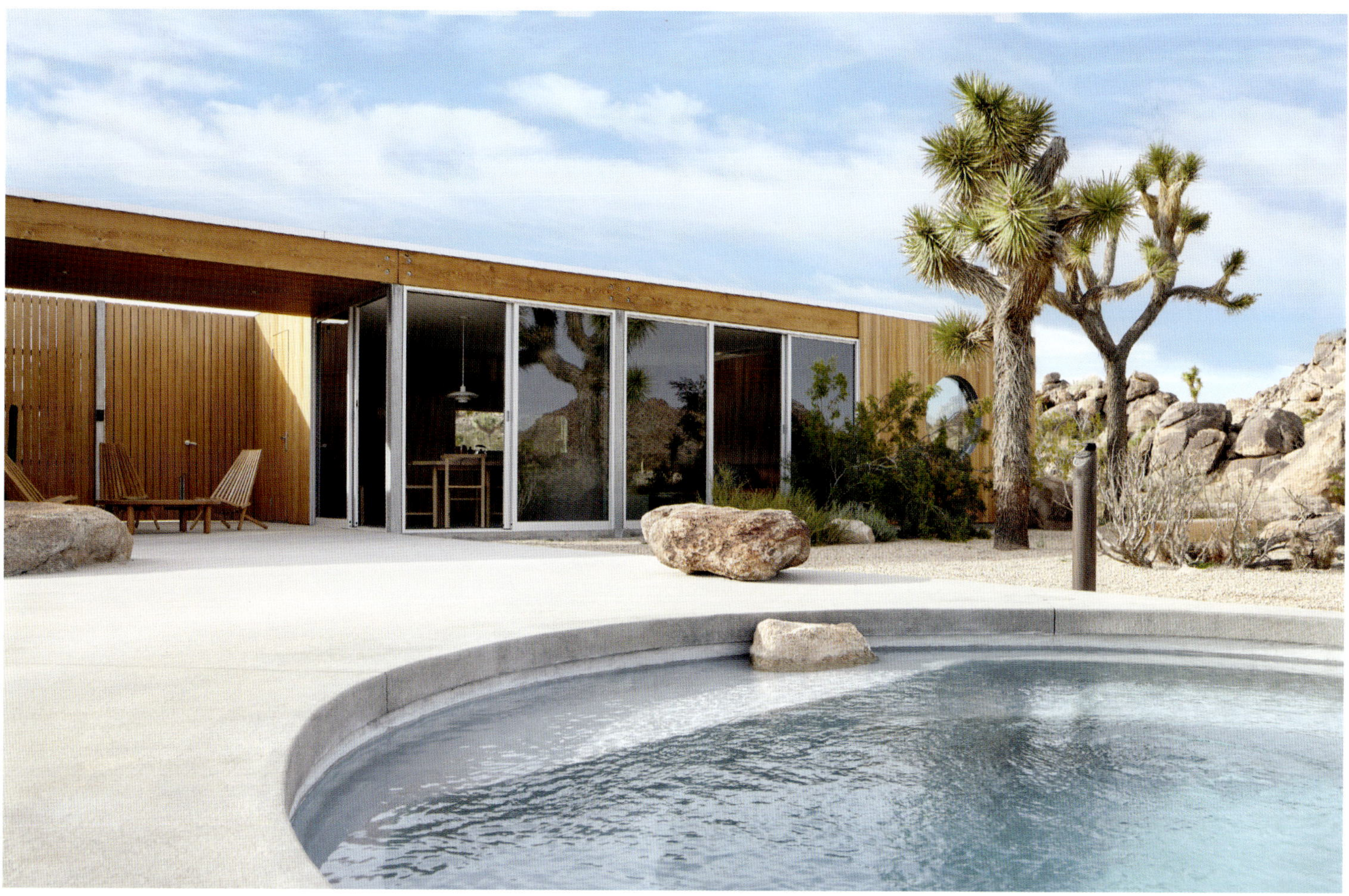

IOAN was founded in 2010 as a research, design, and development office, with a bold mission to rethink methods of production for consumer goods. With products ranging from hand-knit alpaca sweaters from Bolivia to espadrilles from Argentina and naturally dyed basics from India, the goal is to bring the manufacturing back to the regions where products and materials come from. Through collaboration with local communities, IOAN aims to restore the culture and identity of the world's iconic goods, as well as creating new designs in the spirit of environmental and social awareness but also fair trade.

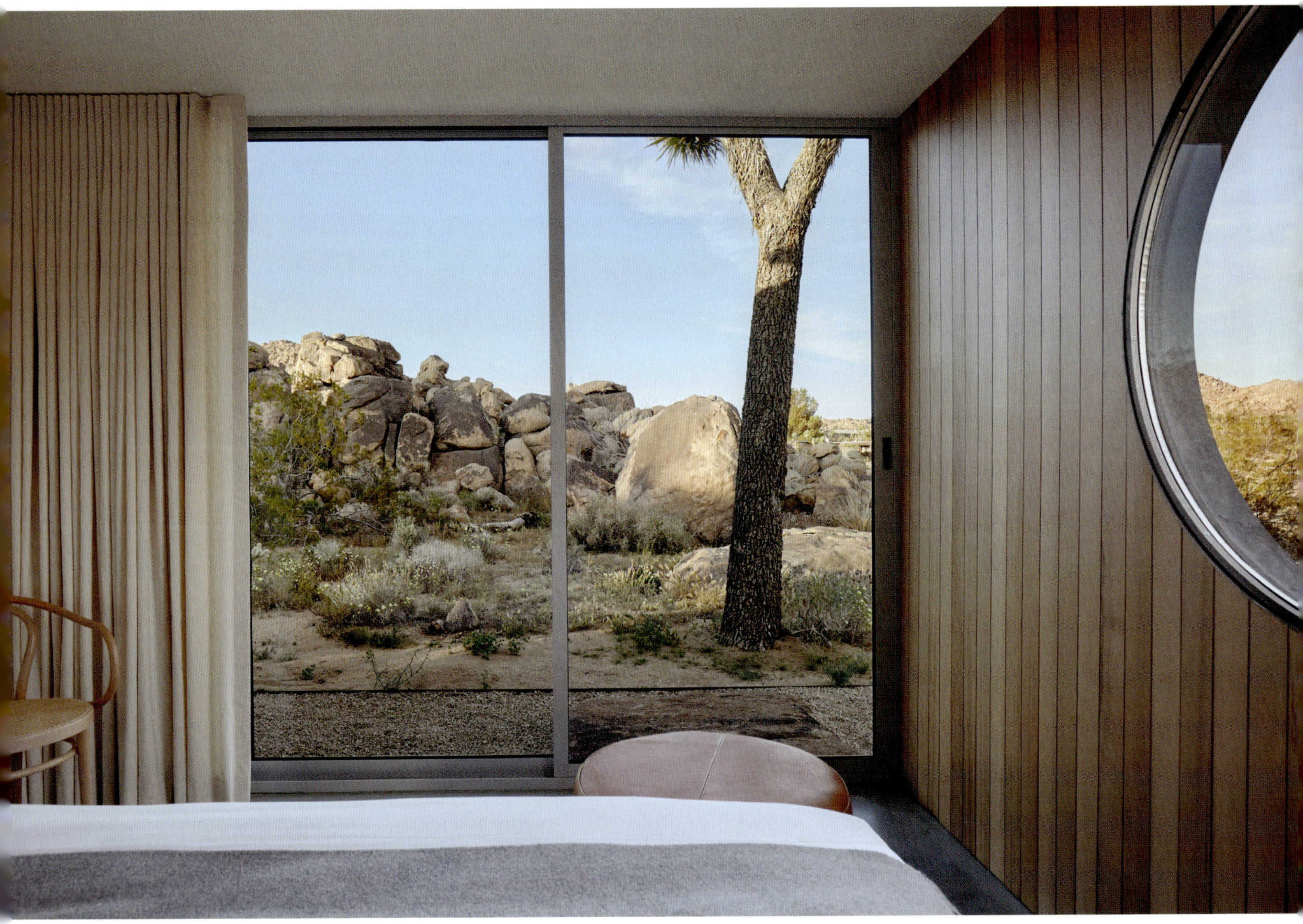

The sustainable wooden pavilion not only merges seamlessly with the desert landscape but also opens onto the majestic views through the openings and mostly the space of the patio.

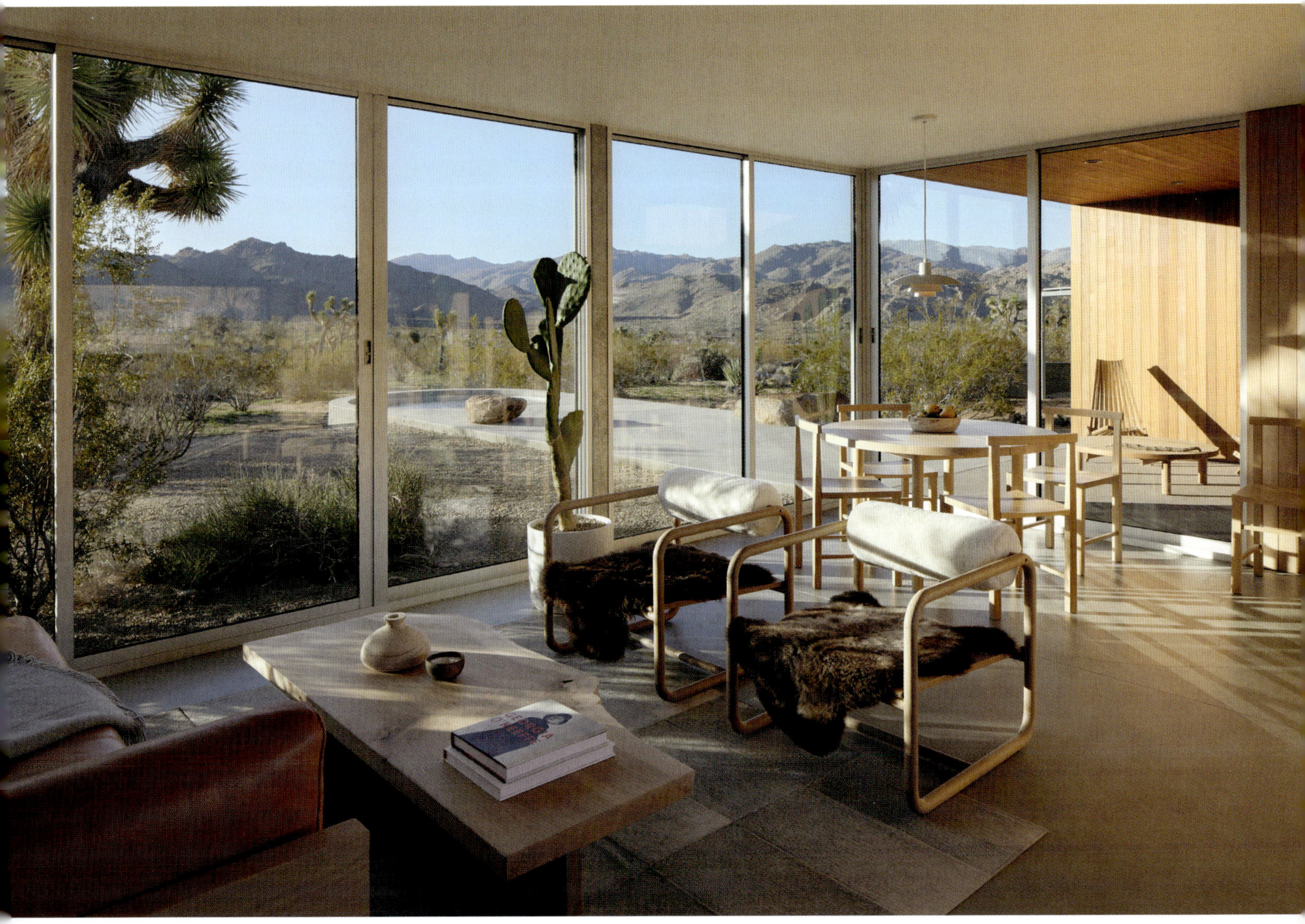

All areas of the house, arranged in a comfortable way, have been designed to invite one to step into the landscape both visually and physically, which is enabled thanks to the floor-to-ceiling sliding glass door in the facade overlooking the patio. The main goal was to nestle the house into the untouched surrounding, which, with its otherworldly views, the presence of iconic Joshua trees, and natural light patterns, has inevitably fueled the design process. The designer chose a modern aesthetic for the pavilion, but its layout and materiality blend well into the context. That thinking starts with the compact and low-profile volumetric space to reduce the intervention into the landscape to the minimum and is enhanced by natural materiality and hues used in the interiors, including cedar wall paneling and white oak furniture. The external shell has been realized with low-maintenance materials, such as concrete, dominating cedar, and glass, with the idea that the house will weather over time and thus fuse with the context even more organically.

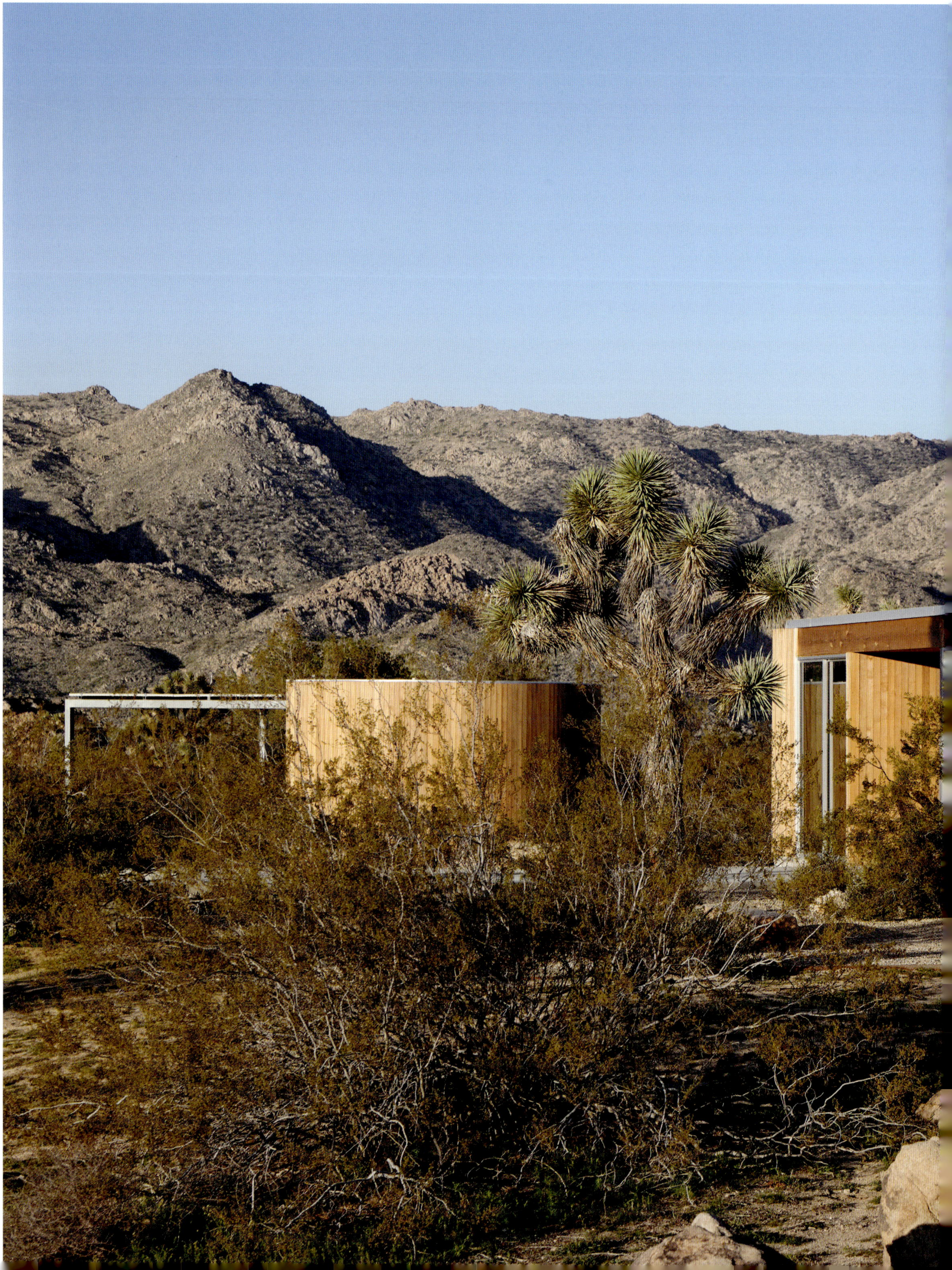

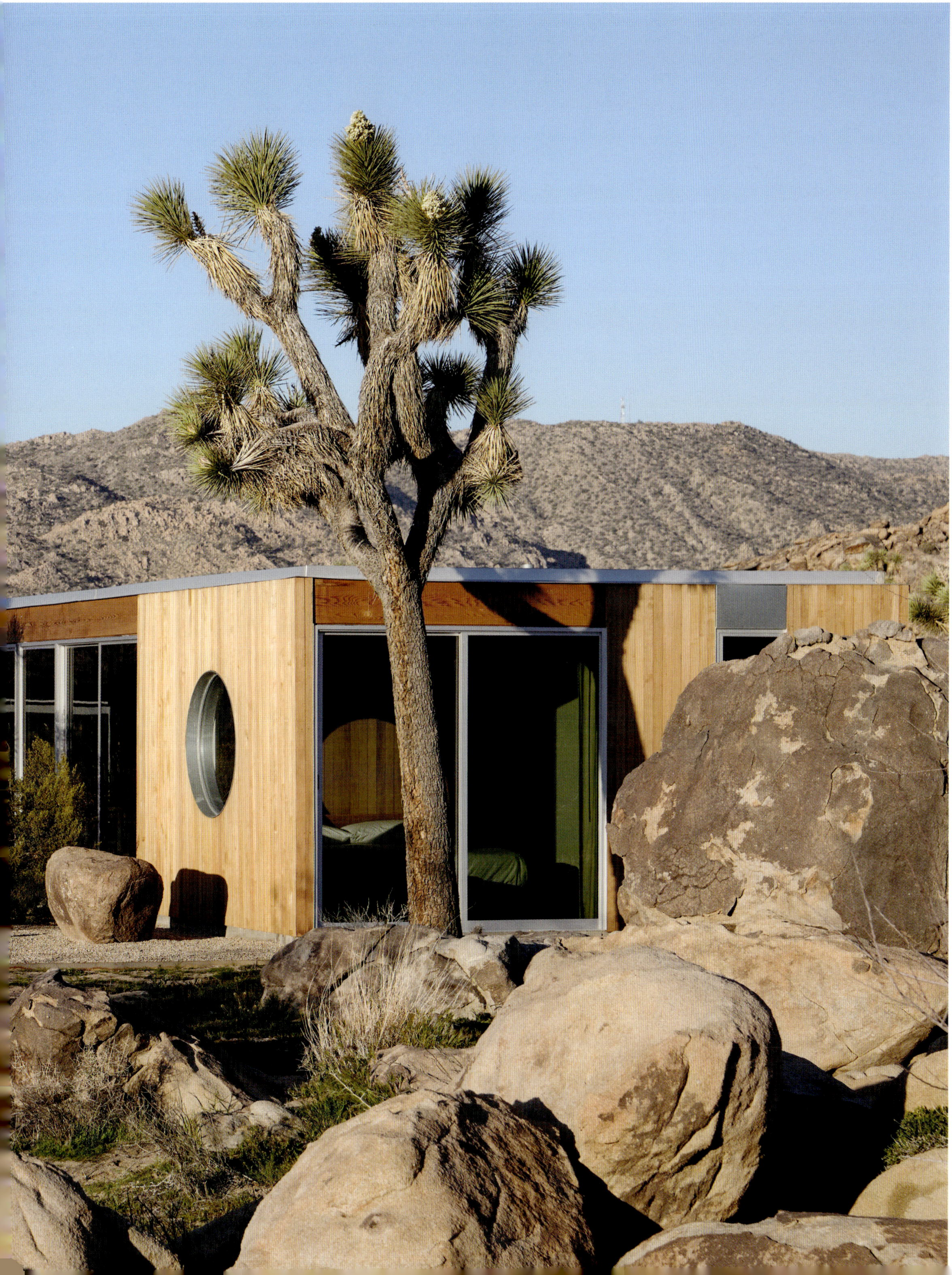

PROJECT: Casa Aspetto
LOCATION: San Francisco, California, United States
YEAR: 2024
ARCHITECTS: Medium Plenty
PHOTOGRAPHY: Shade Degges

Designed for a family of four with two young kids, the three-story Casa Aspetto is striking, with a fancifully shaped facade that frames the views. Its modern expression distinctively stands out against the San Francisco cityscape of iconic townhouses. The project, realized by Medium Plenty, began as a renovation and evolved into a full rebuild, with homeowners taking an active part in envisioning their "forever home" that would be perfect for their needs and wishes. The result is quite refined. Spaces have been organized much more efficiently with many socializing areas, where the family can enjoy spending time together, including a spacious living room that has been fully integrated with the backyard patio and garden. The architects' main objective was to create a common space that is full of sunlight and seamlessly connects indoors and out. This is made possible thanks to fully foldable corner windows, which blur the border and leave an unobstructed view onto the backyard. The outdoor part of this easily expandable living room is partly roofed by the structure of the terrace on the third story, making it very spacious.

The living room, with its stylish arrangement, carefully selected materials and textures, and pared-down yet refined color palette, offers tranquility and comfort. This is enhanced by the sunlight entering through the large openings, which act as interior-exterior connectors. The inside perspective reveals another advantage of this well-planned patio, which is the backyard garden. Designed by MFLA and James Munden, it is filled with original plants and framed with solid stone slabs. This green space turns the whole back courtyard into a true sanctuary of calm, ideal for relaxation and enjoying family life.

Fully integrated backyard patio is a valuable extension to the living room, enhanced by the adjacent garden designed by MFLA and James Munden, which together form a spot of serenity in the townhouse.

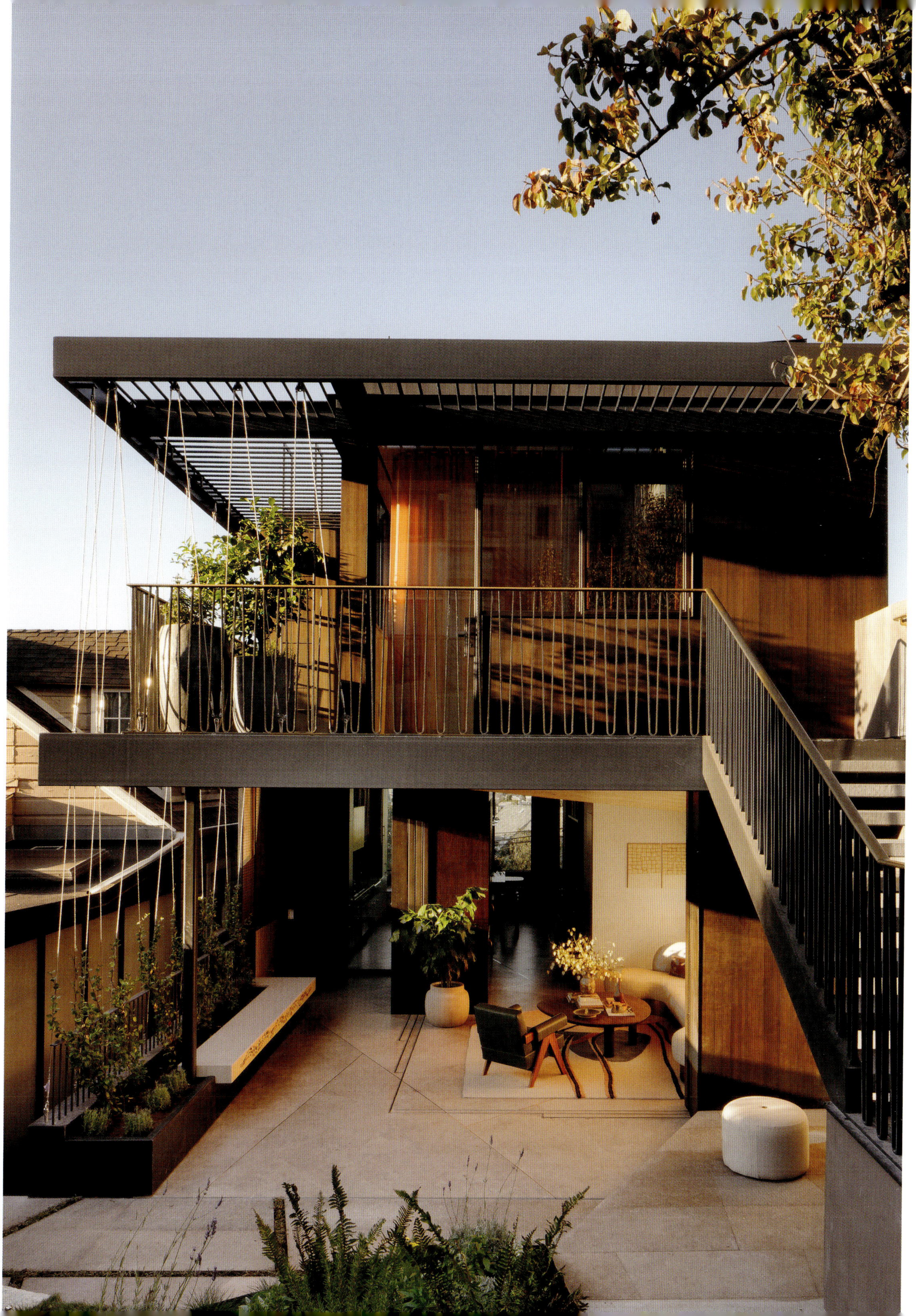

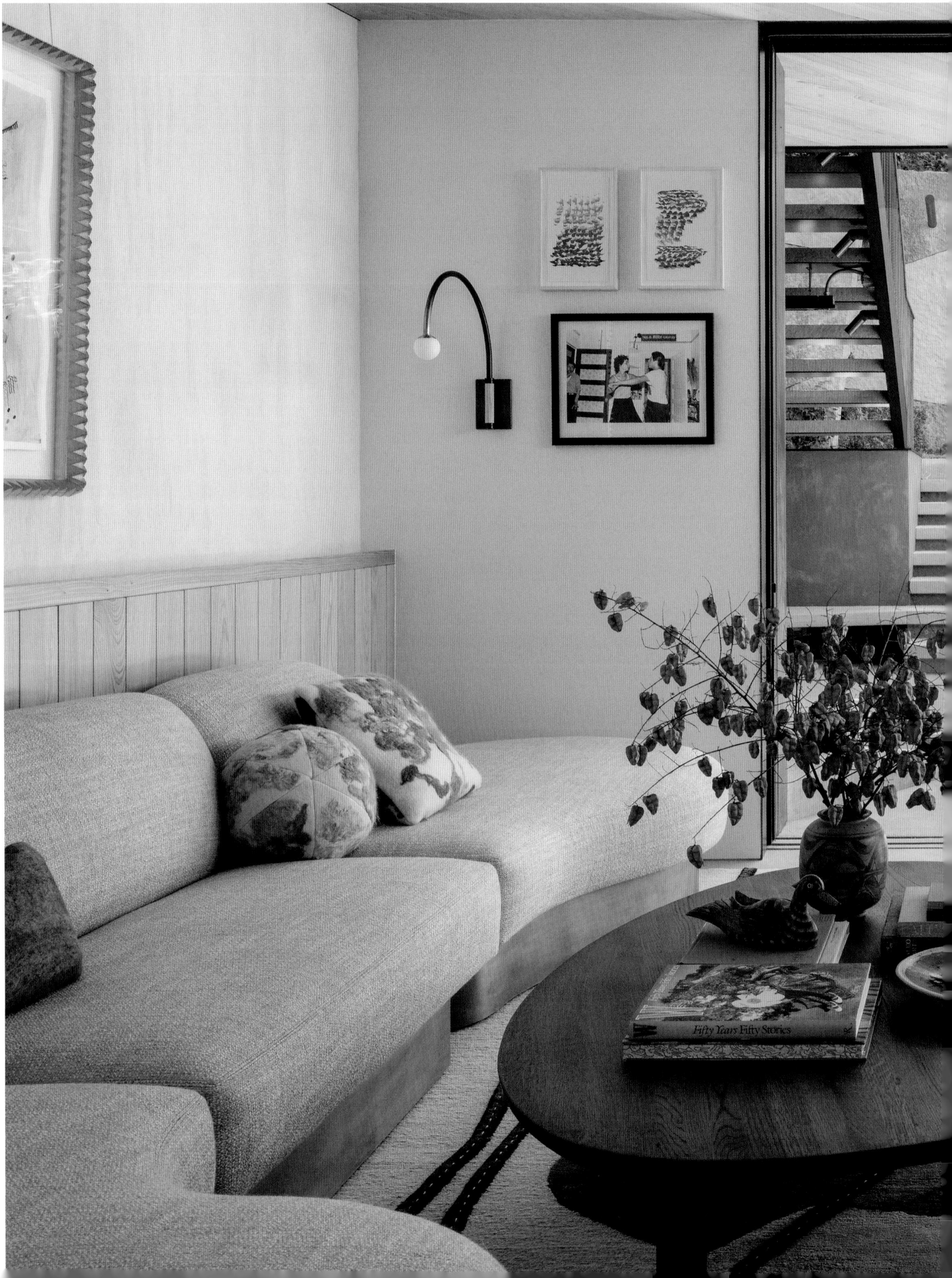
Fifty Years Fifty Stories

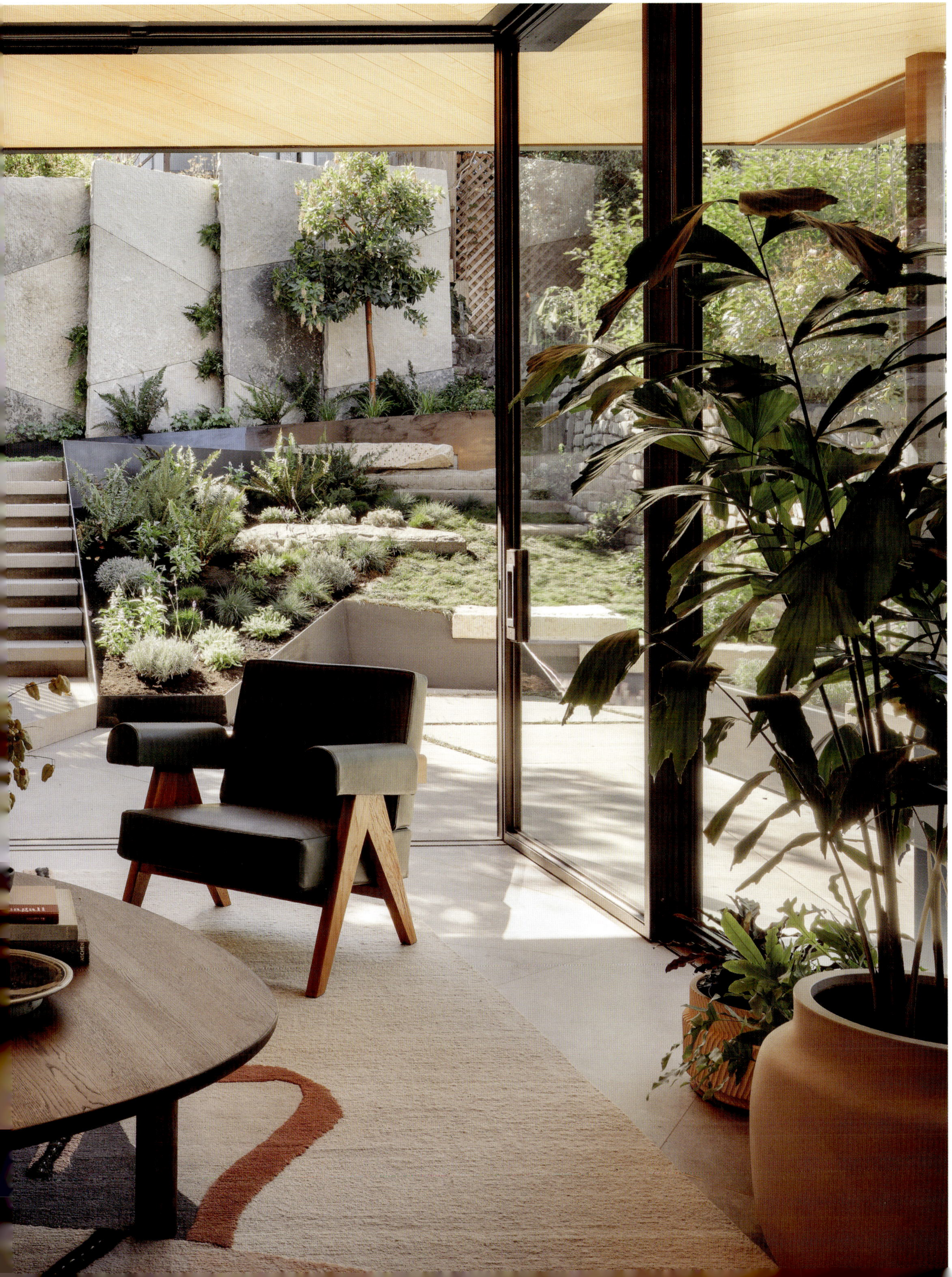

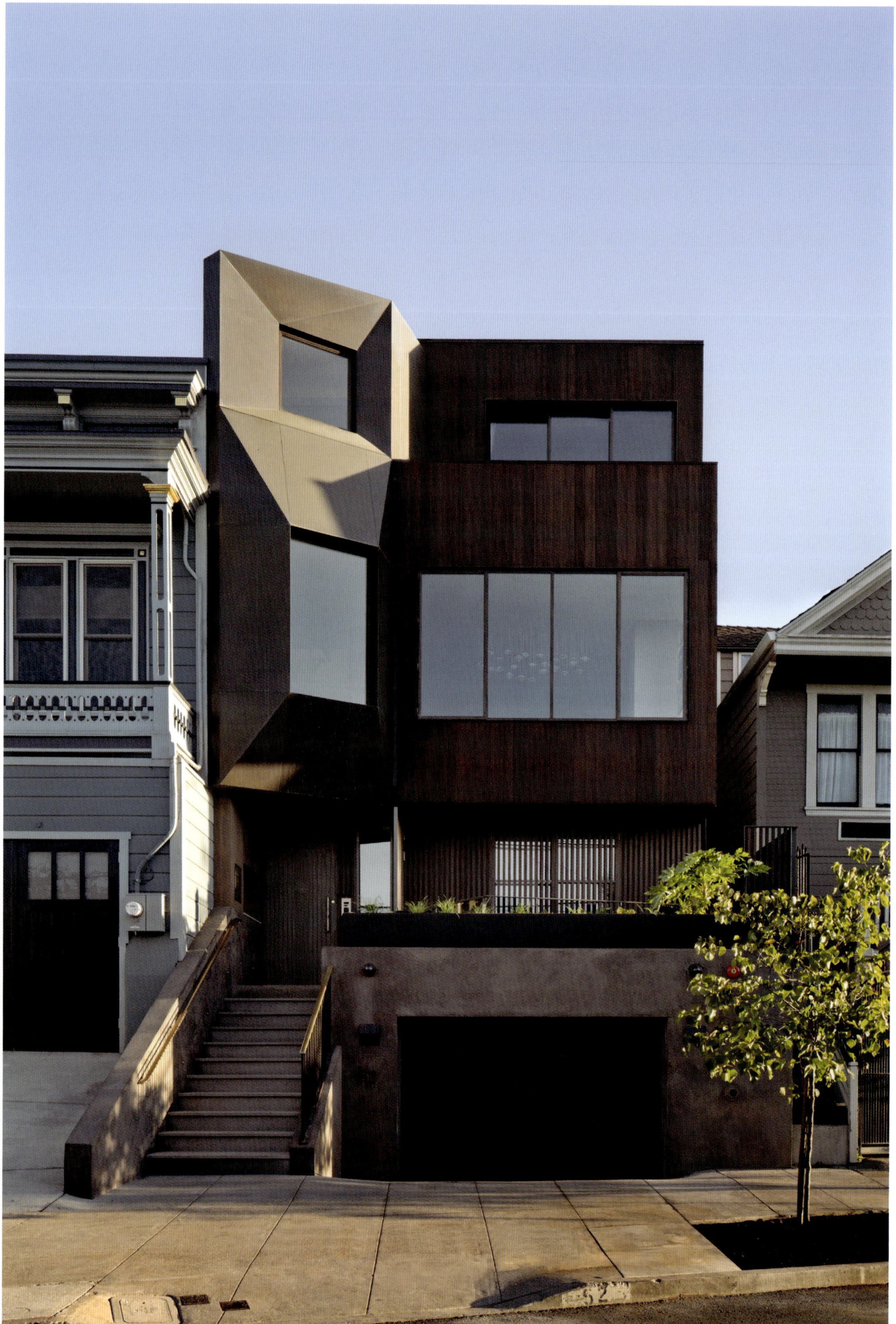

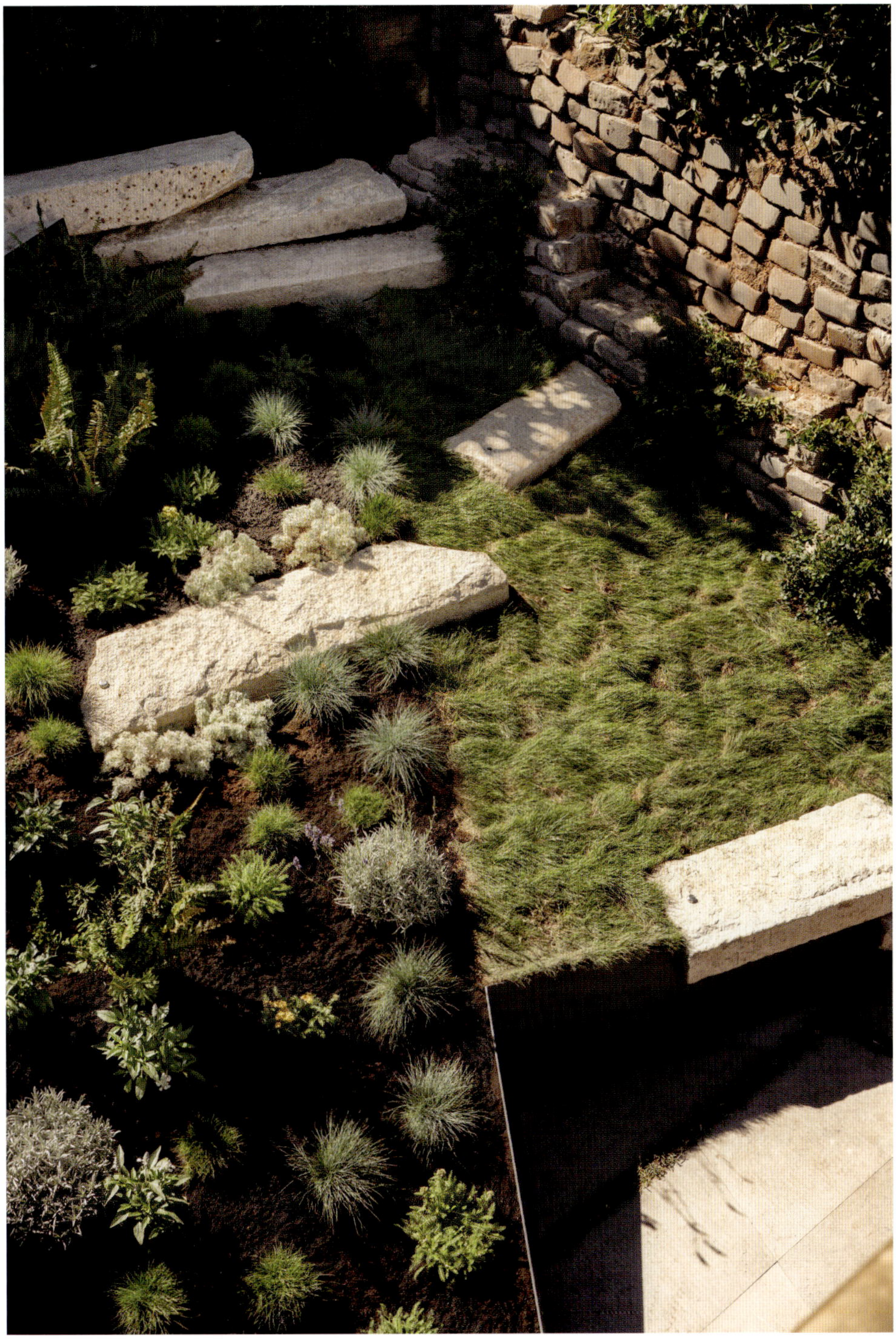

Founded in 2010 by Gretchen Krebs and Ian Read, Medium Plenty is a boutique architecture and interior-design practice with offices in Oakland and Sonoma. Specializing in residential projects, the team employs a holistic approach to design and creates bespoke realizations tailor-made for future residents' lifestyles. "Every detail is always carefully considered, honored, and elevated through an exploration of light, materiality, and space," they stress.

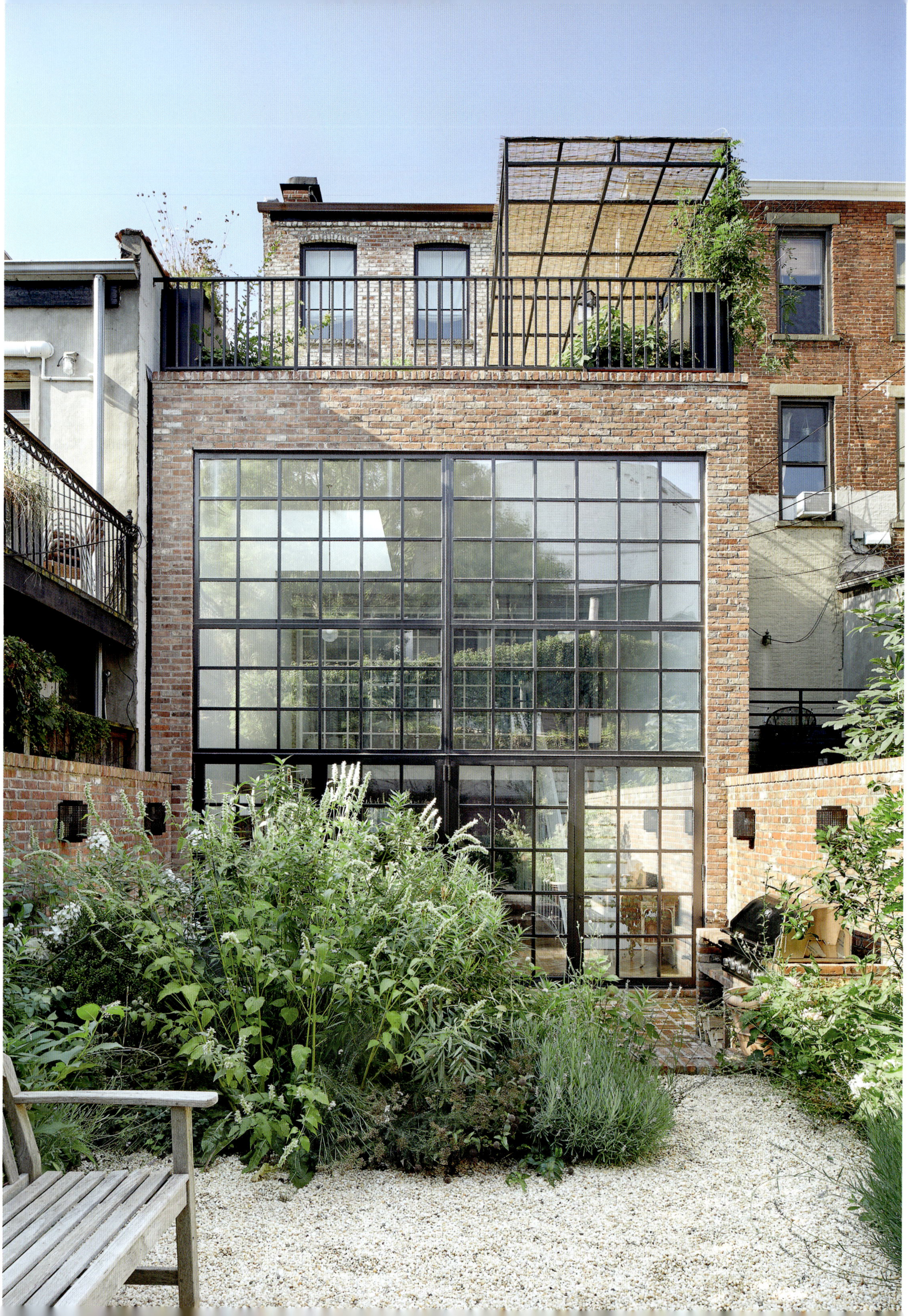

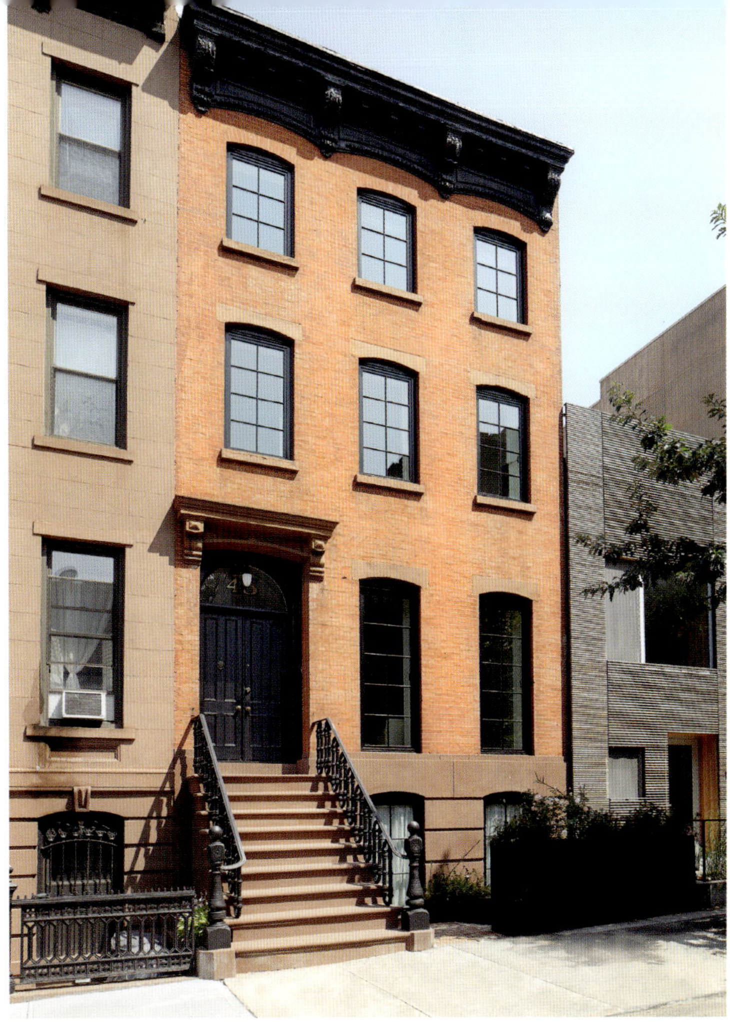

PROJECT: Cube | House
LOCATION: Brooklyn, New York, United States
YEAR: 2022
ARCHITECTS: Palette Architecture
PHOTOGRAPHY: Emily Gilbert

From the outset, the main goal of the renovation of this historical brownstone Brooklyn townhouse from the late 1800s was to bring it back to its original glory. This significant revitalization, however, brought much more. The addition of a new volume, a double-height cube in the rear yard, gave the building contemporary flair. "The form of the cube allows for a variety of outdoor spaces, and the carefully crafted openings accentuate connections to nature," explains Peter Miller, one of the studio's partners. The all-glazed facade connects the house beautifully with the back patio. These openings are also a perfect source of natural light, yet not the only one. A large and asymmetrical skylight in the upper face of this simple architectural volume allows residents to see the sun's trajectory and track weather. It also serves as a connector with the rooftop terrace of the extension.

Cube | House presents two faces, a traditional townhouse facade and a modern cube-shaped addition in the rear yard.

The spacious yet minimally furnished interior of the cube addition is quite stunning. There is not a single superfluous element in the double-height dining space, the kitchen area, or the library-mezzanine above it. The extension is full of light, air, and elegance. The rear face of the cube consists of four full-length doors and a gridded glass curtain wall that puts the full focus on the brick backyard patio and invites the landscape inside. The native grasses and shrubs in the garden also create a relaxing outdoor space, which extends the functionality of the house even beyond the cube. Palette Architecture blended tradition and modernity with a great sense of balance between historical architectural details, which define the higher floors, and the contemporary, clean, and sharp character of the garden level and cube.

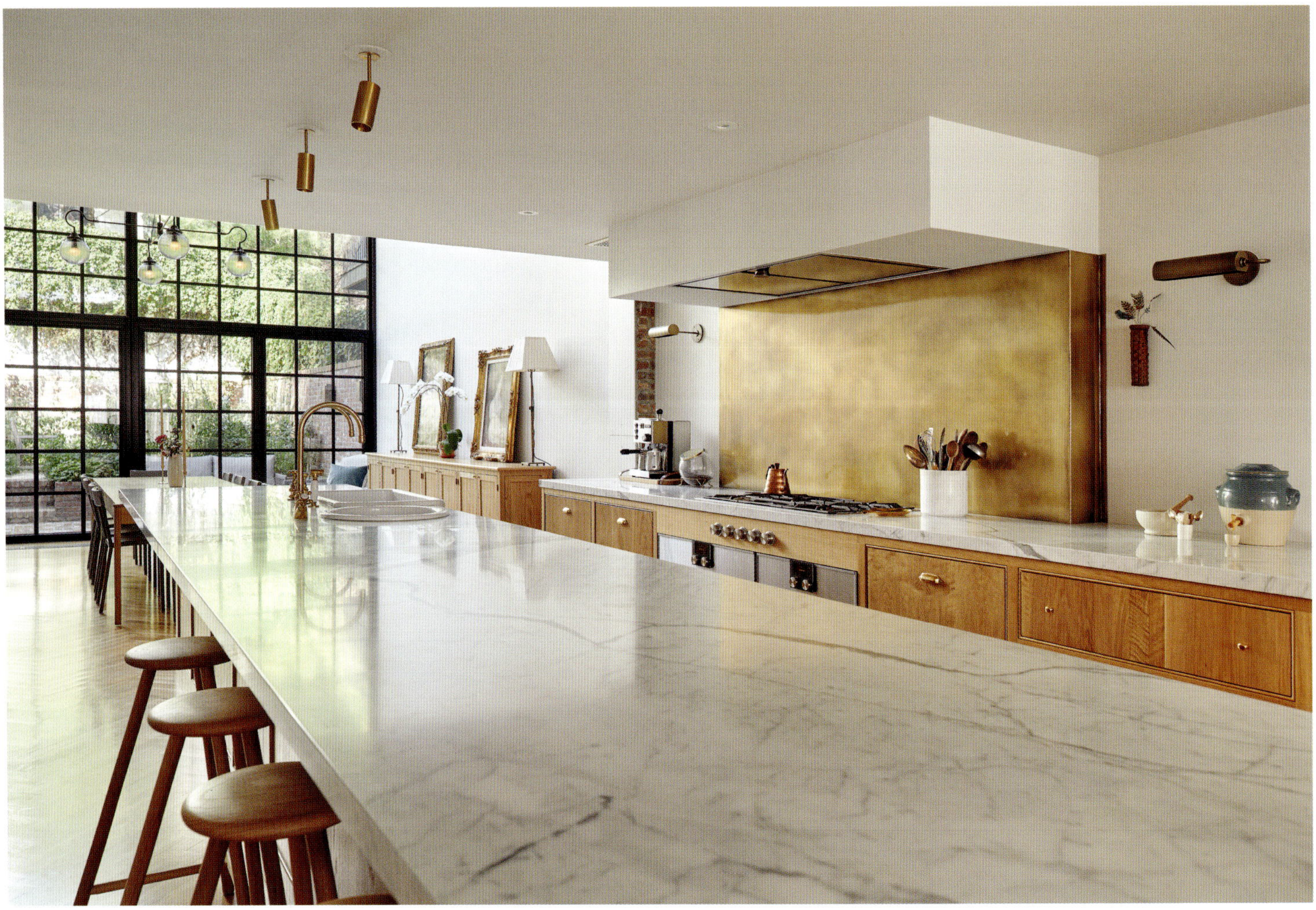

This New York City– and Los Angeles–based architecture and design practice was founded in 2010 by three partners: Peter Miller, John Sunwoo, and Jeff Wandersman. "What ties us together is a shared belief that exceptional design is the product of focused problem-solving," states the team of professionals, with diverse backgrounds. The projects range in scale and typology from education to residential architecture, from facility modernizations to interior retrofits. Each realization aims at creating spaces that enhance everyday experiences.

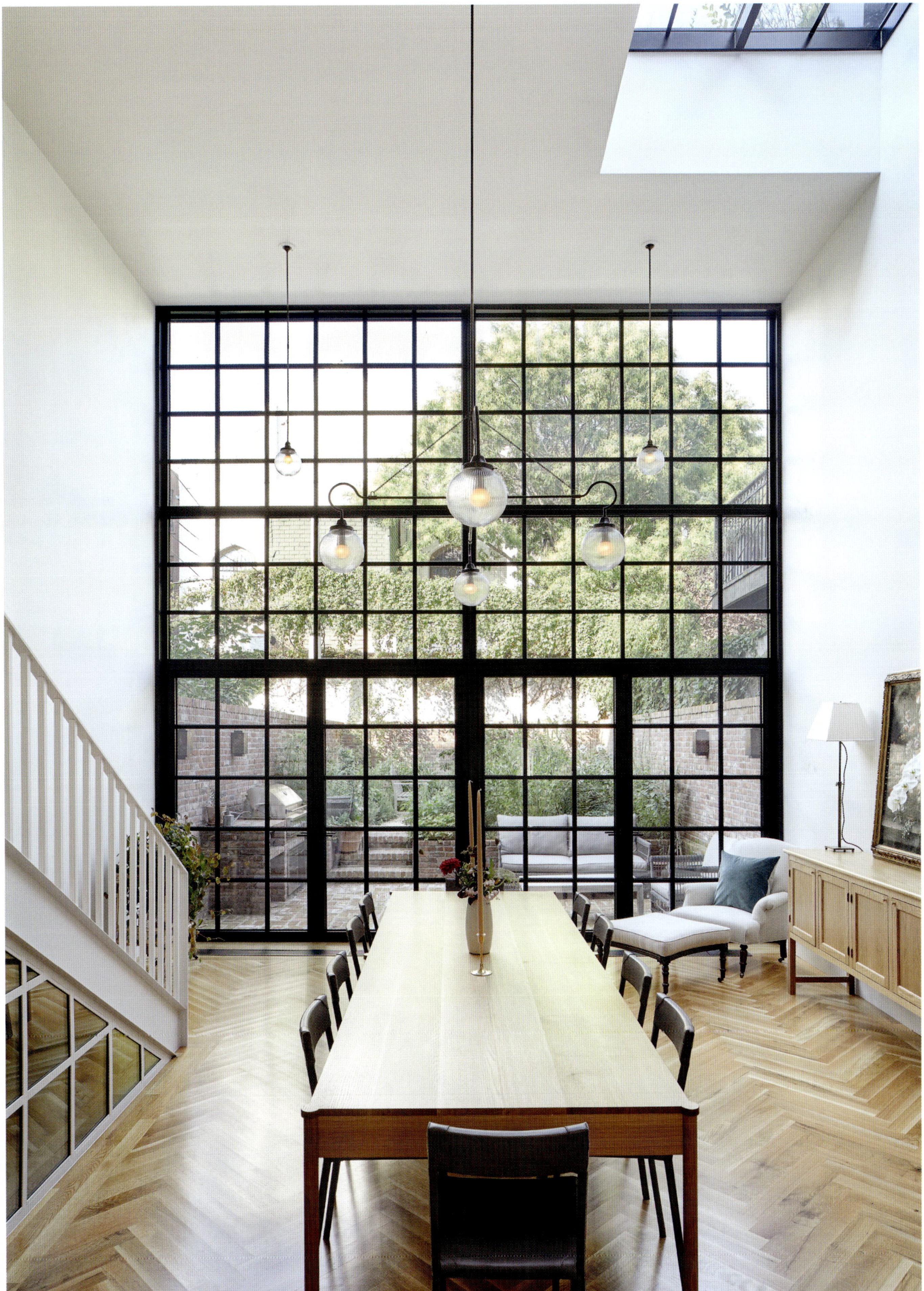

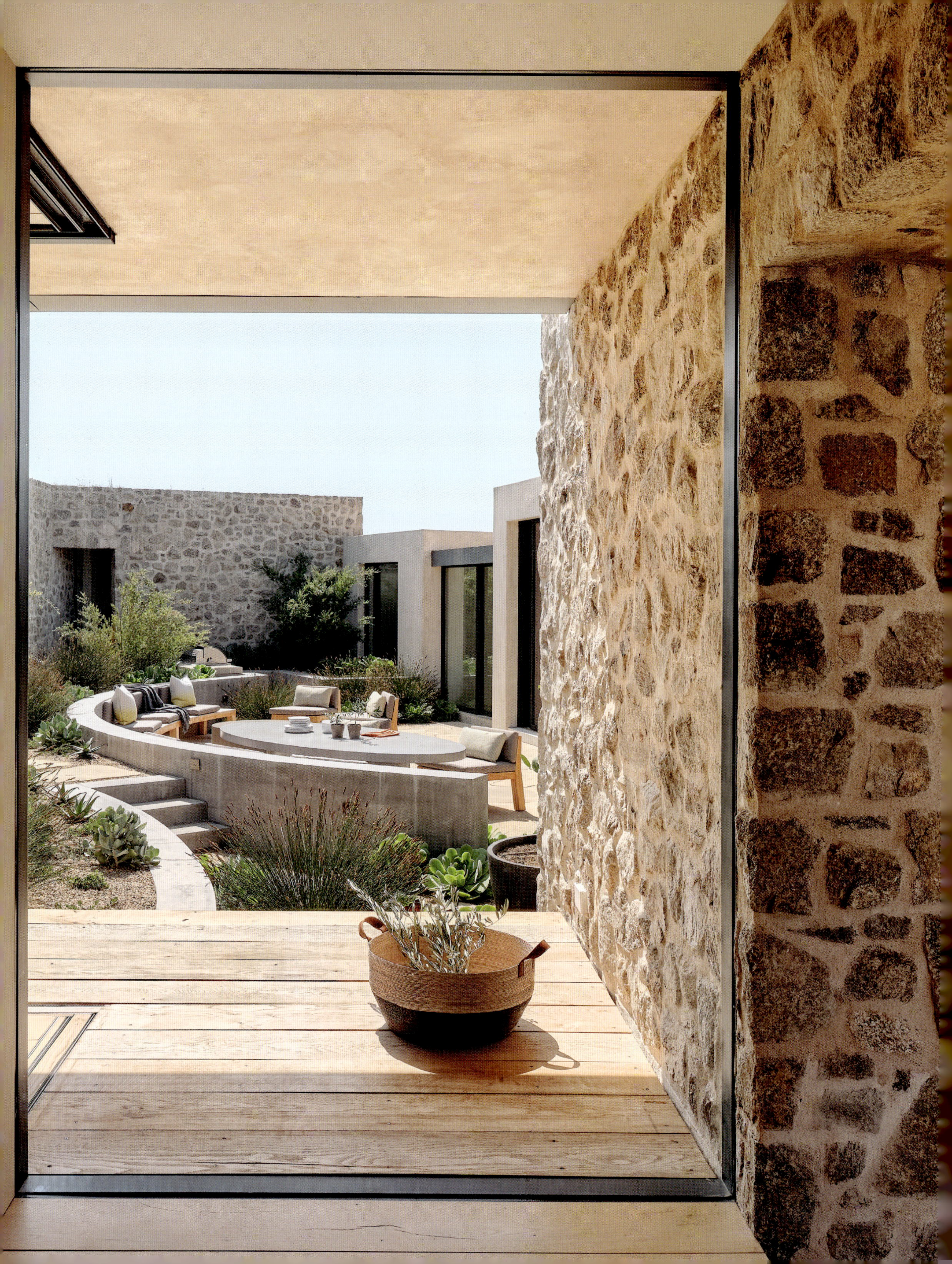

PROJECT: Mal Paso Residence
YEAR: 2022
LOCATION: Big Sur, California, United States
ARCHITECTS: Studio Schicketanz
PHOTOGRAPHY: Joe Fletcher, Tim Griffith

Perfectly integrated with the local topography, Mal Paso Residence is an ideal hideaway. Gabriele Mary Ann Schicketanz and her team, inspired by the stunning landscape, adapted the site by carving a shelf into the slope. Hidden from the main road, Highway 1, the house is nestled into the hillside, surrounded by the unique beauty of nature. Facing west, it offers breathtaking views of the Pacific Ocean, while the central patio provides a sheltered area from coastal winds. To minimize the impact of the architecture on the natural surroundings, the architects chose local granite and a neutral color palette. Achieving harmony between the interior and exterior was a key focus of the project. Another goal was to achieve net-zero energy usage to power the house and charge two electric vehicles, as well as heat up water for the pool. This is made possible through the use of solar panels and, when grid power is not available, Tesla Power Walls.

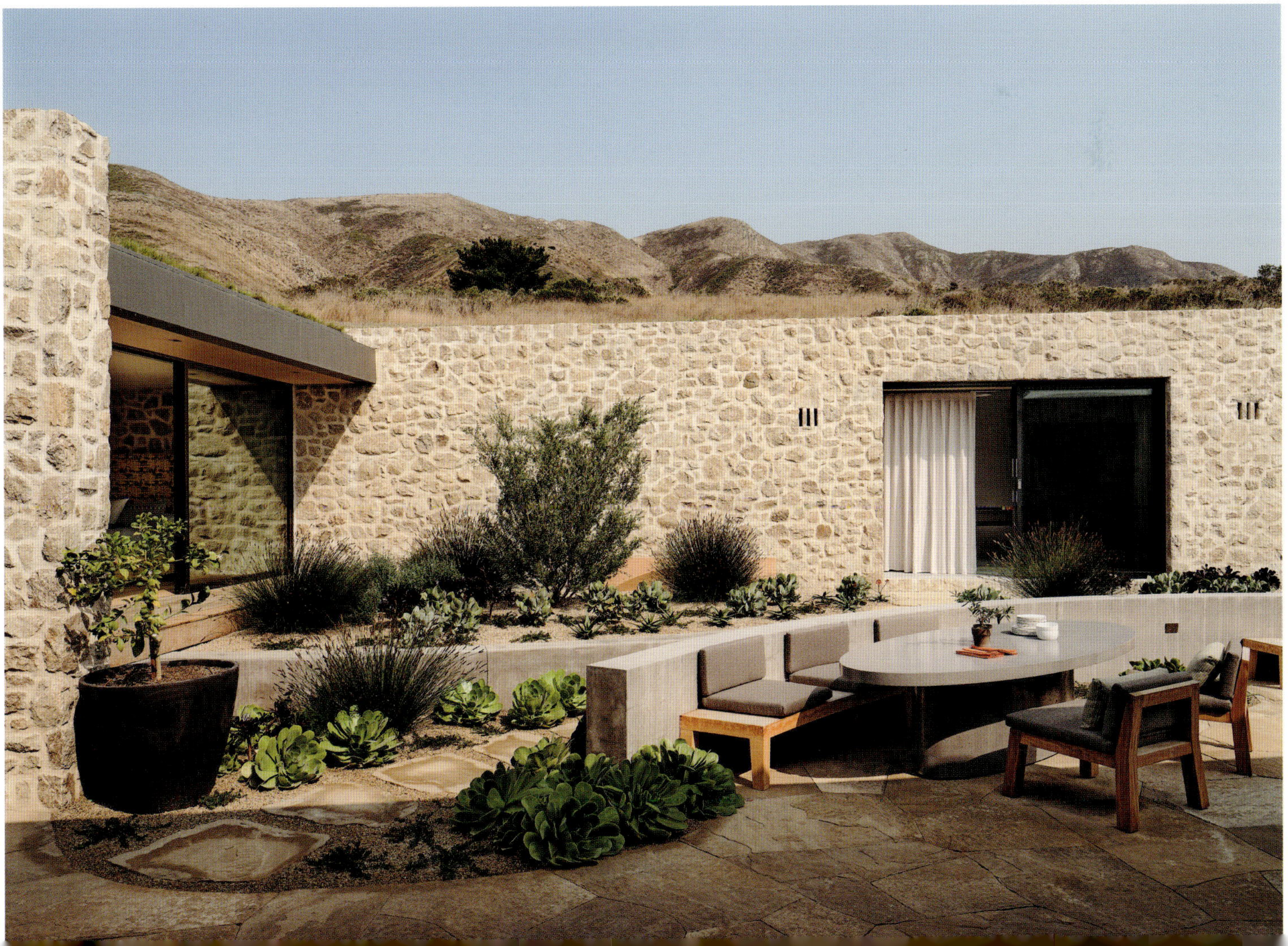

In addition to beautifully designed interiors furnished with custom-made beds and shelves, as well as high-end pieces of furniture, the inhabitants can enjoy the front pool with a view, a game room, and a den. The inner courtyard, with a sinusoid arrangement mimicking the curvatures of the gentle hill, is a place dedicated to relaxation. Large glass openings in the rooms surrounding it allow views into and across this central part from various areas of the house.

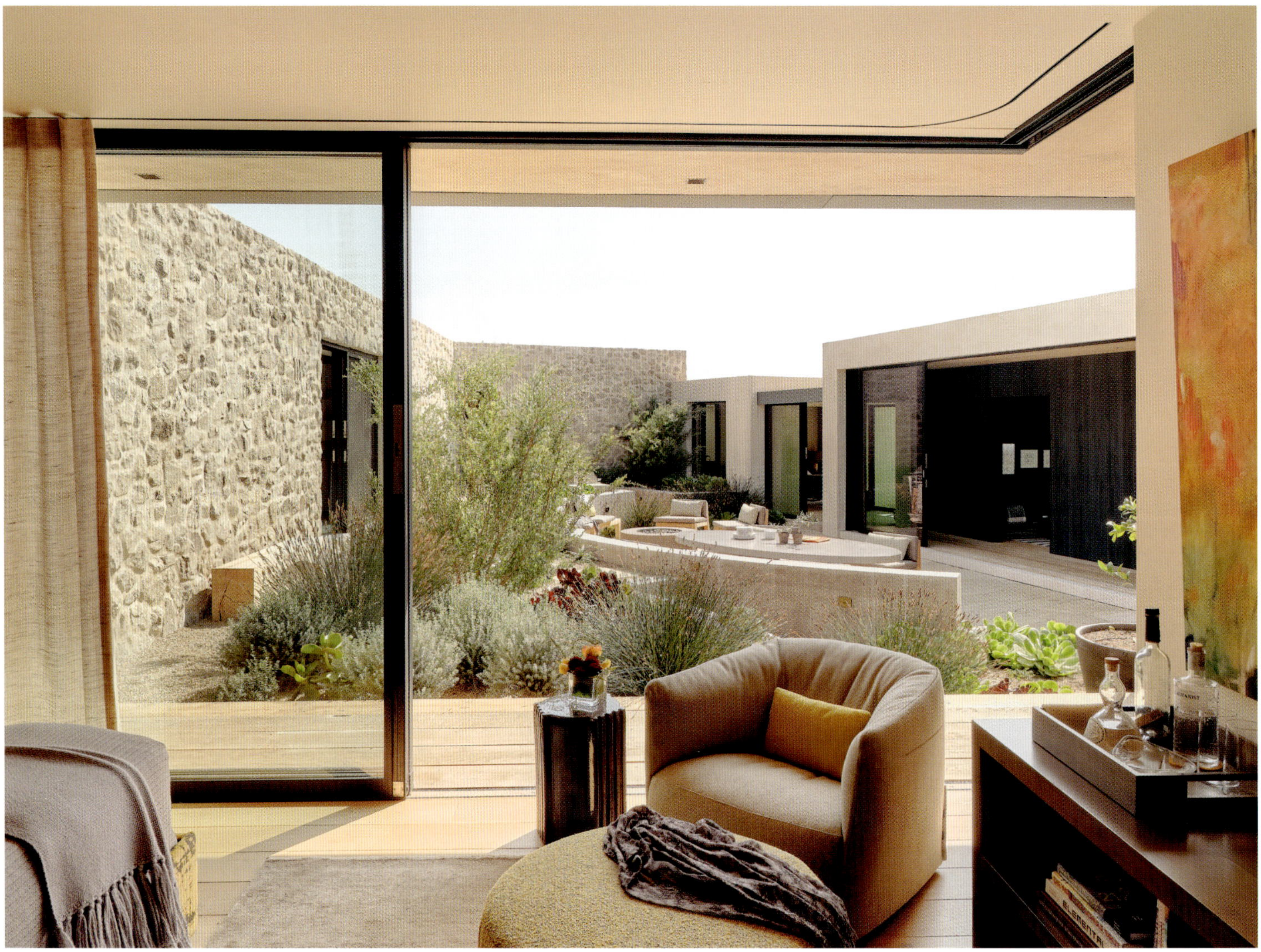

With offices in Bangalore, India, and Carmel, California, Studio Schicketanz is a full-service architecture, interior-design, and consulting firm. The practice combines philosophical perspectives on interior design, architecture, and landscape with a particular focus on livability. Gabriele Mary Ann Schicketanz, the founder, has over thirty years of experience as a professional architect, and her portfolio includes work from both Europe and the Western United States.

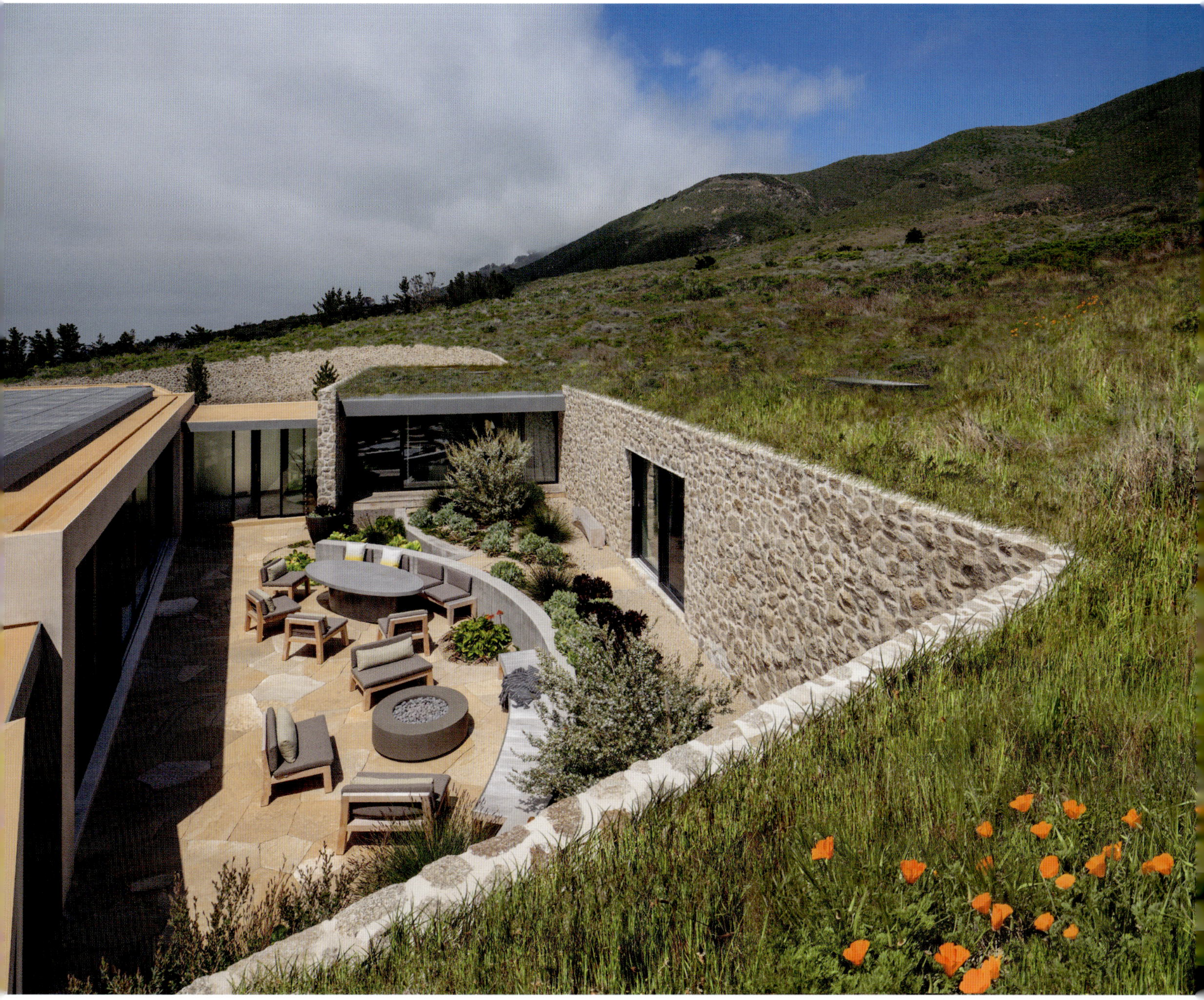

The retreat has been designed as a series of four volumes, three of which face the sea, and the fourth one is connected with the hill, and the courtyard makes a cozy guest quarters. Whenever possible, all walls have been equipped with floor-to-ceiling glazed sliders to make the surrounding views part of the interiors. These openings also smoothly connect the space of the inner courtyard with the surroundings, up to the waterfront. This area is a quintessentially common space, visible and accessible from numerous parts of the house. It has been filled with plants as well as comfortable furniture to offer a striking recreational spot that allows enjoying outdoor living in a cozy and wind-free mode, without compromising on the views. The combination of greenery and earthy hues, but also natural materials, is finely balanced and creates an atmosphere of calmness enhancing the connection with nature around.

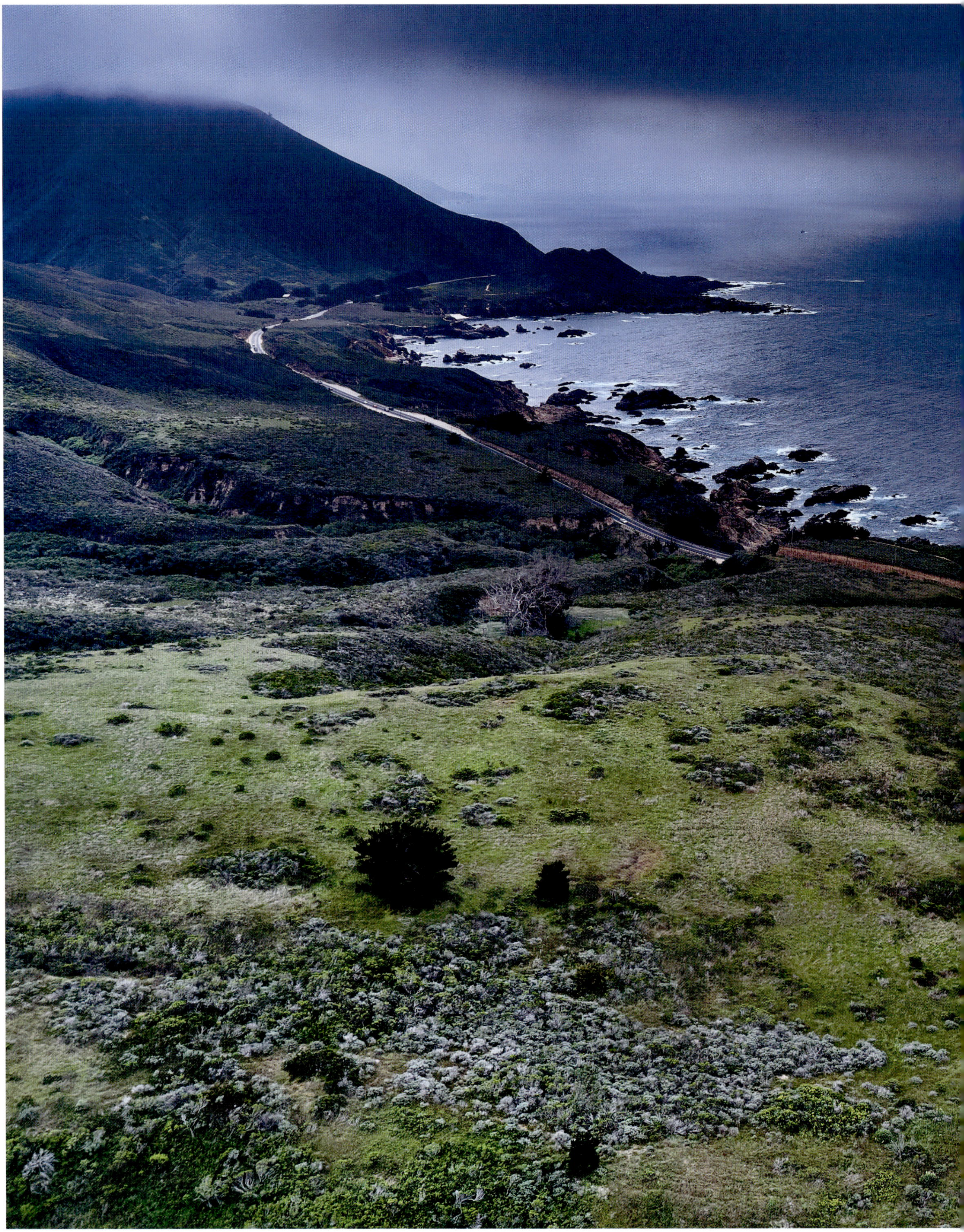

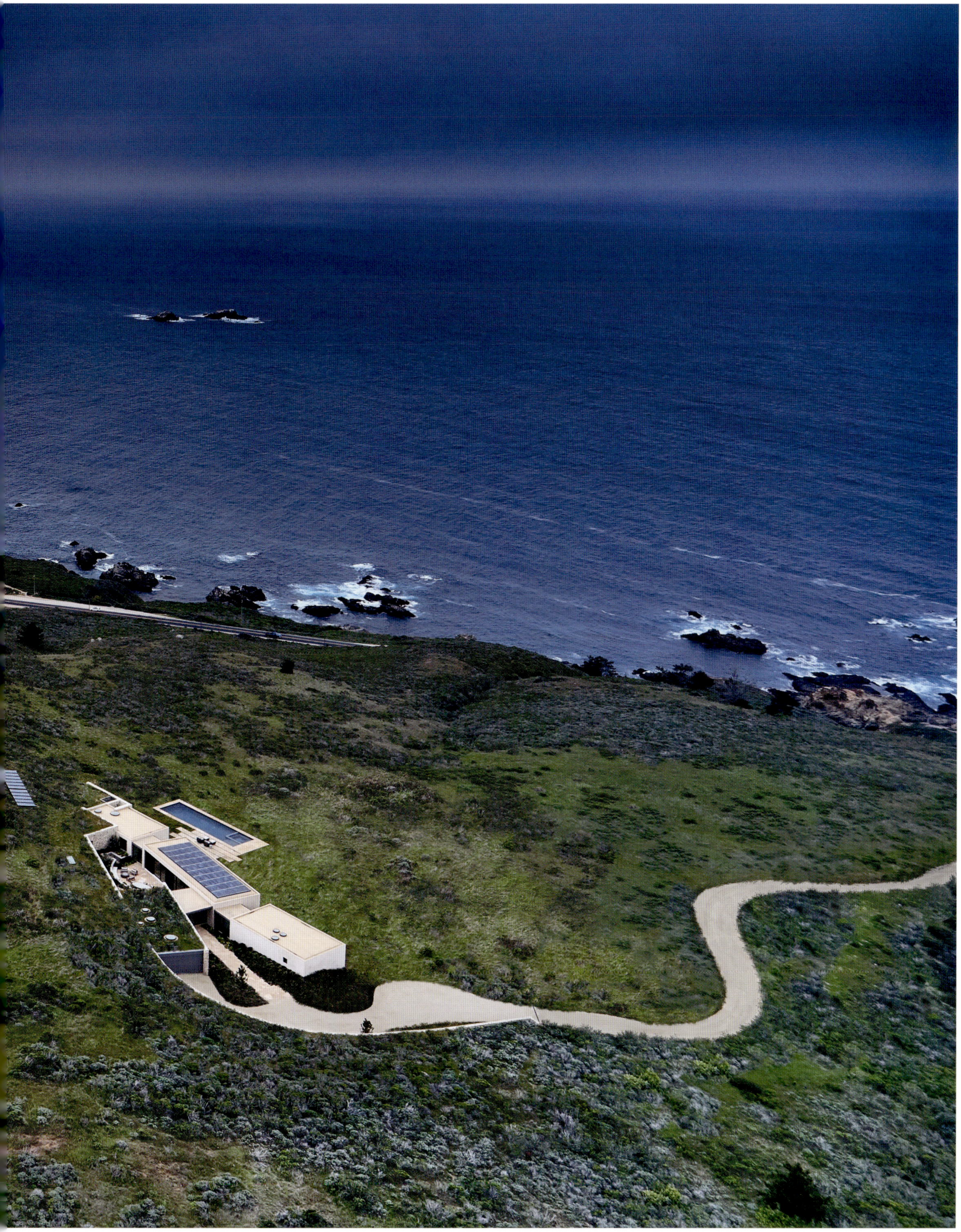

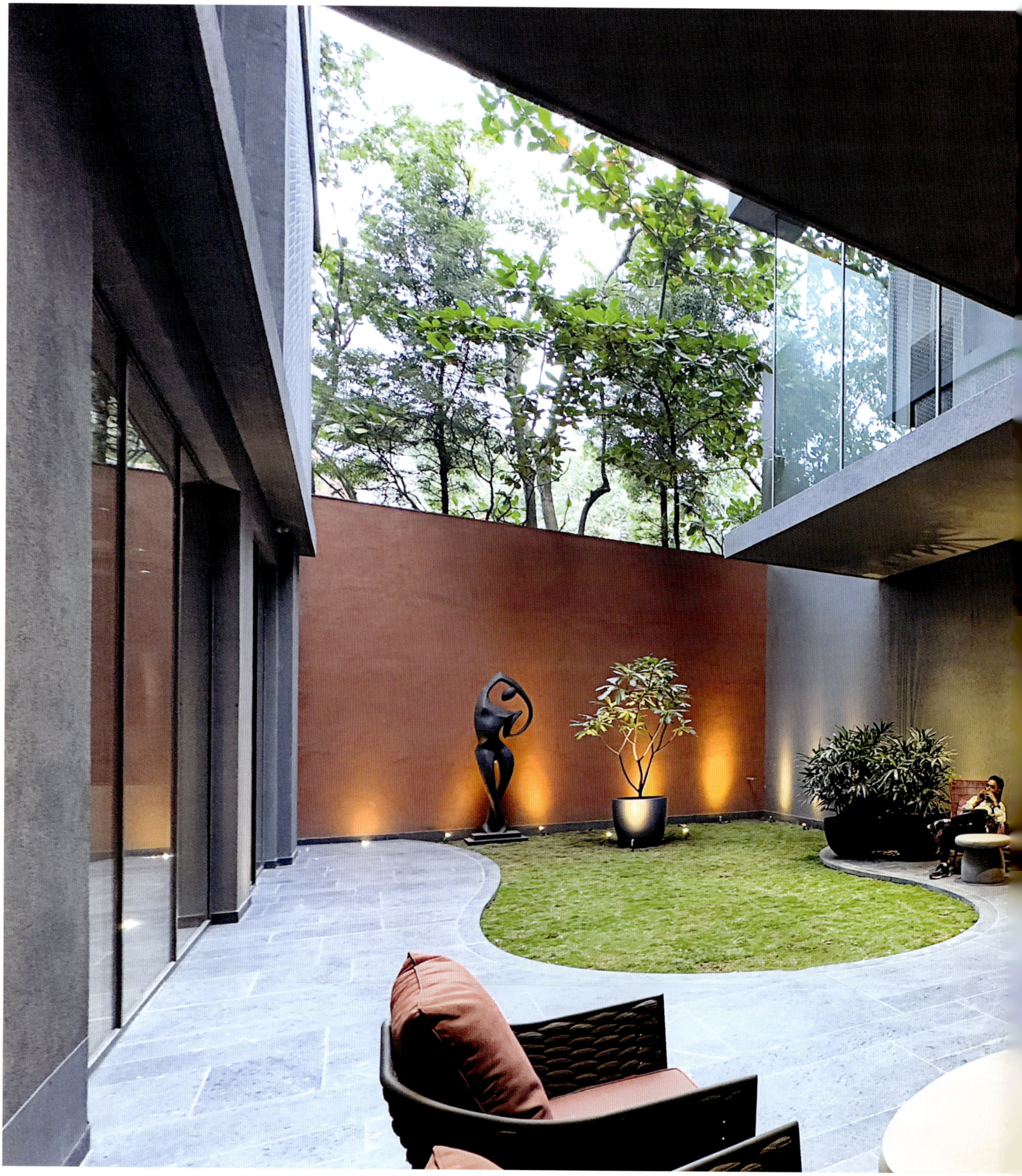

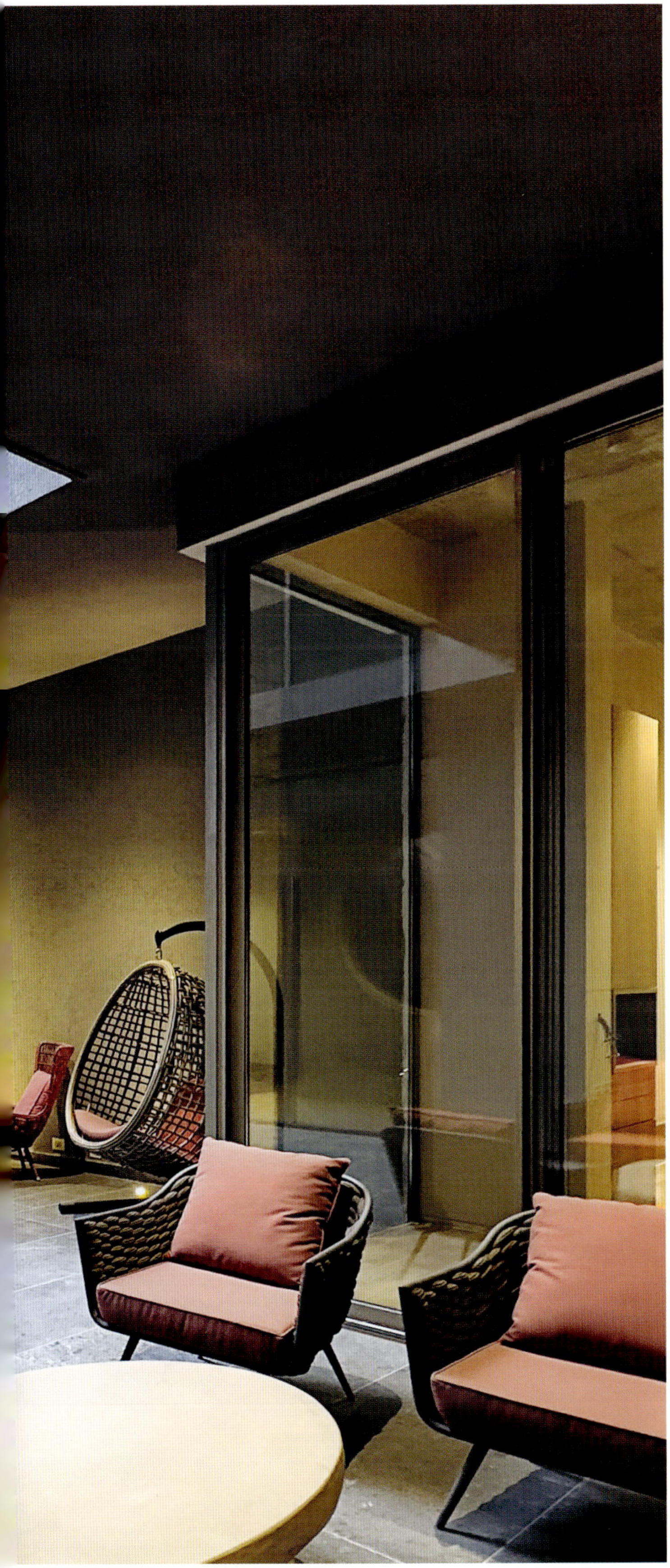

PROJECT: Zen Spaces
LOCATION: Jaipur, India
YEAR: 2023
ARCHITECTS: Sanjay Puri Architects
PHOTOGRAPHY: Mr. Dinesh Mehta

The residence Zen Spaces, harmonized with the existing garden, has been envisioned as a home for three generations living together. Planned on four levels, this spacious residence grows from a subterranean yet naturally lit patio, which features a large lounge, a gym, and a service area. Embraced by the walls of the higher levels, it is simultaneously connected with them and very private. Numerous openings and private outdoor decks owned by each room make the patio visible from all levels, but due to its sunken character, it remains a separated space filled with quietness and privacy. The spot of grass, as well as the view of the lush vegetation, connects the courtyard area with the surrounding landscape and has a soothing effect. "The circulation spine within the house skirts the courtyard, allowing a visual connection to the landscaped spaces while moving within the house," explain the architects. Their goal was to connect various areas of the residence in a way that offers different experiences in each part.

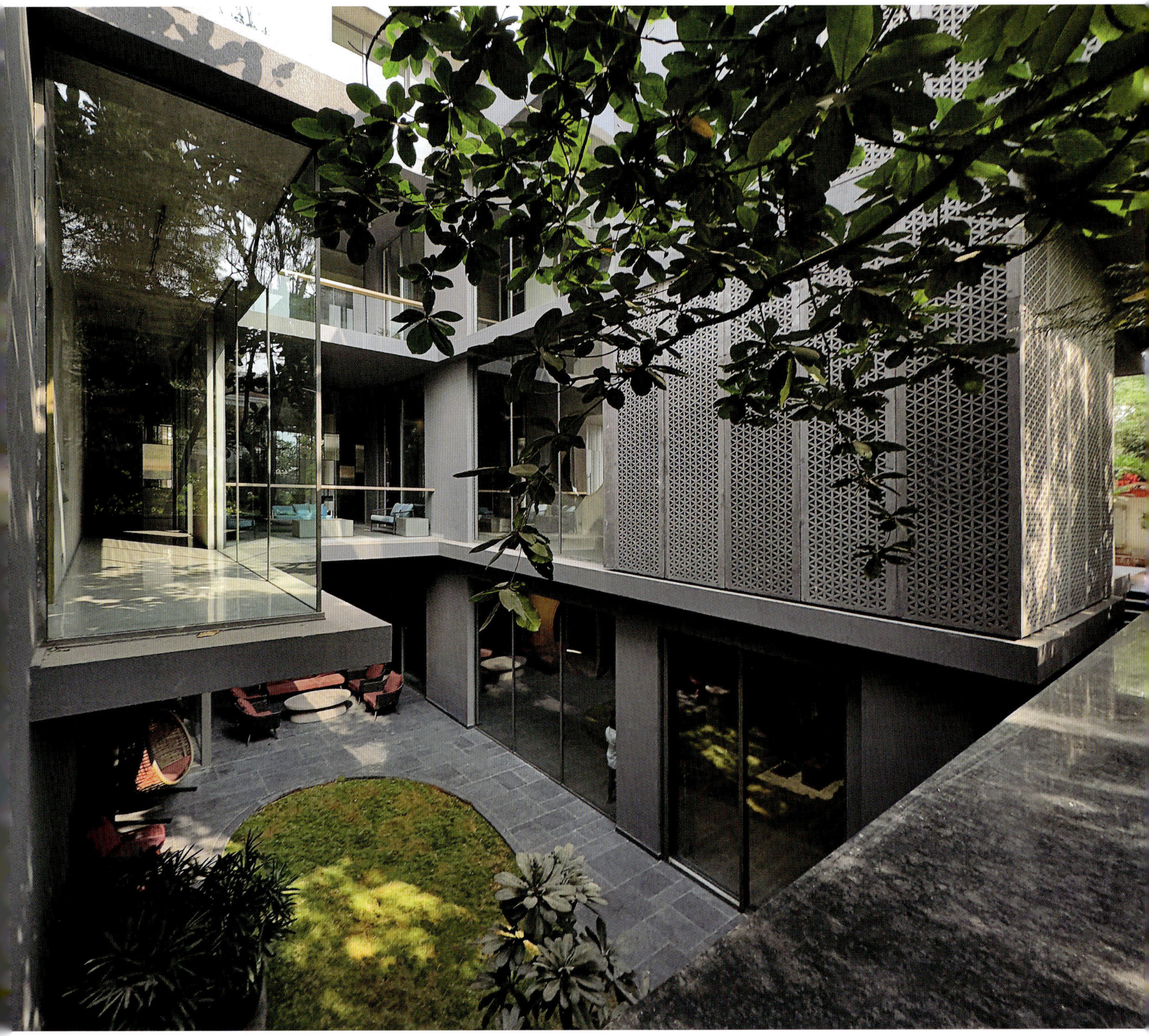

The sunken patio of the house seems like a hidden place in the very heart of the compact volume. The architects also planned a winter deck on the southern side, facing the large garden, and a summer deck in front of the main living area on the northern end, as sheltered outdoor areas for various parts of the year.

The volume of the residence was treated in a sculptural way, where curves and various screenings create a play of light that changes at different times during the day. These screens also reduce the heat gain in the hot months, while being a visual reference to the traditional architecture of Jaipur city and Rajasthan. The architects have chosen numerous environmentally friendly solutions that make the house energy-efficient. Each part of the residence is naturally ventilated, while the courtyard contributes to passive cooling. The house has been equipped with water recycling, rainwater harvesting, and solar-water-heating systems. Last but not least, most of the construction materials have been sourced locally and selected for their eco-friendliness.

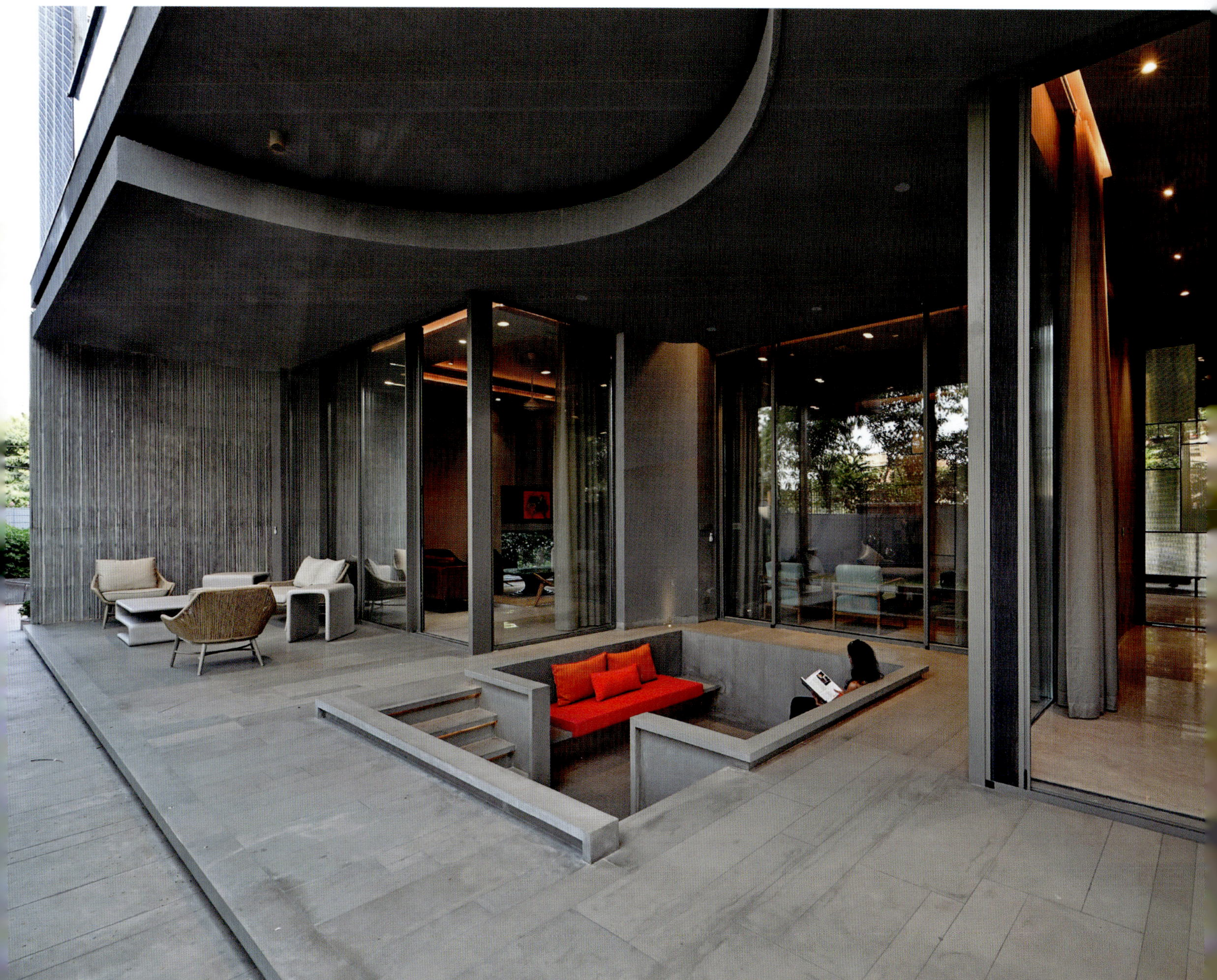

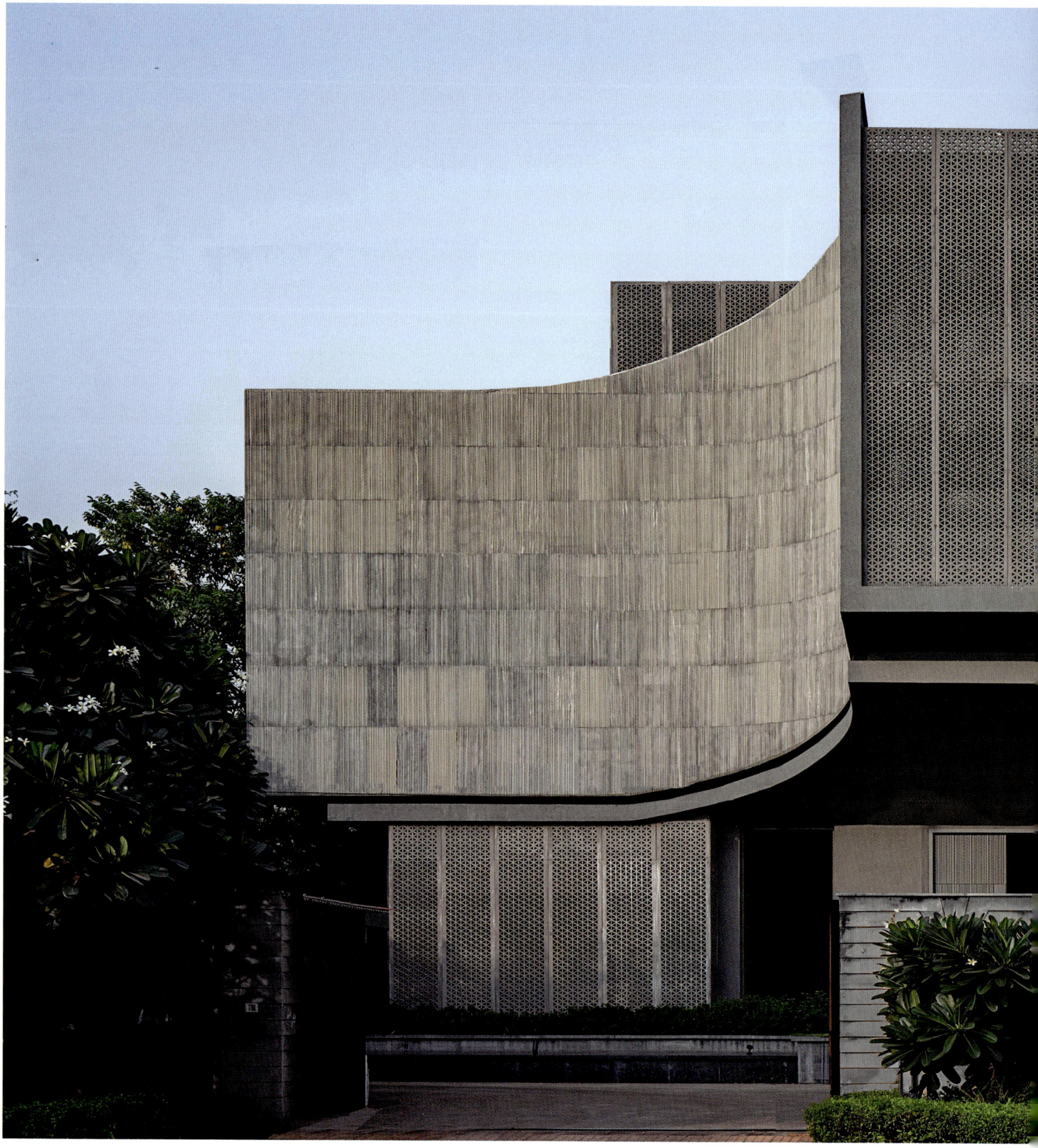

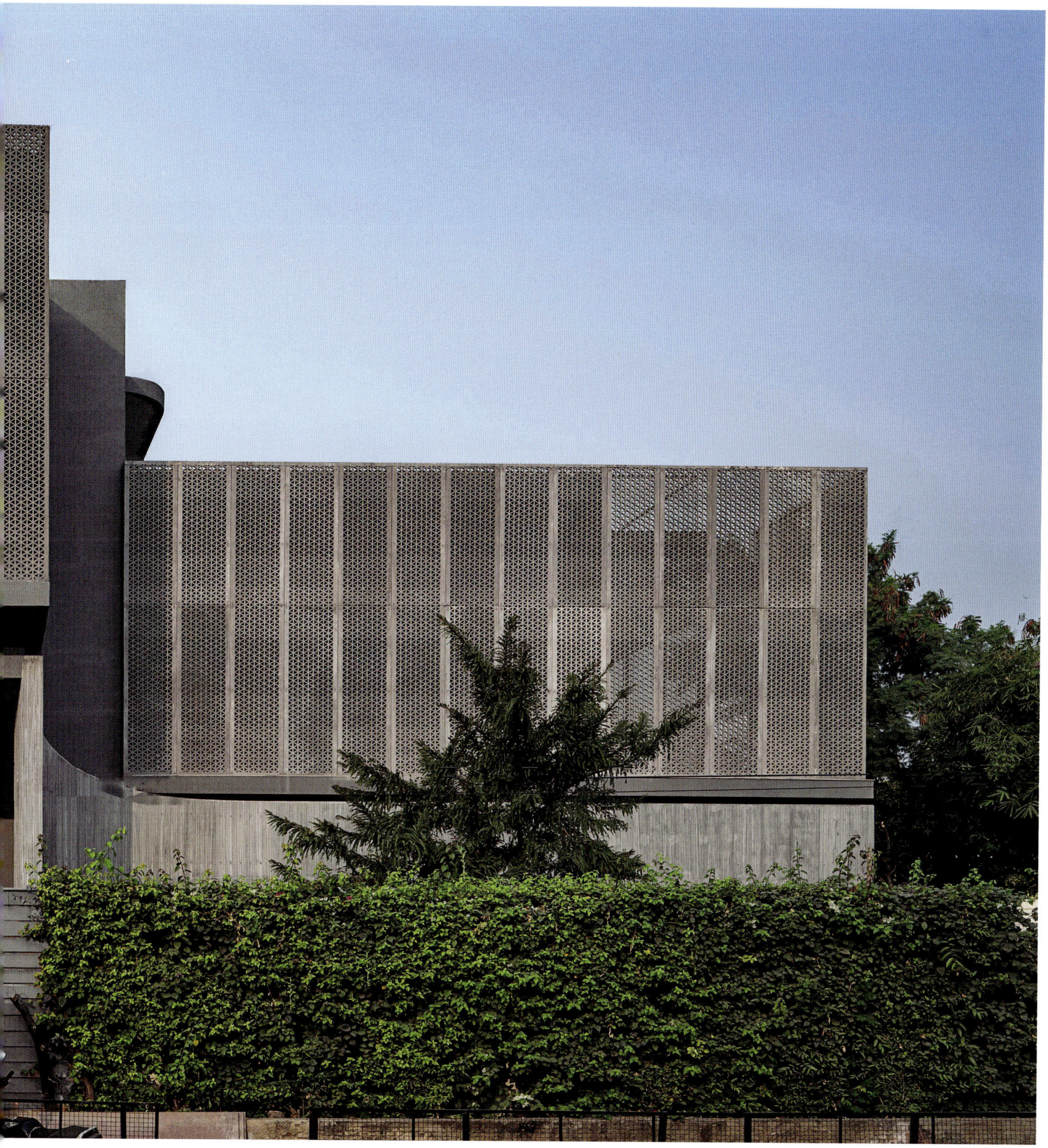

Established in 1992 in Mumbai, Sanjay Puri Architects realizes a wide range of visionary projects across India and internationally. From architecture to interior to product design, the team, led by the founding partners, Sanjay Puri and Nina Puri, pays special attention to the climatic conditions and integrating sustainability in a cohesive way. "Evolving design solutions that are contextual and sustainable and creating spaces that explore spatial perceptions, with new design directions forms the essence of the firm's design philosophy," states Sanjay Puri.

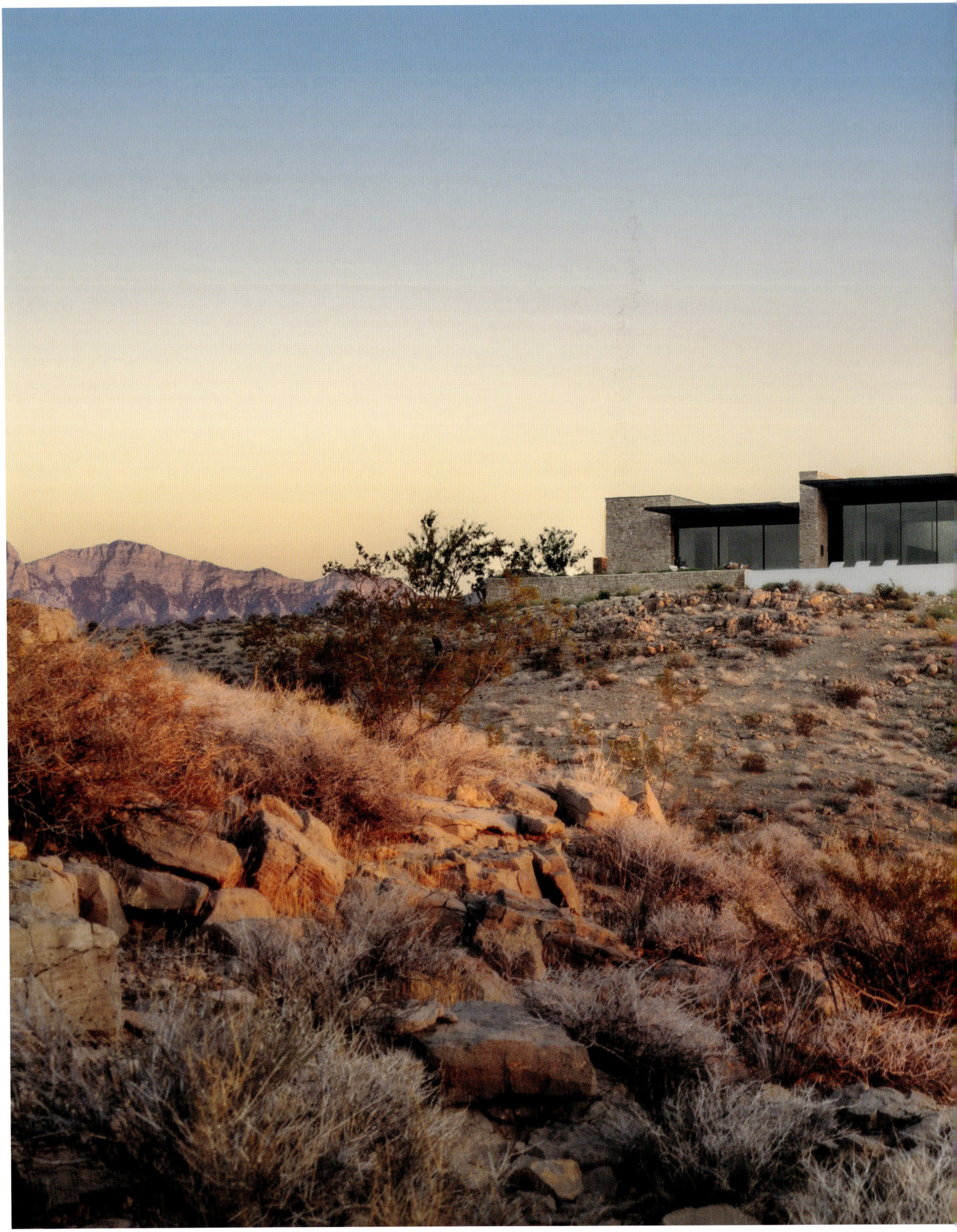

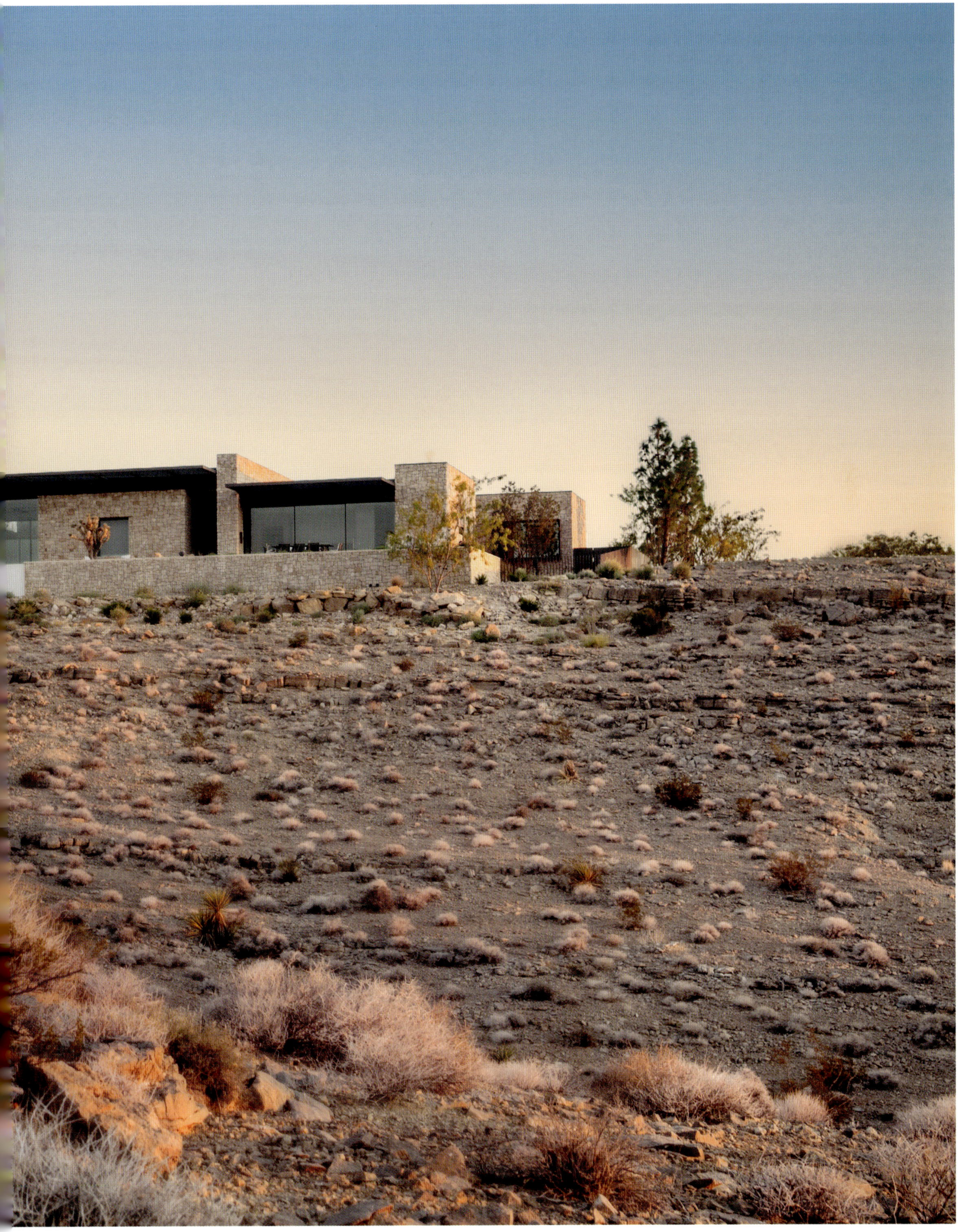

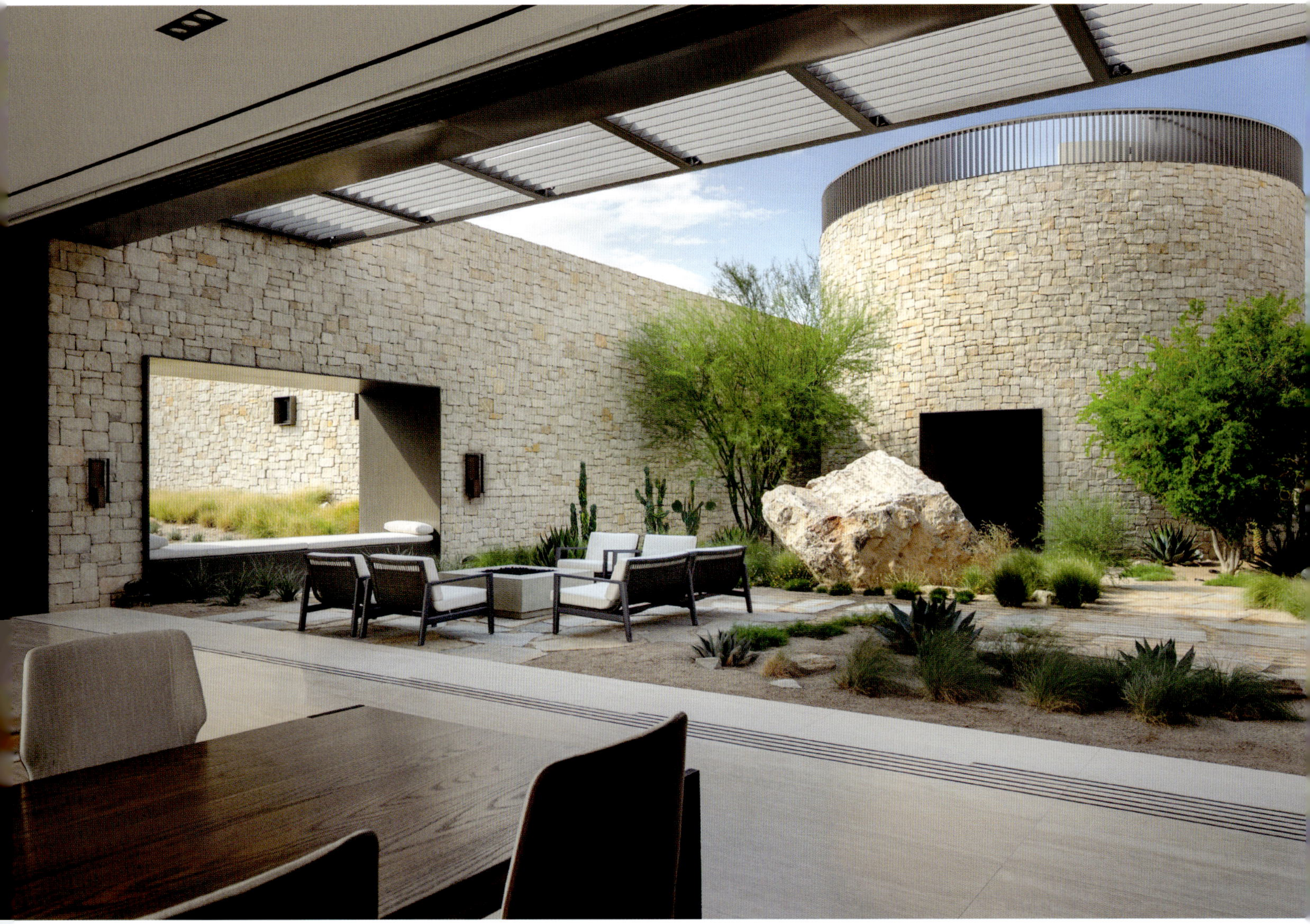

Daniel Joseph Chenin established his multidisciplinary studio in 2014 with the mission to redefine luxury by blurring the lines between design disciplines and project typologies. The team's goal is to create immersive spaces, offer unique experiences, and make architecture, interiors, landscape, and furnishings part of one vision. Sustainable solutions such as passive cooling, indigenous landscapes, and site-sensitive but also long-lasting materials are seamlessly embedded in the architects' process.

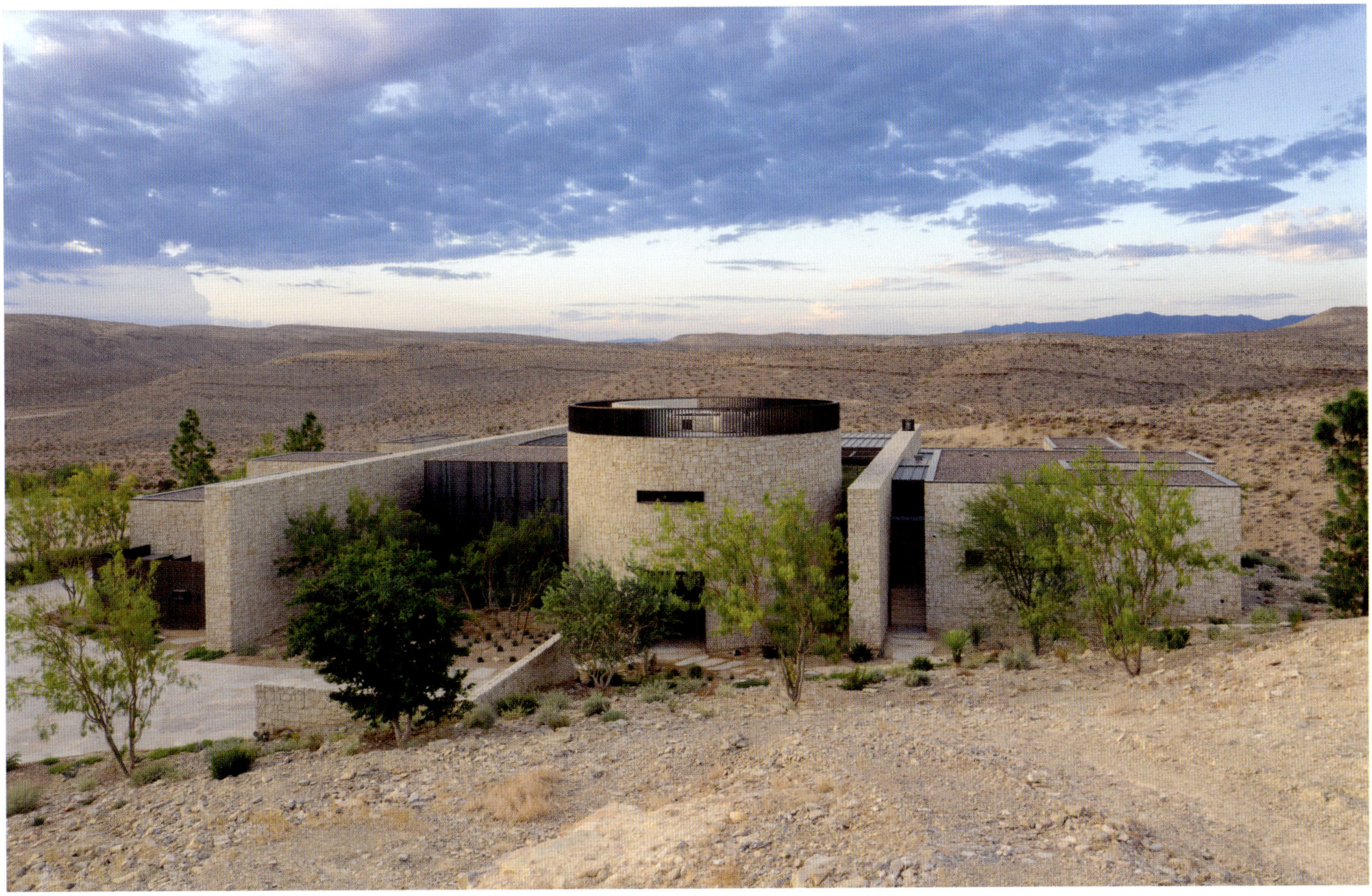

PROJECT: Fort 137
LOCATION: Las Vegas, Nevada, United States
YEAR: 2022
ARCHITECTS: Daniel Joseph Chenin, Ltd.
PHOTOGRAPHY: Daniel Joseph Chenin, Stephen Morgan, Stetson Ybarra

The brief for the Daniel Joseph Chenin studio, responsible for all aspects of the Fort 137 project from architecture to interior design, to installation of the furnishings, was clear: a warm house with contemporary flair that would seamlessly blend into the pristine landscape of the desert. Inspired by the traditional settlements of the pioneers of the Las Vegas Valley in the 1880s, the program of the three complementary volumes prioritized the connection with the rugged context, with the focus on the extraordinary rotunda acting as the entry and a shaded inner courtyard as the beating, and relaxing, heart of the house. The patio is mostly shaded and punctuated with greenery and rocks, including a 75-ton boulder excavated from the site, to re-create the character of the context. Thanks to sliding glass panel walls framing the living area, the patio, together with the house's interiors, can be fluidly connected with the desert landscape, enhancing the experience.

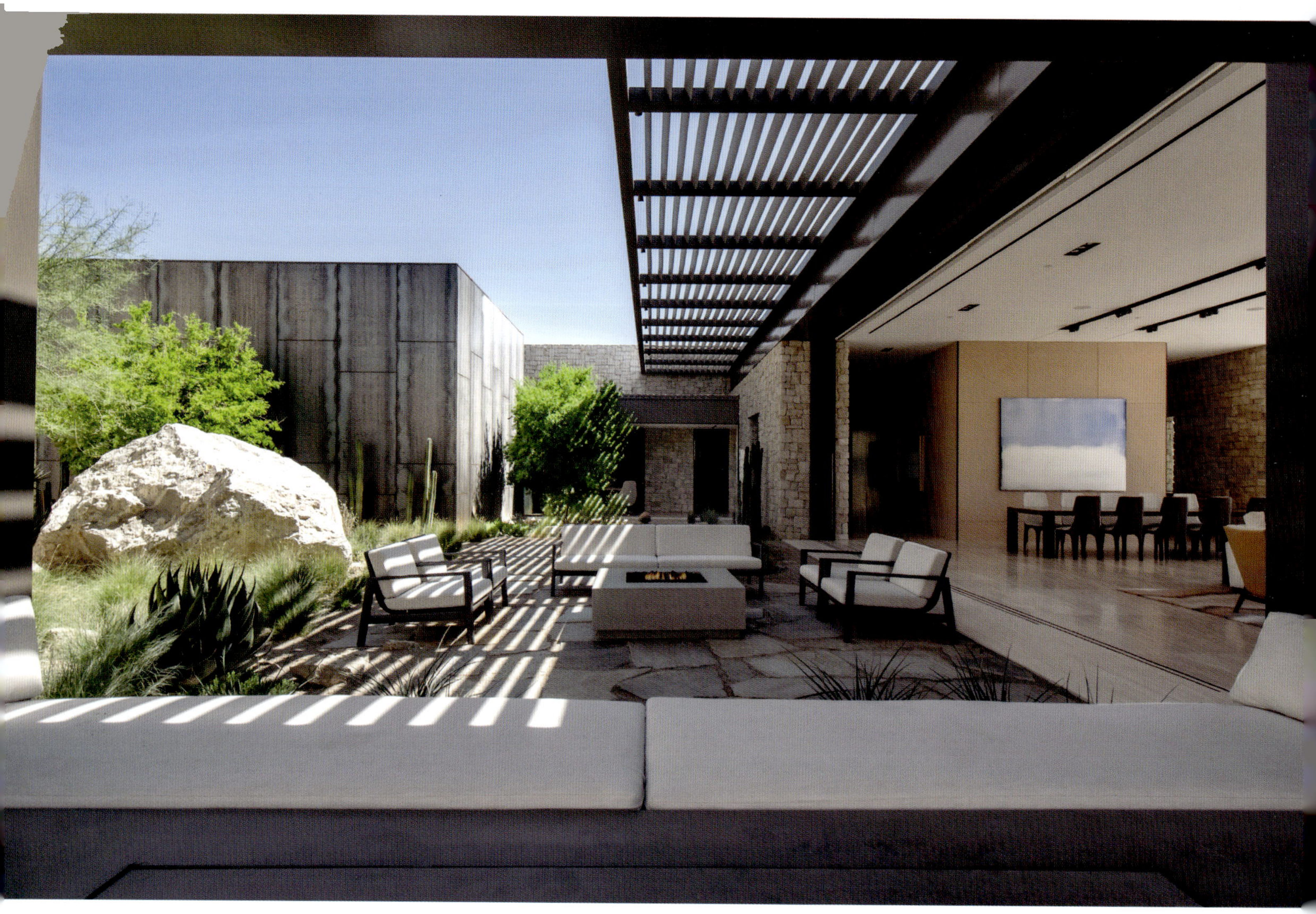

The studio's philosophy reads "For us, architecture is not just about form, it's about designing environments that shape memories, evoke emotions, and leave a lasting imprint. Each project is a crafted journey, a celebration of place, and a reminder of architecture's power to transform." Their desert oasis, Fort 137, located on the edge of the Las Vegas Valley, demonstrates how powerful the realization of this approach is. Structurally, it addresses the desert climate, with extreme sun and wind, while visually echoing the colors and textures of the Red Rock Canyon environment. Maximizing comfort and ambiance, the architects also intertwined efficient features to limit environmental impact. These include a photovoltaic panel infrastructure, passive cooling, thermal mass, and radiant heating, as well as repurposed and locally sourced materials.

Openings, glass walls, and sliding glass panel walls create an unforgettable experience of the desert by framing the panoramic views or directly connecting the interiors with the surrounding landscape.

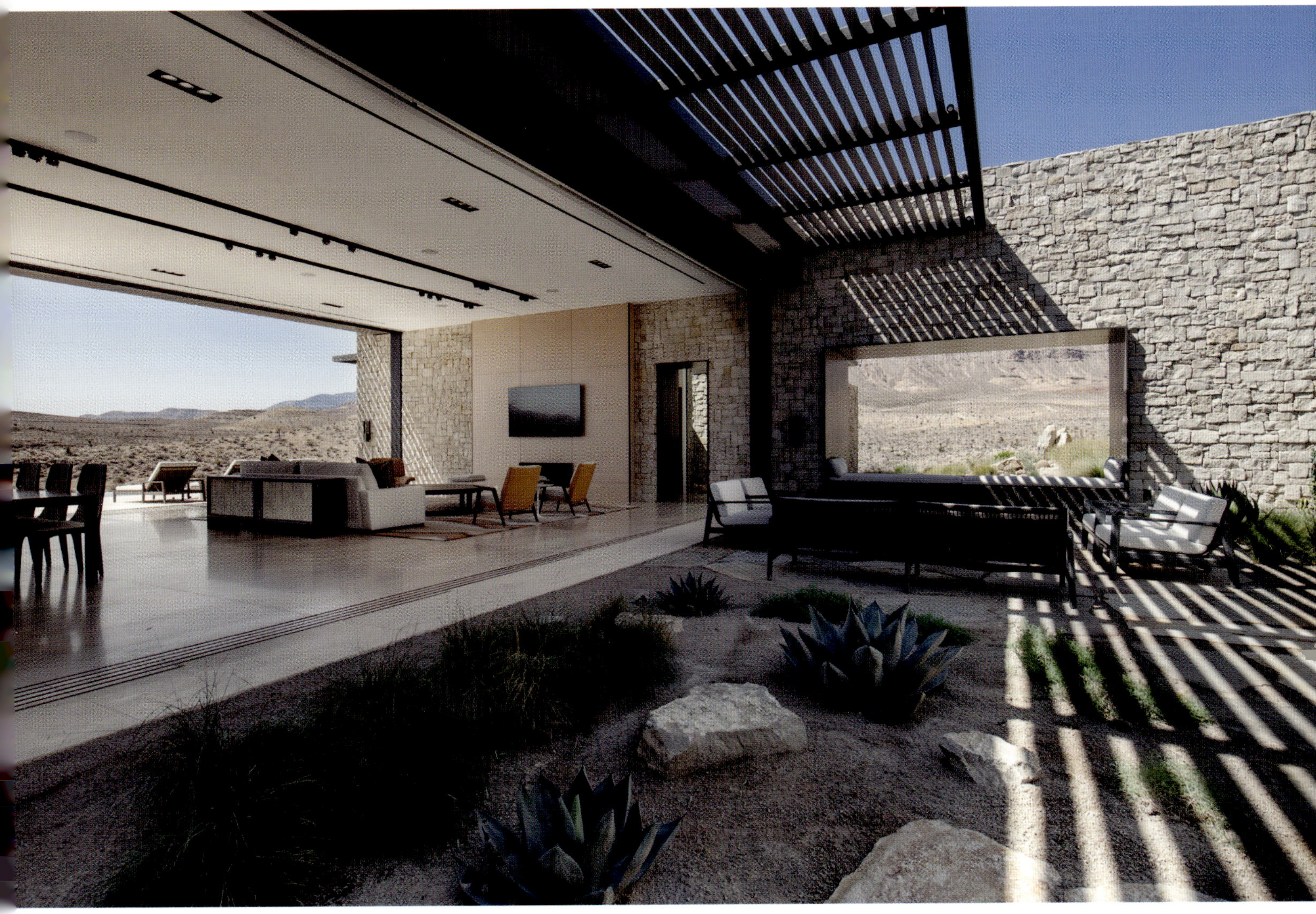

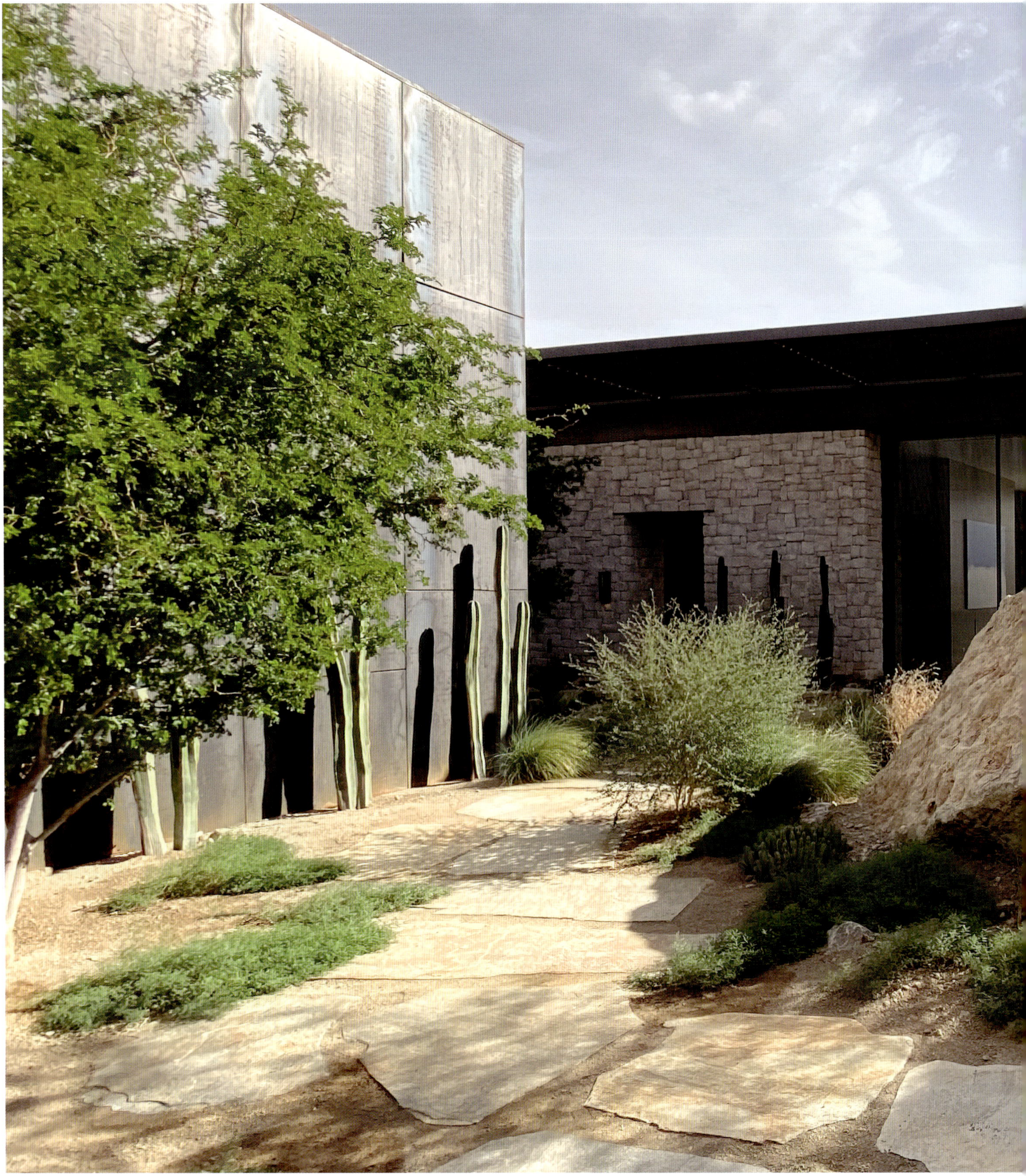

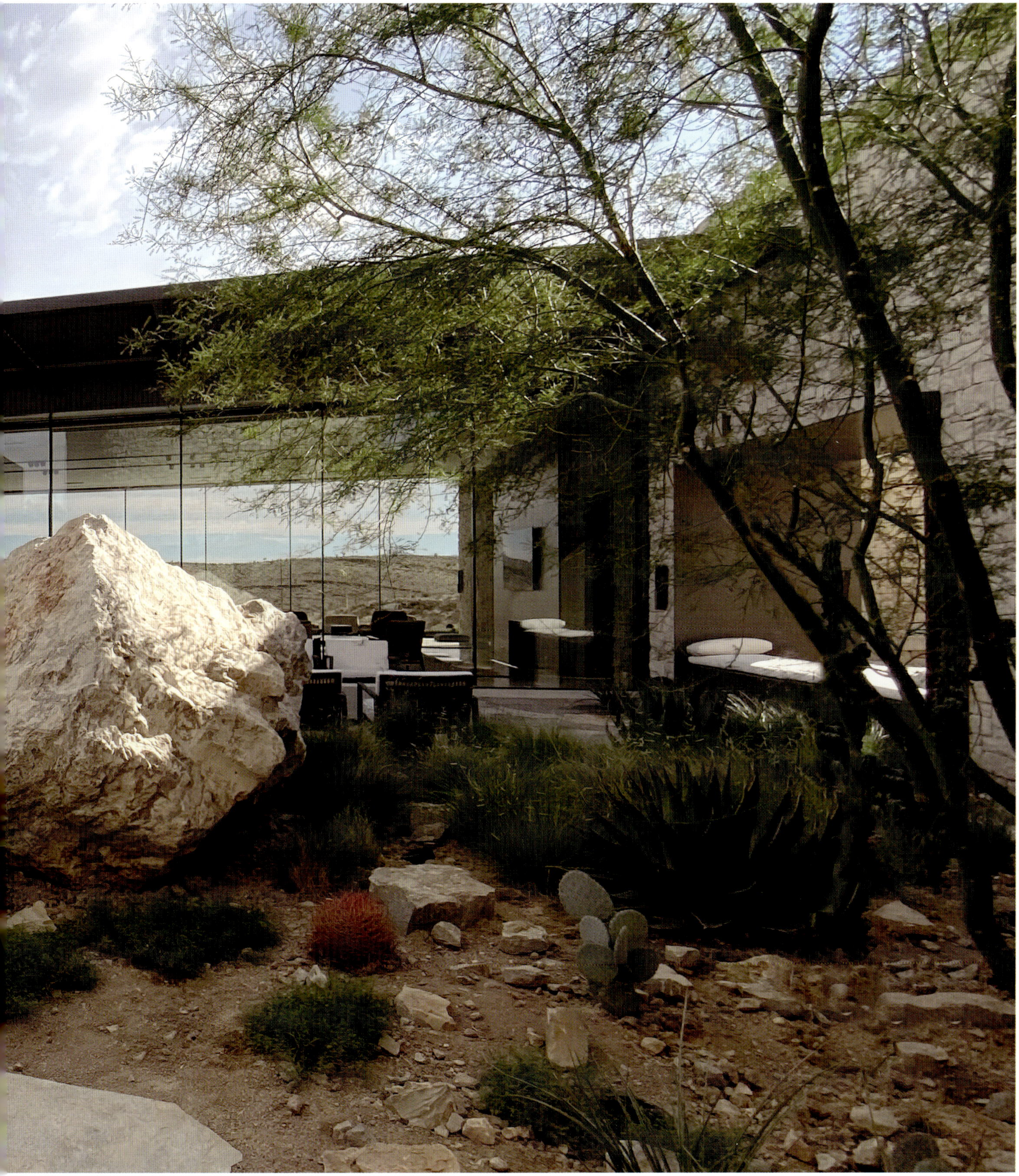

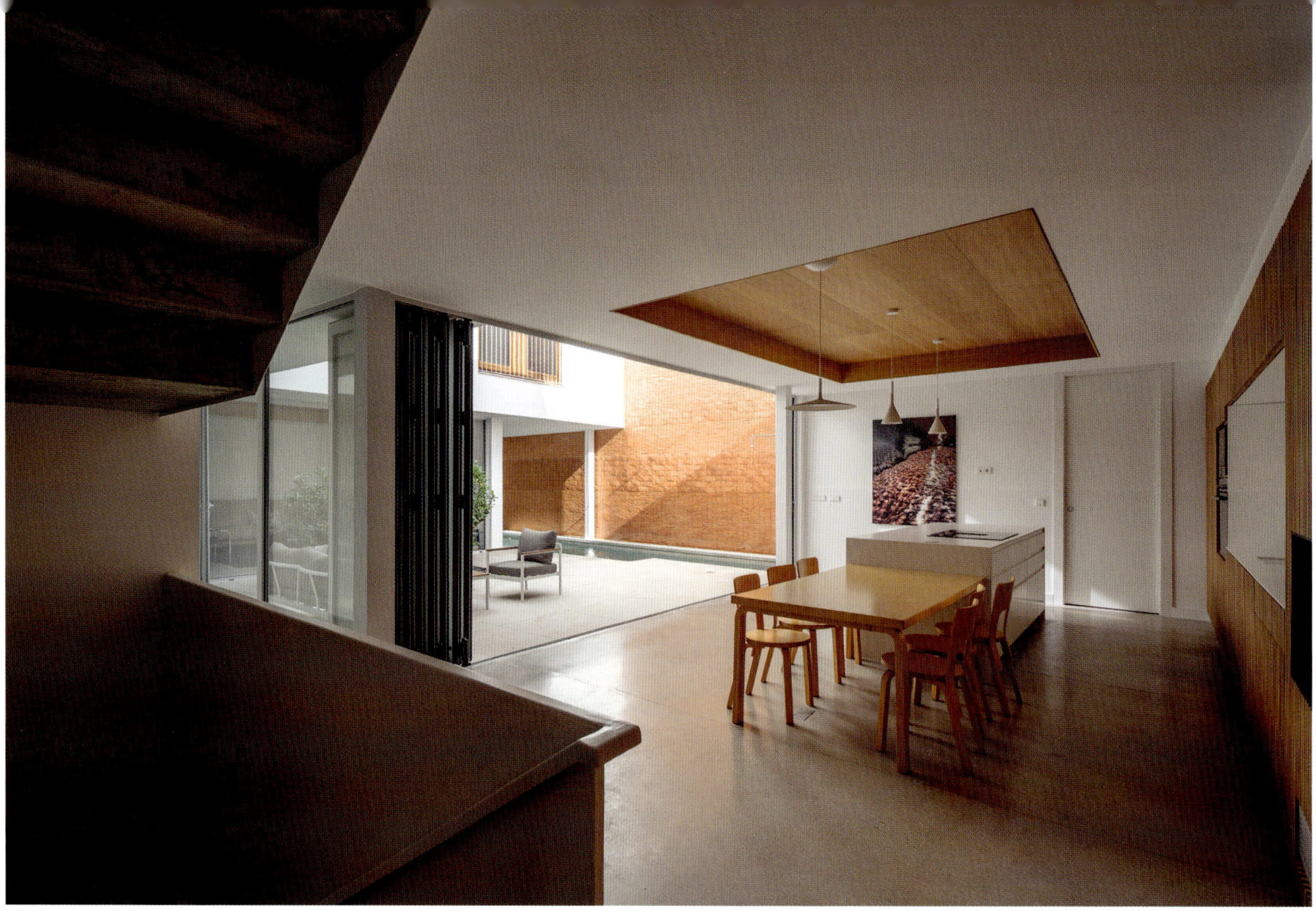

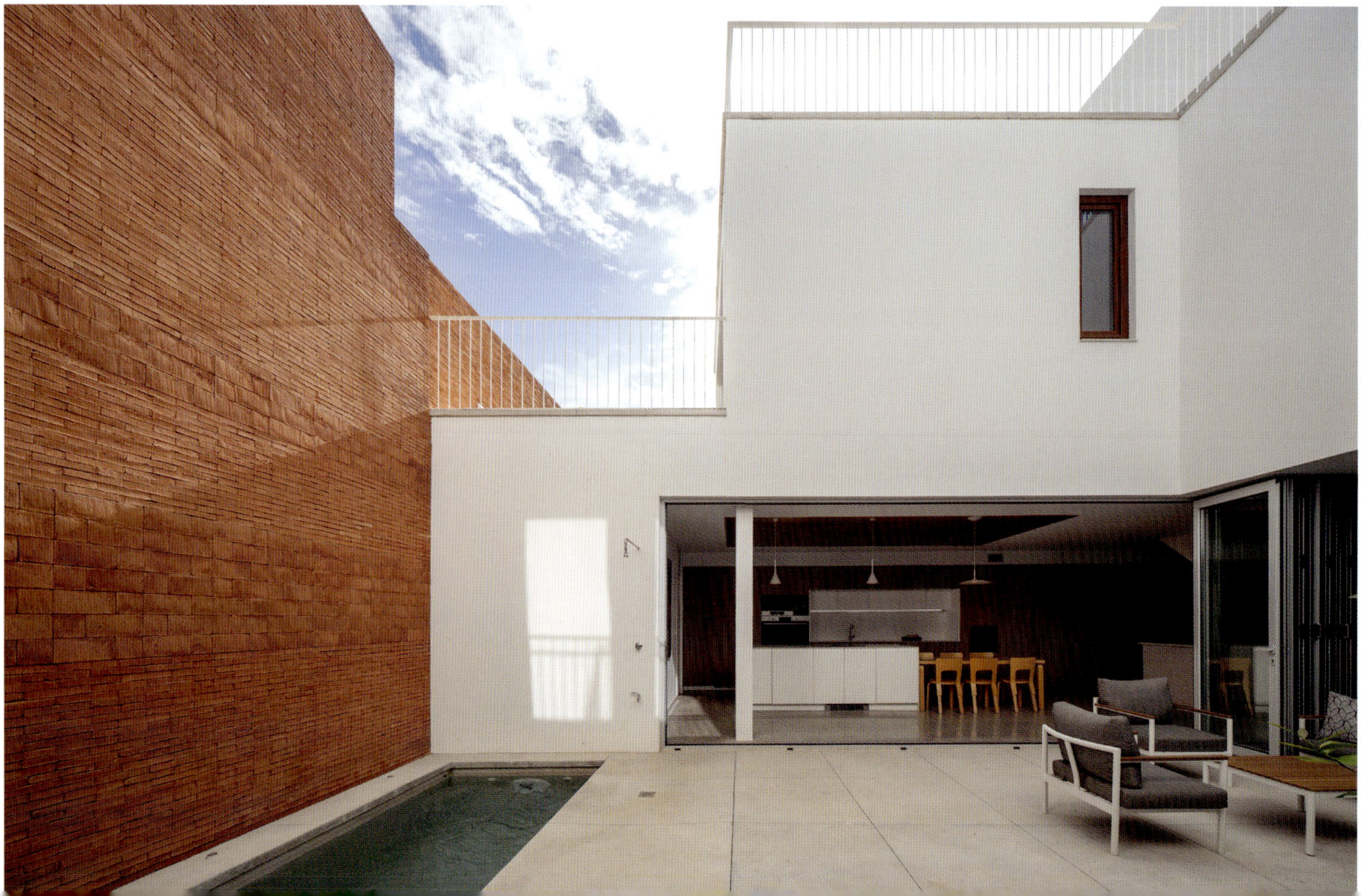

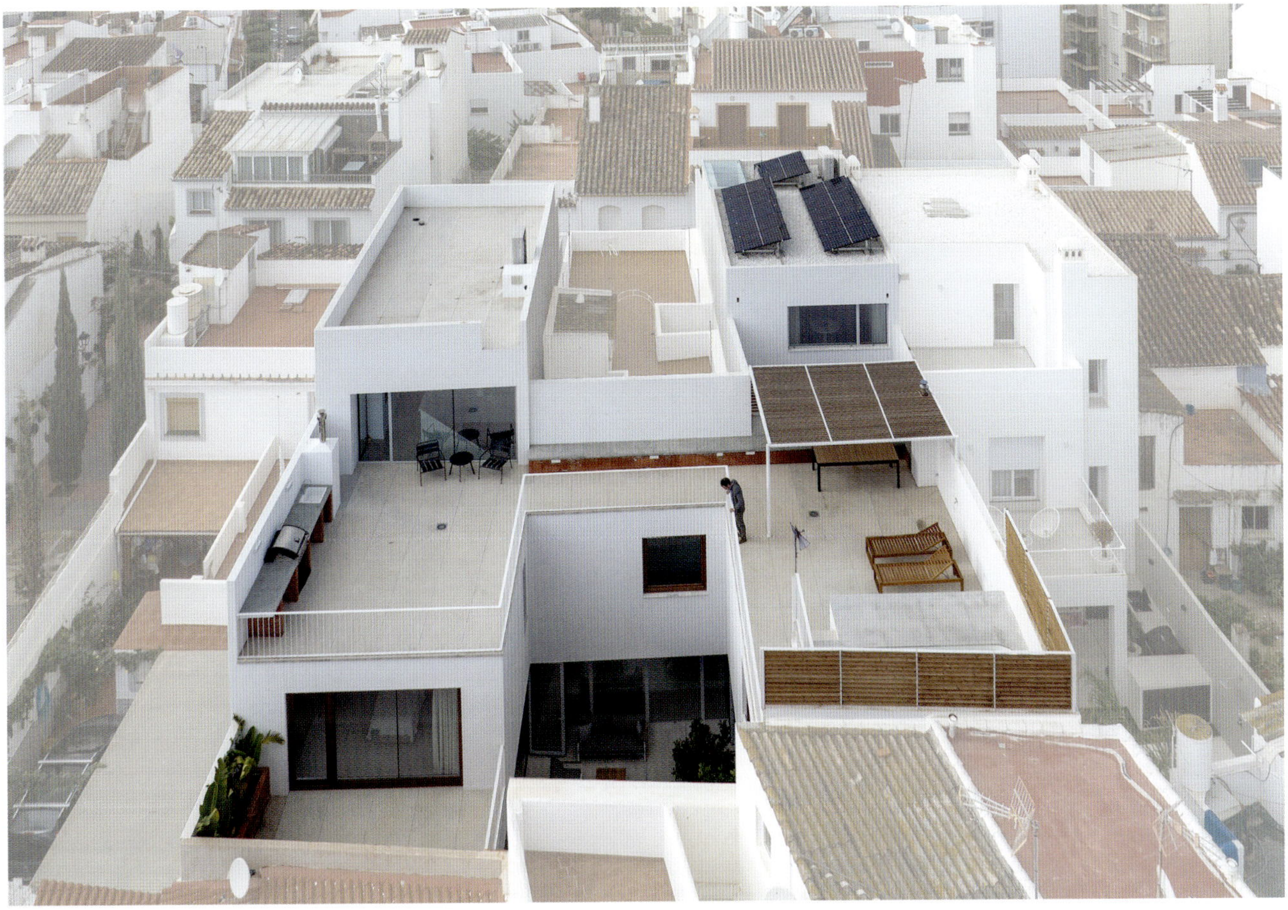

PROJECT: WIIK House
LOCATION: Estepona, Spain
YEAR: 2022
ARCHITECTS: DTR_studio architects
PHOTOGRAPHY: Juanan Barros

When envisioning WIIK House as a summer residence, the architects had to be inventive with the density in Estepona's downtown district. Located on a U-shaped plot, it embraces a central preexisting house. As a result, the new volume forms two independent yet entirely integrated facades that face the same street. The architects used this spatial arrangement to divide the program, placing the main house on one side and the guest headquarters on the other. DTR_studio architects drew inspiration from Arab architecture, emphasizing the need for it to be lived in, inhabited, and walked through, as well as from Mediterranean vernacular traditions. These inspirations resulted in a volume organized around interior patios and the roof, with all areas effectively interconnected.

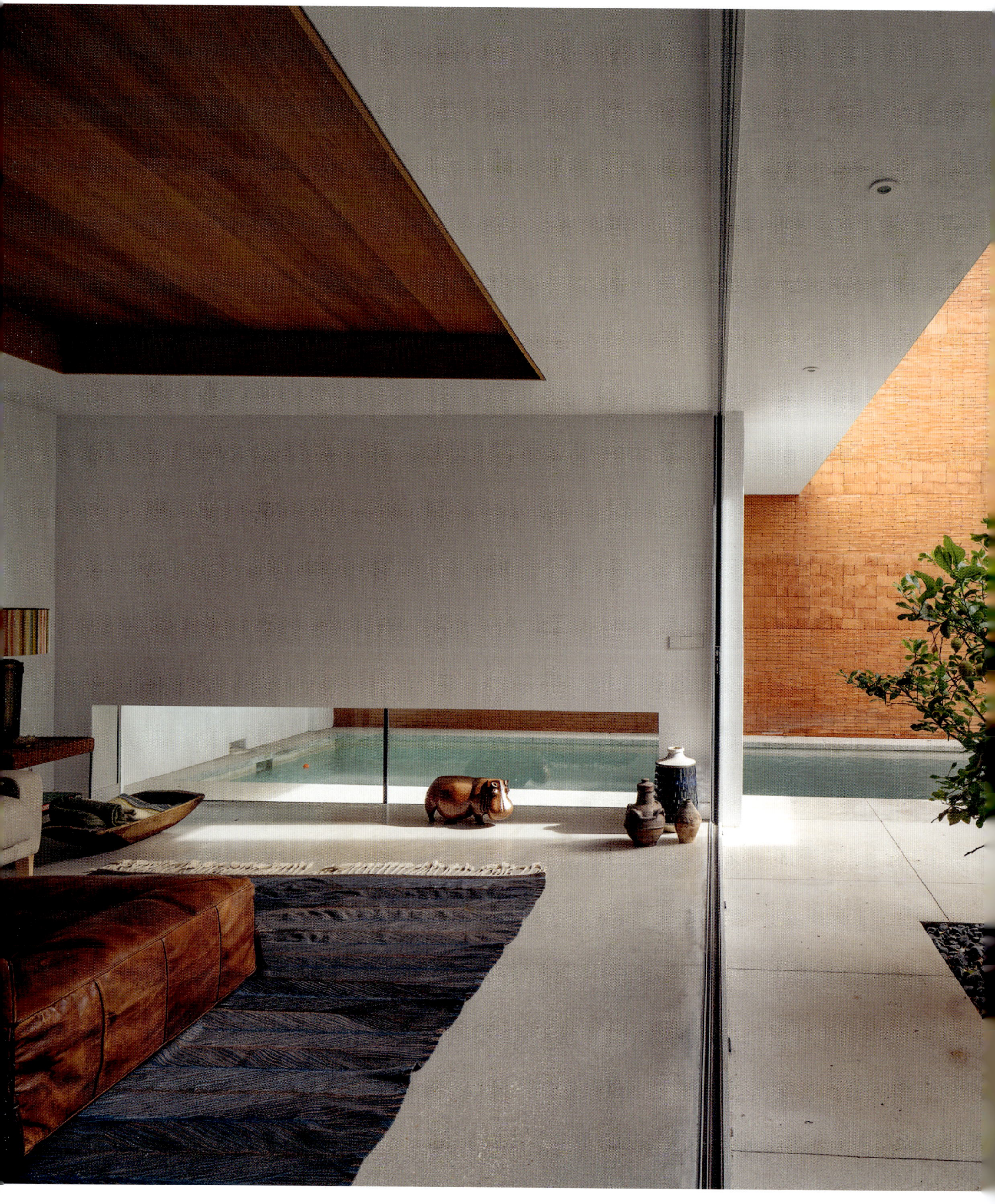

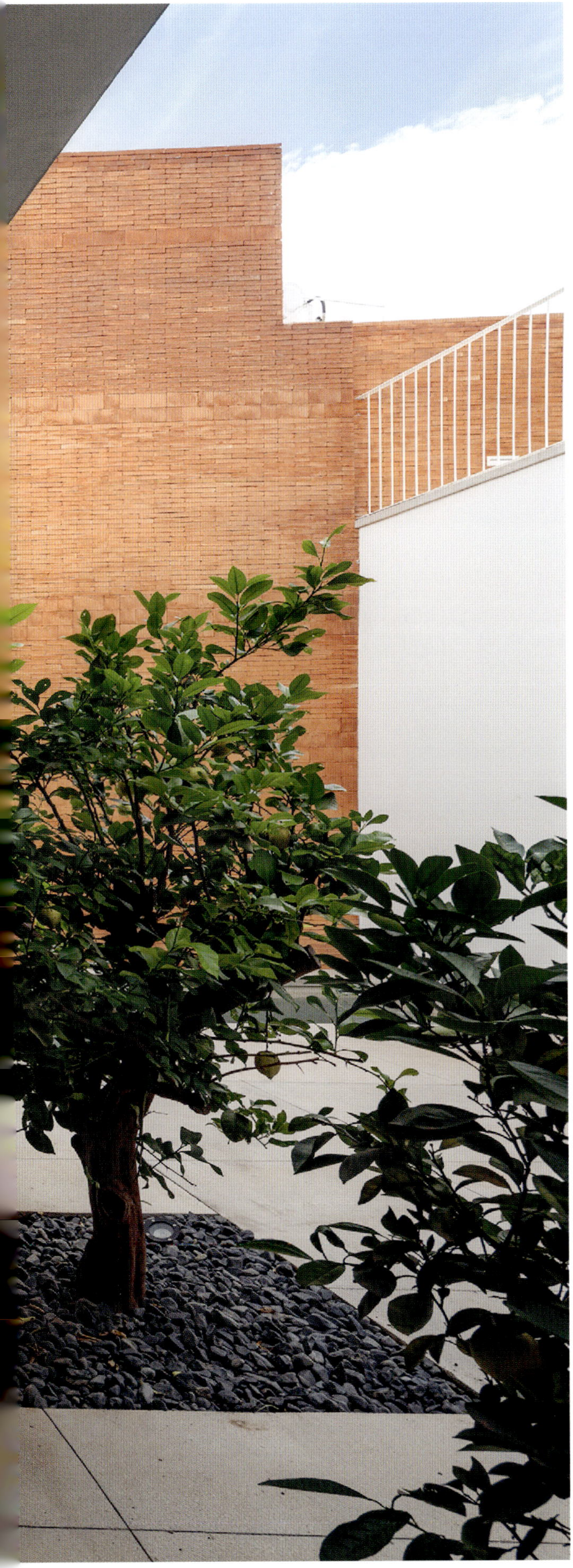

Internal patios, seamlessly fused with architecture, become an important part of the playful relationship between exterior and interior in the elaborate structure of WIIK House.

Based in Granada, Spain, DTR_studio architects was founded in 2003 by José Miguel Vázquez Martín and José María Olmedo Espigares. The practice specializes in residential architecture, often collaborating with individual clients and developers, as well as realizing corporate and retail projects. "The firm also embraces a clear commitment to the inclusion of prefabrication in the construction process," state the architects, whose goal is to make the building stage quicker and deliver better quality standards.

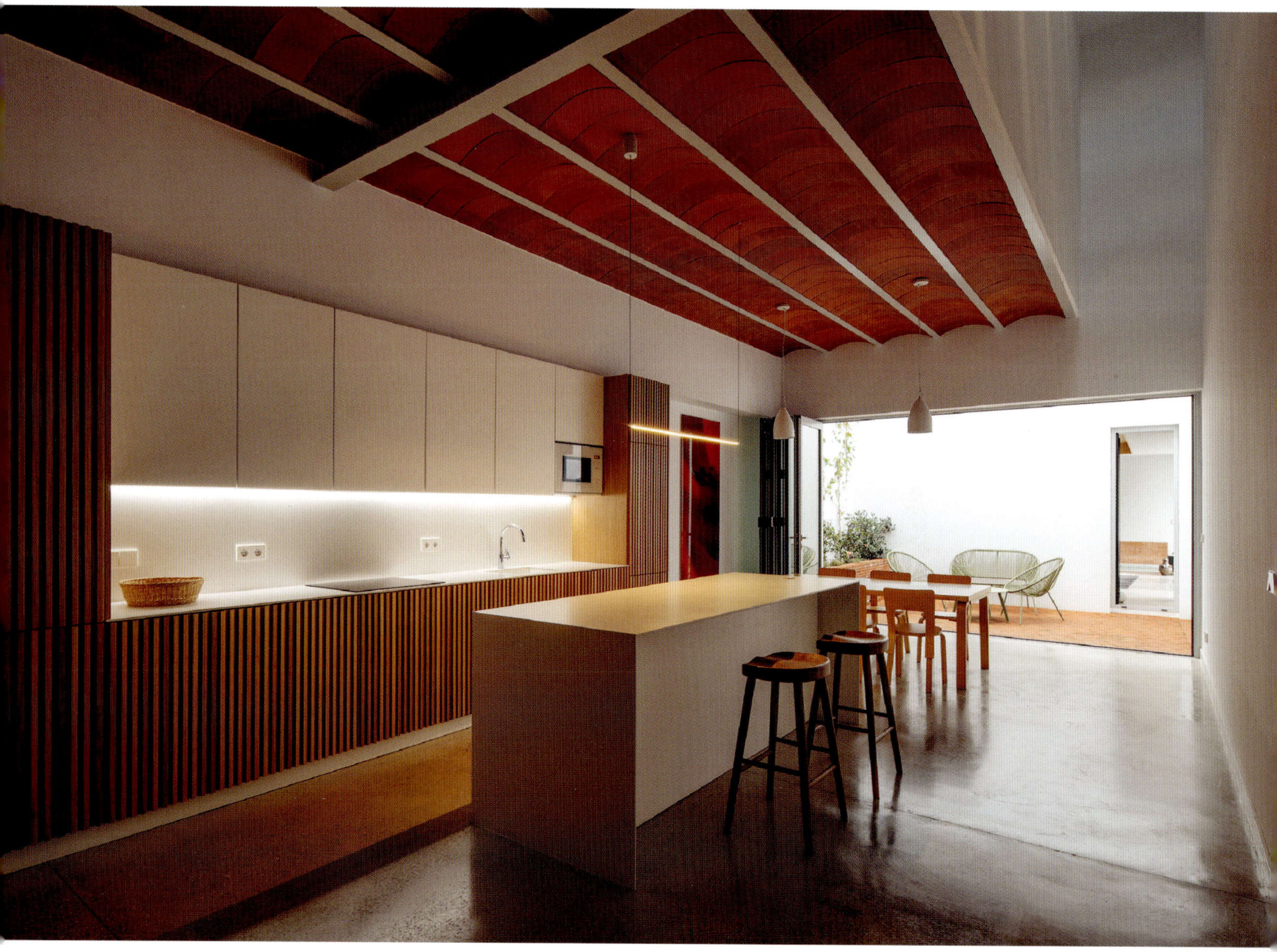

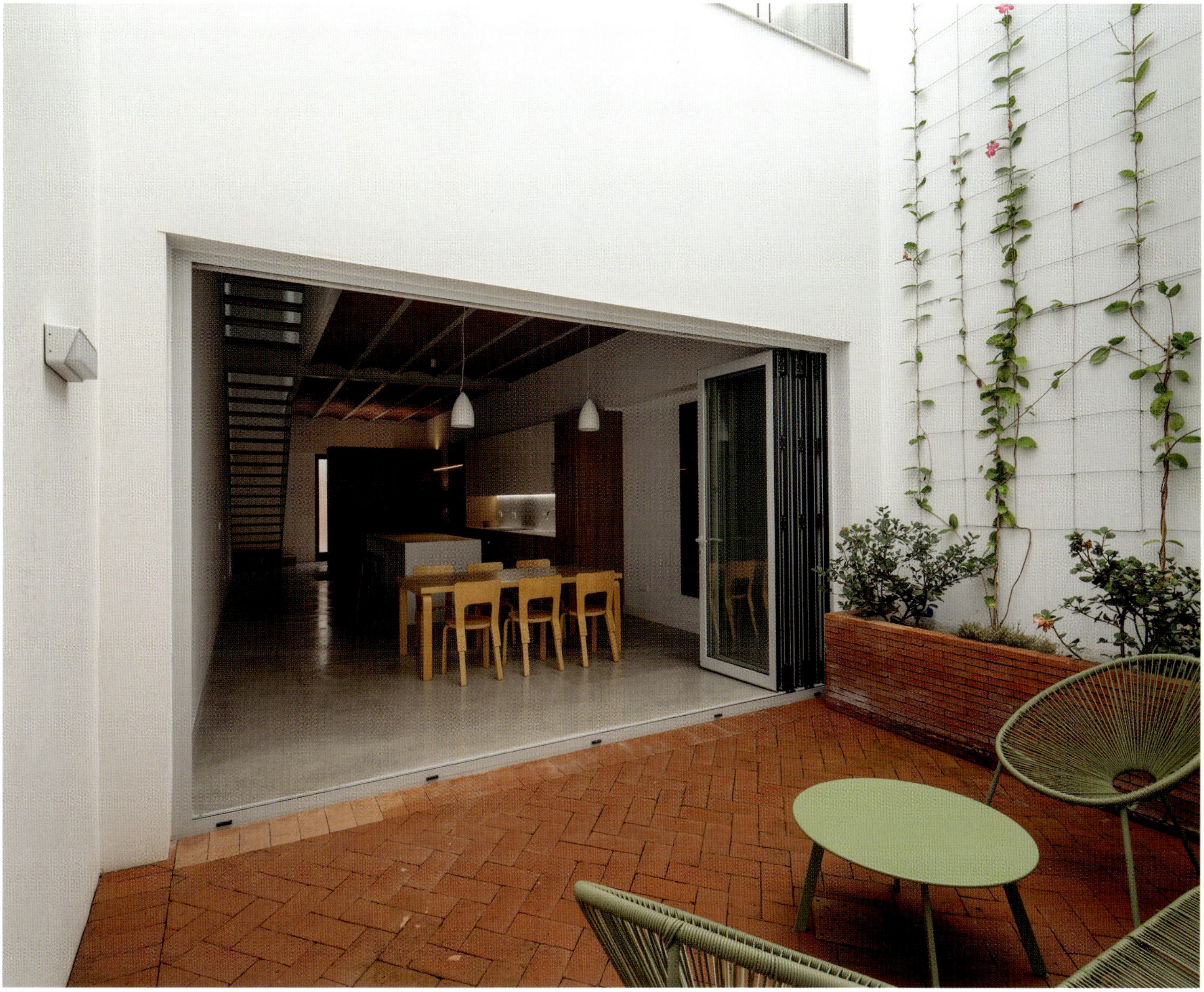

The house has been perfectly adapted to the local mild climate, providing residents the opportunity to enjoy the outdoor lifestyle with shaded lounges, swimming pools, and vegetation around. In the interplay between interior spaces and exterior areas through patios and terraces, the architects introduced numerous ideas to blur the limits between the two. One element providing visual continuity between inside and outside is polished concrete floors in all areas. In this complex and dynamic volume, patios are also a great way to deliver natural light, along with stair-skylights and double-height spaces, to mention just a few strategies employed by the architects. The house has been designed in relation to the passage of the sun during the day, with its light enhancing the palette of colors and materials used by the architects, such as wood and terra-cotta.

PROJECT: Casa LL
LOCATION: Tepoztlán, Mexico
YEAR: 2024
ARCHITECTS: RA!
PHOTOGRAPHY: Mariana Achach Herroz

In the stunning landscape of the slopes of Tepoztlán, the architects of RA! have designed an intriguing Casa LL that mimics the mountainous backdrop. "The house is designed with fragmented prisms that both connect and separate to form its distinct internal spaces, merging to create open areas and dispersing for secluded retreats," remark the architects. The compilation of monolithic cubes reminds one of a labyrinth, but instead of paths in between, there are patios interconnected with paths. What is common with a maze is the sensation of exploring the way, just like while moving across the spaces of Casa LL. The adventure begins upon passing the protective entrance in the form of a concrete block devoid of any openings. The first patio connects two wings of the house. The main one, with the kitchen, living, and dining areas, has been equipped with large openings toward the rear garden to contemplate scenic panoramas of the surrounding mountains.

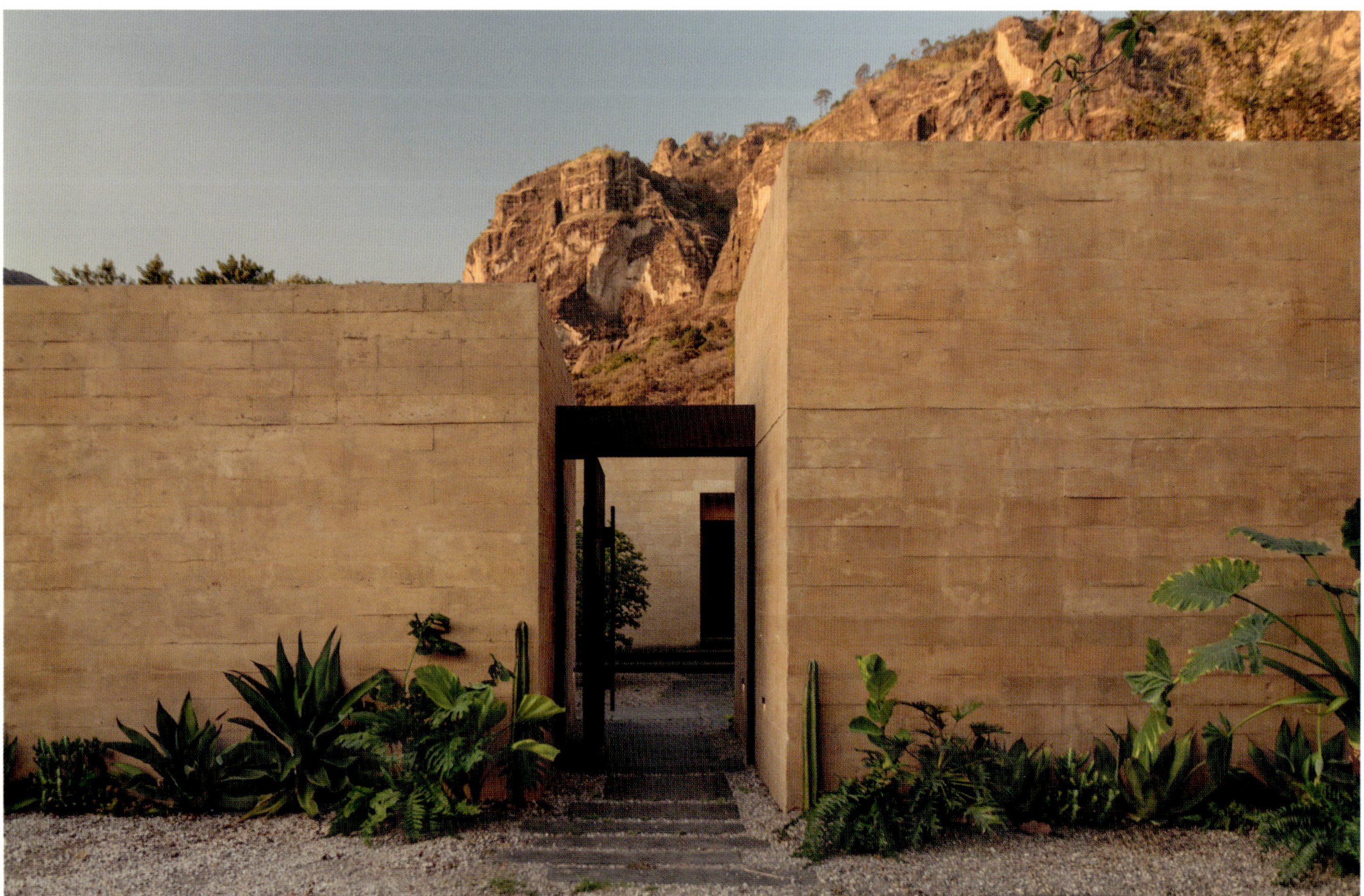

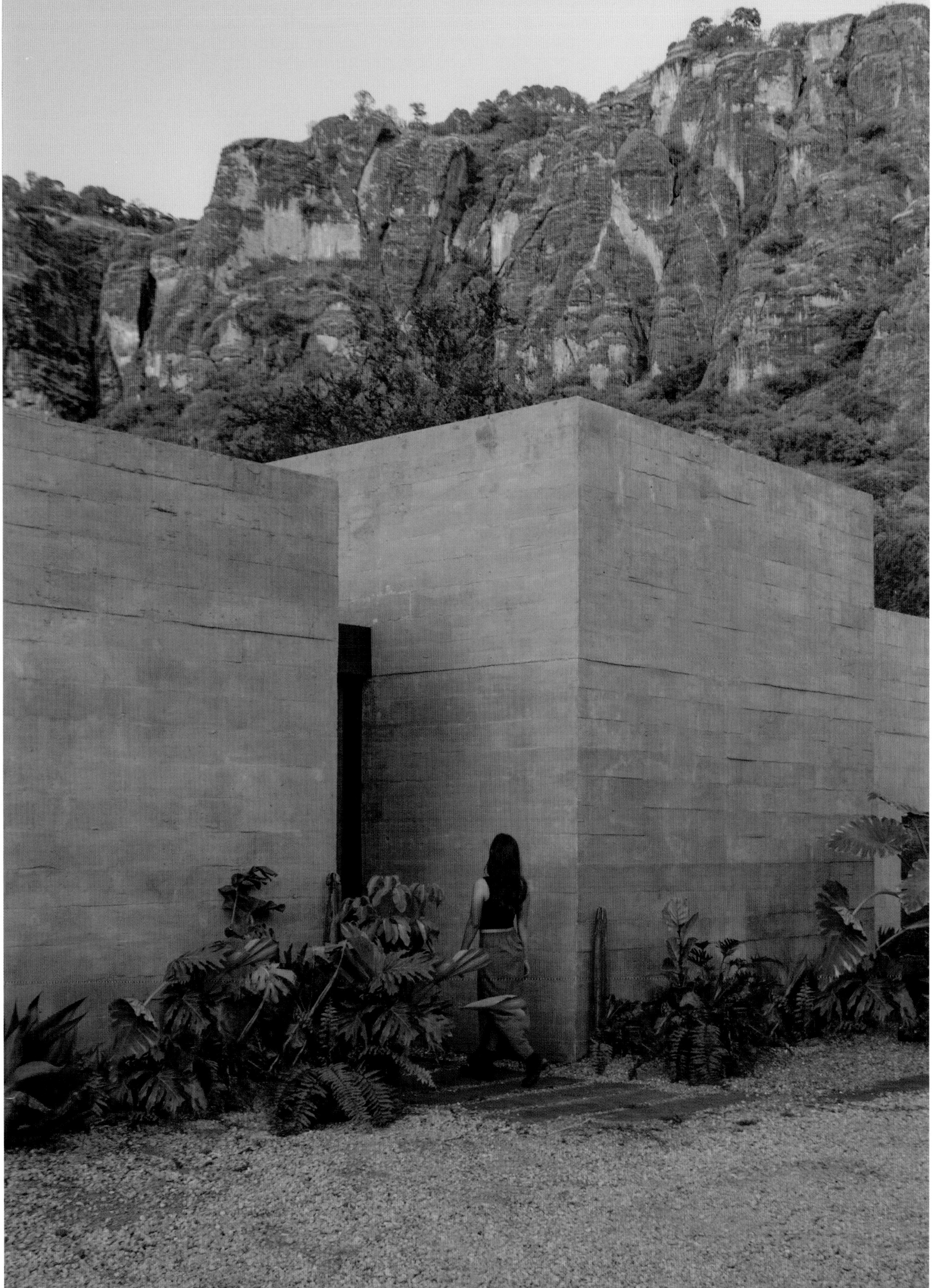

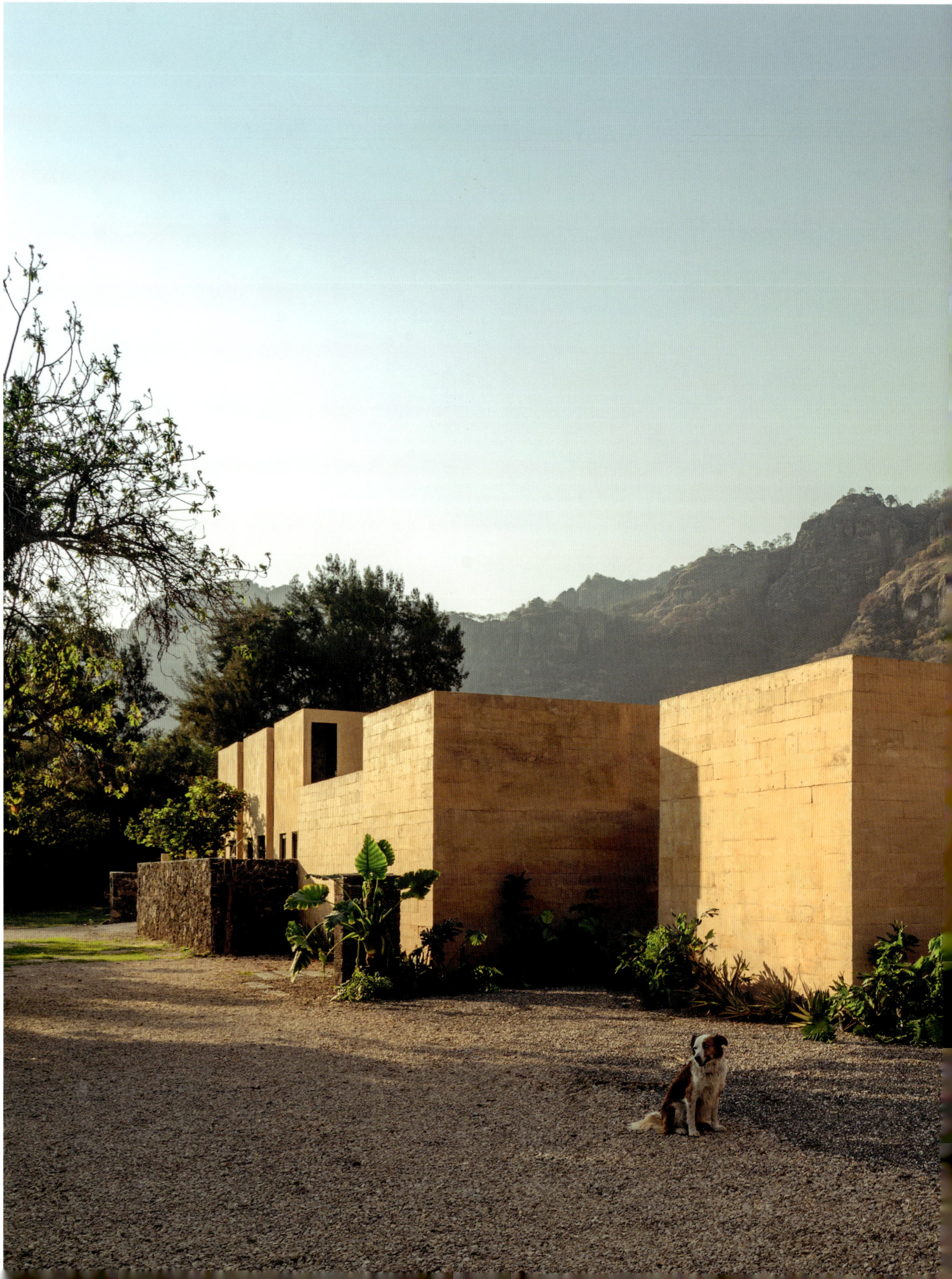

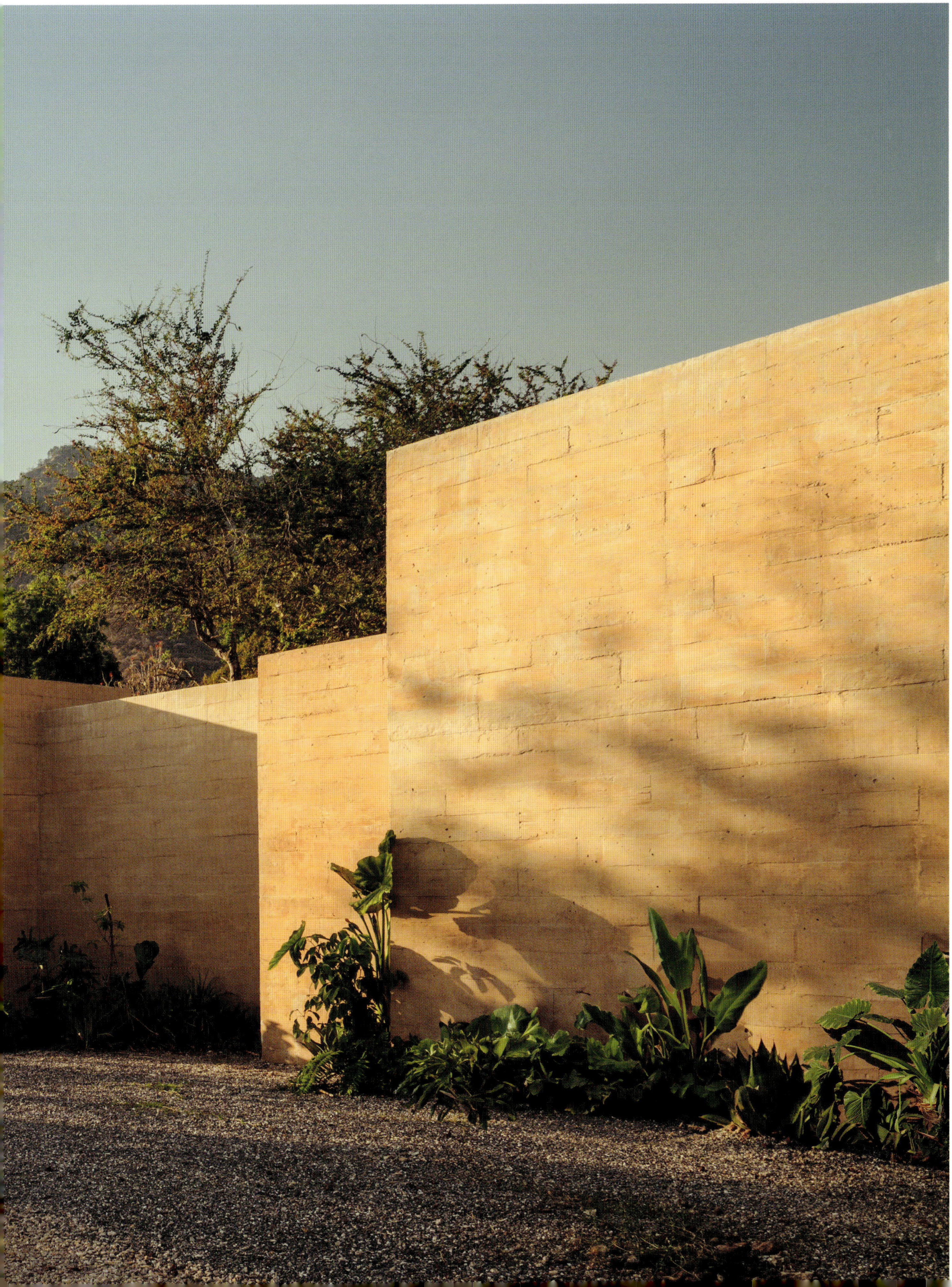

Crucial for the architects was the integration of volumes and open spaces in order to create not only a house but also an intimate connection to the environment, which would enhance the overall living experience.

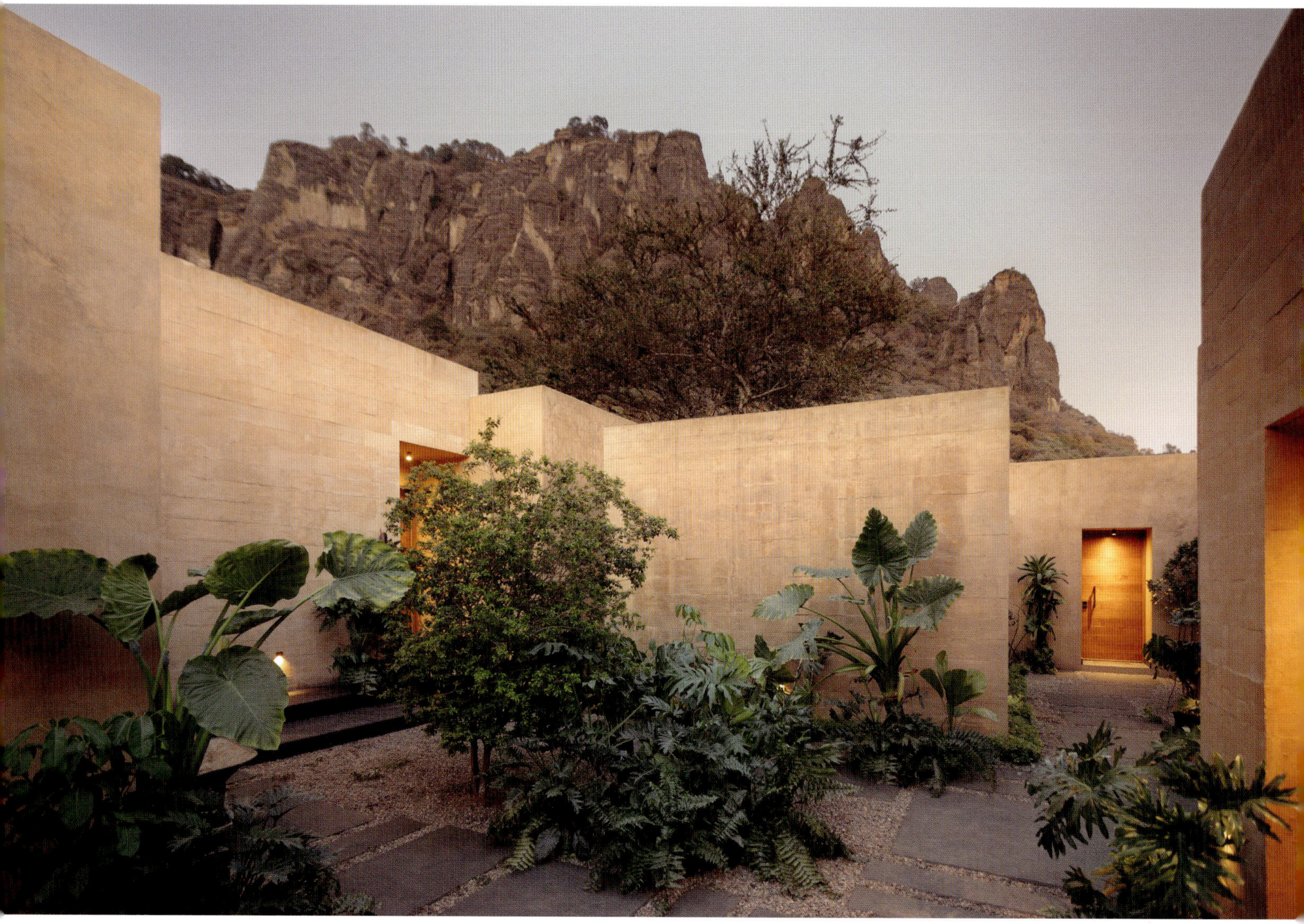

Mexico City–based RA! studio was established in 2017 by Cristóbal Ramírez de Aguilar, Pedro Ramírez de Aguilar, and Santiago Sierra. On the basis of the study of the context and social dynamics of planned spaces, the team's goal is to envision architecture that will establish not only an emotional connection with the residents, but also their relationship with the environment. The architects' designs aim to create atmospheres capable of evoking memory and emotion, prioritizing lived experience over form.

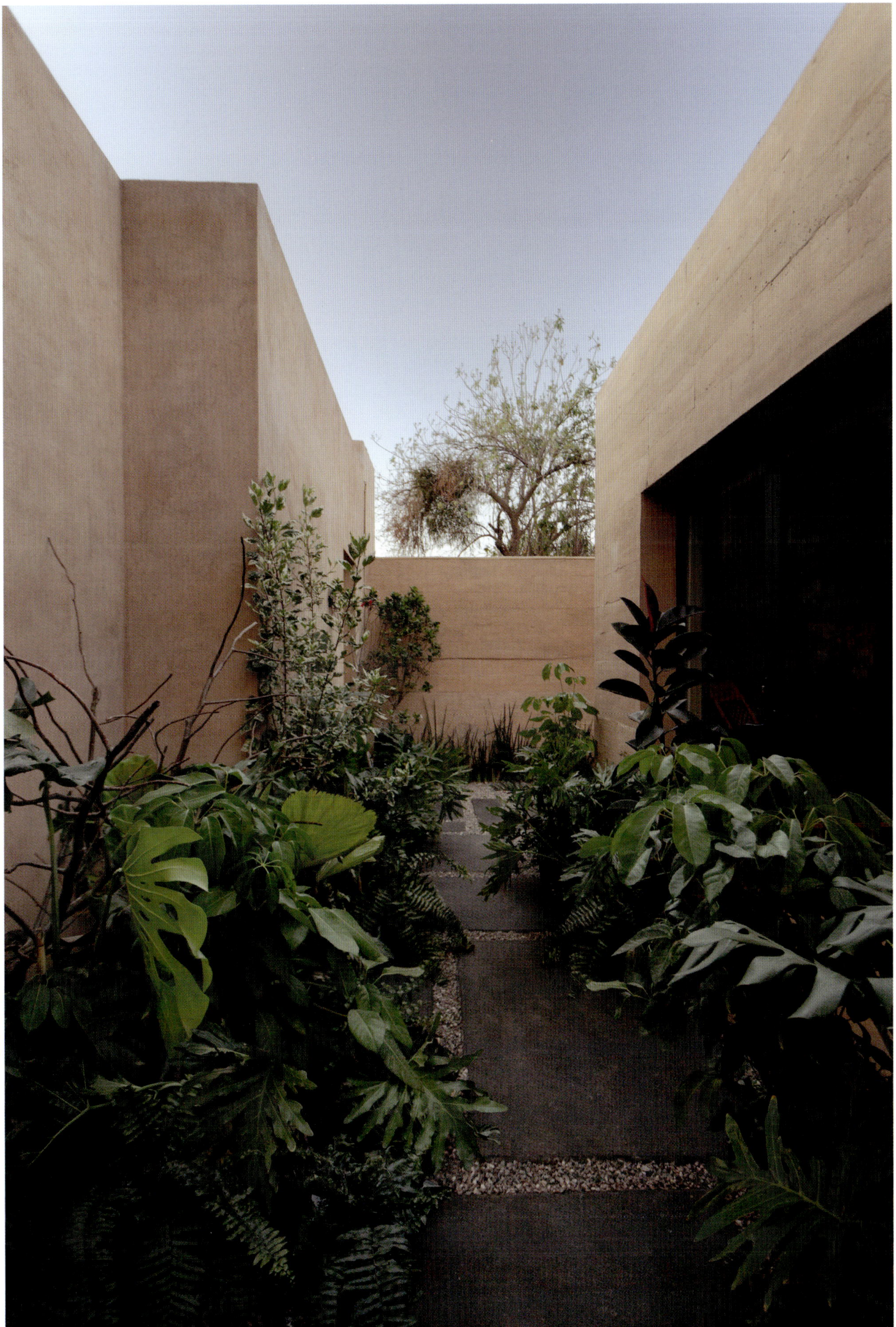

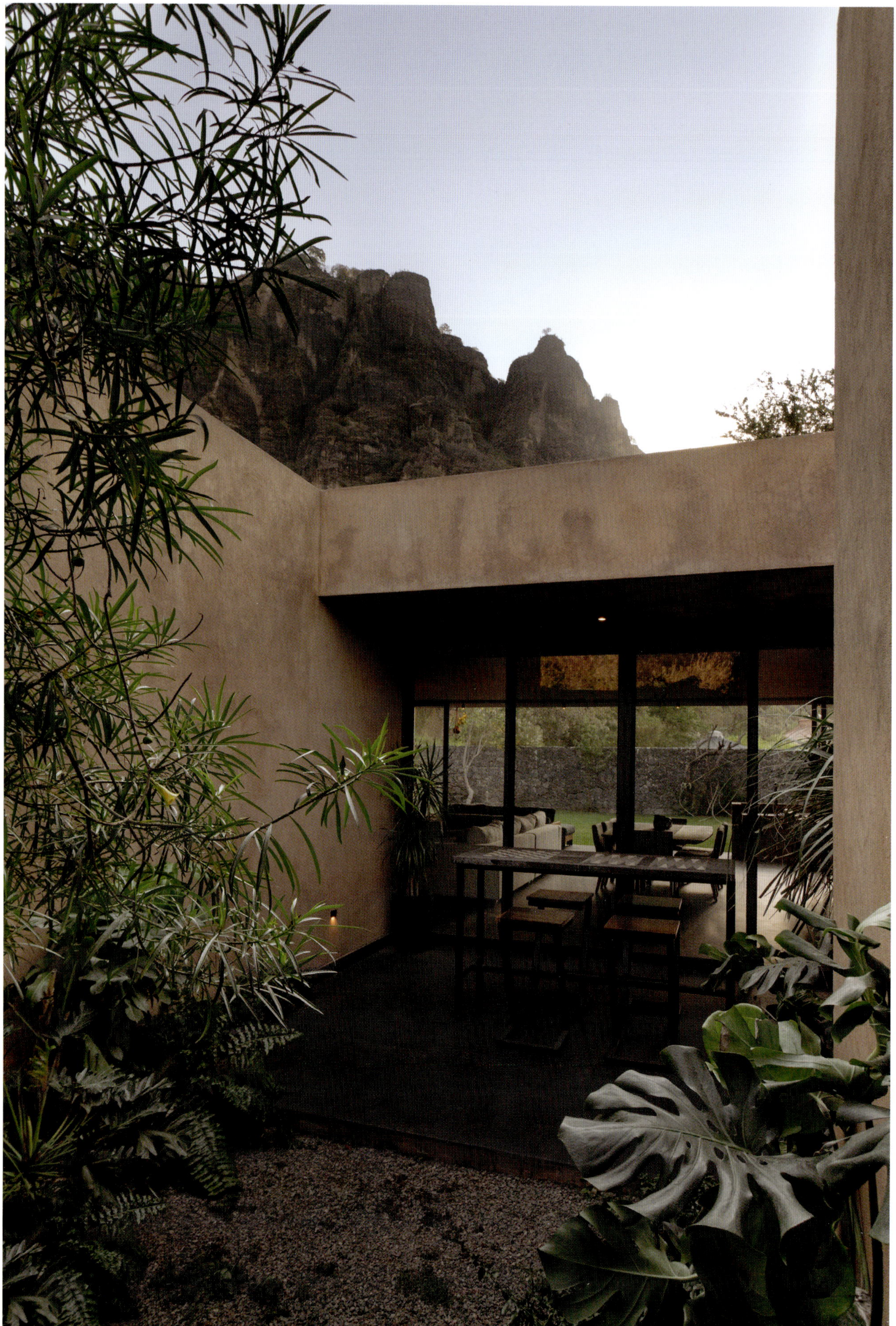

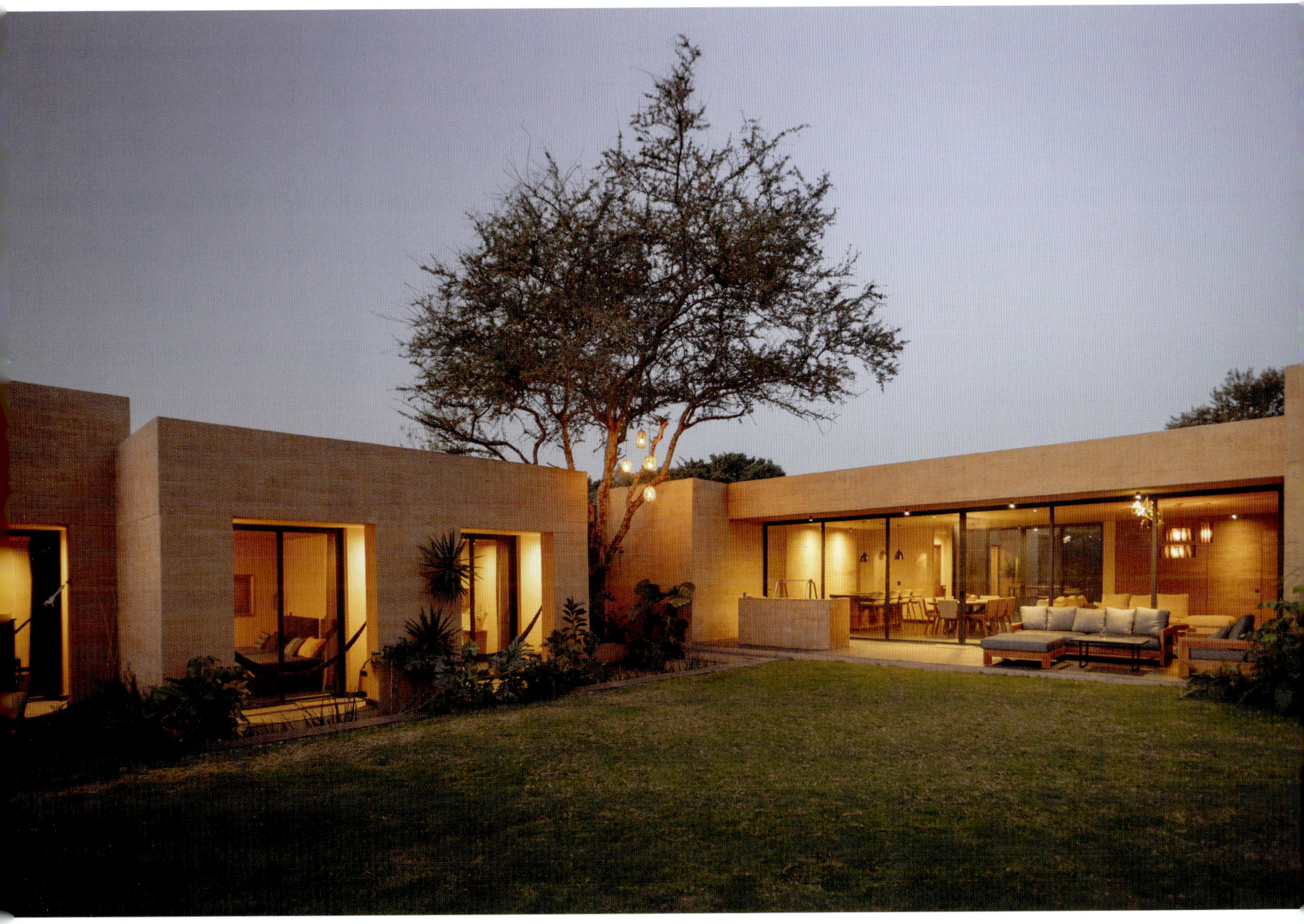

Moving inside the residence, but also between its geometric cubes housing its various parts as well as an art studio, provides a unique experience. It is enhanced by the striking natural context of Casa LL with the landscape, taken into account by the architects. The L shape of the architectural arrangement directs both wings toward the mountains and connects the view with their interiors through an extensive patio. Whether it is the large courtyard, covered with grass and devoted to relaxation, or smaller patios, such as a space for an outdoor dining table, all exterior spaces between the cubes dynamize the experience in the most original way that is intensified by the way the geometrical volumes interact with the passing sun.

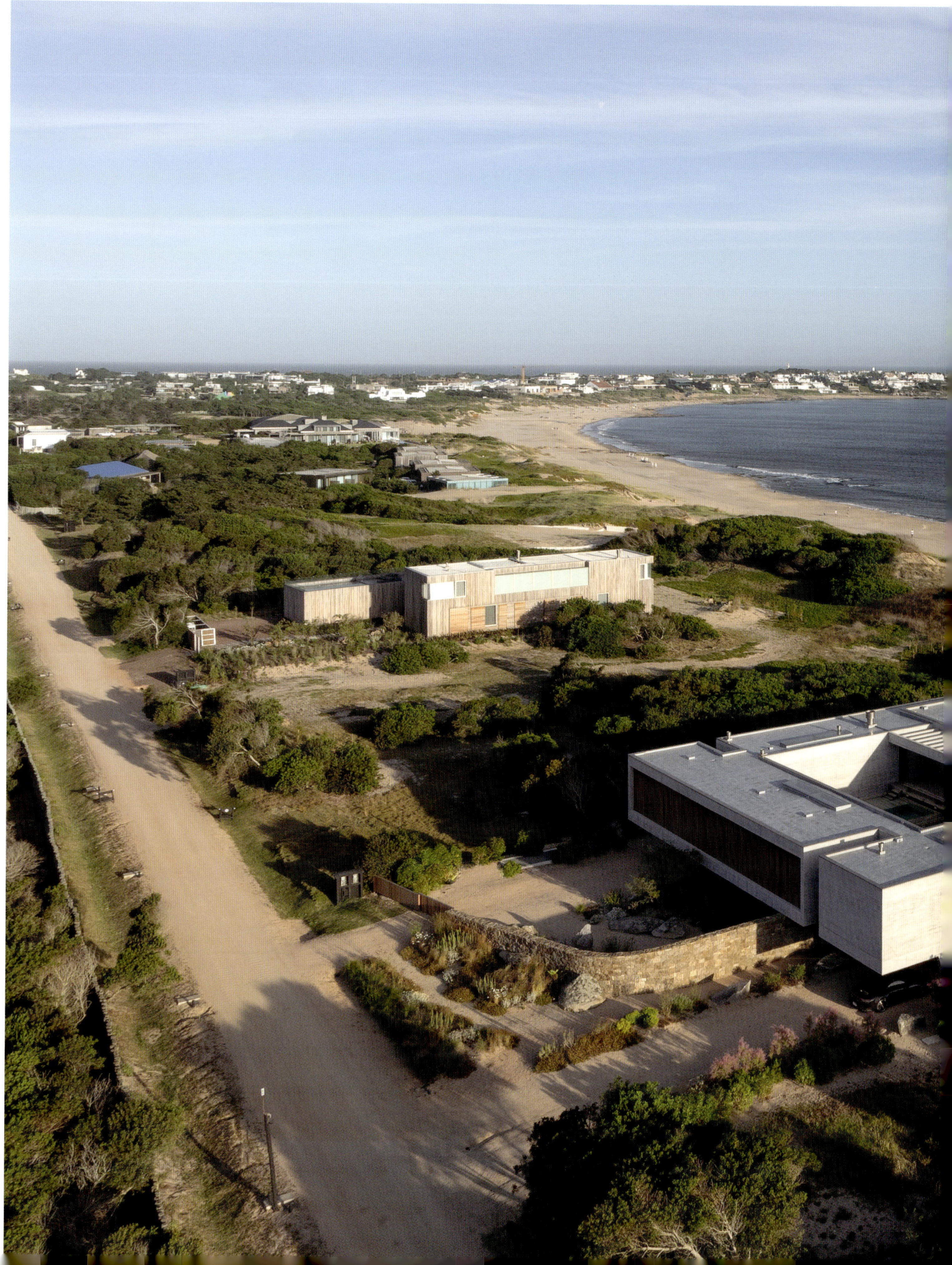

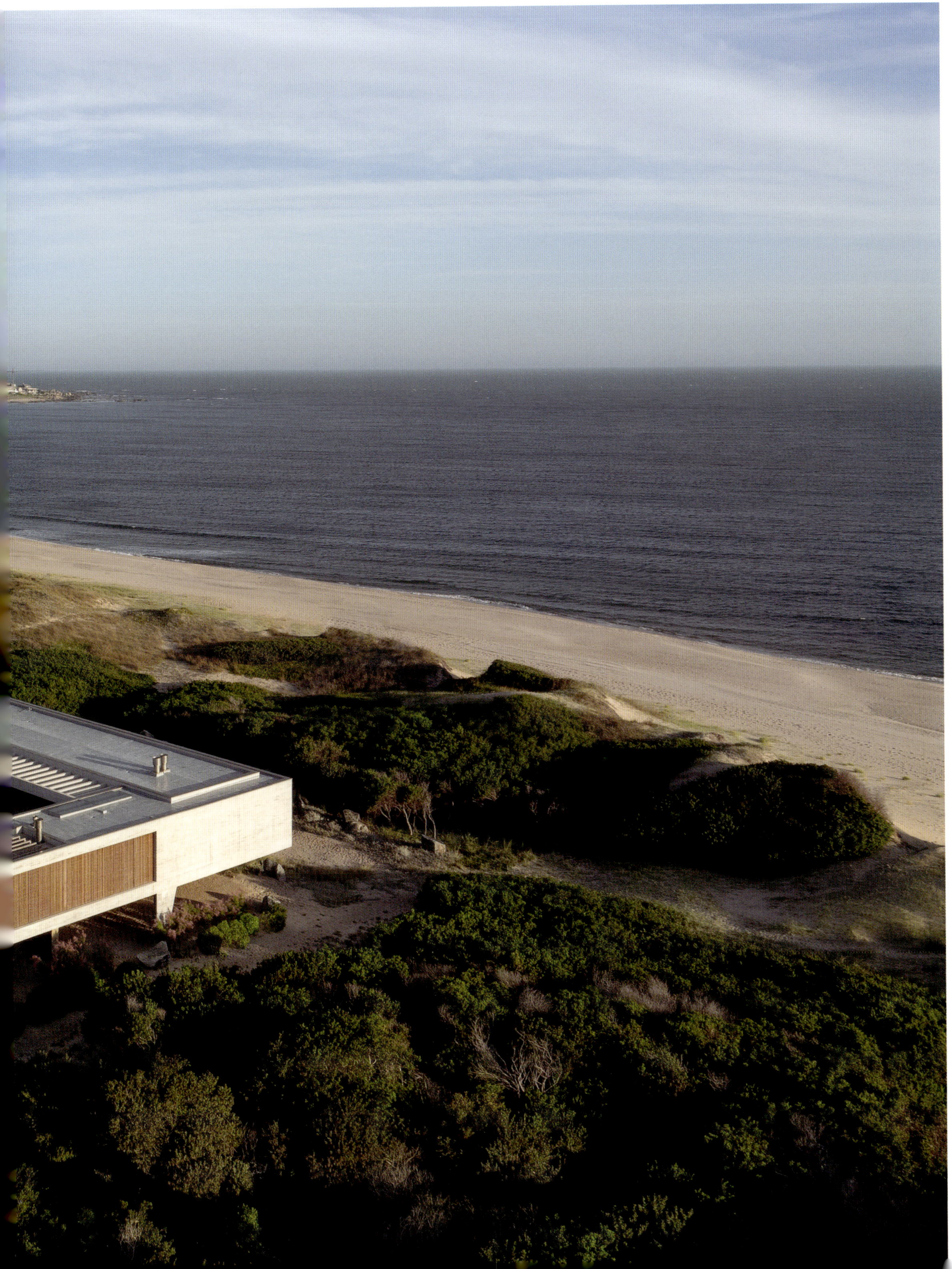

Established in 2011 by Arturo J. Grimaldi and Leonardo M. Nacht, two architects and lecturers with extensive experience, the studio is based in Argentina. Specializing in residential architecture, the duo designs visionary houses across Uruguay and Argentina. In their realizations, distinctive shapes are carefully planned in dialogue with spectacular locations, mostly in natural environments.

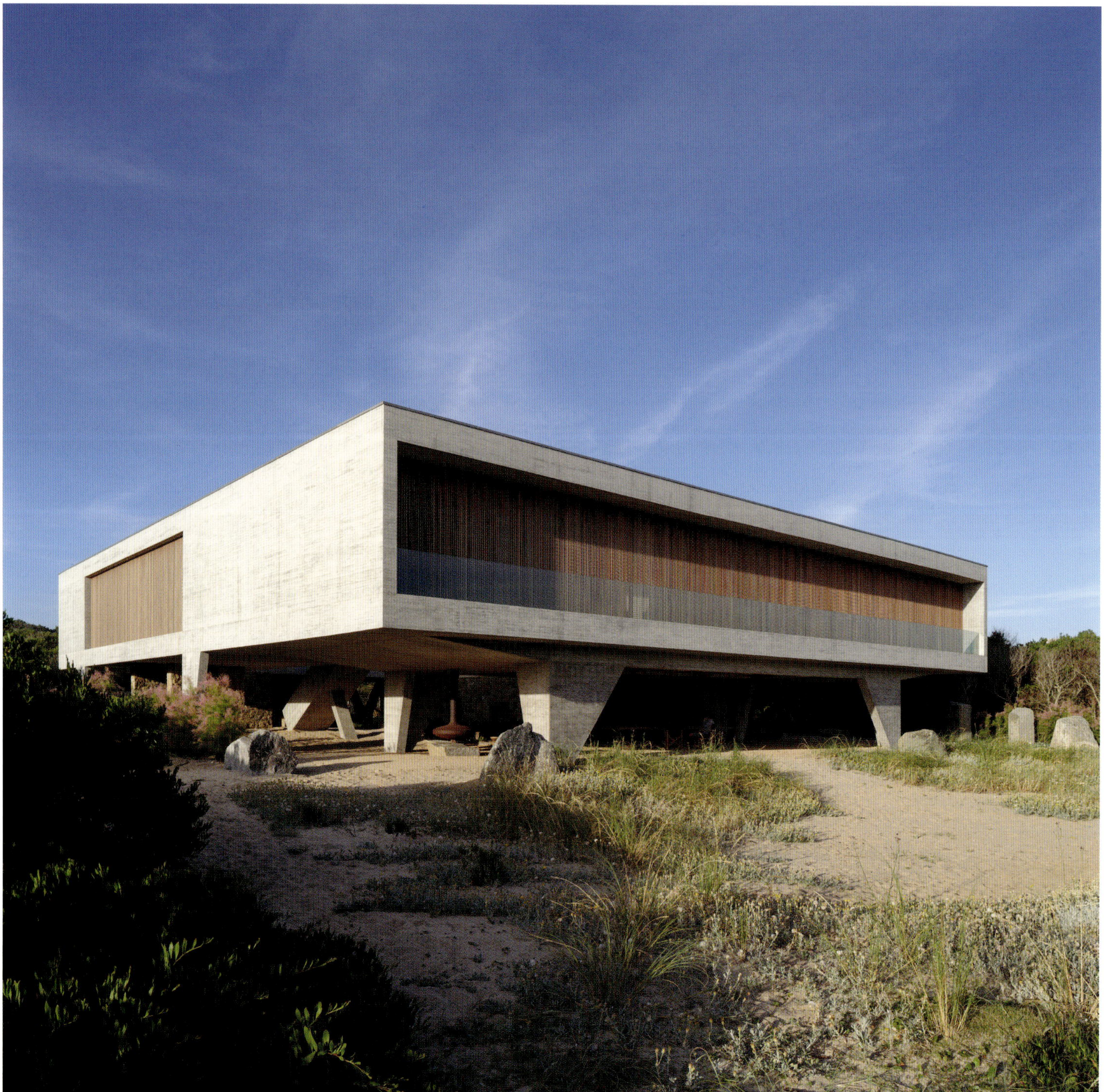

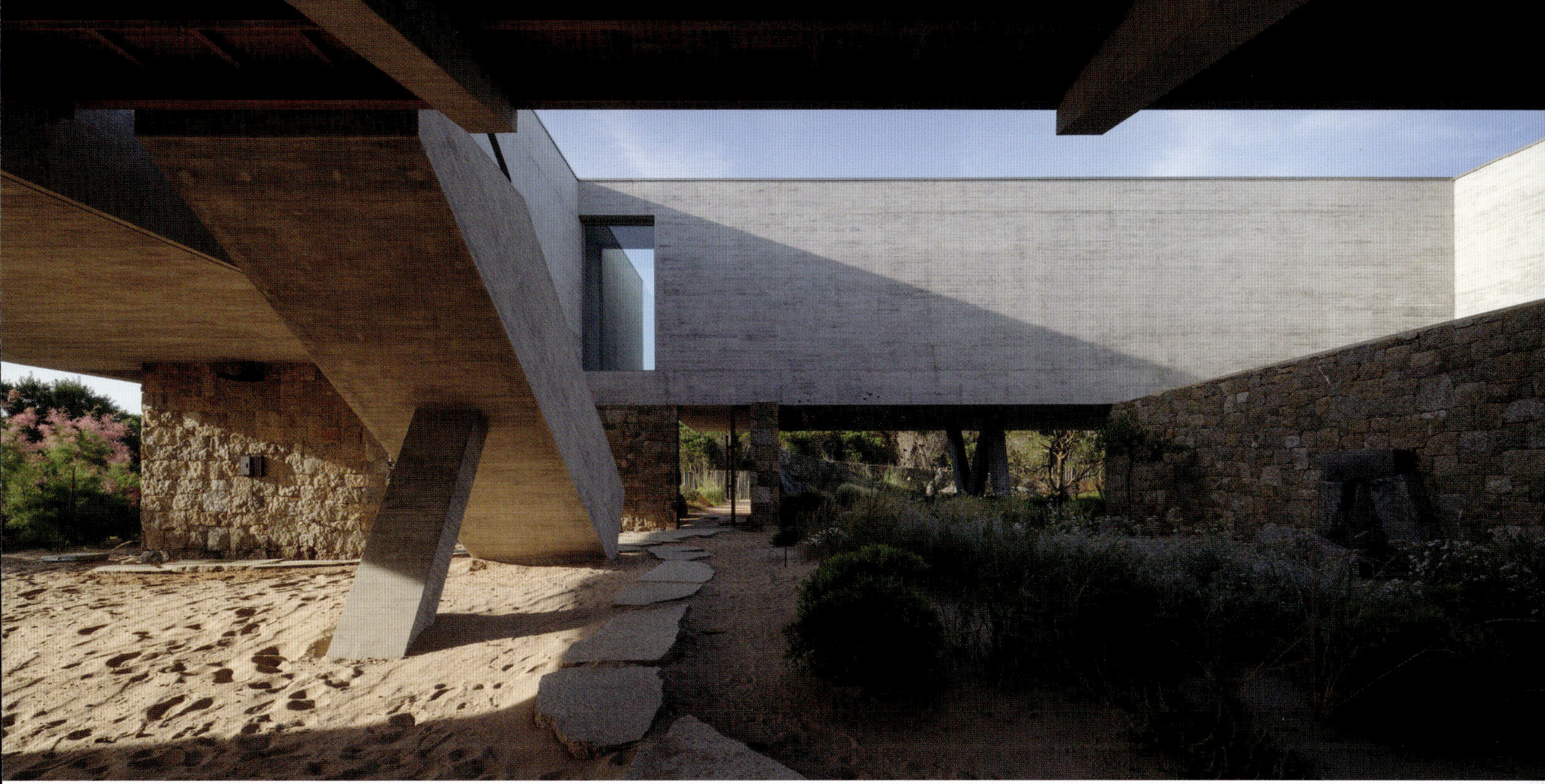

PROJECT: La Secreta House
LOCATION: Faro de José Ignacio, Uruguay
YEAR: 2023
ARCHITECTS: Grimaldi· Nacht Arquitectos
PHOTOGRAPHY: Javier Agustín Rojas

The paradise-like landscape of Mansa Beach in José Ignacio, Uruguay, creates a dramatic backdrop for the equally unique La Secreta House, which is oriented toward the sea. Designed by Arturo Grimaldi and Leonardo Nacht, the villa incorporates several ingenious solutions to connect with its surroundings. The geometric volume has been elevated above the ground, resulting in a spectacular patio that one arrives at along a curved stone wall leading from the main entrance. While the building appears as a simple cube from the outside, approaching the courtyard reveals a complex system of connections between the ground and various parts of the house. The dynamism of the inside-outside relationship animates the space enveloped by concrete walls, responding to the surrounding landscape.

Inspired by the topography of the dune, the architects decided to create two spheres—a recreational area on the ground, featuring a dining room, a grill, and a fireplace for gatherings, and a more private space on the upper level, with a stunning living room facing the seafront. Thanks to hidden openings in pockets, this space can open entirely to the outside, since the dialogue between the spaces and the sea was one of the architects' objectives. Elevating the house also helped reduce the impact on the site and minimize alterations to the natural landscape. All interiors have been organized around the central patio, with the open-air yet sheltered swimming pool area blending visually with the courtyard.

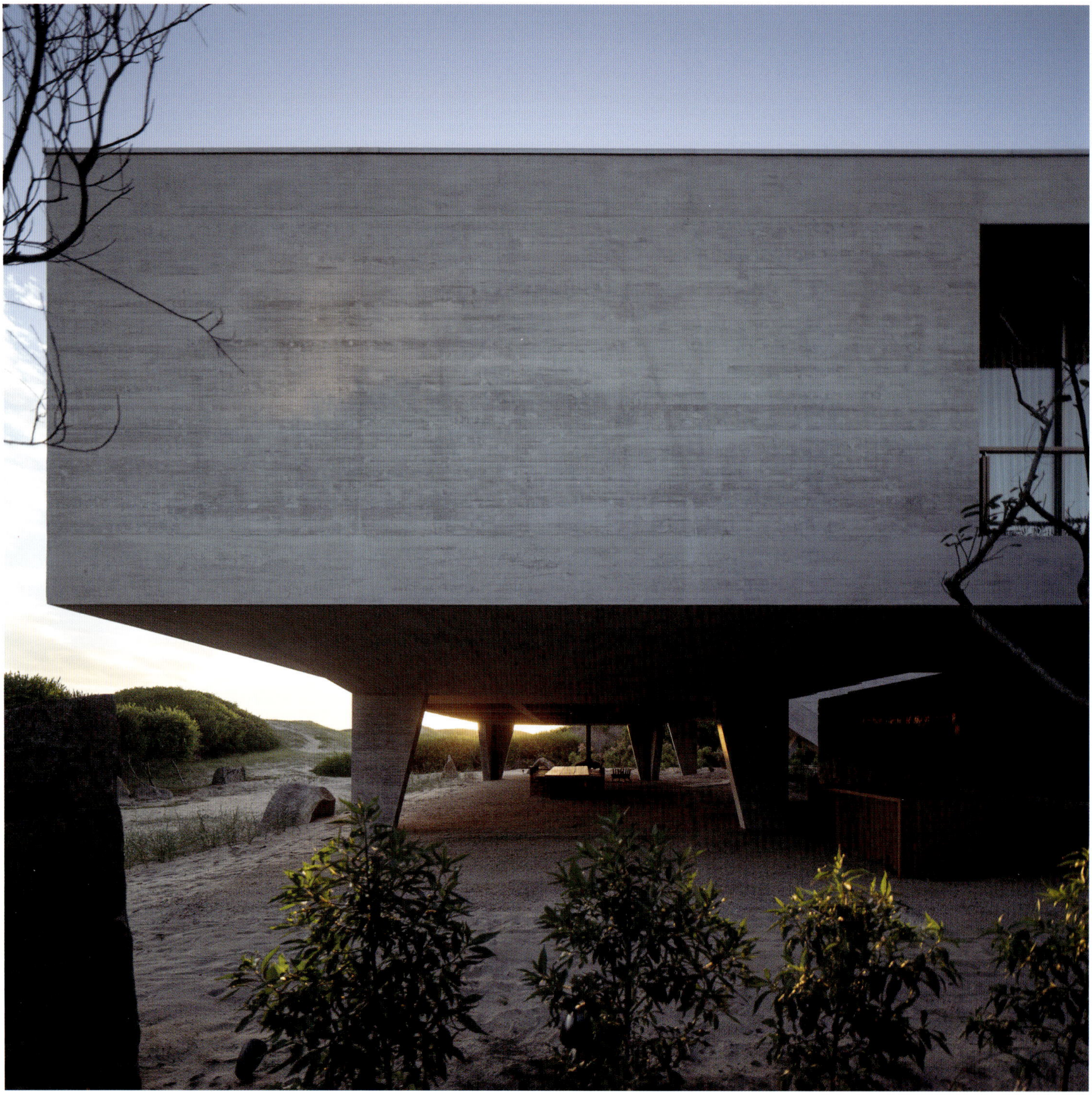

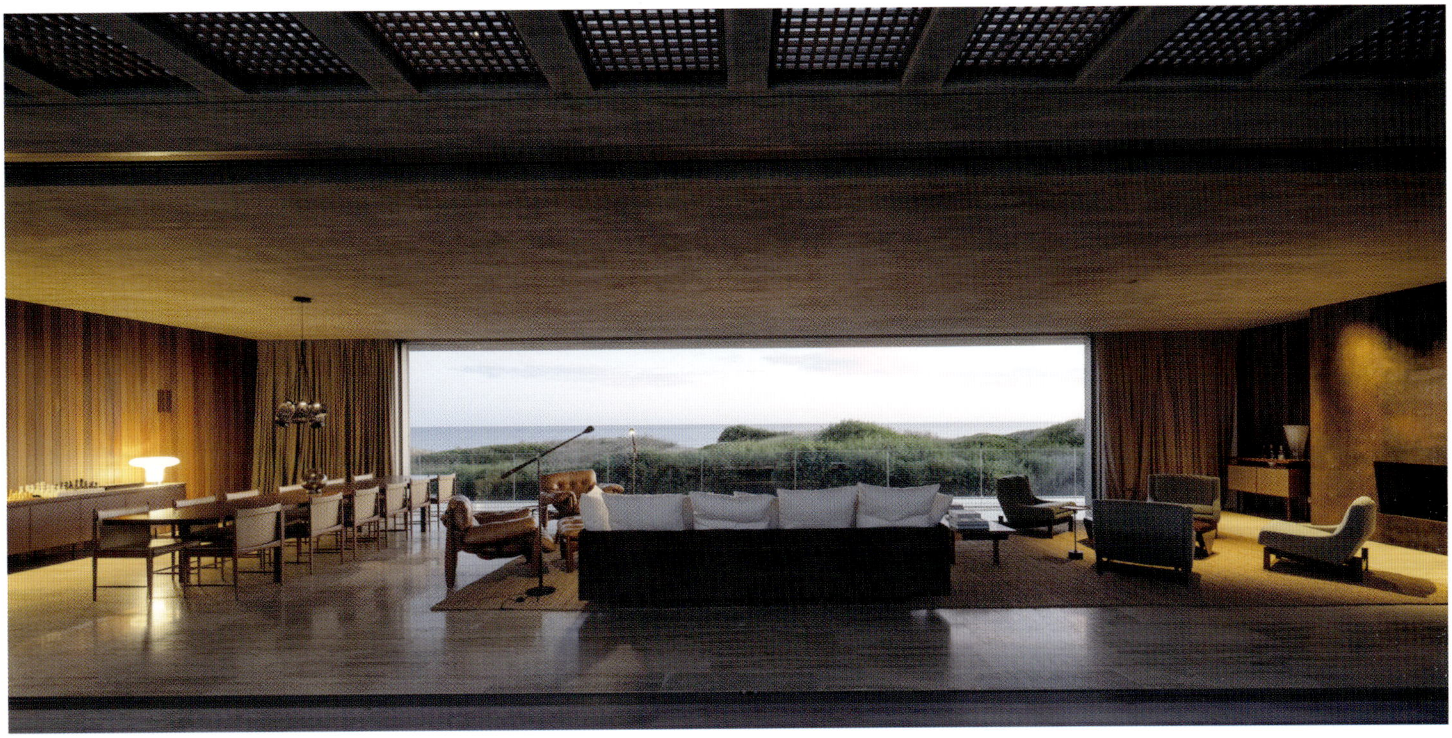

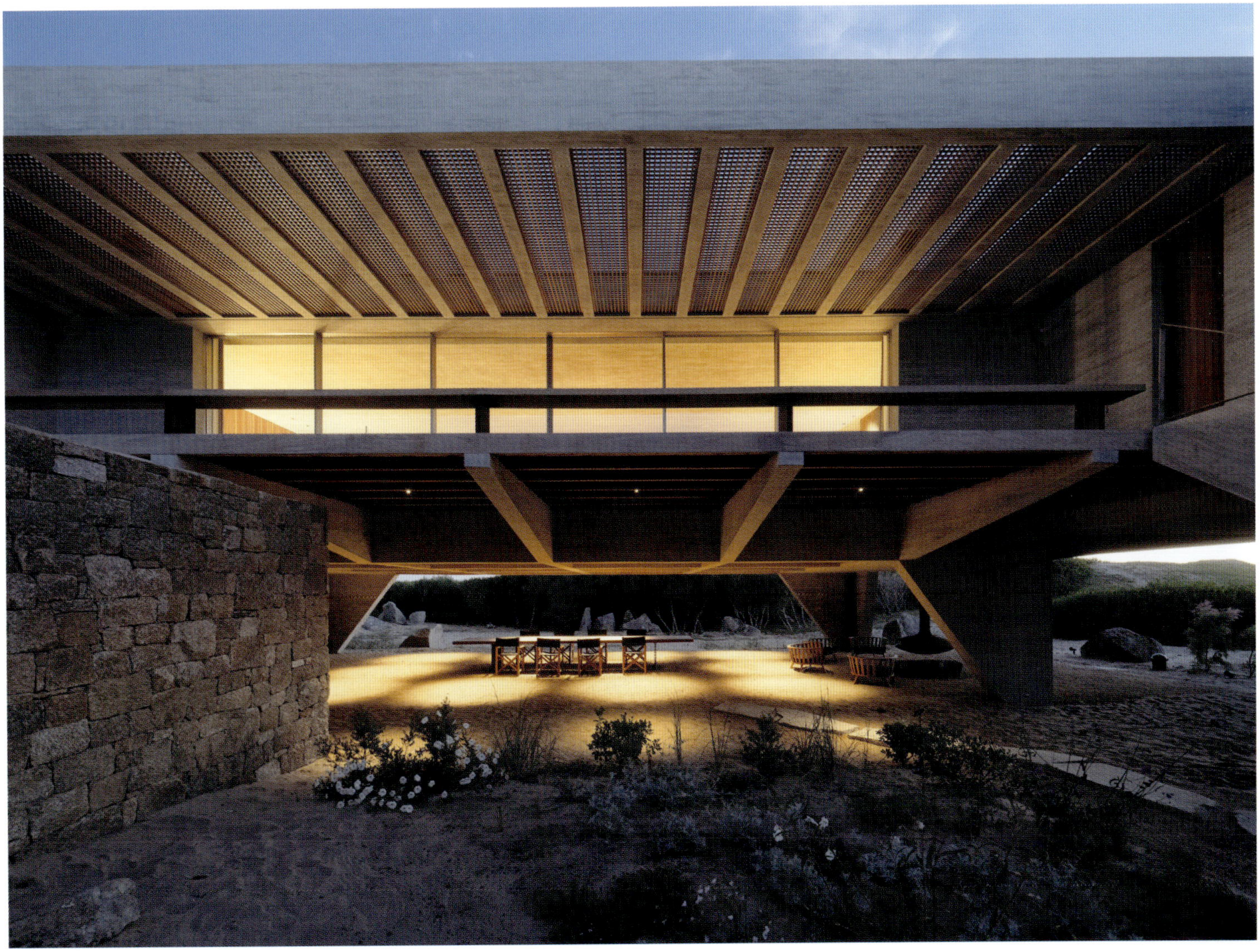

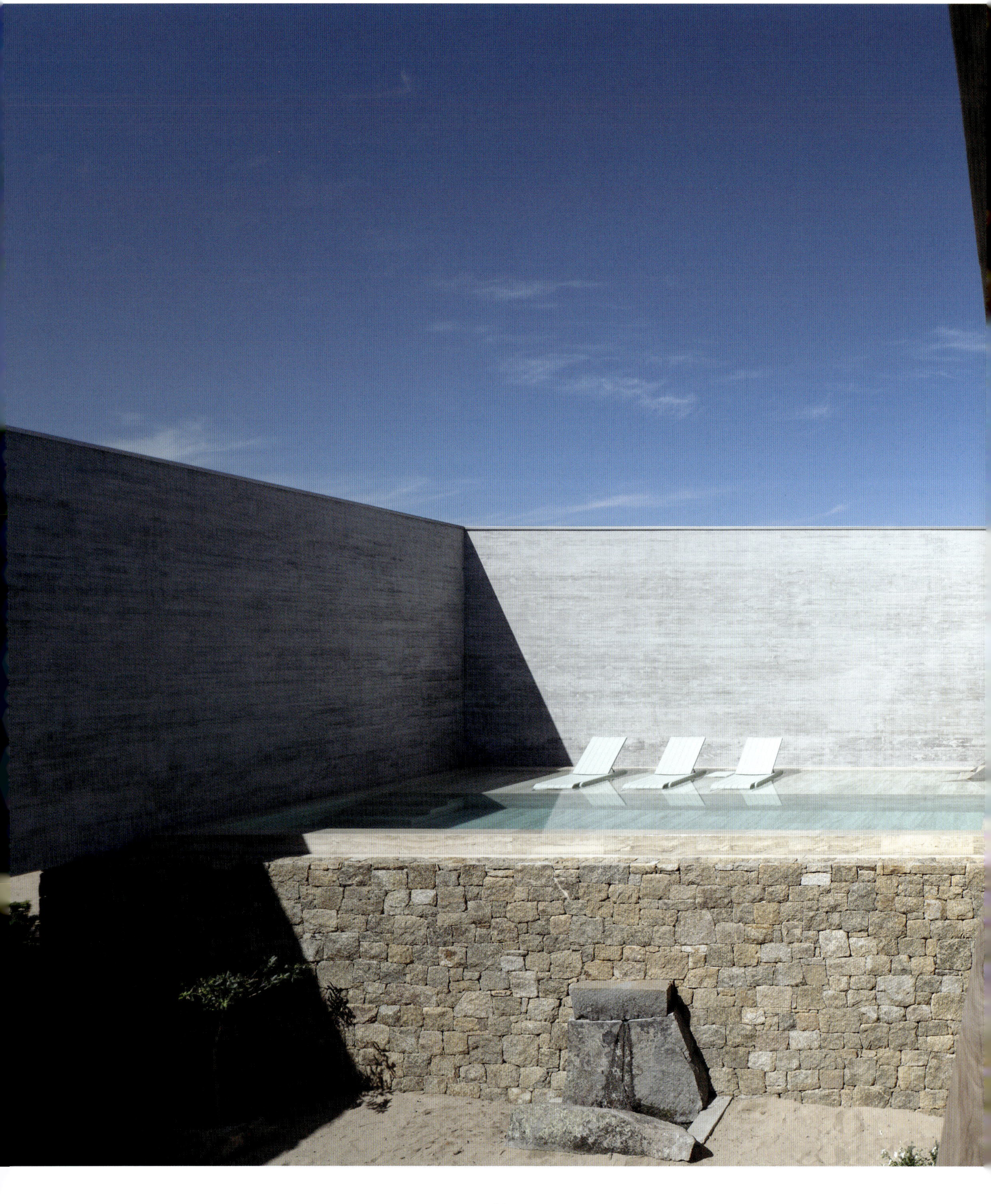

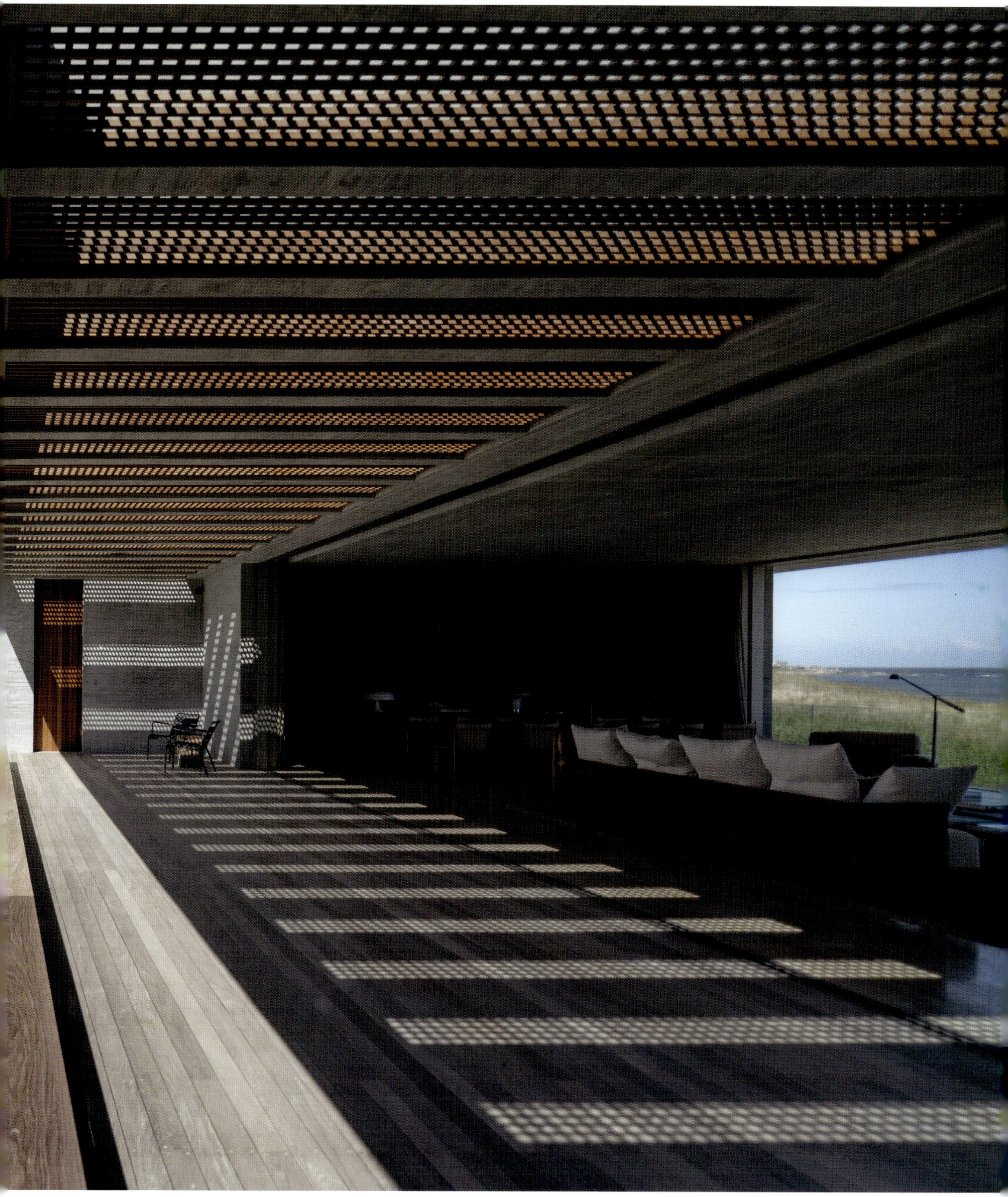

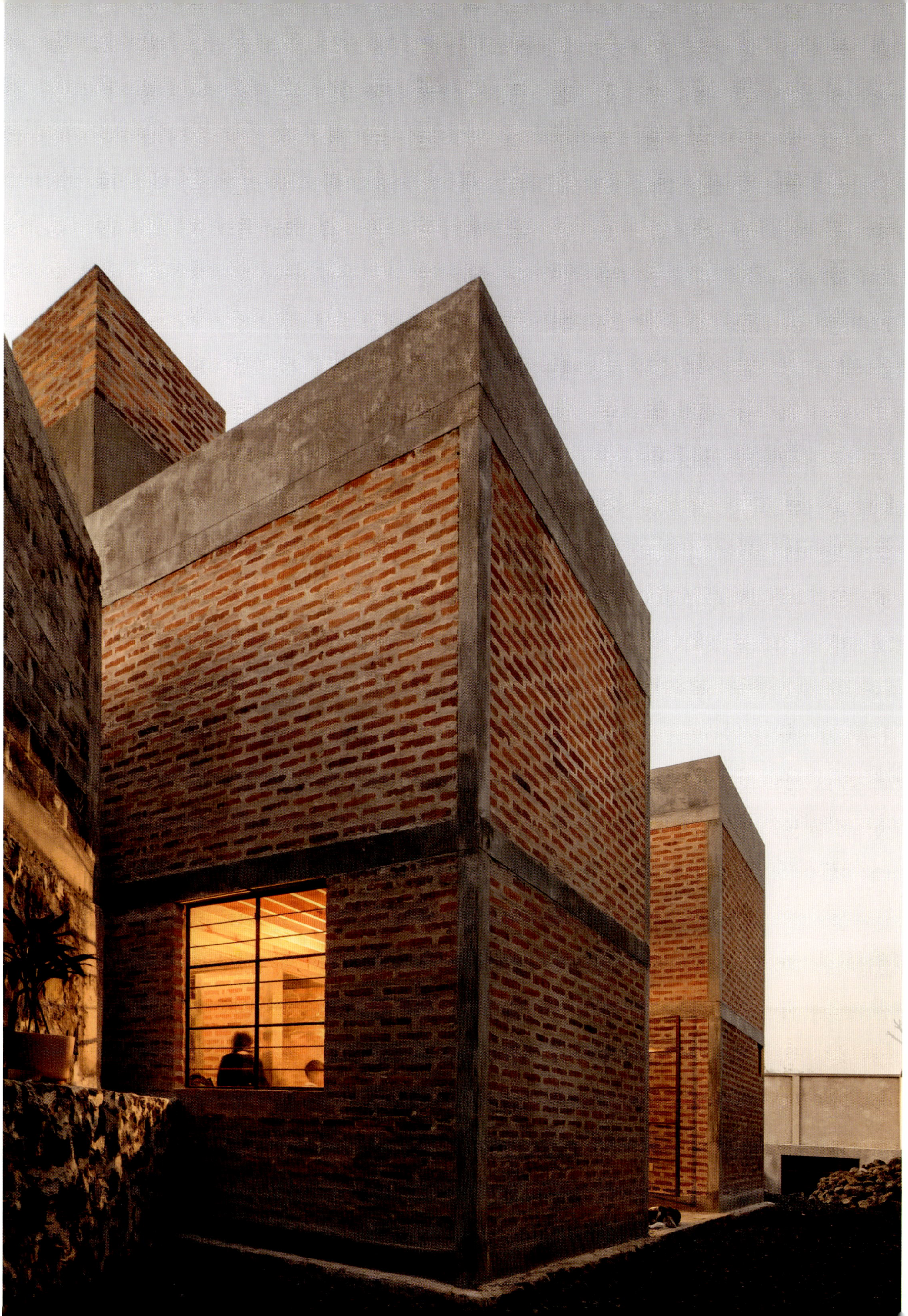

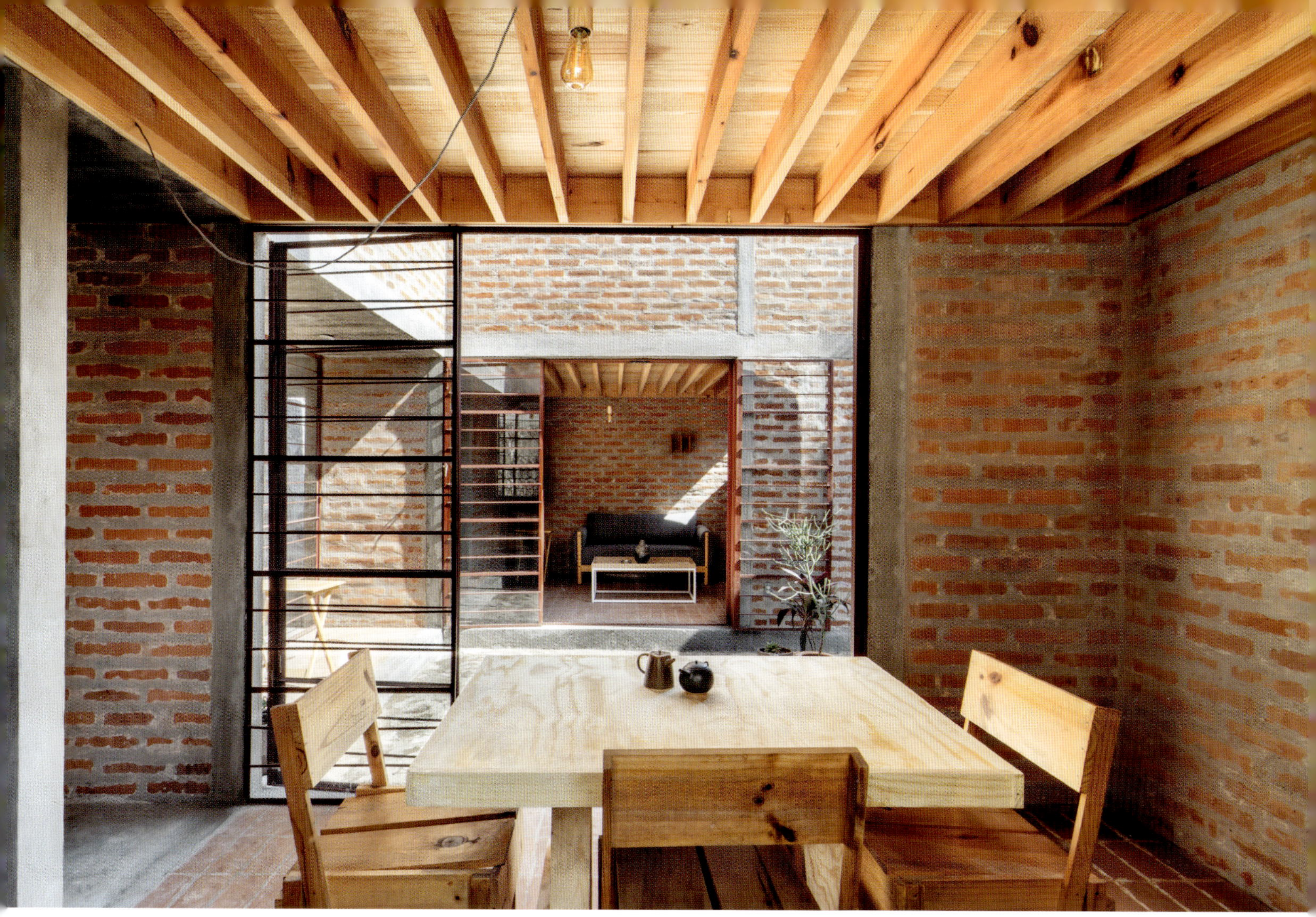

PROJECT: Nakasone House
LOCATION: Mexico City, Mexico
YEAR: 2020
ARCHITECTS: Escobedo Soliz Studio
PHOTOGRAPHY: Ariadna Polo

Nakasone House, designed by Pavel Escobedo and Andrés Soliz, demonstrates the architects' fascination with materials and their textures. Made of brick framed by the concrete skeleton (to strengthen the structure in case of common earthquakes), the geometric U-shaped volume speaks a sensorial language. Achieving such a powerful rough texture was possible thanks to the skillful use of common material, following traditional masonry construction techniques. "By using the simple running brick bond and a thick joint of mortar, we were able to build walls with less material in less time," emphasize the architects. The final smoothing touch was polishing the surface with another brick block when the mortar was fresh.

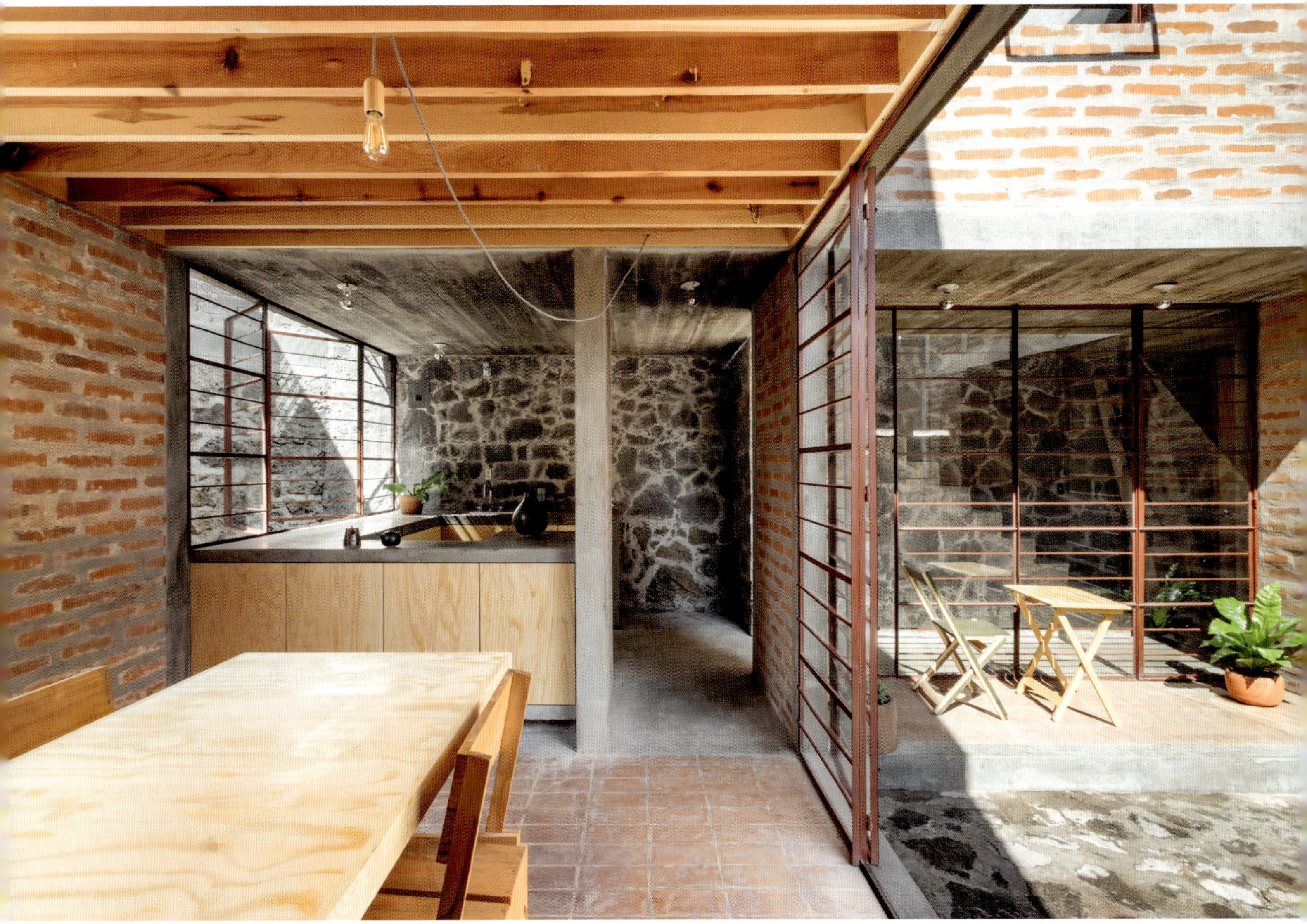

The patio, located intimately between two wings—one housing the kitchen with the dining area and the opposite consecrated to a living room—is the heart of the project. Connected with various interiors through large openings, this courtyard provides privacy and becomes a comfortable extension of the first floor. The visual continuity is strengthened by the same method of finishing the walls, which is identical on the outer skin and inside the house. Playing with the sun throughout the day, this rough texture is yet more expressive. Another material the architects used was the volcanic stone found on-site, which, like the brick, helps regulate the temperature of the house. Additionally, the central patio also effectively supports the ventilation of the main spaces.

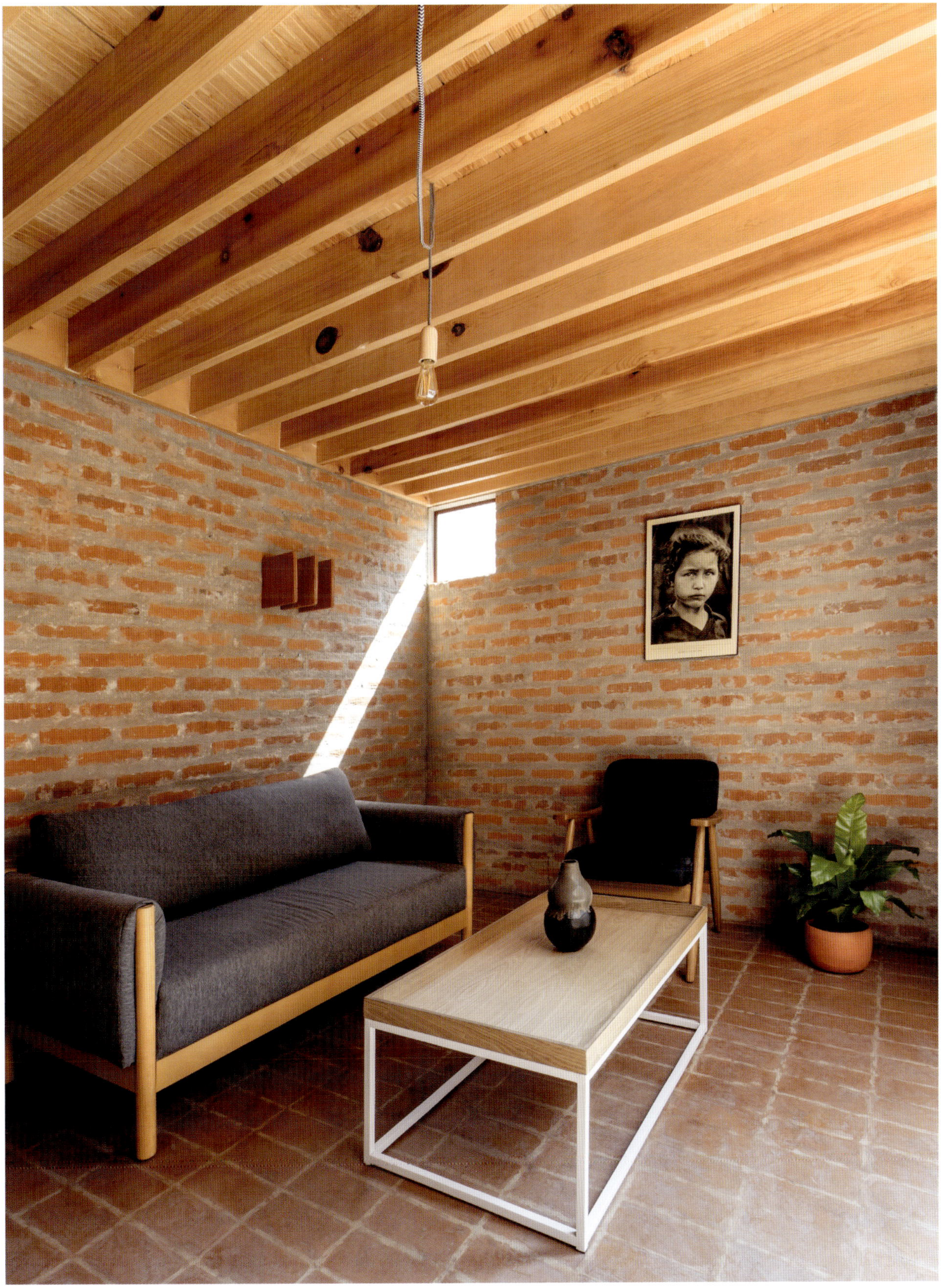

This Mexico City–based studio was founded in 2016 by Pavel Escobedo and Andrés Soliz. As they state, doing more with less time, fewer resources, and less environmental impact is the constant objective in their practice. Dedicated to continuous exploration of materials and structural solutions, the architects result in an expressive language that triggers senses. The architects are also dedicated academic teachers and lecturers worldwide.

PROJECT: Casa Aguilar
LOCATION: Querétaro, Mexico
YEAR: 2024
ARCHITECTS: Taller Segovia Molina
PHOTOGRAPHY: Diego Vázquez Mellado, ZAICKZ

The monolithic volume is impressive with its grand scale and striking geometry of its facades, constructed in exposed concrete. "Casa Aguilar emerges with the idea of creating an interior oasis where a family can experience introspection and contemplation while inhabiting their home," explains the studio. Since the house is located in a dense neighborhood, this task was challenging, and only wrapping the volume in a solid shell made it possible to create such an intimate and protective space. Introducing patios planned on each of three levels to this particular solution not only enhances the atmosphere but is also functional, since they become an important source of natural light.

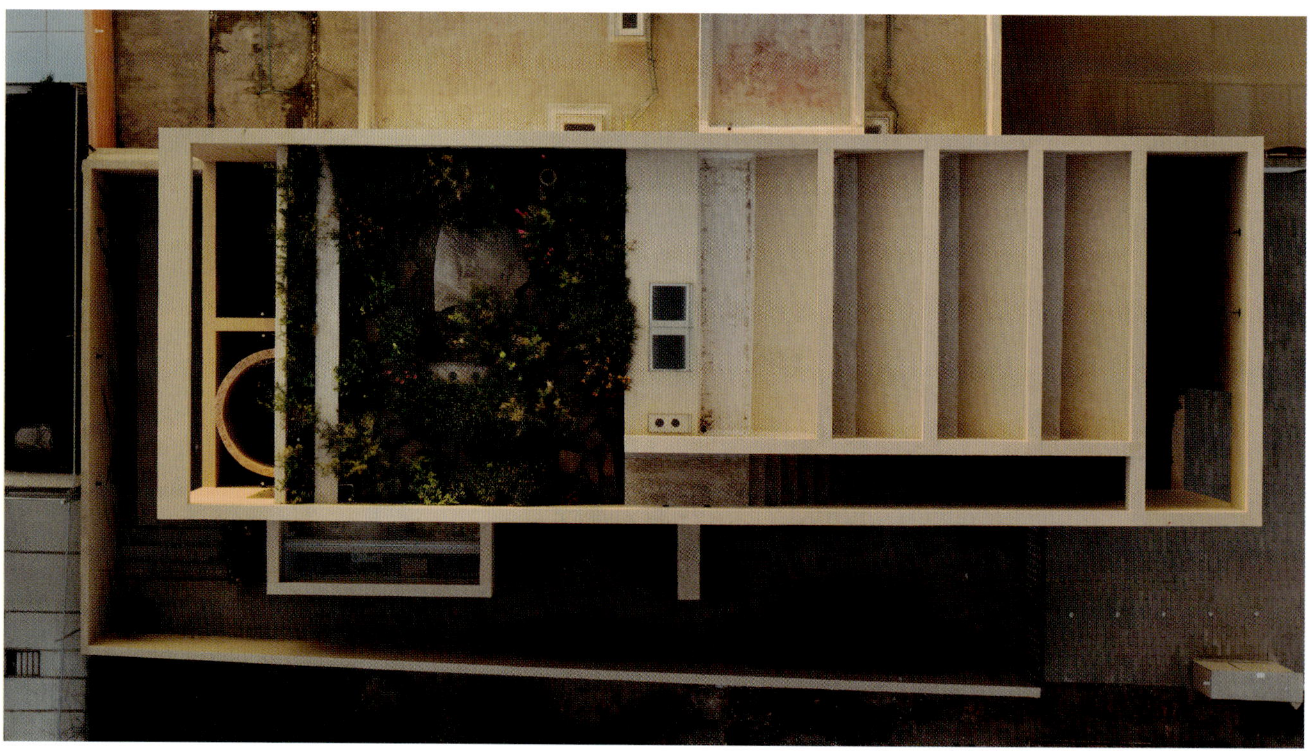

The aerial view of Casa Aguilar demonstrates how a big part of the volume has been dedicated to the internal patios, including the stunning rooftop garden.

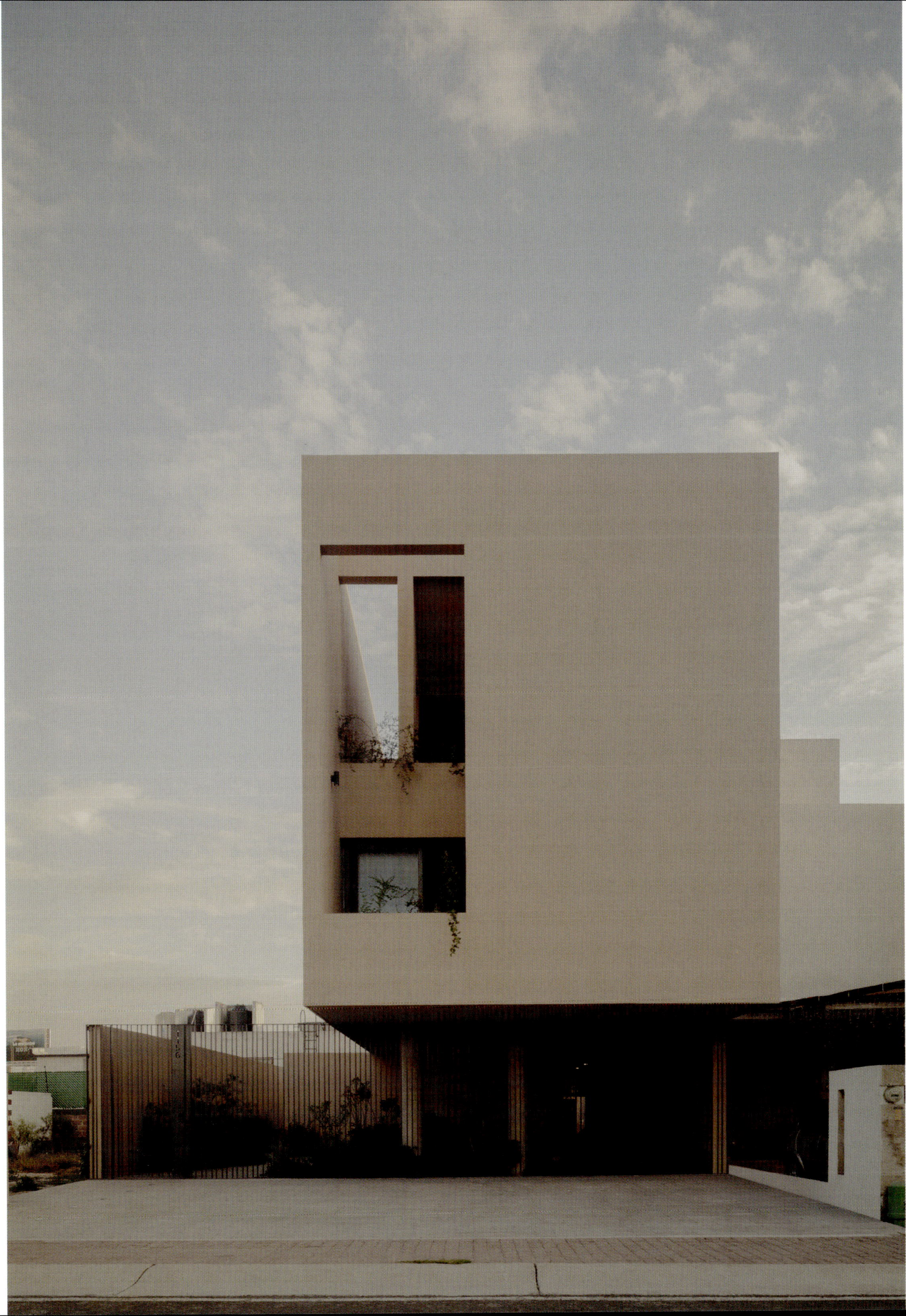

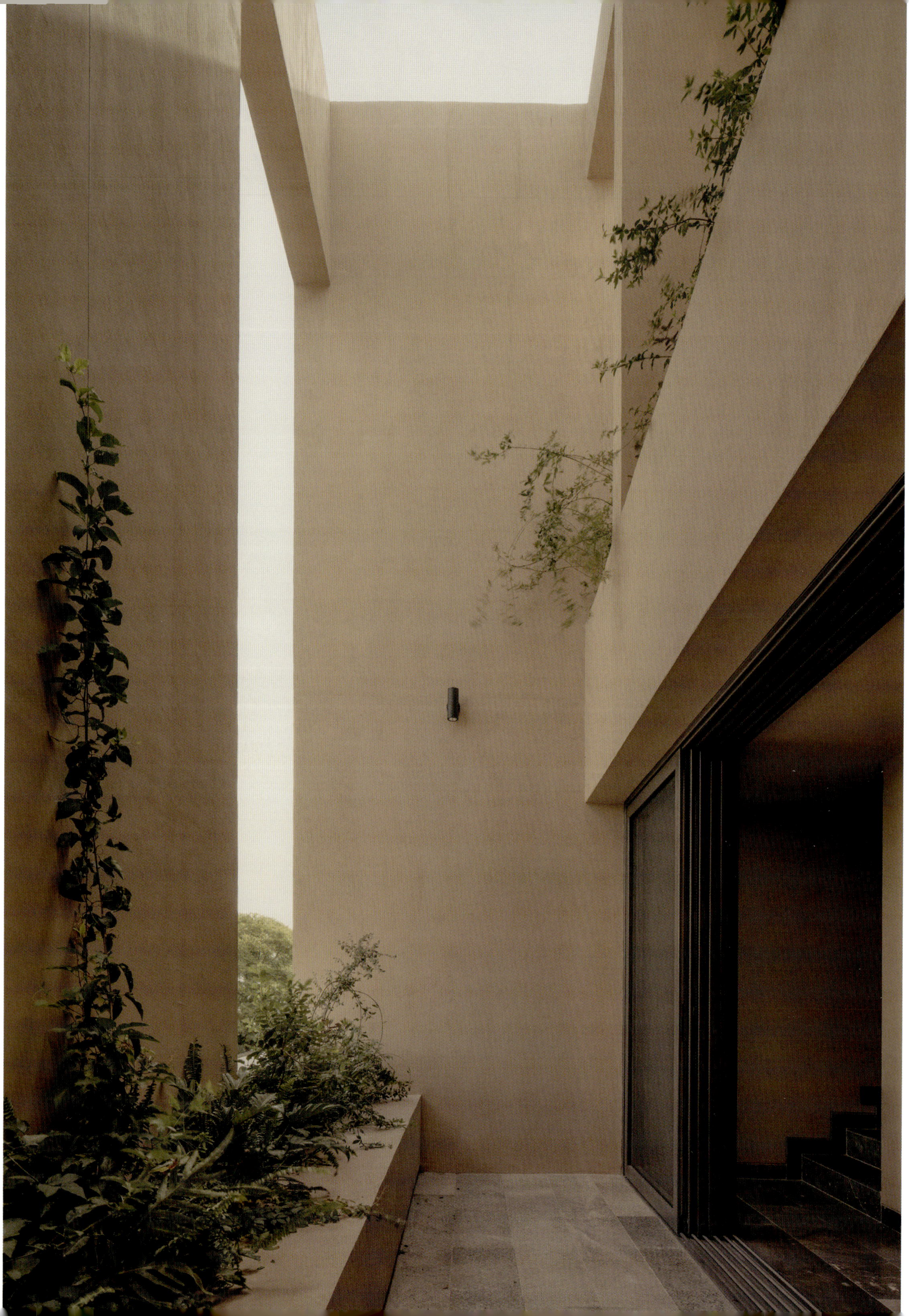

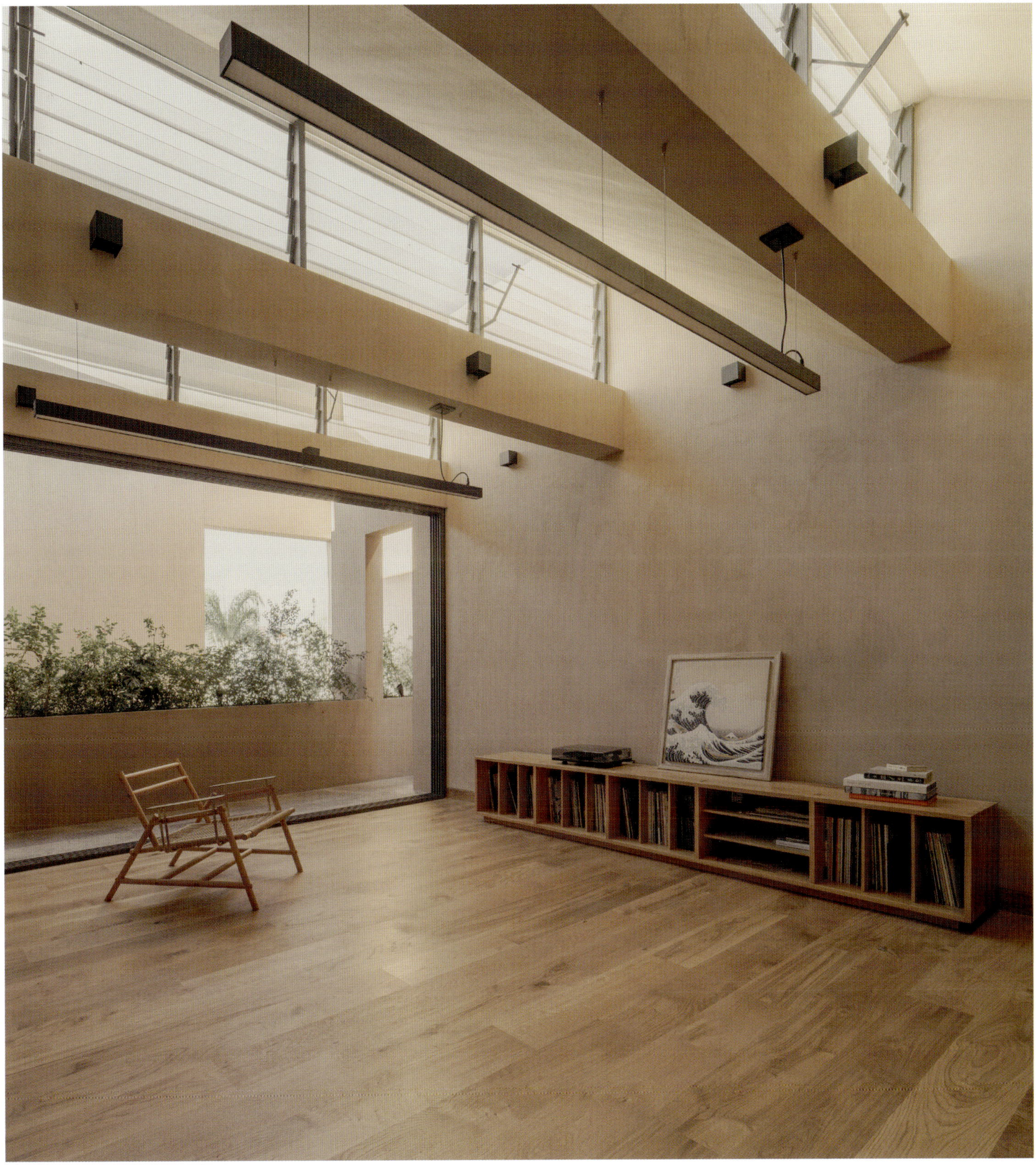

Established in Mexico in 2015 by architect Daniel Segovia Molina, the architecture and design firm Taller Segovia Molina specializes in single- and multifamily housing. The practice's approach is to combine functionality with sustainability, based on a careful examination of the context. Unique solutions are enhanced by distinctive architectural language.

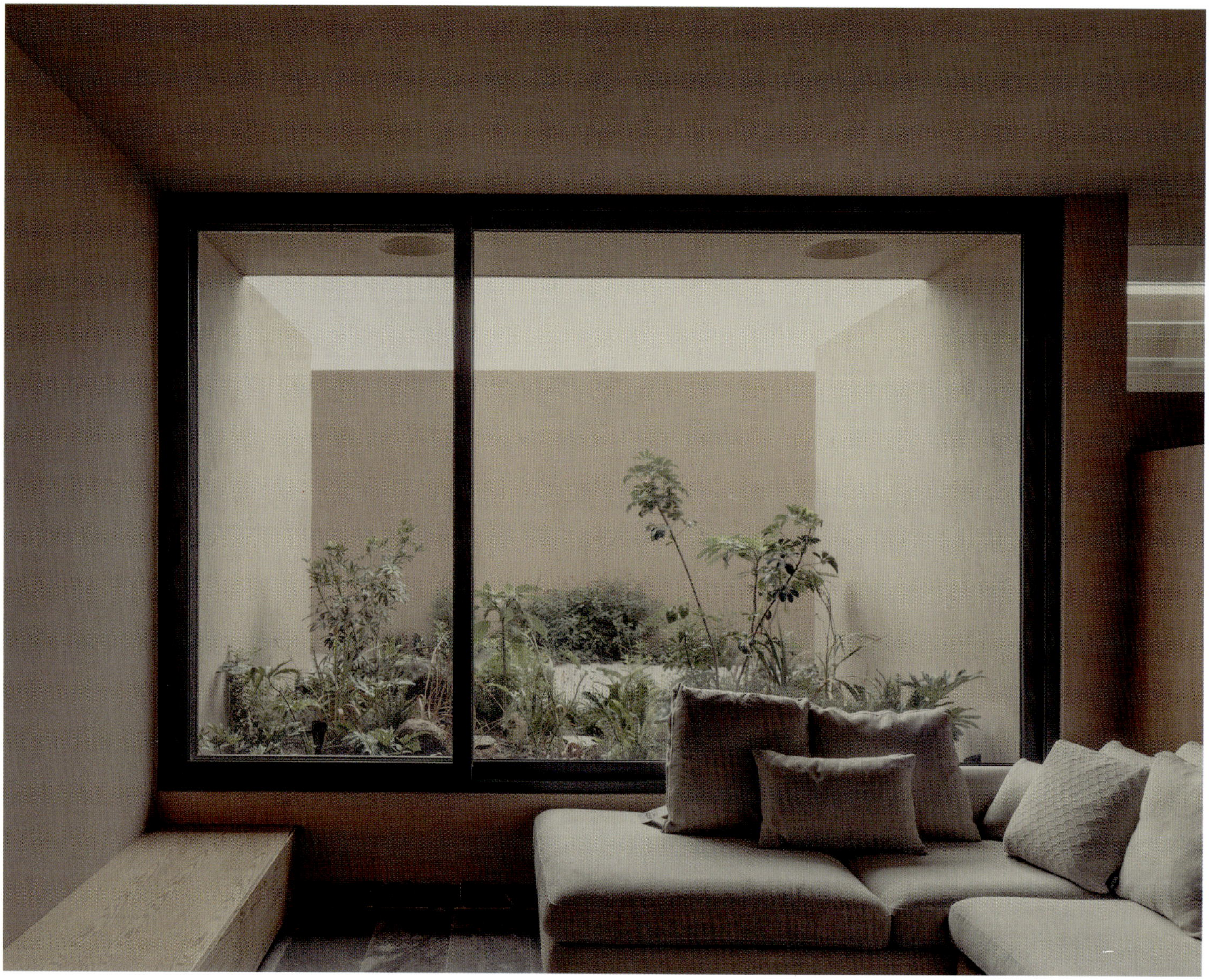

One of the architects' goals was to create an intriguing interplay between private spaces and expansive areas. This is why each level is designed as an open space that is intertwined with smaller areas. Stark contrasts between open and closed, just like on the exterior, generate unique spatial experiences. Patios in the fabric of the residence are crucial for this strategy. As internal spaces of quietness, they are softly embraced by greenery and filled with filtered light, quintessentially intimate. Yet again, the design creates an interesting relation between numerous smaller patios as well as terraces and the striking garden located on the rooftop. The project has been realized in collaboration, with Andrés Casal responsible for the structure and Matorral in charge of landscaping.

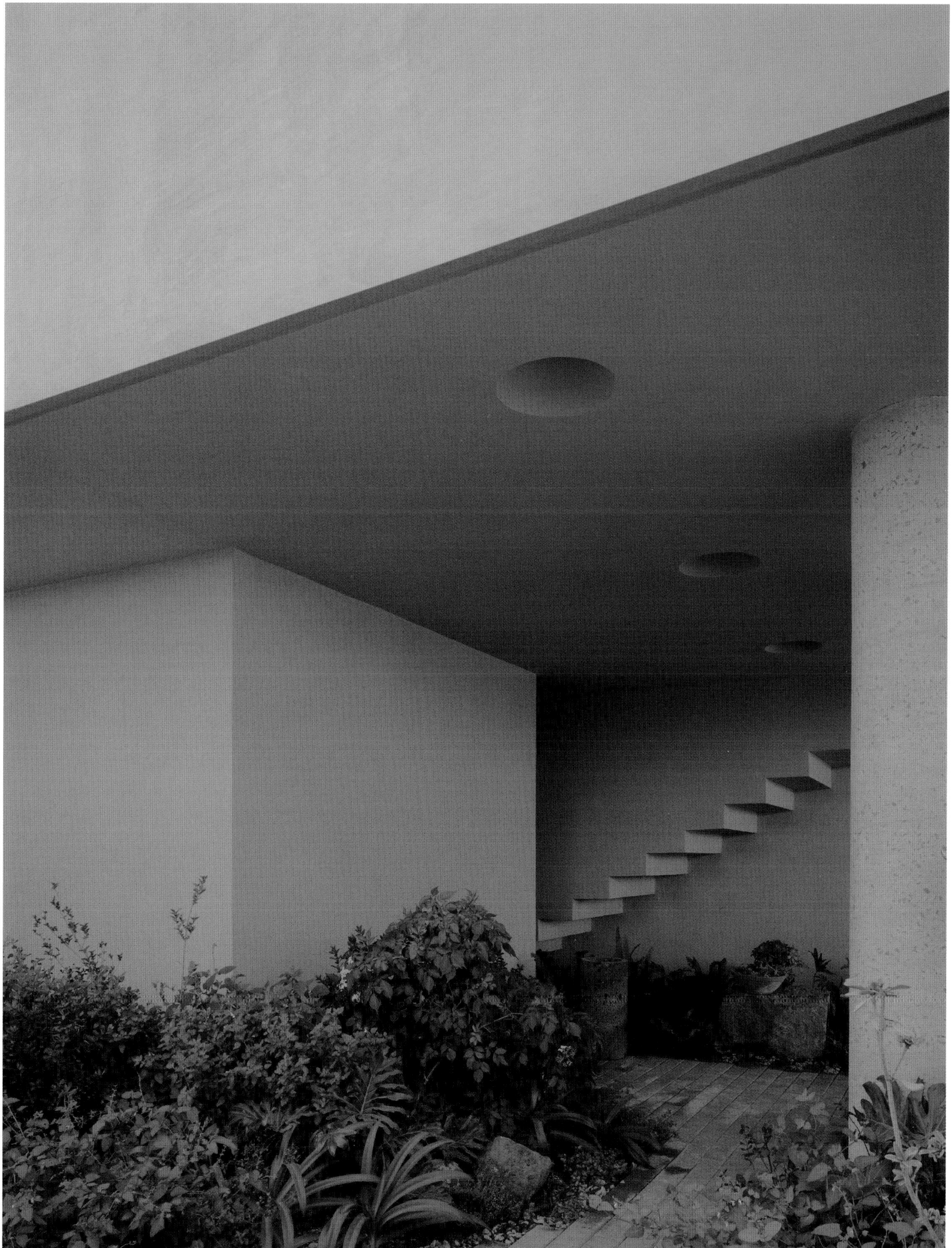

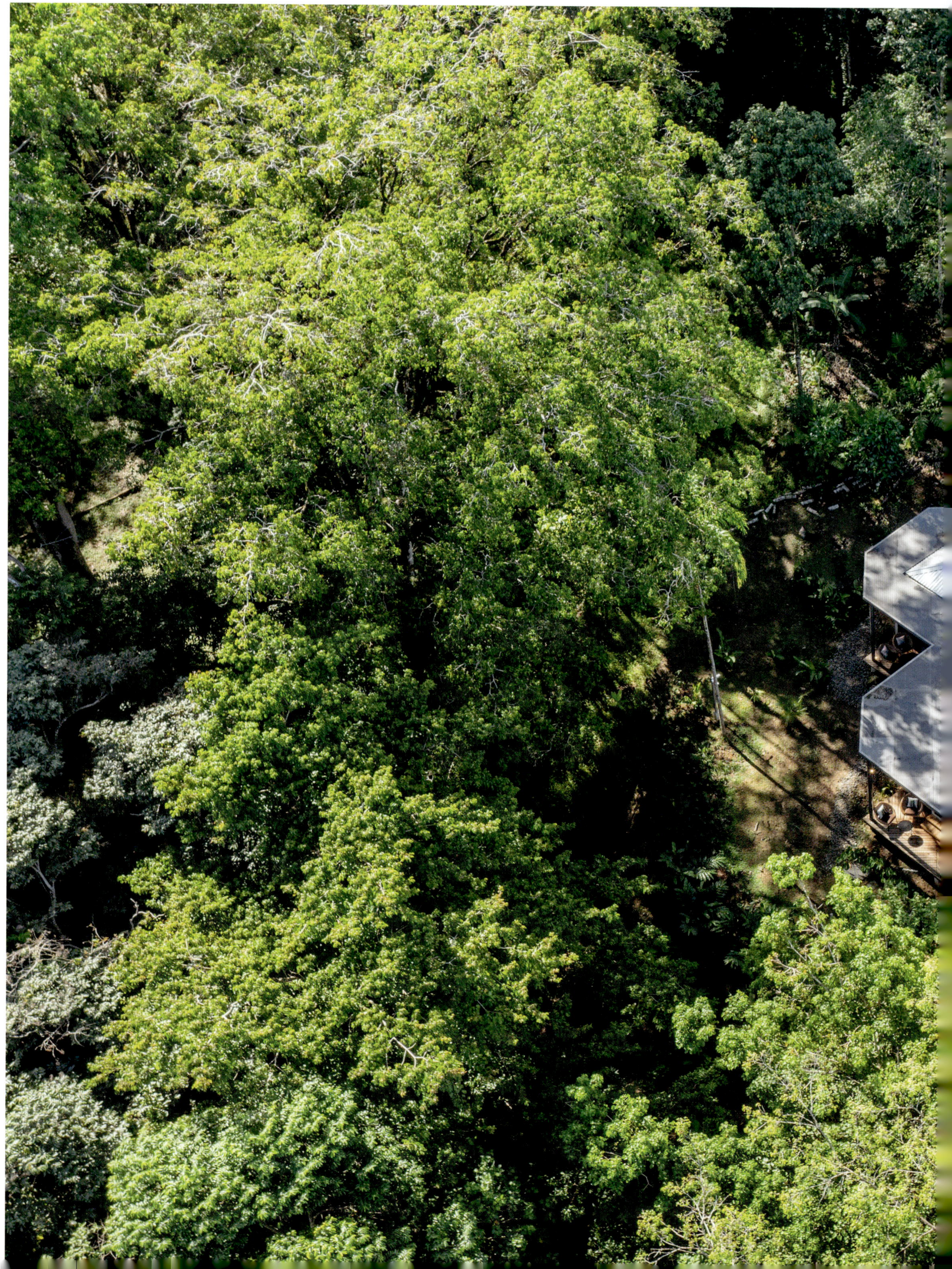

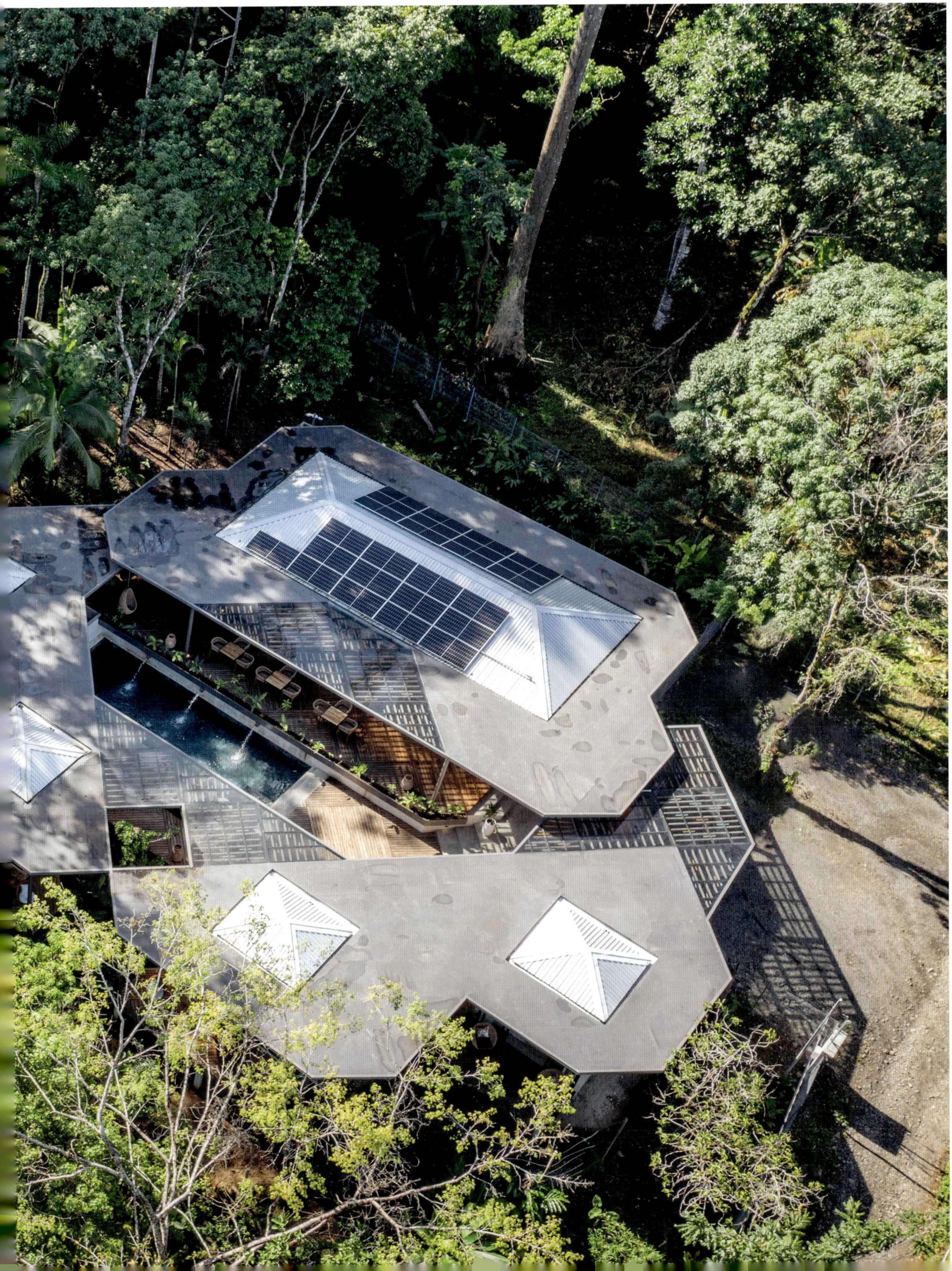

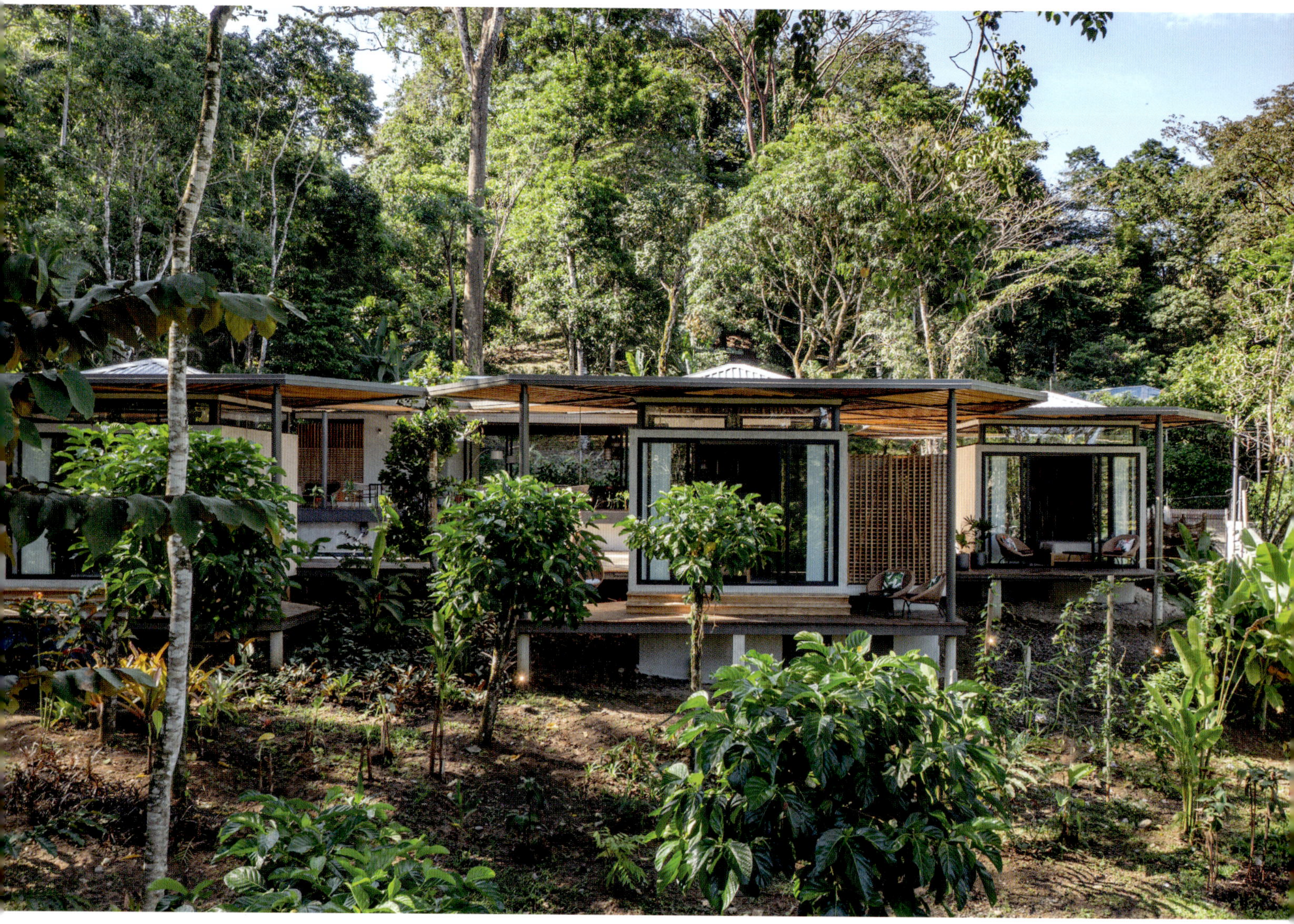

Light wooden structures permeate the rich and dense jungle in a way that allows architecture and the natural environment to coexist harmoniously while minimizing the footprint of the extensive villa.

PROJECT: Caribbean Courtyard Villa
LOCATION: Puerto Viejo, Limon, Costa Rica
YEAR: 2021
ARCHITECTS: Studio Saxe
PHOTOGRAPHY: Andres Garcia Lachner

Studio Saxe's design process has been built from scratch on the basis of the strong belief that regardless of the environment, buildings must connect to their landscape. This philosophy is particularly crucial when architects work in the context of virgin wilderness, such as the splendid nature of Costa Rica, which challenges the boundaries between natural habitats and inhabited spaces. Innovative forms and well-adjusted functions are at the core of the architects' projects. The Caribbean Courtyard Villa, in the middle of the jungle on the coast of Puerto Viejo, Limon, takes the form of triangular pavilions dynamically embracing a spacious courtyard. The architects refer to the pavilions as "a woven network of pergolas," which they chose as the perfect shape to blend with the natural surroundings. Light structures built in wood and generous windows allow these enclosed rooms to intertwine with the lush vegetation around.

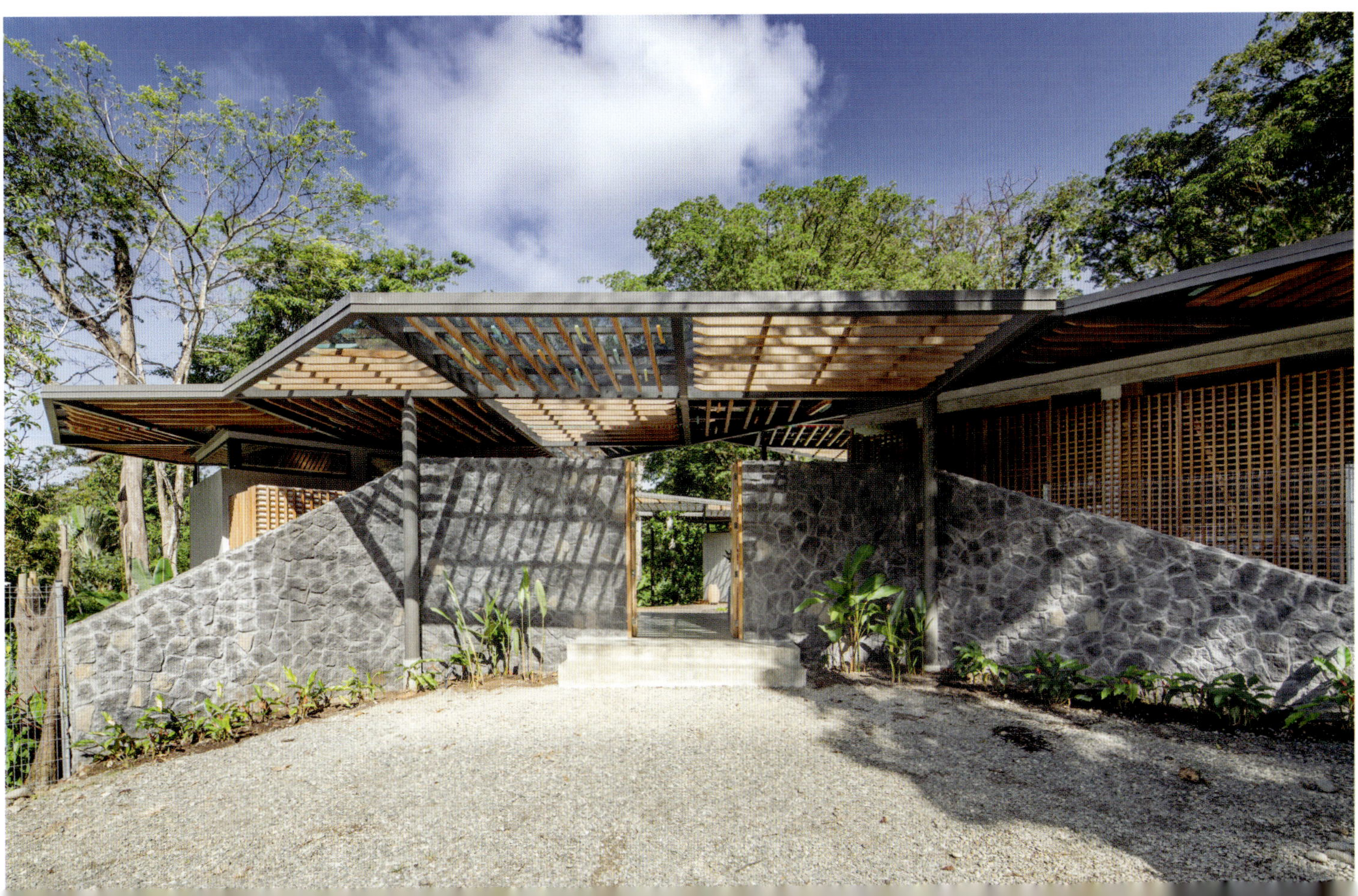

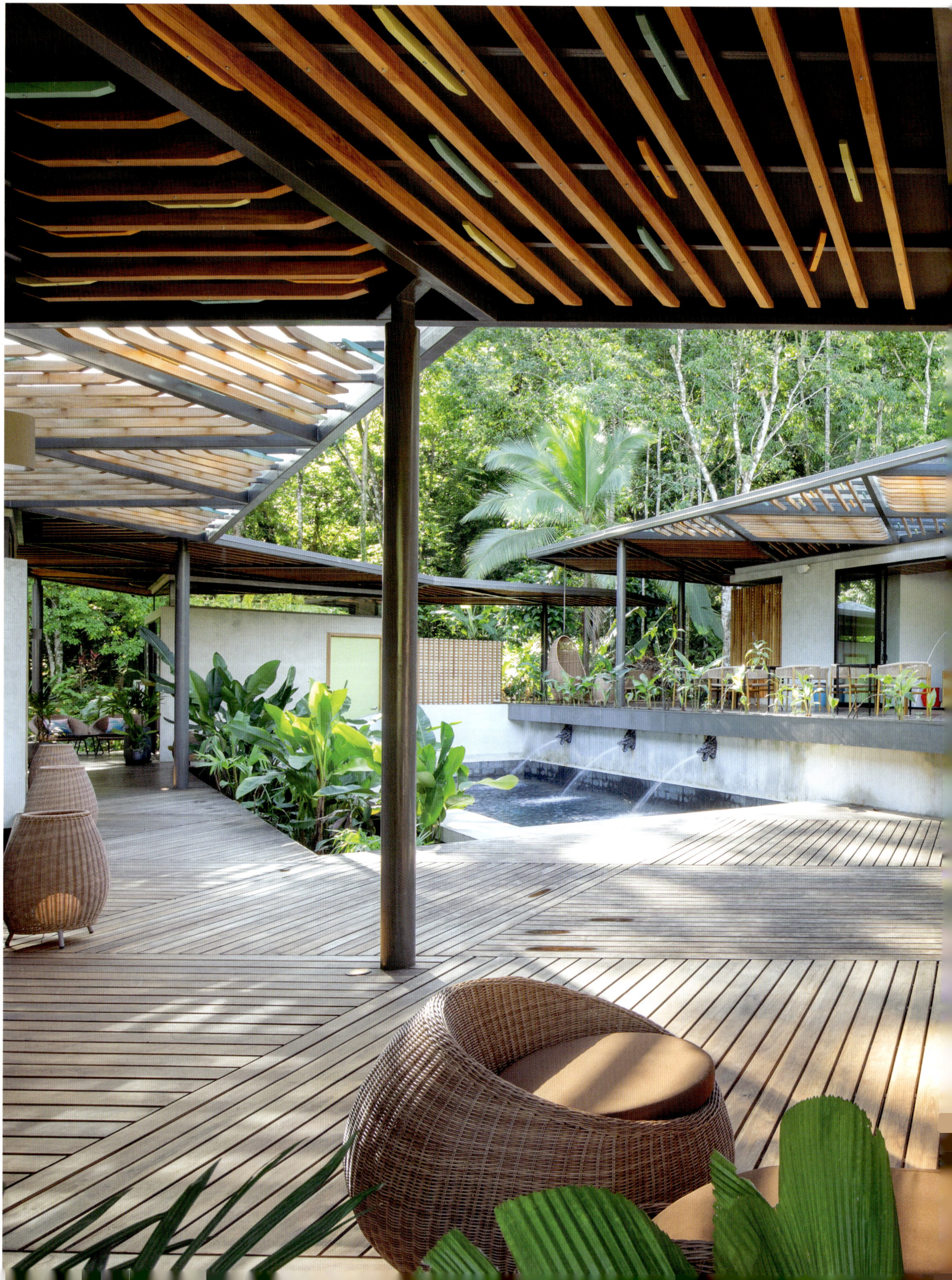

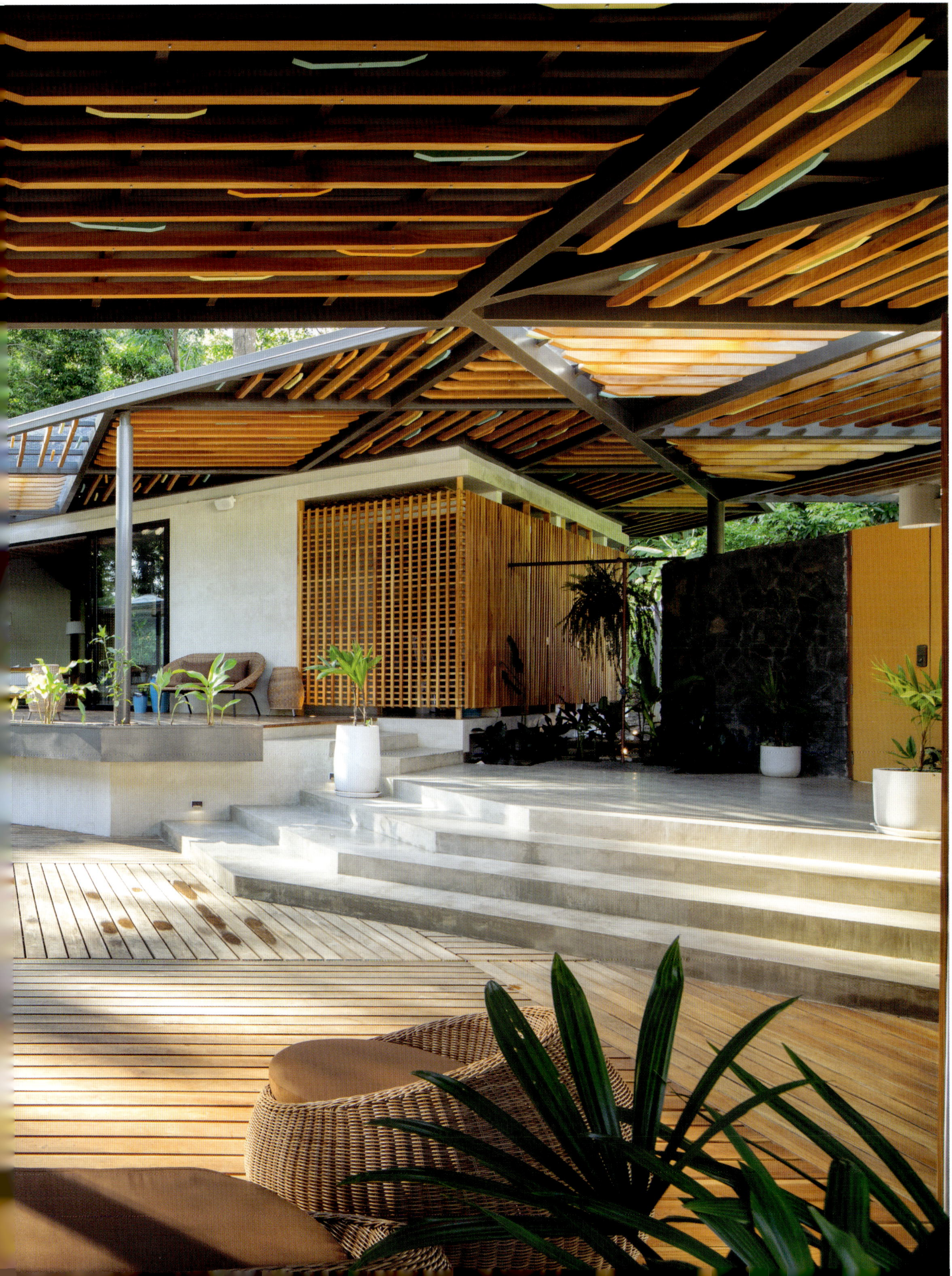

The rooms, placed in triangular pavilions, are accessible through the central patio but are open to the enveloping jungle, with large openings, sliding doors, and private terraces.

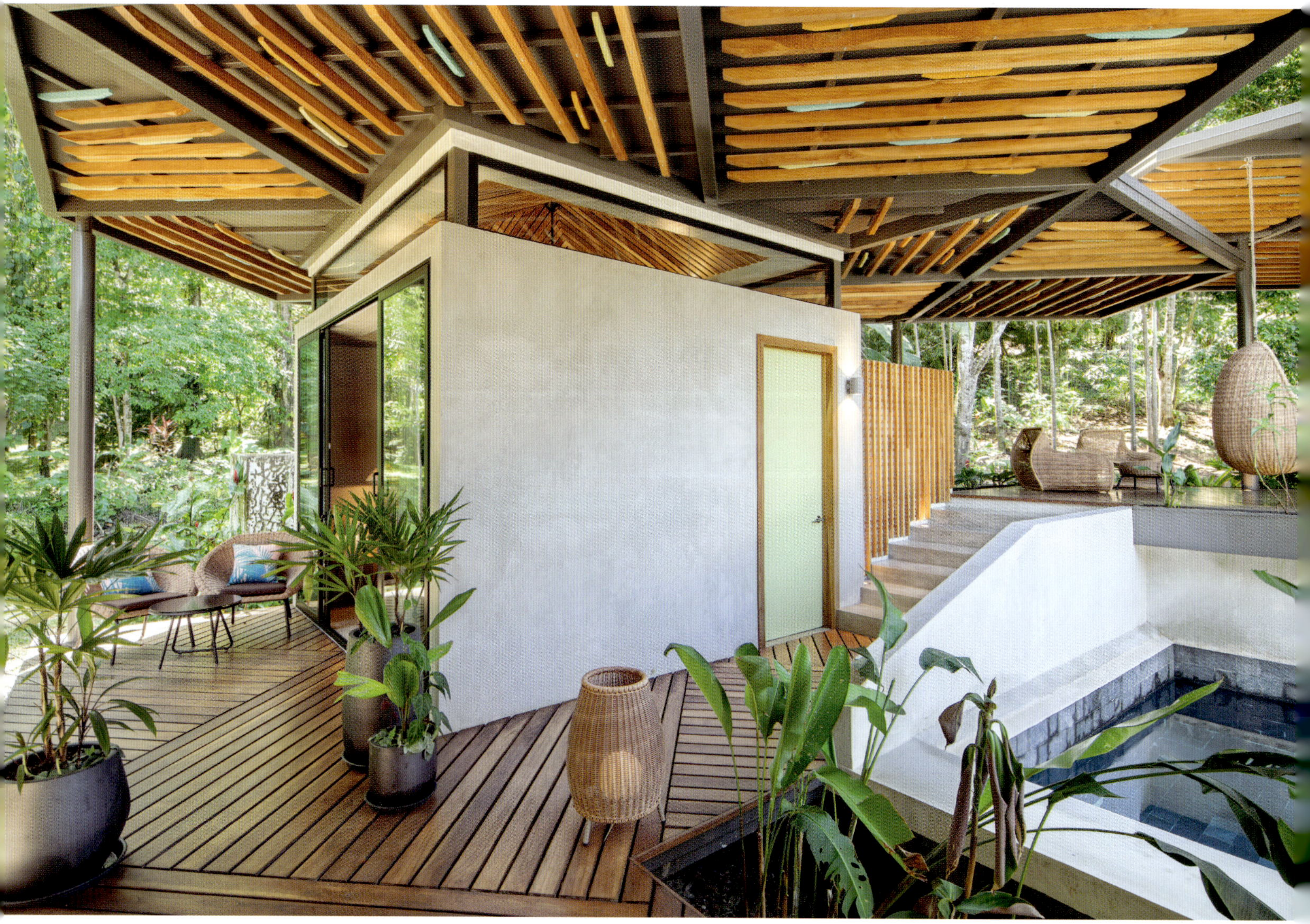

Established by Benjamin G. Saxe in 2004 in San Jose, Costa Rica, the practice now has two other offices in London and Los Angeles. The founder's main goal was, as he states, to explore our relationship with the natural environment through architecture. Working internationally, the multidisciplinary team continually works on new design solutions that are quintessentially sustainable by marrying advanced technology and handcrafted techniques, often drawing from local traditions.

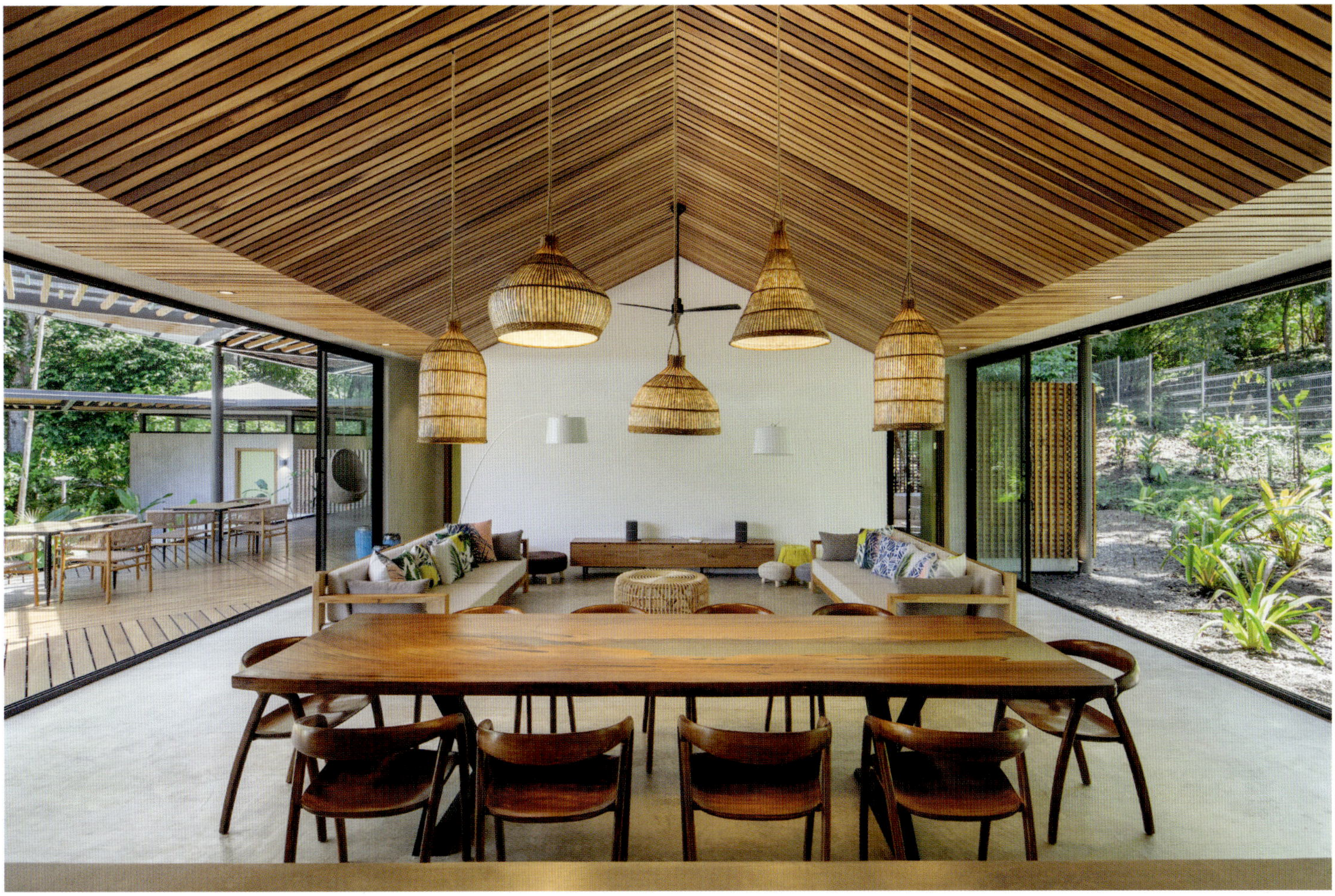

The inner patio, consolidating all parts of the retreat, serves as both a comfortable communication hub and relaxation spot. Inhabitants can circulate freely between all private and common spaces, as well as enjoy the outdoors. Two elements are crucial in the structure—one being the roof canopy, organized around the whole complex of volumes, which creates a perfect shading system to soften the strength of the tropical sun. While the triangular rooms open to the jungle surrounding the house rather than toward the patio, the large living quarters have been equipped with fully openable sliding doors that blur the line between the outside and inside. The modular structure of this tropical house has been harmoniously placed within existing trees and the hilly topography of the plot, making it sustainable. Solutions including solar energy generation, water-efficient systems, and passive bioclimatic design reduce the impact of architecture in a pristine location.

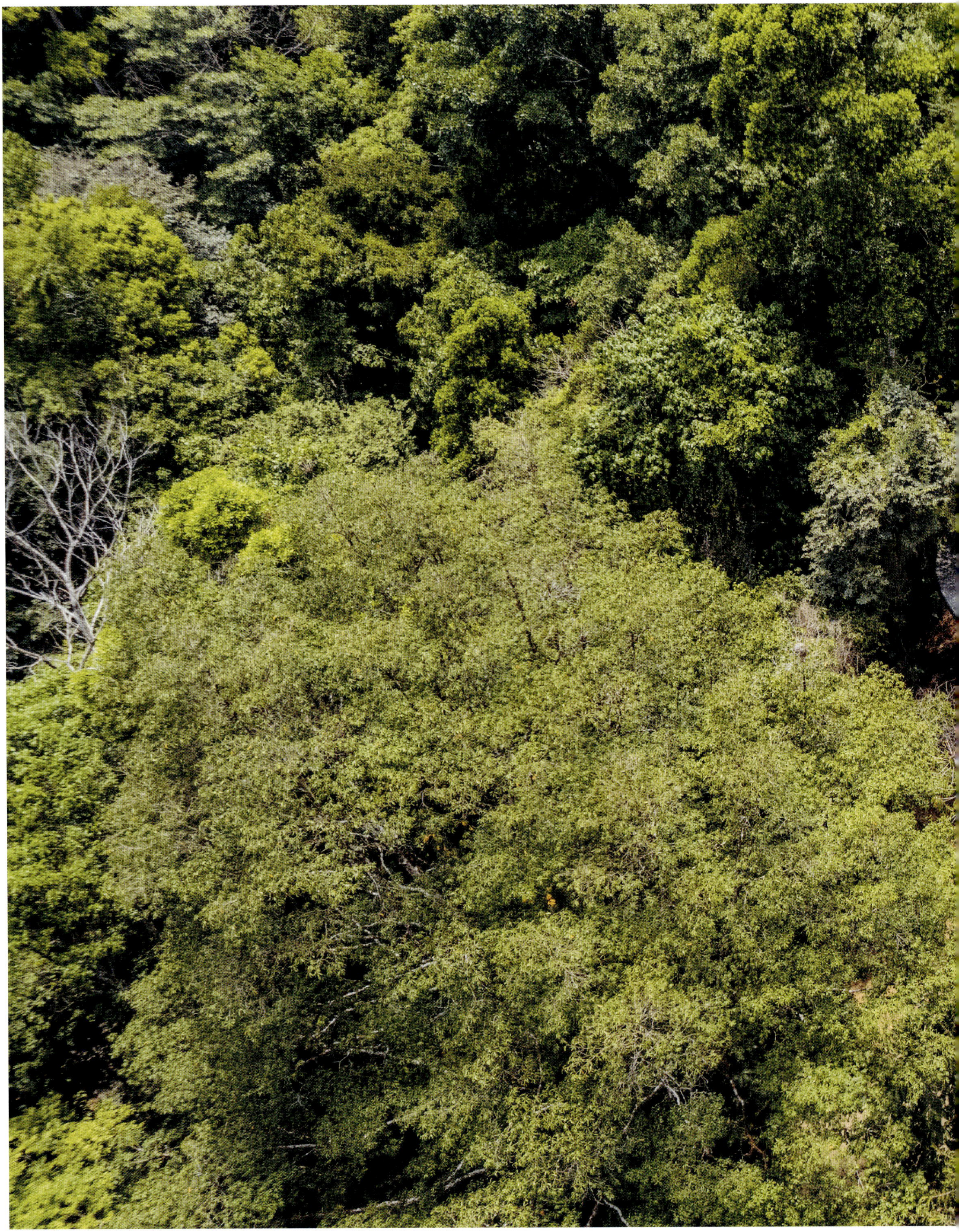

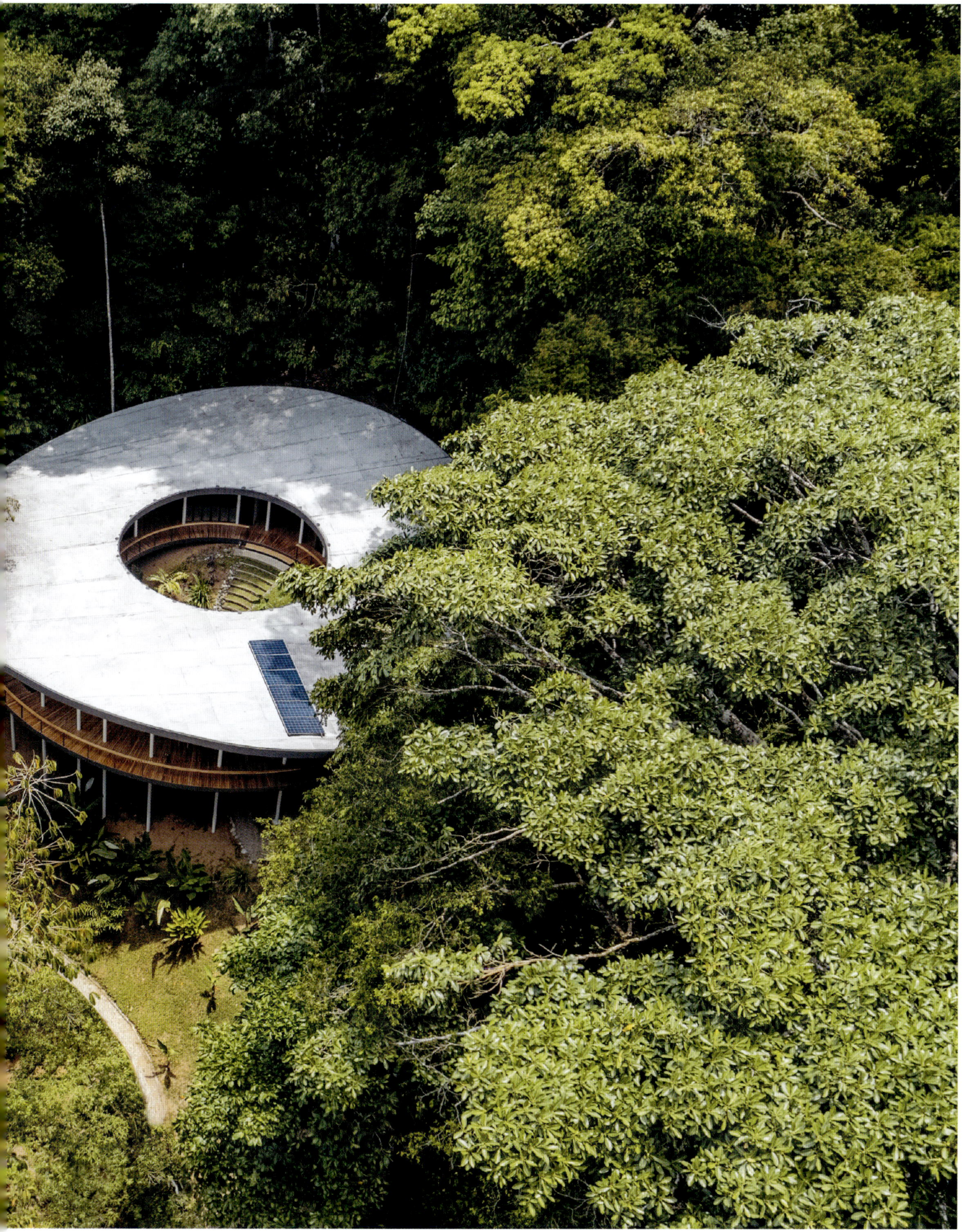

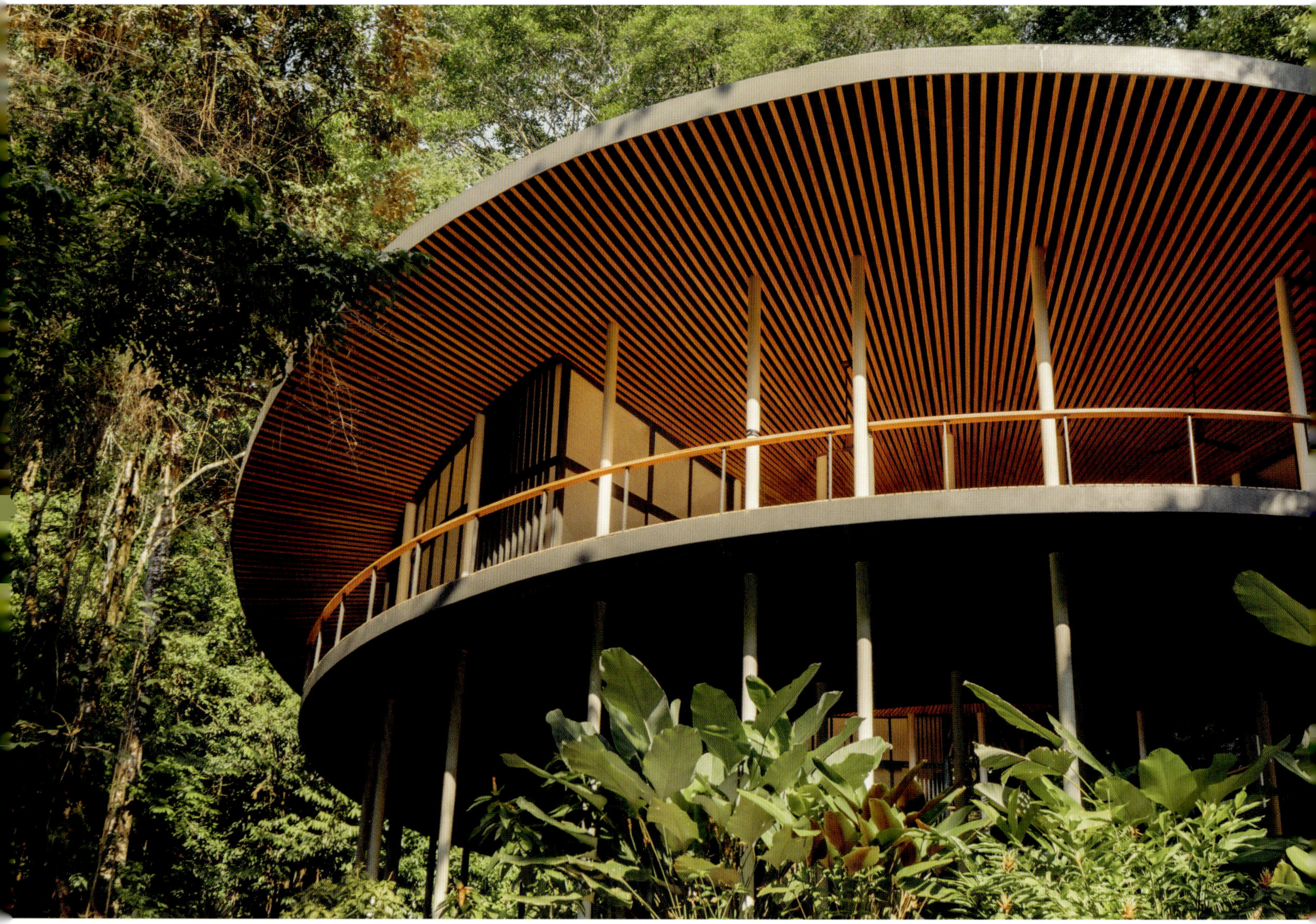

The light structure placed on pillars helps preserve the native vegetation and biodiversity of the ancient rainforest, effectively reducing the impact of the architecture on the pristine location.

PROJECT: Sinfonía Verde
LOCATION: Península de Osa, Costa Rica
YEAR: 2022
ARCHITECTS: Studio Saxe
PHOTOGRAPHY: Alvaro Fonseca-Depth Lens

Sinfonía Verde is another of Studio Saxe's visionary projects in an extraordinary location. The context of the rainforest on the Osa Peninsula was stimulating to create an unusual structure in the place where a giant tree fell. The architects filled the space it left in the dense vegetation in a highly sensitive way, choosing a ring form for an off-grid home for two researchers. Future owners were initially hesitant about the round form, but they quickly realized that it would be a way to plant the house into the natural sounds, vibrations, and lighting of the forest's biodiversity. "A walk along the 360 degrees of the platform constantly shifts your attention: from skyline to secondary forest, to earthy terrain, to primary forest, and back again to skyline," they remark. While this concept allows the residents to immerse themselves in the environment, the curvaceous shape also echoes a tree trunk and, being devoid of sharp edges, blends softly into the surrounding nature.

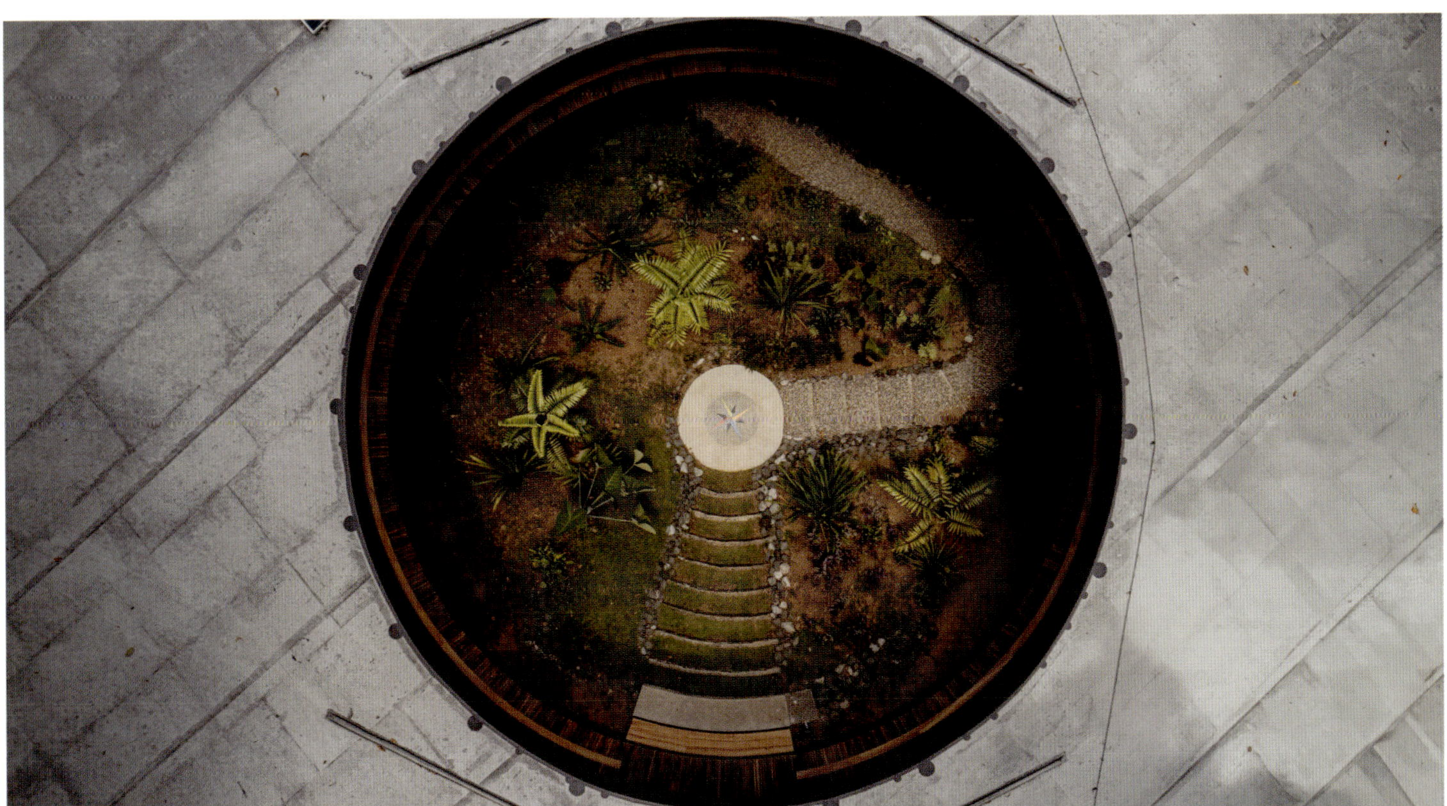

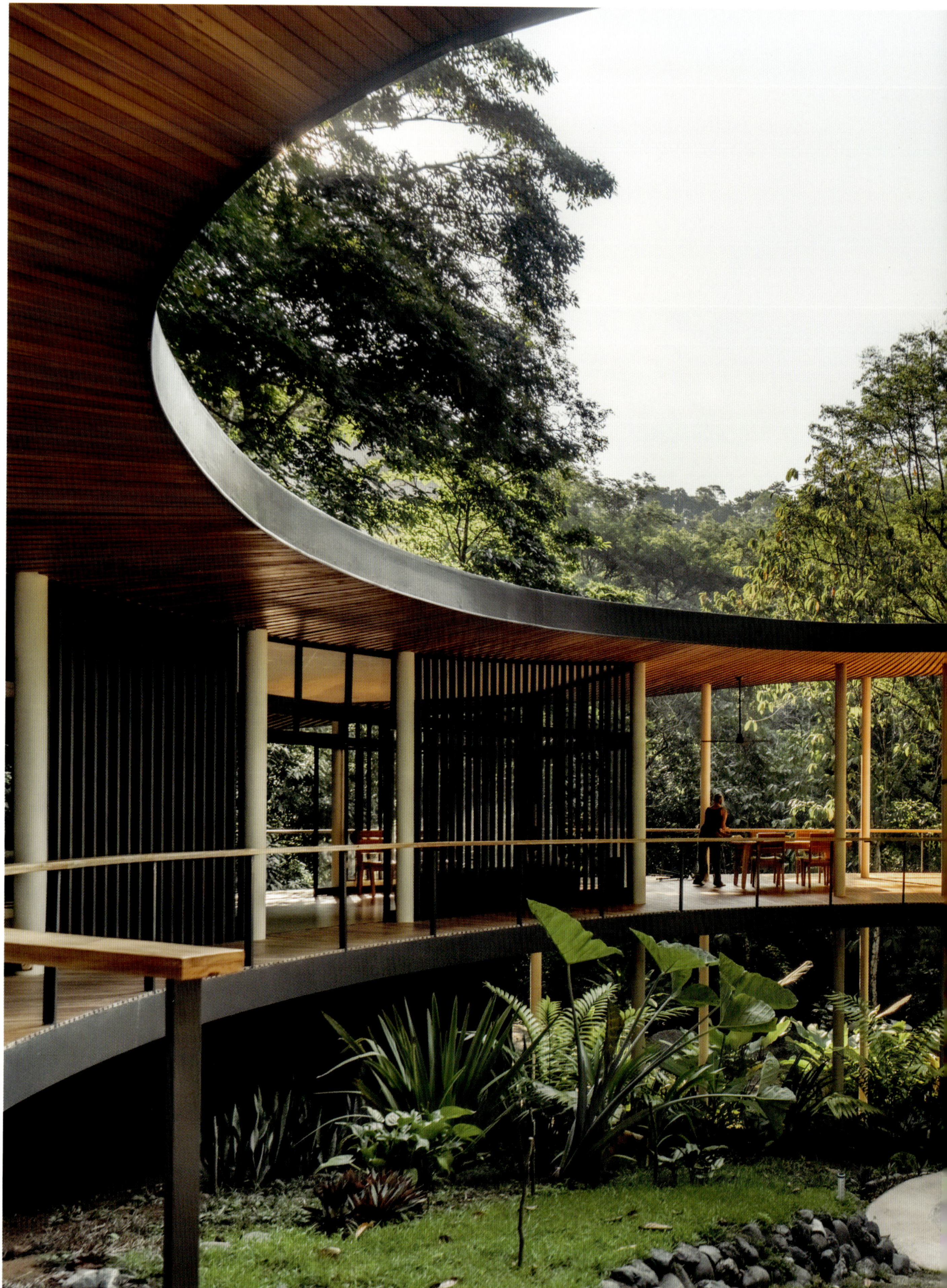

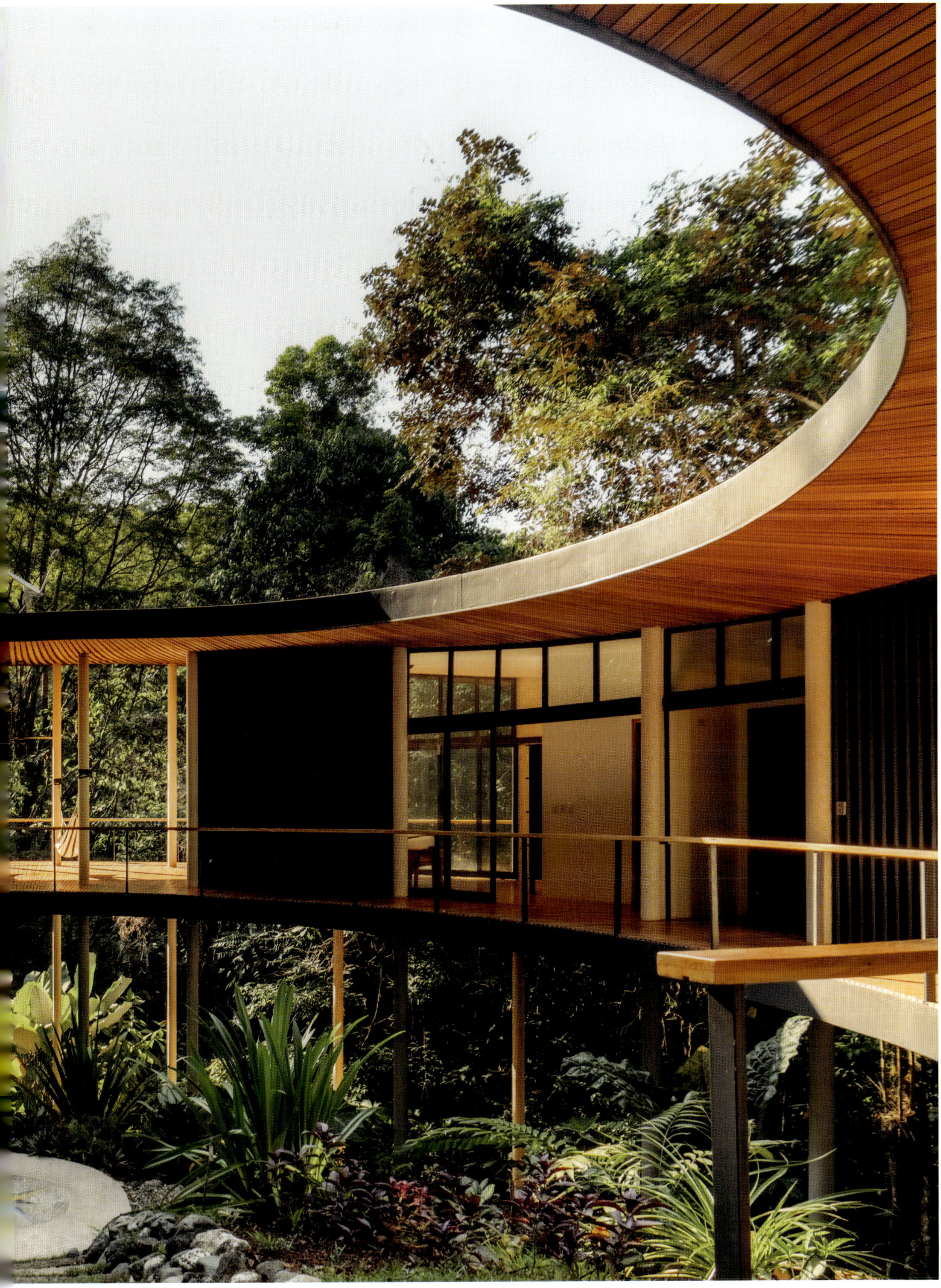

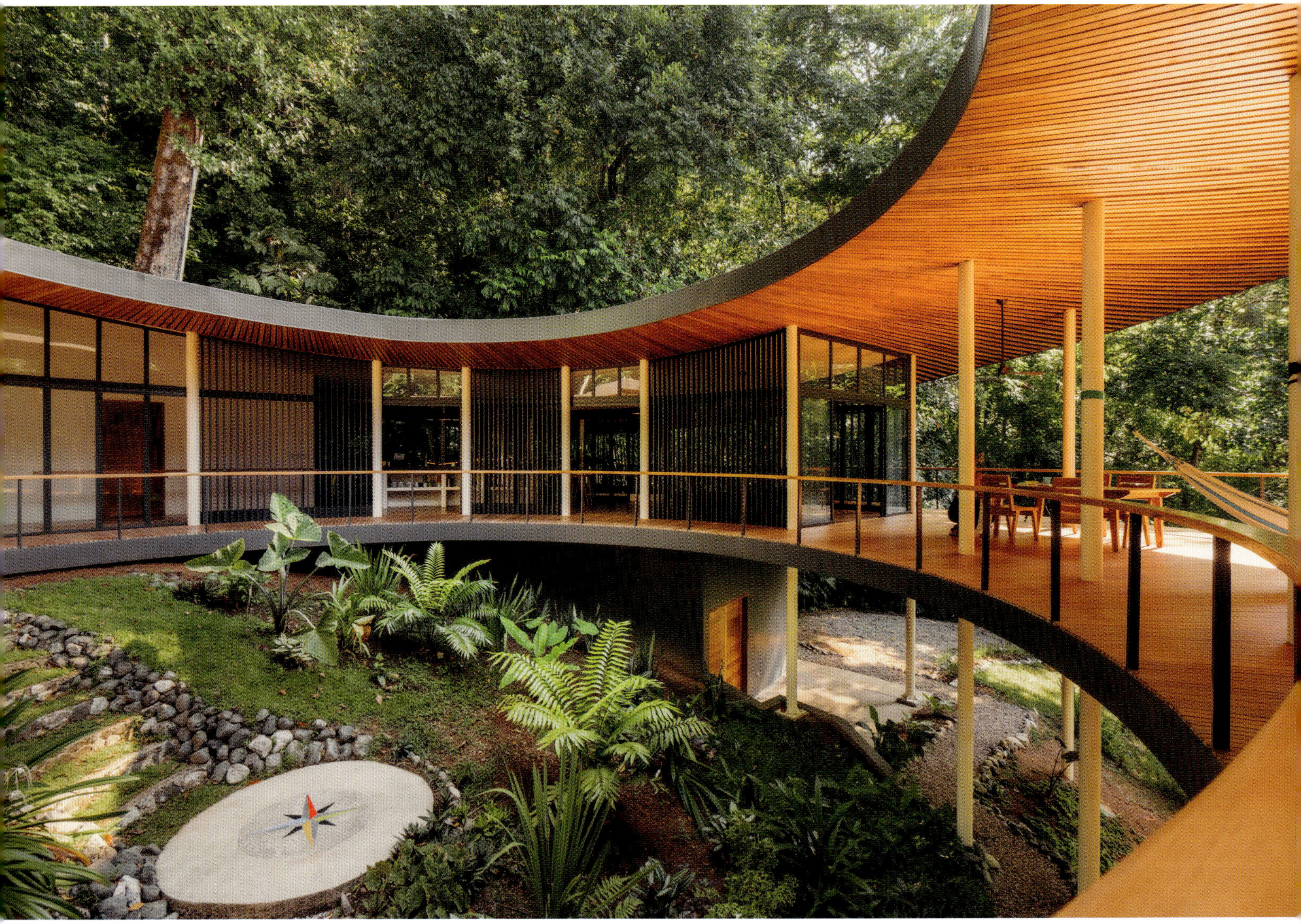

The architects used an opening in the foliage by inserting a light volume, intertwining rooms and shaded terraces, in response to the multilayered structure of the rainforest. The main goal was to enhance the experience of the wilderness in proximity to Corcovado National Park, which is said to host approximately 3 percent of the planet's biodiversity. This interaction with the vegetation is initiated around the periphery as much as in the central patio, filled with replanted native vegetation that seamlessly develops the house as yet another connection between built and natural environments. The total immersion into the context through the circular shape also means that the house takes over the daily rhythm of nature. The secluded location in an earthquake zone, with intense rain and sun, drastic temperature differences, salt in the air, and wildlife, required a minimal footprint, smart selection of materials, careful construction planning, and lots of sustainable solutions. With a photovoltaic array and a hydroturbine in a nearby stream, which generate power and supply drinking water, the home is entirely self-sufficient.

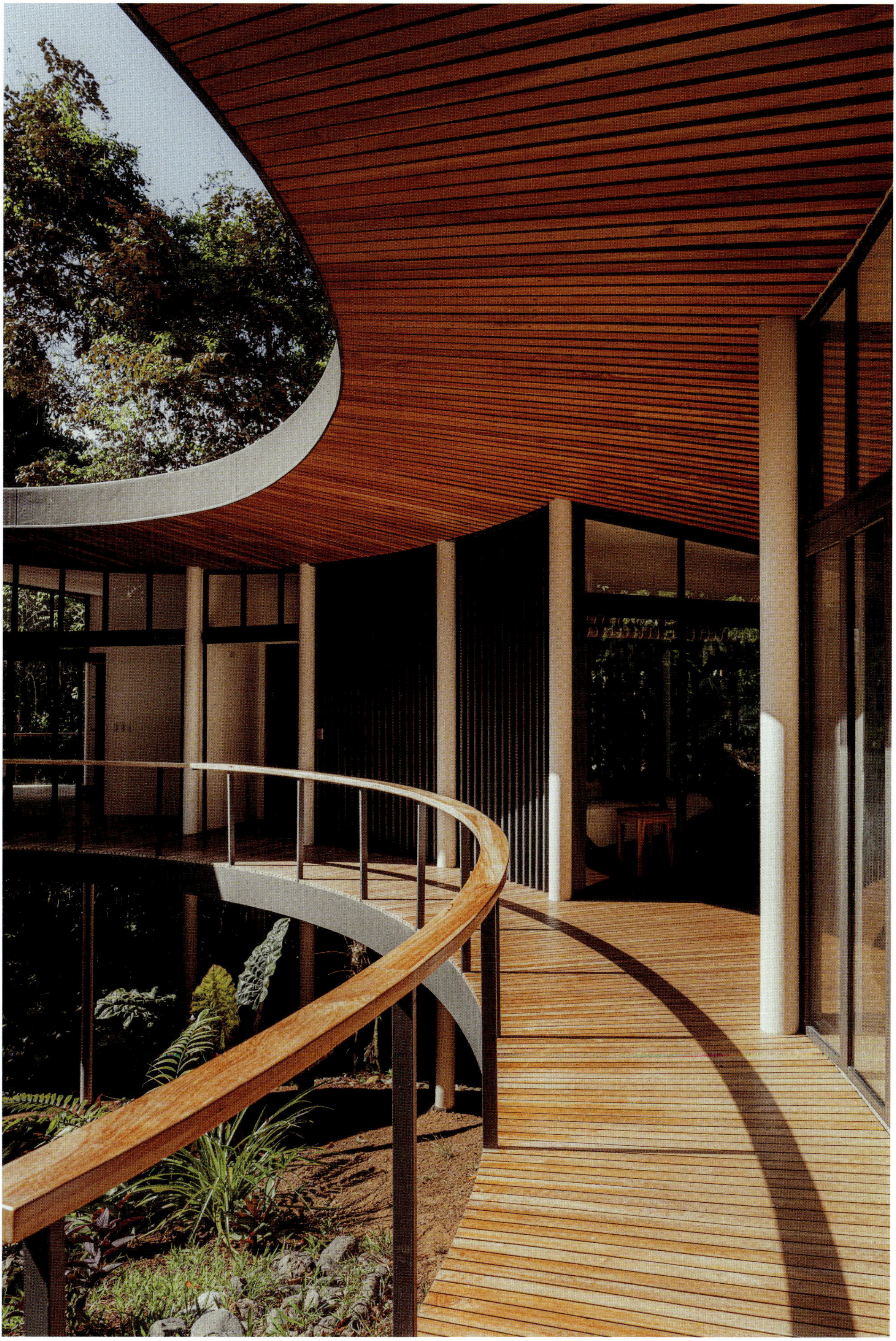

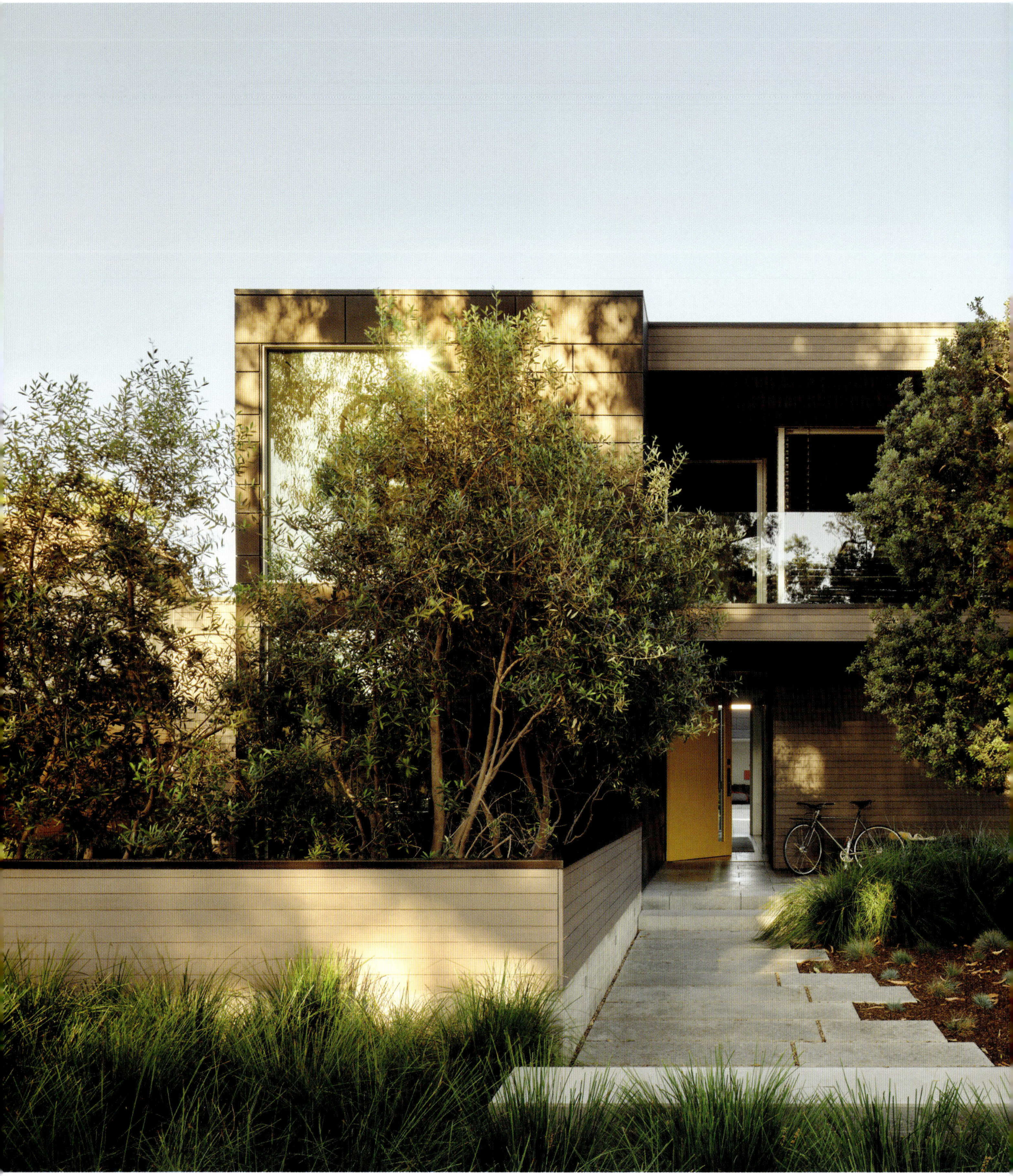

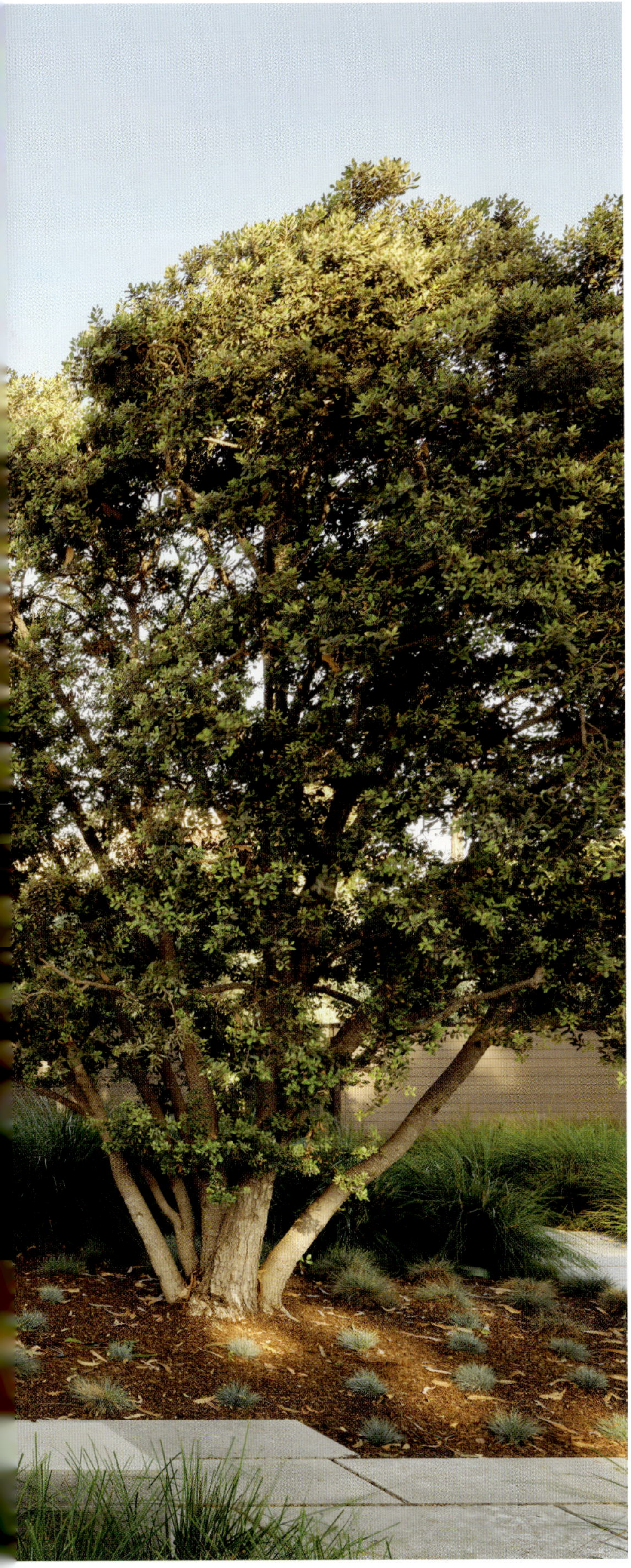

PROJECT: Santa Monica Modern
LOCATION: California, United States
YEAR: 2023
ARCHITECTS: Walker Warner
PHOTOGRAPHY: Matthew Millman

One of the mottoes of the architects of Walker Warner reads "Thoughtful design heightens your way of life. It invites you to feel at ease, at peace, at home." Santa Monica Modern shows this philosophy perfectly in practice. Despite the practical urban location, the residents can have a feeling of being surrounded by nature in a kind of enclosed green oasis. Invisible from the perspective of the street, the highlight of the house is an extensive patio with trees, including eucalyptus and lush vegetation. The serenity of this space creates a stark contrast with the busy city life starting just in front of the protective facade. Inviting greenery and several areas for different activities such as dining or sitting at the fire pit offer the family ultimate relaxation or entertainment, making it the true center of the house. The scenic garden, designed by Fiore Landscape Design, was envisioned to bring shade, privacy, and also the beauty of changing seasons, which the residents can observe while enjoying the outdoors, practically all year round thanks to mild temperatures.

The facade of the house, partly camouflaged by lush vegetation, is an elegant barrier preserving the privacy of the residents and leaving the spacious green patio entirely out of sight.

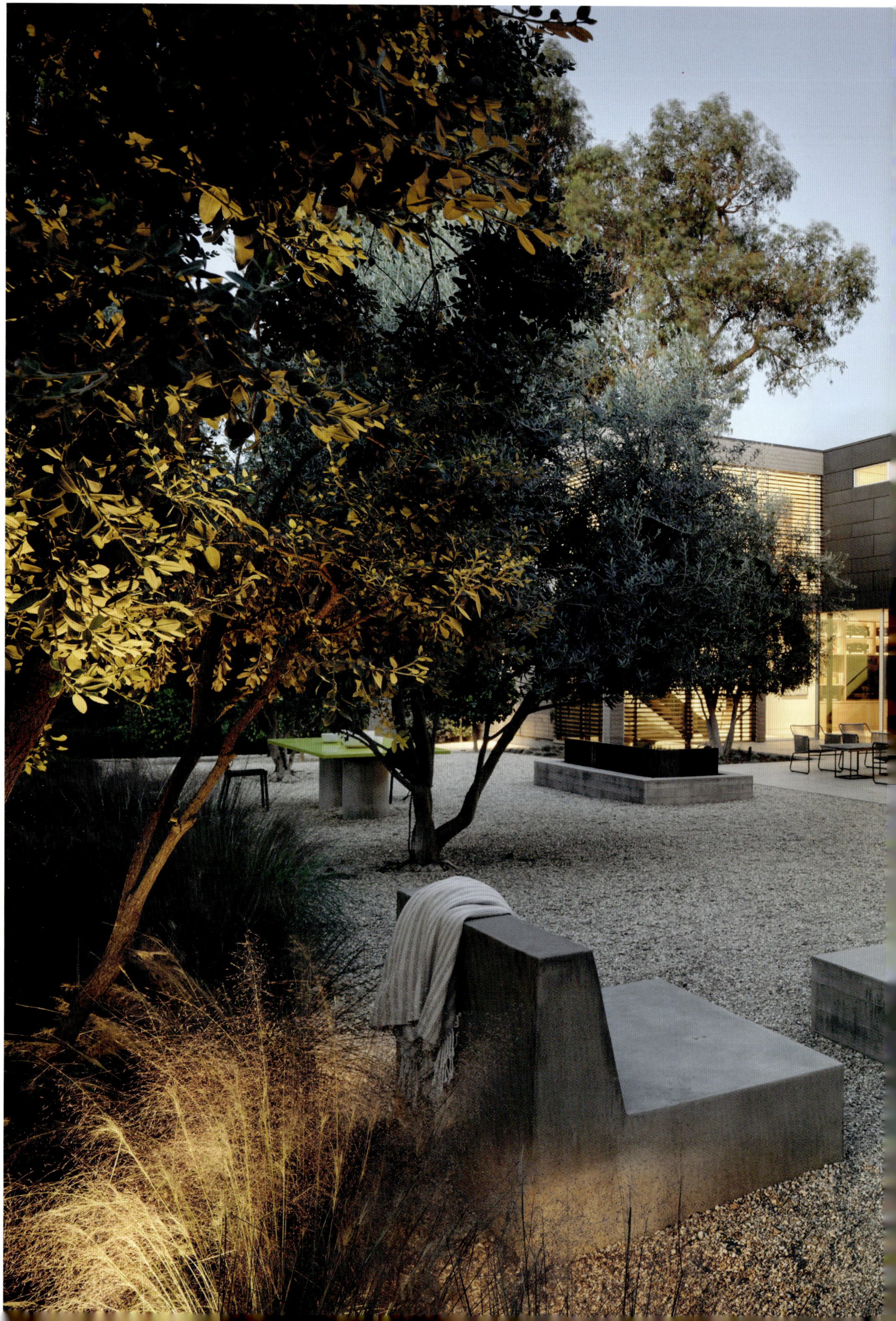

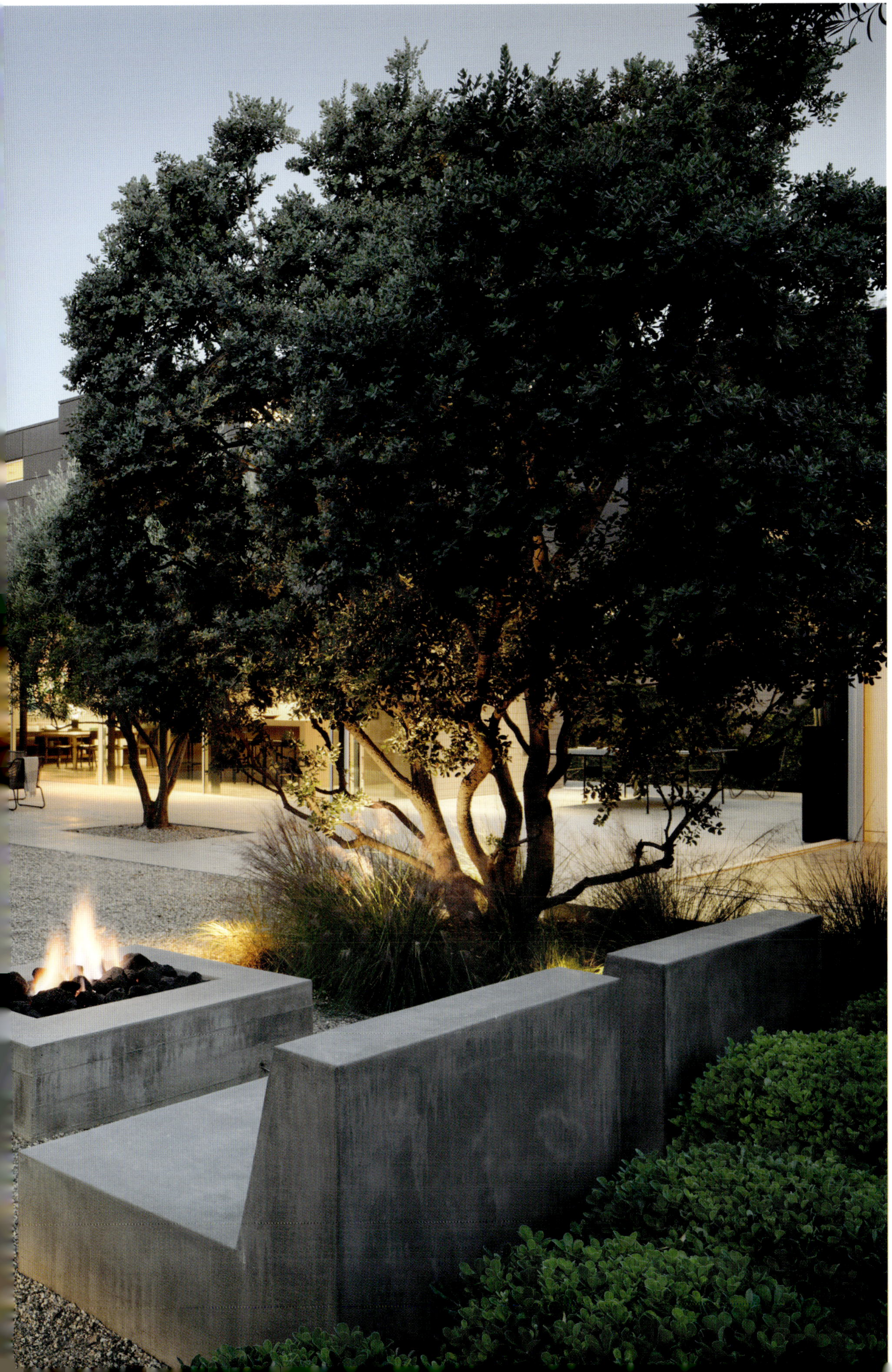

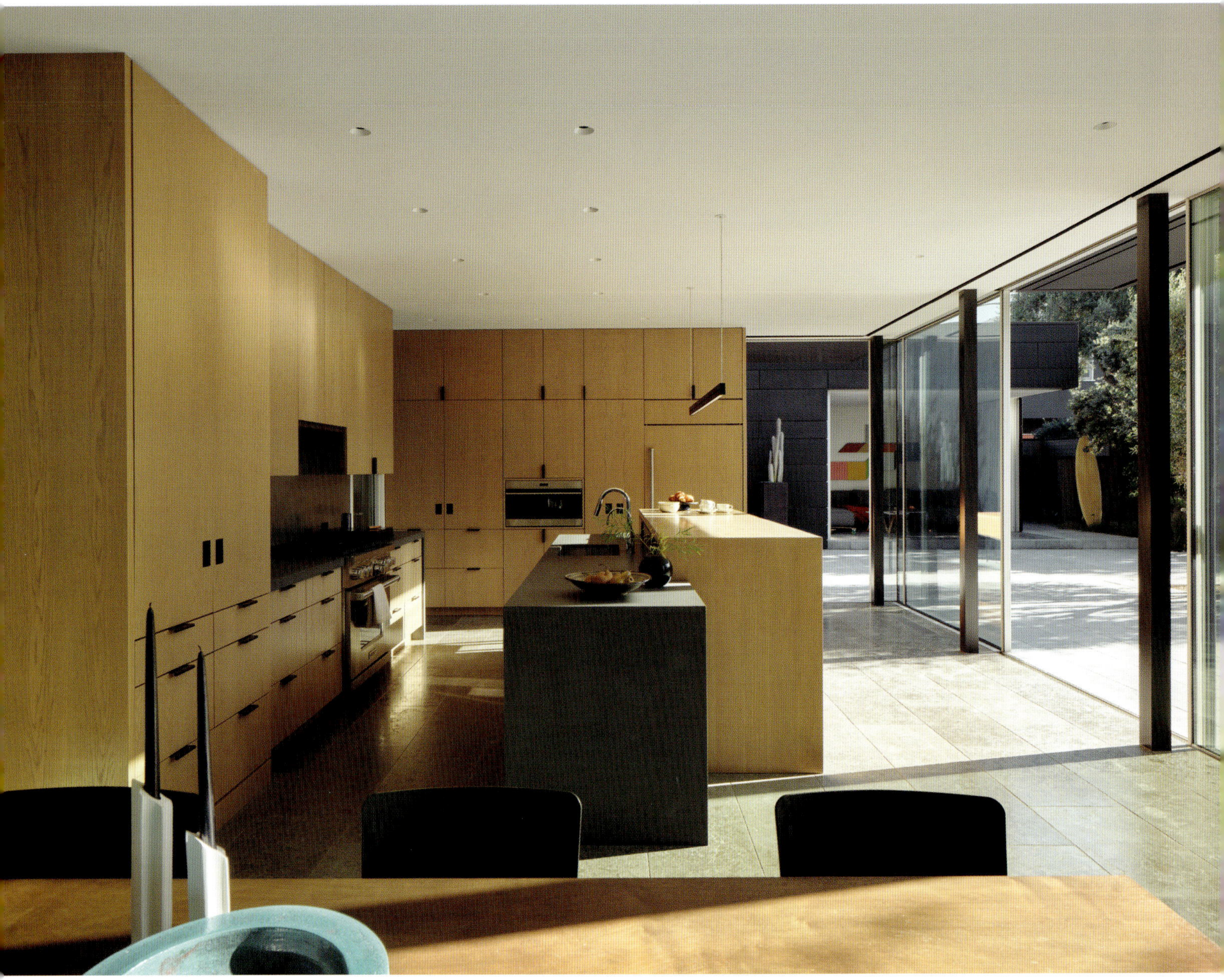

The minimally yet stylishly designed interiors seem to create an addition to the spectacular courtyard. This impression is enhanced by the full-height glazing and numerous sliding doors, which form a smooth connection between inside and outside. This is particularly striking in the kitchen area, which can open entirely onto the dining table on the patio. An important part of the architect's design process is the choice of materials, which have to not only be suited to their purpose but also engage the senses. White oak and limestone in the interiors are beautifully complemented with red cedar and zinc on the exterior shell, additionally highlighting the transition between indoors and outdoors and creating a lovely parenthesis between the living quarters and the courtyard with the garden.

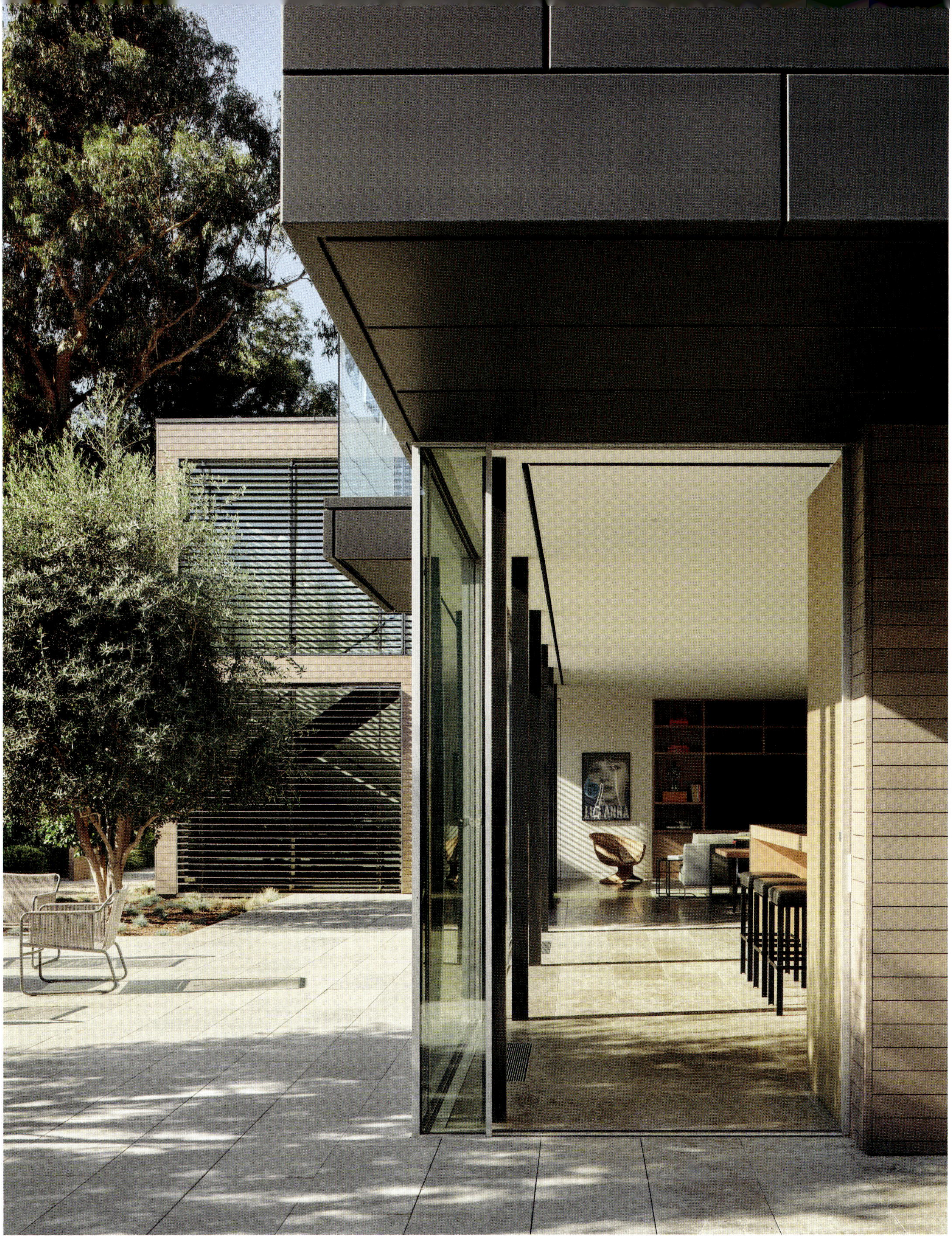

Established in 1989, Walker Warner is led by partners Greg Warner, Kathy Scott, Mike McCabe, Greg Mottola, and principal Brooks Walker. The firm focuses on custom residential and hospitality architecture. The starting point of all projects is the context—the history and culture of the place as well as the landscape, blended with the client's vision. Responsible and environmentally friendly solutions are as important as the choice of materials—durable and aesthetic at once.

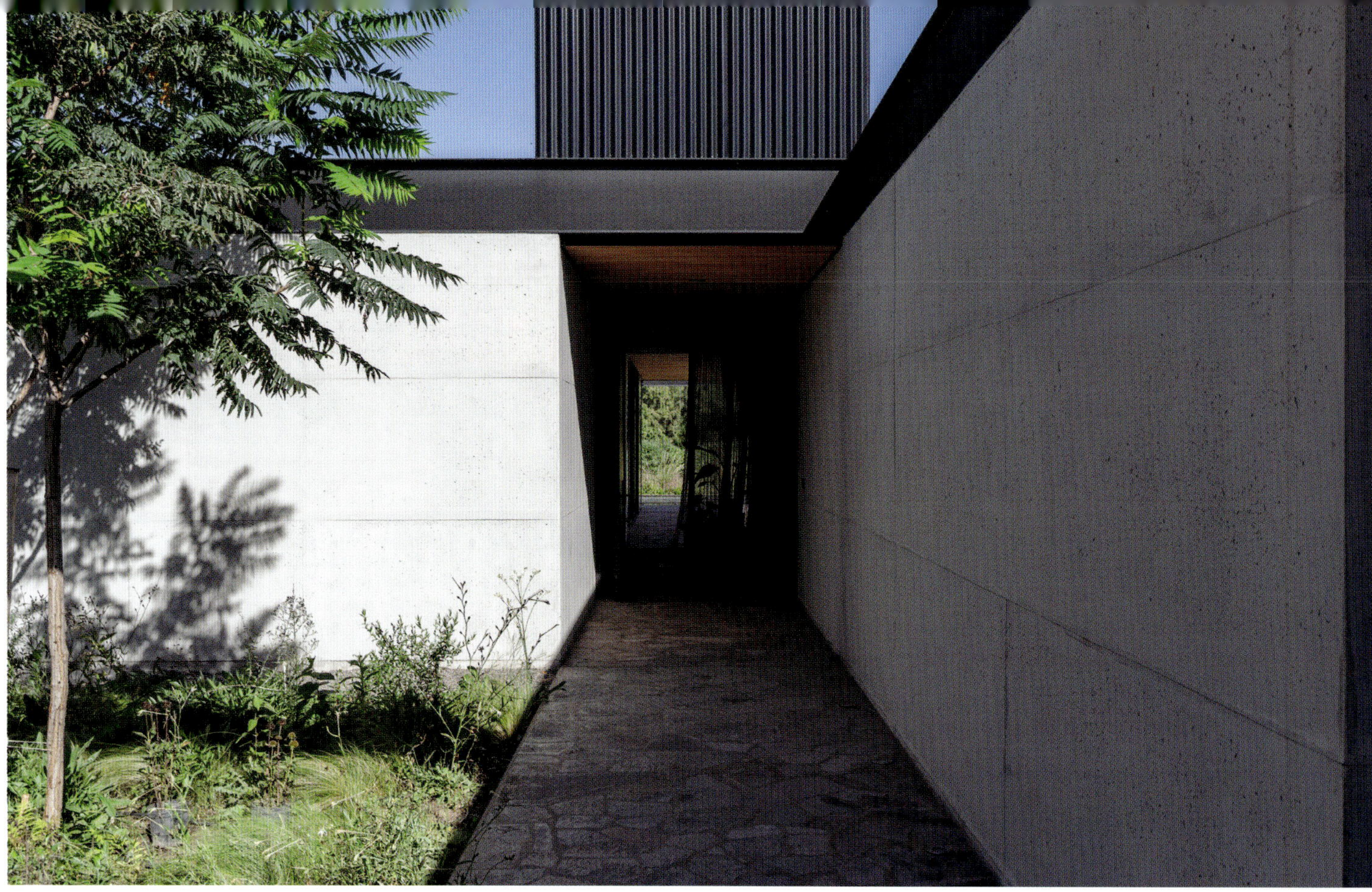

PROJECT: Casa Cañuelas
LOCATION: Cañuelas, Córdoba, Argentina
YEAR: 2023
ARCHITECTS: 31 64 estudio,
sdf Arquitectos
PHOTOGRAPHY: Juan Cruz Paredes

Located in a residential area of Córdoba, Argentina, Casa Cañuelas is a carefully planned constellation of metal profiles and concrete walls. The way the architects arranged the structural elements depended on whether they wished to provide the inhabitants privacy or, on the contrary, offer them views. And this is how the house has received not only distinctive character but also interesting patios. A smaller one includes a gallery and a pool, and the larger one is playfully filled with greenery that is a perfect counterbalance to the minimalistic architectural language of the house and omnipresent exposed concrete.

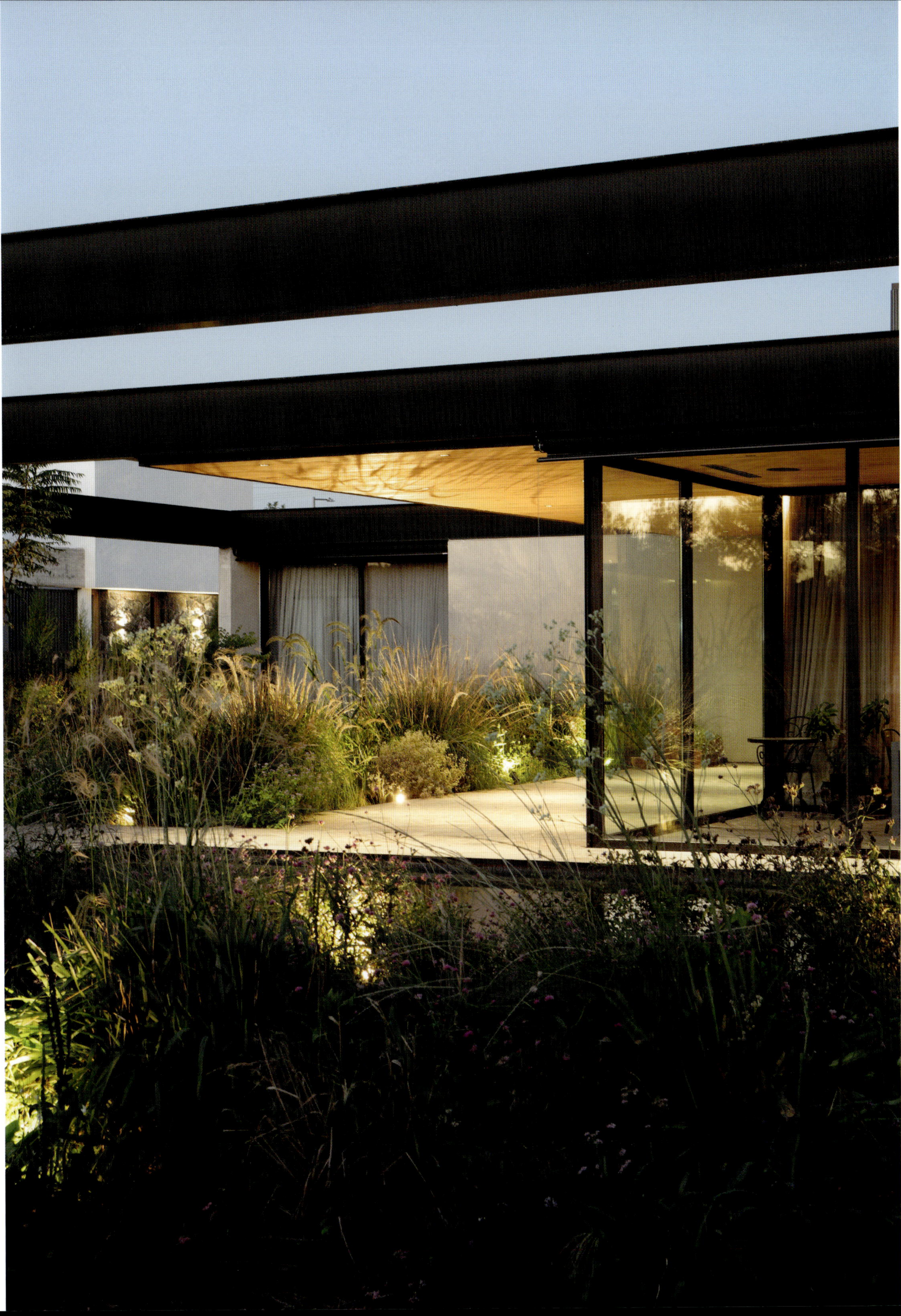

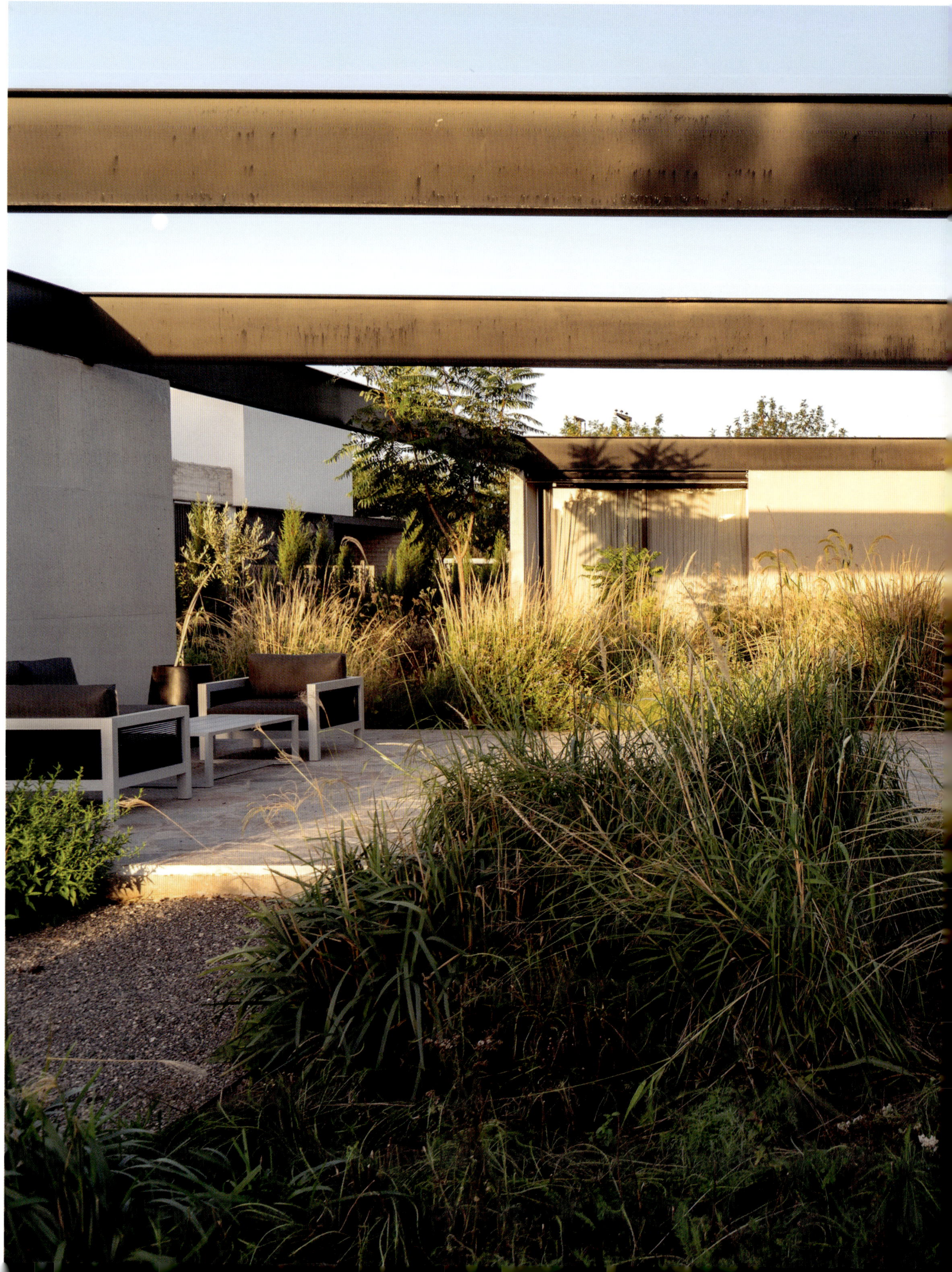

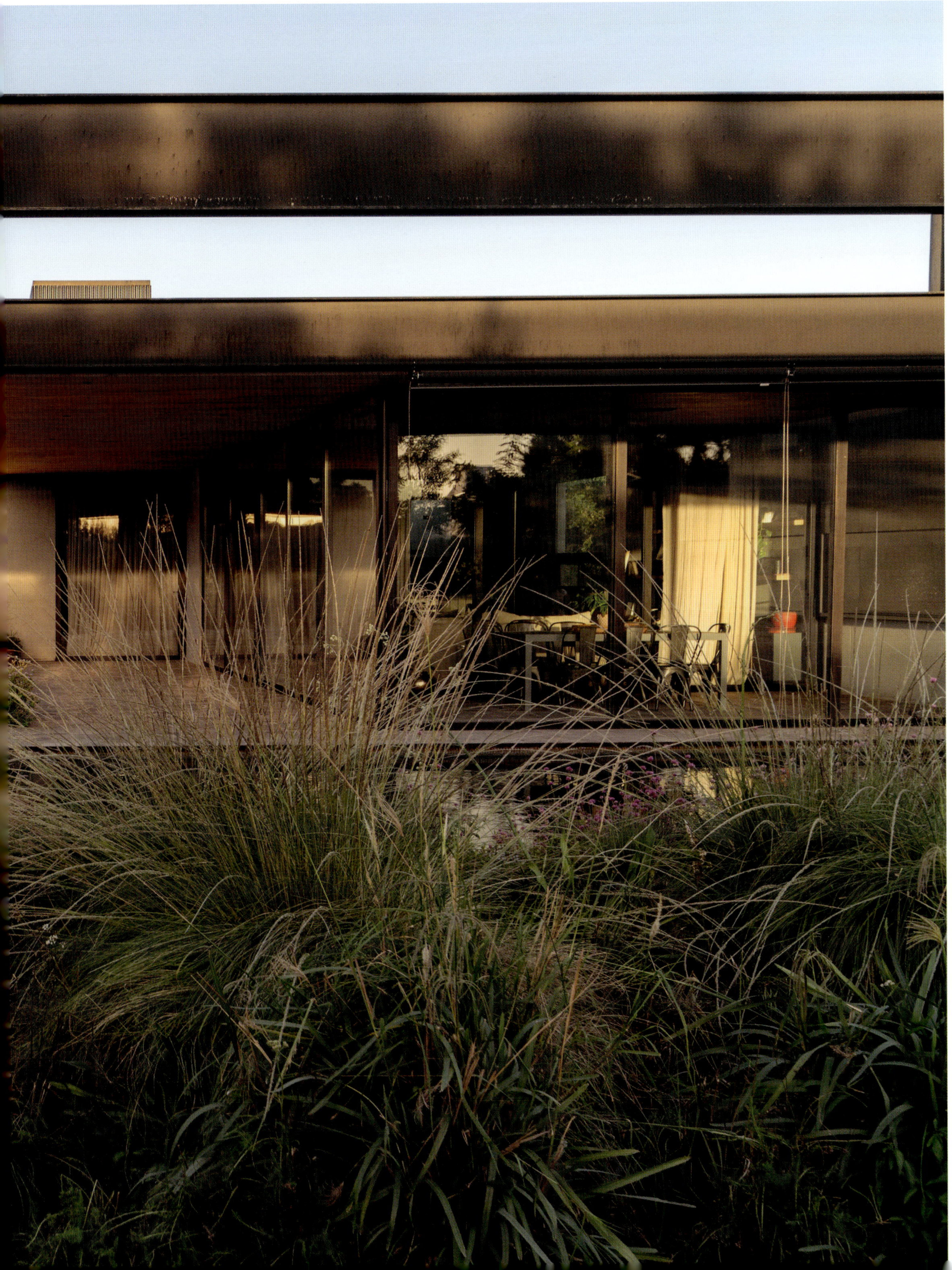

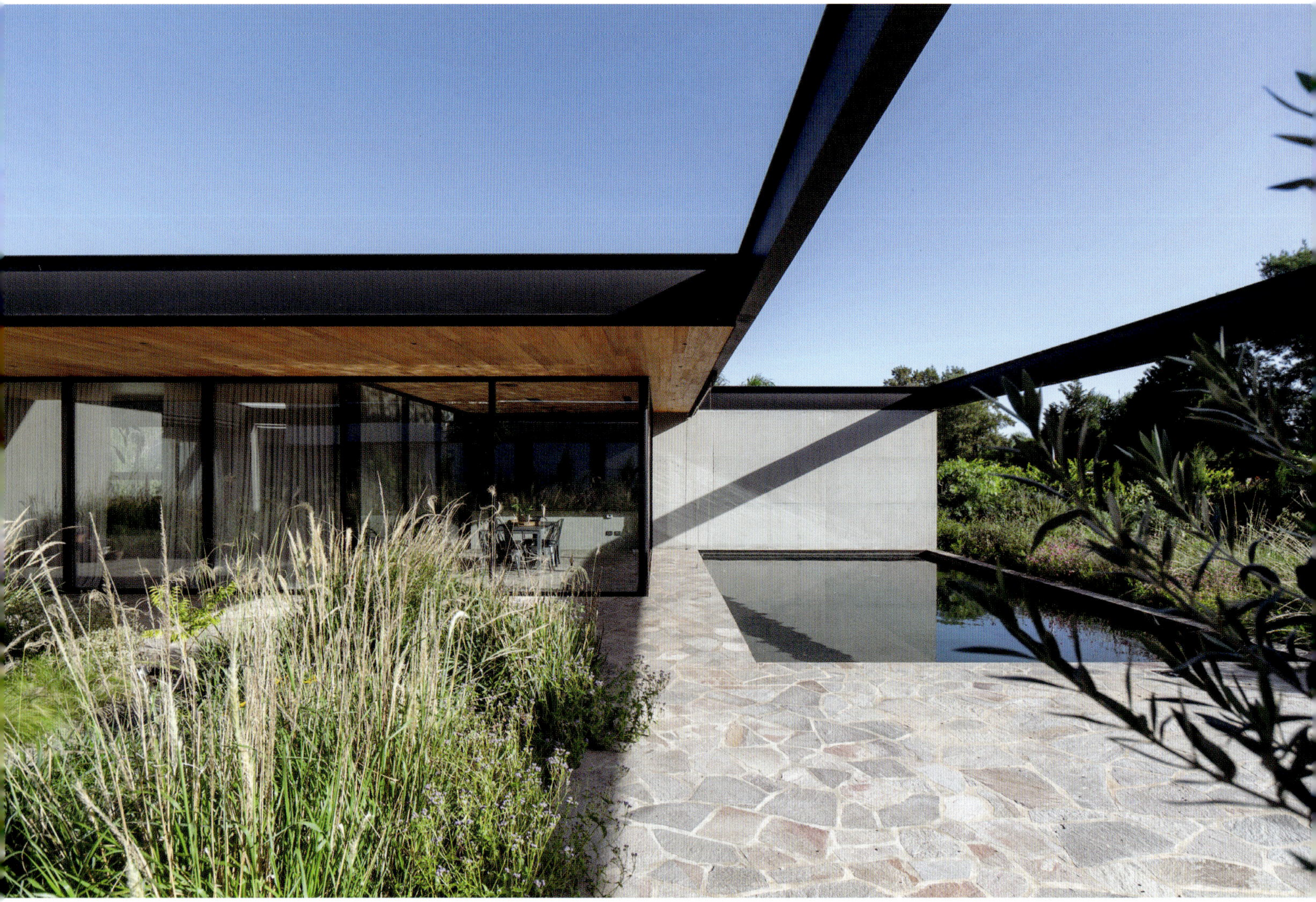

31 64 estudio, established in 2024, is a team of three architects: Ignacio De Biasi, Mariano Pognante, and Francisco Taravella, who are dedicated to designing residential buildings. The name of the practice refers to the geographical coordinates of 31° south and 64° west, to highlight the importance of the context.

sdf Arquitectos, founded in 2011, is led by Leandro Darsie and Lucas Fantini and works on a large scope of projects in different scales and typology. The team of the architecture and design studio is also devoted to the academic world, blending practice and research in their work.

Both studios are based in Córdoba, Argentina, and successfully collaborate on various projects.

As the courtyards and paths around both volumes of the house enhance its unique character, so does the vegetation used in the landscape of the closest surrounding. A selection of native local species have been chosen to alternate the blooming across the seasons. The interiors have been organized in two volumes connected through the central axis; the first one houses common areas, and the second one private rooms. While the one for social activities has an open plan and is smoothly connected with the recreational outdoor space, the structure of the privacy volume has been divided into three bedrooms.

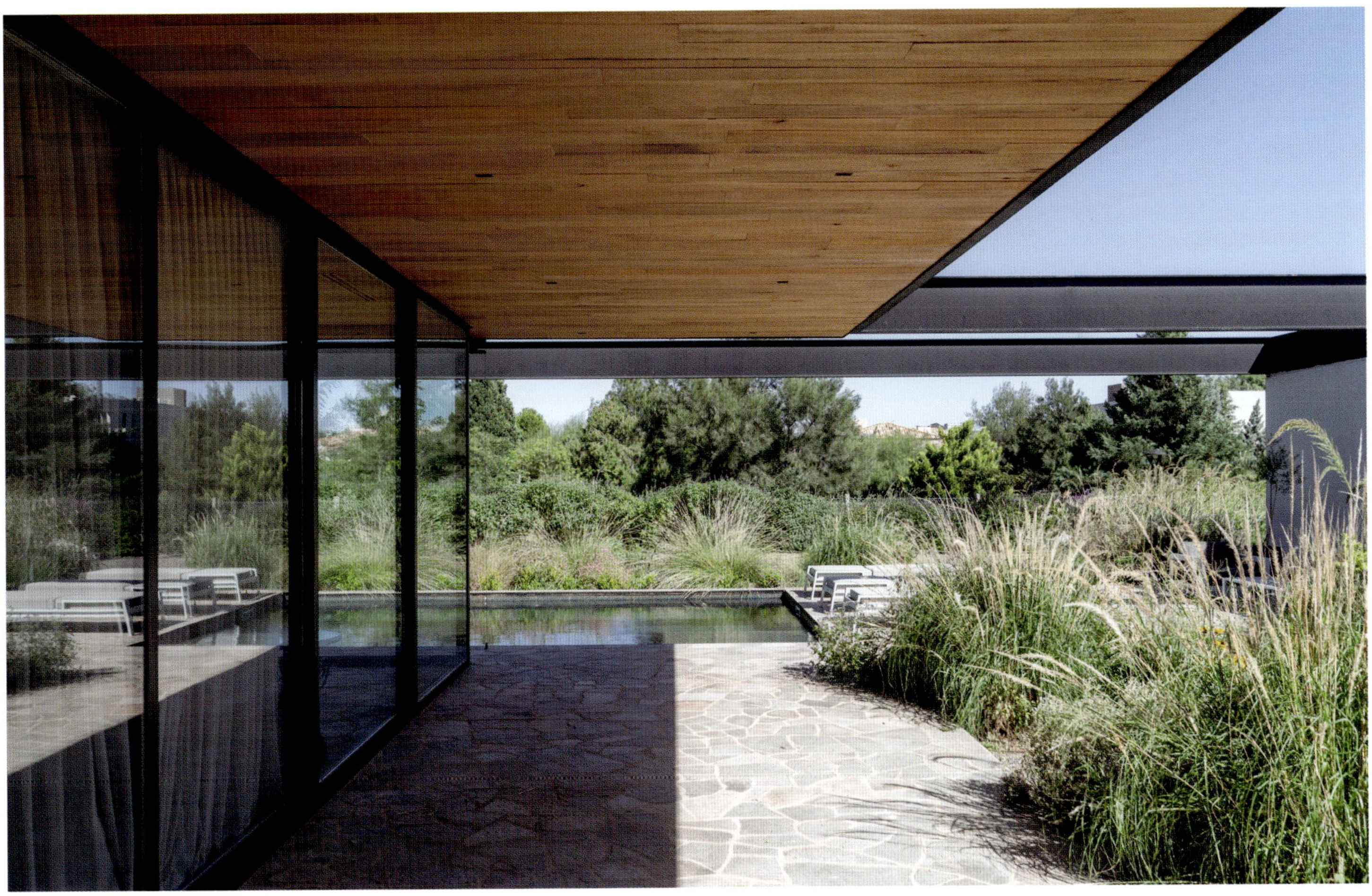

The minimalistic juxtaposition of visually distinctive metal profiles, walls in exposed concrete, and wood used in the ceilings adds a timeless flair.

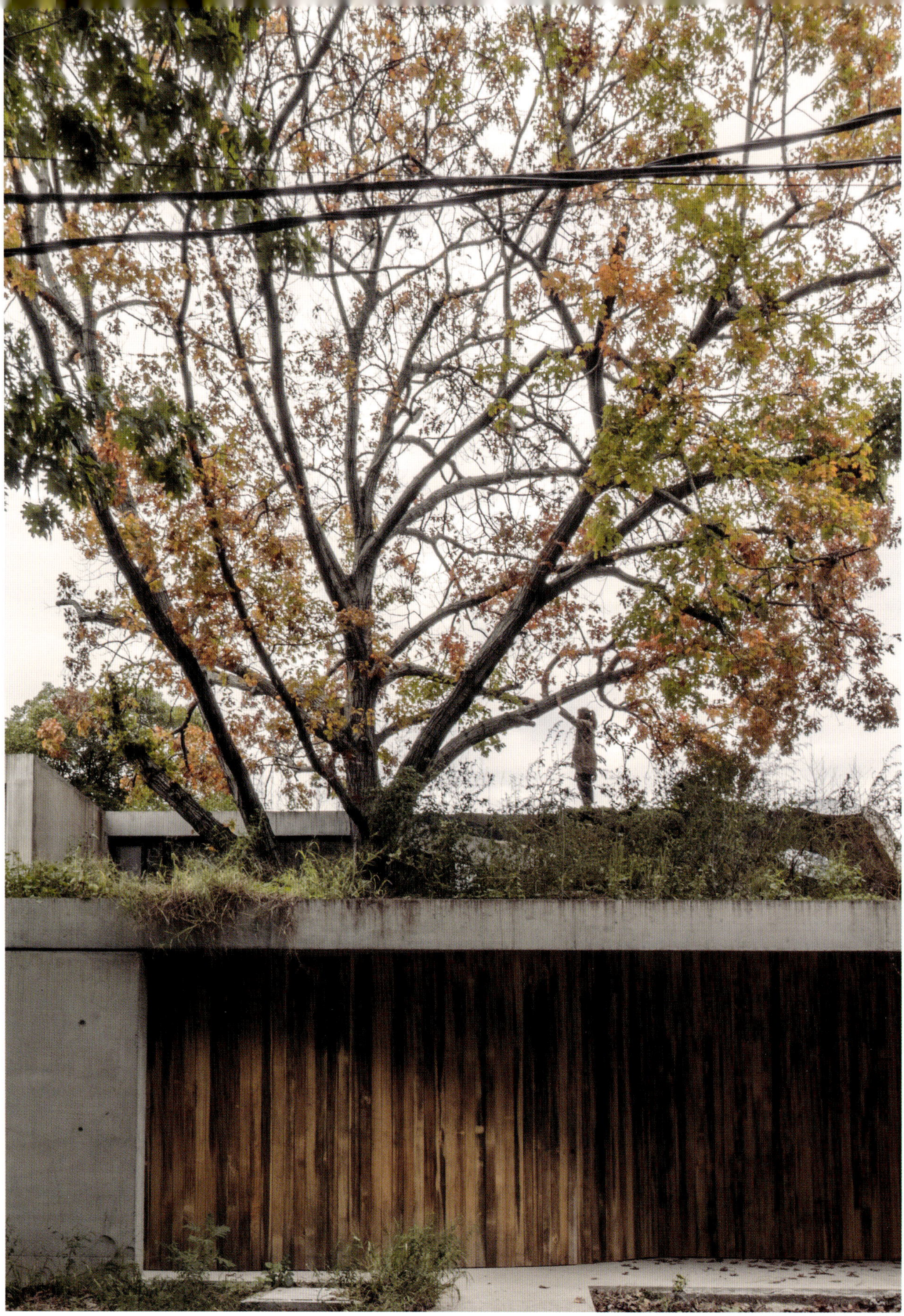

AtelierM is a Buenos Aires–based studio founded by Argentine architect and musician Matias Mosquera in 2020, after a decade of gaining professional experience among others in Denmark. The team's philosophy has three main pillars—design based on the circular economy, experimentation in pursuit of constant creative search, and working in a collaborative spirit where multiple disciplines, inspirations, and traditions meet.

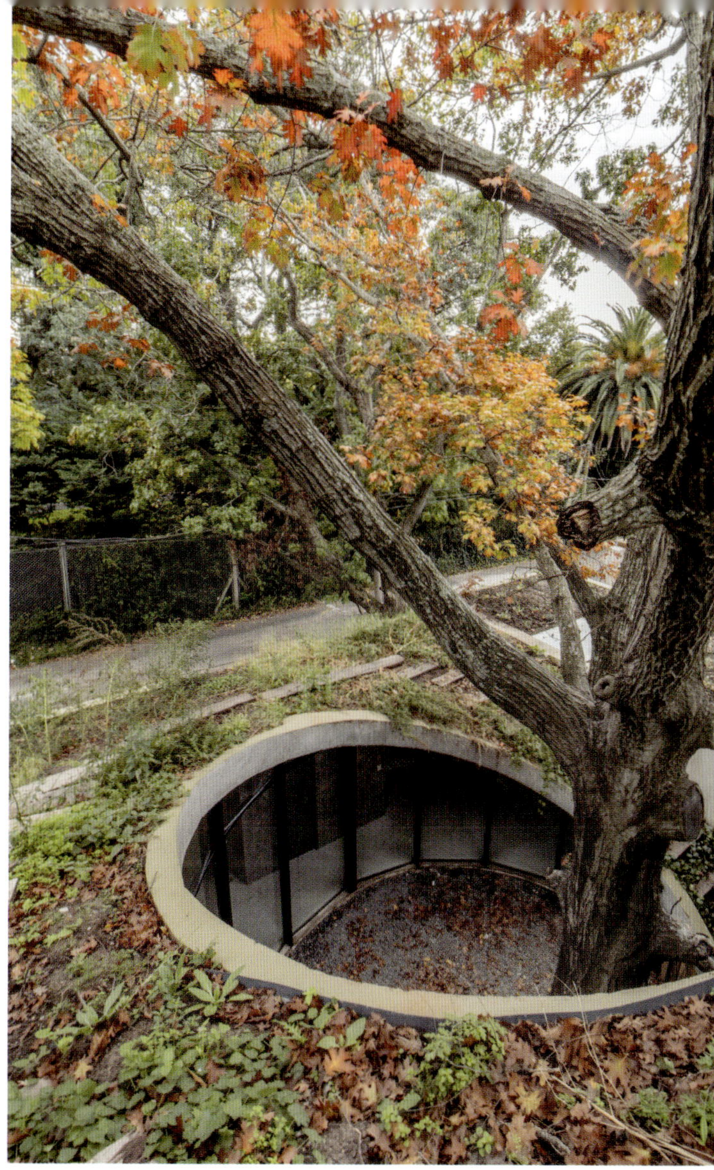

PROJECT: LuMa House
LOCATION: Martínez, Argentina
YEAR: 2020
ARCHITECTS: AtelierM
PHOTOGRAPHY: AtelierM

Advocating for more-human and more-personalized architecture that would be at its core sustainable, the architects of the Argentinian firm AtelierM envision unique projects. LuMa House shows how the team makes conscious decisions based on the analysis of the context. Challenging was not only a typologically unusual plot but also a hundred-year-old oak in the very heart of it. The goal was to establish a harmonious relationship with the place and, most of all, the old tree. Yet another objective was to deliver enough natural light to the interiors. The architects resolved this complex task in a highly inventive and poetic manner. The blind entrance facade on the north preserves the inhabitants' privacy, features the majesty of the tree, and opens to a magic residence.

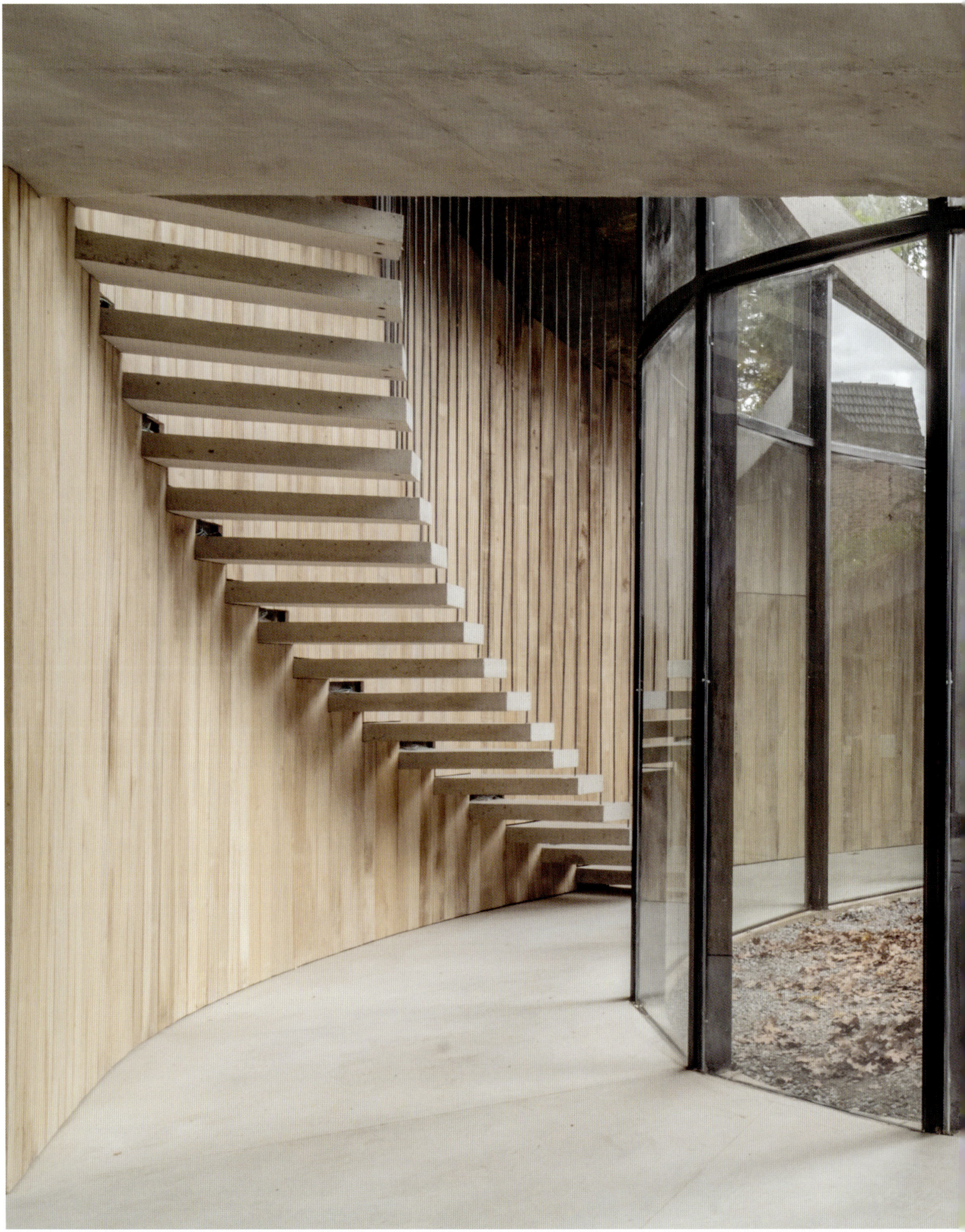

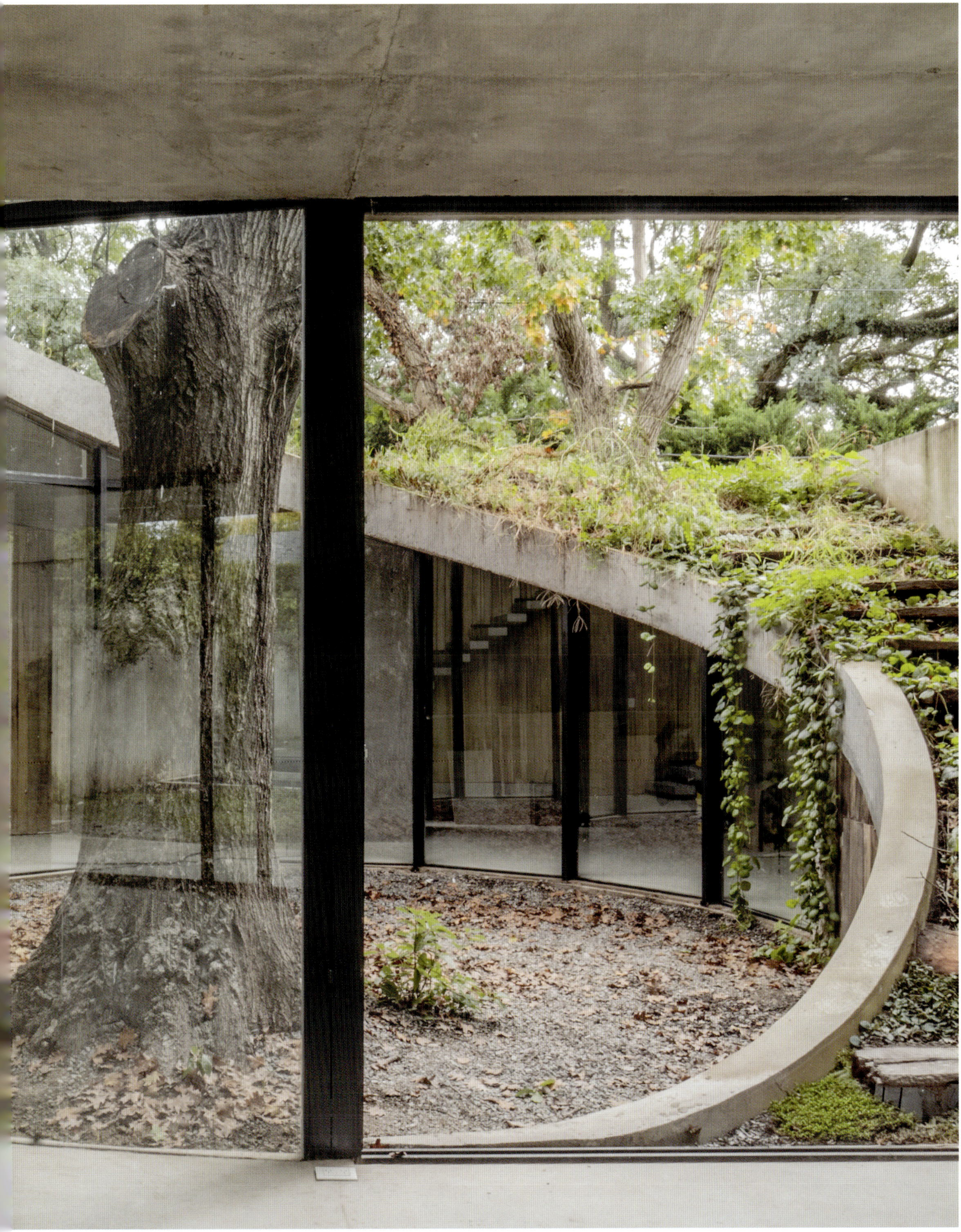

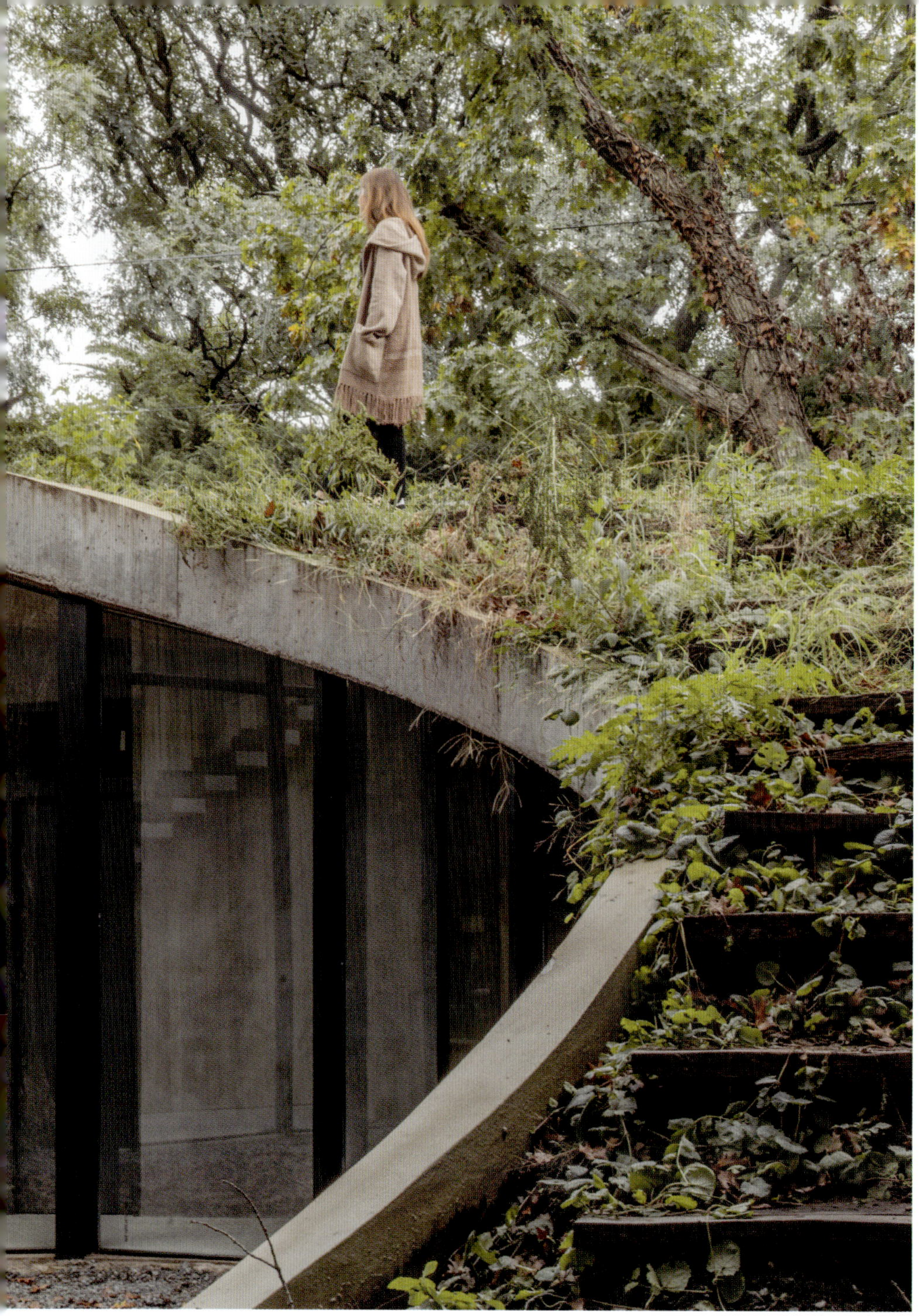

Entirely hidden from the street view, the inventive structure of LuMa House has been designed in relation to the solar cycle. Crossing the entrance door, one enters onto a circular patio sculpturally embraced by a curvaceous wall. This surprising inner courtyard, visually connected with the common spaces on the first ground, creates a space perfectly harmonized with the old tree. They coexist also in terms of the light—while in the winter it allows brighter interiors, in the summer its leaves have a cooling effect. The house is designed to deliver a unique experience of space, with numerous paths dynamically communicating various areas. One of them leads outdoors from the living room up to the garden located on the roof. In stark contrast, the private rooms have been planned on the second story, intimately disconnected from the exterior of the patio or the roof garden.

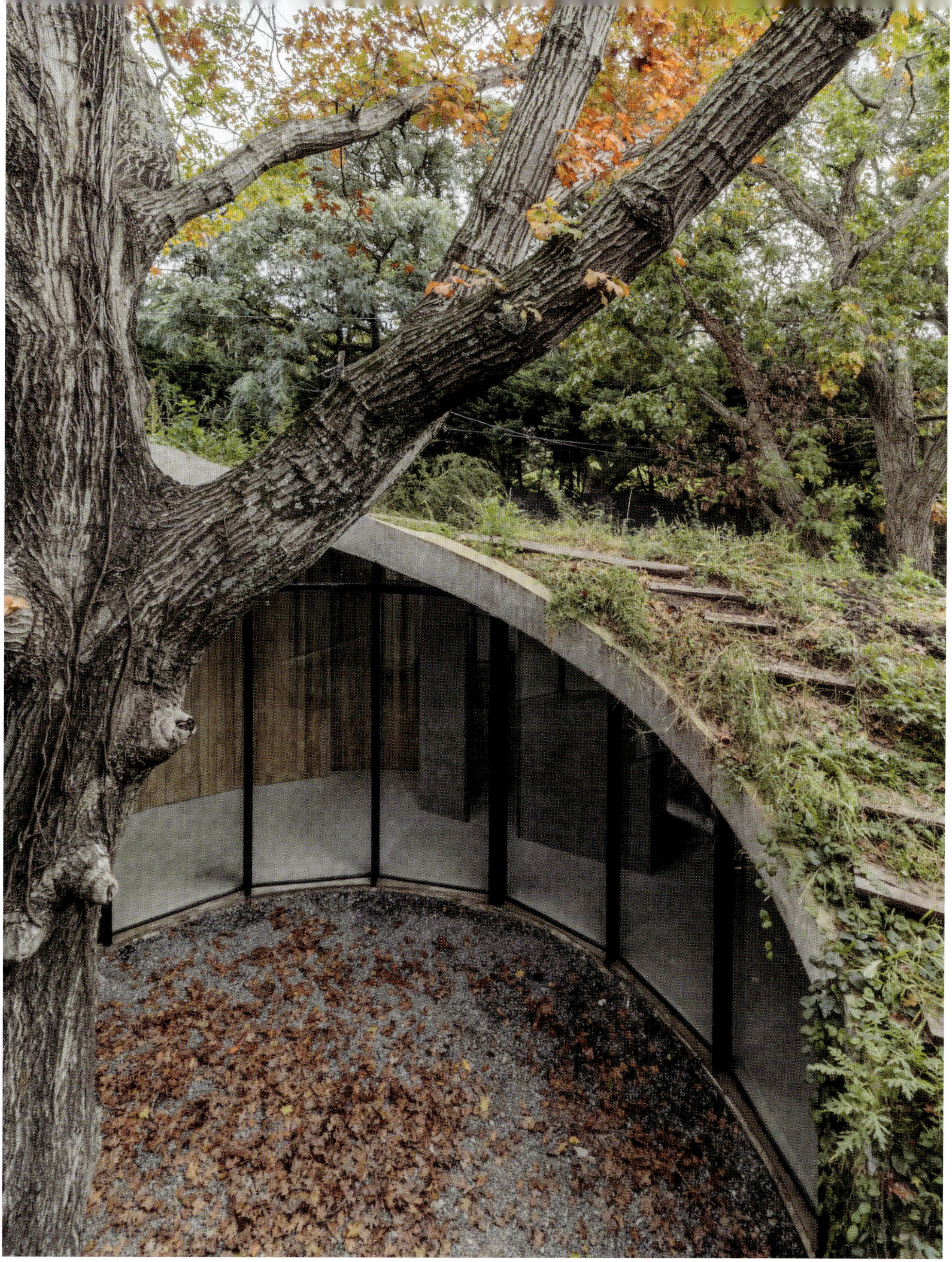

The curvaceous stairs hidden in lush vegetation are a discreet invitation to experience architecture by walking up to the garden with a view.

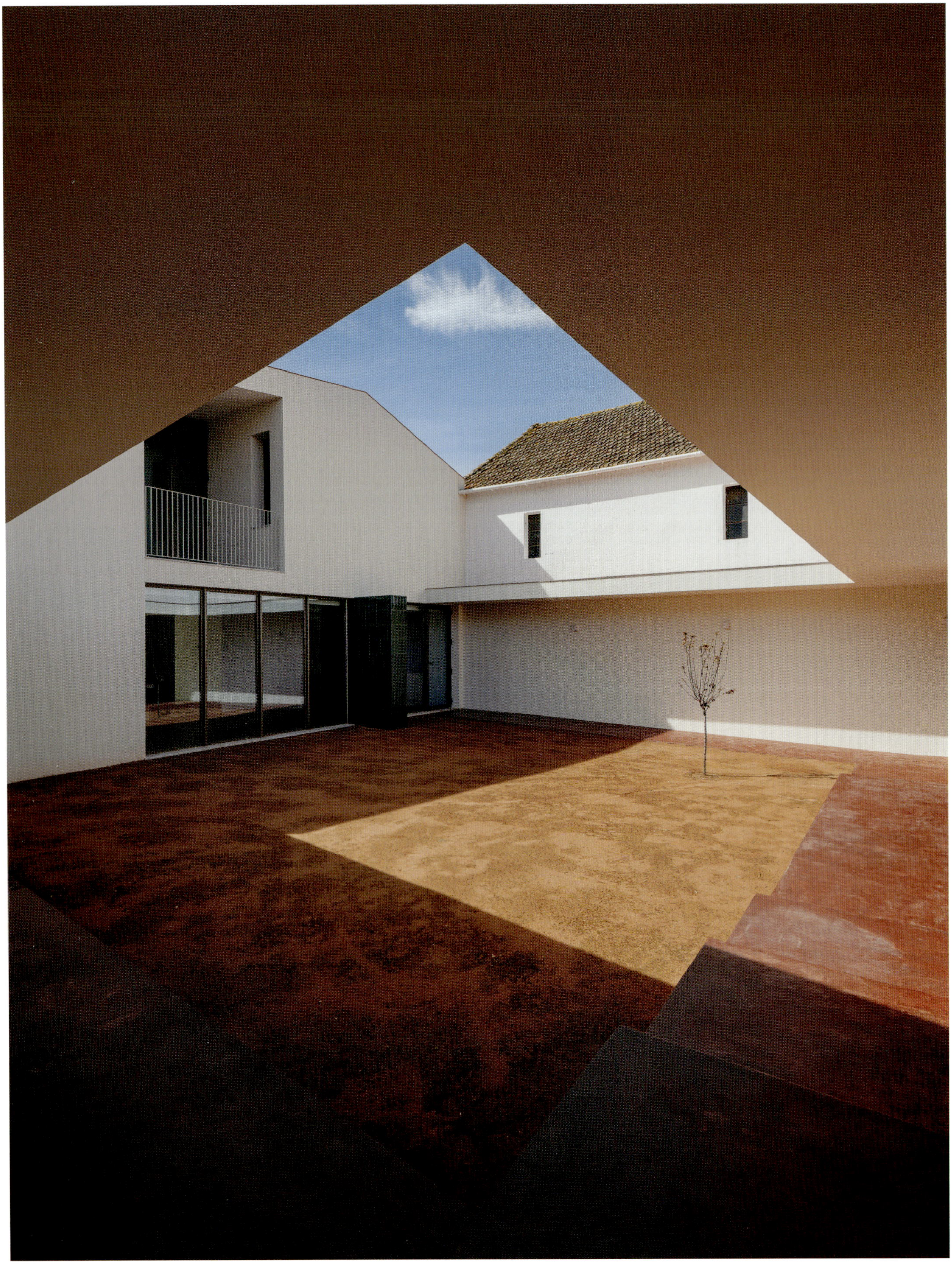

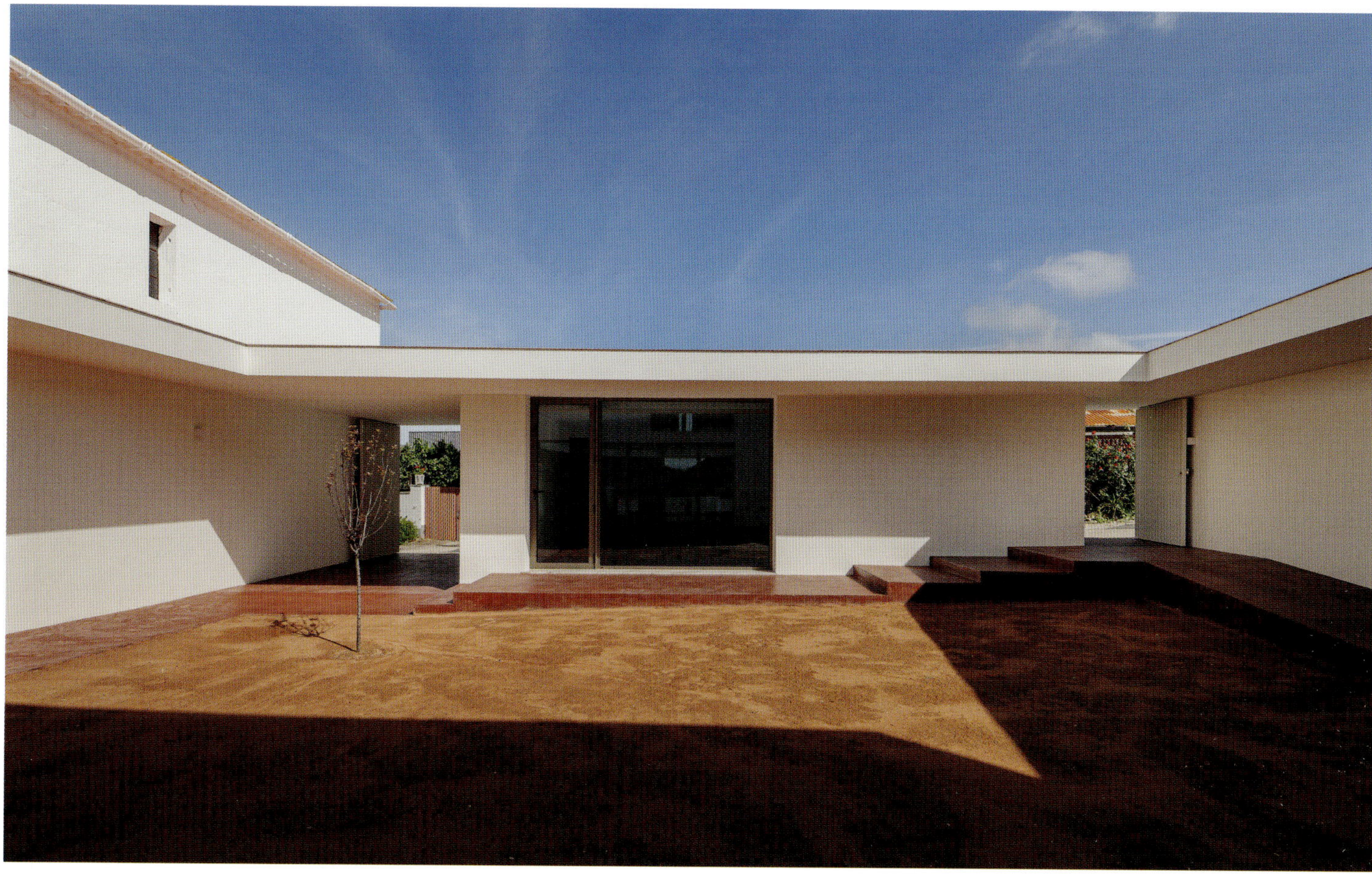

PROJECT: Casa Pátio IV
LOCATION: Painho, Portugal
YEAR: 2024
ARCHITECTS: Volume Architecture Lisbon Studio
PHOTOGRAPHY: Eduardo Nascimento

The scale and color palette of Patio IV House have been carefully planned in relation to the district's context. The entrance from a less frequented street opens directly to the spectacular inner patio, which plays an important role in the program of the residence in Painho. Envisioned as a space for receptions, socializing, and family gatherings, it is a large yet intimate area that is filled with sunlight from the east. Another interesting aspect is a roofed path around the patio, smoothly adjusted to various parts of the volume and serving as a harmonizing element. The architects used traditional iron oxide pigmentation technique to refer to the natural tones of the roofs and the patio's surface.

This spacious courtyard is also a transitional space between the office space, located in the entrance wall, and the residential quarters. Moving up from the low volume toward the house on a ramp creates an interesting experience of changing scales—"The moment you enter the house is accentuated by a double-height ceiling, which reveals the staircase leading to the bedrooms," explain the architects. The common spaces have been planned on two levels to create a communication with the garden to the south through a semiunderground part in the lower area. The smooth relation facilitates generous openings and another, covered, patio envisioned as a more intimate reading area.

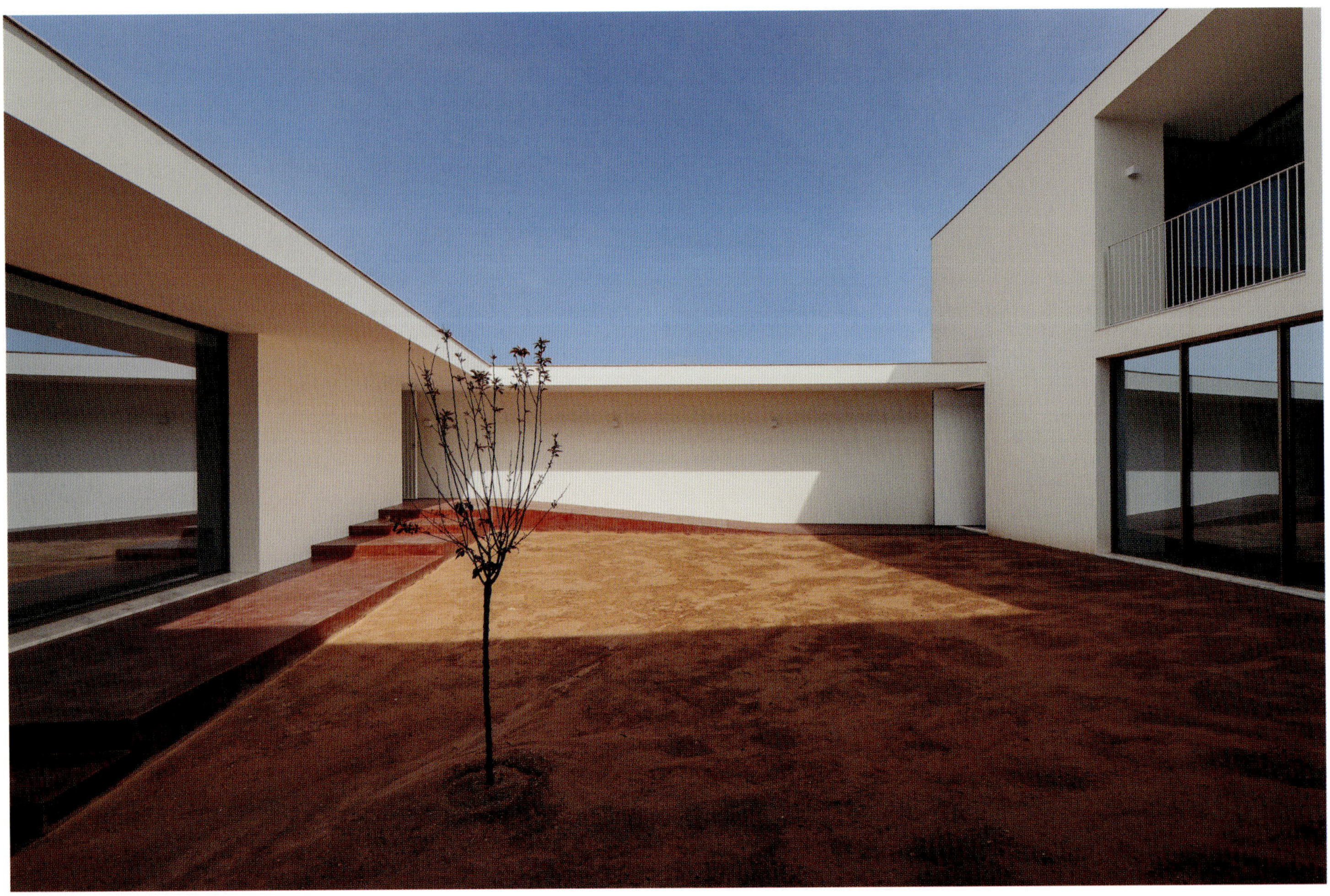

After working for various studios, João Caria Lopes and Rodolfo Reis decided to establish their practice Volume in 2021. The Lisbon-based firm works on a large scope of projects in various scales as well as typologies, such as renovations, urban planning, and residential and institutional buildings and offices, but also product design. They aim at delivering stimulating spaces that are designed in a holistic way.

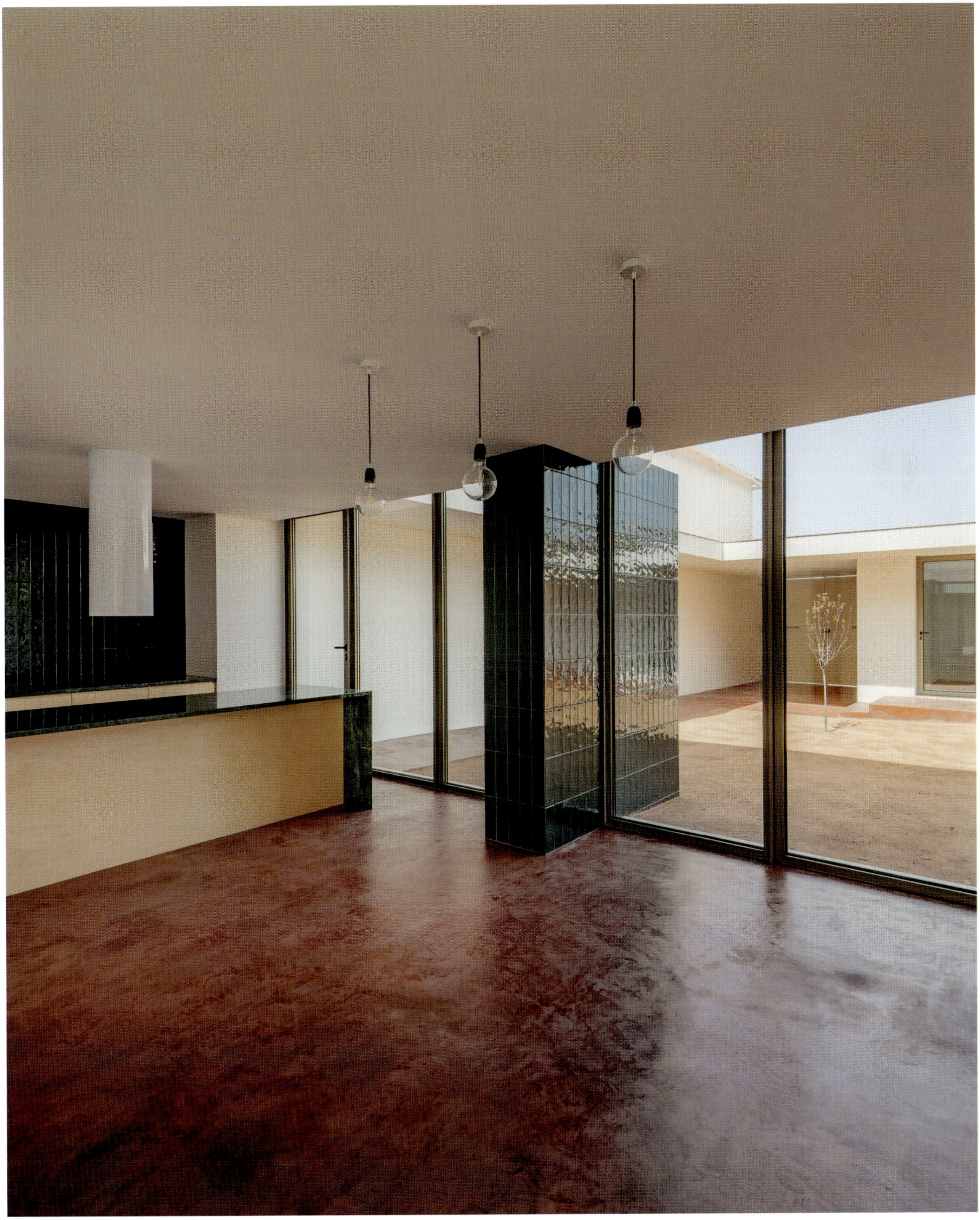

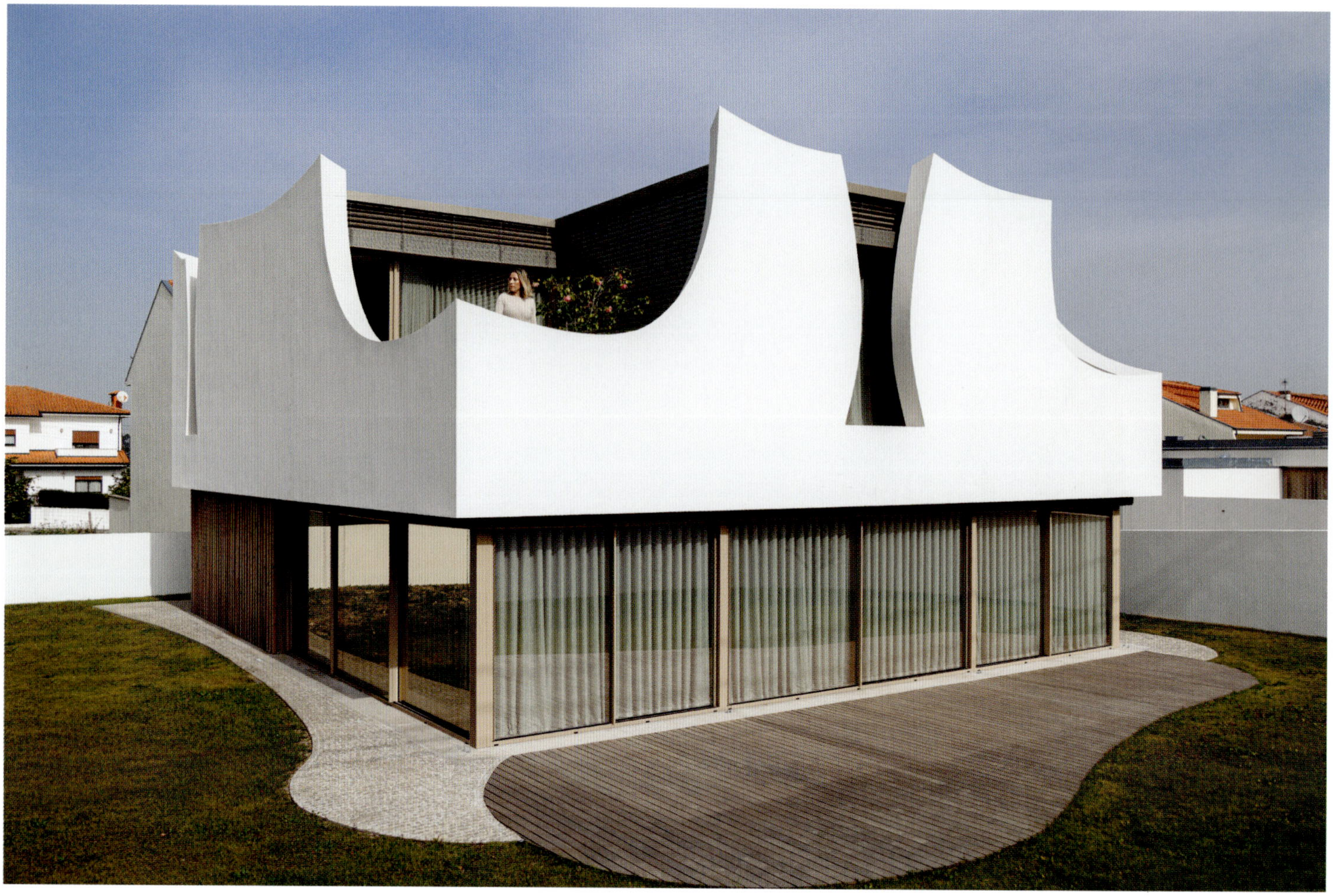

PROJECT: Casa Pátios de Pétalas
LOCATION: Porto, Portugal
YEAR: 2023
ARCHITECTS: Sandra Micaela Casinha Atelier
PHOTOGRAPHY: Ivo Tavares Studio

Drawing from both art and nature, Sandra Micaela Casinha translates her creative visions into extraordinary residences. Embracing innovative technologies and methods allows for truly playful results. Casa Pátios de Pétalas—House Patios of Petals—is an exquisite example of this philosophy. Located in an urban context but inspired by the natural landscape, the volume combines a simple geometric base with a more extravagant curvaceous structure that envelops the second story. The petallike wrapping, with curves suggesting movement, acts as protection from the sun and provides privacy, especially from the street perspective. It is also like a curtain that opens to intimate patios accessible from the rooms and looking out onto the back courtyard, with the garden on the ground level.

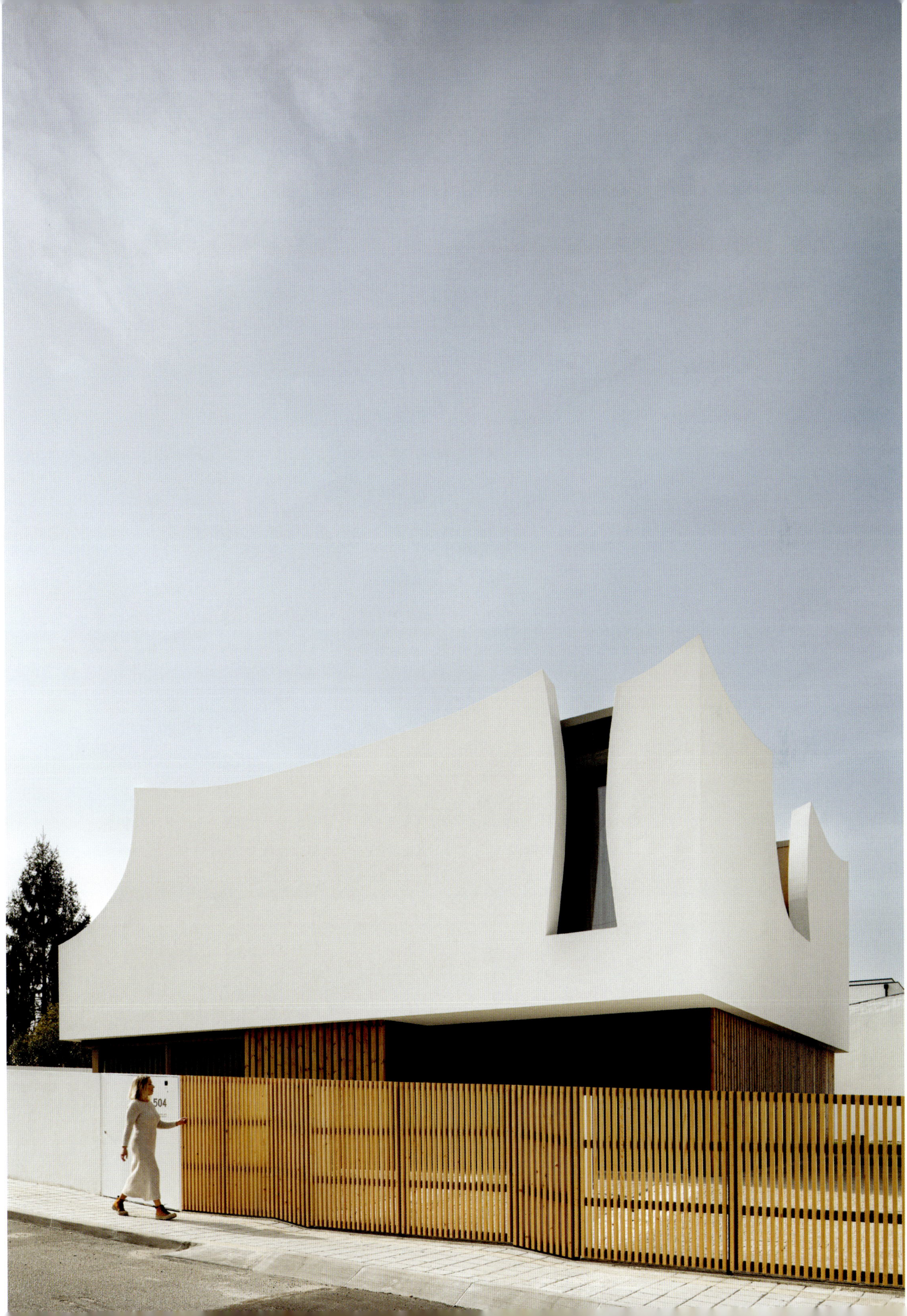
504

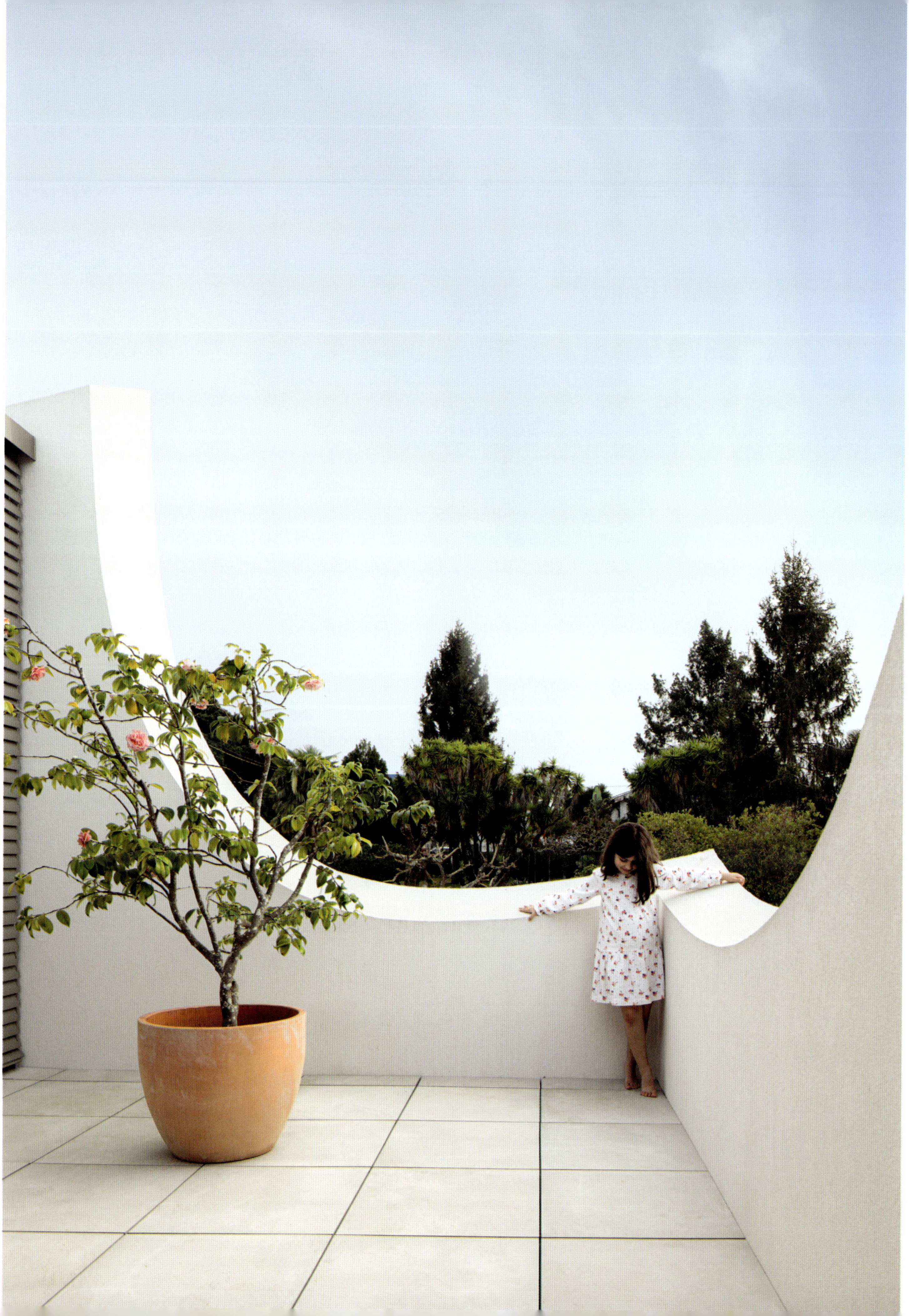

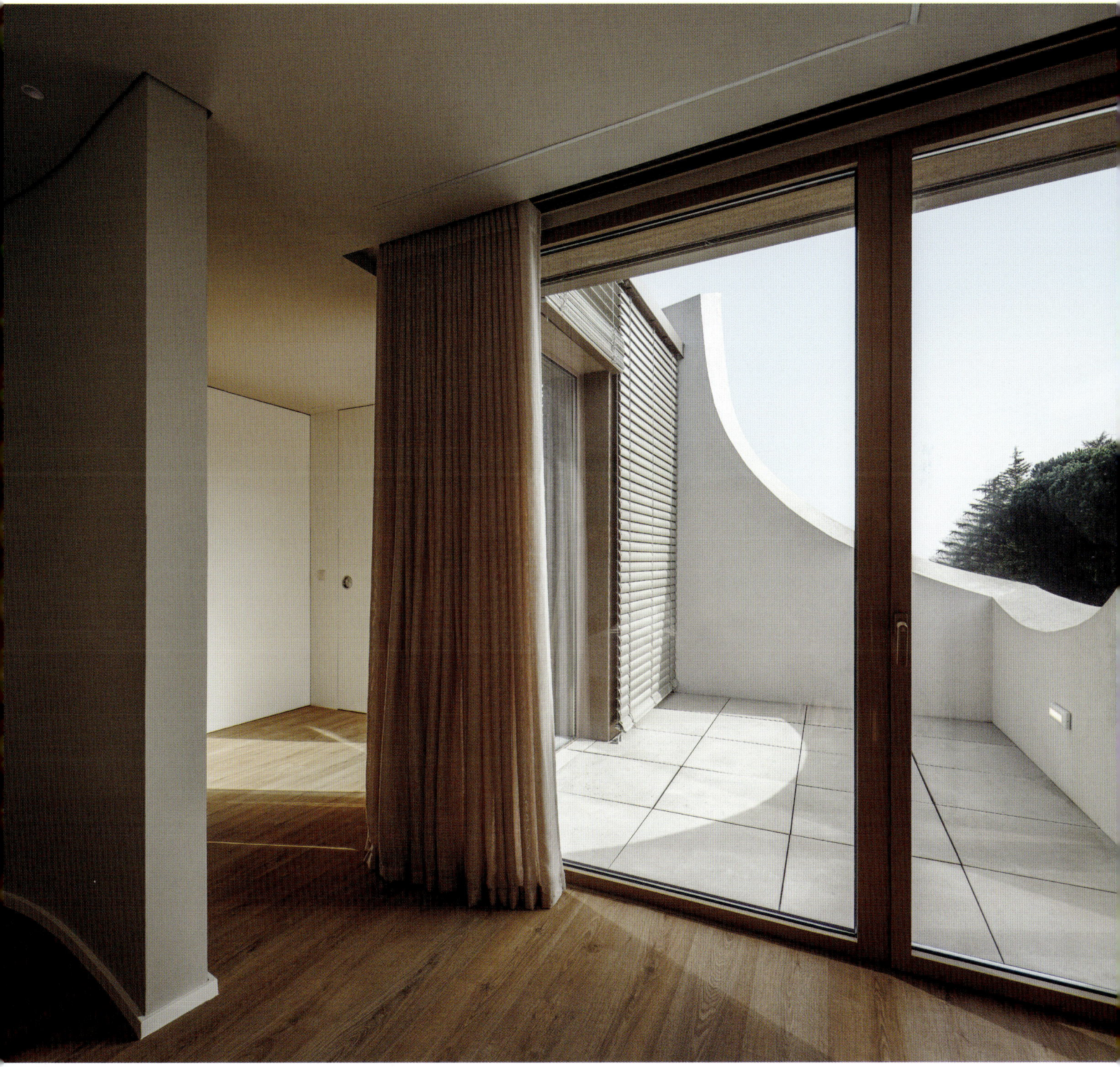

Sandra Micaela Casinha began her professional career as an engineer but quickly dedicated her Porto-based practice to architecture in 2005. Inspired by art and with a creative approach, the architect designs visionary residential single- and multifamily housing. The goal is to enhance the quality of life through innovative and aesthetically original architecture.

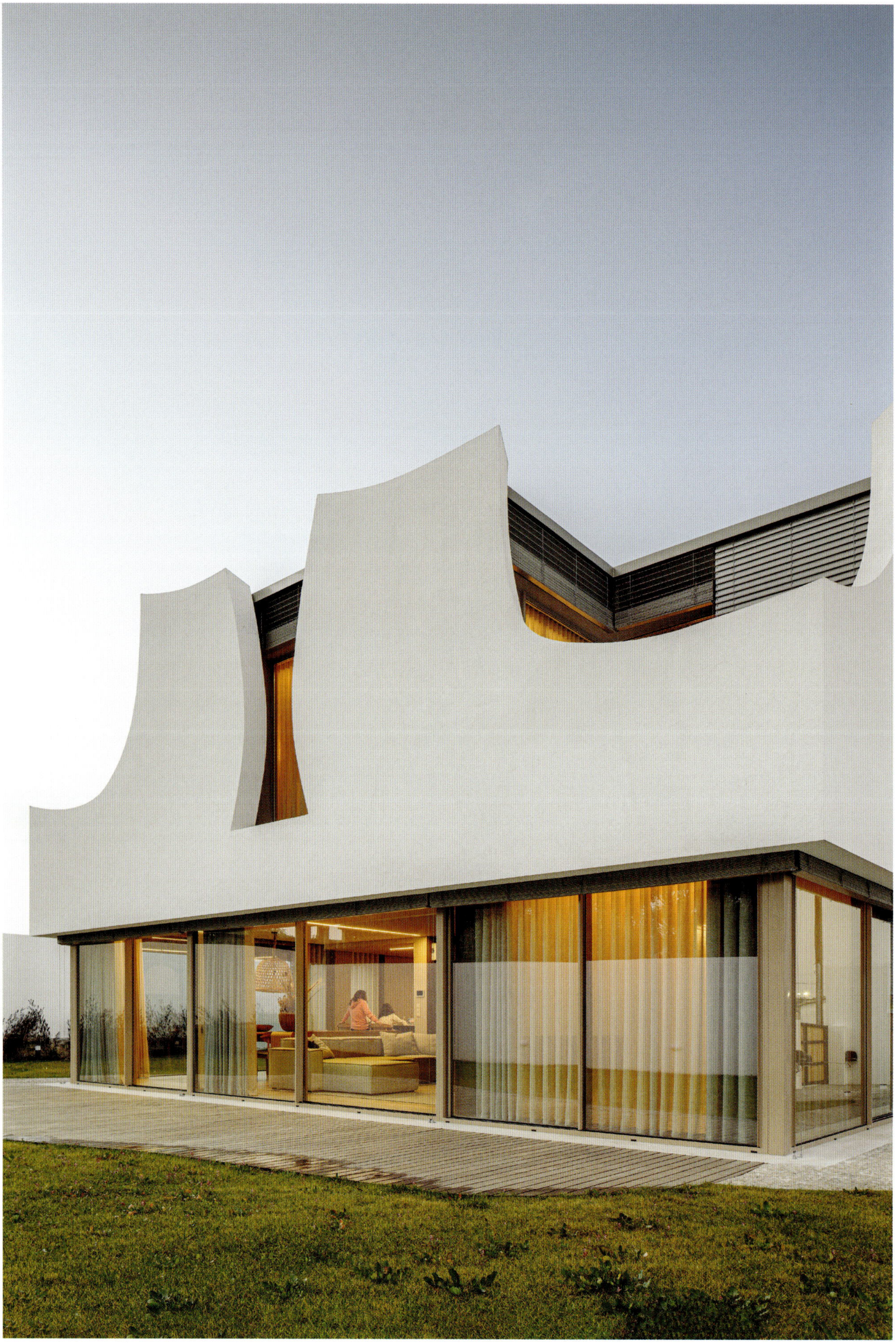

The residents of the house can decide, depending on the occasion and mood, between more-intimate patios on the upper level and a larger courtyard adjoining the garden, inviting one to socialize on the ground floor.

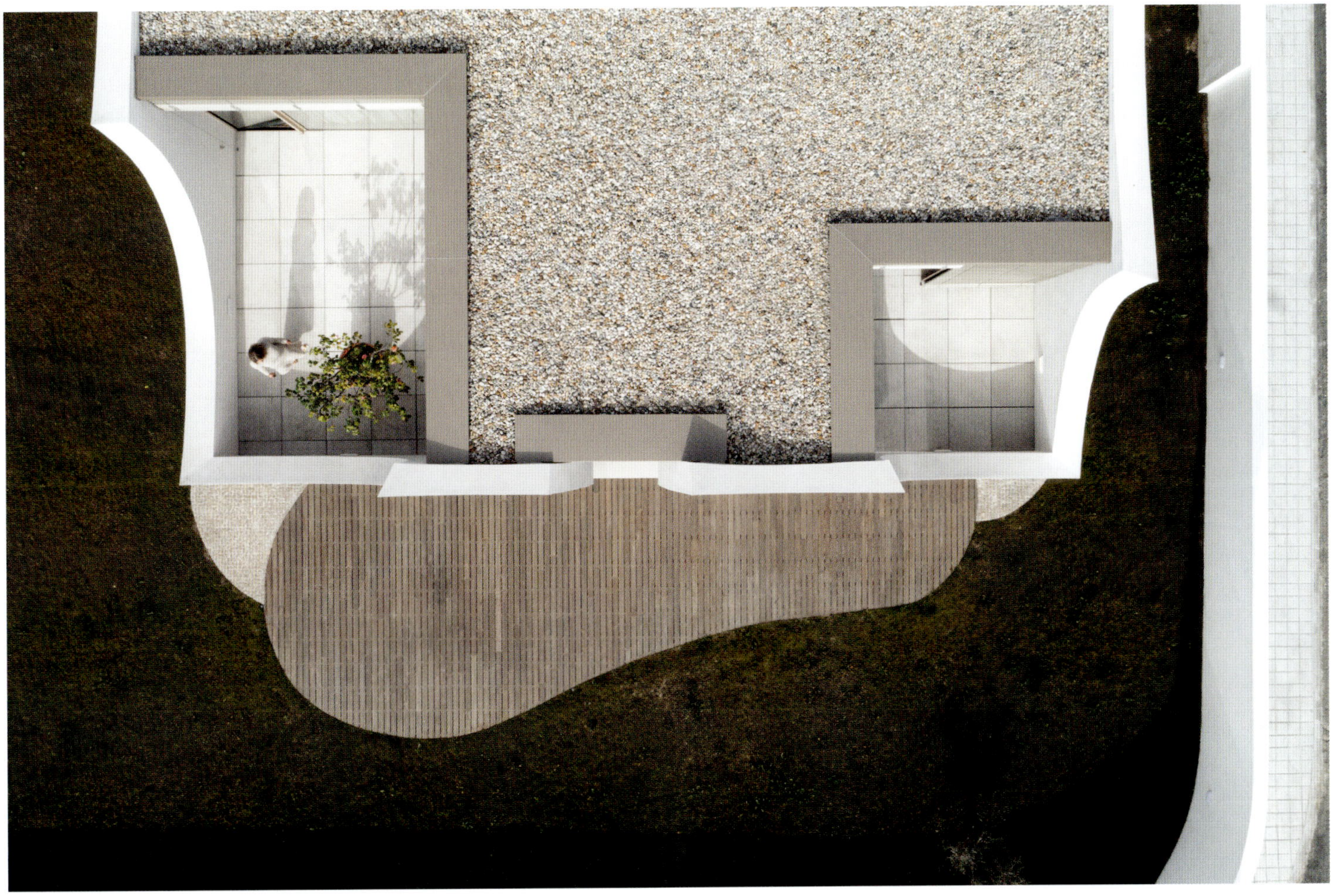

To highlight the expressive power of this organically shaped "crown" within the volume, the architect decided to limit the palette of materials to aluminum, glass, and wood. The interior is equally theatrical, with a spectacular curvaceous staircase at the very heart of the house, fluidly connecting the two levels—common area located on the lower one and private spaces on the upper one. Generous openings allow for smooth communication between all patios and the interiors. Whether in the intimate courtyards on the top or the extensive social space on the bottom, residents can enjoy the outdoors in two entirely different modes. The neutral hues of the interior design are in perfect balance with the distinctive petal-inspired structural elements.

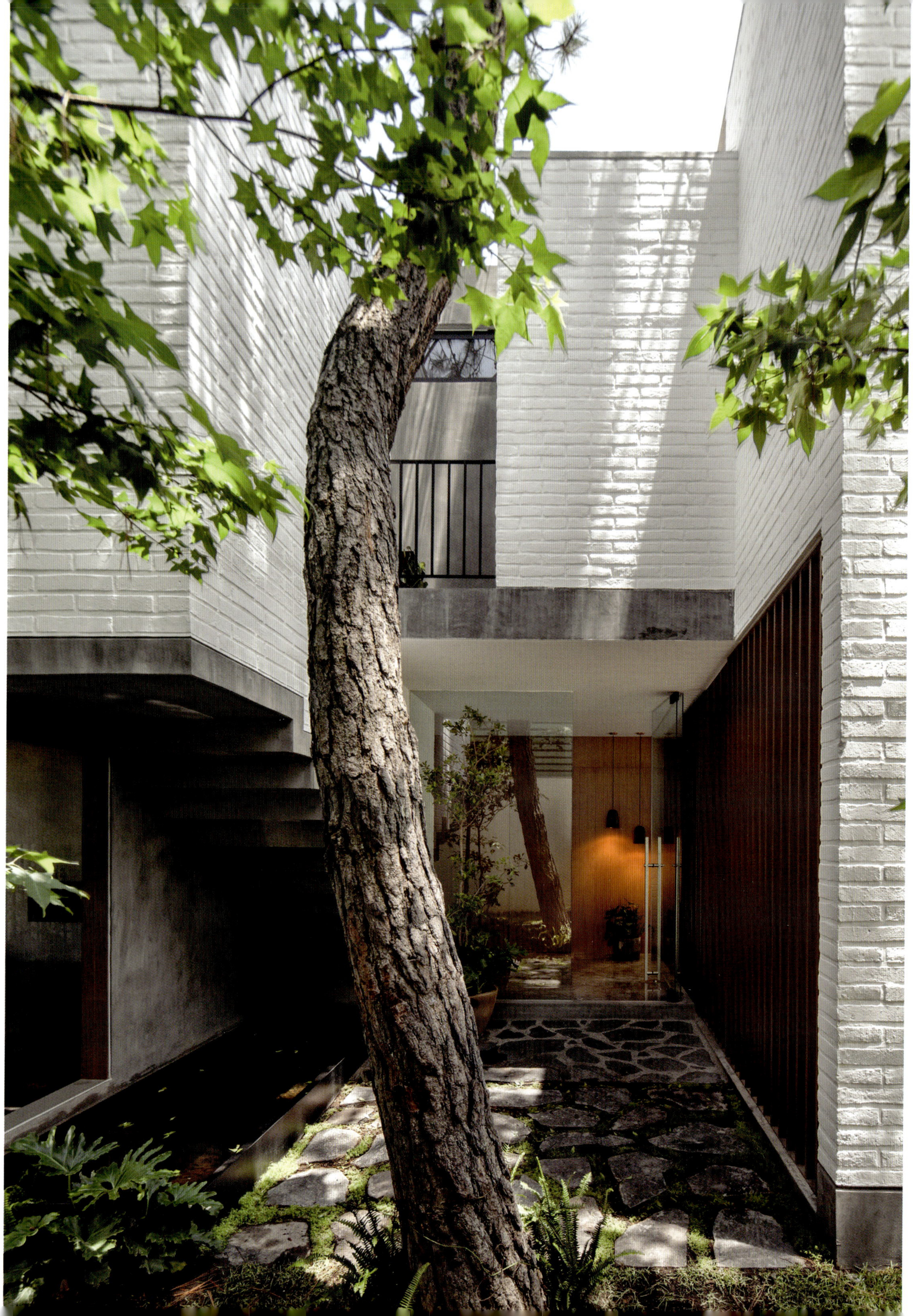

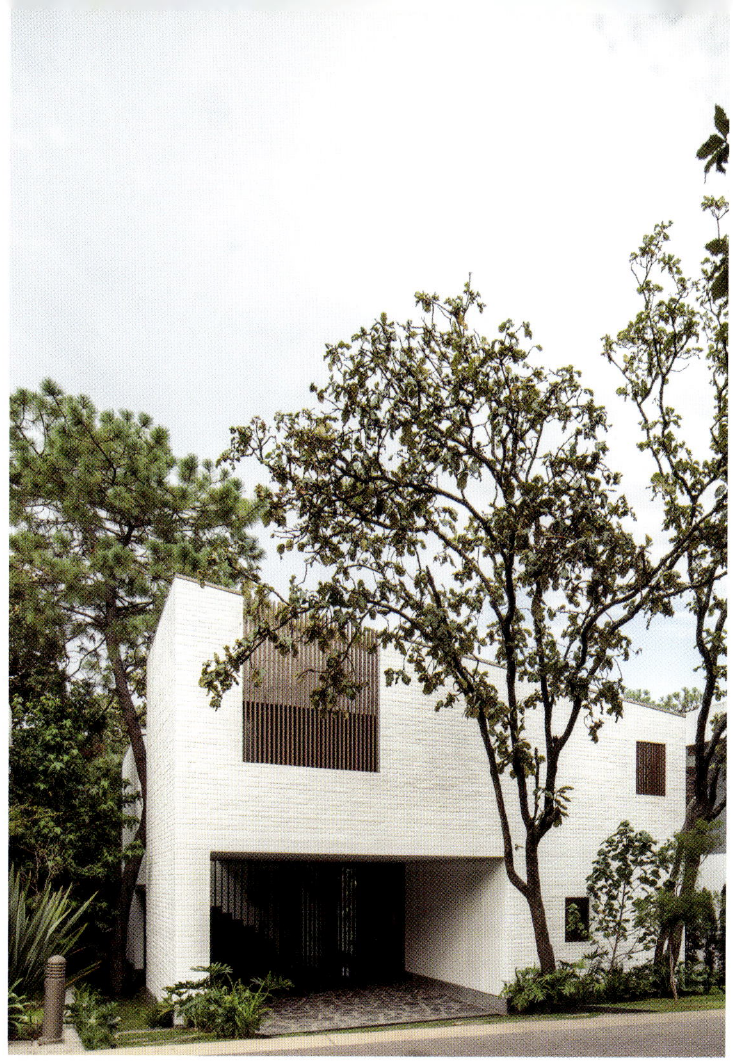

PROJECT: Casa R.A
LOCATION: Guadalajara, Jalisco, Mexico
YEAR: 2020
ARCHITECTS: Estudio Radillo Alba
PHOTOGRAPHY: César Belio

The work of Mexican architect and lecturer Edgar Radillo Alba beautifully demonstrates how to connect the past with the future in architecture. Together with his small team, he decided to focus on rethinking the ways of living, which is particularly interesting in the dynamically evolving housing design in Mexico. Through careful analyses of the traditional styles, techniques, and materials, the architects approach new projects with a quintessentially modern twist. This means combining long traditions with innovative concepts that express new lifestyles and contemporary aesthetics. One of the best examples is the way the studio plans patios in new residential architecture, including Casa R.A. Internal courtyards, common in Mexican traditions since the seventeenth century and still very functional, are reduced in size and programmed in private spaces such as bedrooms rather than social common areas.

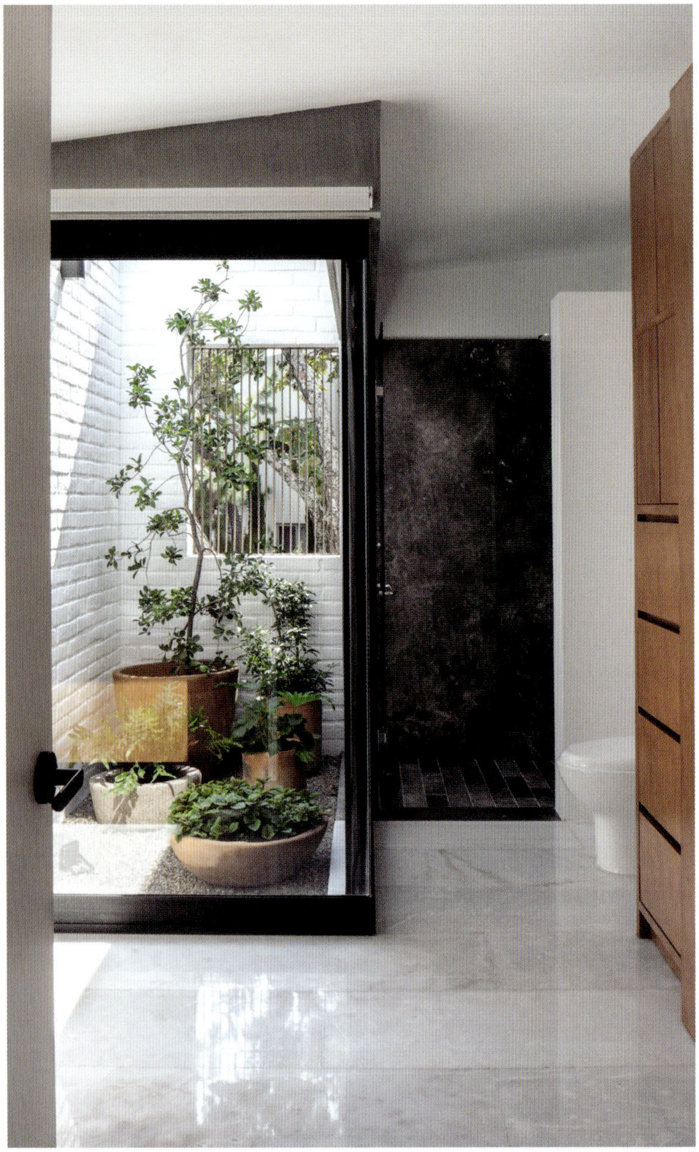

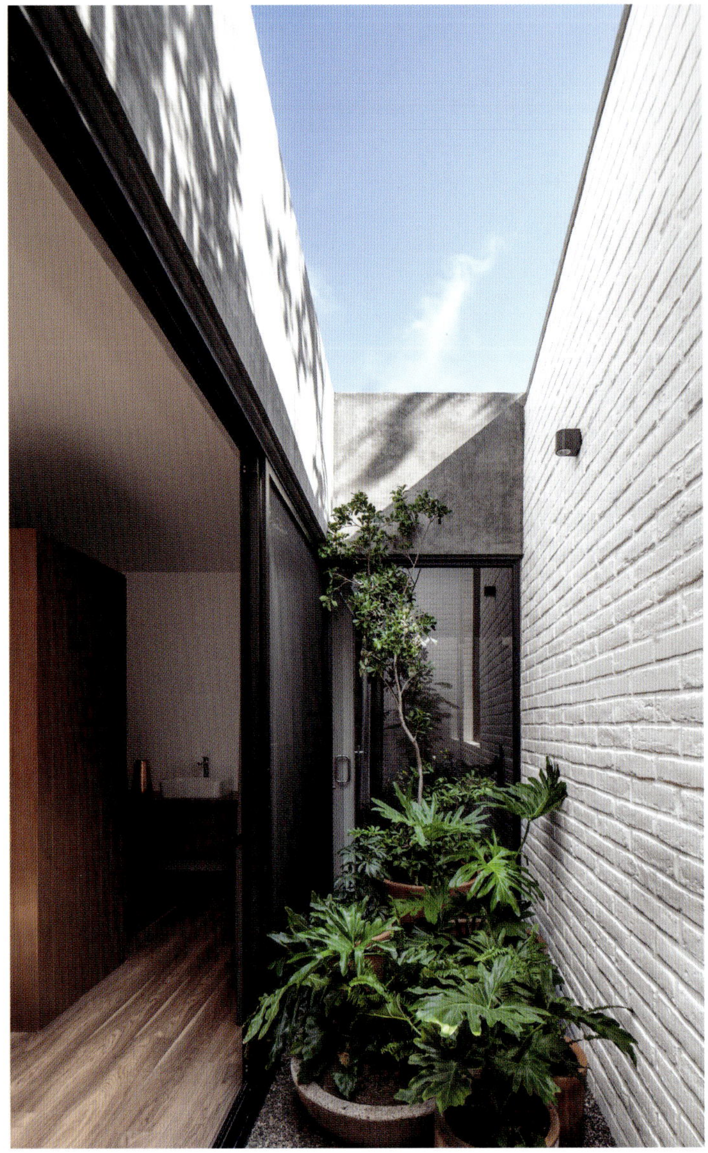

Innovative patios become in this project a perfect opportunity to bring nature into the house, with a variety of plants in pots standing out against white brick walls.

Architect and lecturer Edgar Radillo Alba established his practice, Estudio Radillo Alba, in Guadalajara, Jalisco, Mexico. The architectural studio focused on residential projects, which marry local craftsmanship and materials with innovative visual language and new forms of living. The architect draws from traditional artisanal methods while reinventing spaces with a special focus on new kinds of patios.

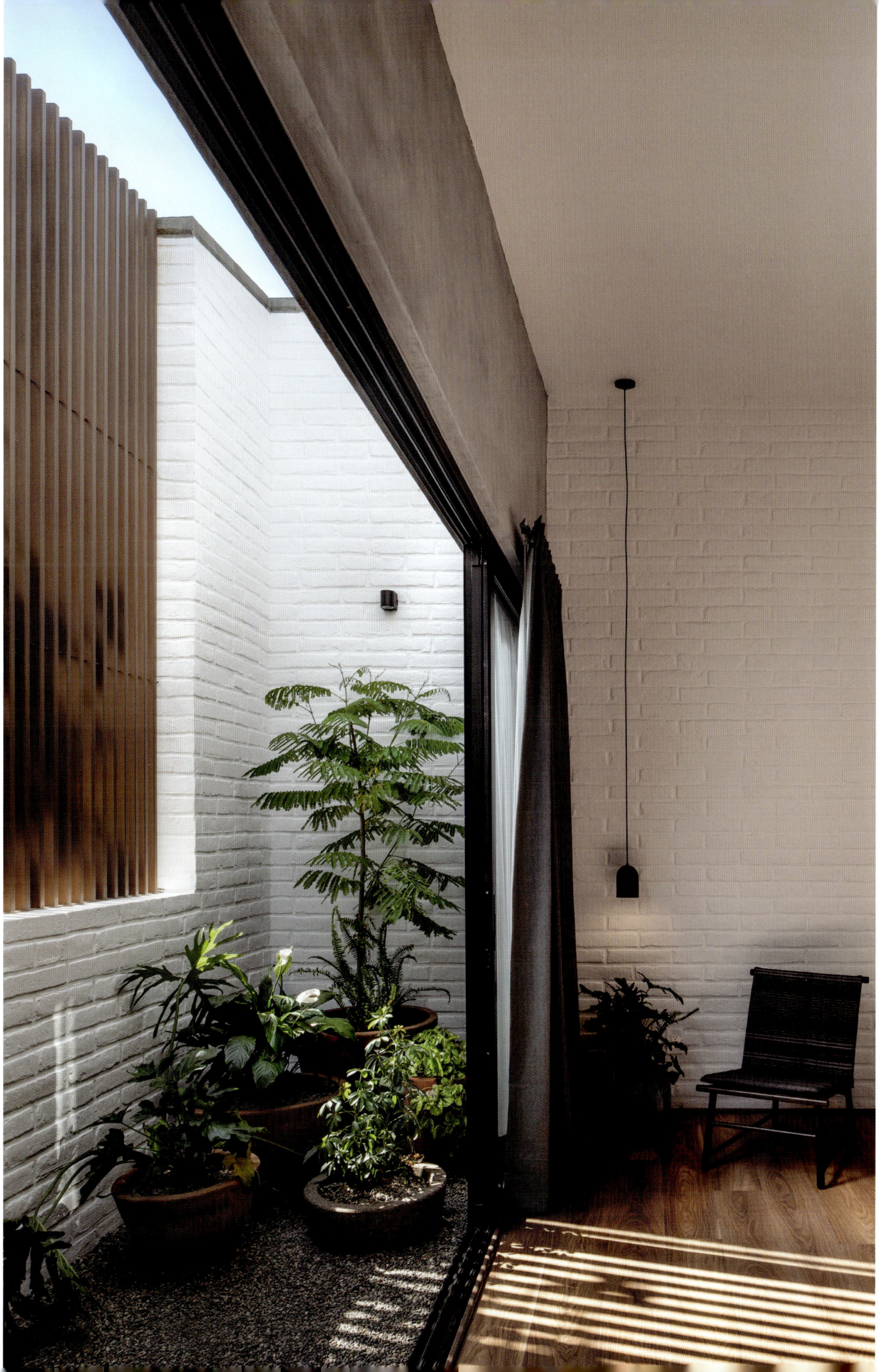

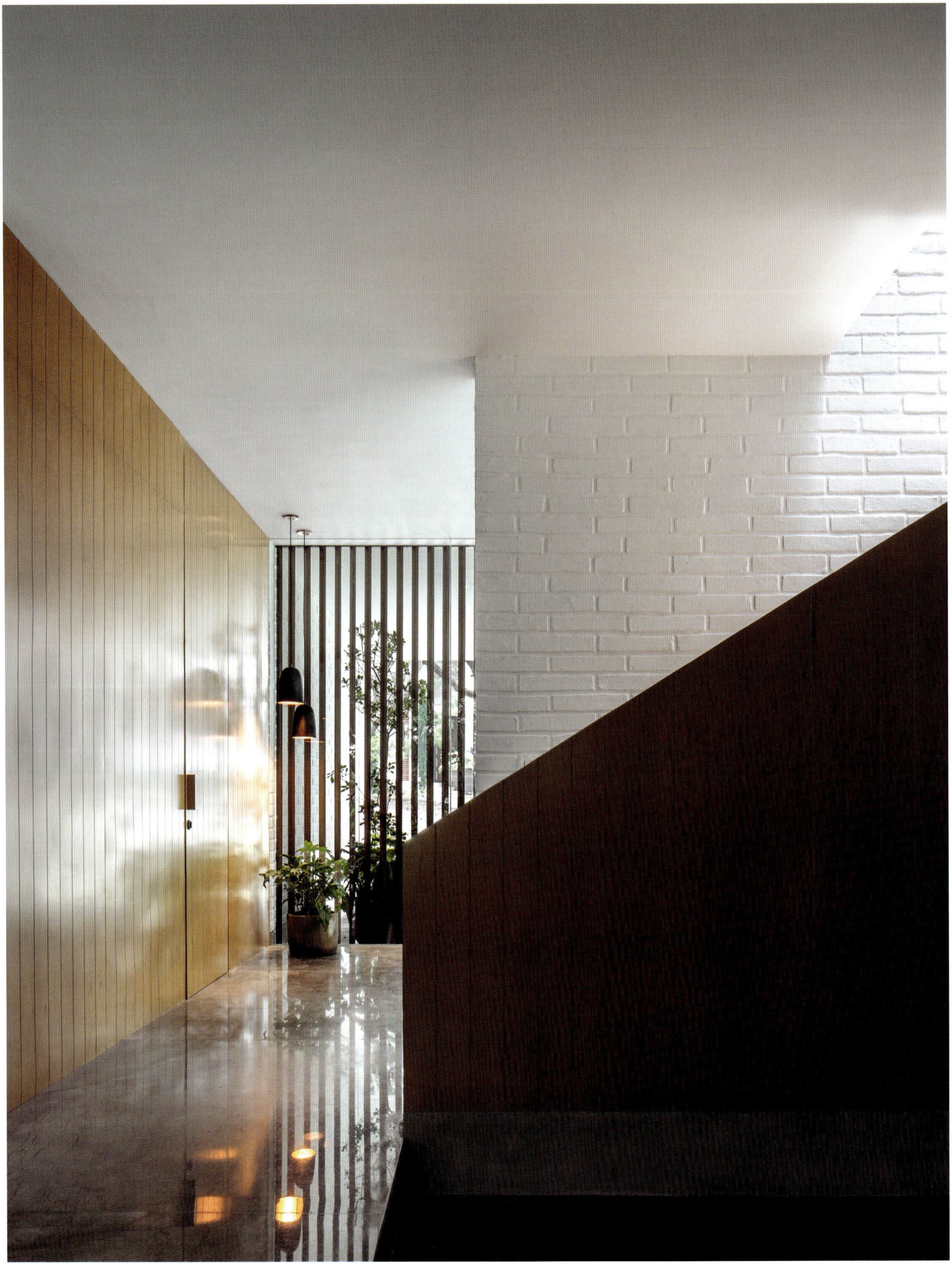

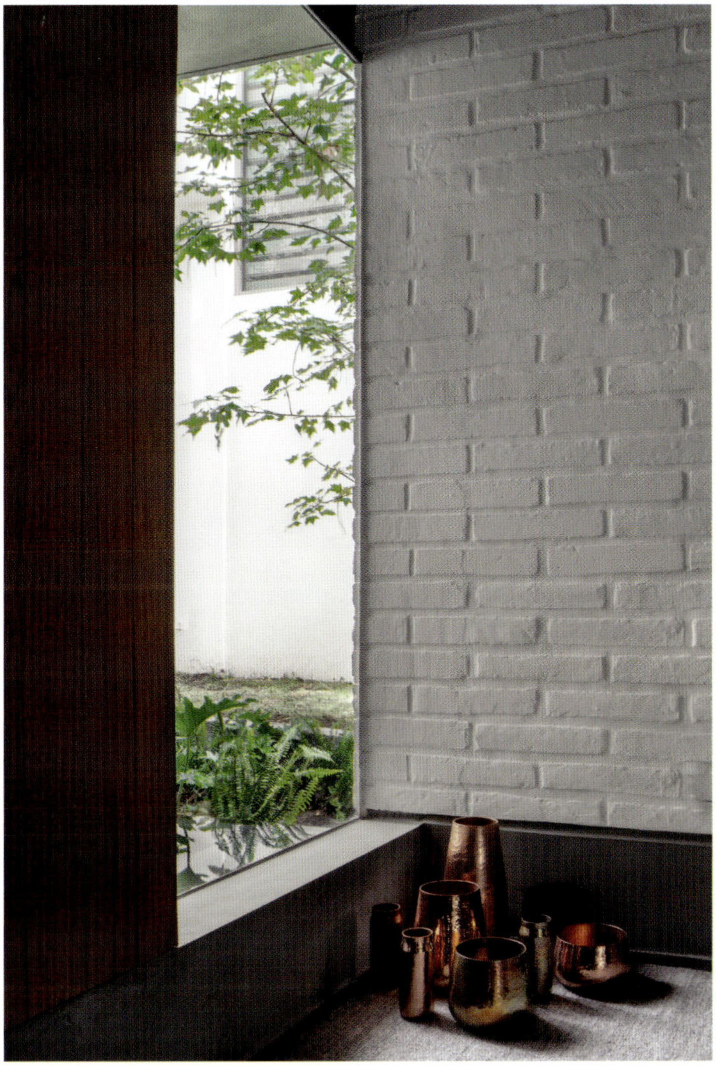

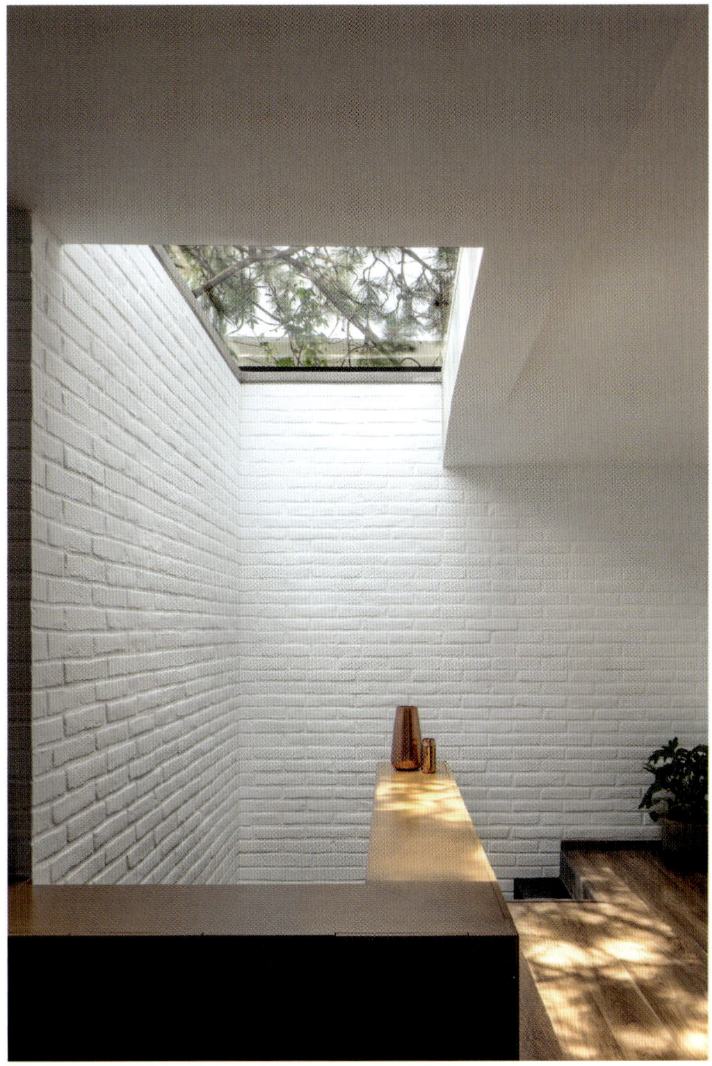

"We aim to take this traditional concept and adapt it to contemporary designs," remark the architects when speaking about reinventing the traditional patio. A family residence in Guadalajara was designed in response to five trees on the plot. Preserving them gave an opportunity to play with the volume and leave spaces for patios, accesses, and terraces. The patios, originally located next to spaces such as rooms, bathrooms, and showers, create an interesting relationship between intimate interiors and exterior, additionally enhanced by vegetation. Edgar Radillo Alba, known for using artisanal methods, selected locally produced mud brick as the building material. Customized for the project, it is proudly featured on the external shell, celebrating Jalisco's heritage and valuable traditions with a modern touch.

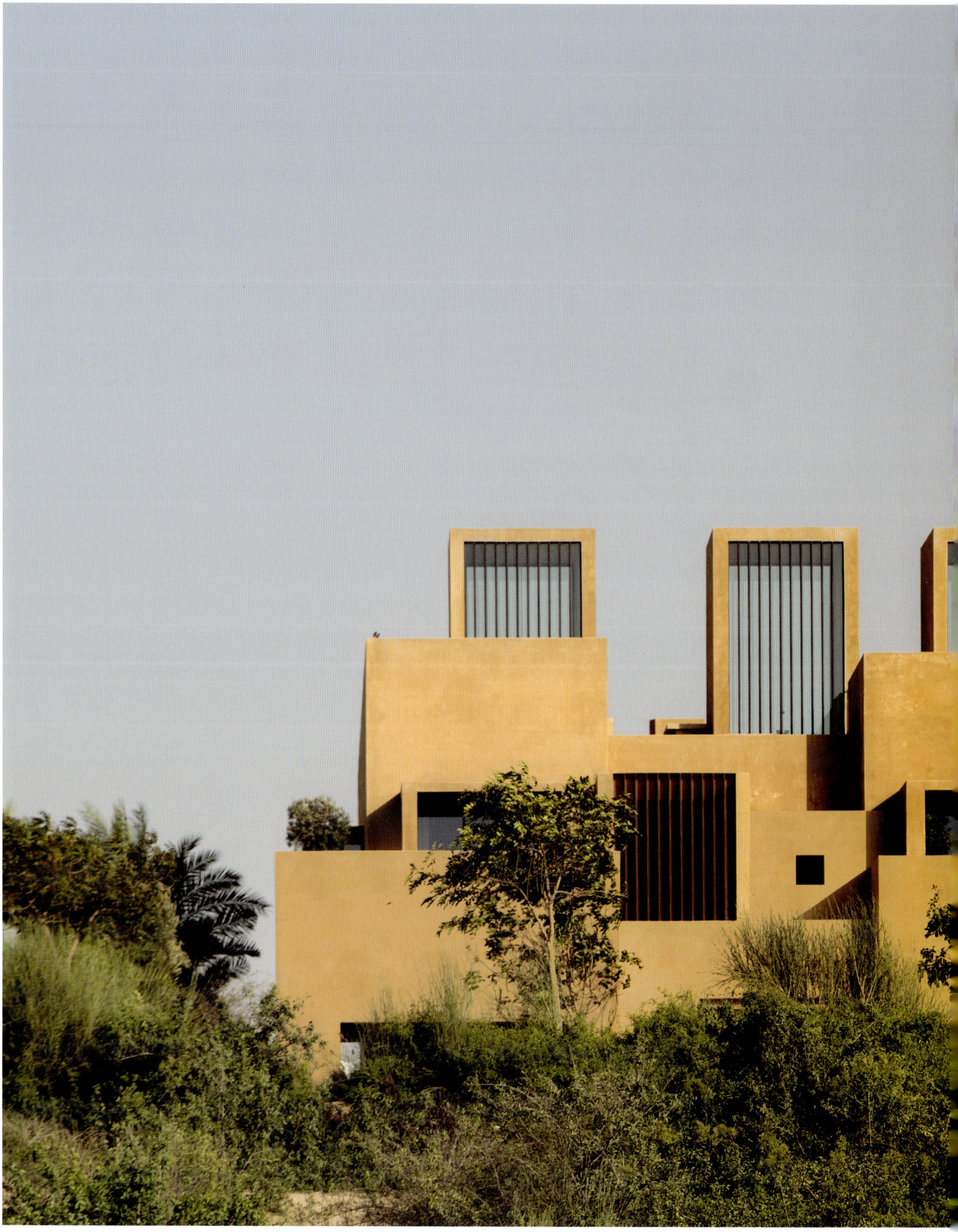

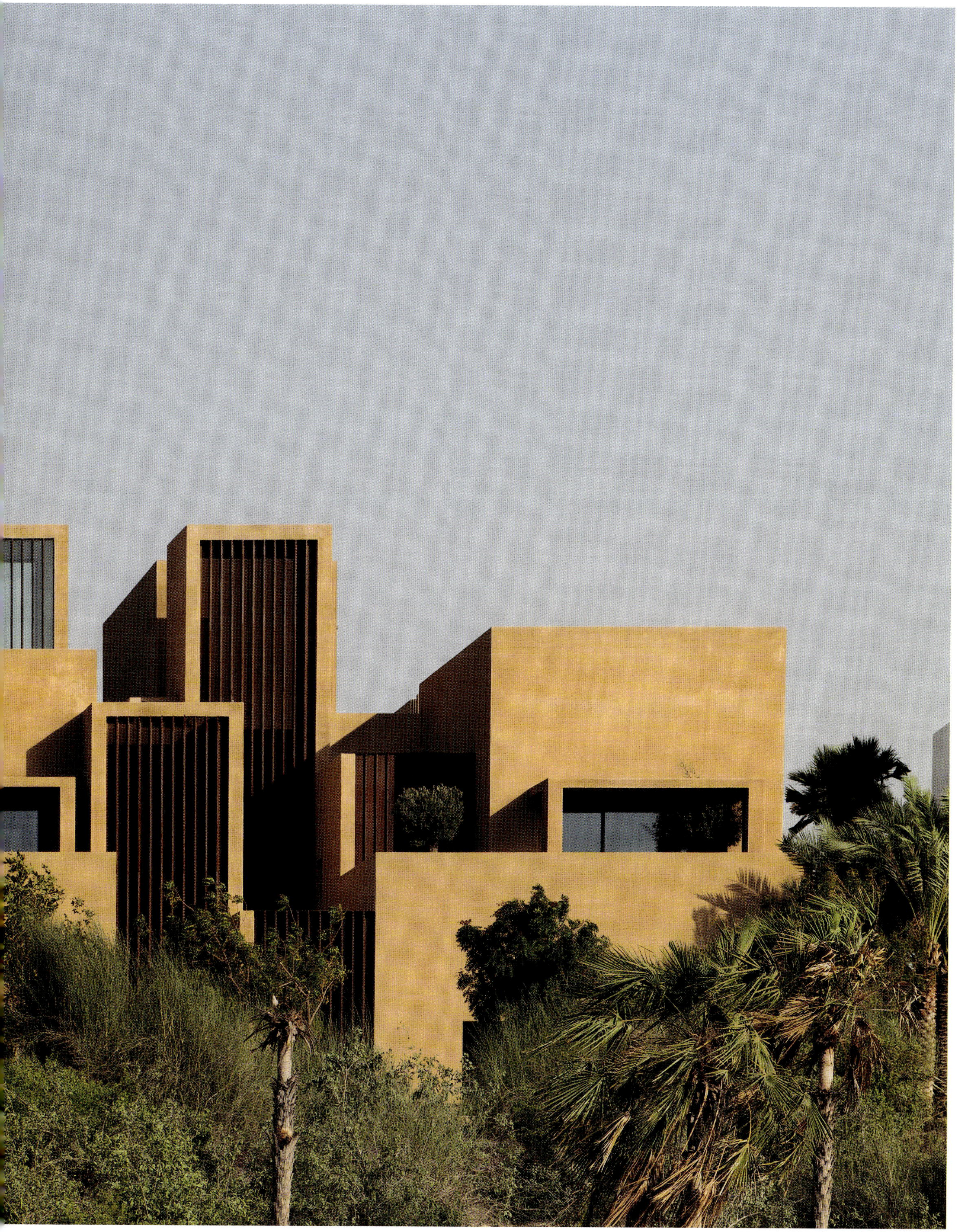

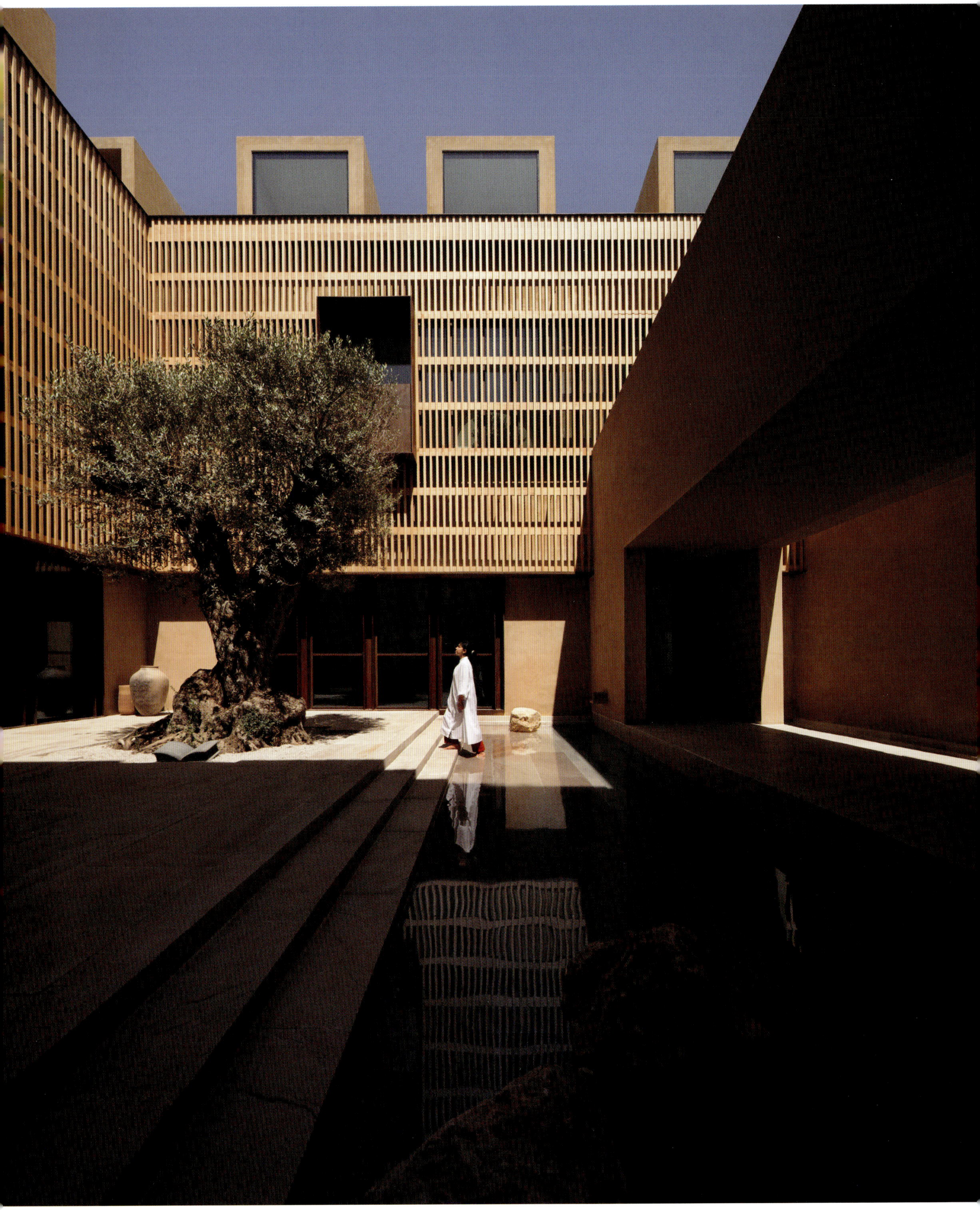

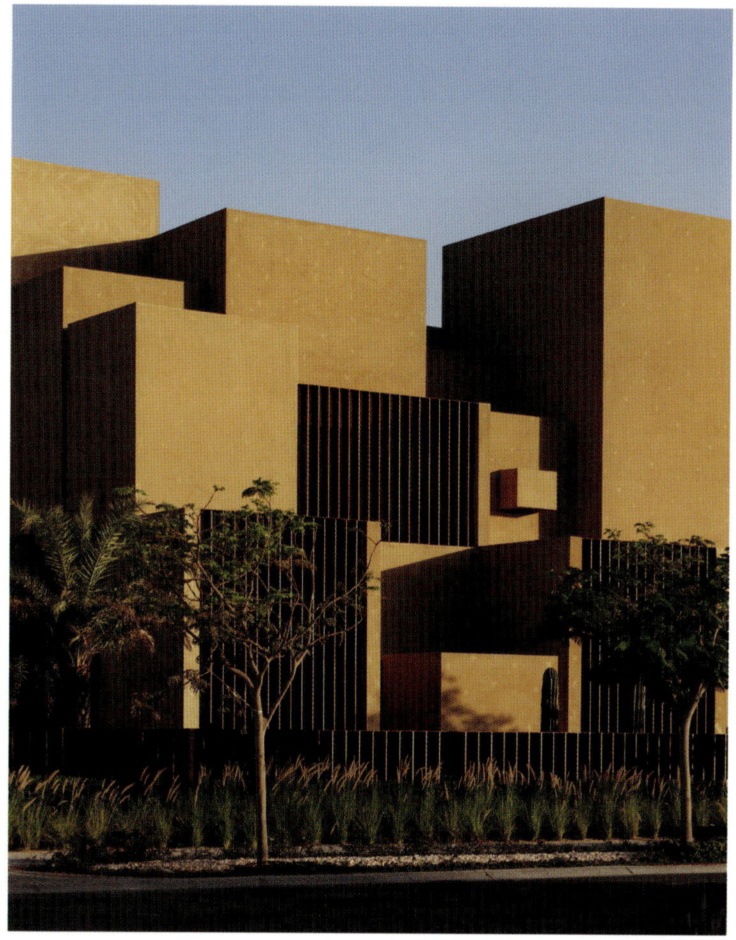

PROJECT: House of Courtyards
LOCATION: Dubai, United Arab Emirates
YEAR: 2023
ARCHITECTS: Studio VDGA
PHOTOGRAPHY: Ema Peter,
Shoayb Khattab

A distinctive sequence of geometric volumes, enhanced by natural color, strikes with the scale. House of Courtyards has been inspired by the complex and diverse urban fabric of the city of Dubai and is envisioned as a form that mirrors desert architecture. The high turrets, providing interiors with natural light, together with the lower parts, create a dynamic interplay between solid and transparent, which highlights the sculptural character of the house. In search of a perfect balance between functionality and aesthetics, the architects at Studio VDGA planned a complex and extensive residence, which embraces numerous courtyards that breathe life into the spaces, as they remark. All patios feature olive trees, whose soft green color creates a lovely combination with the color of the walls.

The way the volumes have been stacked and openings planned across the vast residence is based on the study of the sun path in various seasons. Since the goal was to create a climatically conducive environment, the structure is, to a large extent, self-shading, including the courtyards remaining shadowed during the hottest hours, which makes spending time outdoors possible all year round. Thermal regulation of the interior is also supported by numerous Corten perforated screens visually resonating with the facade walls. These screens, like patios, provide ventilation for various spaces across the large residence, which is crucial given the hot local temperatures. Radiation of the sun has been limited by leaving the south facade without any windows.

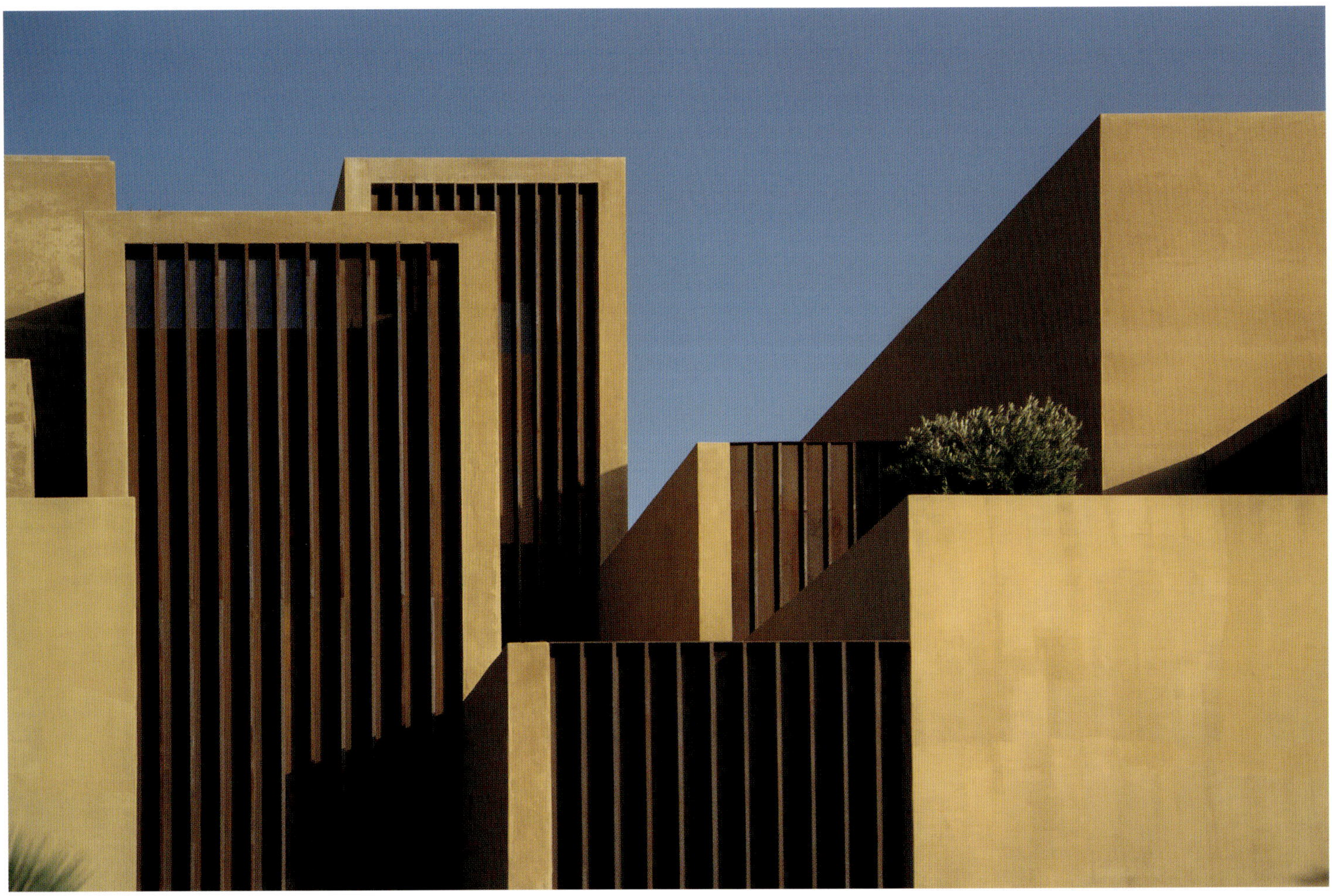

Studio VDGA was established in 2003 and is based in Pune, India, specializing in residential and hospitality architecture as well as offices and campsites, realized across India, Vietnam, and the Middle East. The team aims at designing soul-enriching experiences and states that "architecture, we believe, is a journey of spaces, manifested through various mediums: sun, shadows, air, and form being just a few premises on which it is built."

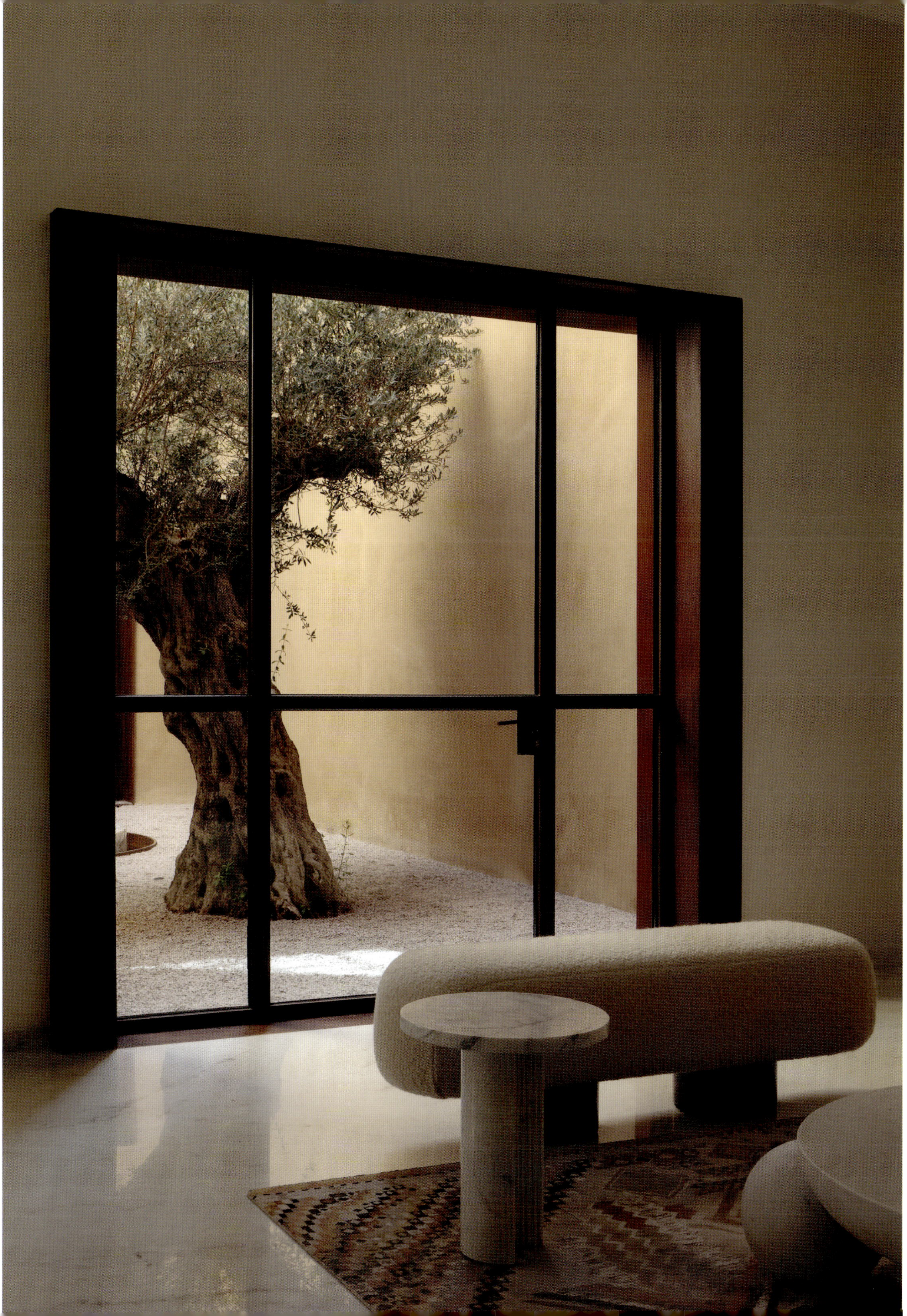

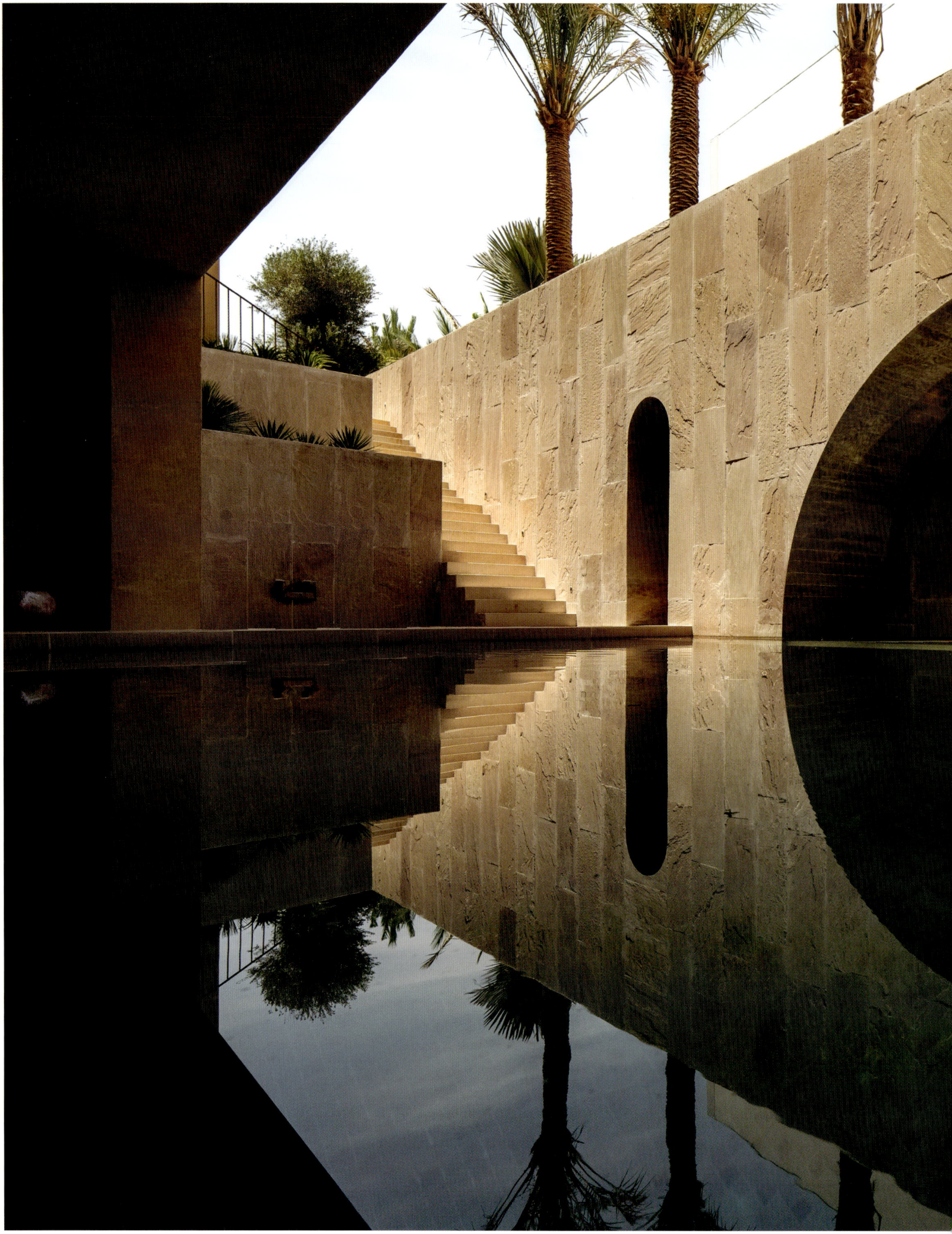

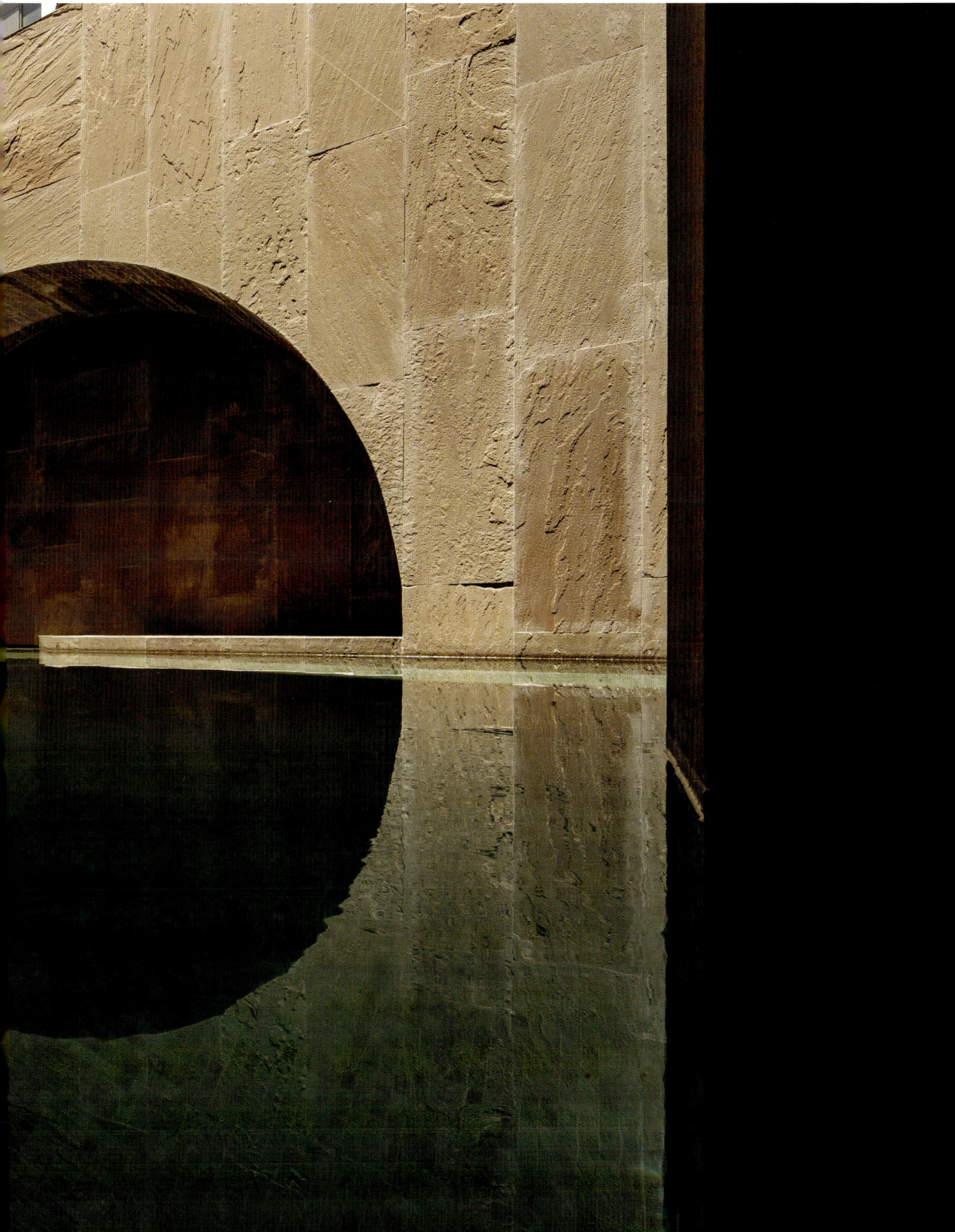

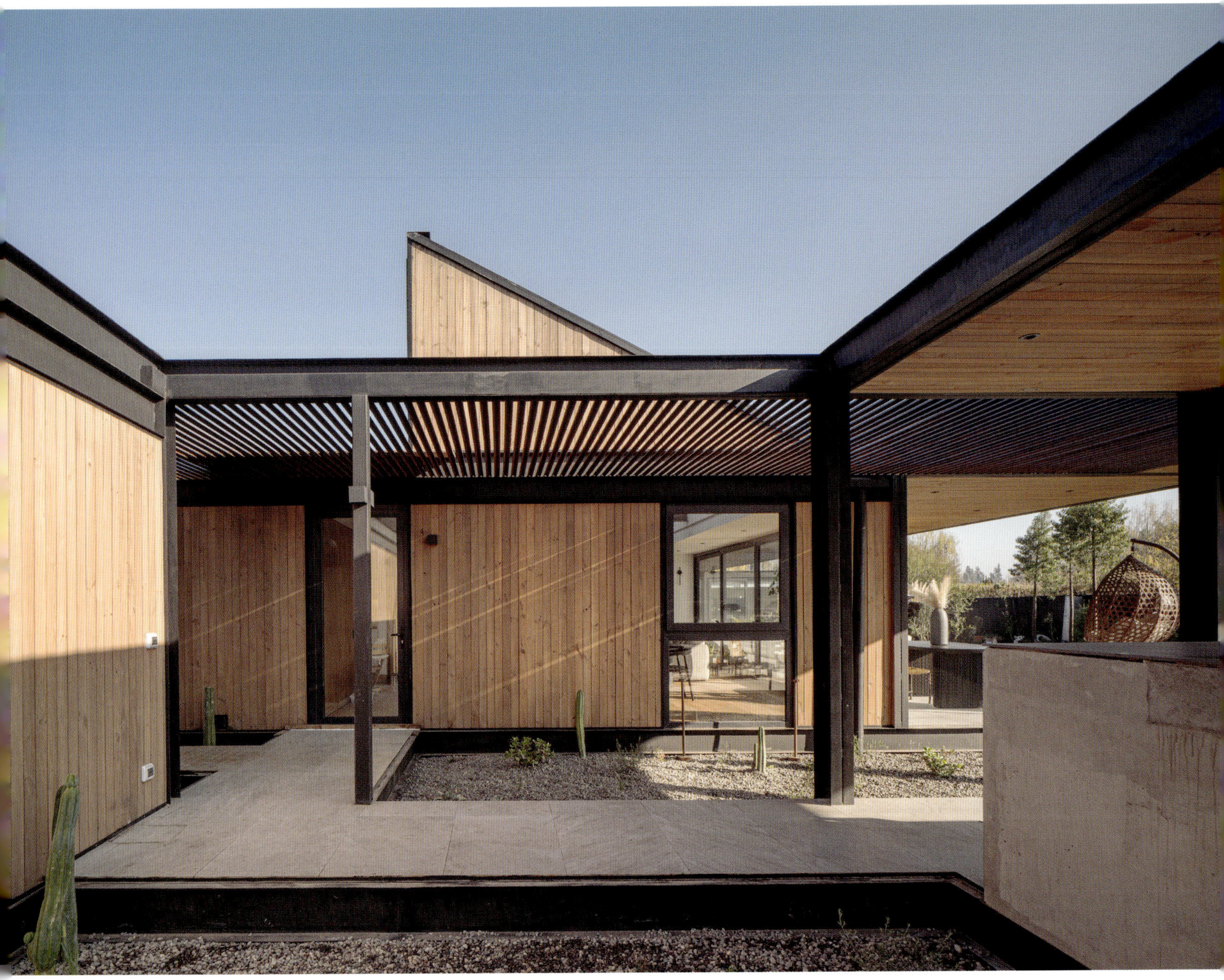

The distinctive "lucarna" skylight facing south is an element that visually breaks an otherwise regular volume. It is also an important source of natural light in the common spaces—the living and dining areas, and the kitchen.

Paralelo Transversal is an architecture studio based in central and southern Chile, working across the country but also internationally. Their main domains are residential, urban, and territorial projects that are driven by the context. The firm also offers consulting and management services in legal and technical matters related to the development of architectural projects throughout Chile.

PROJECT: House with Lucarna
LOCATION: Santiago, Chile
YEAR: 2024
ARCHITECTS: Paralelo Transversal
PHOTOGRAPHY: Marcos Zegers

House with Lucarna demonstrates how employing a patio in a residential project can make a building sustainable. Located on the outskirts of Santiago, with a hot climate, the house needed a carefully planned cooling system that would minimize the use for mechanical air-conditioning. The architectural team at Paralelo Transversal decided to design the residence with passive strategies. An important part is played by patios and gardens that have been playfully integrated into the structure. Not only do they open the interiors onto the direct surroundings and mark divisions between various parts of the house, but most of all they support both thermal regulation and ventilation in all spaces.

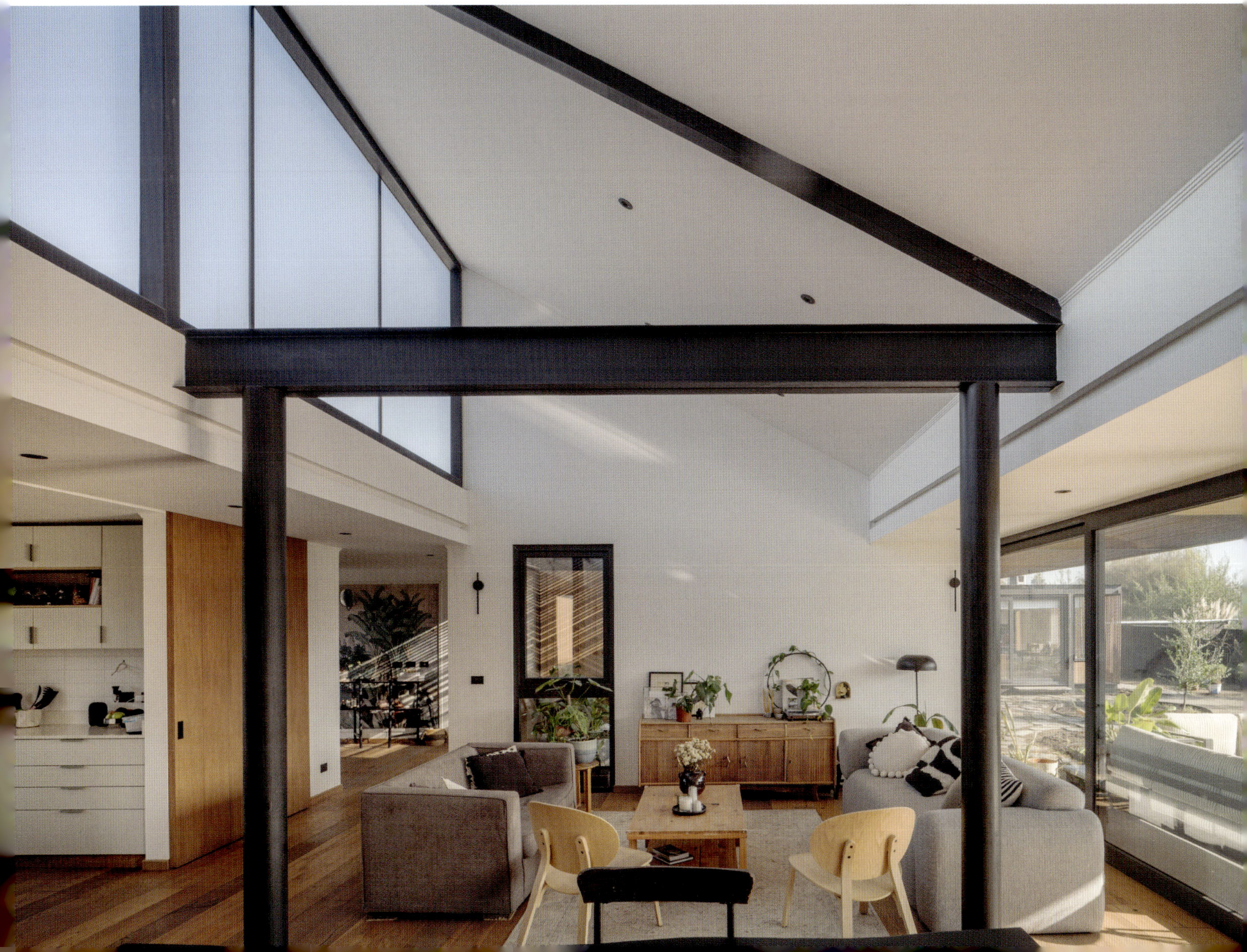

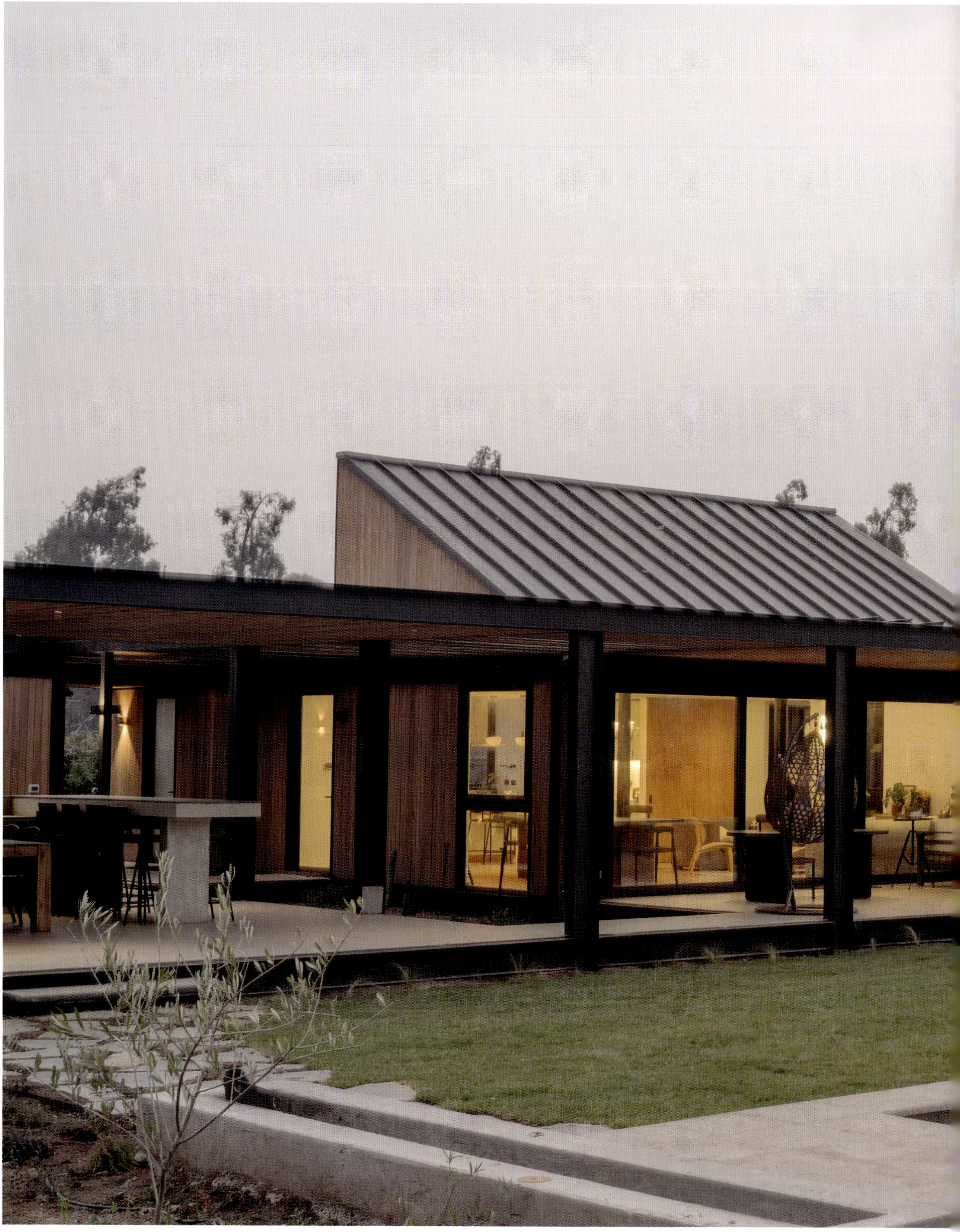

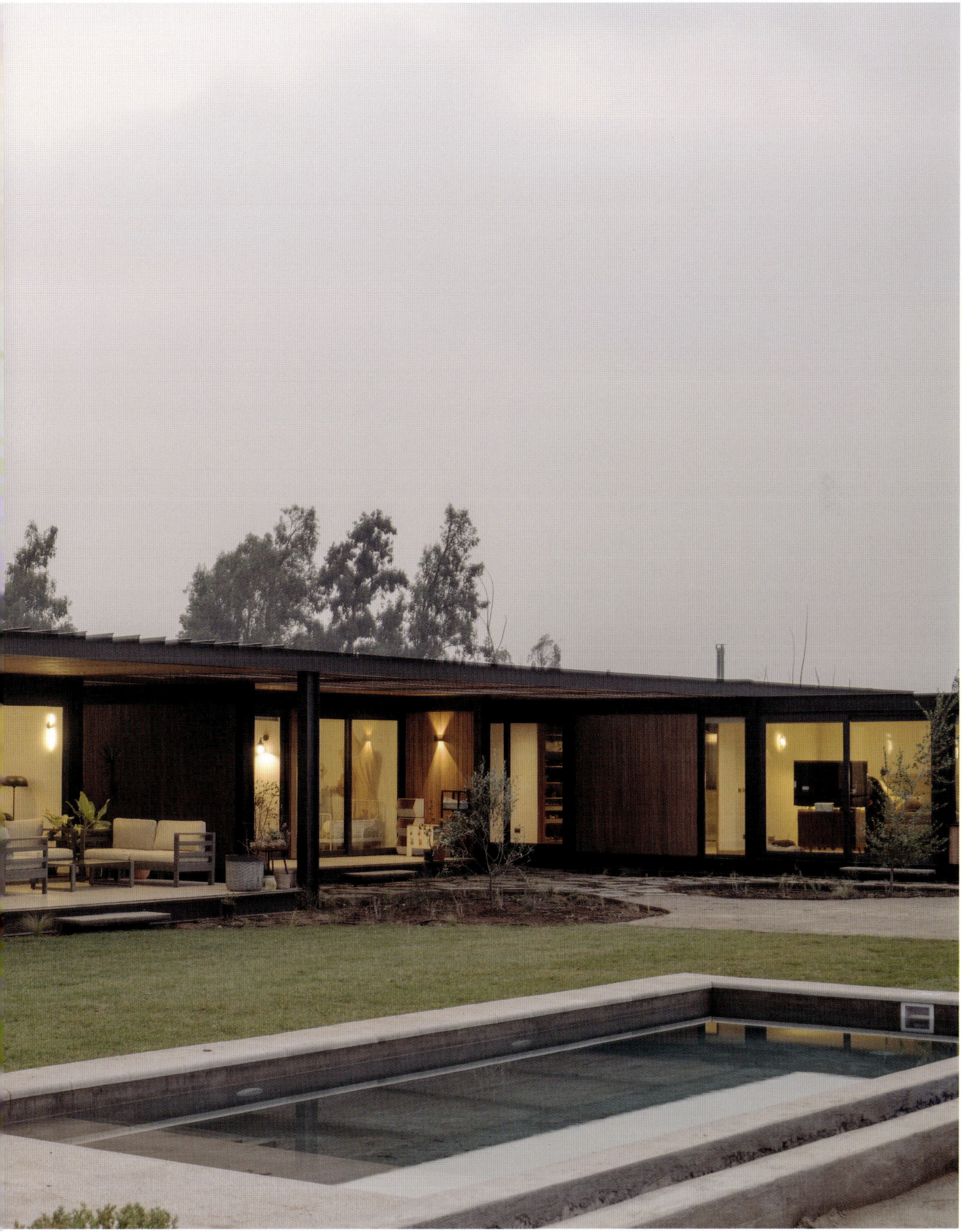

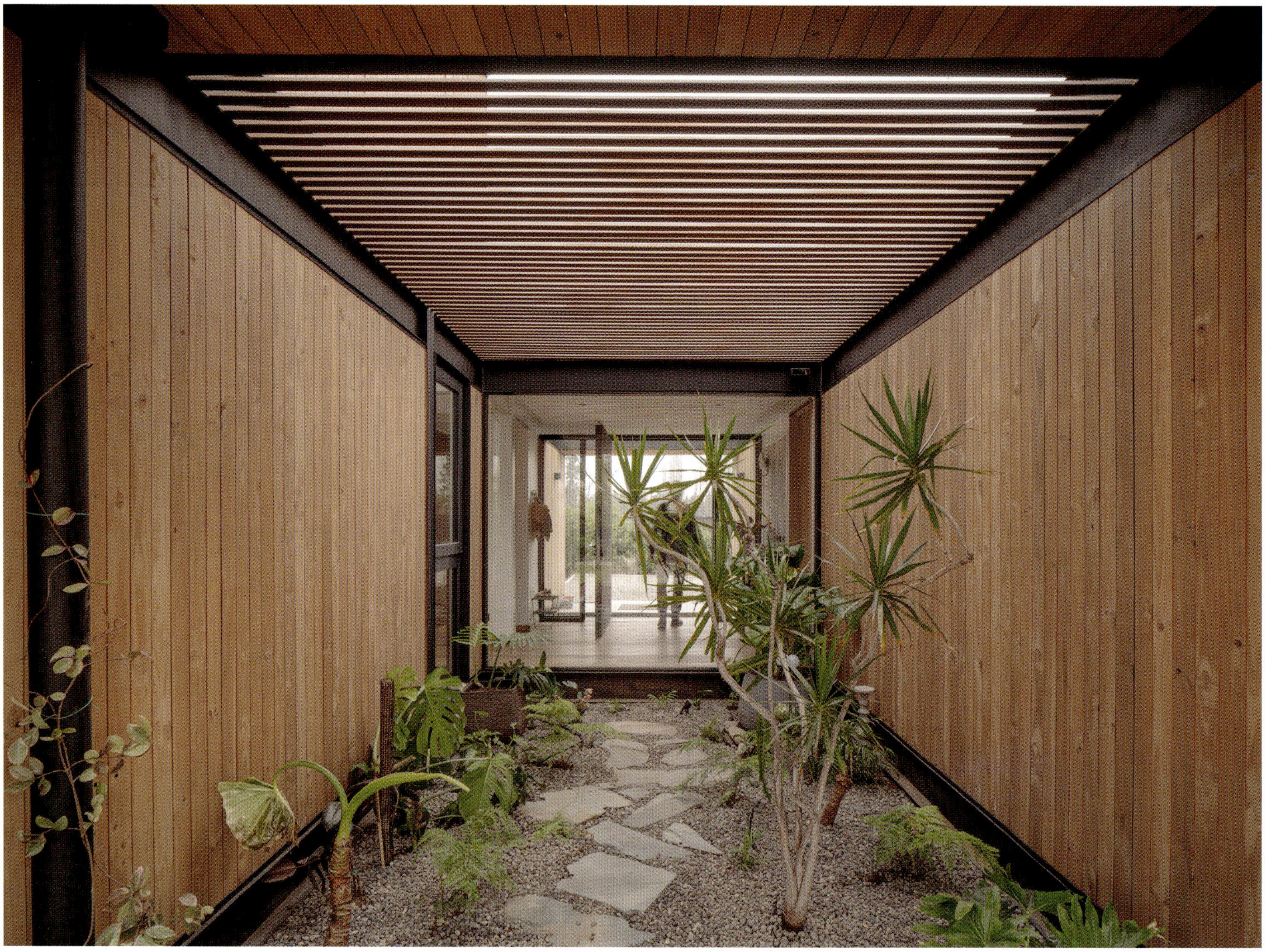

While the structure of the house is made of steel, natural wood has been used for external walls. This well-chosen duo of materials gives a sense of stability and lightness. Additionally, the volume sits slightly above the ground, which is yet another way the architects improve natural ventilation. Another solution that effectively cools down the interiors is a semitranslucent overhang along the linear shape, envisioned to soften the power of the sun accessing through all height openings. It also allows spending time outdoors, where the residence extends with comfortable lounge and dining areas. The skylight over the common spaces, which opens to the south, is certainly a visual highlight of the volume, just like numerous patios. The latter, often filled with vegetation and acting as cooling zones, create an interesting play of voids and transparencies that make the project sustainable on many levels.

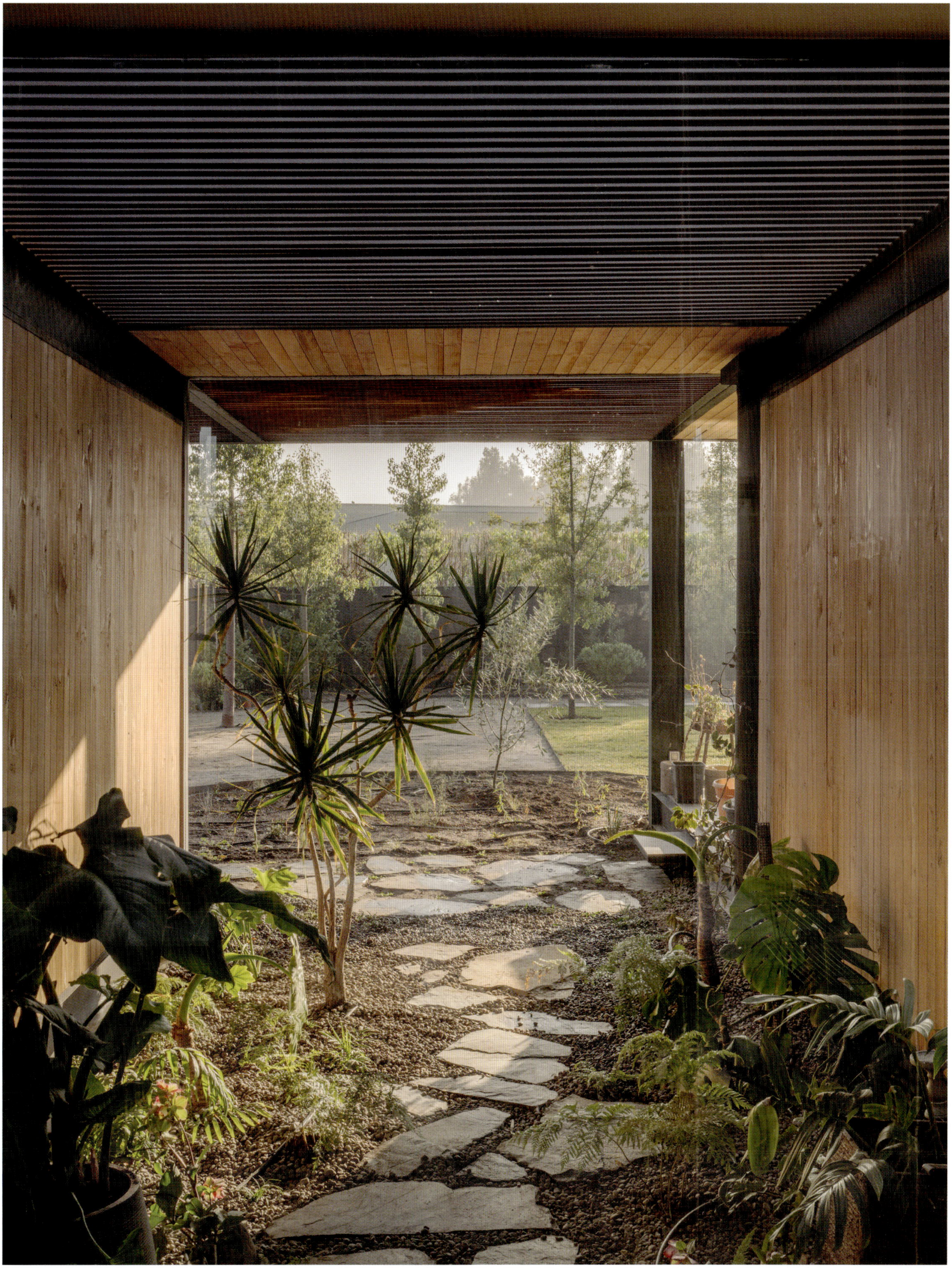

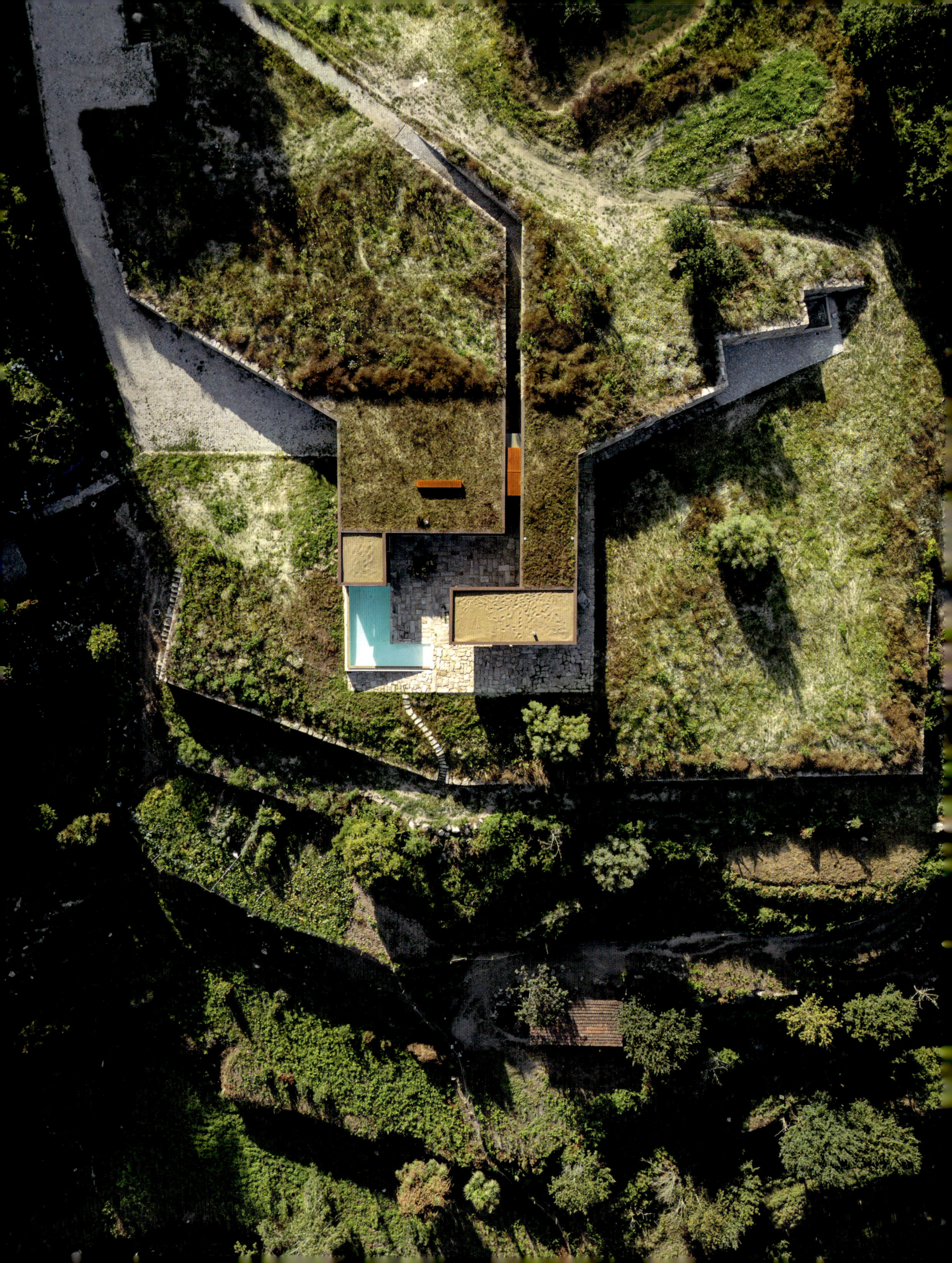

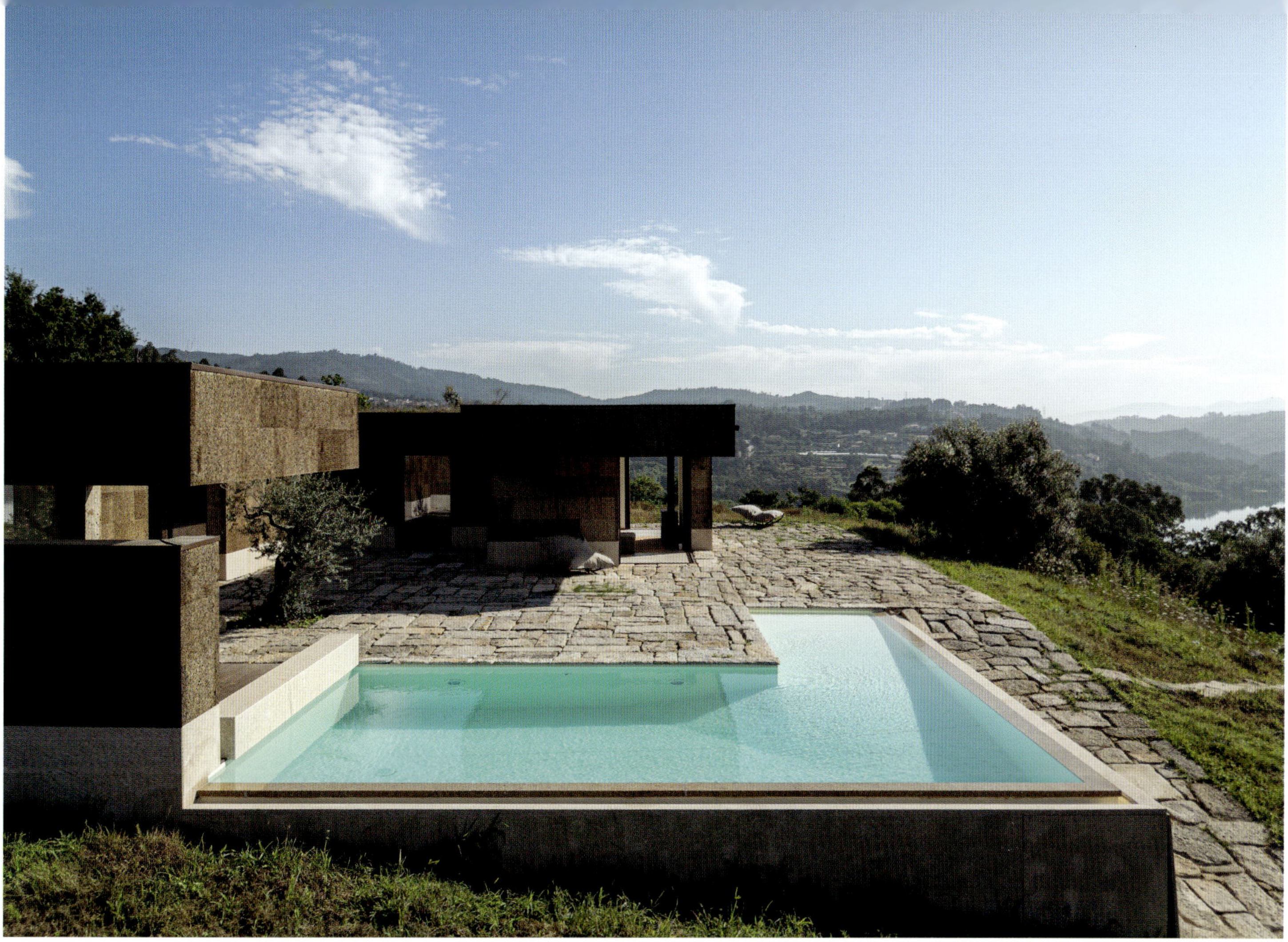

PROJECT: Casa de Levada
LOCATION: Penafiel, Portugal
YEAR: 2024
ARCHITECTS: Tsou Arquitectos
PHOTOGRAPHY: Ivo Tavares Studio

The team at Tsou Arquitectos is dedicated to envisioning projects that establish a dialogue with their context, making the best of the scenic location of Casa de Levada. Located in Portuguese Penafiel, on a plot atop a terraced hill with a striking view of the river Tâmega, it is an ideal spot to construct a family house. The architects celebrate this landscape by carefully selecting materials and perfectly adapting the structure to the site's topography. The integration with the surrounding nature extends to making the house literally grow out of the slope, enhanced by the greenery covering the roof in a camouflage-like way. The visual and physical continuity between the building and the context also plays a functional role in improving the energy efficiency of the villa.

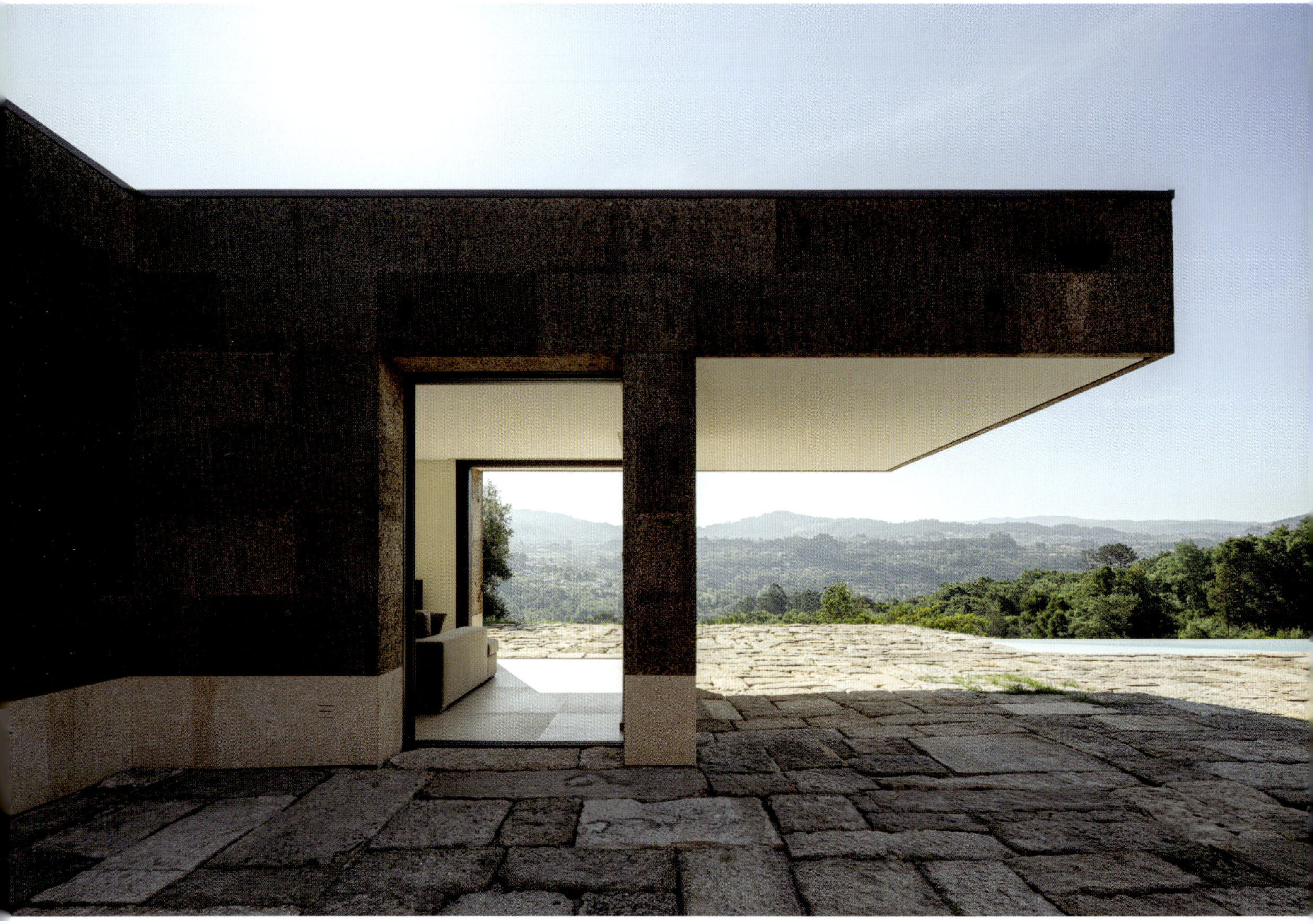

Based in Porto, Portugal, Tsou Arquitectos was established by Tiago Tsou in 2010. "We believe in meaningful architecture, attentive to the essence of the place, designed feasibly, and built responsibly" reads the statement. In their projects, ranging from residential to industrial to commercial buildings, the architects aim to enhance the surroundings by fitting new designs sustainably into the unique characteristics of each location.

The interesting choreography of the spaces begins with an intriguing entrance path designed as a paved groove over the green surface of the land. This leads to the central courtyard, which connects two parts of the house—clearly separated volumes with common spaces on one side and private rooms on the other. The patio, accessible from both, with generous roofs creating shaded areas to enjoy outdoors, acts as a panoramic platform merging architecture with the surrounding hills and riverbed. The architects made numerous sustainable choices, from selecting materials such as cork cladding and stone for the patio, to solutions providing the comfort of living. This includes a heat pump for heating and cooling, and glazing with exterior protection to optimize thermal solar gains.

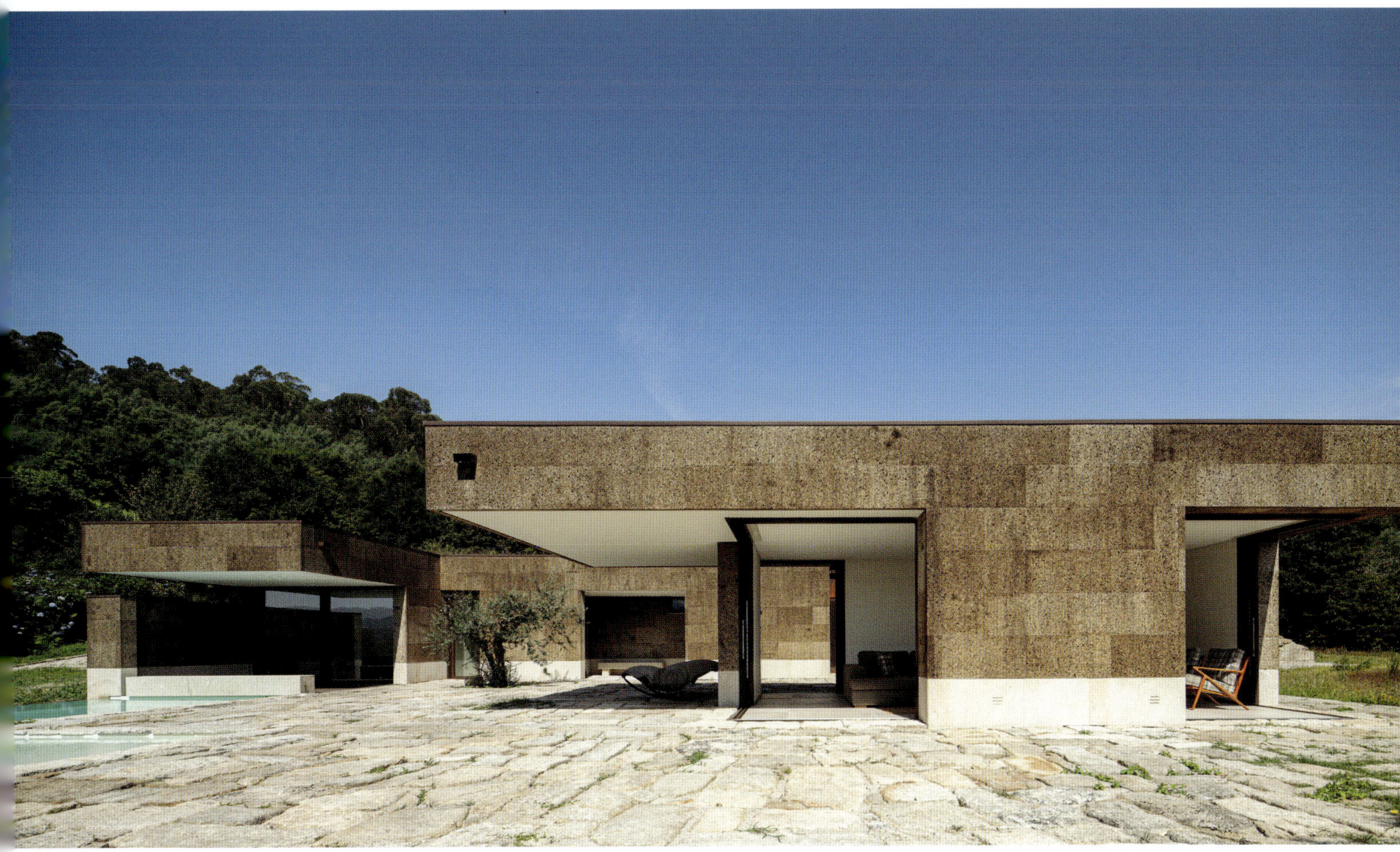

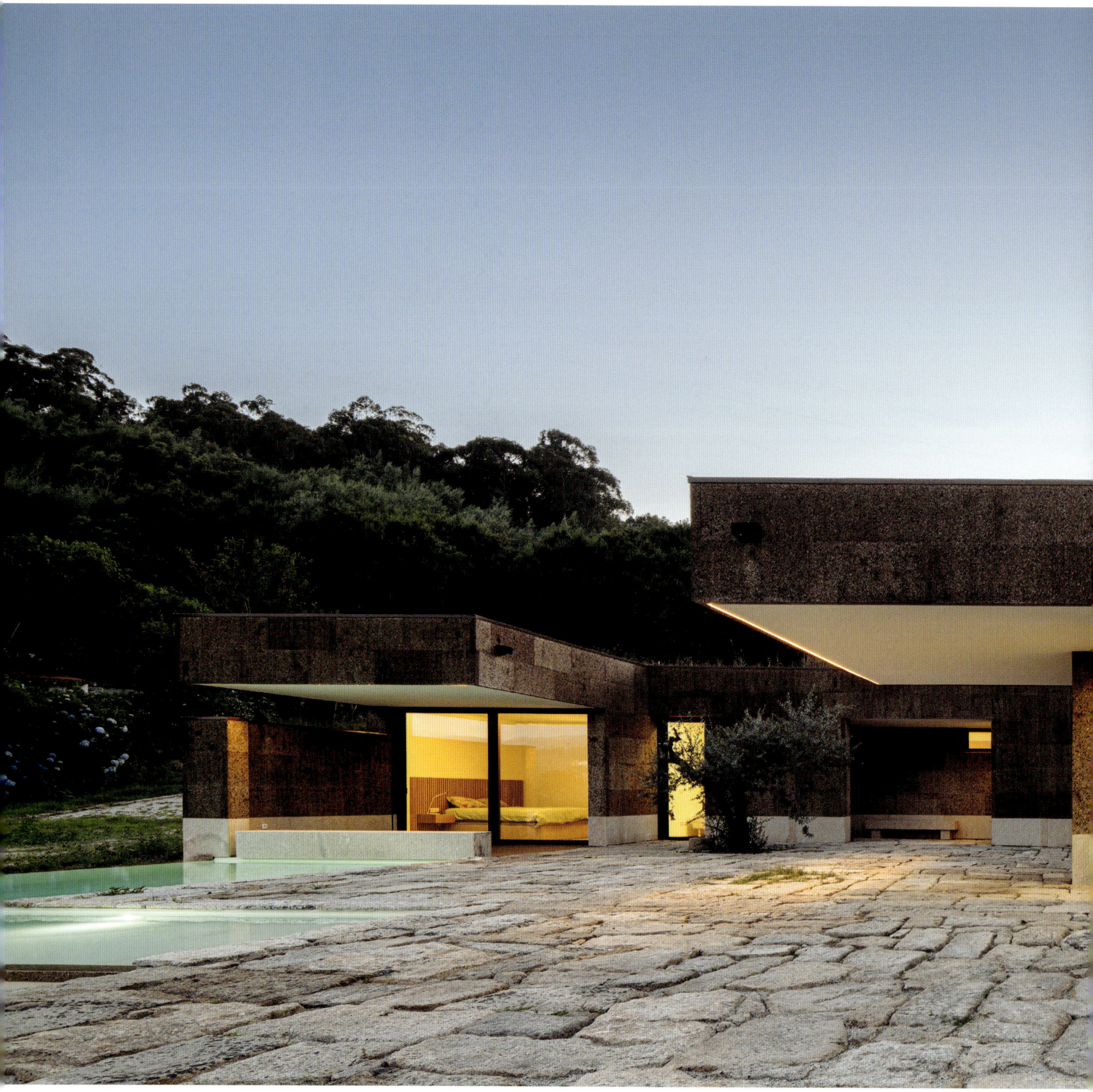

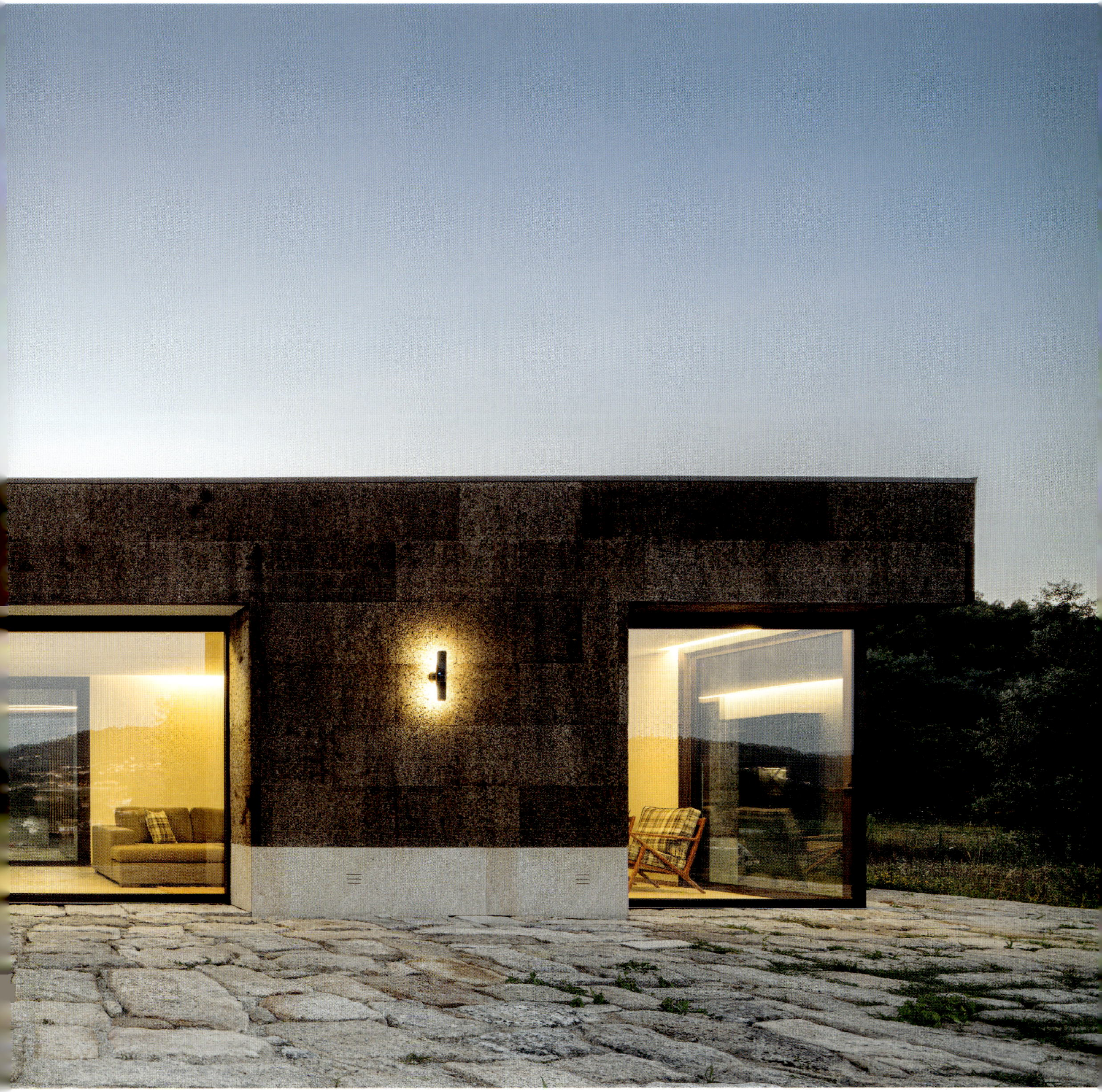

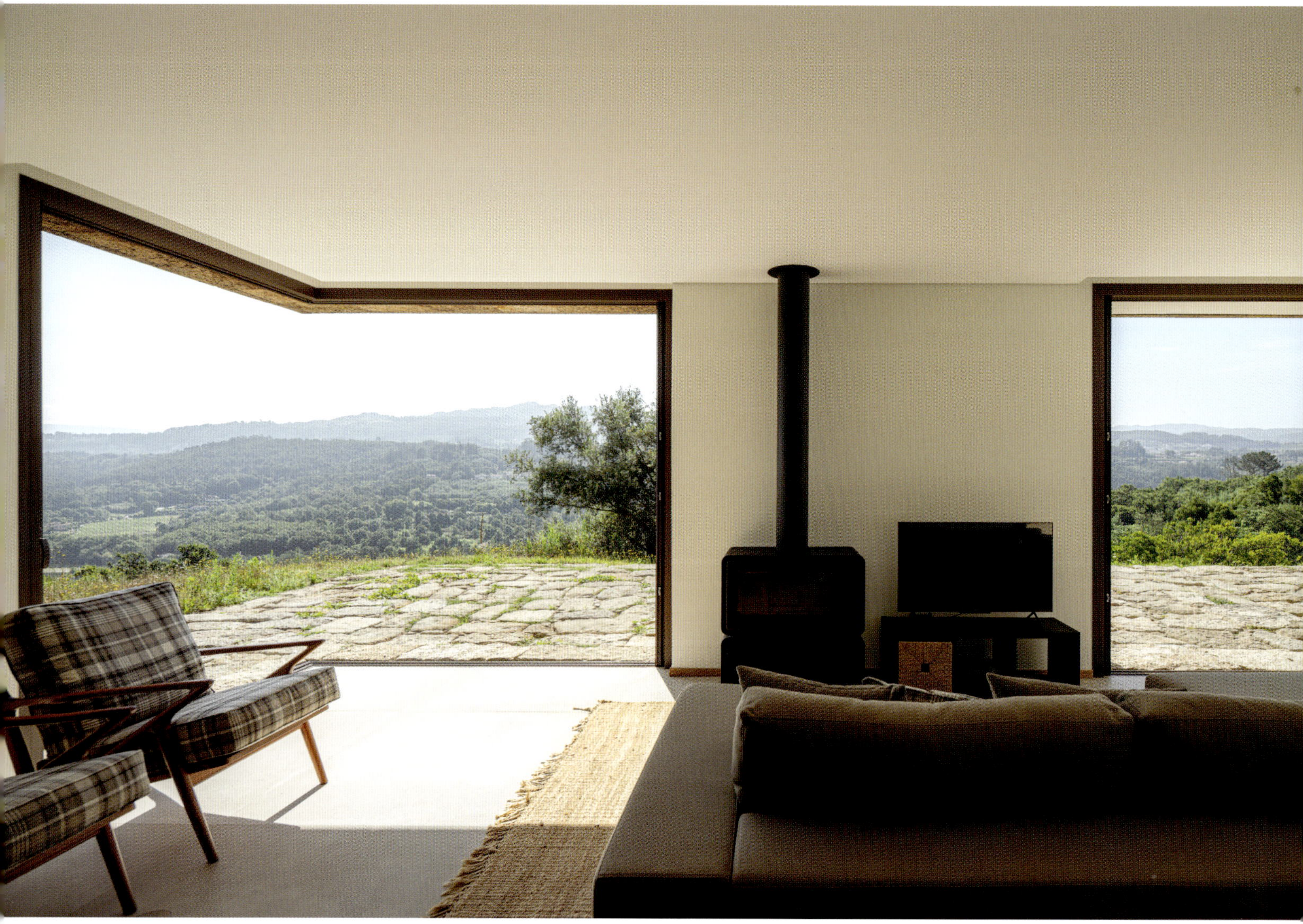

The ingenious system of sliding windows, which can be opened entirely, creates a unique living room that seamlessly connects with the outdoor spaces. This solution, with a particularly striking effect on the corners, opens the interiors to stunning vistas and provides natural ventilation.

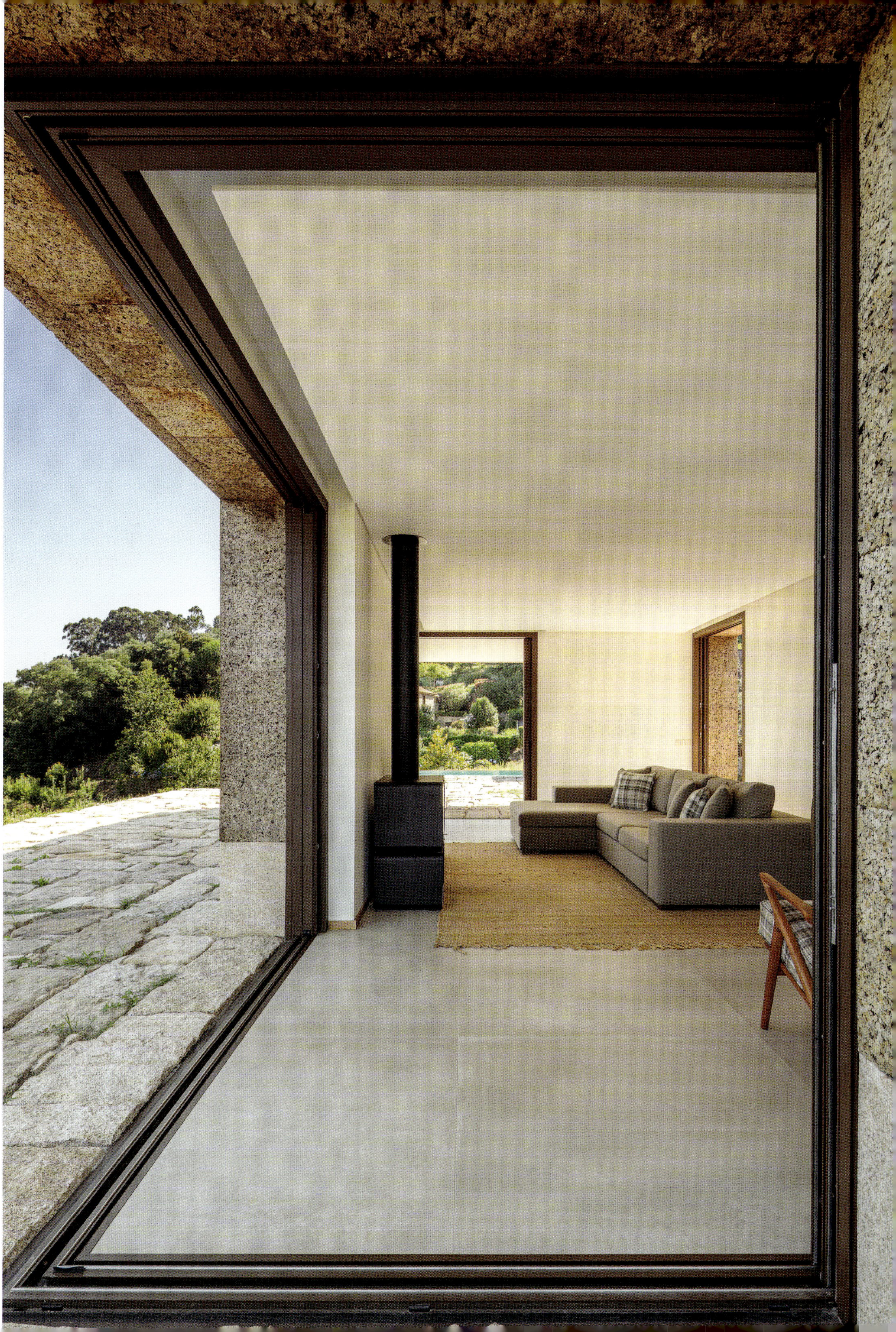

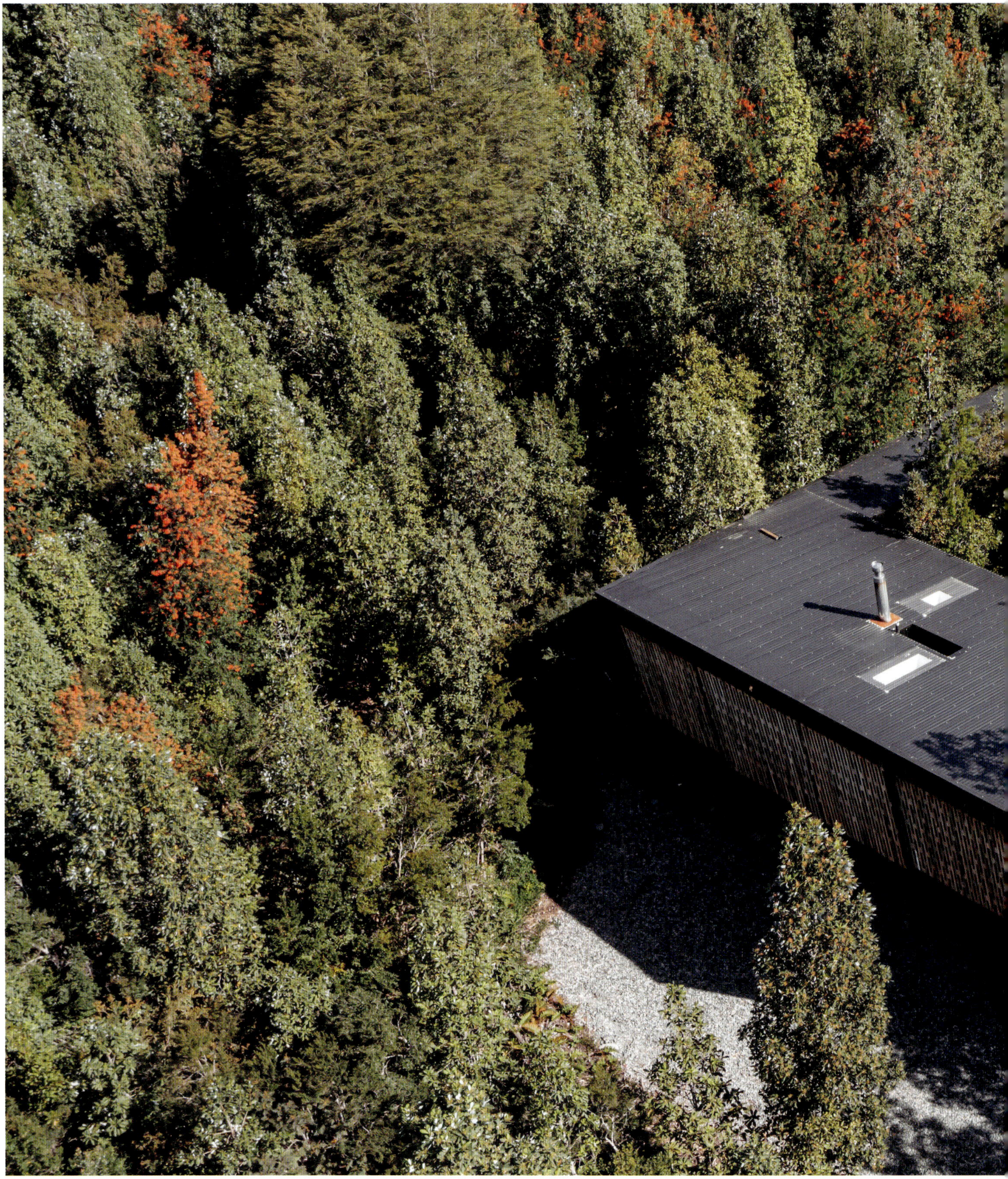

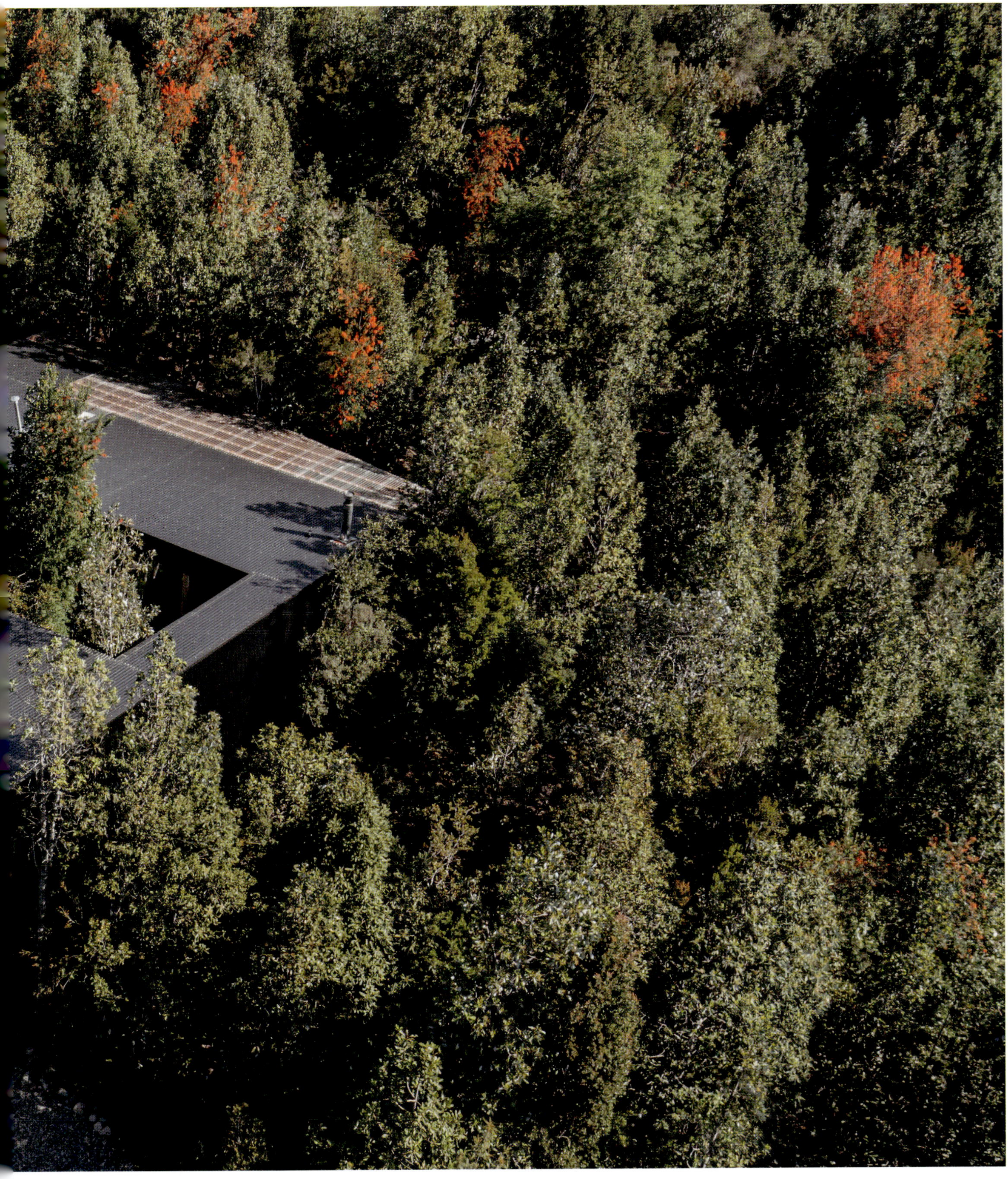

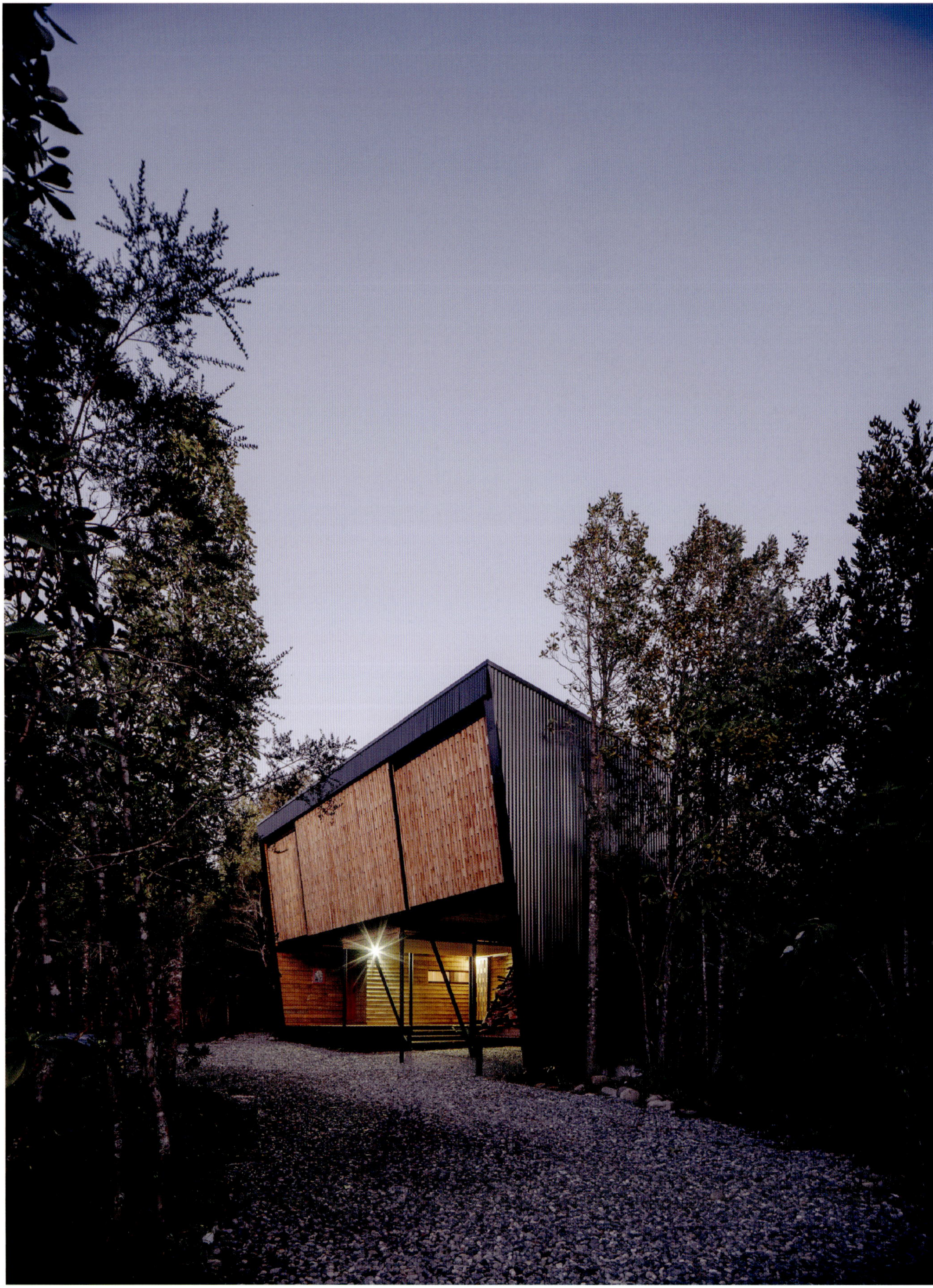

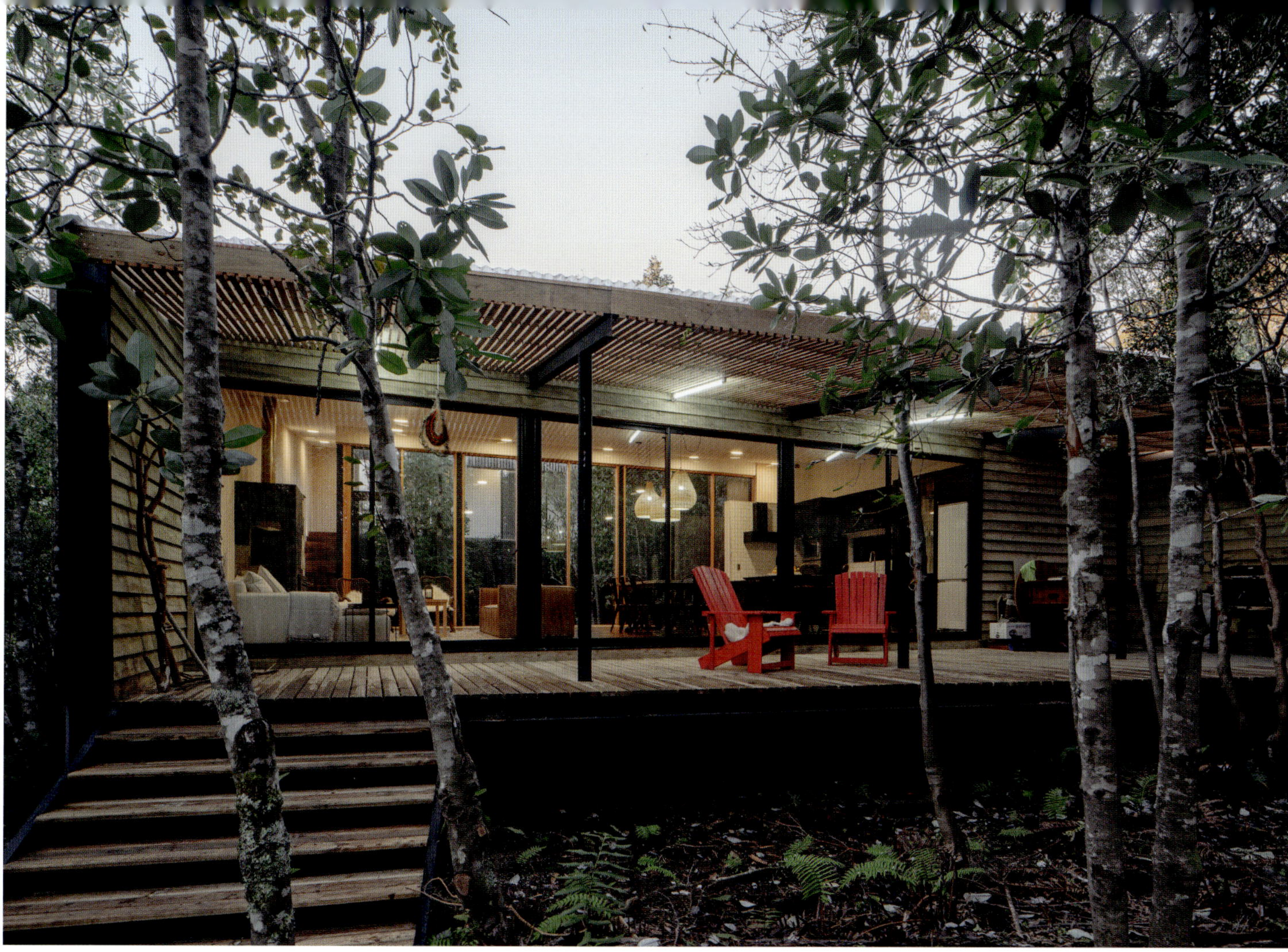

PROJECT: Casa Un Patio
LOCATION: Molco, Chile
YEAR: 2022
ARCHITECTS: Lucas Maino Fernández Arquitectos
PHOTOGRAPHY: Marcos Zegers, Fernando Alarcon

The aerial view of Casa Un Patio, designed by Lucas Maino Fernández Arquitectos in Chilean Molco, perfectly captures the beauty of the untouched location at the foot of the north slope of the Villarrica volcano. It also shows how masterfully the architects connected the built and natural environment, since their main goal was to initiate a dialogue between the house and the landscape. The density of the forest presented a challenge and an advantage at once. Part of the strategy to preserve the native species and minimize intervention into the plot was creating a central patio that frames a portion of vegetation. The house and surrounding forest are harmoniously intertwined, thanks to the use of wood as a building material, which will weather with time to blend the volume into the context.

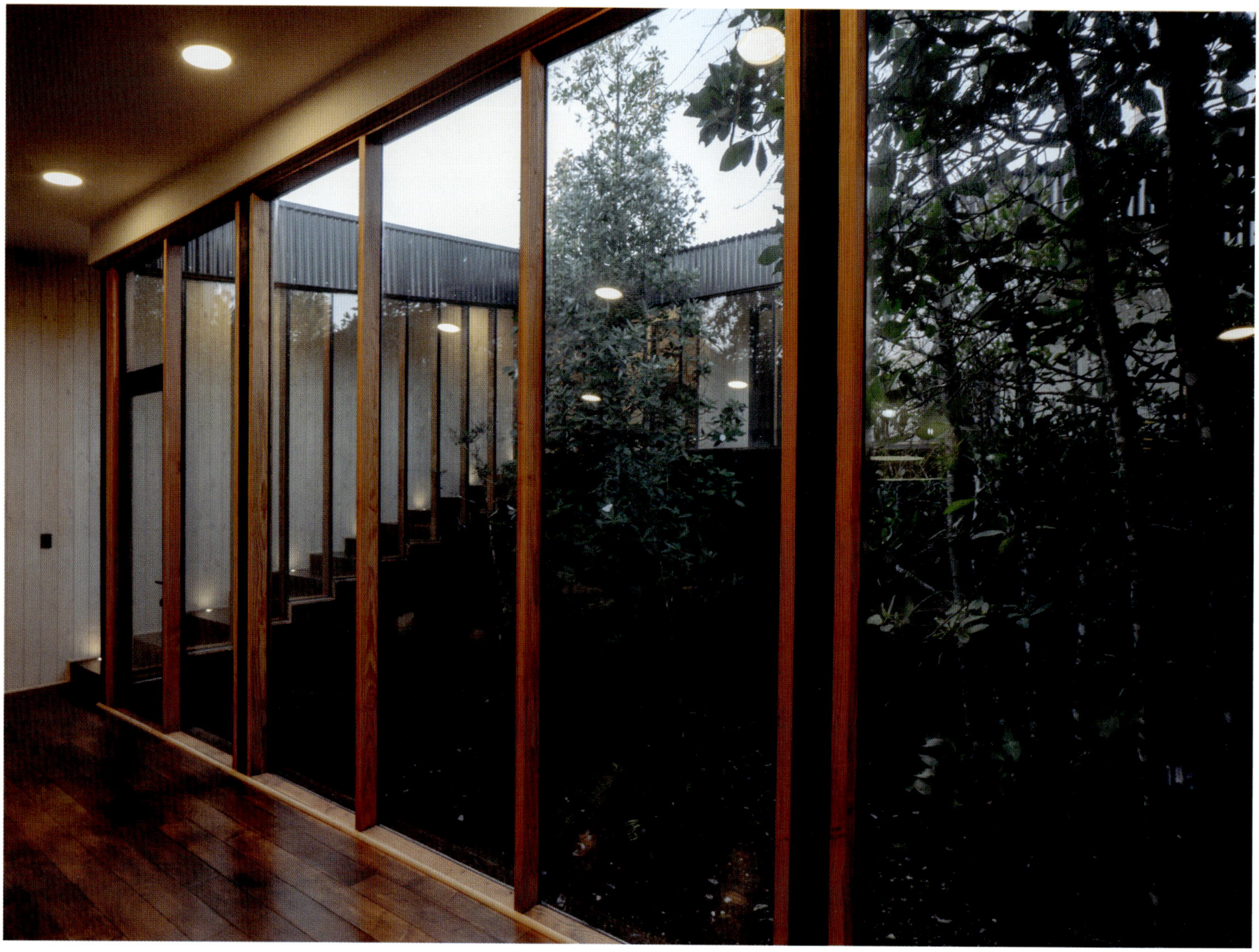

Through glazed walls, the vegetation in the patio becomes visually part of the house, enhancing the experience of living immersed in the dense forest.

Lucas Maino, an architect and lecturer, founded his practice, Lucas Maino Fernández Arquitectos, more than a decade ago. Based in Santiago, Chile, the firm specializes in wood construction. The team, which also includes Josefina Echaíz, Samuel Carmona, and Macarena García, focuses on the design of residential and commercial architecture with projects spanning from central to southern Chile.

The internal patio blends the interiors with the fabric of the forest, and the integration of the house into the context has been planned from various angles. The architects' main goal was to create continuity between both, as in the common areas of the house, including the living and dining rooms, as well as the kitchen. These are all sandwiched between the interior and exterior forest, giving a sense of being embraced by the vegetation and limiting the visual presence of architecture in the native forest through transparencies. Thanks to this solution, the rooms are filled with natural light, and the power of the sun also supports heating the spaces. While the south facade, housing the everyday life quarters, opens to the forest with a large opening, the shaded entrance on the north is solid in contrast.

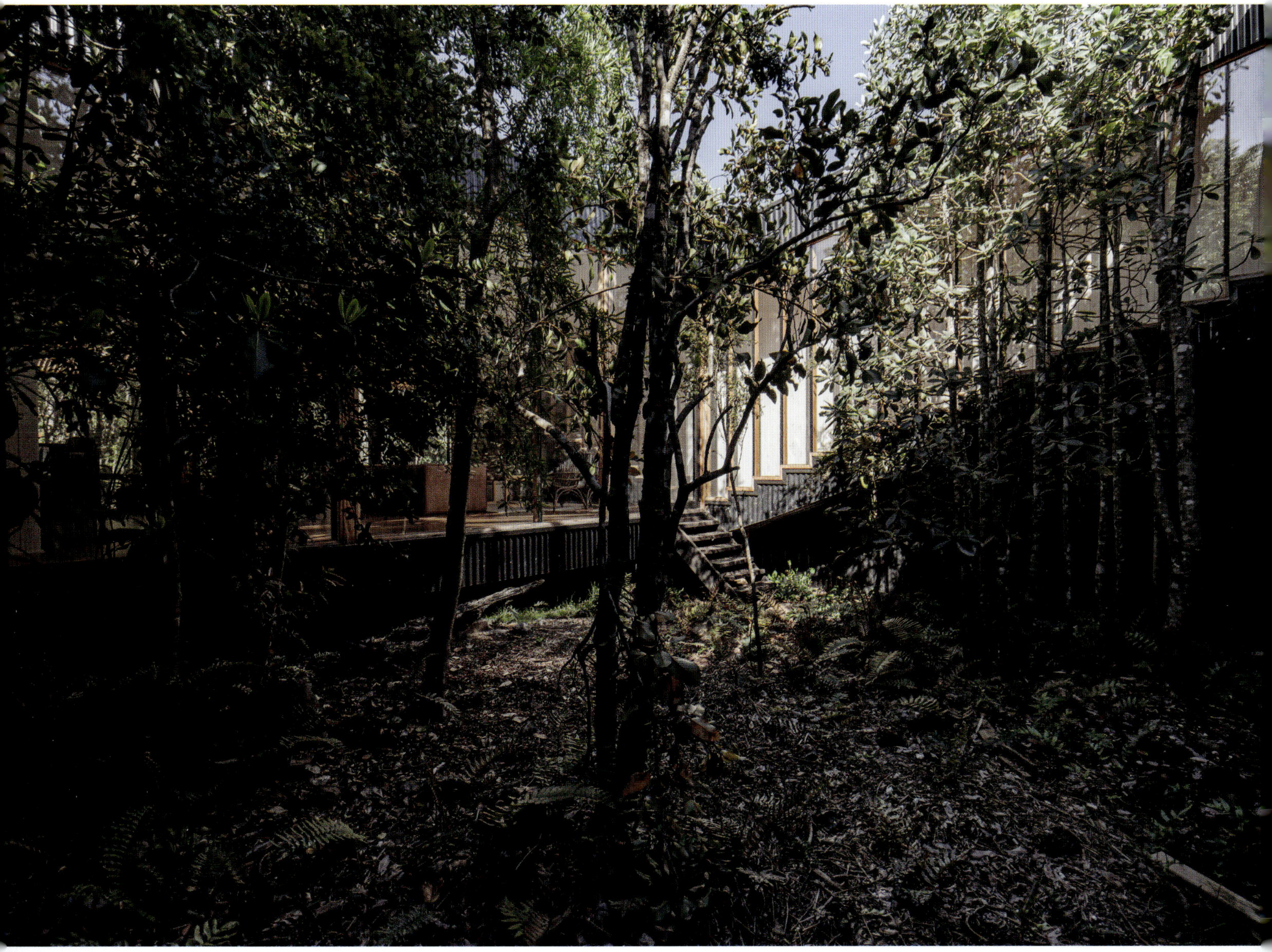

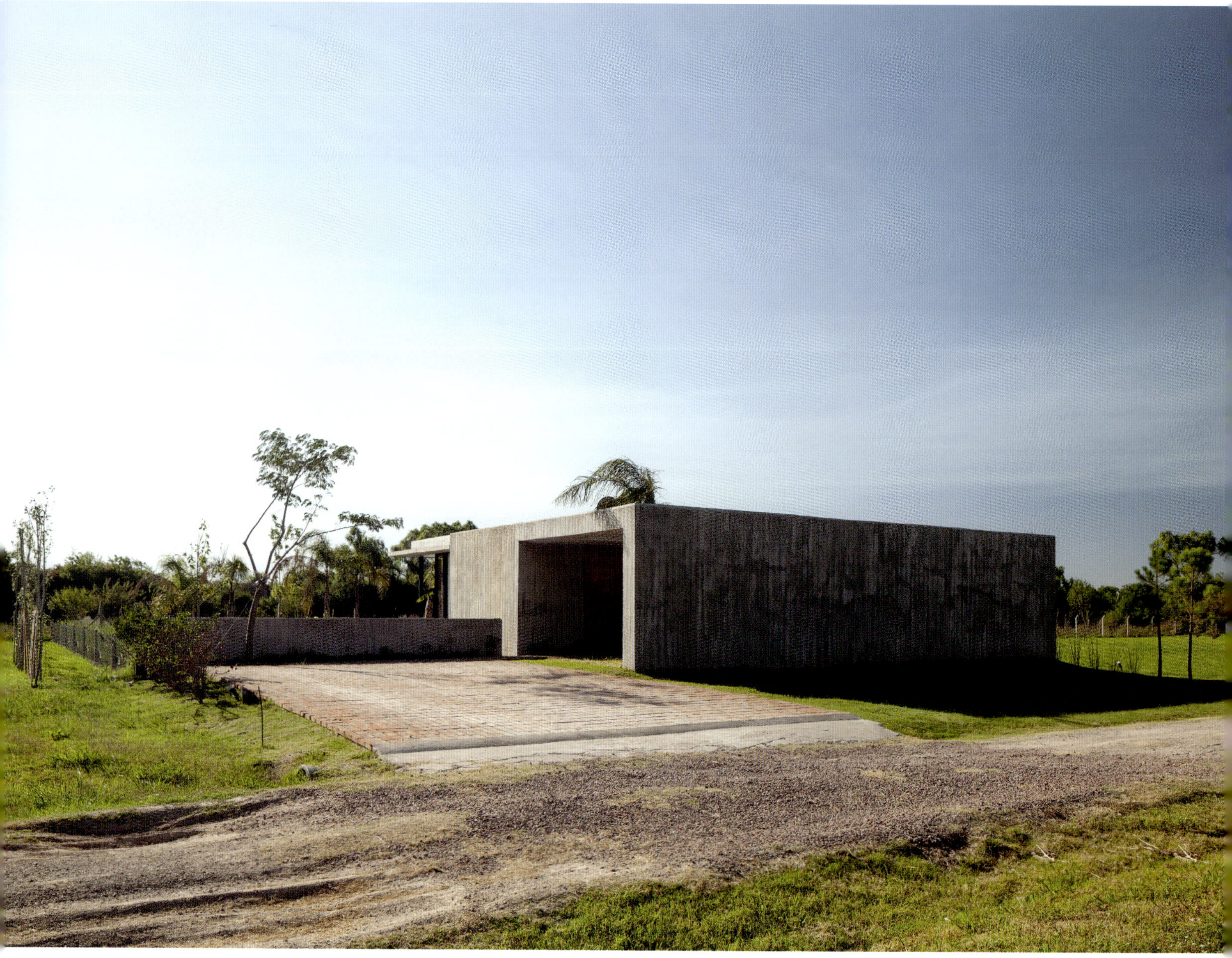

Over a decade ago, Felipe González Arzac established his studio in Buenos Aires. The team has realized more than 150 residential projects. With projects of complex residential neighborhoods, country estates, and gated communities in La Plata, Gonnet, City Bell, and the Atlantic coast, the practice's signature style is a minimalist language of pure geometric forms enhanced by the use of exposed concrete combined with glass.

PROJECT: Casa Closed
LOCATION: La Plata, Argentina
YEAR: 2019
ARCHITECTS: Felipe González Arzac
PHOTOGRAPHY: Javier Agustín Rojas

Casa Closed, boldly designed by Felipe González Arzac, is a house of exciting contrasts. The entrance perspective demonstrates the practice's signature elements—modern shape, clean form, rough material, and conceptual approach. Massive solid walls made in exposed concrete give the minimalistic shape a strong presence. Defending the privacy of the inhabitants, the blind entrance facade stands in stark contrast with the opposite side of the residence, which is nearly entirely glazed and is in dialogue with the surrounding. This exciting interplay between closed and open, solid and transparent, culminates in two patios—one central and one exterior, which are quite different in character.

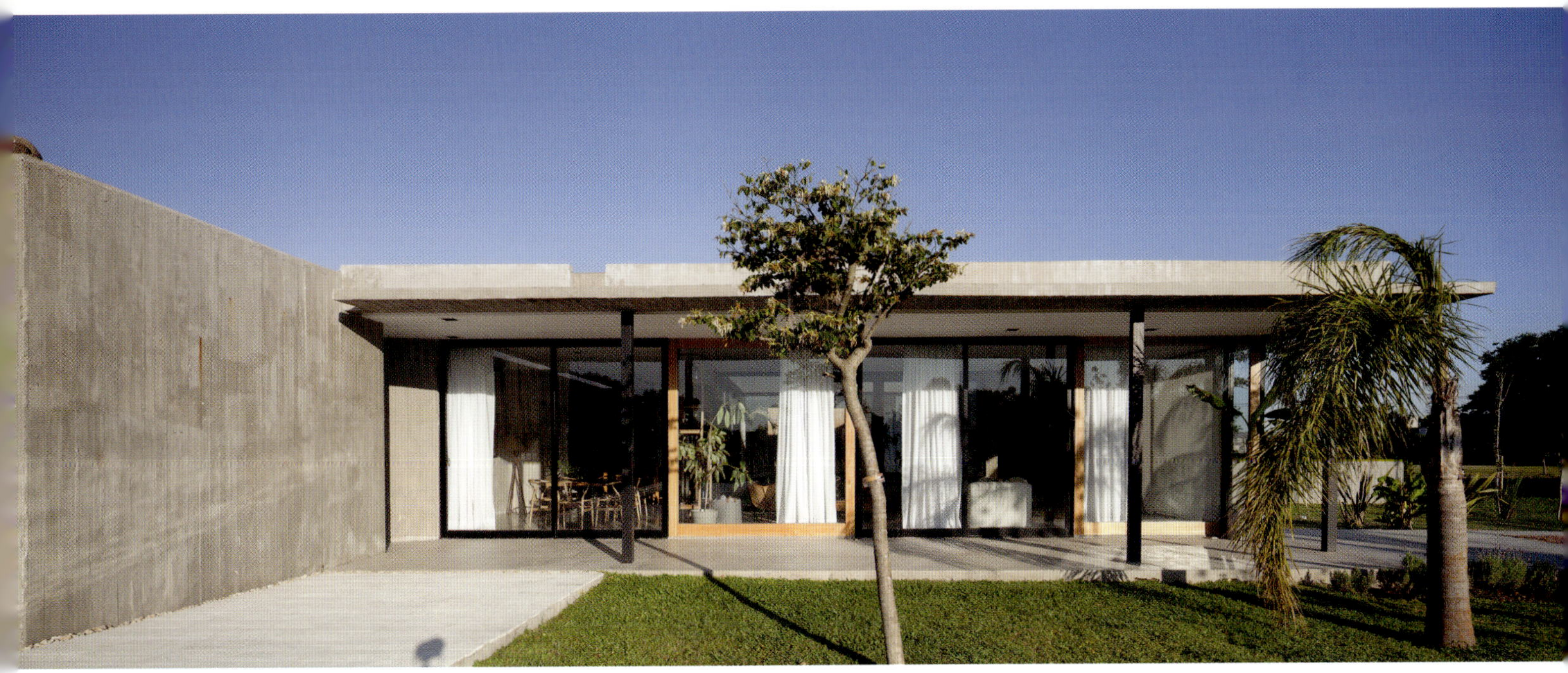

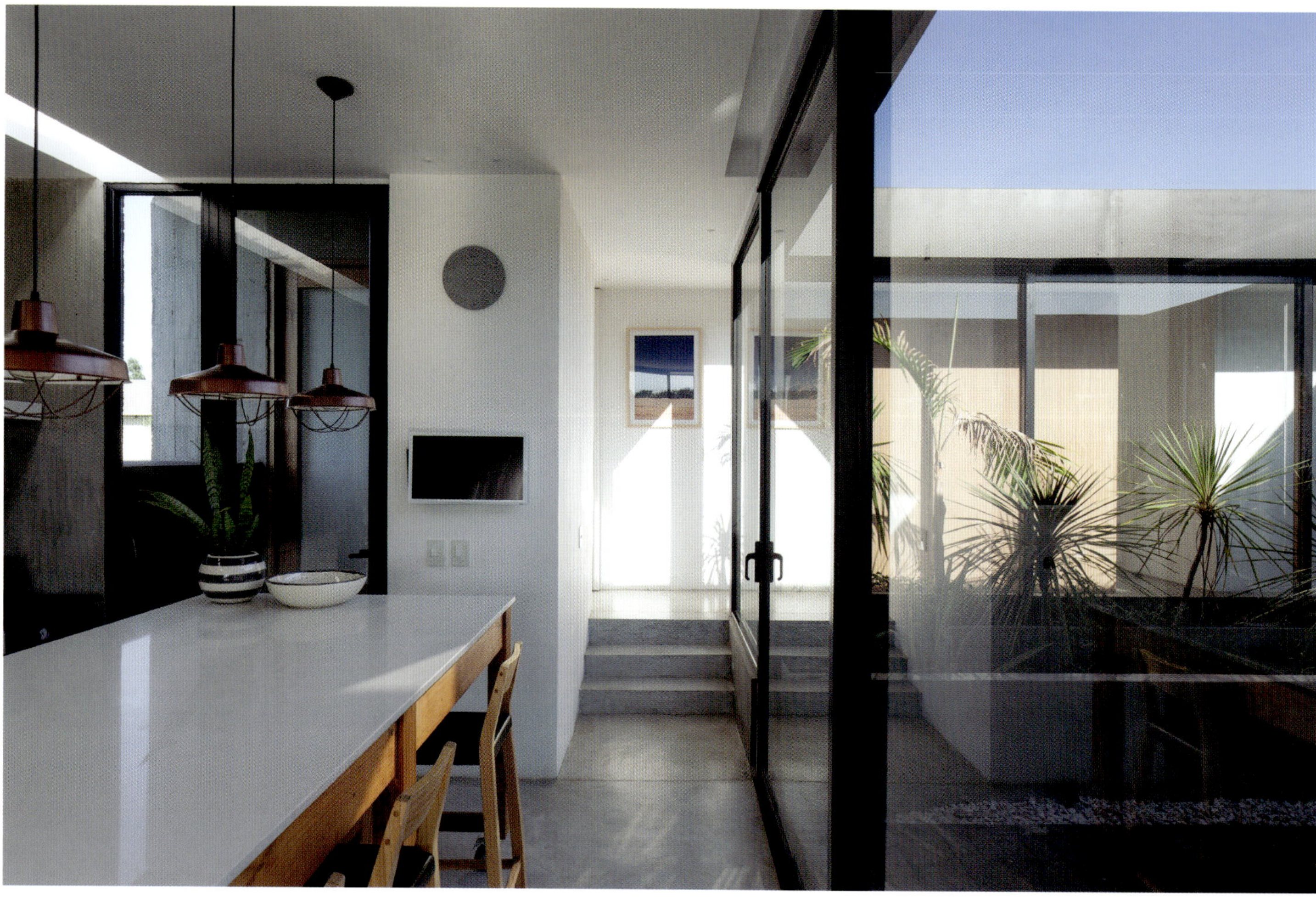

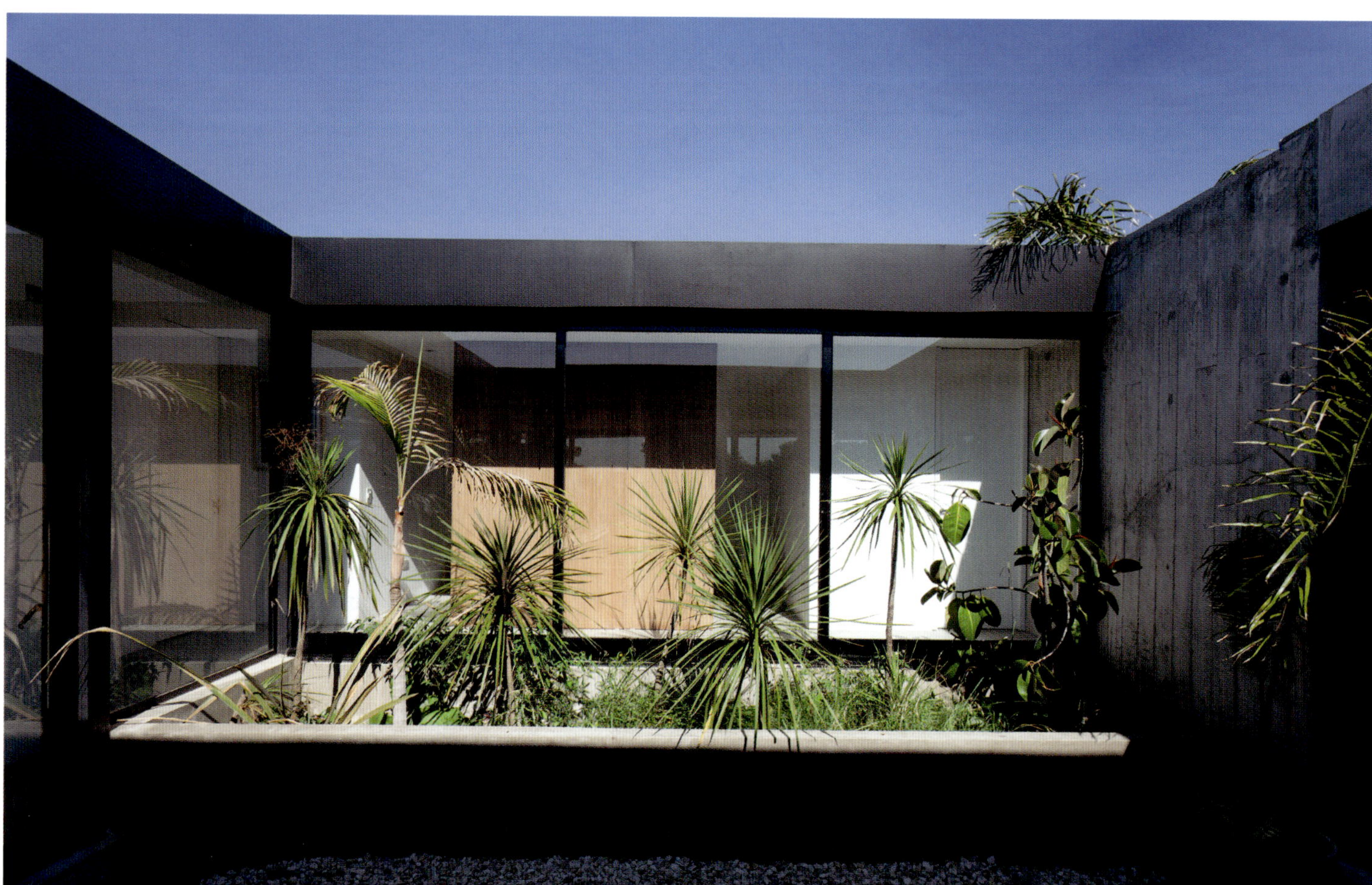

The internal patio, filled with vegetation, is the orientation point for the common areas organized around it and has a calming effect thanks to the visual connection with social spaces through all-height openings.

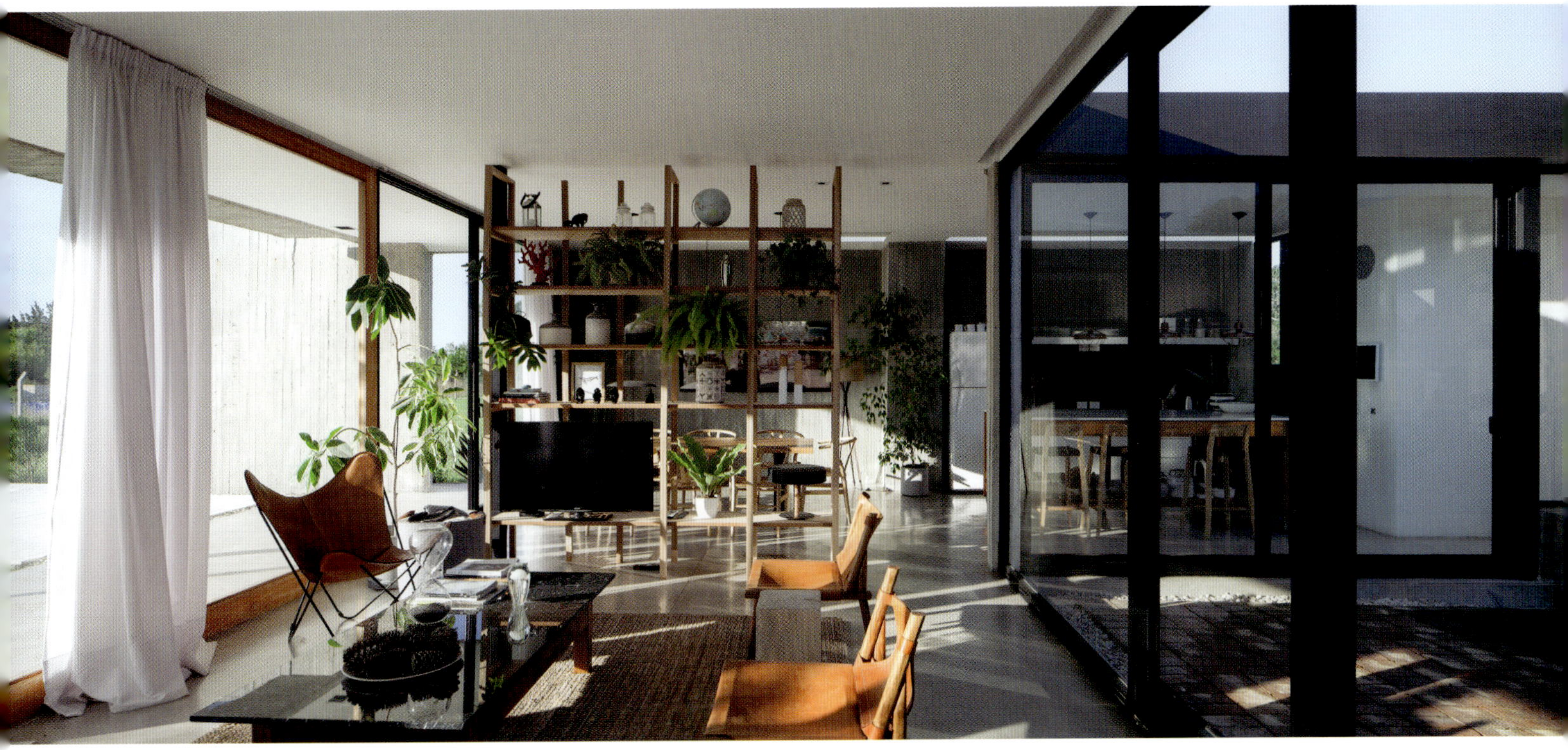

Another interesting surprise is that the volume, which seems to be a simple cube, is much more complex inside the house, which has been planned along two crossing axes. Thanks to the generous glazing, the interiors are filled with natural light and spacious through the connections created between the interior and exterior patios. The living room, looking out at both, is a particular communicative hub. The small scale of the central patio together with its geometry makes it a quiet and atmospheric space adorned with plants. The exterior courtyard is extensive and open to the adjacent garden, meant for bigger gatherings and outdoor activities. These contrasting moods are enhanced by the amount of sunlight, which is limited in the central patio and ample on the outside one.

PROJECT: Casa un Patio
LOCATION: Mérida, Yucatán, Mexico
YEAR: 2017
ARCHITECTS: P11 Arquitectos
PHOTOGRAPHY: Eduardo Calvo Santisbon

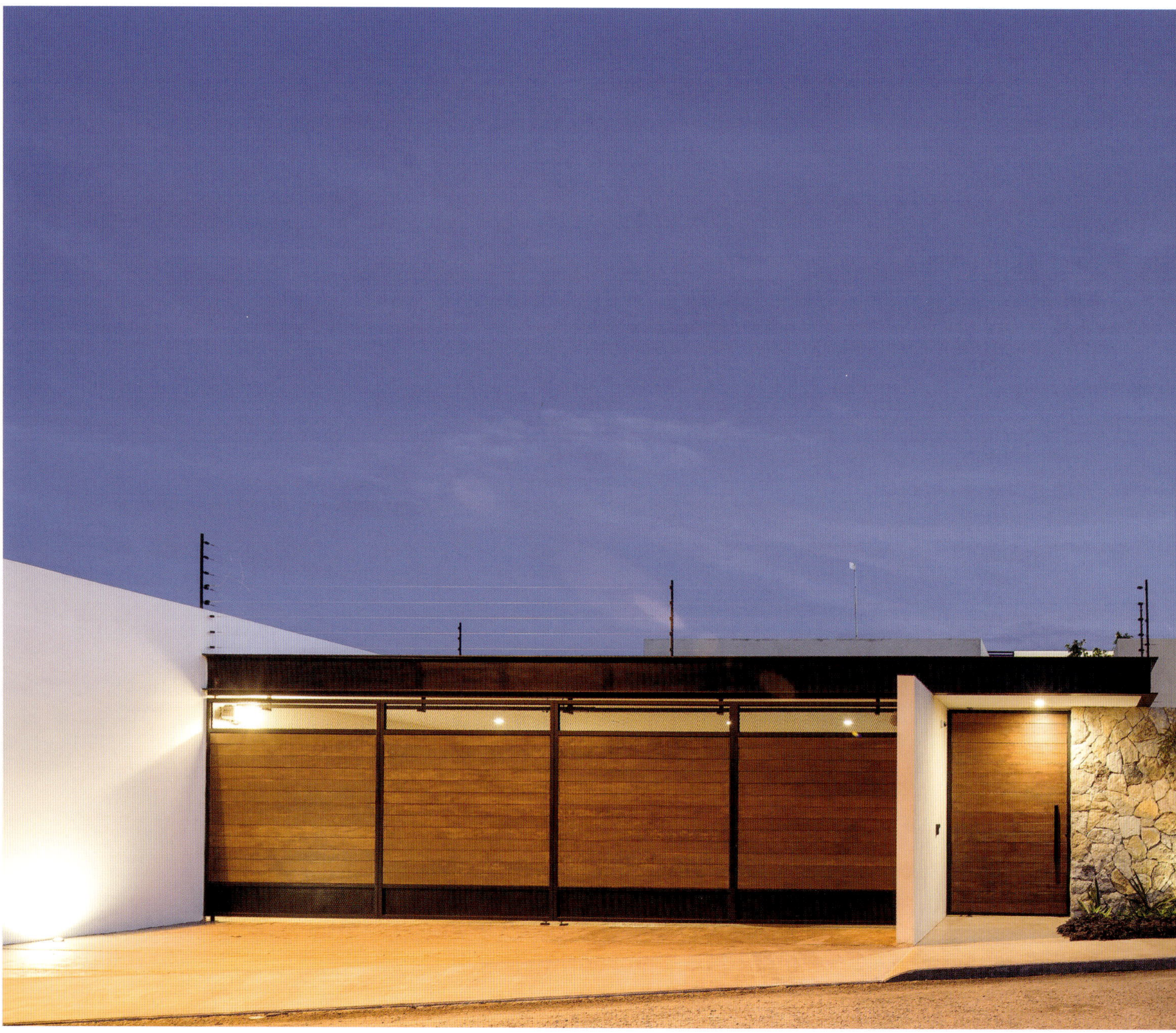

An entirely inconspicuous street entrance leads to a complex residence on a rectangular plot. Designed by P11 Arquitectos in Mérida, Yucatán, this extensive villa has been envisioned for a family and their art collection. The villa takes a quadrangle shape made of intersected volumes with a central patio and a leisure courtyard with a grand terrace and pool surrounded by greenery. The architects have marked the meeting points between various parts by using different materials. The main one consists of loose volumes inside and houses private areas, while a double-height volume, intersecting the quadrangle, contains the common spaces.

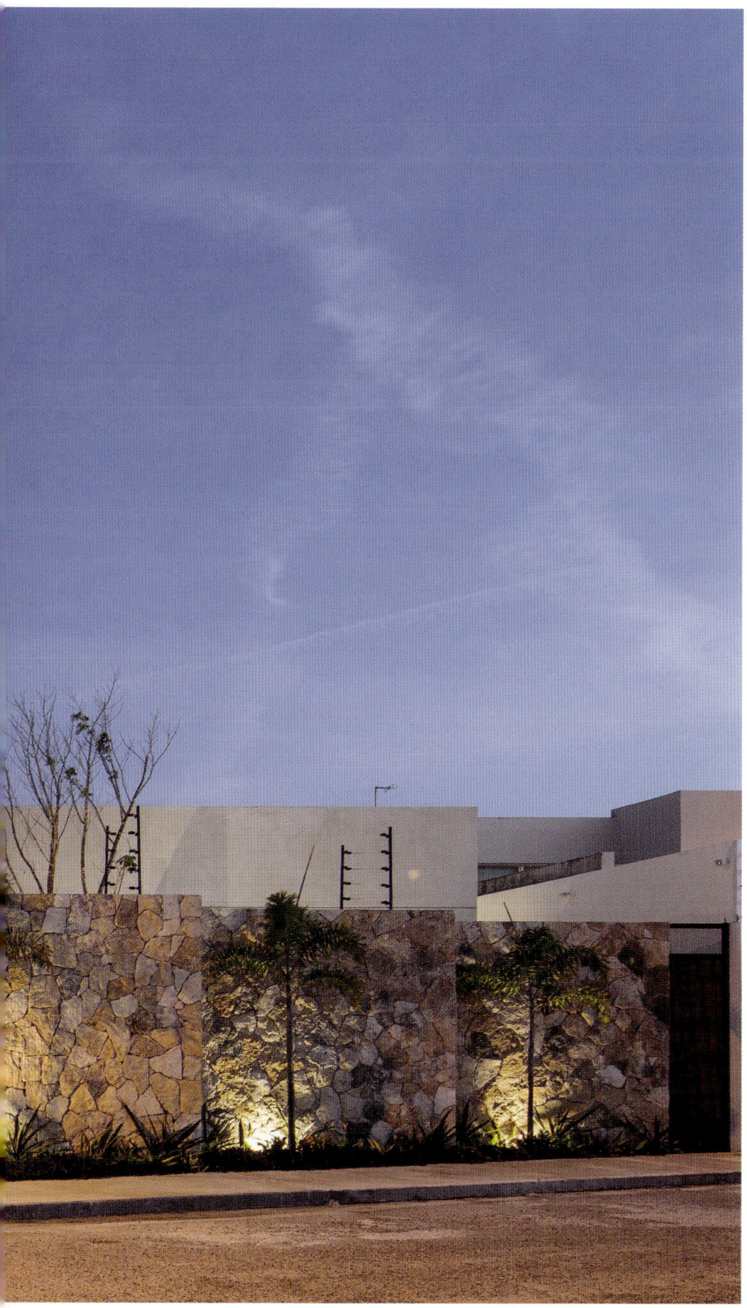

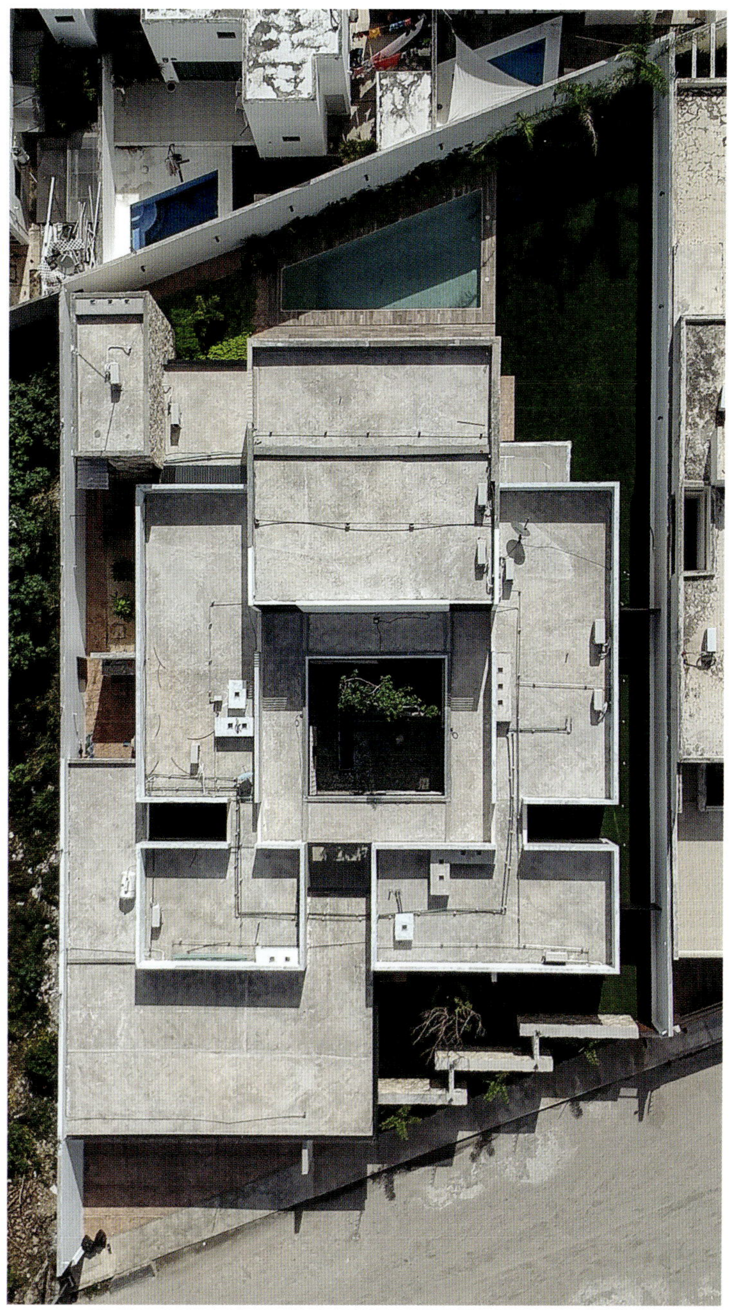

This minimalistic patio, adorned with aspen, is the very center of the spacious family residence, creating an interesting contrast with the complex intersection of volumes.

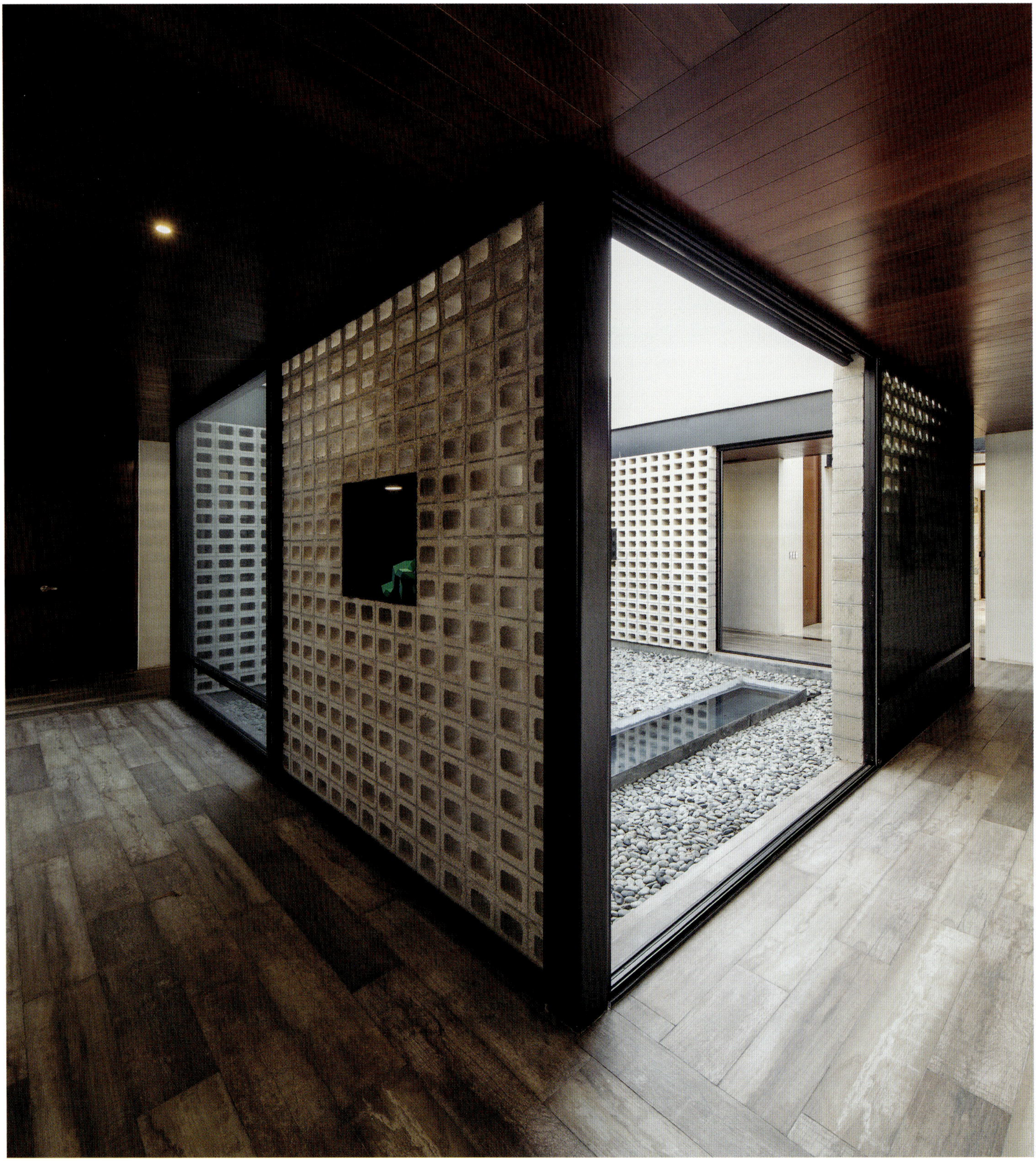

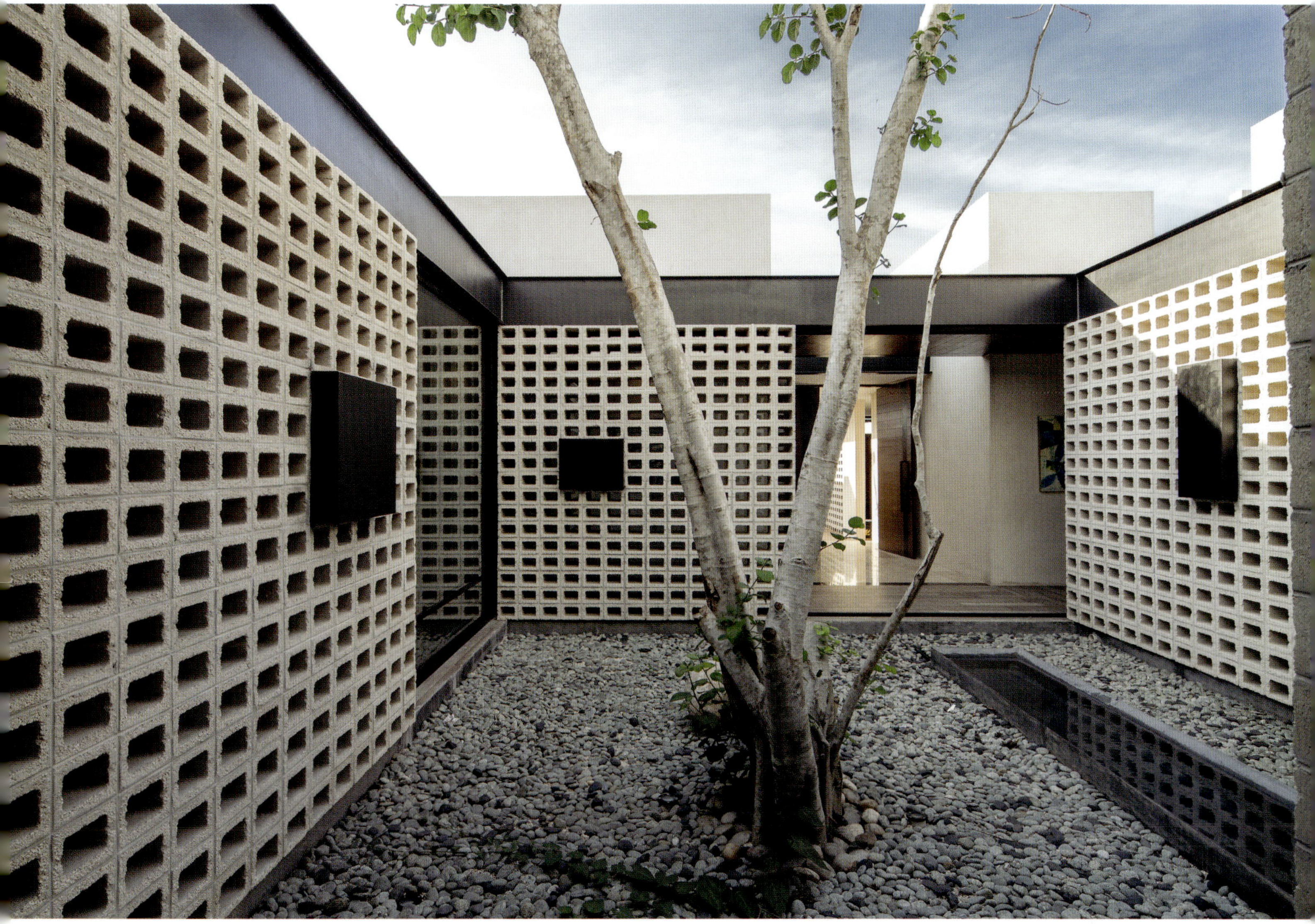

Both courtyards play an important role in the relation between exterior and interior. The central patio, as the heart of the house, is marked with an aspen tree. Wrapped with an interplay of concrete blocks and large openings, it creates a quiet space sculpted throughout the day by the passage of the sun (providing natural light, supporting ventilation, and controlling humidity). Around this meditative space, the architects planned a concentric vestibule, which creates a dynamic communication between various parts of the house. The second courtyard is quite the contrary—a large open space accessible from the double-height living room, with a shaded terrace and opening to a pool surrounded by greenery. A steel beam carries a massive concrete celosia wall, which is a visual reference to the internal patio.

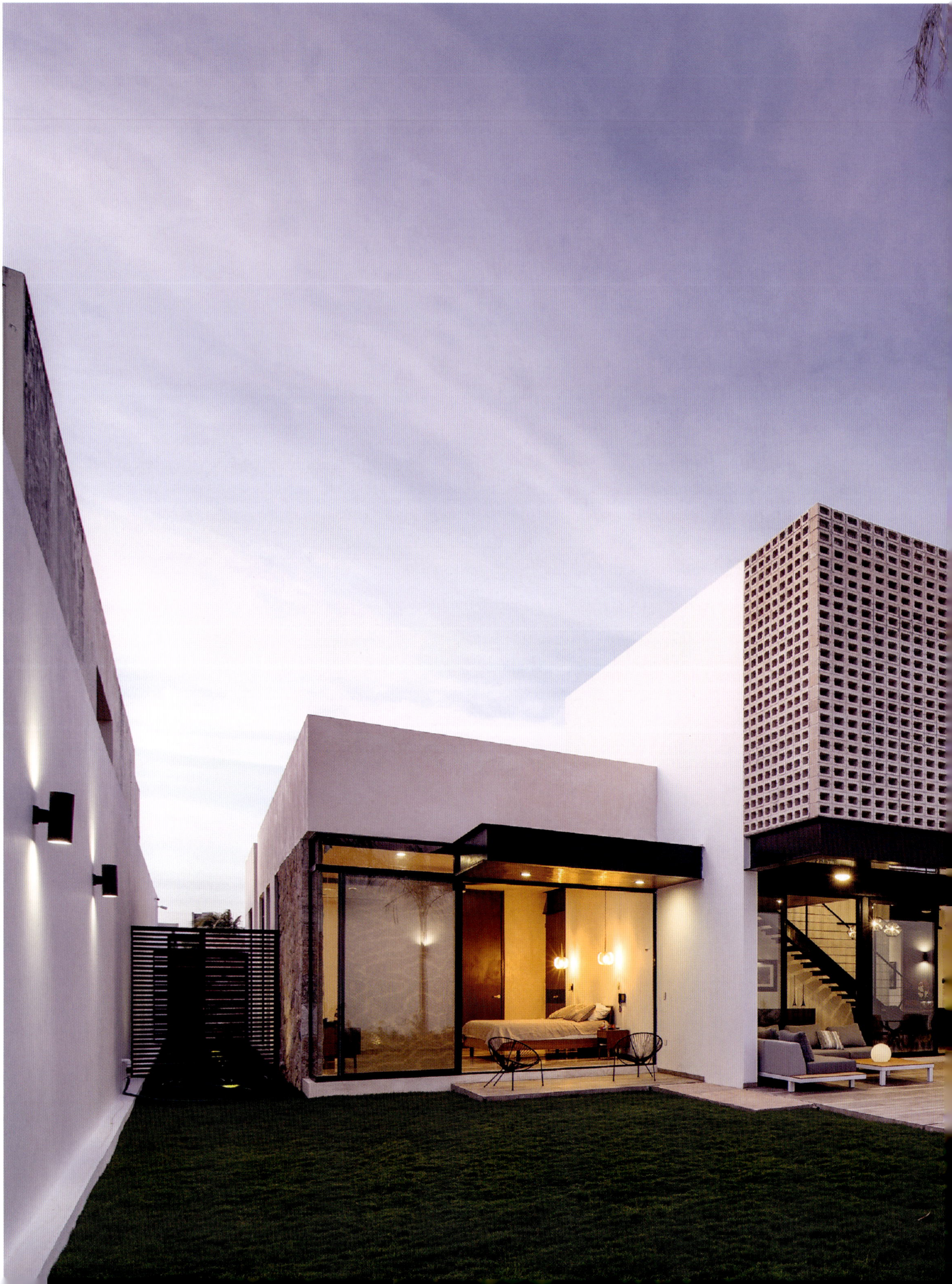

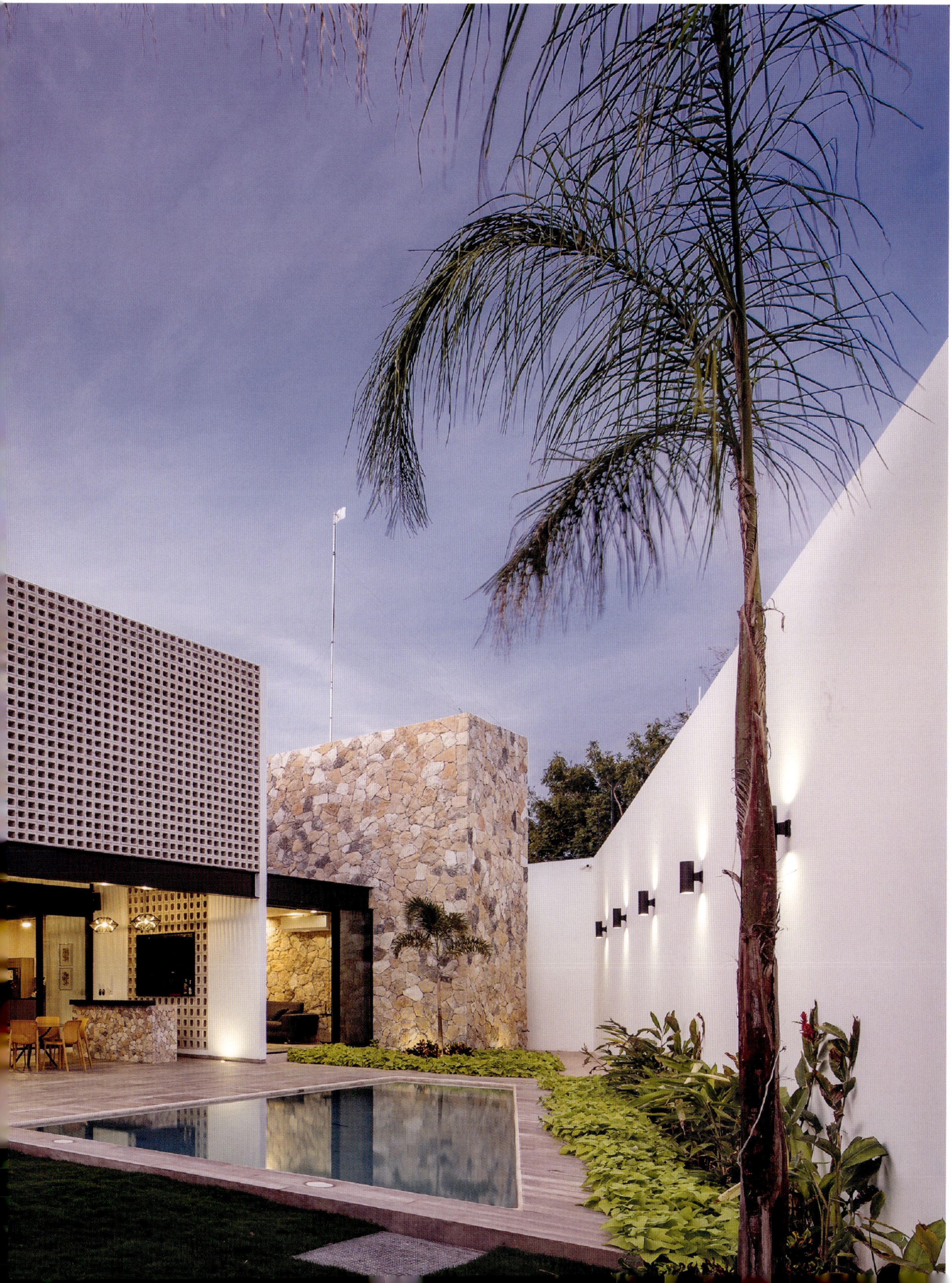

The concrete celosia used in the structure is the common element distinctively marking the patios and creating in both cases a spectacular play of light.

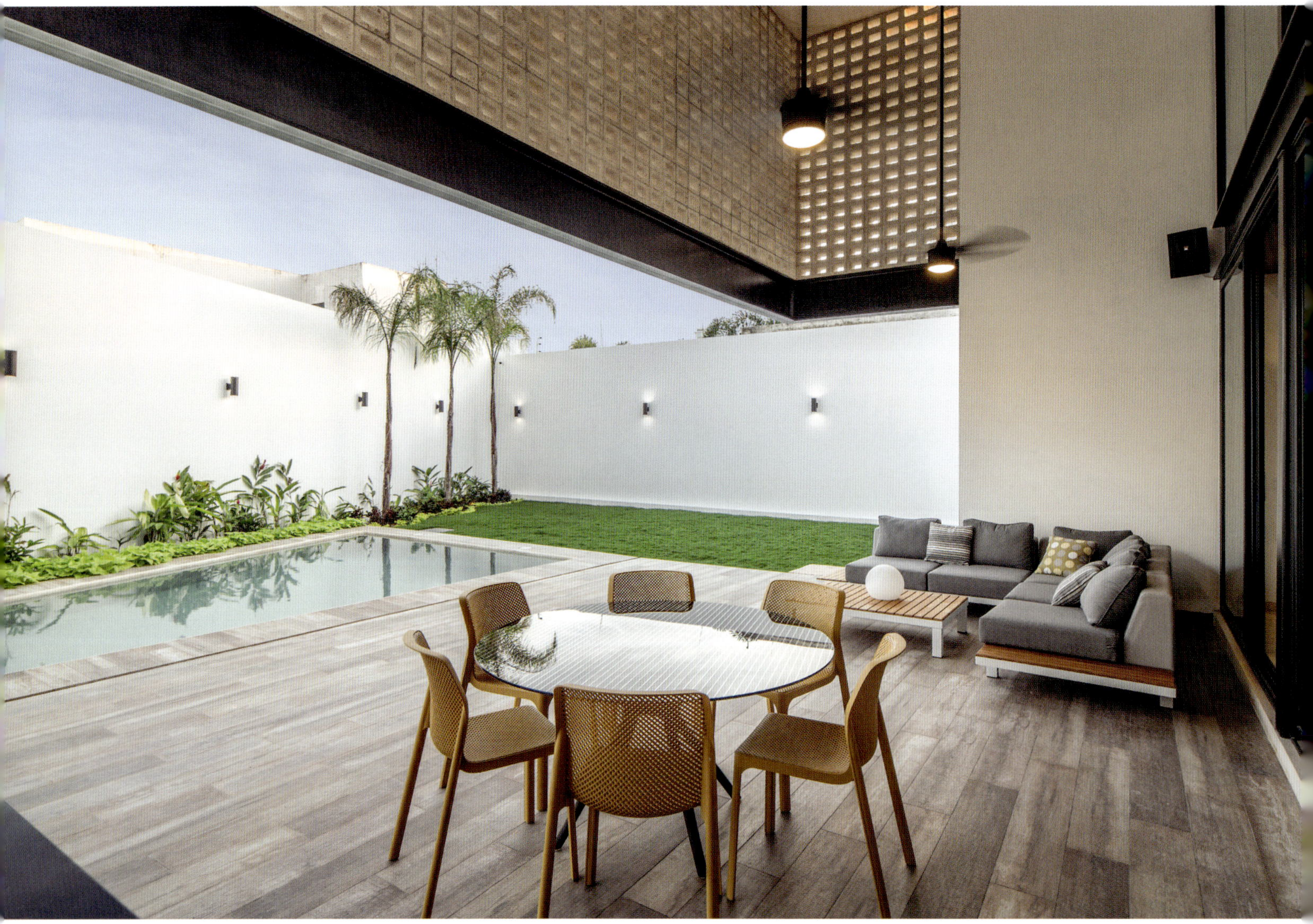

After working at other studios, Arturo Carrillo Ponce founded his own practice, P11 Arquitectos, in 2005. Based in Mexican Mérida, Yucatán, the firm specializes in residential architecture and office buildings. A team of young architects dedicated to the development and supervision of each realization aim at distinctive concepts that are practical as much as they offer unique solutions.

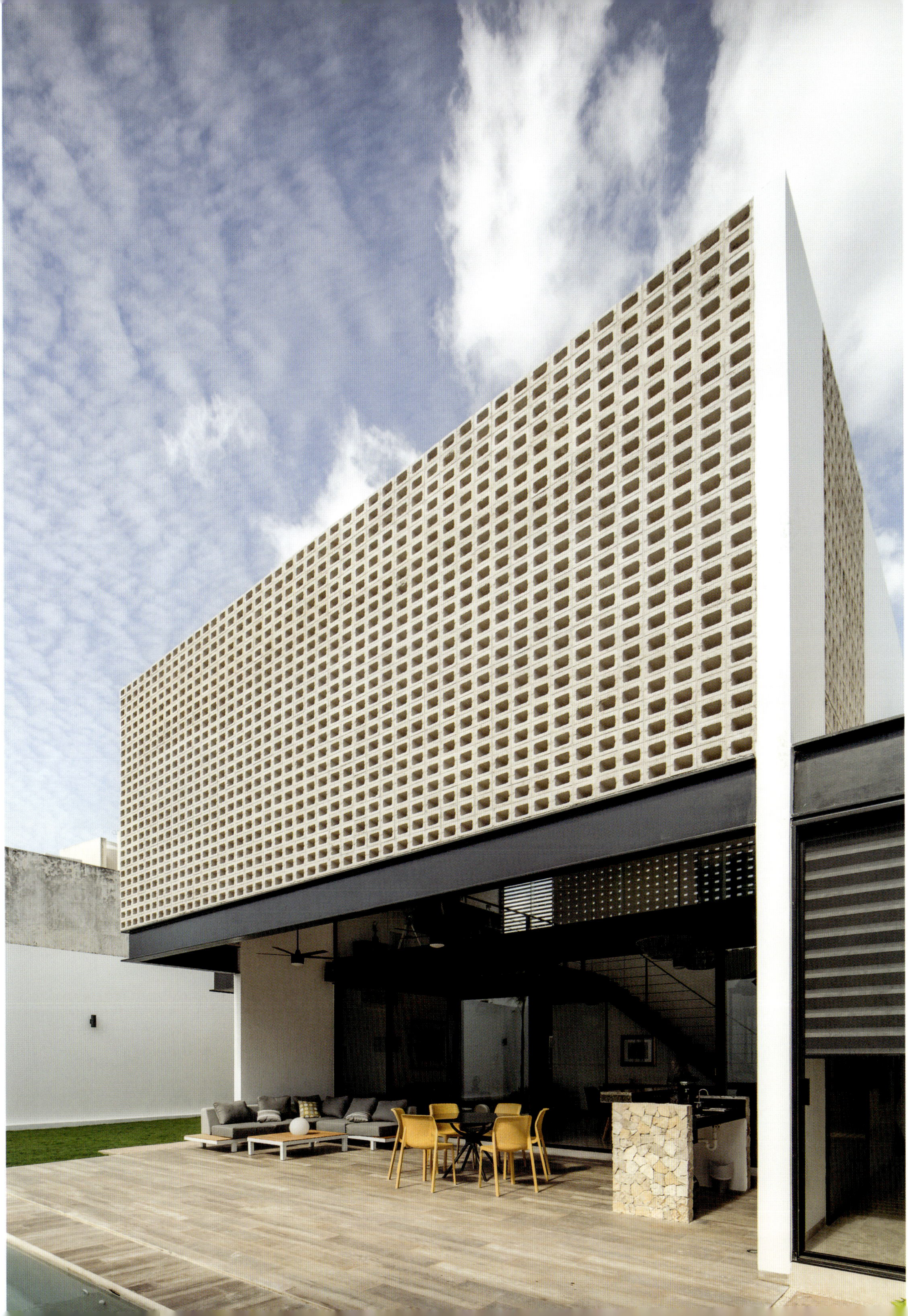

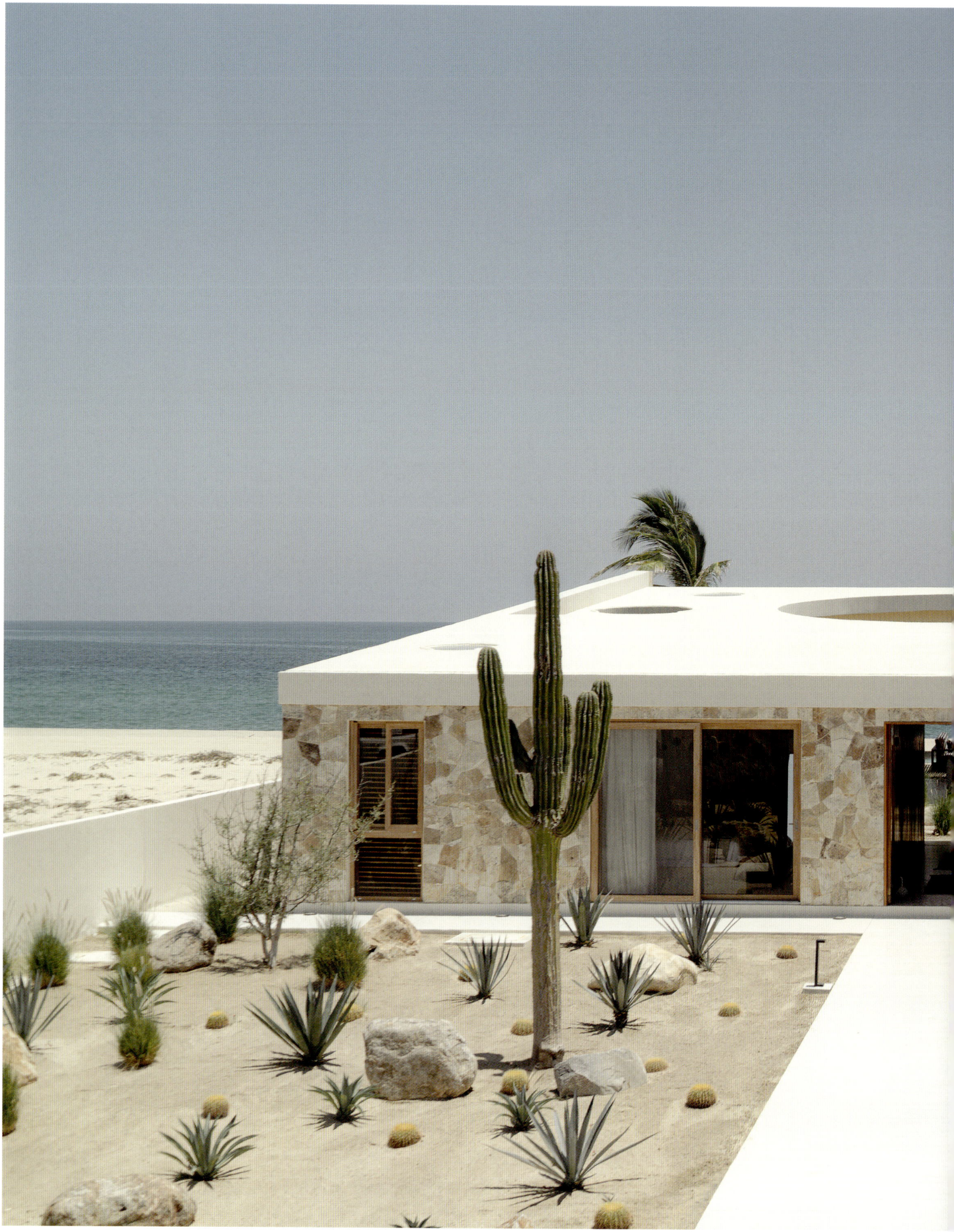

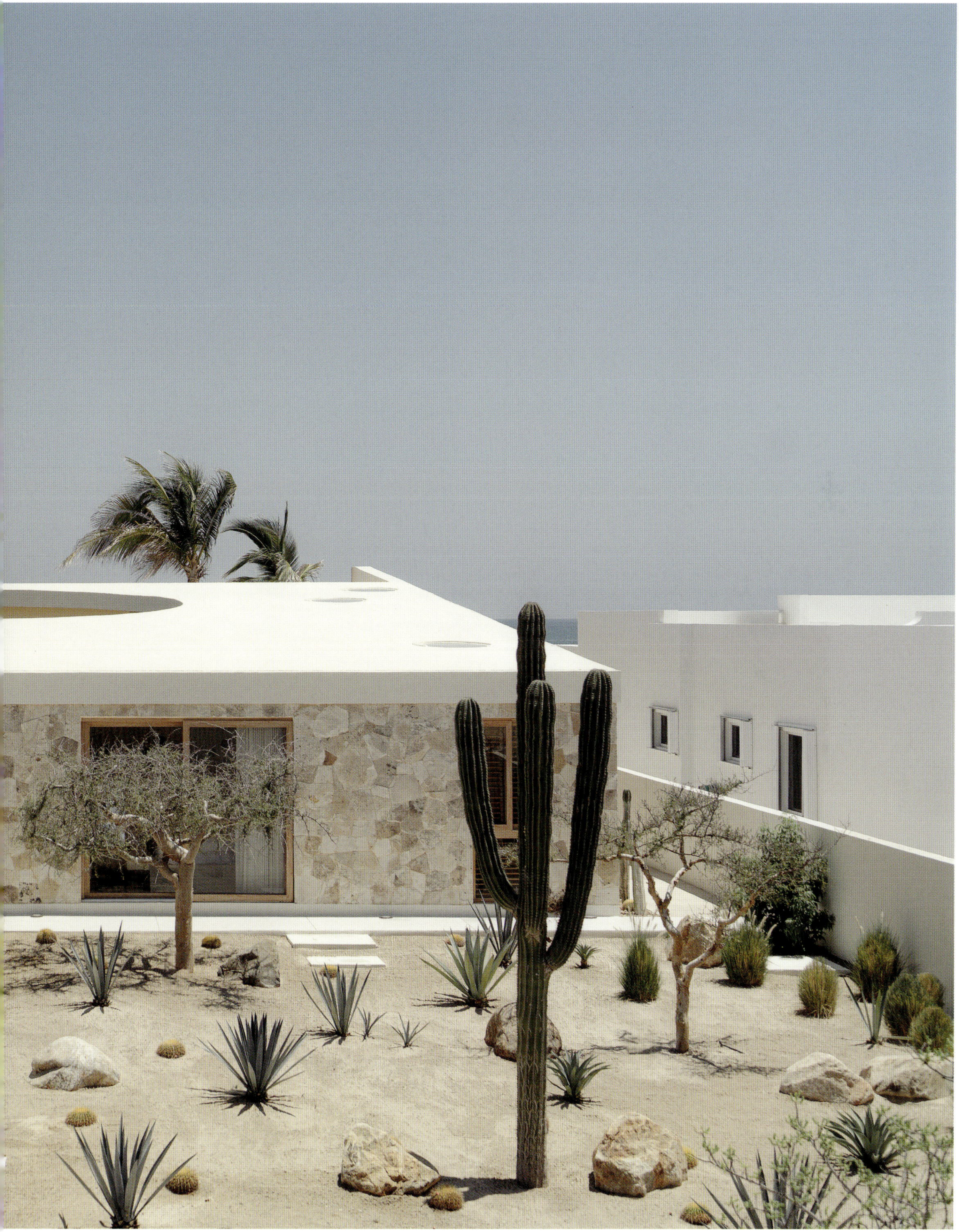

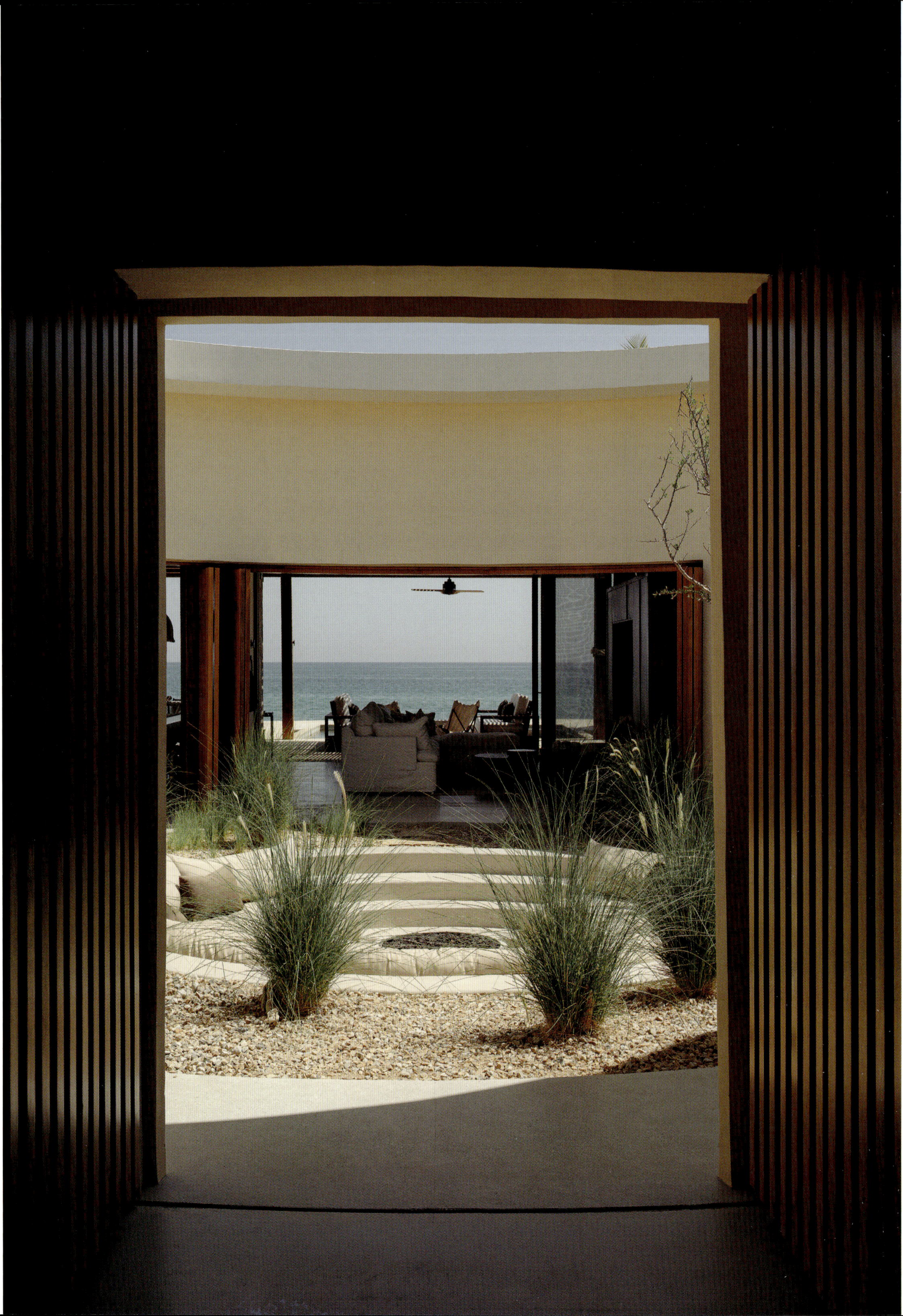

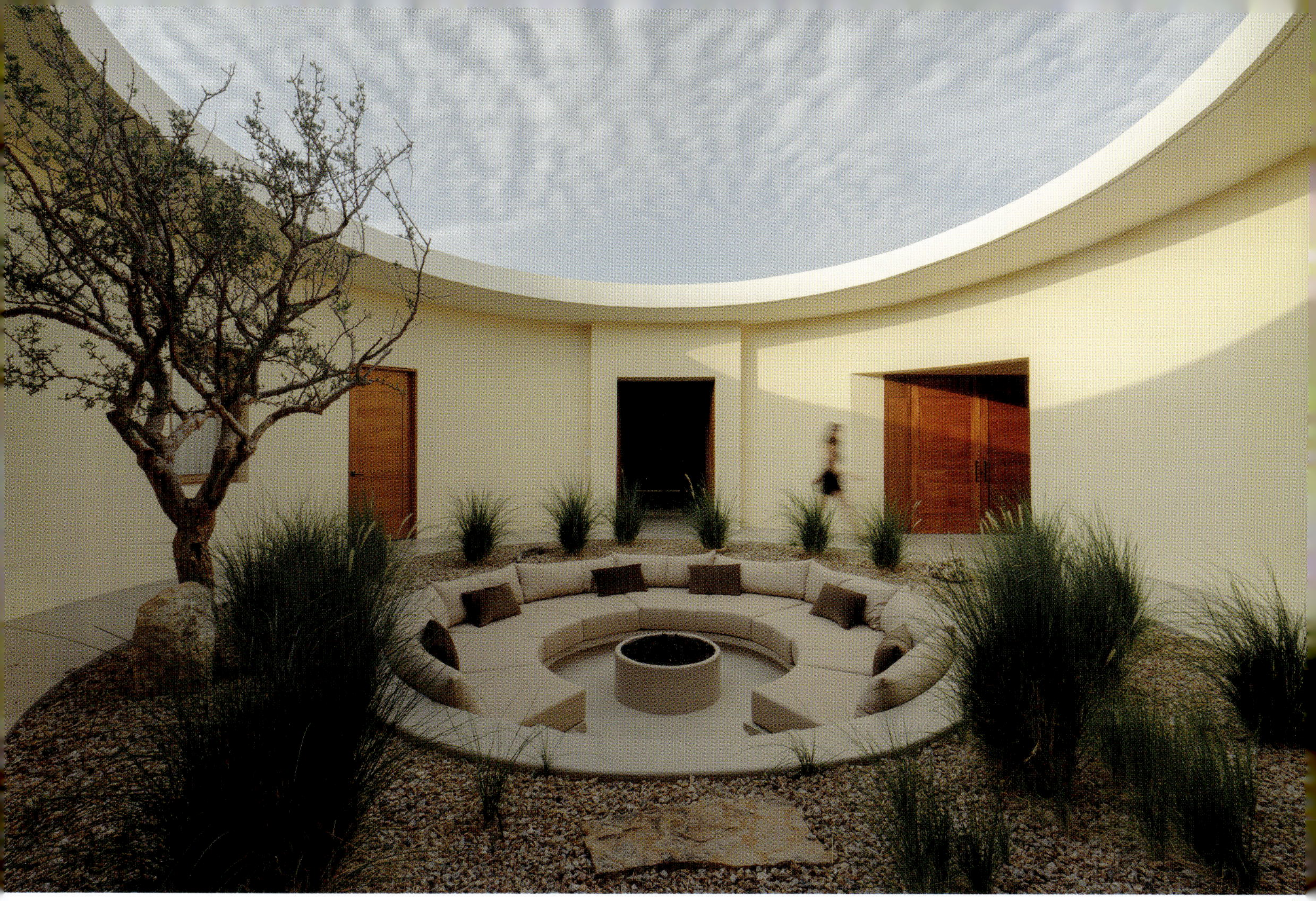

PROJECT: Suna House
LOCATION: La Ribera, B.C.S., Mexico
YEAR: 2024
ARCHITECTS: YDR estudio
PHOTOGRAPHY: Luz Imelda Castillo

The beautiful location of the Suna House, nestled between a stunning beach and rugged mountains, inspired architect Yolanda De Rueda to create a holiday villa that harmonizes perfectly with its surroundings. The one-story volume does not overpower the landscape; instead, through the use of local stone, beige concrete, and natural wood, the vacation home blends seamlessly into the natural color palette of the area. The minimalistic entrance, adorned with a courtyard garden featuring cacti, leads to the center of the house—a circular patio marked with an oculus in the white roof, perfect for stargazing at night (the fire pit in the center also invites gathering around the fire). A centrally placed round sofa, nestled in a cozy spot below ground level, creates a comfortable socializing area.

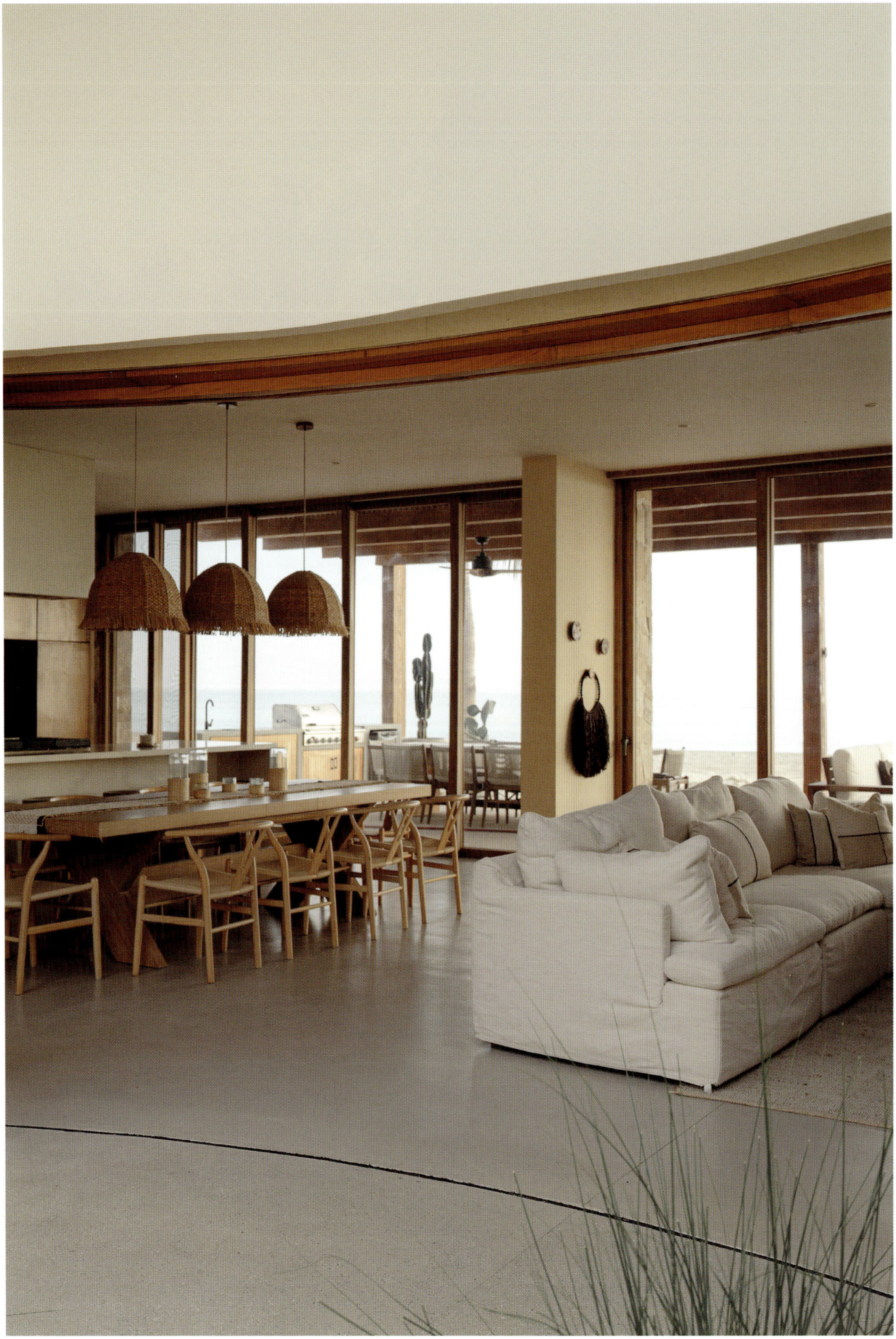

The part of the house facing the lovely beach is connected to the patio through entirely openable, full-height windows. This design fosters a smooth communication between the interior and exterior spaces, as well as visual continuity with the coastline view. The open-plan kitchen, dining, and living-room areas further open onto an extensive terrace that extends to the sandy beach. This layout not only integrates all common spaces with each other and the landscape but also supports cross-ventilation effectively. An outdoor kitchen, a large table for meals, a pool, and a jacuzzi create an entertaining space for relaxation. The interior design aesthetic features a neutral color palette with a calming effect that perfectly complements the atmosphere of the location and the relaxing purpose of the house. The architect's goal, successfully achieved, was to combine recreation with luxury and offer a serene experience in this exceptional place located among the sea, the sky, the desert, and the mountains.

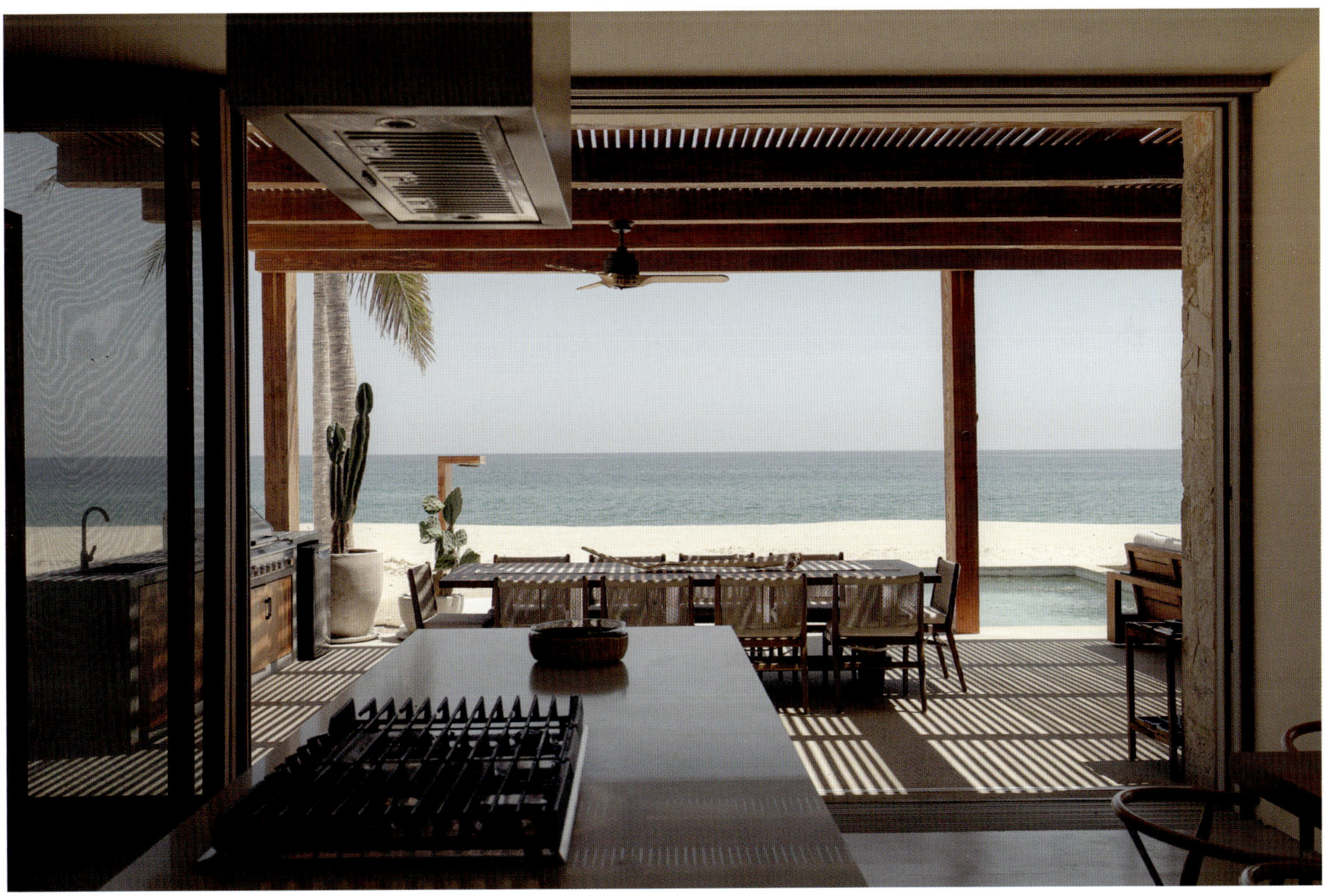

The fully glazed beachfront offers breathtaking views of the coastline that can be enjoyed both from the interiors and the large shaded terrace with a pool and jacuzzi. This area effectively doubles the living space.

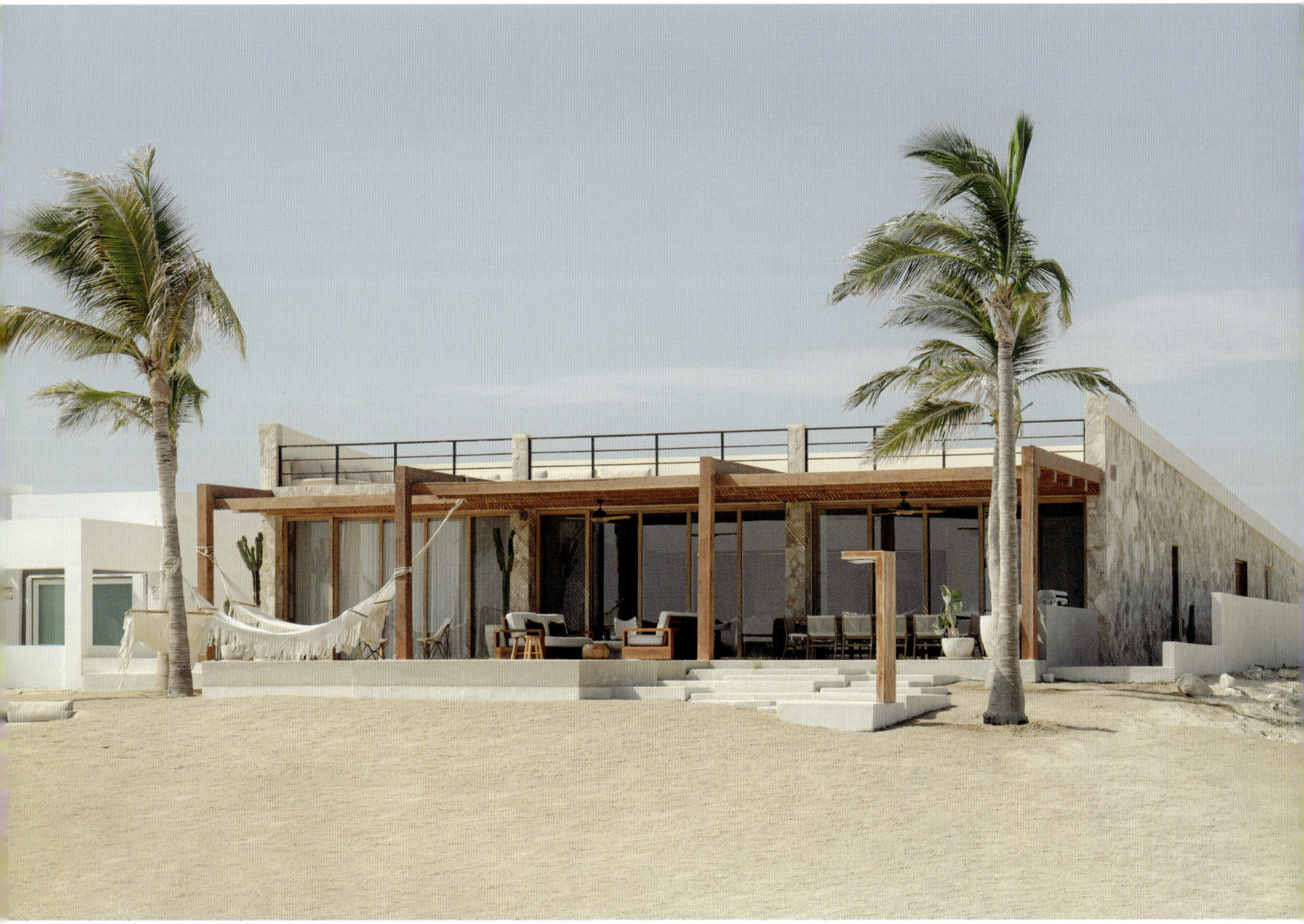

After working with Tatiana Bilbao Studio in Mexico City and Herzog & de Meuron in Basel, Switzerland, Yolanda De Rueda established her own studio. With headquarters in Guatemala, the firm focuses on residential architecture with a portfolio of striking residences across Mexico and Guatemala. Other projects include Plaza, envisioned for the botanical garden in Culiacán, Mexico, a master plan for the Mexican Puerto Vallarta, and the Feltrinelli Foundation in Milan, Italy.

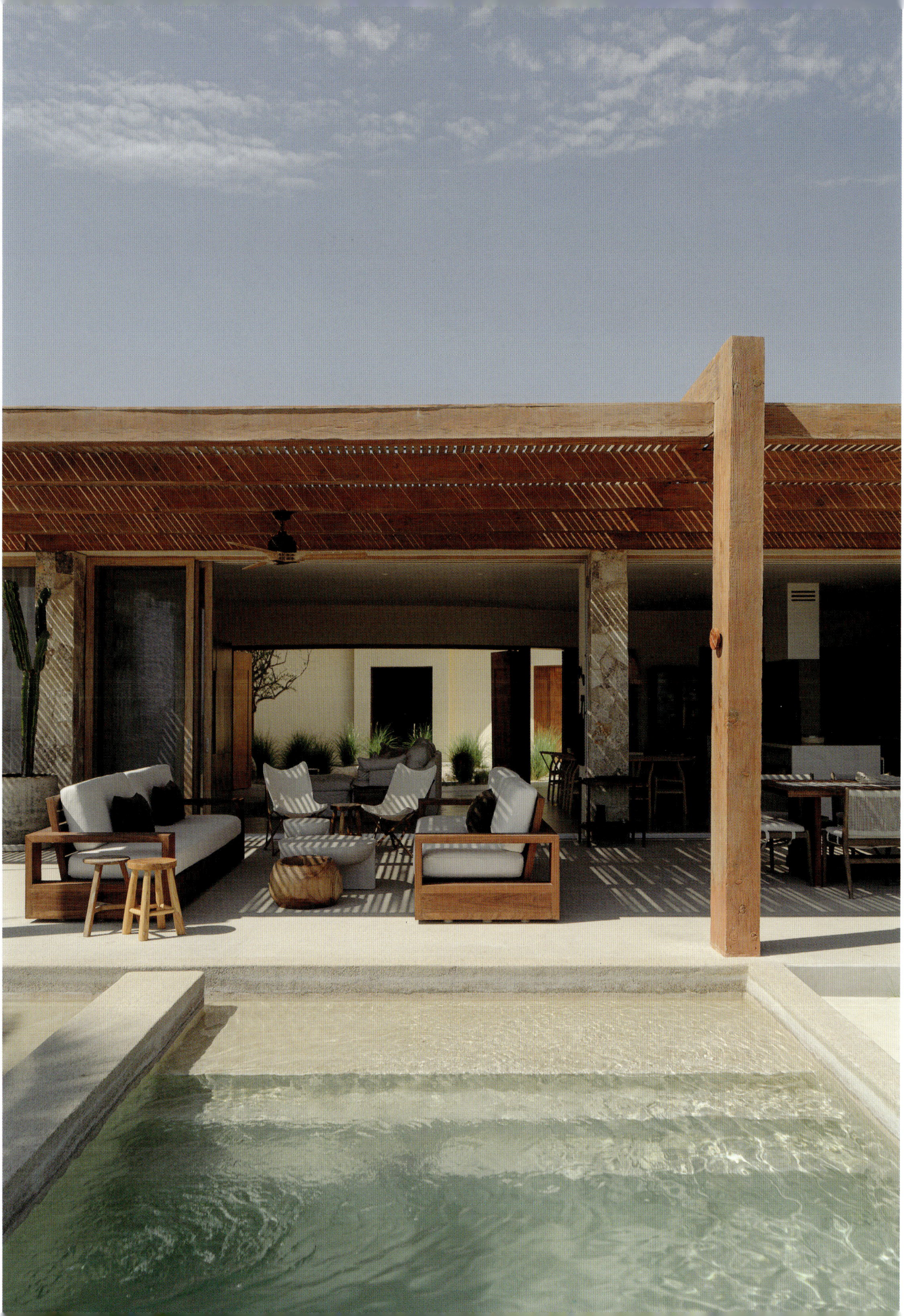

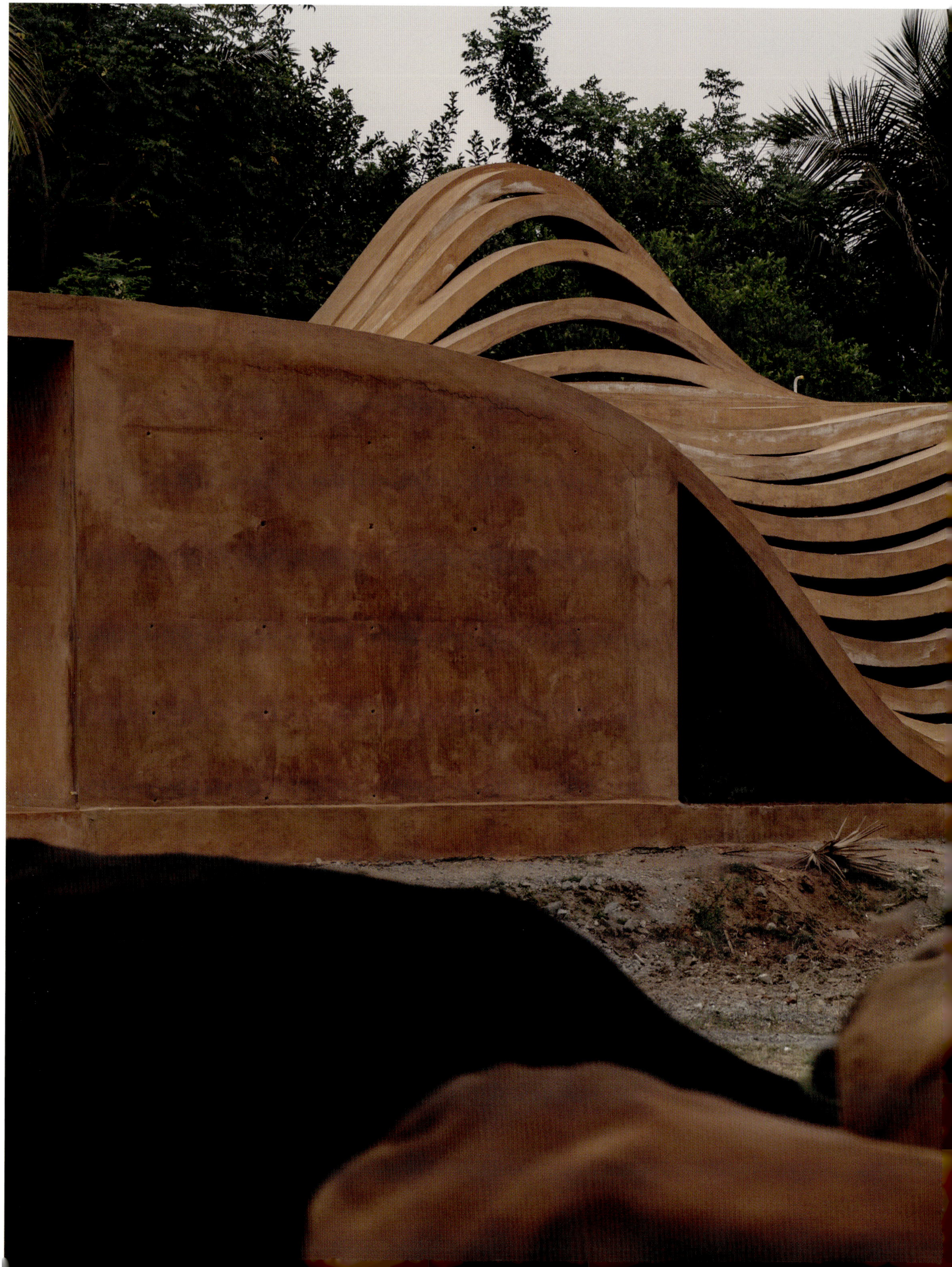

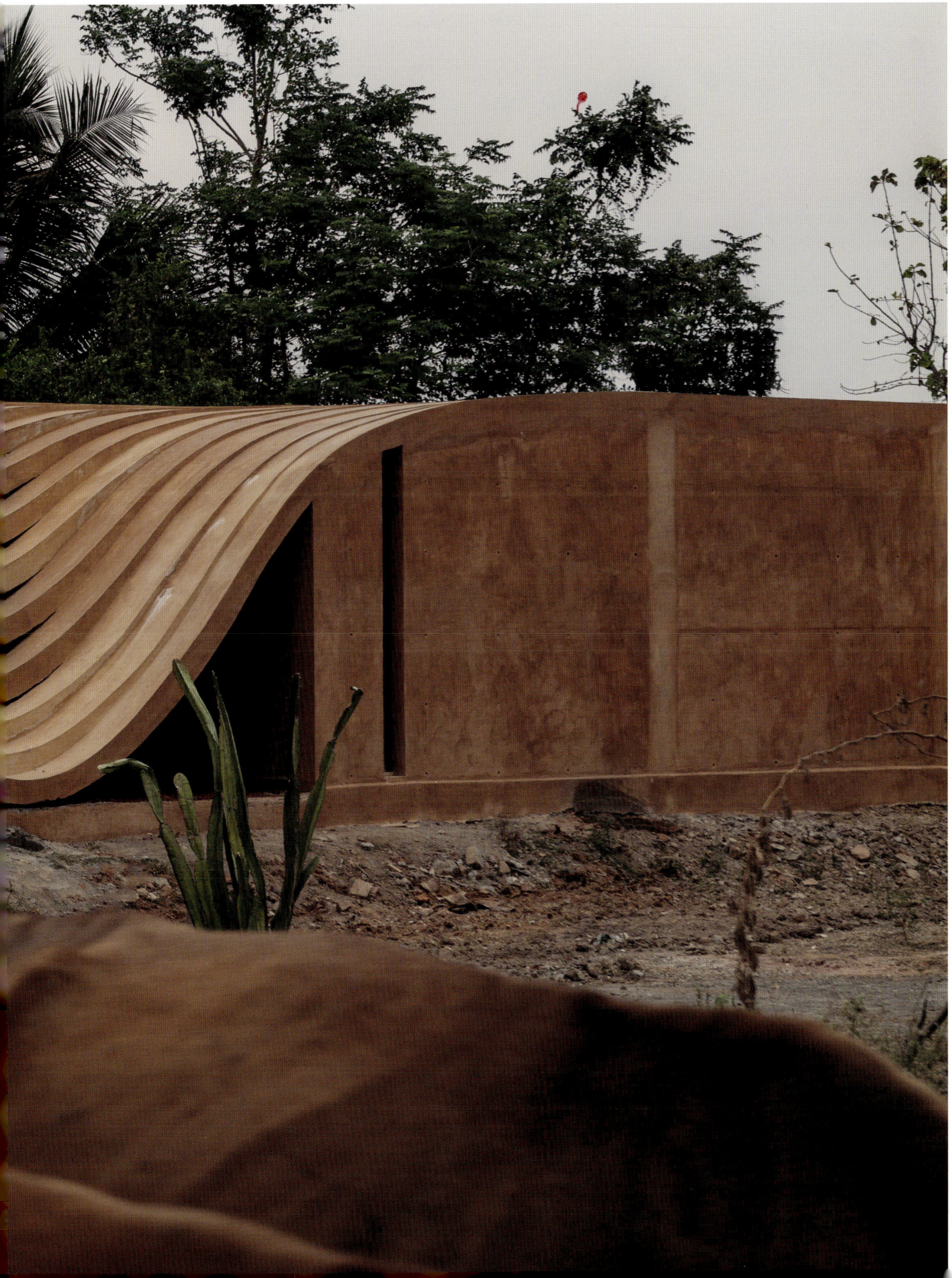

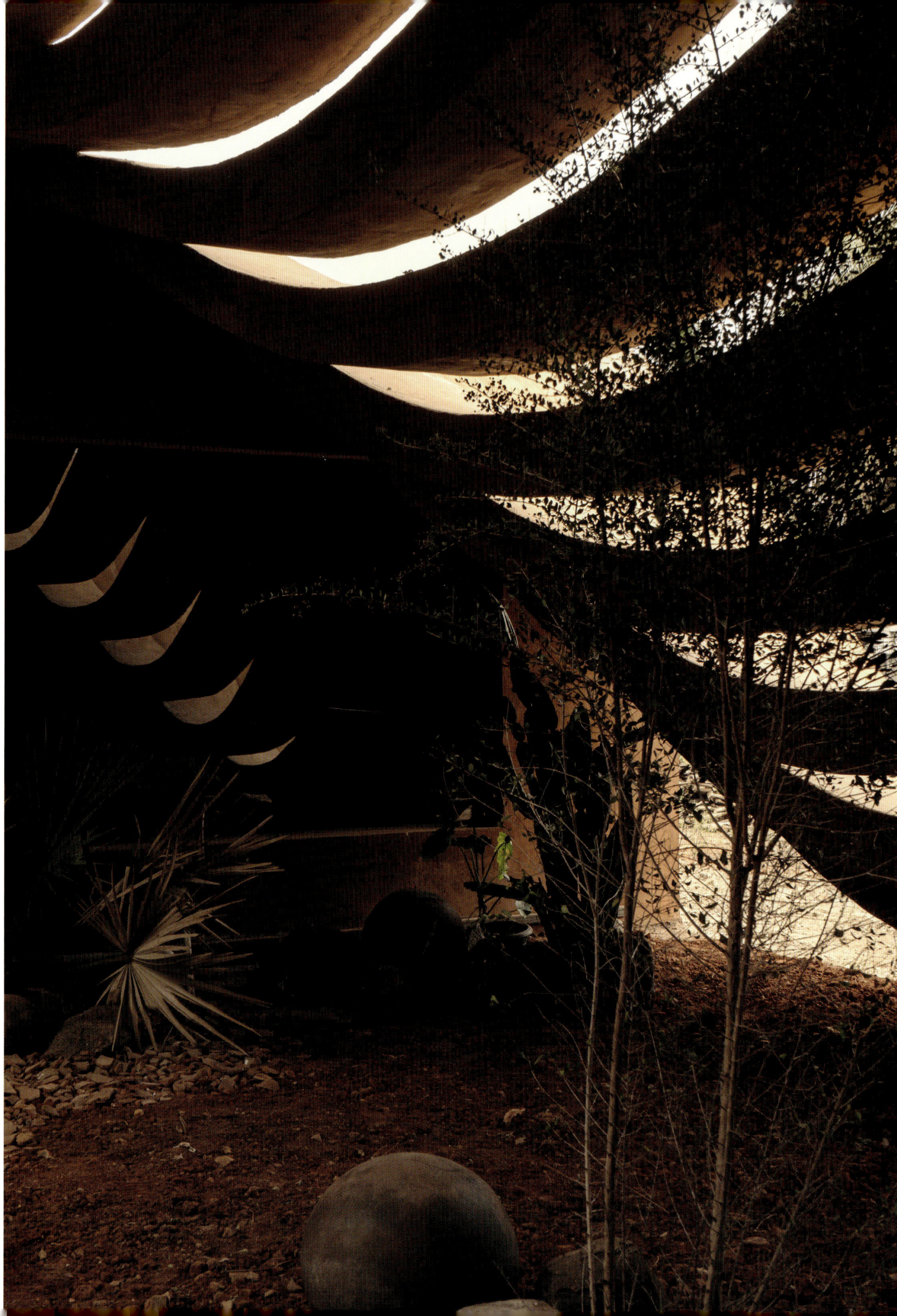

PROJECT: Vaazh House
LOCATION: Vedanthangal, Tamil Nadu, India
YEAR: 2024
ARCHITECTS: Vy architecture studio
PHOTOGRAPHY: Syam Sreesylam

The Vaazh House, in Vedanthangal, India, features one of the most remarkable patios ever. While it organizes all spaces around it, it also remains in visual relation with each of them, especially the living and dining areas, connected with the courtyard through a glazed wall. The dynamically curved cover of the courtyard is not merely a visually striking feature but also plays a functional role. In the first place, it protects against the strong rays of the sun, with sculptural perforations creating a beautiful play of light and shadow. The patio has been designed to draw hot air up and out of the living spaces, acting as a thermal chimney. During the monsoon season, it becomes a collection point for rainwater. On the exterior, this curved wall turns into a staircase leading to the roof, serving as a recreational outdoor space itself.

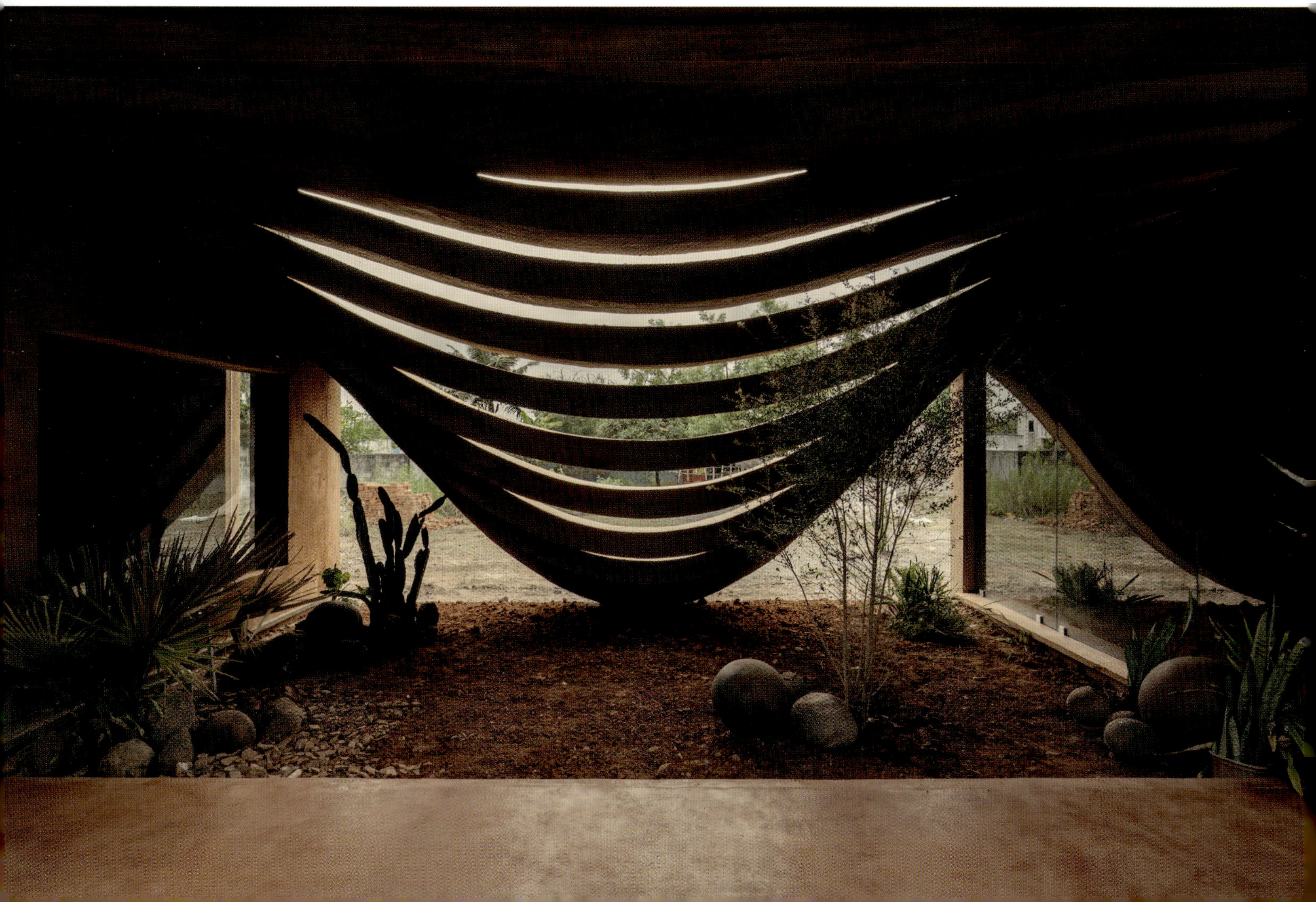

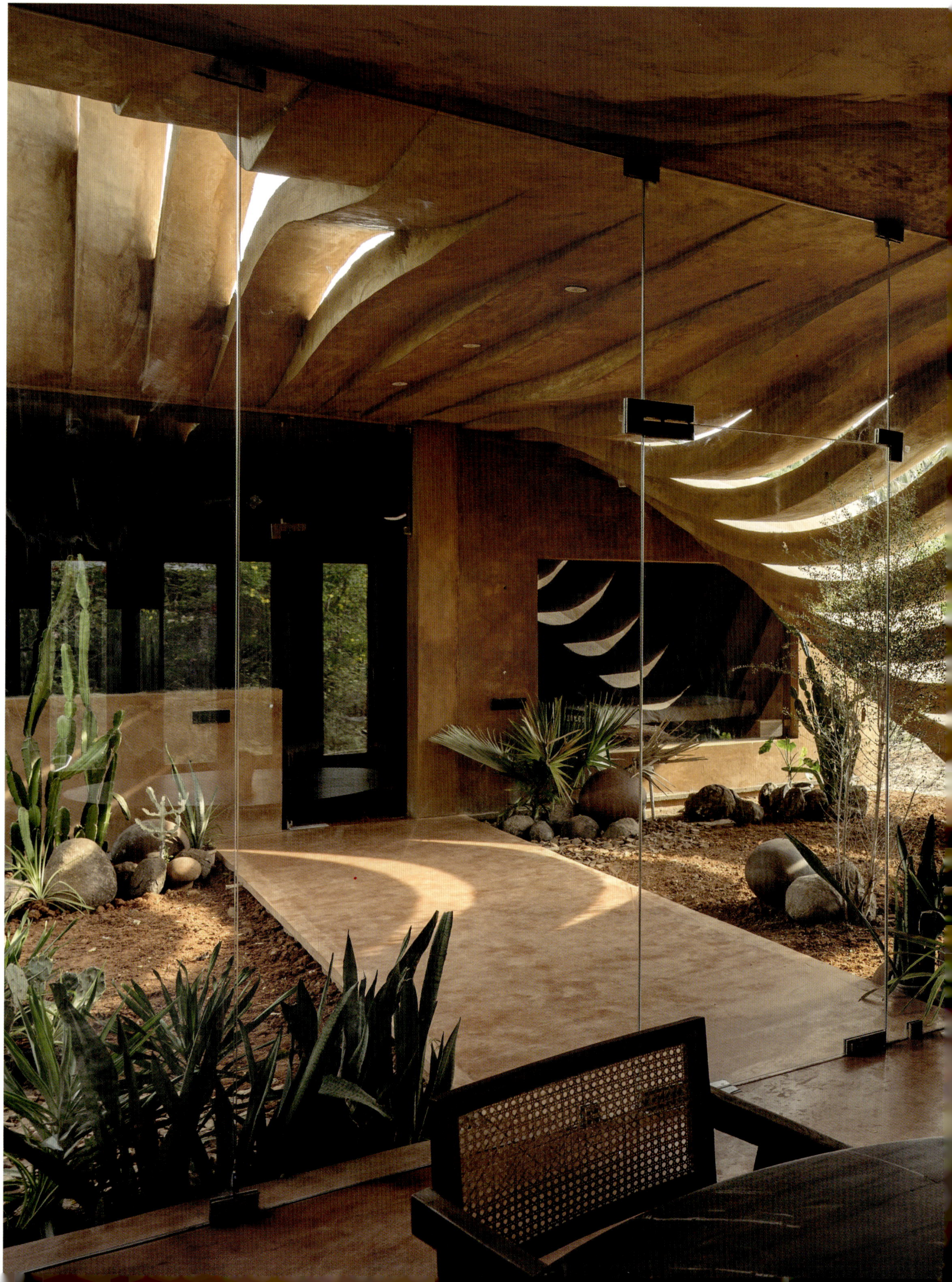

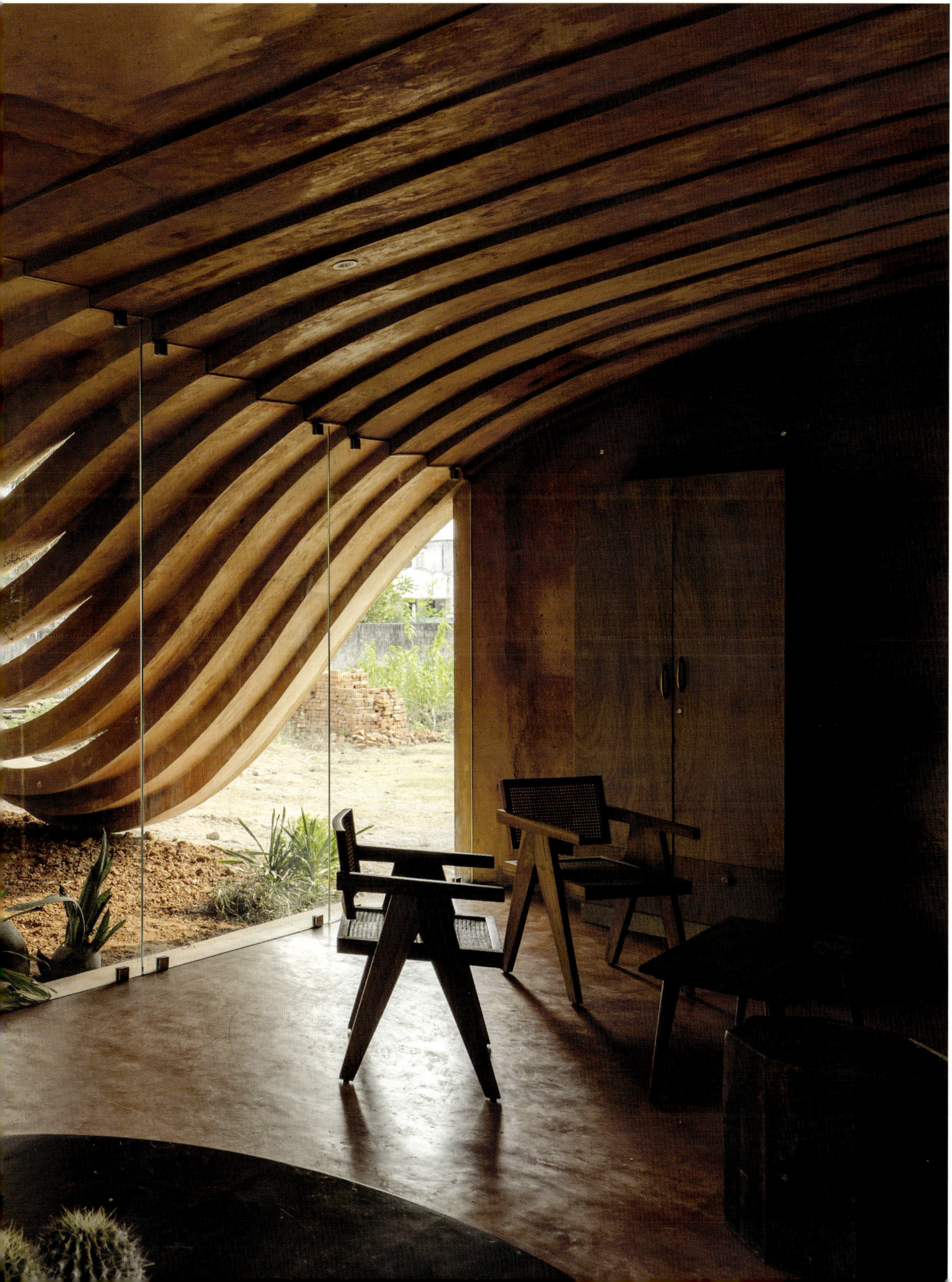

Carefully planned openings, facilitating cross-ventilation, fill the interiors with natural light, create a connection with the internal patio, and frame views of the landscape.

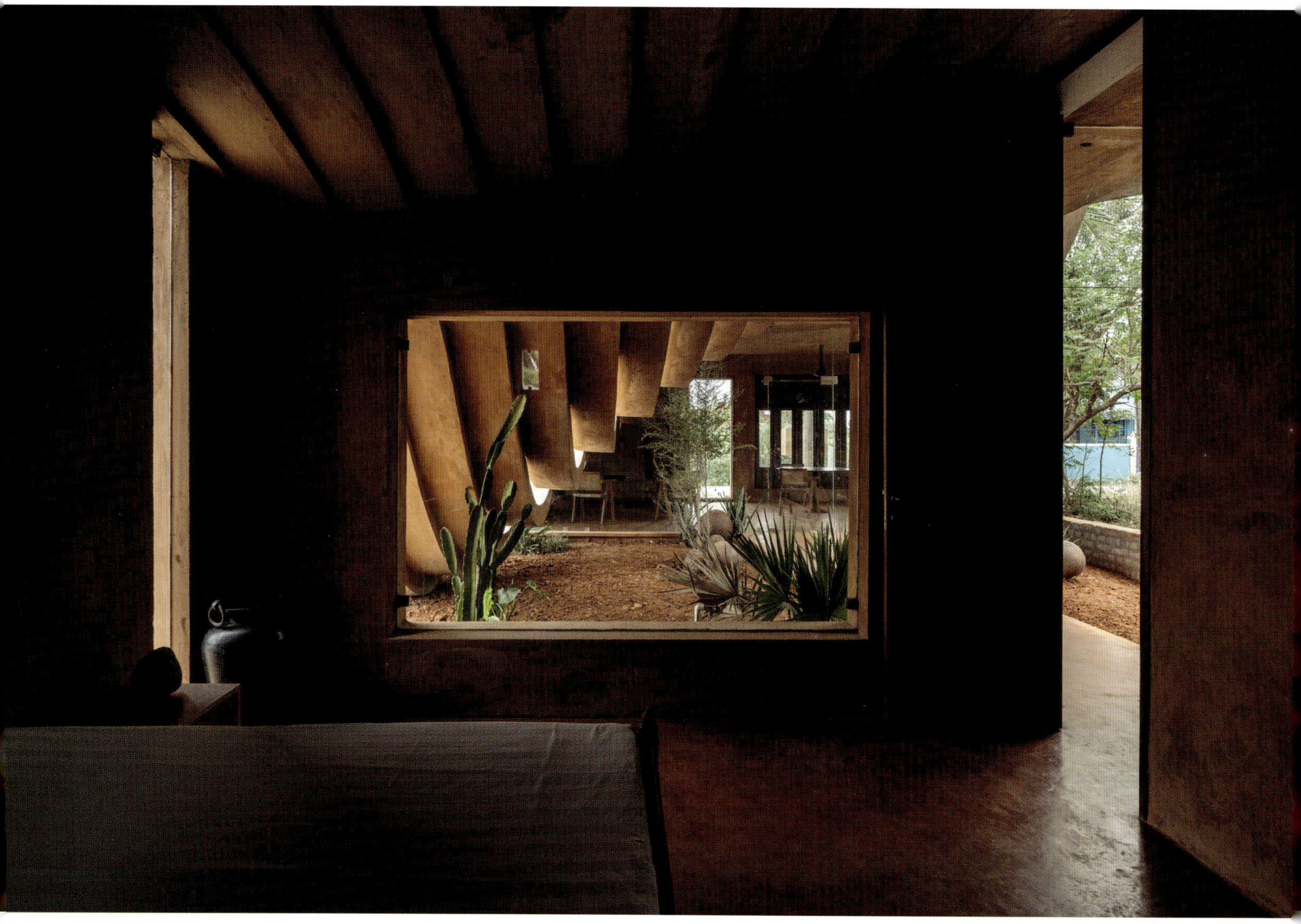

Vy architecture studio was established by AR Venkatesh and AR Yogalakshmi in Chennai and Mahindra World City. The core of the practice is eco-parametric architecture, focusing on innovative sustainable solutions in residential projects. While the main goal for the duo of principal architects is designing livable spaces with a minimal carbon footprint, their work is also visually captivating. "Our unique architectural language, which is simultaneously artistic, is an ode to the earth," the architects state.

Envisioned as a blend of urban lifestyle and rural serenity, the house takes on a modern shape, built with local mud and river rocks. The construction technique combines traditional mud architecture with modern structural systems, using compressed-earth blocks for the walls to enhance thermal mass and minimize the carbon footprint. Natural materials, mixed with vegetation planted on the patio and an earthy color palette in the interior design, create an atmospheric residence. In every aspect, the architects aimed to connect the inhabitants with the surrounding nature. The palette of hues and materials is part of this strategy, as well as making the roof an additional outdoor space for the residents to enjoy the vistas, watch birds, or stargaze.

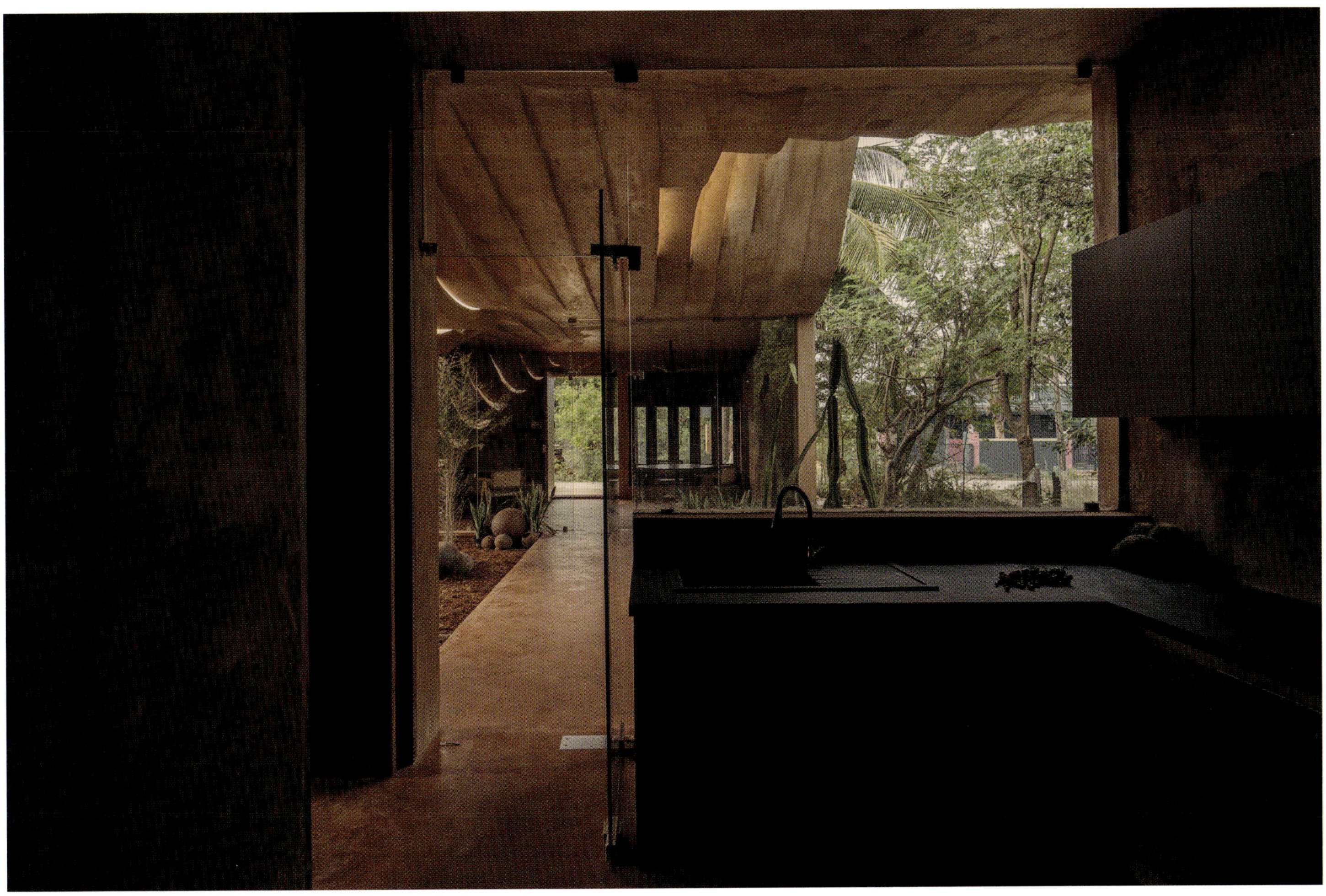

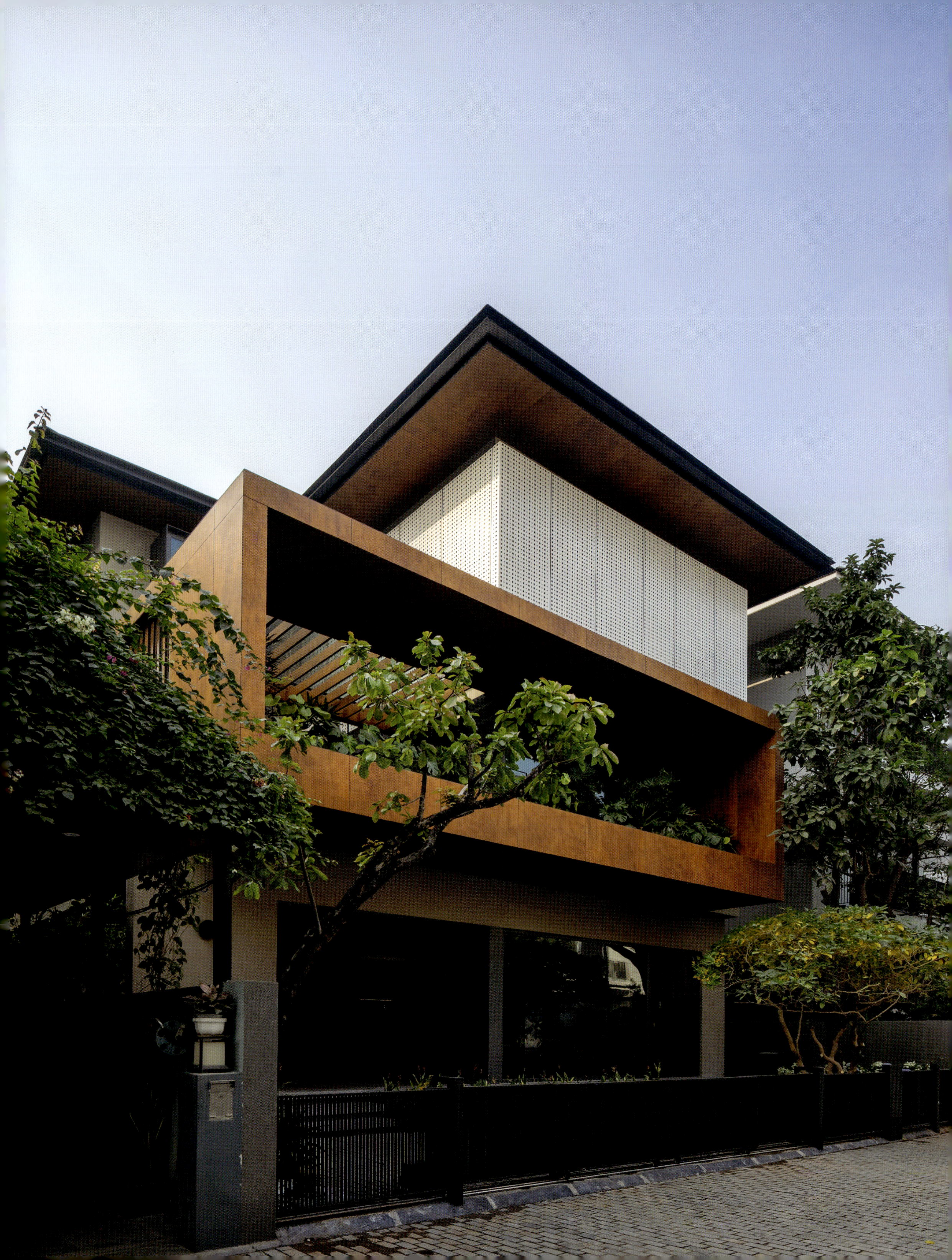

PROJECT: BT5 Villa
LOCATION: Lakeside Splendora, Hanoi, Vietnam
YEAR: 2024
ARCHITECTS: APDI Architecture
PHOTOGRAPHY: Trieu Chien

When envisioning the BT5 Villa, the team at APDI Architecture placed special emphasis on incorporating greenery into various outdoor spaces throughout the house, from patios and gardens to pathways and balconies. The presence of plants not only connects with nature but also reflects the stunning Lakeside Splendora neighborhood, where the house is surrounded by water features and natural landscapes. The standout feature is the landscaped rooftop garden, designed as a serene retreat. The architects maximized natural light by employing generous openings, which also aid in natural ventilation. The goal was to seamlessly integrate the surrounding landscape with the interiors, creating harmonious, minimalistic spaces that are open and vibrant.

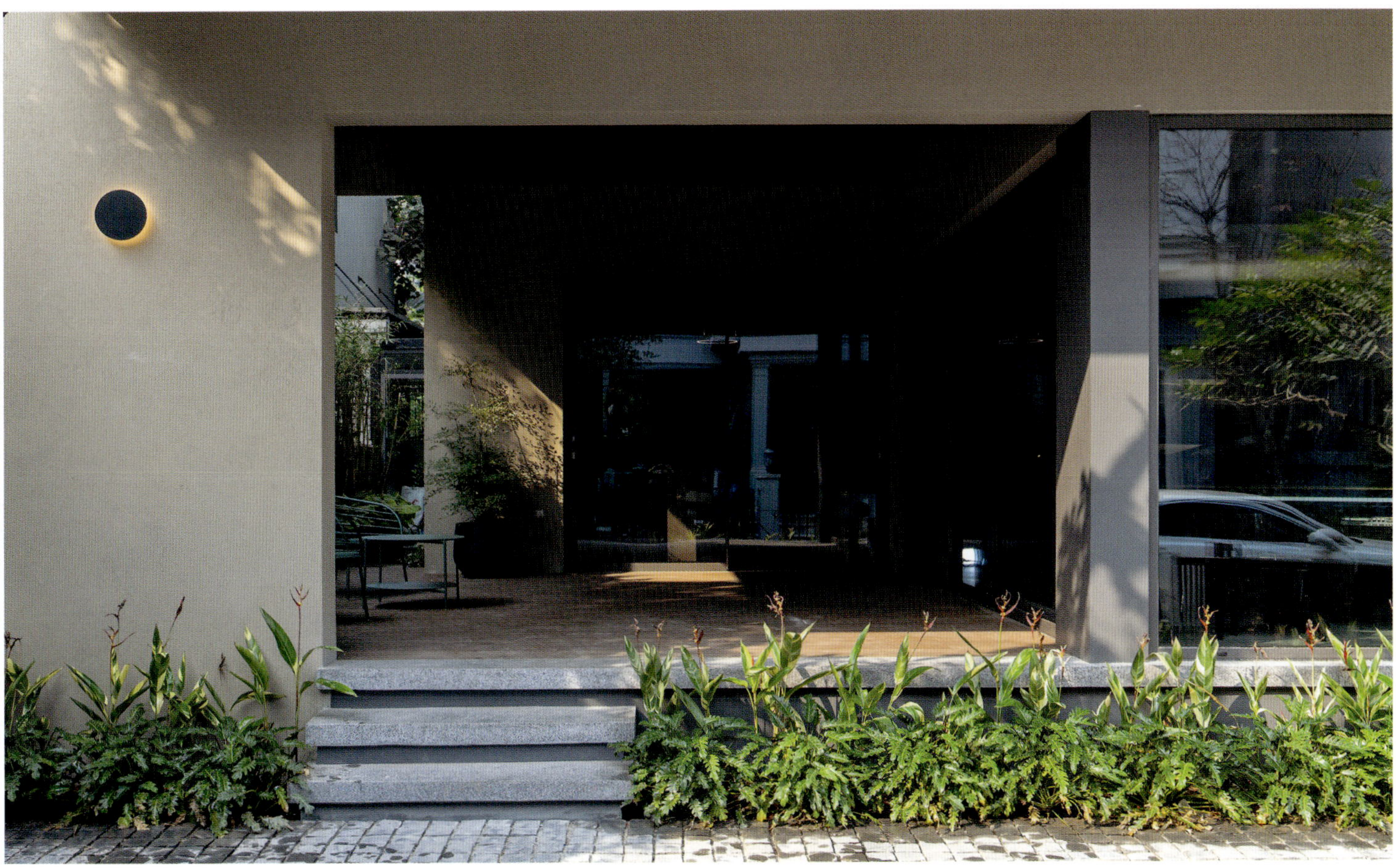

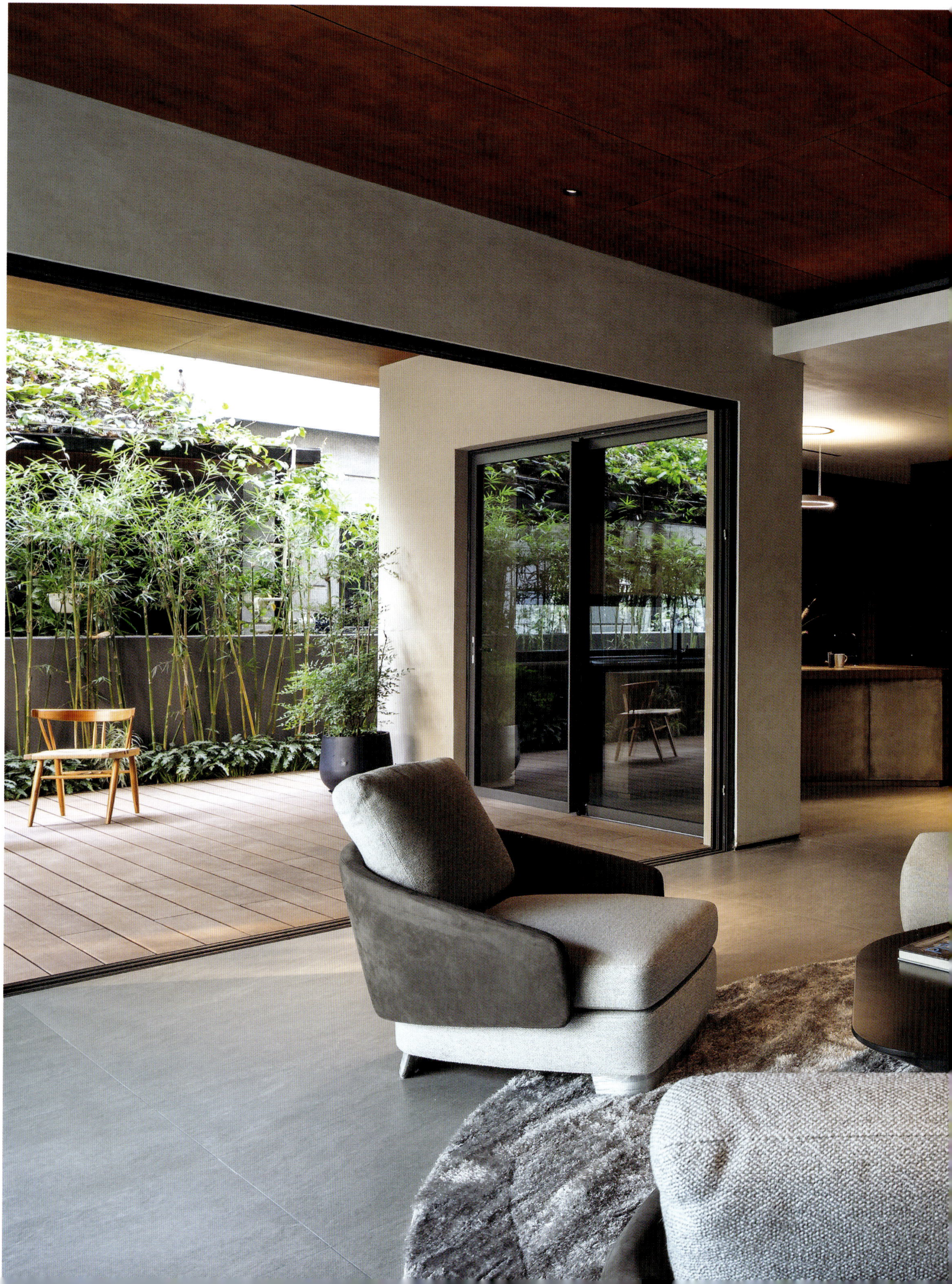

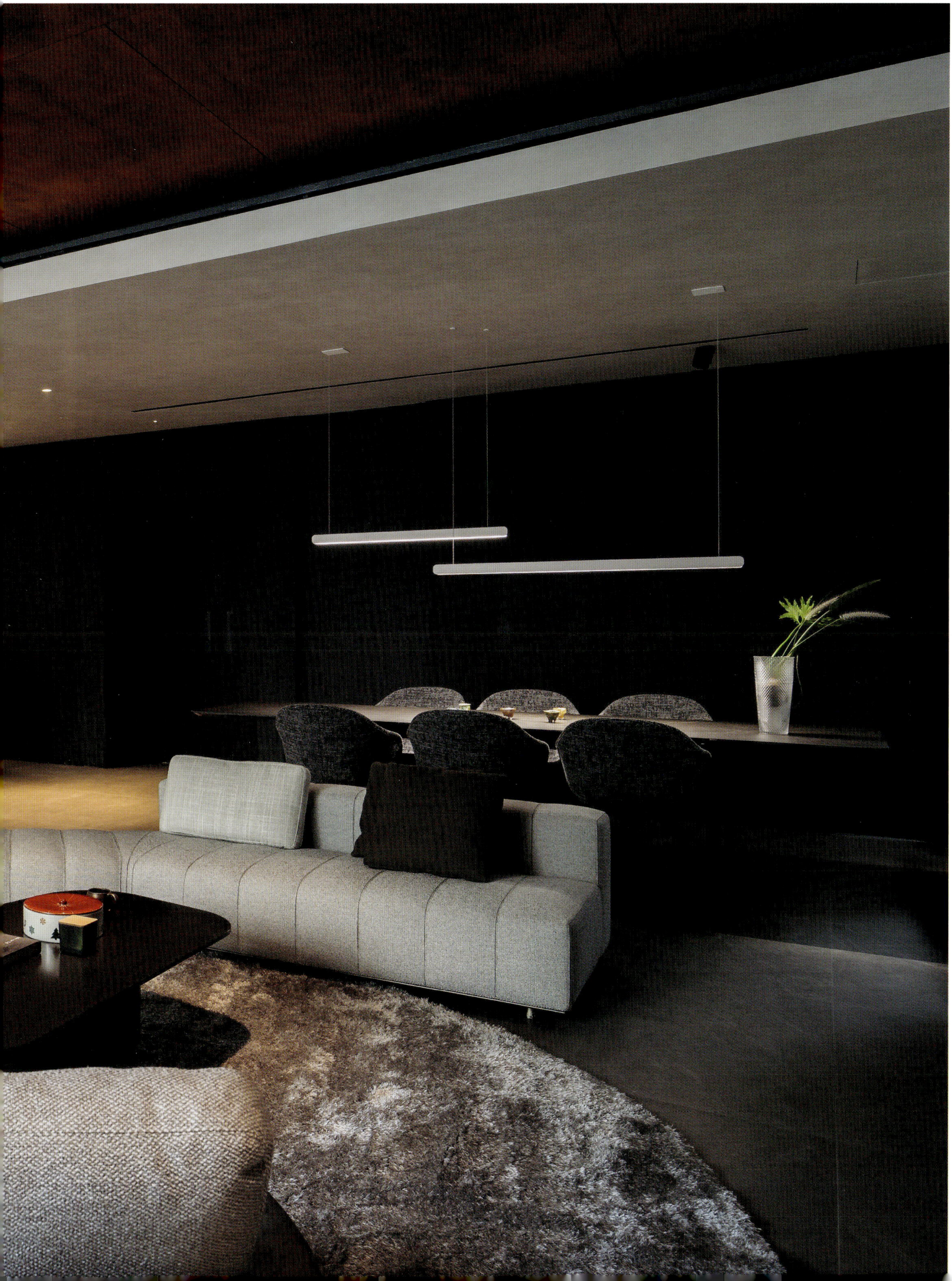

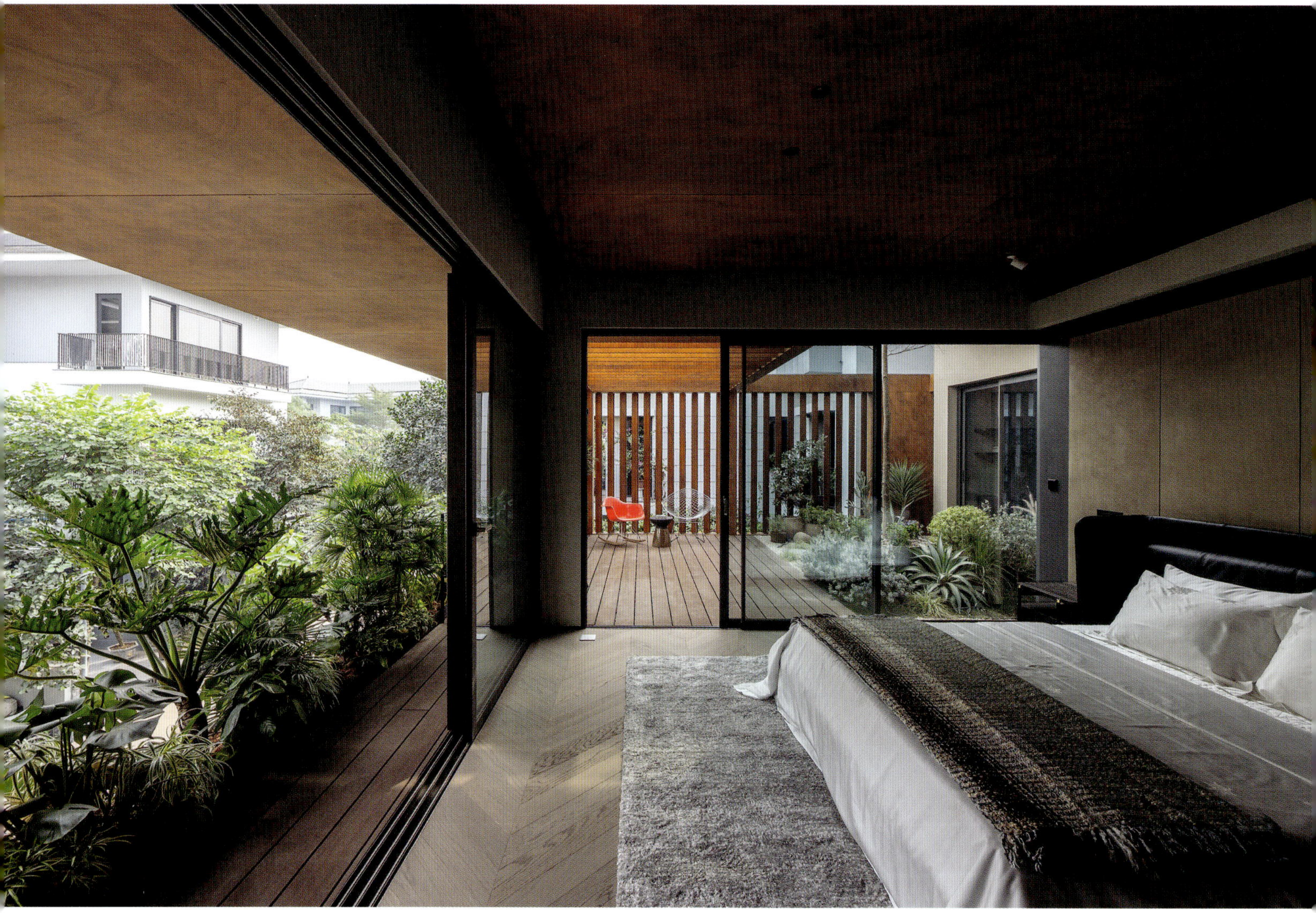

The objective was to design a house that offered comfortable living space while allowing the owner to express themselves. A professional in the audio and lighting field, and an architecture enthusiast, inspired a dedicated space on the third story featuring a multipurpose room with excellent soundproofing and optimized audio experience for watching movies, listening to music, and socializing. The house's layout provides unique spaces for all family members to enjoy and spend time together, such as the spacious and comfortable living room, connected to the dining and kitchen areas, opening onto a covered green patio. All private bedrooms are located on the second story, which leads to the atmospheric rooftop garden adorned with vegetation.

The architects have designed all outdoor spaces with a clear mission to create a closer connection with nature in the middle of a bustling city, visible in all parts of the house, including patios, pathways, and terraces.

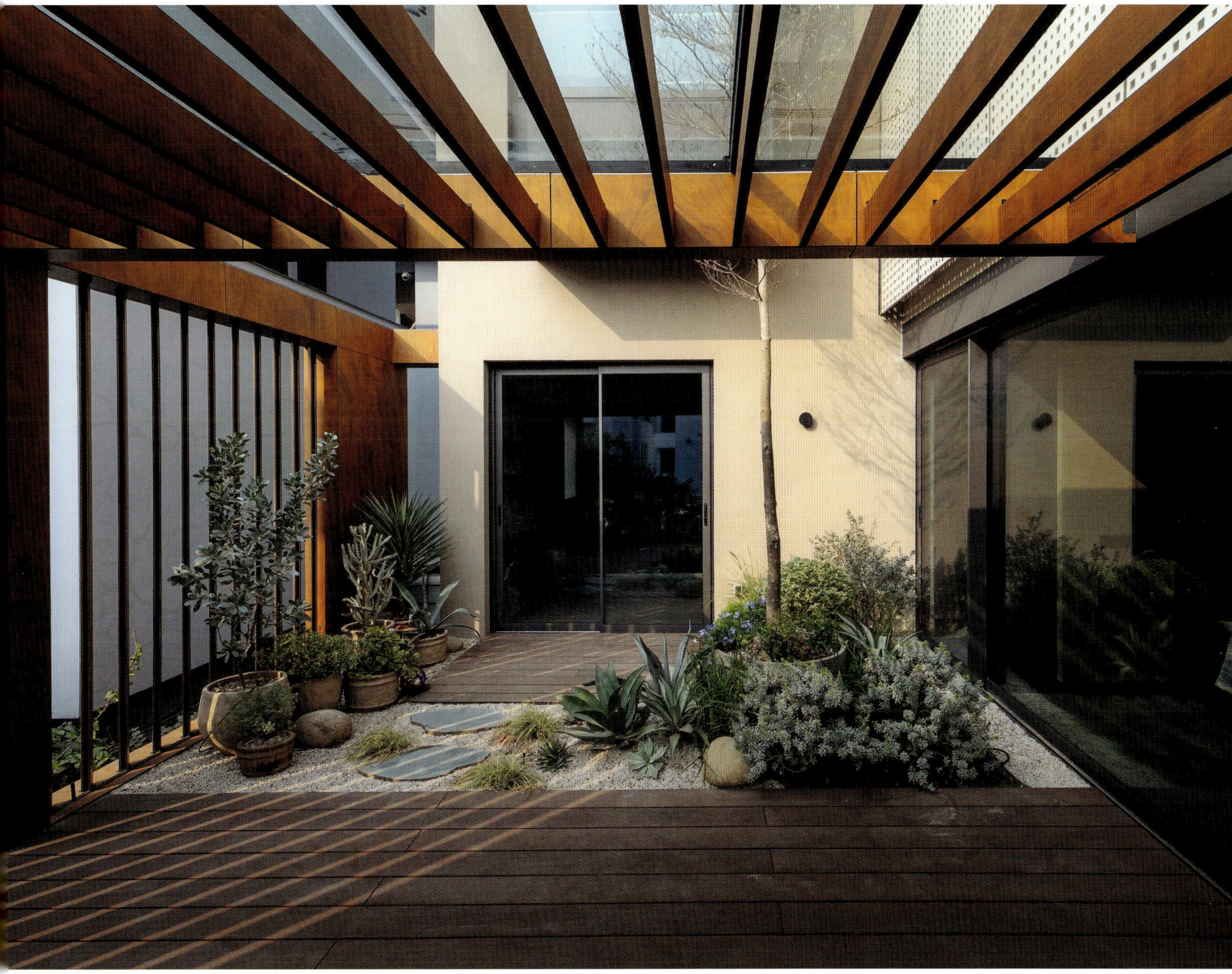

Hanoi-based APDI Architecture was established by architect Nham Chi Kien in 2015. The founder and his associates use their extensive experience in architecture, planning, landscaping, and interior design to envision innovative residential and hospitality buildings. All projects are carefully planned to intertwine aesthetics and functionality within optimal budgets. The primary goal is to employ energy-saving solutions and optimize the use of natural light to make each realization truly sustainable.

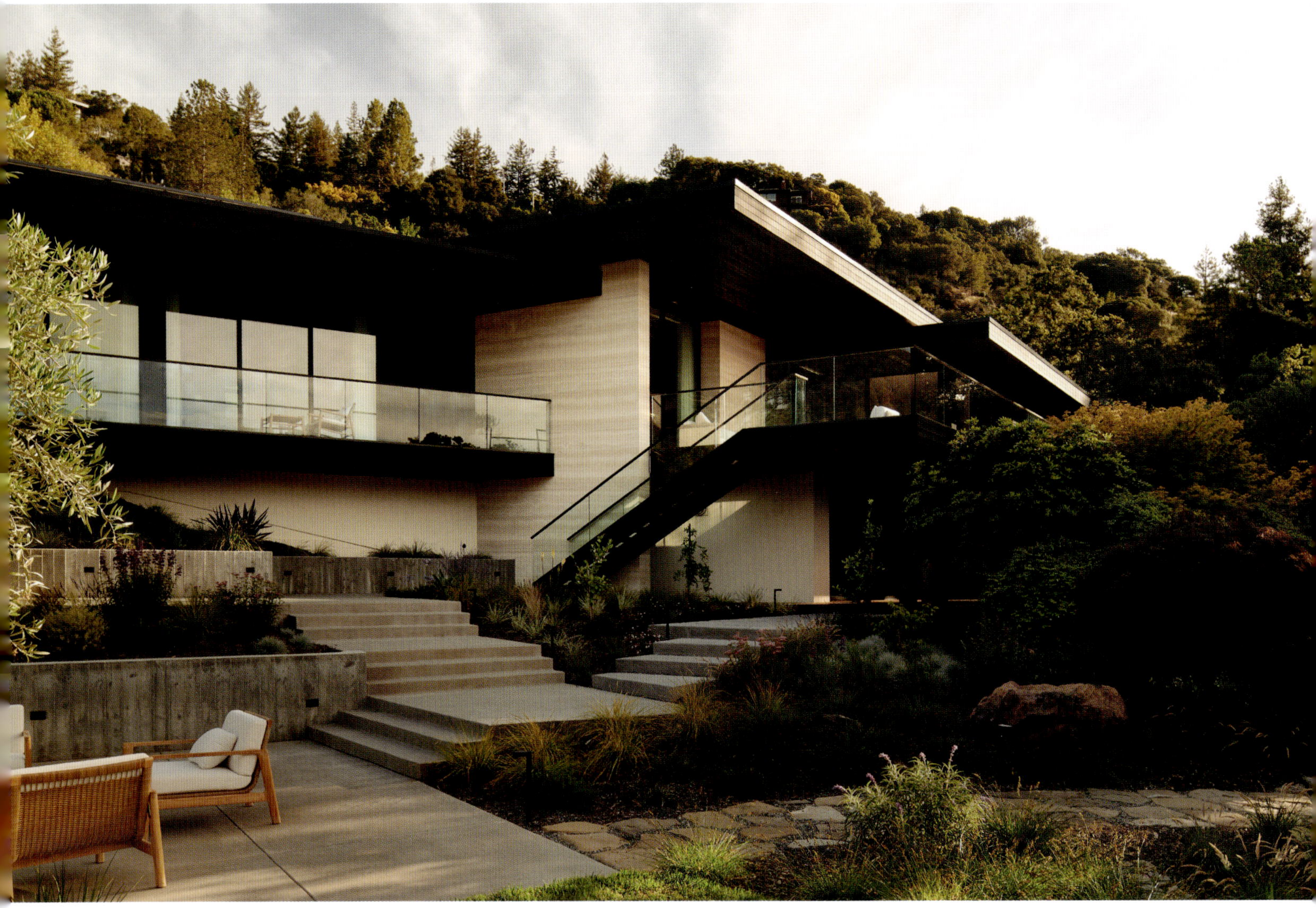

The connection with the surrounding nature is at the core of the project, with the visual relation unfolding in various parts of the house—from the entrance area, overlooking a koi pond, to the common spaces, enveloped by woodland trees on higher levels.

PROJECT: Kojima House
LOCATION: Kentfield, California, United States
YEAR: 2022
ARCHITECTS: Swatt + Partners
PHOTOGRAPHY: Nils Timm

As the inspiration for the design of the Kojima House, the architects of Swatt + Partners refer to the fusion of influences from the American Midwest and East and Southeast Asia. This extraordinary renovation and expansion of the house from the 1950s, realized for homeowners who spent two decades in Japan and Singapore, brought unique results. The house is located in the scenic landscape of the San Francisco Bay Area, and its sculptural structure has been divided into two volumes to separate private and common areas. The main objective was to harmonize architecture with the landscape and create, as the architects remark, a structure that poetically embraces the land. All this without compromising on the comfort, aesthetics, or quality to create well-lived-in spaces that stand the test of time.

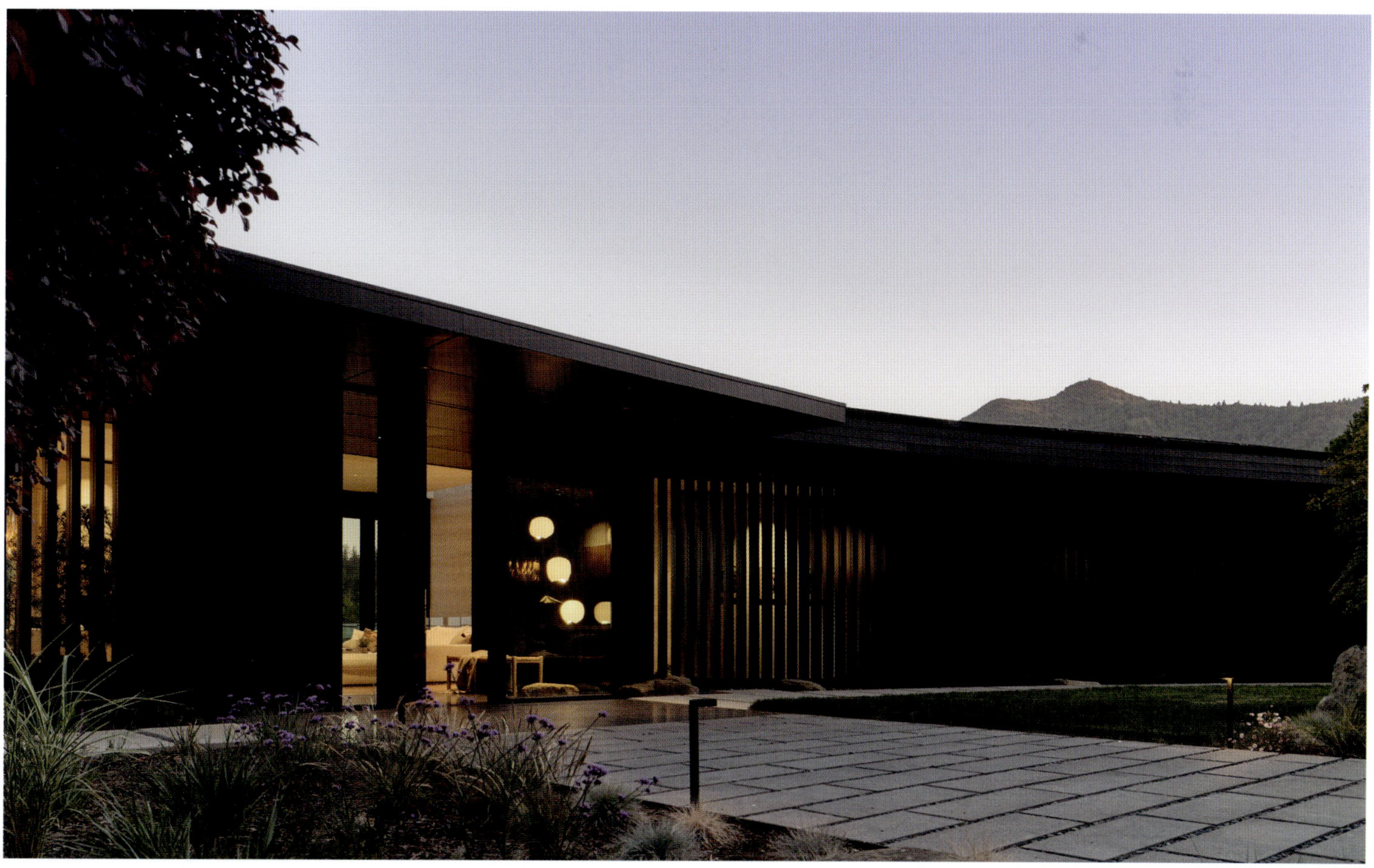

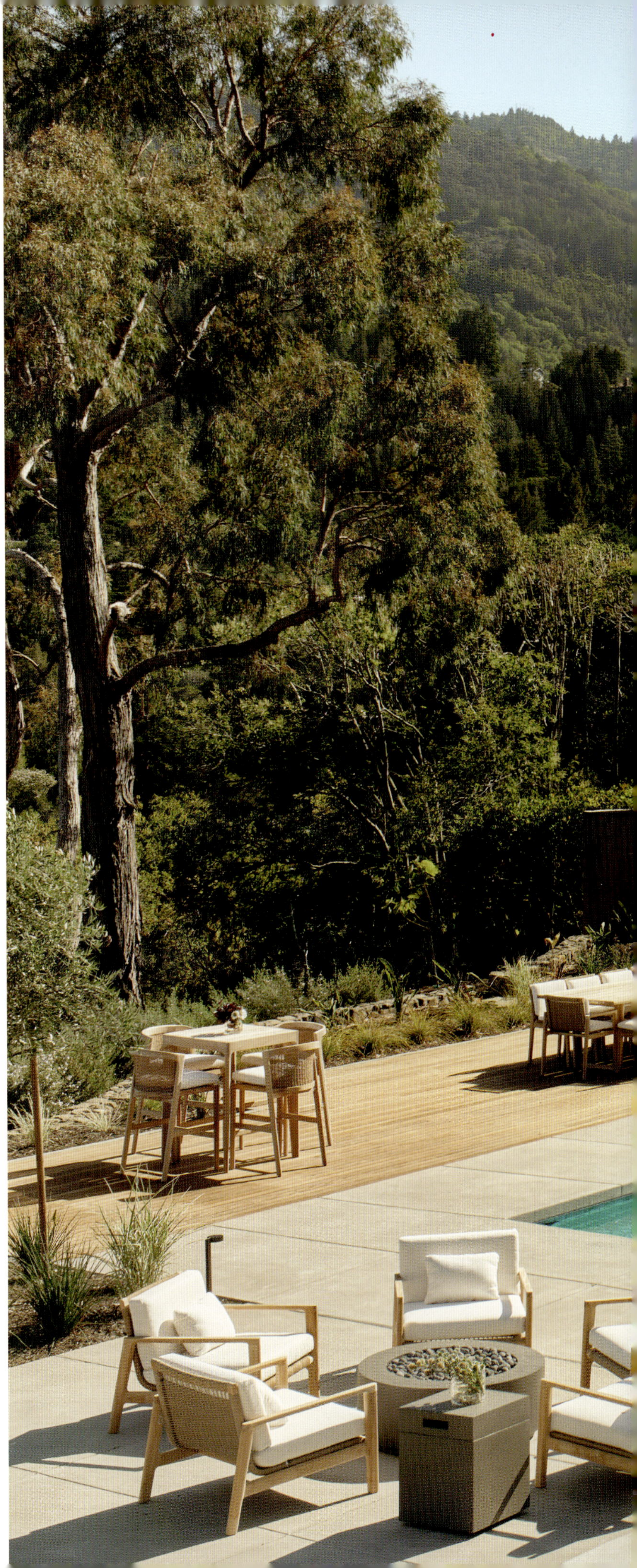

The spectacular back patio, with the pool nestled between the lush greenery and the sculptural volume of the house, is the highlight of common spaces and the ultimate relaxation spot.

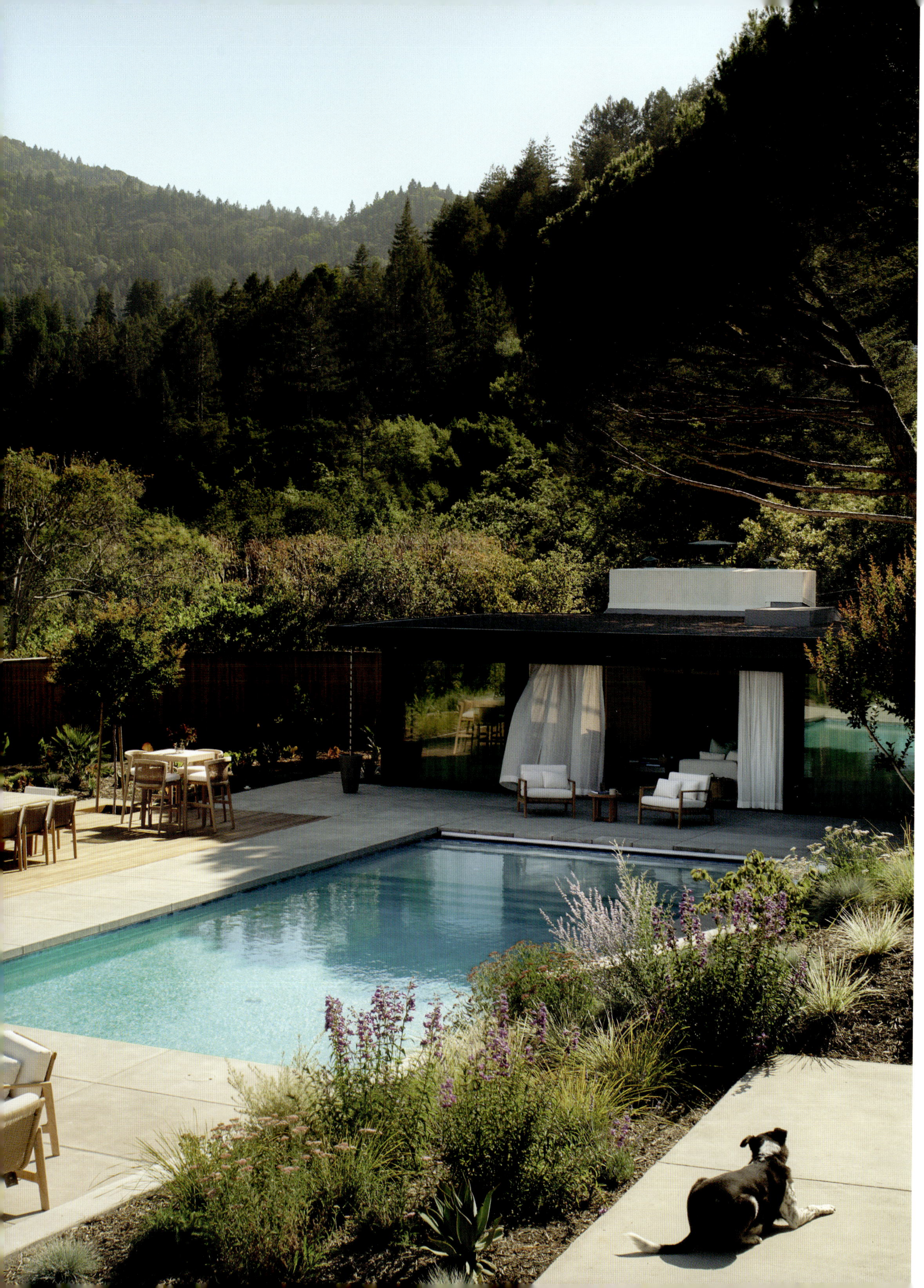

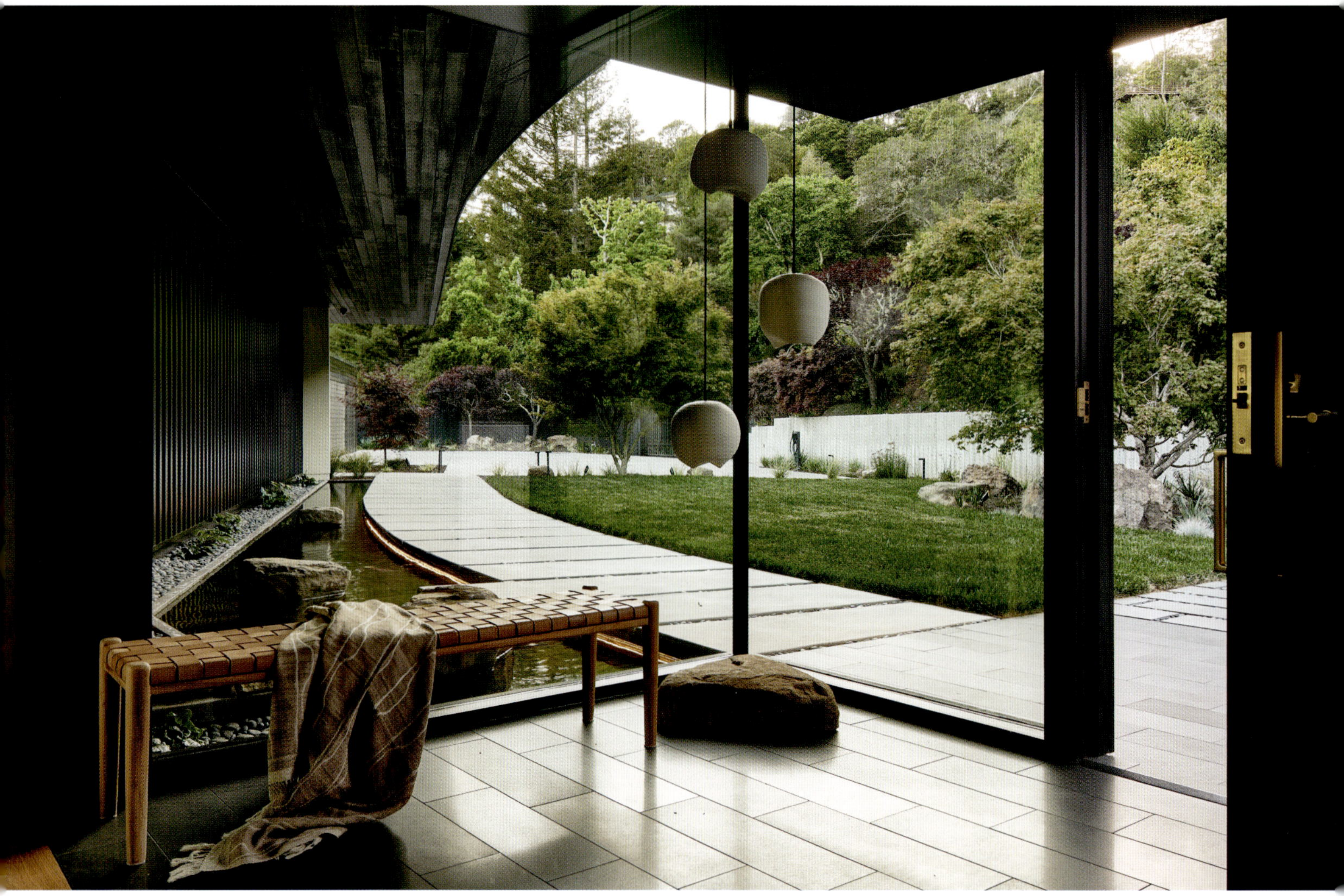

Swatt + Partners is an architectural practice based in the San Francisco Bay Area and specializing in envisioning one-of-a-kind homes throughout California, and in Colorado, Nebraska, Hawaii, Canada, India, and Spain. The firm was established by Robert Swatt and is run with partners Miya Muraki and Phoebe Wong-Oliveros, and the multidisciplinary team pays special attention to create designs that are carefully tailored to the topography of the sites, even the most challenging, in order to create special relations between architecture and nature.

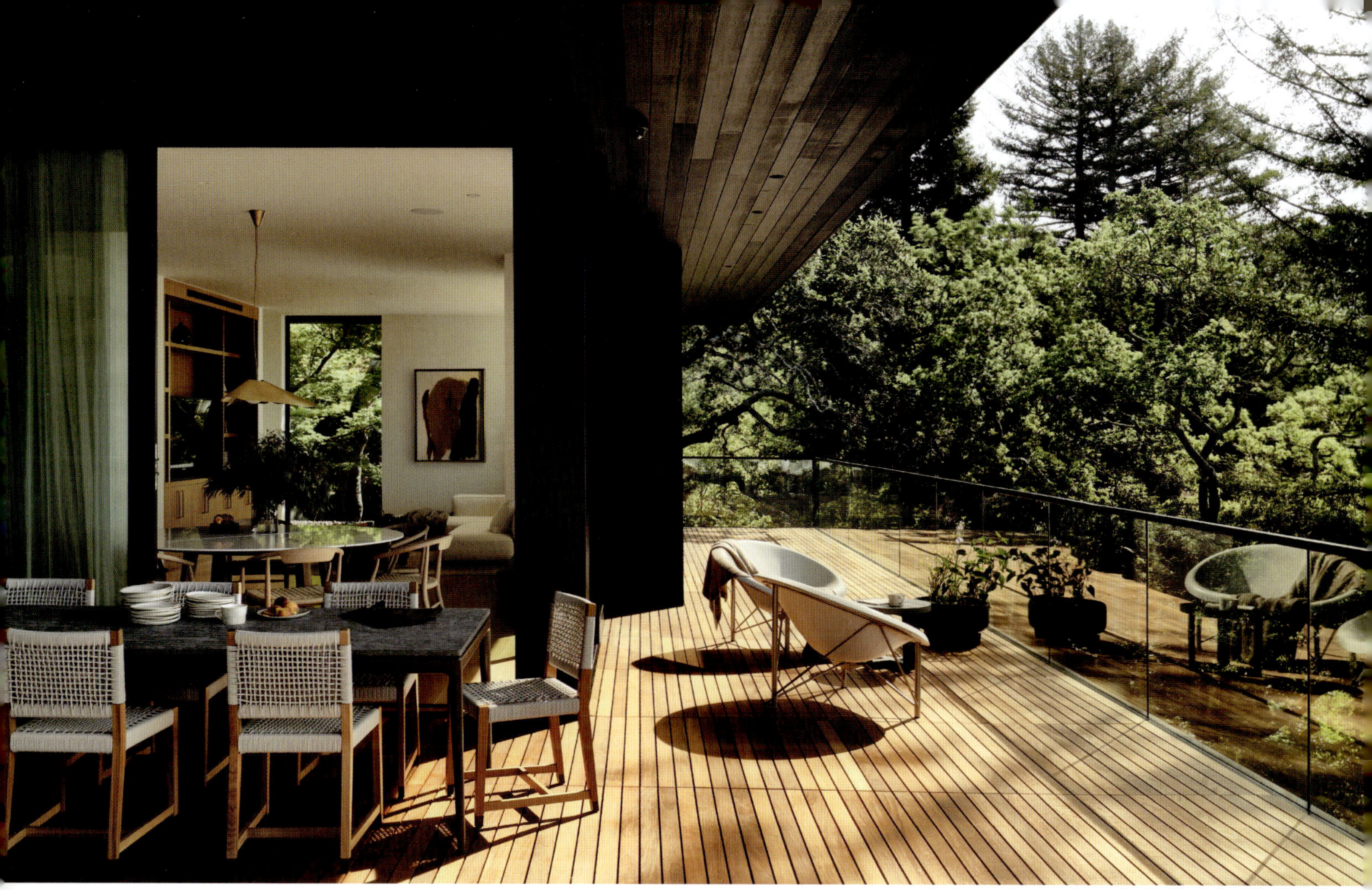

The Kojima House proves true the bold statement saying that "the studio goes beyond framing the views to ally structures with land, sea, and air." The architects have planned openings and numerous floor-to-ceiling glass walls to maximize the connection between outdoors and the interiors in various parts of the house. With the Kent-Woodlands valley to the south and with views of Mt. Tamalpais and the Marin Hills, the location creates a truly exceptional setting skillfully interwoven with architecture that is designed as a response to the natural characteristics of the land. From the entrance to the various levels of the facade overlooking the back patio, the relation with architecture is visibly at the core of the design. The culmination is the enormous patio nestled between the stunning vegetation and the house, with various zones for relaxation, eating, and socializing as well as the pool. The project was completed in collaboration with MOMO WONG DESIGN studio, responsible for the interior design, and landscape architect Huettl Landscape Architect.

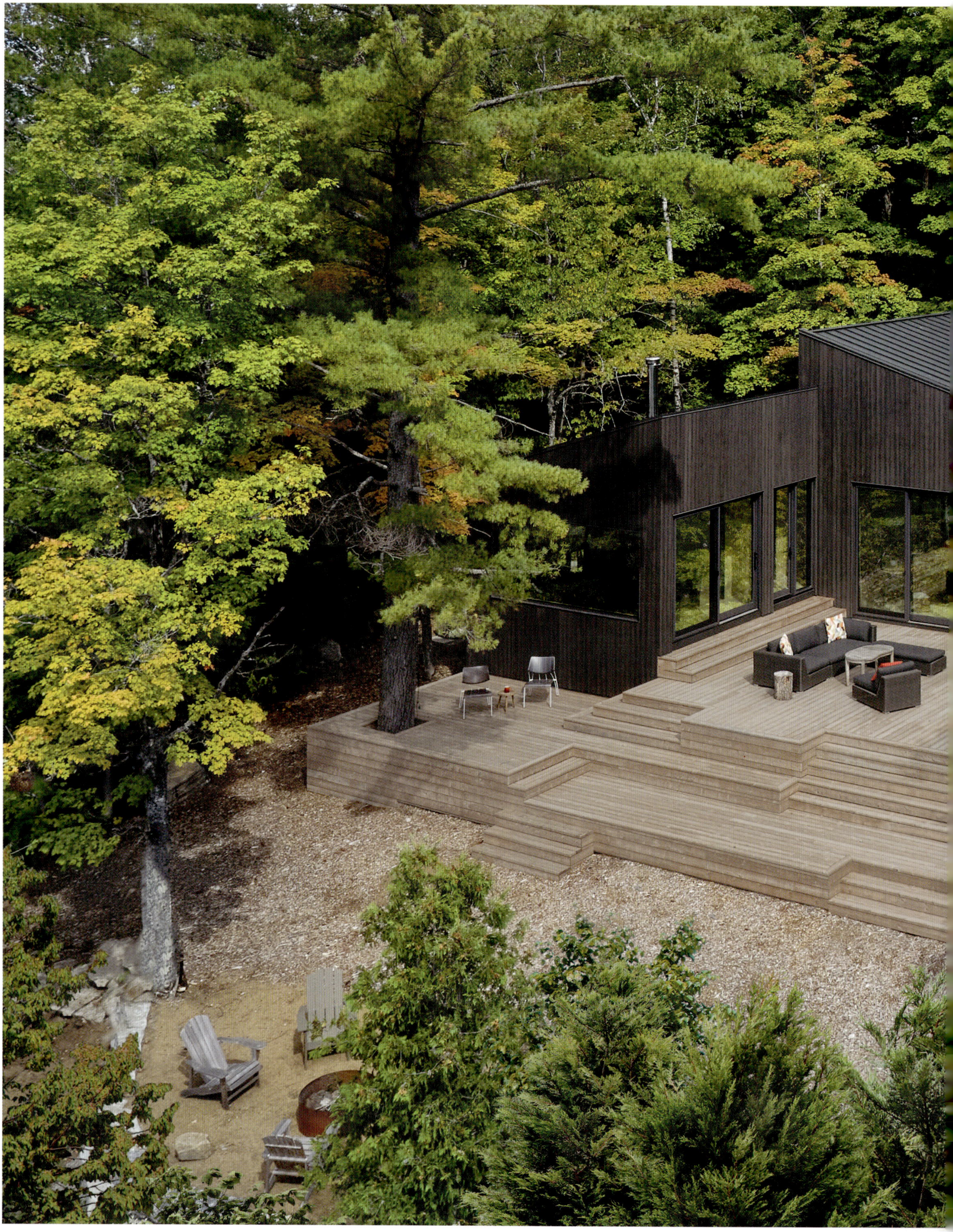

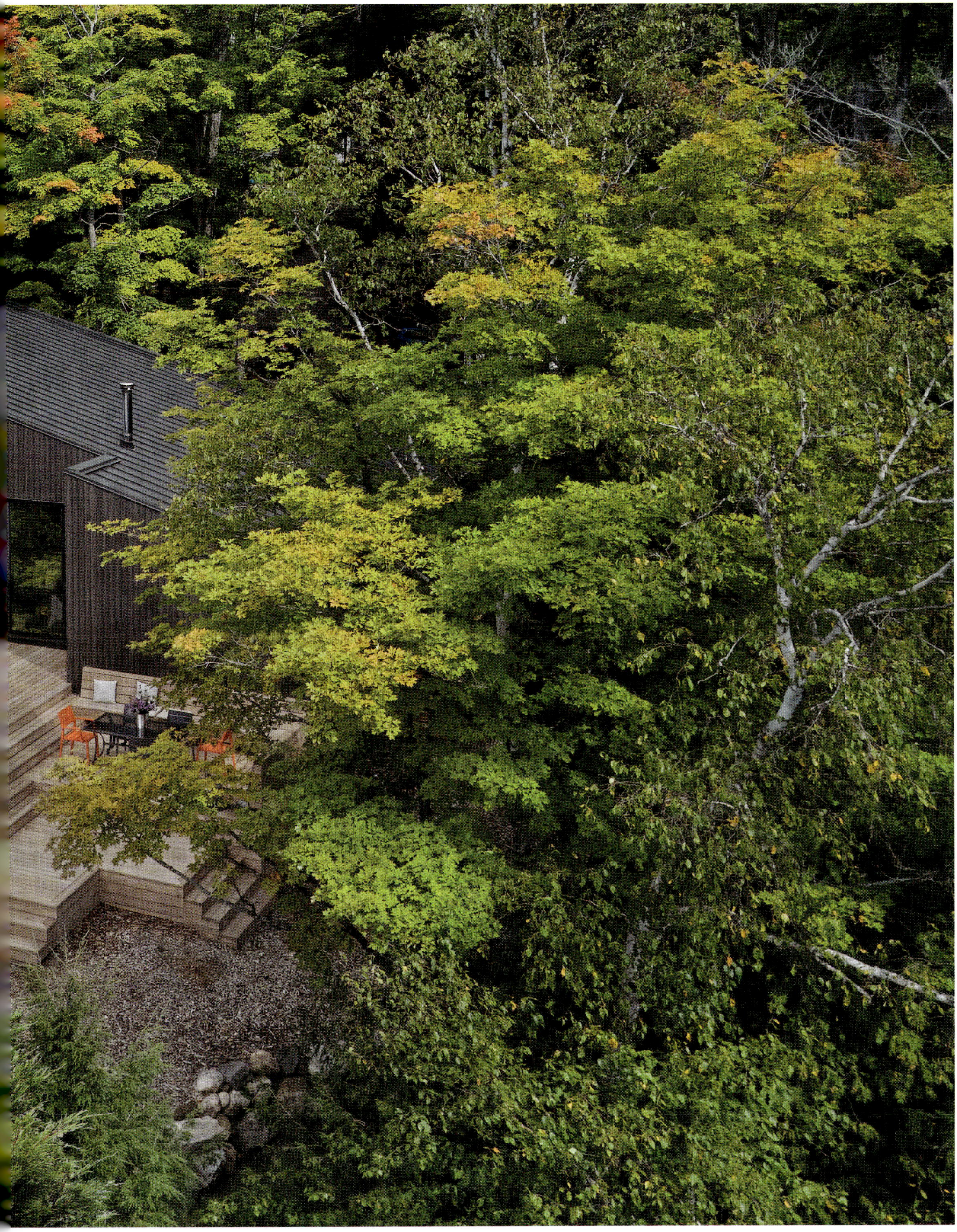

Founded by architect Heather Dubbeldam, Dubbeldam Architecture + Design is a multidisciplinary studio based in Ontario, Canada. The team focuses on designing residential and hospitality architecture and workspaces as well as interiors and landscapes. Their innovative and holistic approach is based on ongoing research into progressive sustainable design. "We believe in the transformative power of high-quality design to enrich people's lives," the team states.

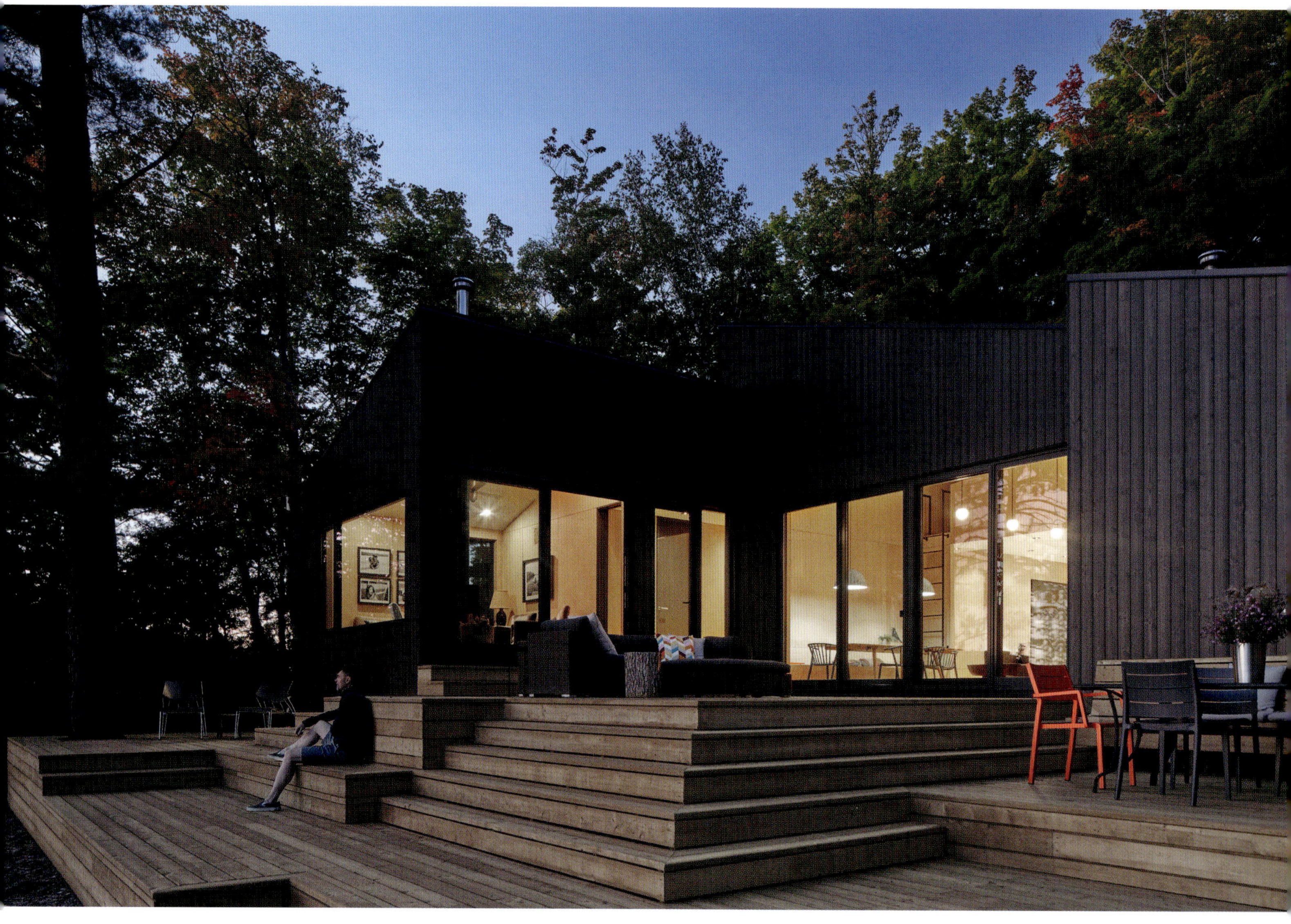

The terraced deck meets various volumes of the cottage while providing a spacious area for outdoor relaxation. It also acts as a transition between the built and natural environments, adjusting to the site's topography as it leads toward the lakeshore.

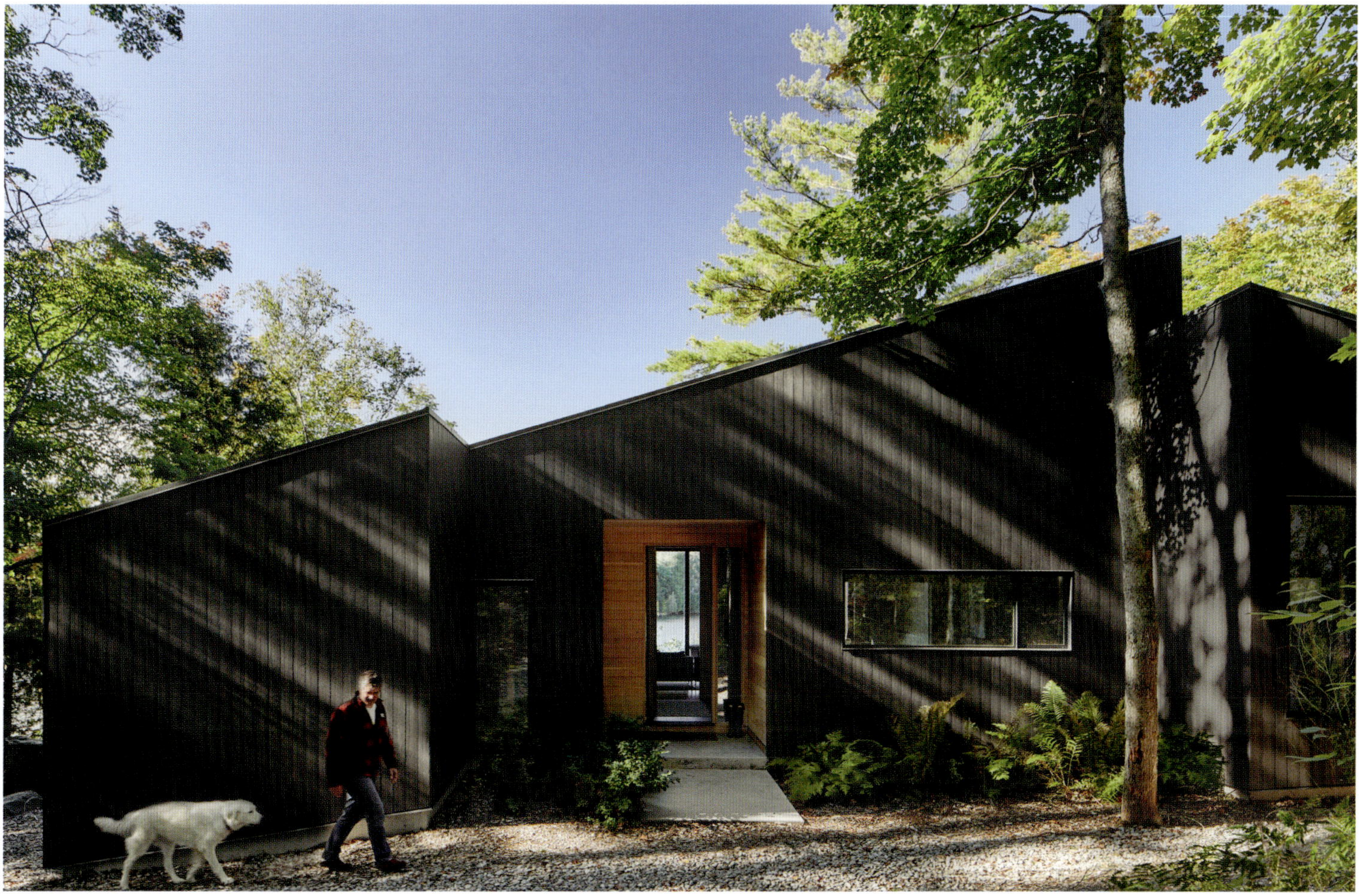

PROJECT: Catchacoma Cottage
LOCATION: The Kawarthas, Ontario, Canada
YEAR: 2023
ARCHITECTS: Dubbeldam Architecture + Design
PHOTOGRAPHY: Riley Snelling

Located in an extraordinary spot with a scenic view over Lake Catchacoma, this four-season cottage has been designed for an extended family of three generations. The house, which replaced a previous structure within an opening of a dense forest, blends into the context with its one-level volume, which has been divided into three dynamically juxtaposed parts. The living area in the center is enveloped by the main and guest bedroom wings. The common space for all of them is the semisheltered deck, with separate relaxation and eating areas that merge gently through cascades of stairs with the water's edge. Enveloped cozily by the trees, all of which have been preserved, the retreat is visible mainly from the lake. This relation to the surrounding is highlighted by the walls of both facades—more solid on the entrance side and generously glazed on the one facing the water.

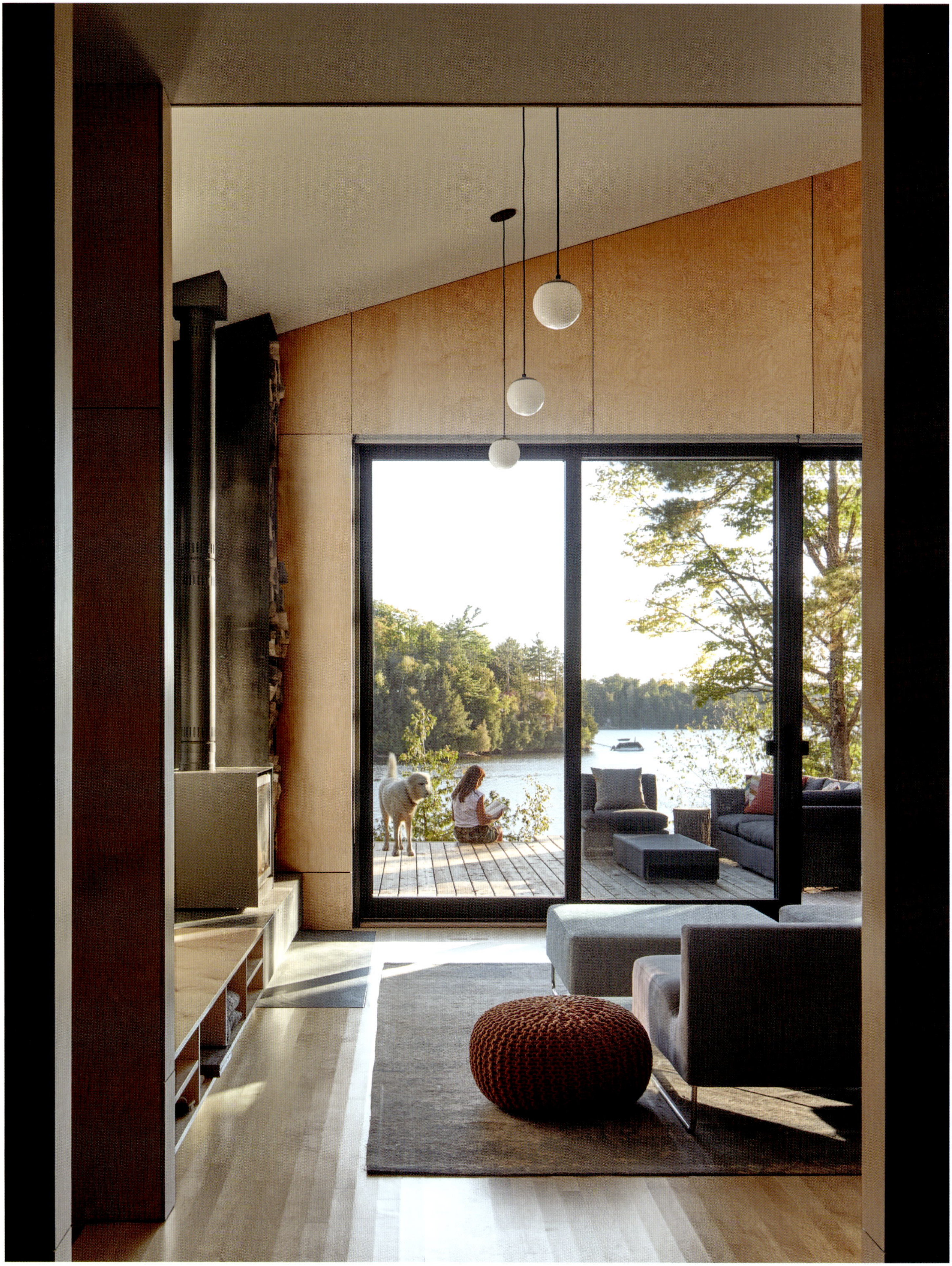

Maximizing the visual connection with the surrounding environment was the architects' main goal. This begins at the entrance to the cottage, where the perspective of the deck and the lake is revealed through expansively glazed sliding doors in the central living area. The openings in other parts of the house have also been planned to frame the views and integrate nature with the interiors. These spaces have been designed with natural materials and a neutral color palette, further blurring the boundaries between inside and outside. The courtyard created between the house and the lakeshore on the multilevel deck is the heart of the house and the point where architecture meets the landscape. Through the arrangement of the volumes, the steeply sloped roofs, and the use of wood in the structure, the cottage blends into the surrounding environment.

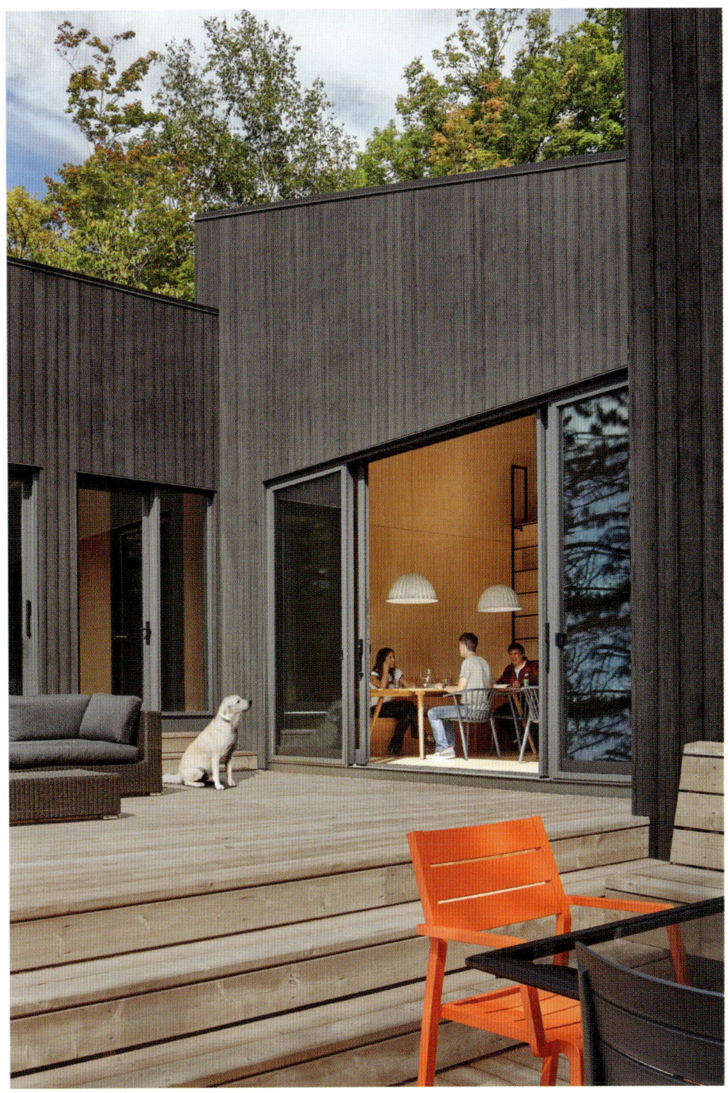

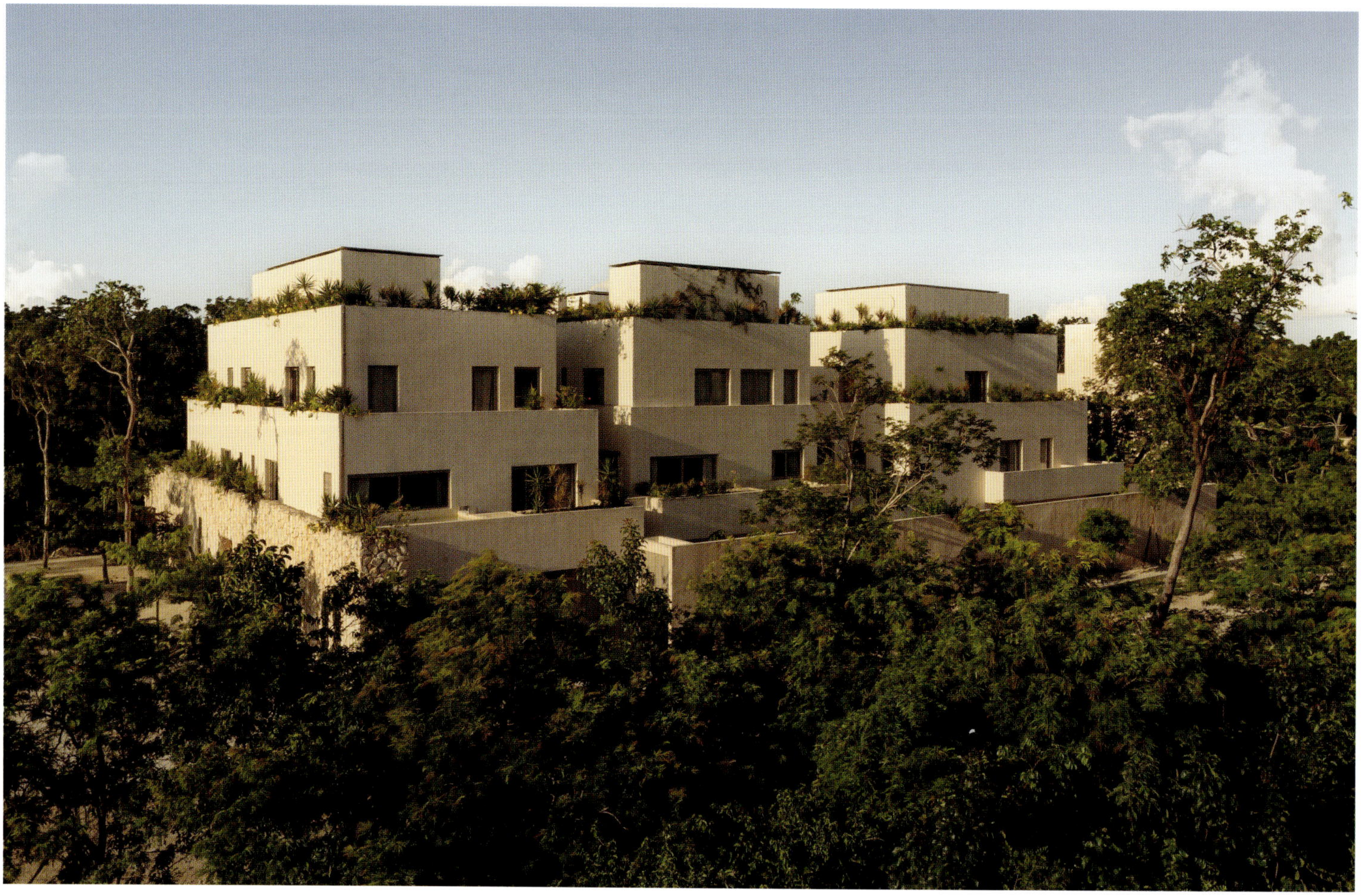

PROJECT: Hacienda Wabi
LOCATION: Tulum, Quintana Roo, Mexico
YEAR: 2023
ARCHITECTS: RA!
PHOTOGRAPHY: Ariadna Polo, Christian Velasco

Hacienda Wabi, nicknamed "a residential complex in the jungle," is an excellent example of how patios can bring life to a multifamily house. Nestled in the lush natural surroundings, the hacienda was designed by RA! and developed by a Tulum-based developer, Namus, as an intriguing combination of volumes intertwined with numerous outdoor spaces in the form of inner courtyards and terraces. "Its design draws inspiration from the aesthetics of ruins to reinterpret the passage of time and evoke the ancient settlements that once occupied the region," explain the architects. The omnipresence of vegetation across the stepped building was essential in creating a visual connection with the pristine landscape. The playful configuration of volumes overgrown with plants was employed to gain natural light and enable cross-ventilation in each unit.

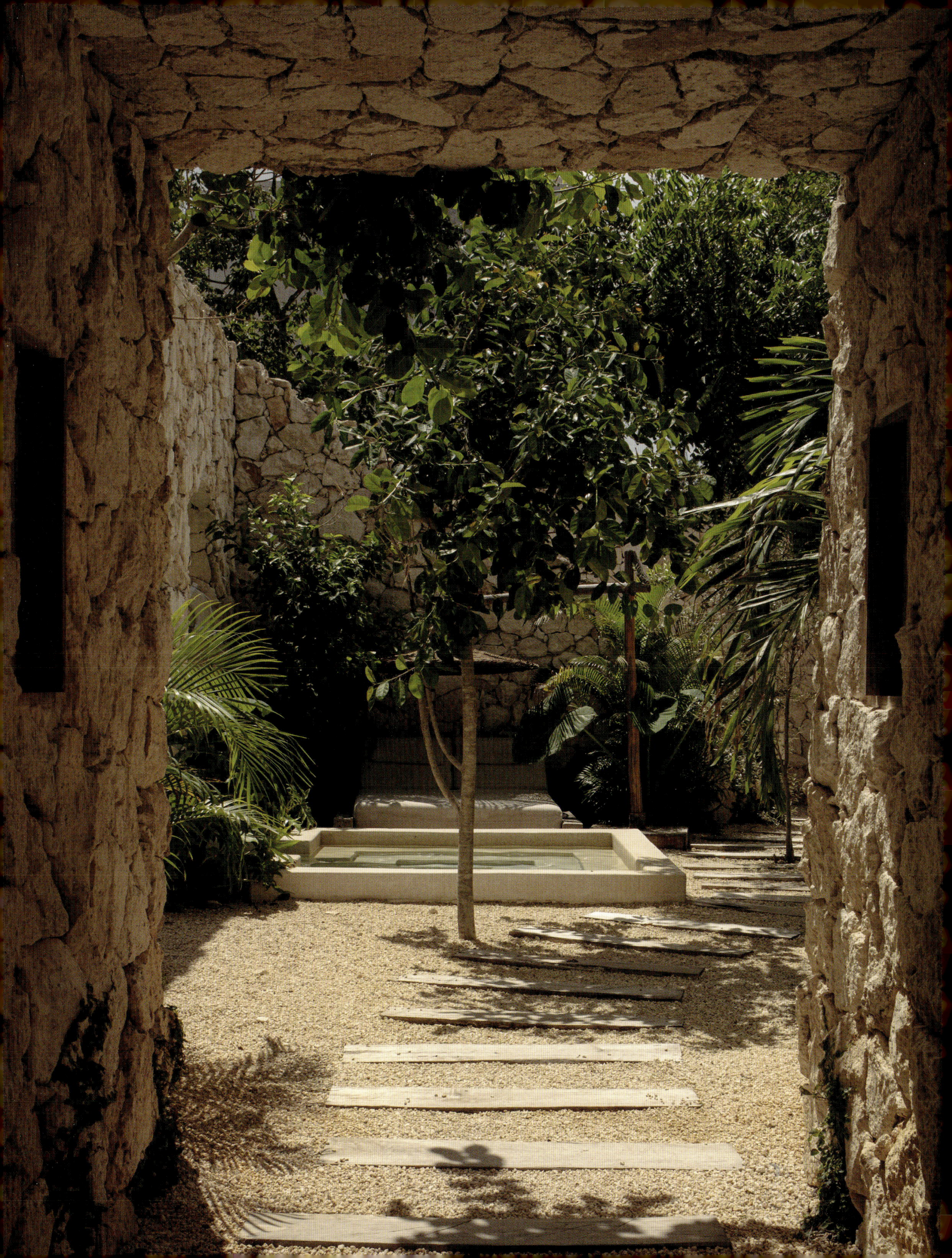

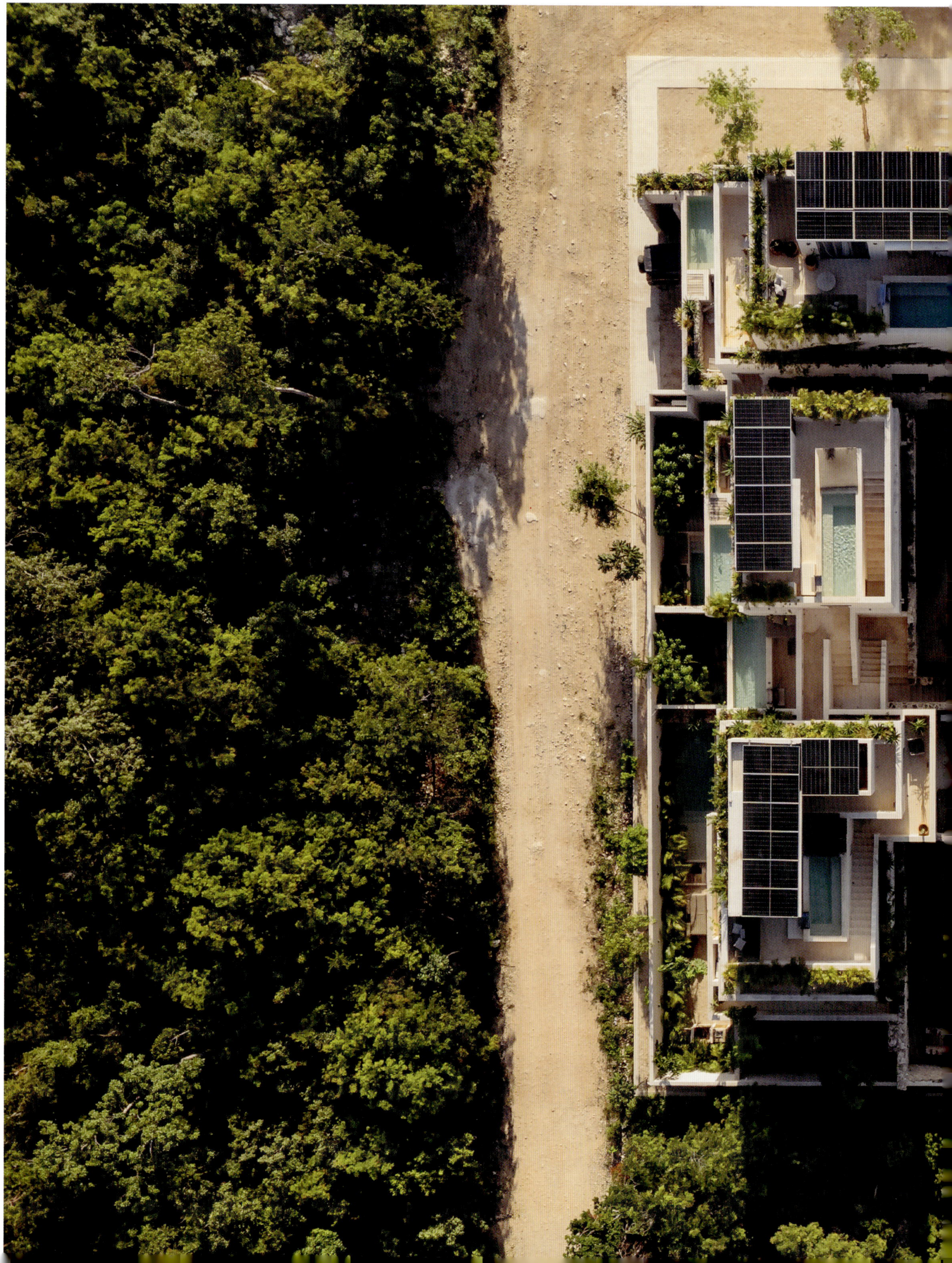

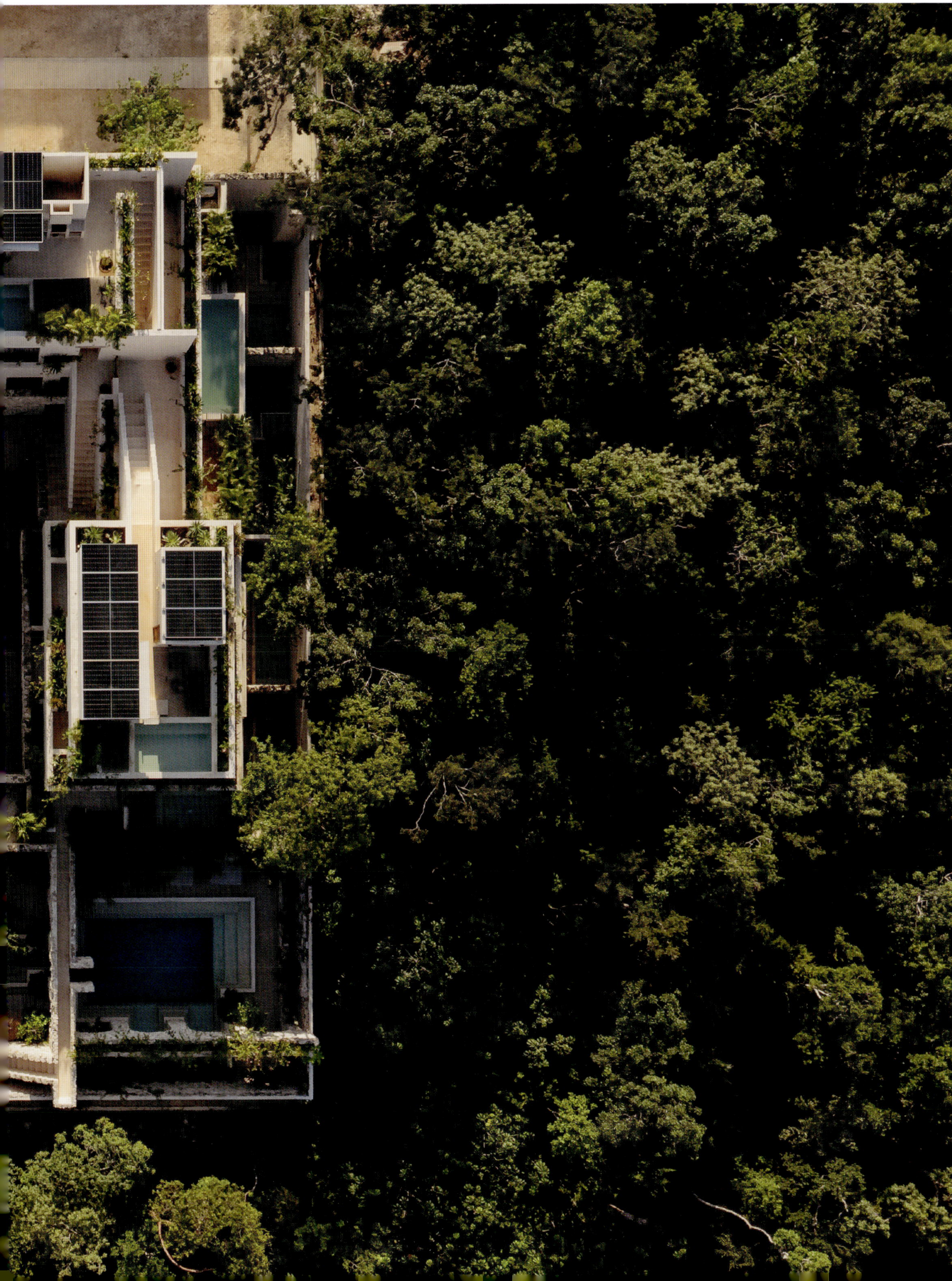

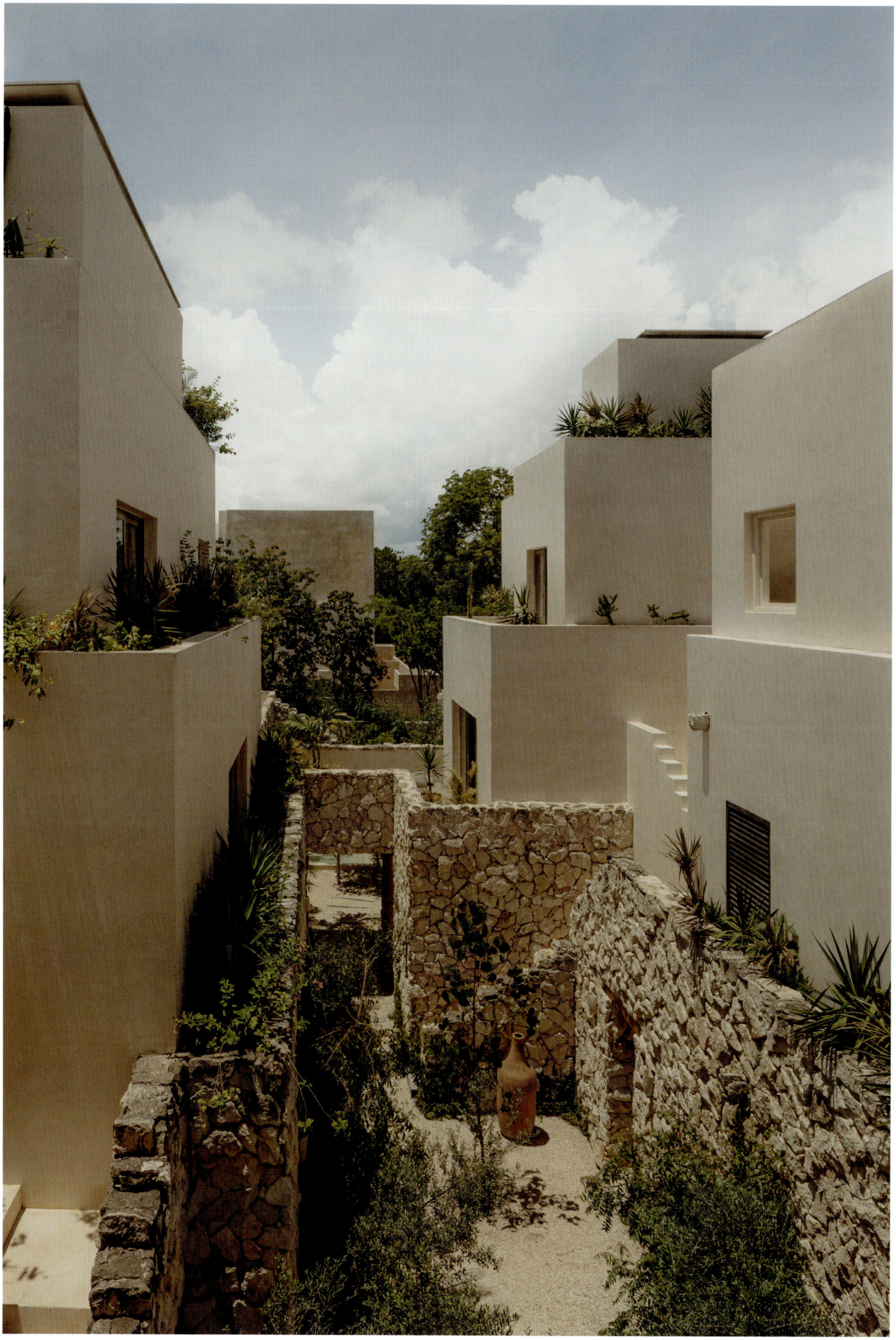

Numerous internal patios of Hacienda Wabi, varying in ambiance and size, collectively create a common thread across the sculptural building.

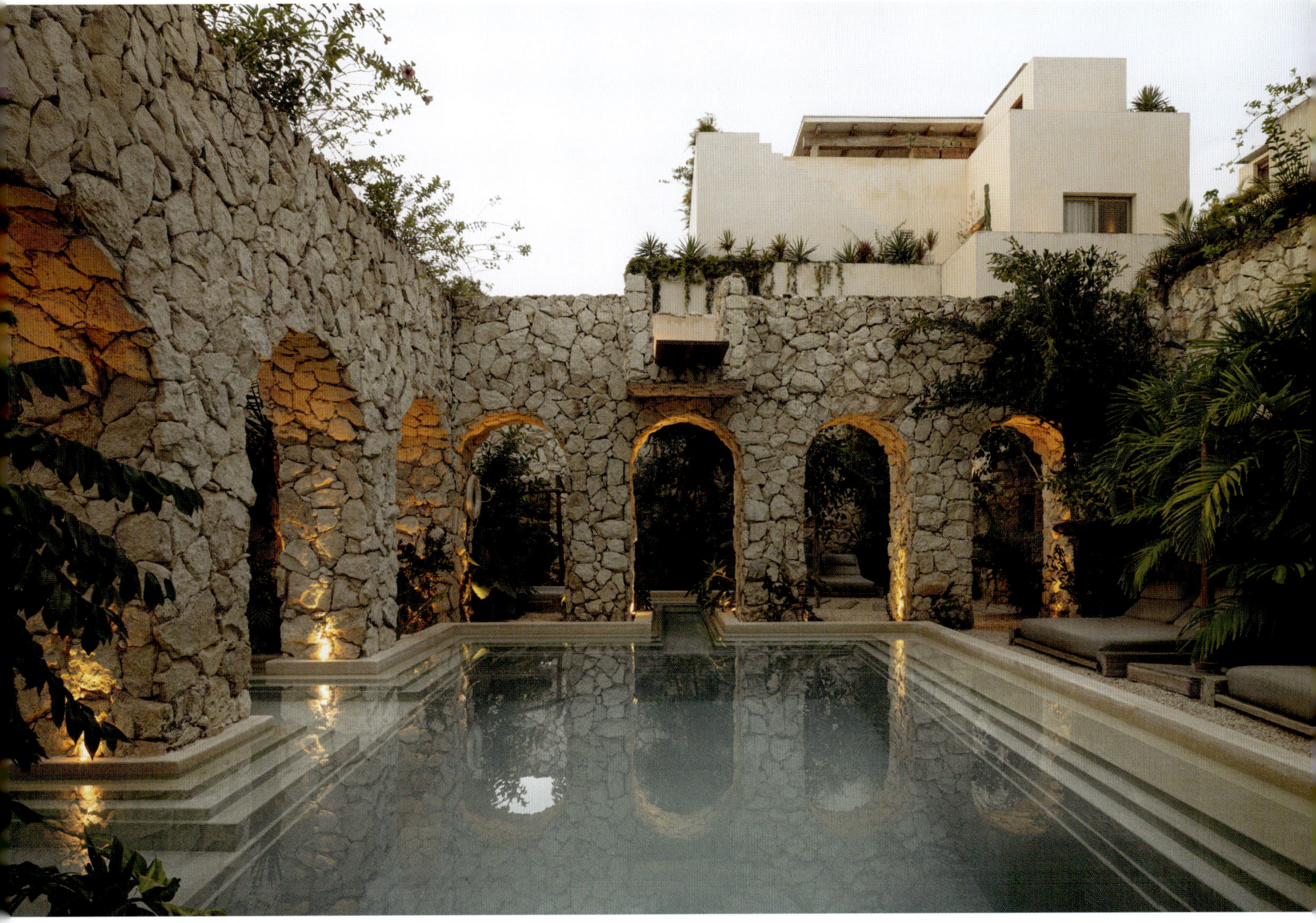

At the very center of Hacienda Wabi is the central patio, a hub that provides access to fifteen flats on three different levels, each of which features different amenities: gardens and private pools on the first story, terraces and jacuzzis on the second, and terraces as well as roof gardens with stunning treetop views on the top level. The centrally located courtyard is then divided into smaller patios connected by pathways that lead to a semipublic area, a recreational space with a swimming pool. All outdoor spaces have a distinct character thanks to the materials selected by the architects. While the base has been built with regional stone, the walls are finished with a natural, plant-based and sand coating called Chukum. Their beige hues are beautifully emphasized by the sunlight and create a sense of tranquility.

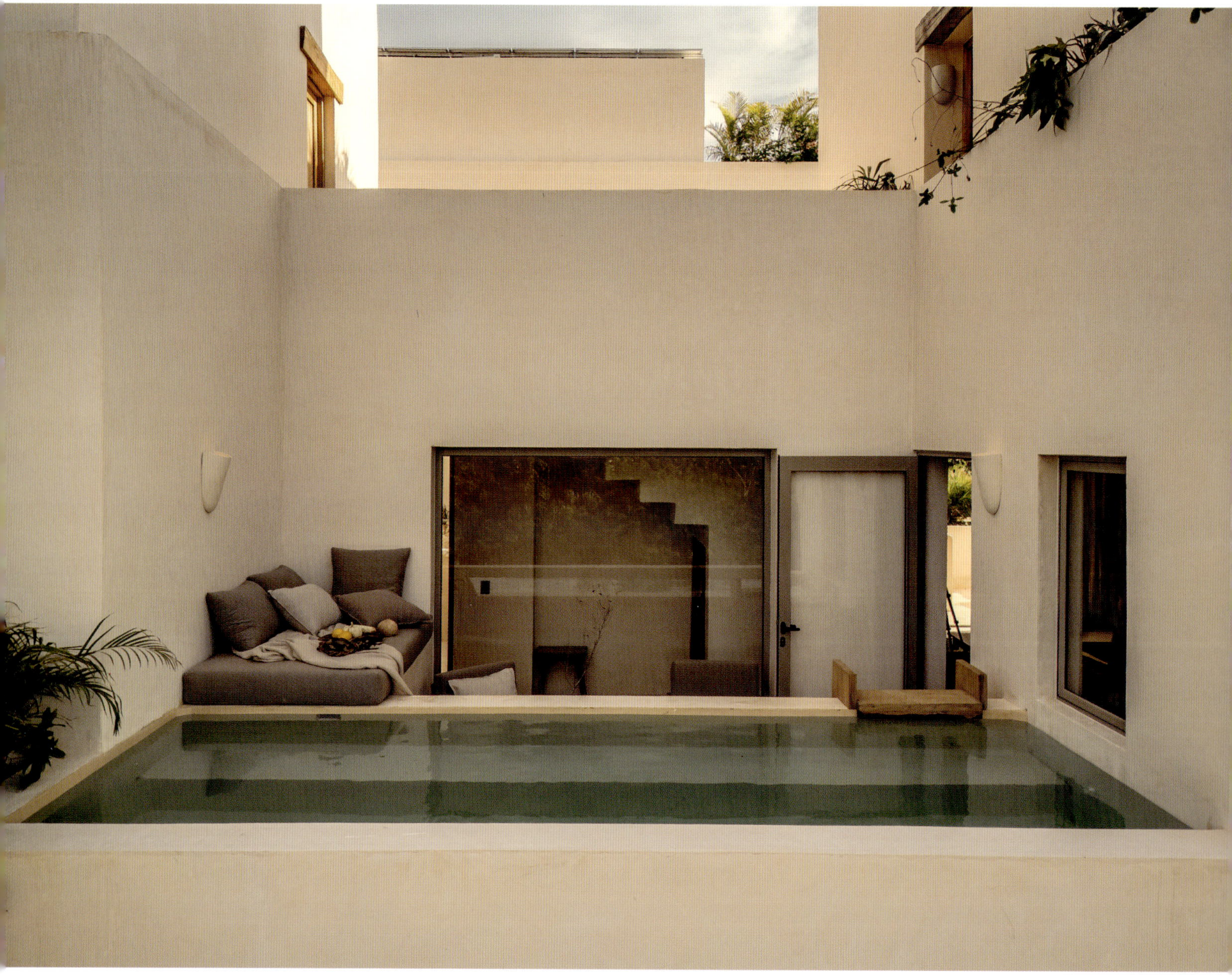

Framed with stones, adorned with vegetation, and featuring water reservoirs, the patios create serene areas both in-between the individual residences and as entirely private spaces.

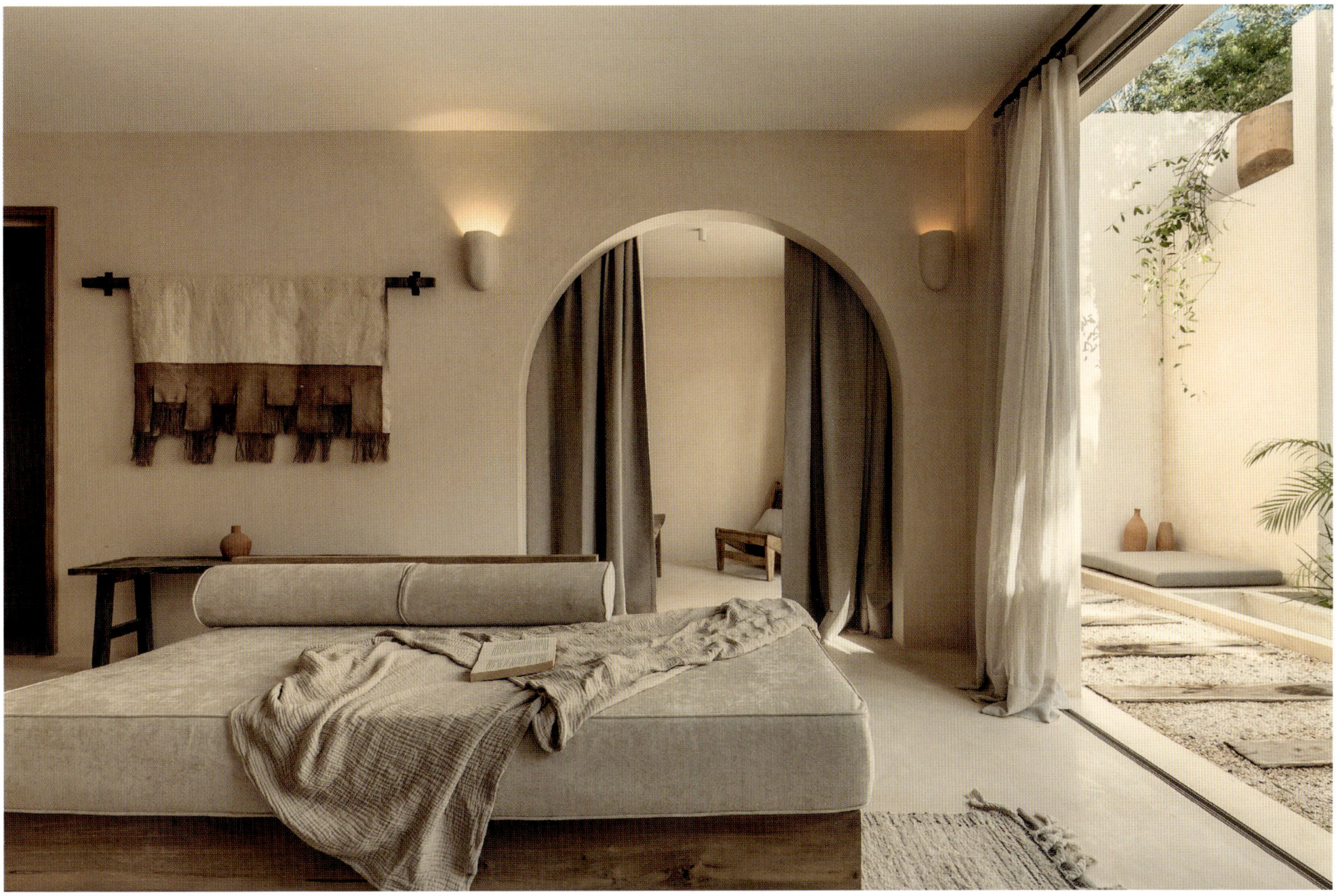

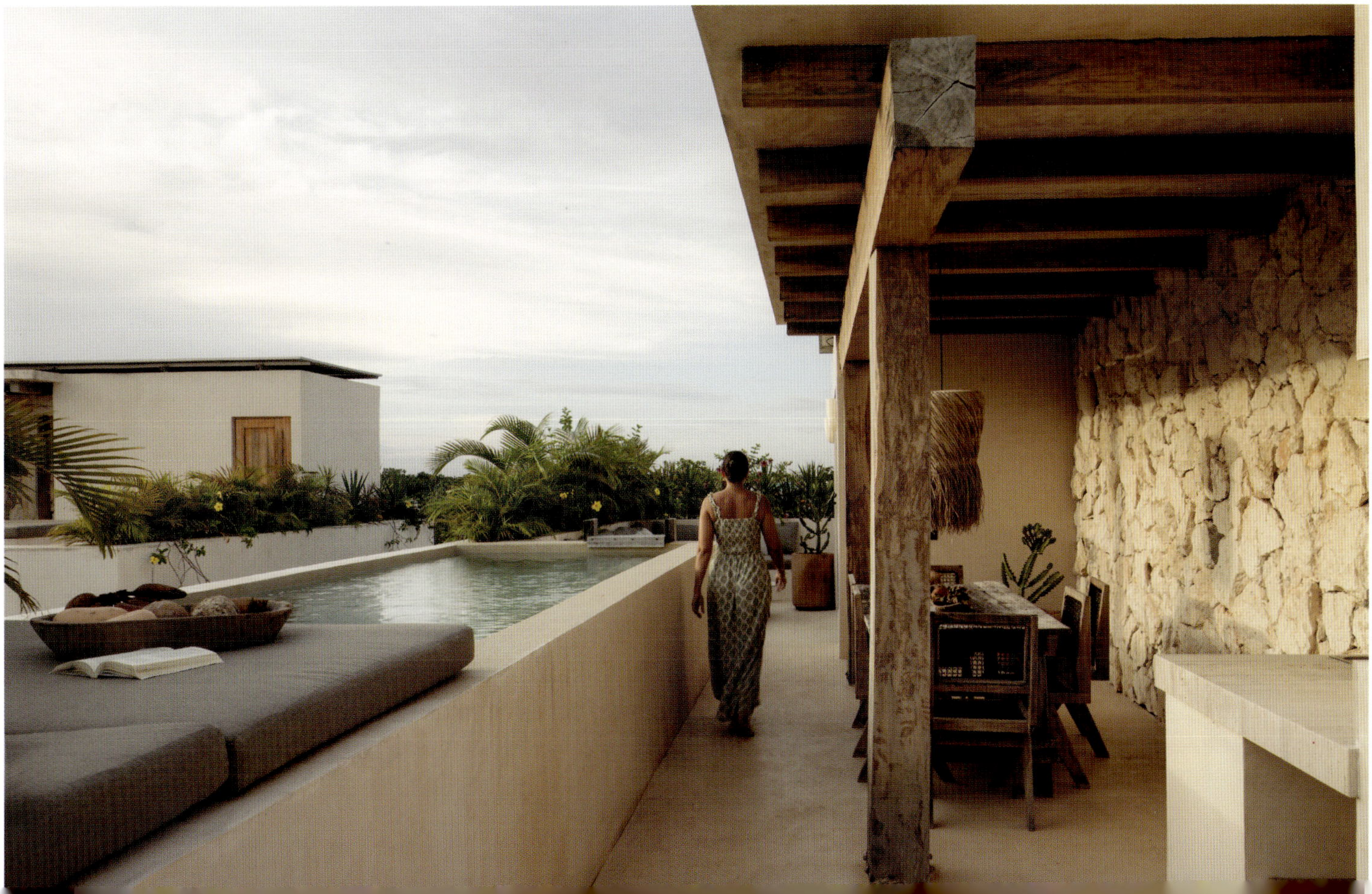

PROJECT: Casa Jardín Escandón
LOCATION: México, Mexico
YEAR: 2020
ARCHITECTS: CPDA Arquitectos
PHOTOGRAPHY: Jaime Navarro

Casa Jardín Escandón is another example of a multifamily house with a central courtyard at its core, completely hidden from street view. The entrance through the uniquely shaped facade leads to a large patio filled with greenery adapted to the climate and easy maintenance. This spacious and bright courtyard provides access to fourteen apartments, ten of which are three-story townhouse-style units. Ensuring natural light and cross-ventilation in all living spaces was a top priority, achieved in large part through the internal patio space, but also generous window openings of various shapes. These openings create a dynamic relationship between common and private areas. The central patio, designed as a hidden garden, aims to enhance residents' living experience within the urban context.

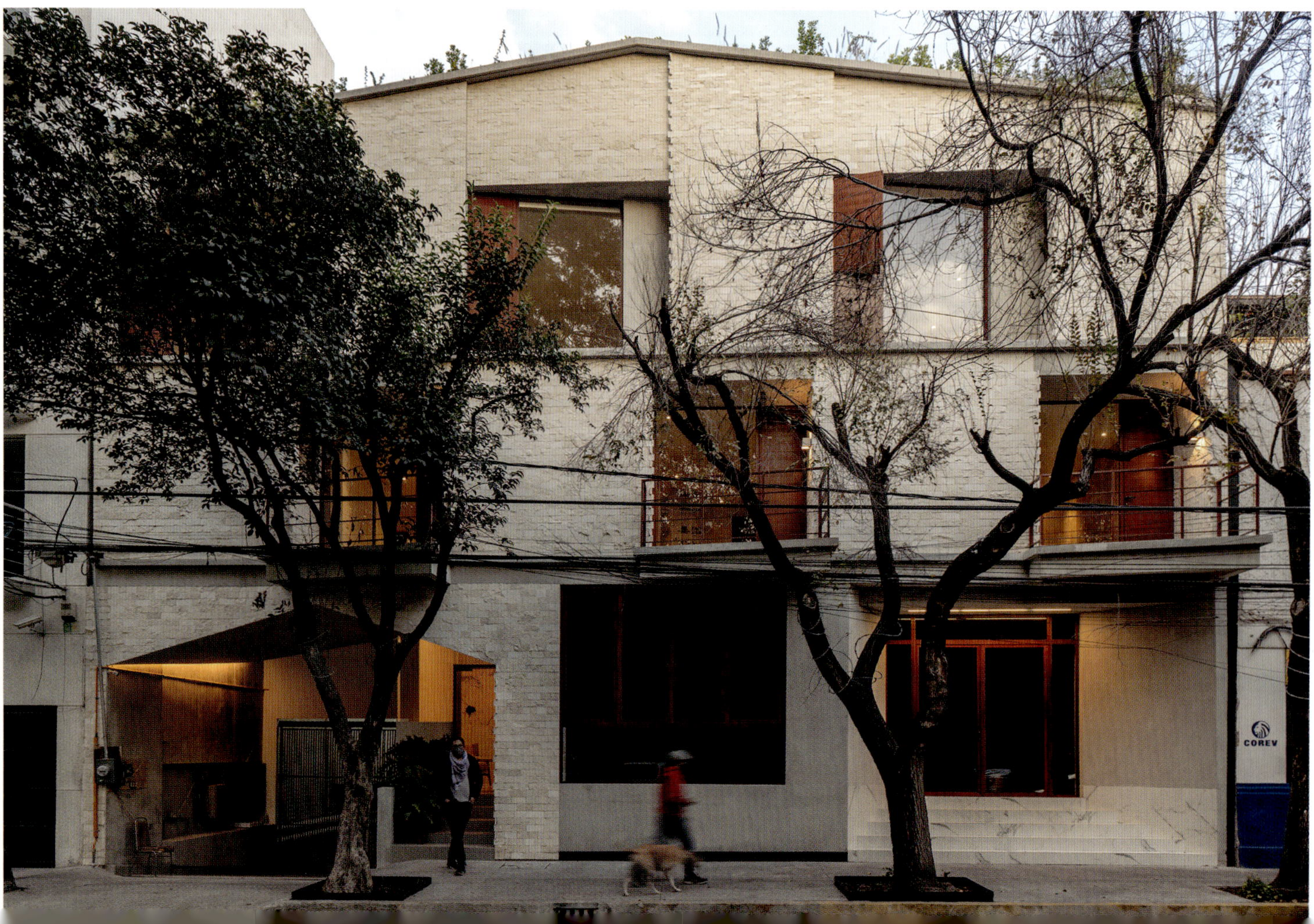

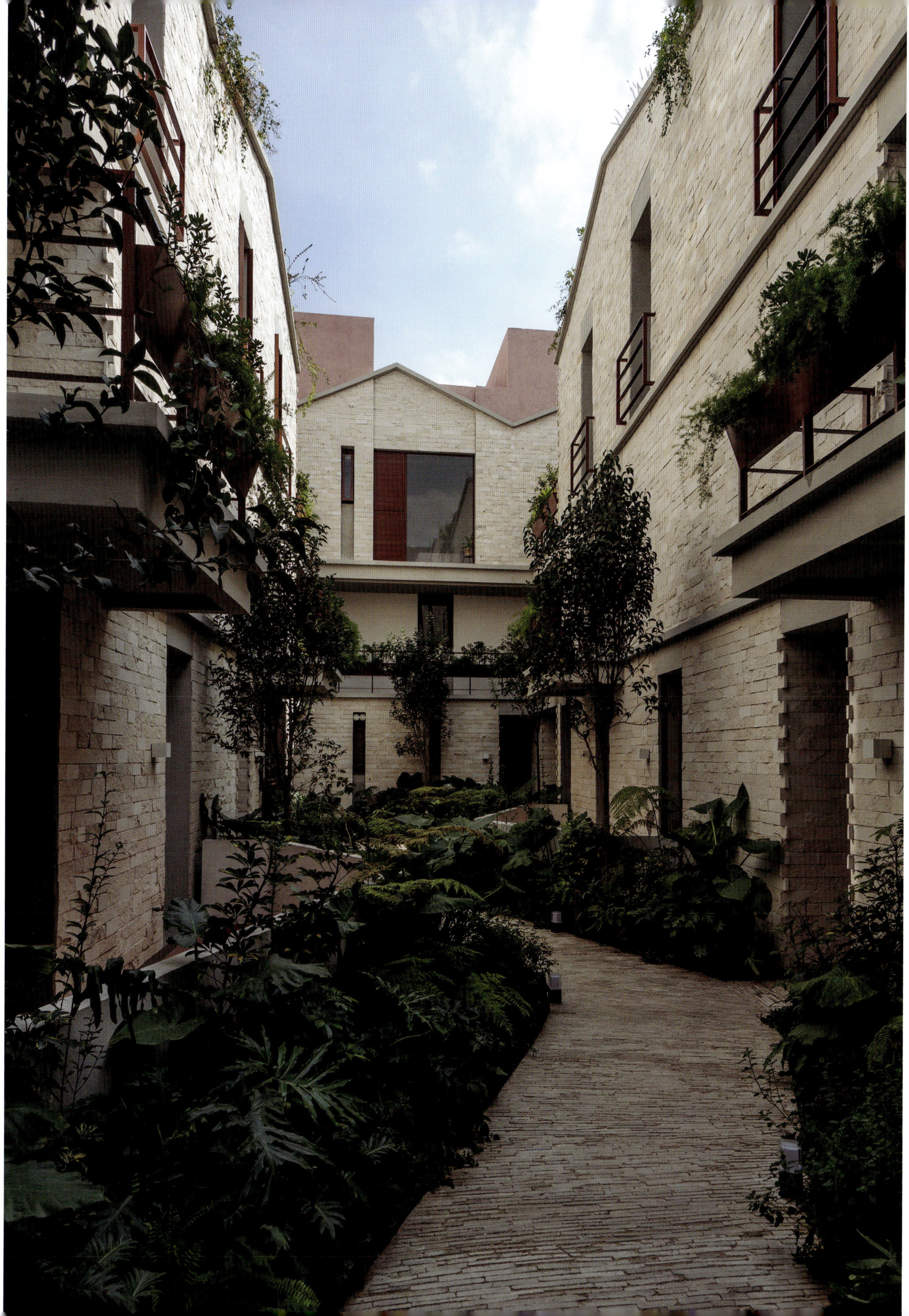

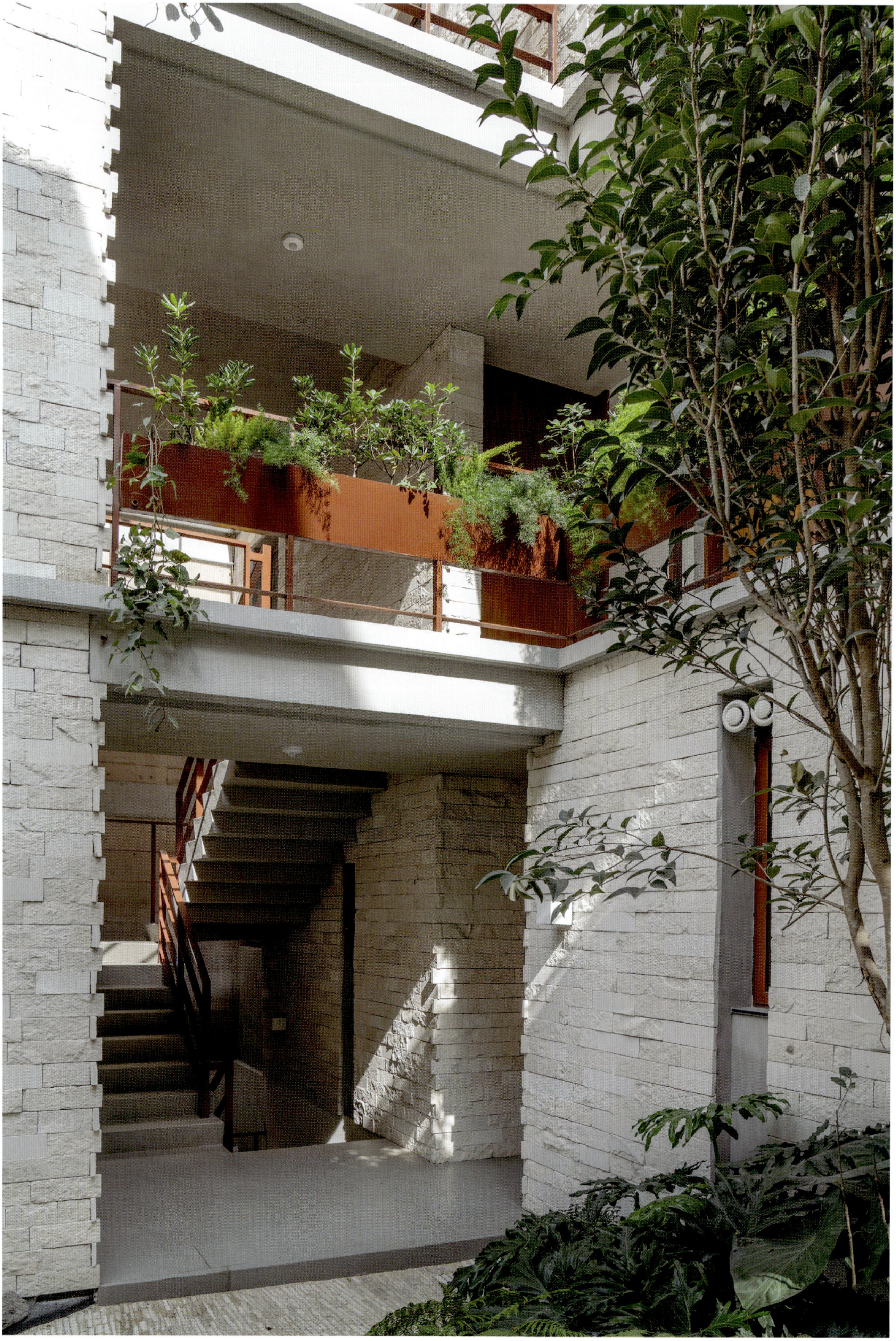

Casa Jardín Escandón blends perfectly into the rapidly developing neighborhood, where historical buildings coexist harmoniously with contemporary architecture. Traditional gable roofs of the complex are juxtaposed with original windows, and modern lines of the building are clad in galarza stone, creating a visually striking fusion of old and new. The multifamily residence serves as the architects' statement on successfully combining natural and built environments in the urban landscape. Native vegetation in the courtyard serves as a tranquil transition between the bustling city and the apartments. Additionally, smaller courtyards on the roof offer residents intimate private spaces, highlighted with a soft pink hue.

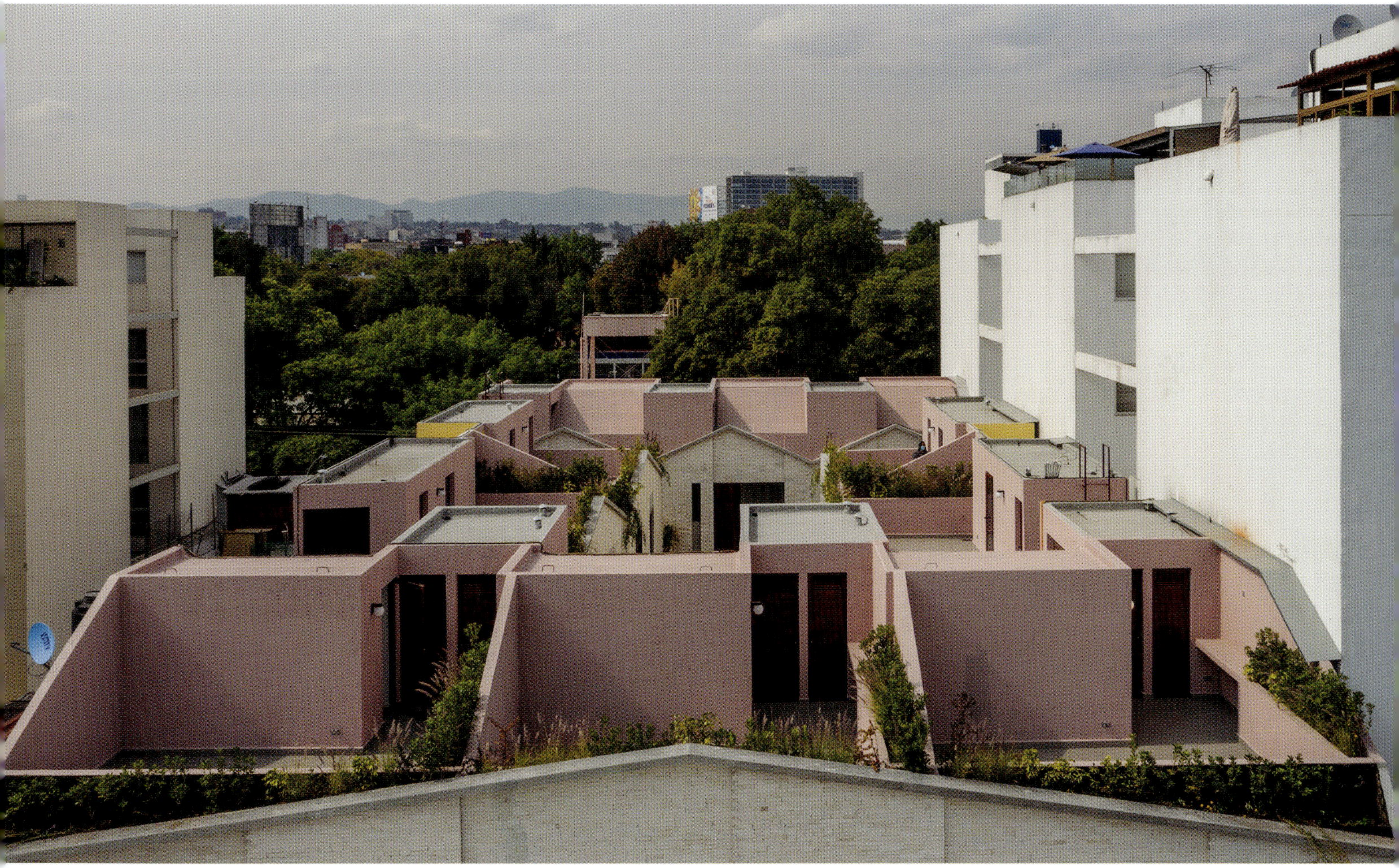

CPDA Arquitectos, based in Mexico City, is a multidisciplinary practice founded in 2016 by Juan Pablo Cepeda. Their portfolio includes projects of varying scales and typologies, all emphasizing innovative solutions integrated with urban, social, and cultural contexts. The architects prioritize creating a city by adapting to the context, respecting the historical process, and acknowledging the site's transformation. Their goal is to facilitate a dialogue between new and traditional architecture, honoring the legacy of Mexican design to create lasting, sustainable structures.

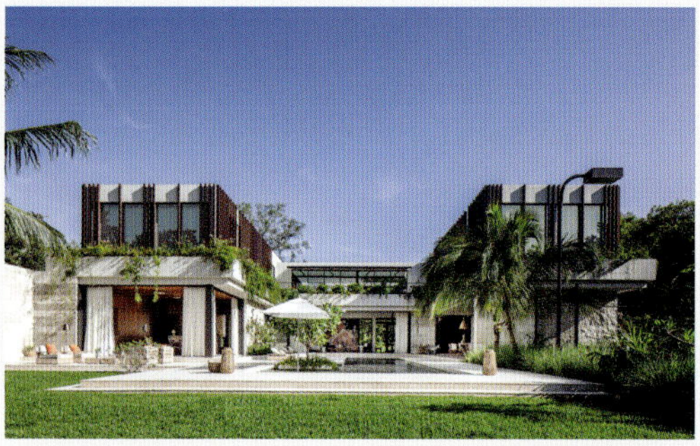

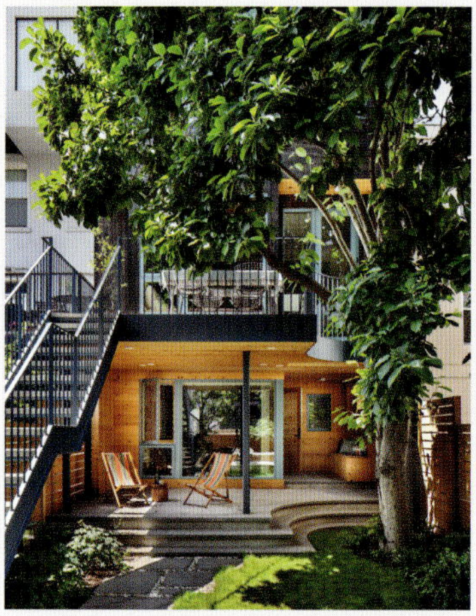

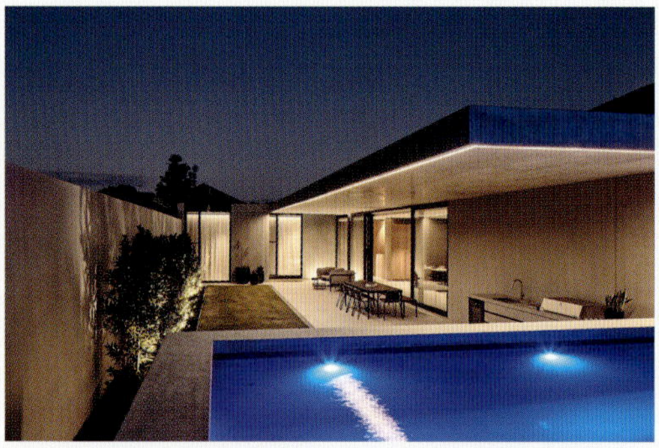

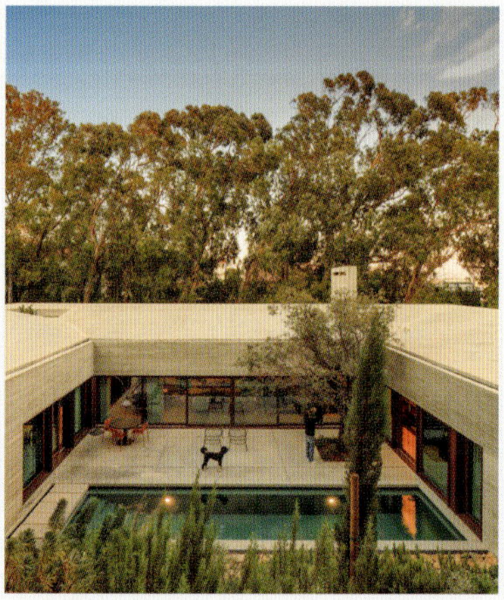

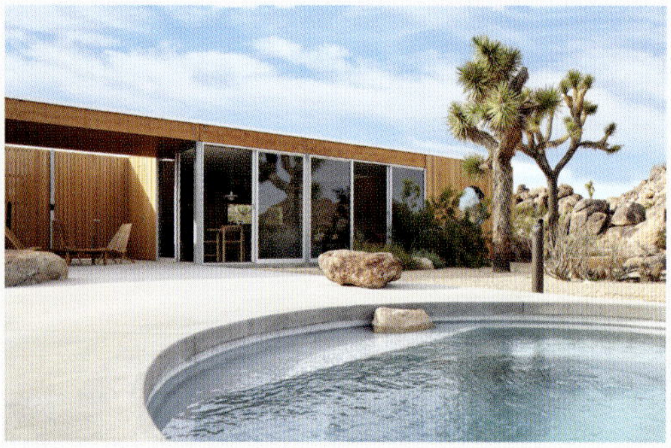

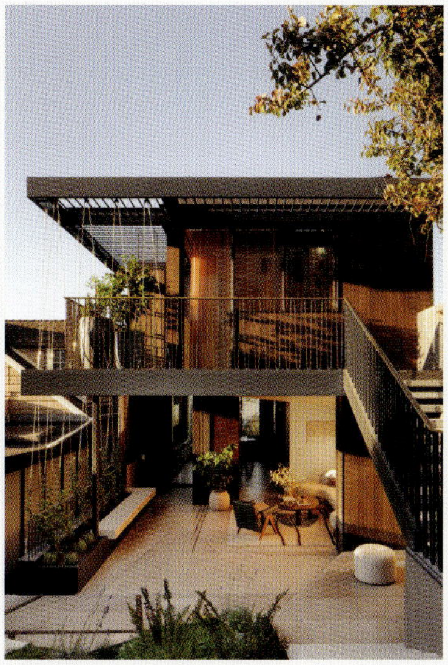

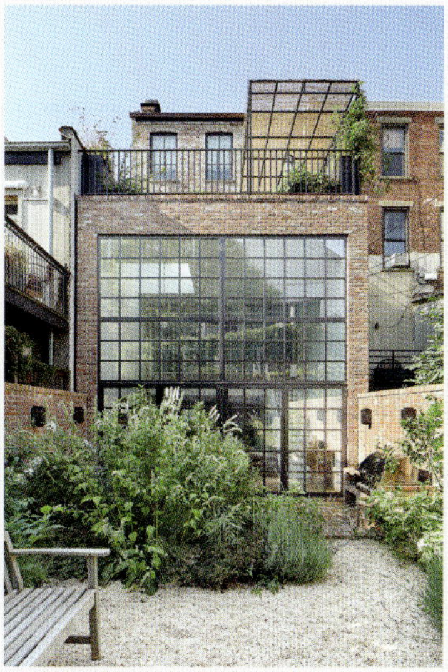

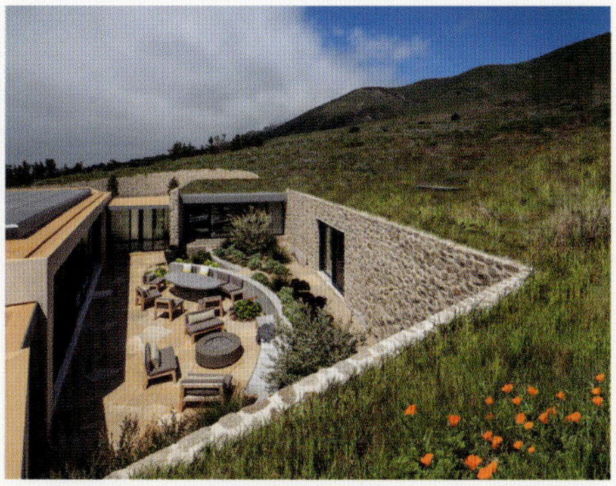

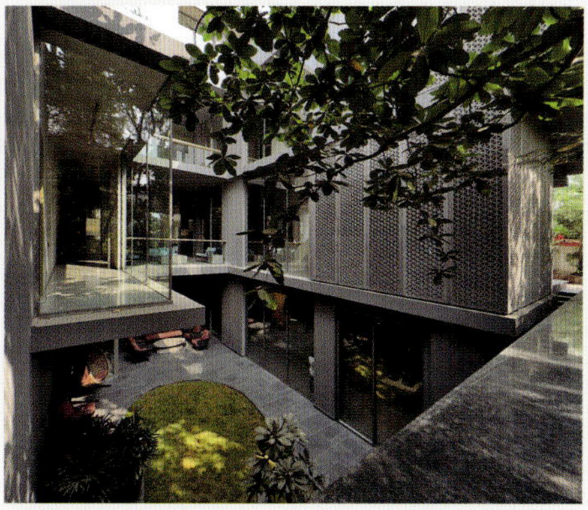

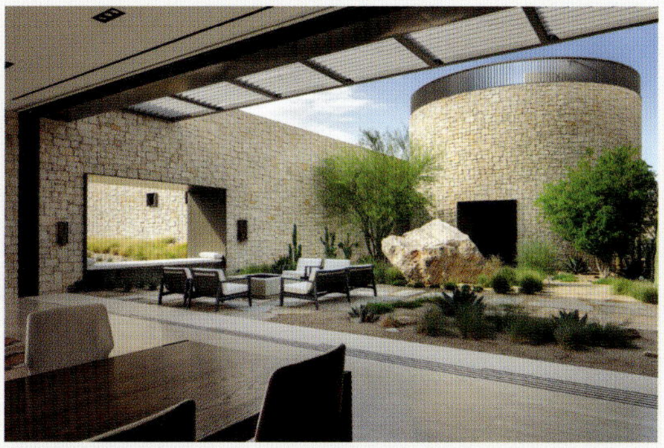

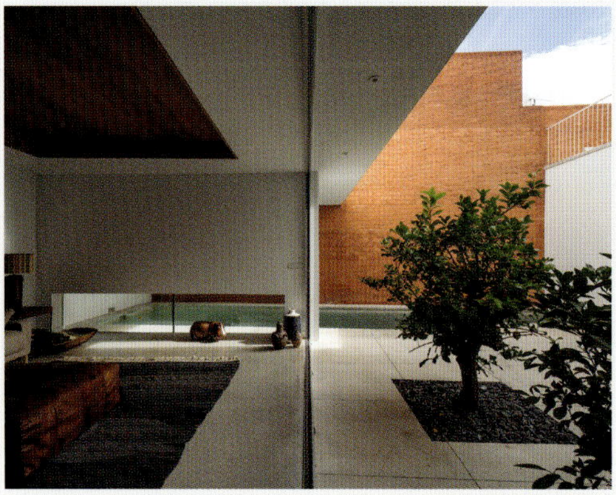

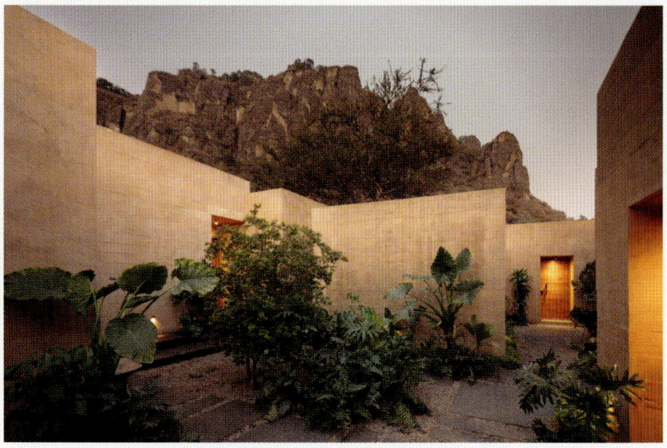

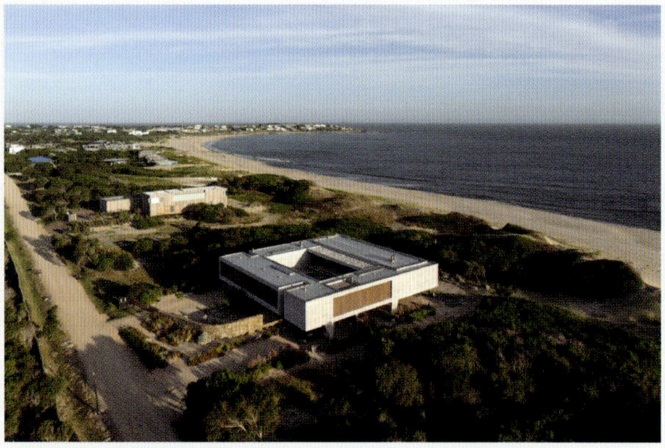

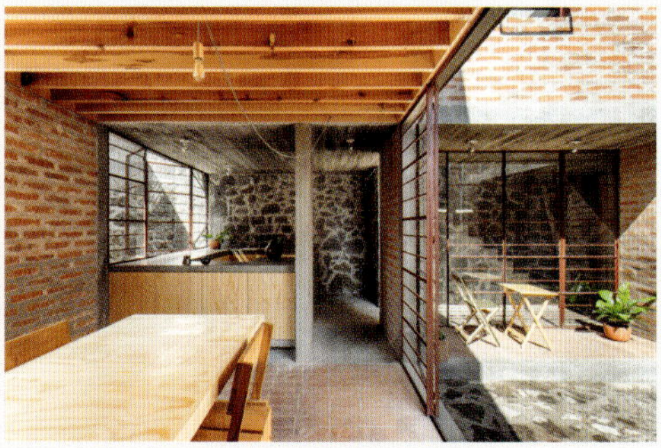

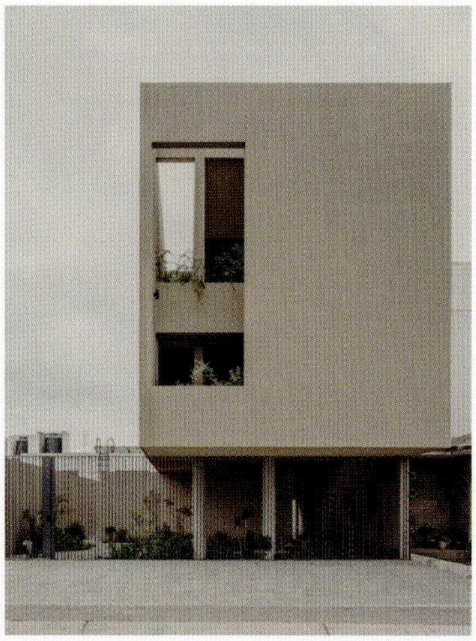

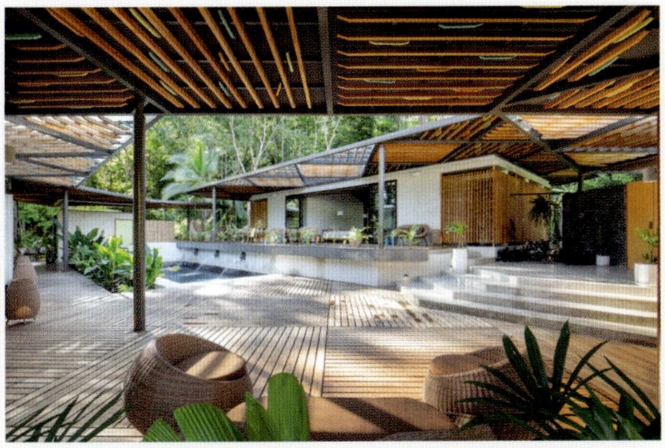

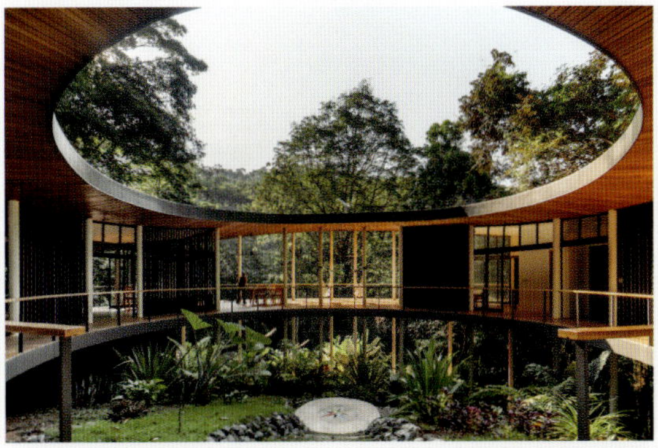

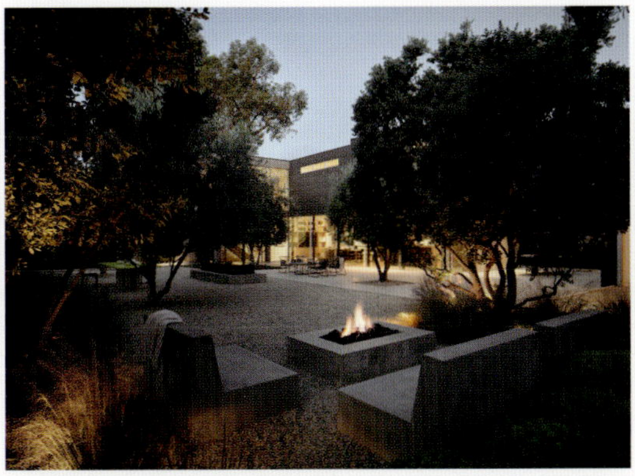

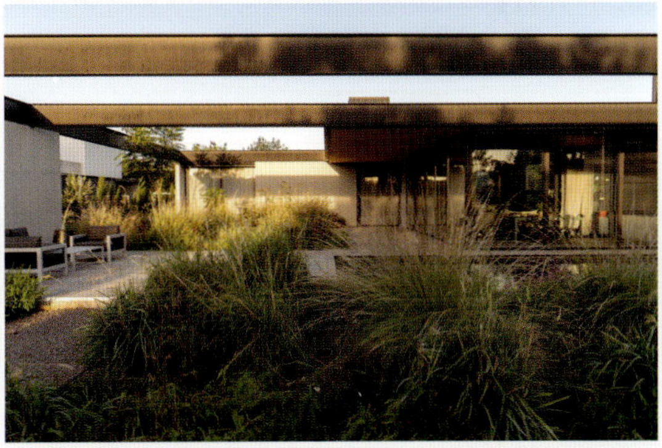

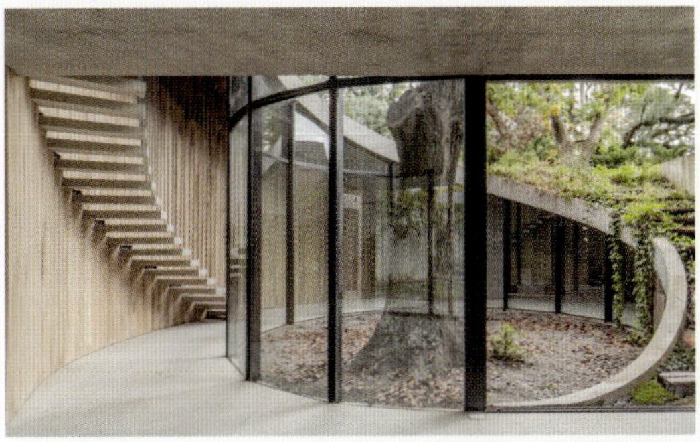

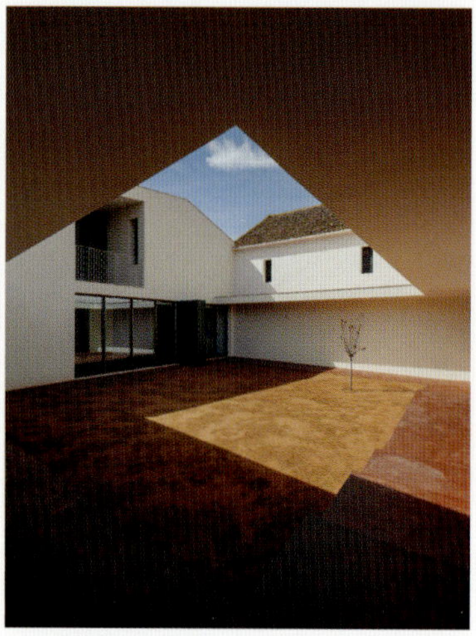

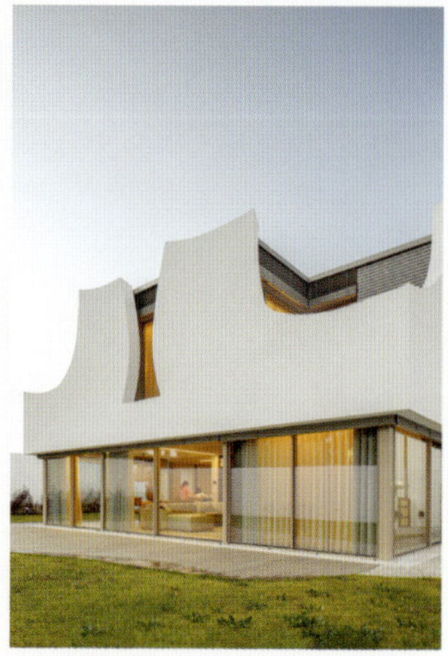

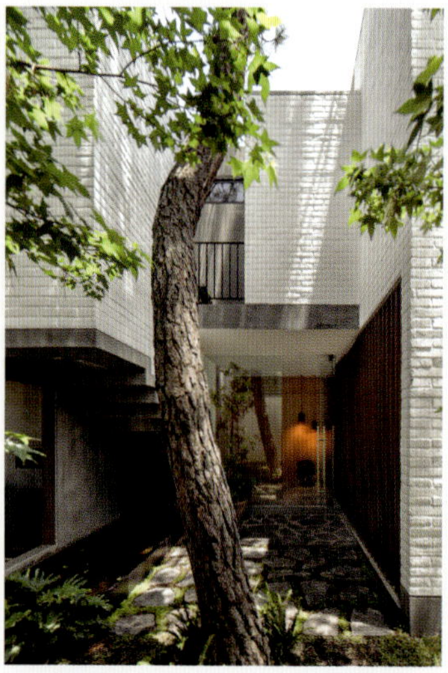

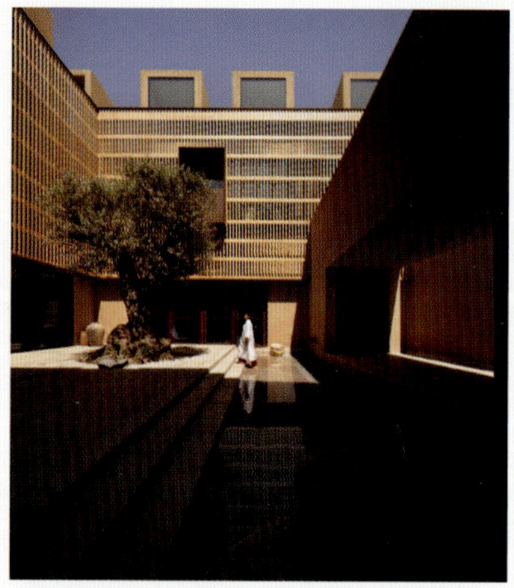

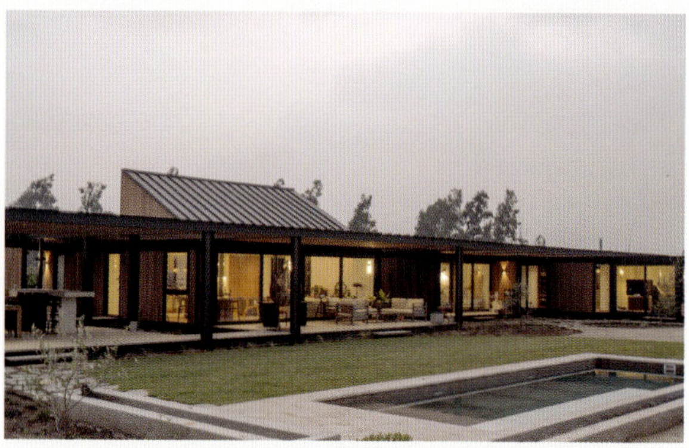

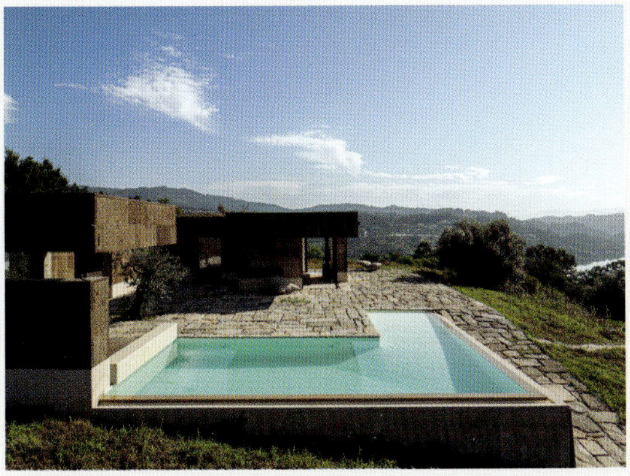

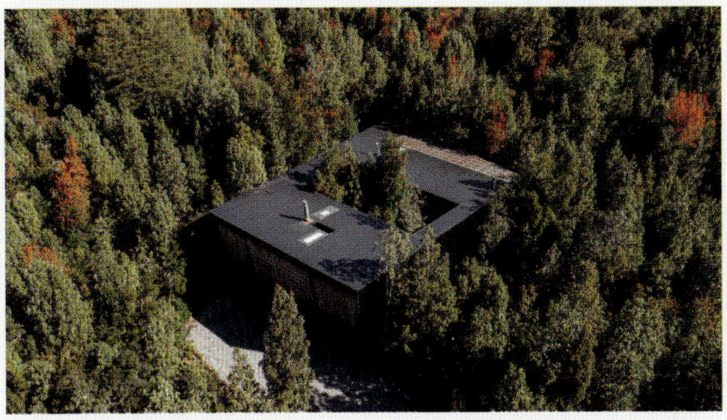

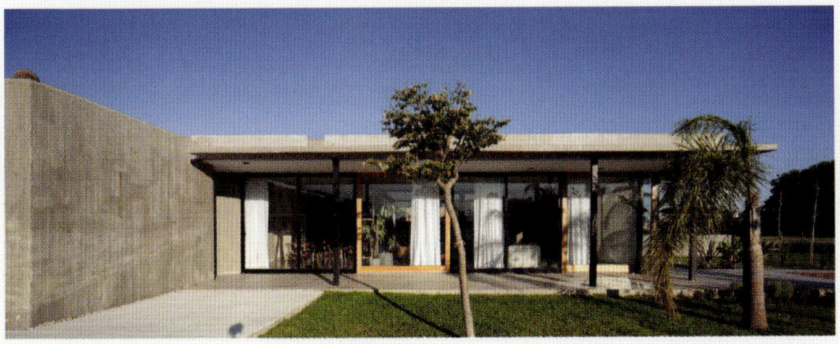

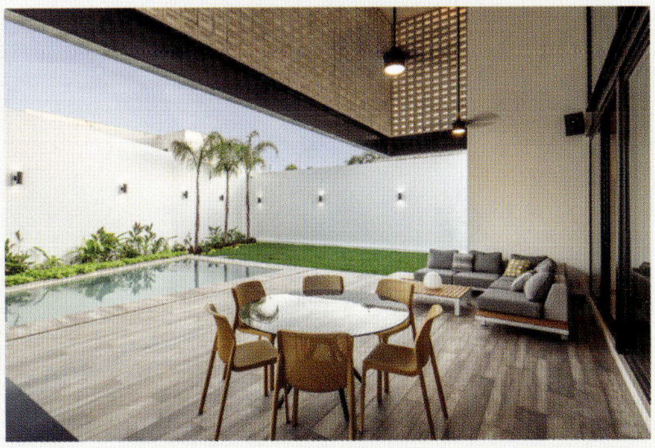

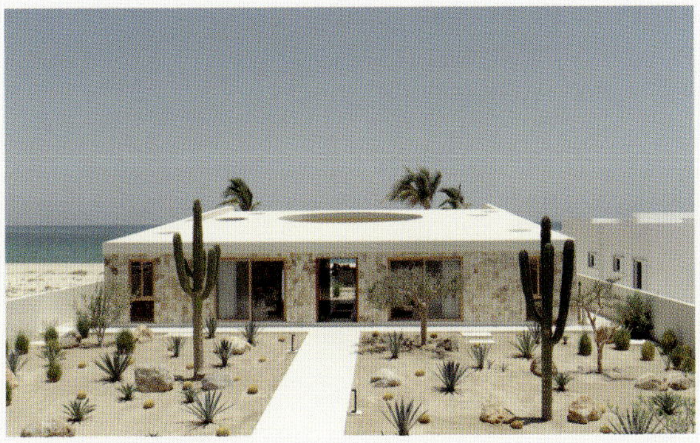

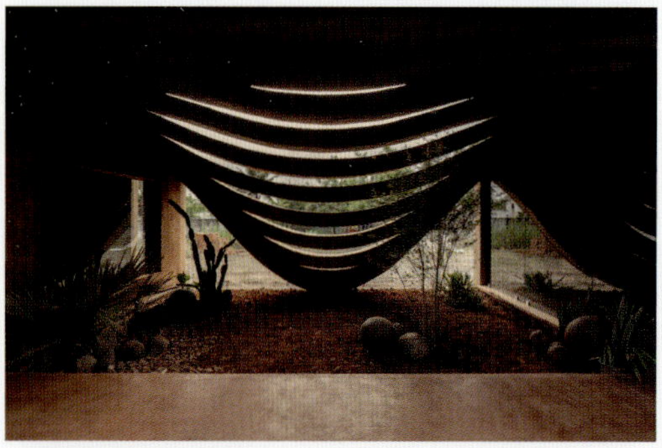

Vaazh House
Vy architecture studio
www.vyarchitecturestudio.com
pp. 206–213

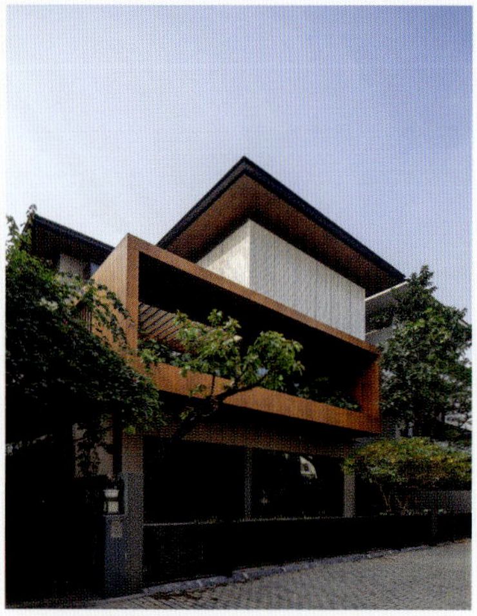

BT5 Villa
APDI Architecture
www.apdi.com.vn
pp. 214–219

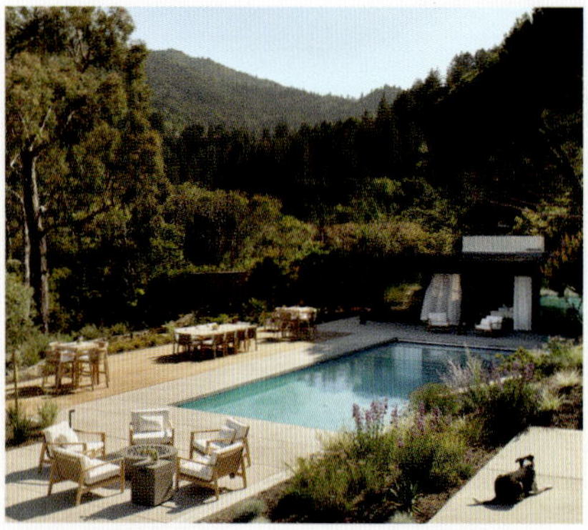

Kojima House
SWATT + PARTNERS
www.swattpartners.com
pp. 220–225

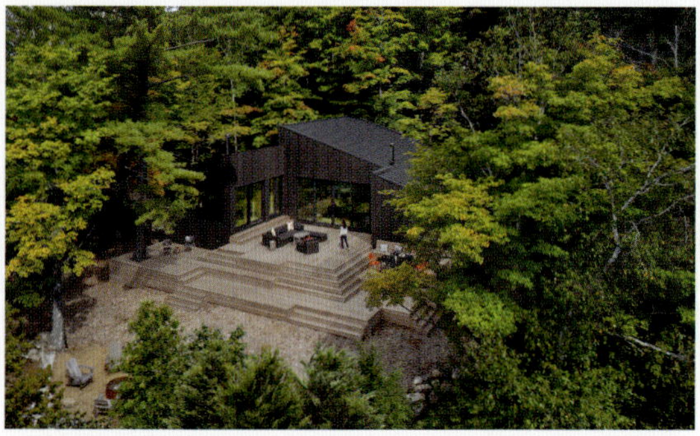

Catchacoma Cottage
Dubbeldam Architecture + Design
www.dubbeldam.ca
pp. 226–231

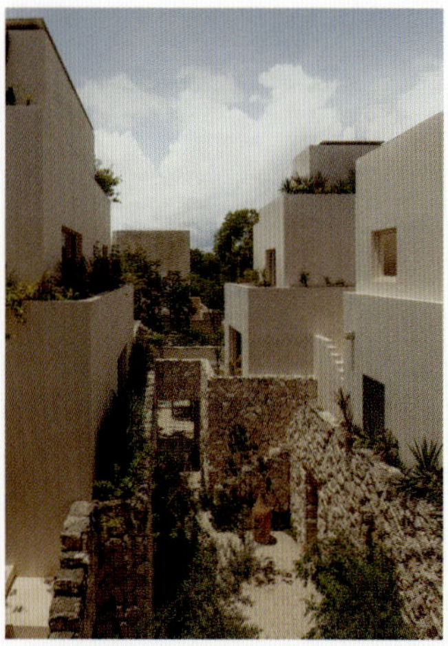

Hacienda Wabi
RA!
www.raarq.com
pp. 232–239

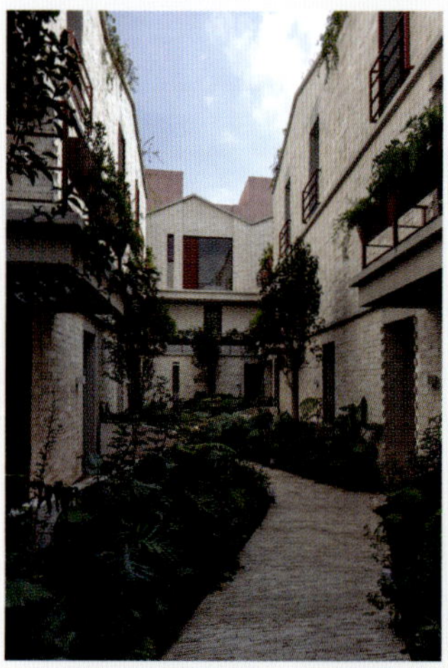

Casa Jardín Escandón
CPDA Arquitectos
www.cpda.mx
pp. 240–243

Acknowledgments

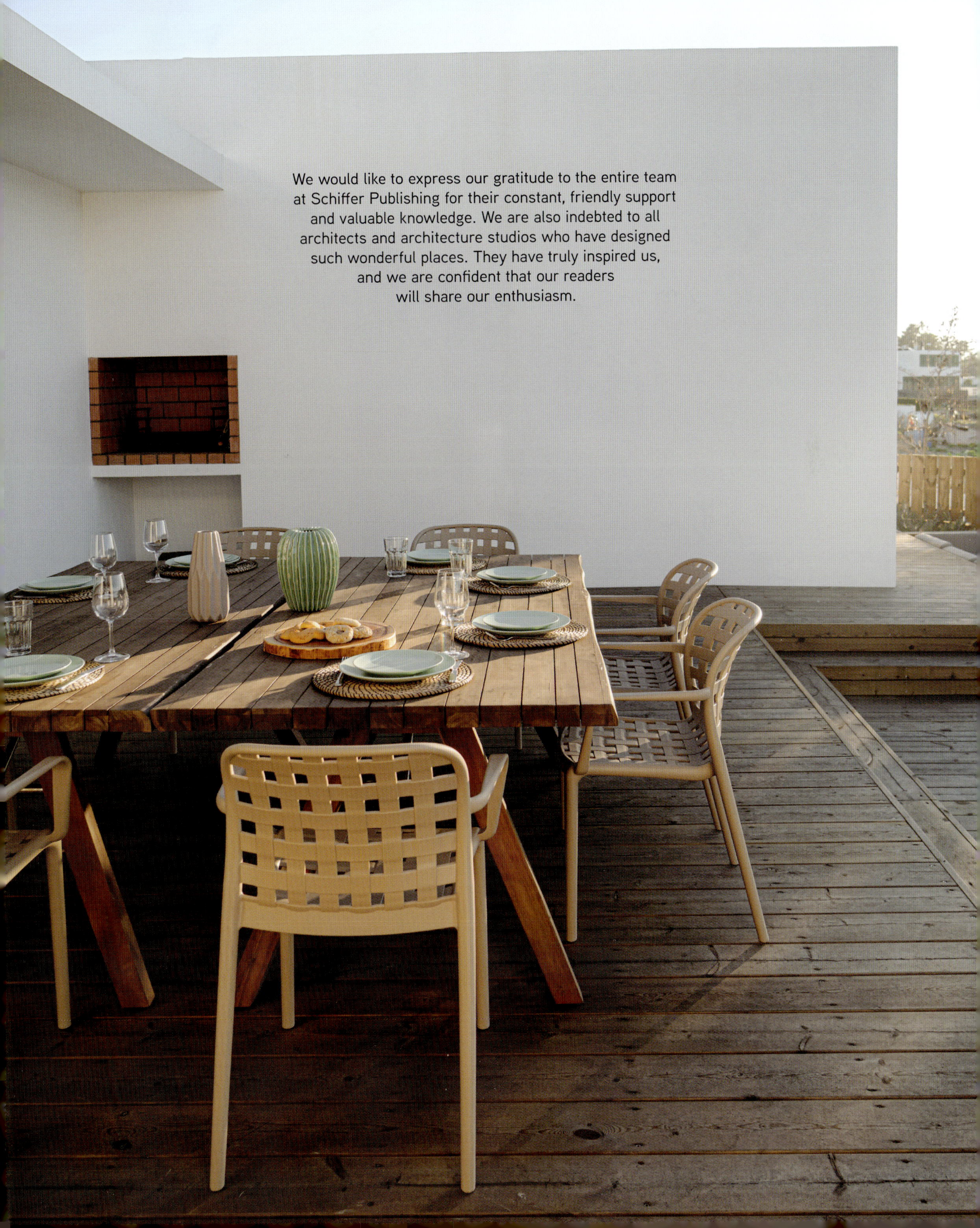

We would like to express our gratitude to the entire team at Schiffer Publishing for their constant, friendly support and valuable knowledge. We are also indebted to all architects and architecture studios who have designed such wonderful places. They have truly inspired us, and we are confident that our readers will share our enthusiasm.

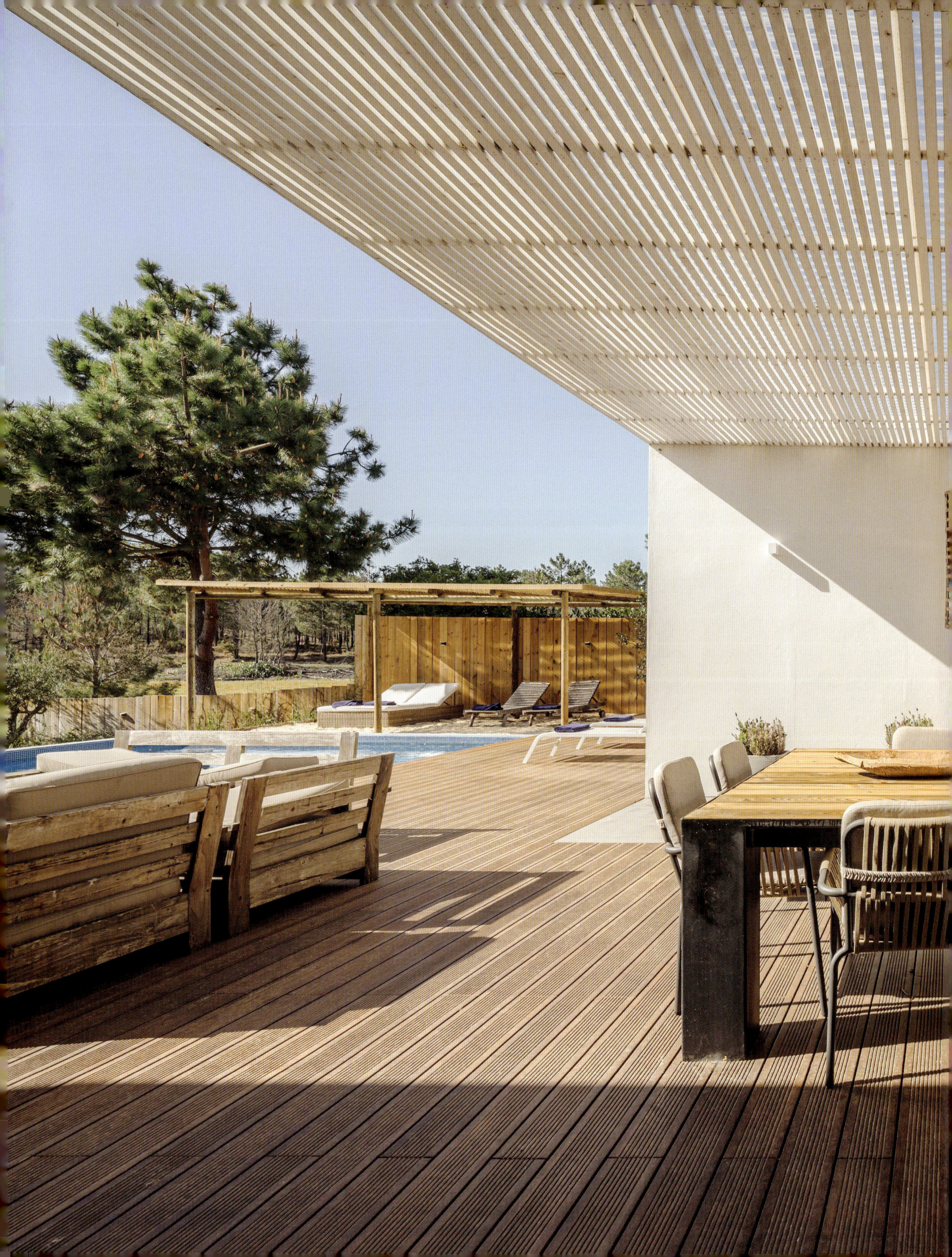

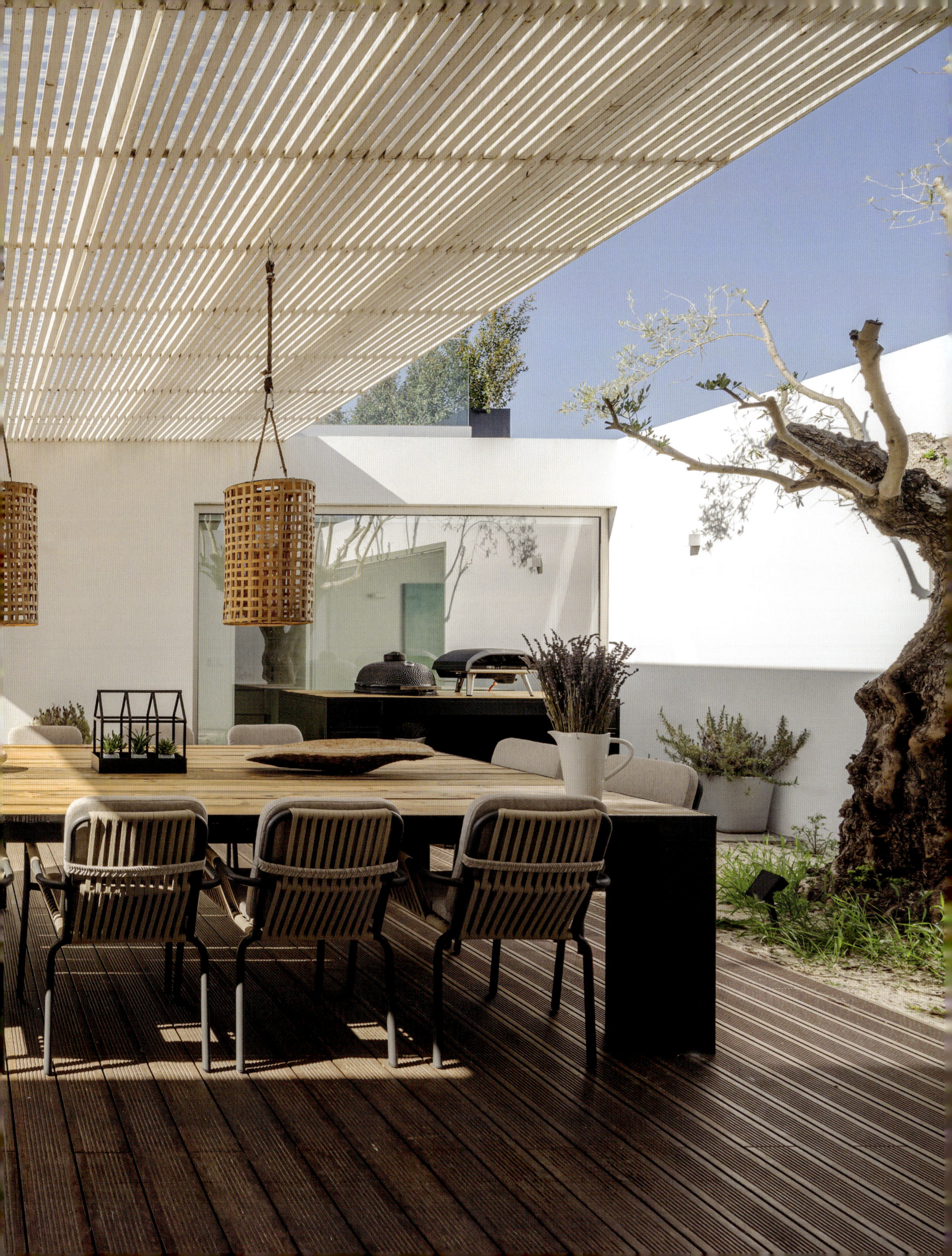

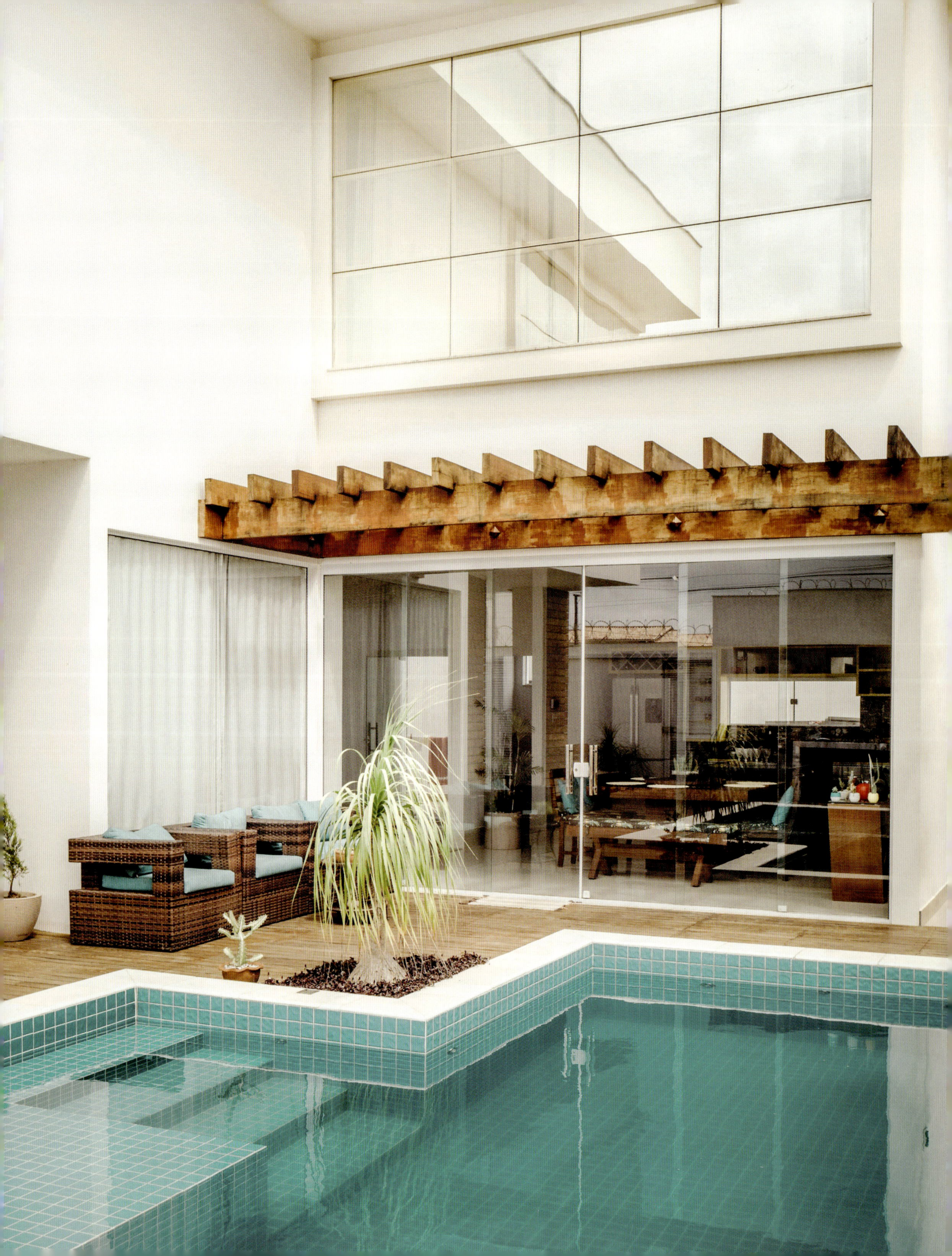

PHOTO CREDITS

pp.:
2 © Vincent Rivaud / Pexels
4 © Hutomo Abrianto on Unsplash
7 © Lianhao Qu on Unsplash
8 © Tonet Gandia / Shutterstock
10–11 © Tom Fisk / Pexels
14–21 design © STRANG, photography © Kris Tamburello / courtesy of v2com
22–25 design © Barker Architecture Office, photography © Francis Dzikowski/OTTO / courtesy of v2com
26–33 design © FGR Architects, photography © Peter Bennetts / courtesy of v2com
34–37 design © OODA, photography © Fernando Guerra / courtesy of v2com
38–45 design © Industry of All Nations, photography © Ye Rin Mok / courtesy of v2com
46–51 design © Medium Plenty, photography © Shade Degges / courtesy of v2com
52–55 design © Palette Architecture, photography © Emily Gilbert Photography/ courtesy of v2com
56–61 design © Studio Schicketanz, photography 56–58 © Joe Fletcher Photography / courtesy of v2com; 59, 60–61 © Tim Griffith Photography / courtesy of v2com
62–67 design © Sanjay Puri Architects, photography © Mr. Dinesh Mehta / courtesy of v2com
68–75 design © Daniel Joseph Chenin, Ltd., photography 68–71 © Stetson Ybarra / courtesy of v2com; 72–73 © Stephen Morgan / courtesy of v2com; 74–75 © Daniel Joseph Chenin / courtesy of v2com
76–81 design © DTR_studio architects, photography © Juanan Barros / courtesy of v2com
82–89 design © RA!, photography © Mariana Achach Herroz
90–97 design © Grimaldi· Nacht Arquitectos, photography © Javier Agustín Rojas
98–99 design © Escobedo Soliz Studio, photography © Ariadna Polo
102–107 design © Taller Segovia Molina, photography 102, 103, 107 © ZaickzMoz; 104, 105, 106 © Diego Vázquez Mellado
108–115 design © Studio Saxe, photography © Andres Garcia Lachner
116–123 design © Studio Saxe, photography © Alvaro Fonseca-Depth Lens
124–129 design © Walker Warner, photography © Matthew Millman
130–135 design © 31 64 estudio and © sdf Arquitectos, photography © Juan Cruz Paredes
136–141 design © AtelierM, photography © AtelierM
142–145 design © Volume Architecture Lisbon Studio, photography © Eduardo Nascimento
146–151 design © Sandra Micaela Casinha Atelier, photography © Ivo Tavares Studio
152–157 design © Estudio Radillo Alba, photography © César Belio
158–165 design © Studio VDGA, photography 158–159, 162, 164–165 © Shoayb Khattab; 160, 161, 163 © Ema Peter
166–171 design © Paralelo Transversal, photography © Marcos Zegers
172–179 design © Tsou Arquitectos, photography © Ivo Tavares Studio
180–185 design © Lucas Maino Fernández Arquitectos, photography 180–181, 185 © Fernando Alarcon; 182, 183, 184 © Marcos Zegers
186–189 design © Felipe Gonzalez Arzac, photography © Javier Agustín Rojas
190–197 design © P11 Arquitectos, photography © Eduardo Calvo Santisbon
198–205 design © YDR estudio, photography © Luz Imelda Castillo
206–213 design © Vy architecture studio, photography © Syam Sreesylam
214–219 design © APDI Architecture, photography © Trieu Chien
220–225 design © Swatt + Partners, photography © Nils Timm / courtesy of v2com
226–231 design © Dubbeldam Architecture + Design, photography © Riley Snelling / courtesy of v2com
232–239 design © RA!, photography; 232–237, 239 bottom © Ariadna Polo / courtesy of v2com; 238, 239 top © Christian Velasco / courtesy of v2com
240–243 design © CPDA Arquitectos, photography © Jaime Navarro / courtesy of v2com
244–250 © All copyrights as mentioned above
251, 252–253 © Luis Viegas / Shutterstock
254 © Jonathan Borba / Pexels

Library of Congress Control Number: 2026932903

Typeset in Aaux Next

ISBN: 978-0-7643-7211-7

Printed in China

Published by Schiffer Publishing Ltd., 4880 Lower Valley Road
Atglen, PA 19310
Phone: (610) 593-1777; Fax (610) 593-2002; Email: info@schifferbooks.com
Web: www.schifferbooks.com

FSC
www.fsc.org
MIX
Paper | Supporting responsible forestry
FSC® C104723

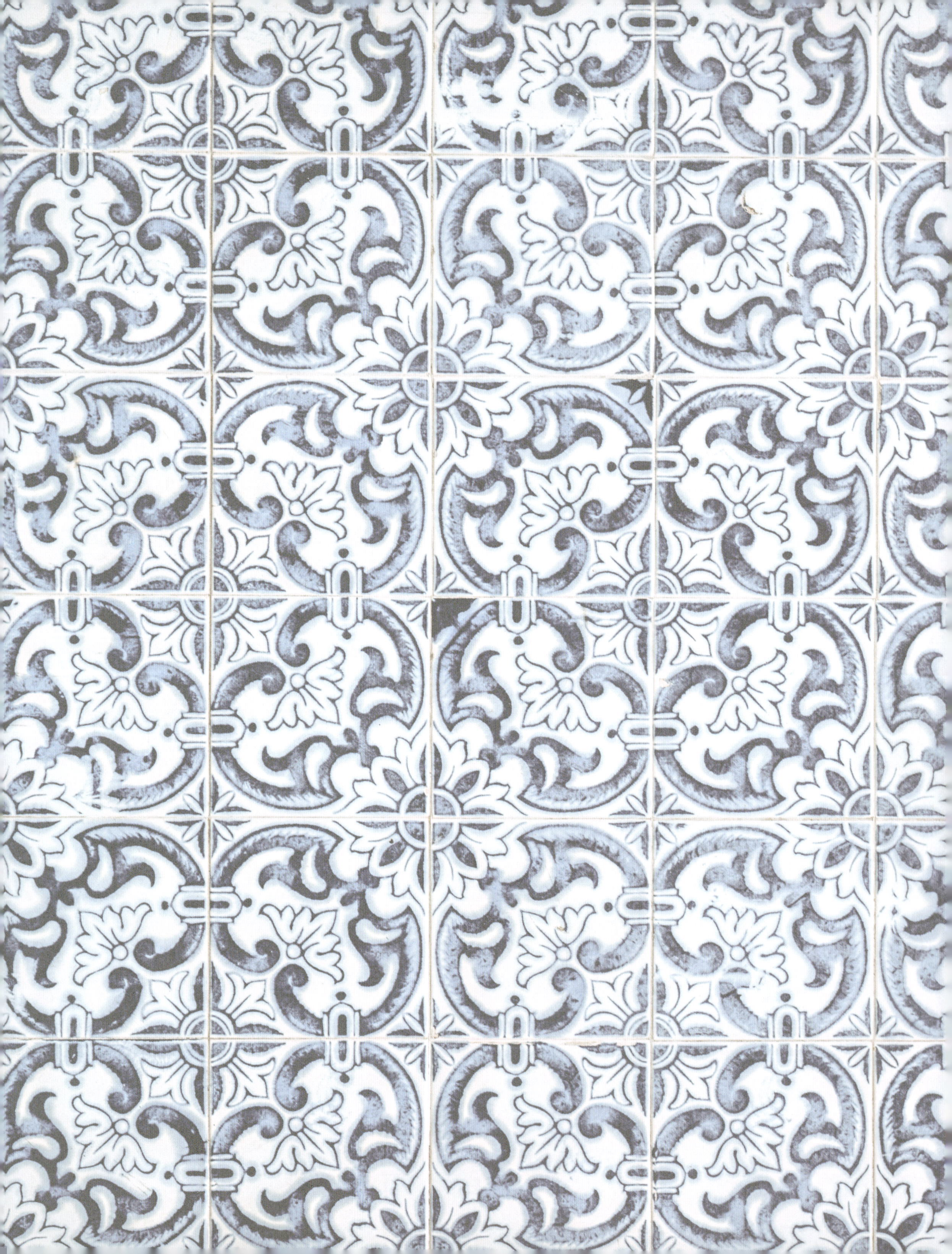